CW00547771

Praise for *Apartheid's Stalingrad*

'It's a lovely read, with lively energy and great detail.'
– Albie Sachs, twice winner of Sunday Times Literary Awards, and retired Judge of the Constitutional Court of South Africa

'From the 1950s through to the 1990s, the black communities living around Port Elizabeth would fight the main battles against apartheid, in scale and in duration unmatched elsewhere in South Africa. From the middle of the 1980s this resistance would deliver the decisive actions that would bring about the advent of a democratic state. Rory Riordan can tell this story with unusual authority for he was there when this struggle reached its climax. To this story he brings the investigative skills of a superb journalist, the industry and care of a trained academic researcher, and the passion of an engaged witness.'
– Tom Lodge, Emeritus Professor of Peace and Conflict Studies, University of Limerick, author of Black Politics in South Africa since 1945; All, Here, and Now: Black Politics in South Africa in the 1980s *(with Bill Nasson), and many others including most recently,* Red Road to Freedom: A History of the South African Communist Party 1921–2021

'For those of us who were in the struggle, enduring as we did countless years of detention and many periods of brutalisation and torture, and to have seen so many of our friends killed so tragically, it is heartening now to read Rory's manuscript that puts so much from those years into one document.

'And to see so many "unsung heroes", Dr Njongwe, Ernest Malgas, Henry Fazzie, Ivy Gcina and others, all less well-known than the Mandelas, etc. – to see them also now placed clearly in the picture of our struggle – this is great.'
– Mkhuseli 'Khusta' Jack, author of To Survive and Succeed, *businessman, former president of the Port Elizabeth Youth Congress (PEYCO), and spokesperson for the Port Elizabeth consumer boycott*

'Rory Riordan's manuscript shows "why" and "how" the Eastern Cape was the bedrock of black opposition to apartheid from the earliest times.

'Drawing from many sources, including the archives of the Human Rights Trust and *Monitor* magazine – both of which he founded – Riordan shows how the apartheid security juggernaut was stopped by the black township communities of Port Elizabeth and Uitenhage.

'Powerfully argued, and a compelling read, this work is a major contribution to our understanding of the end of white minority rule in South Africa.'
– *Peter Vale, Senior Research Fellow, Centre for the Advancement of Scholarship, University of Pretoria, and Nelson Mandela Professor of Politics Emeritus, Rhodes University*

'The Eastern Cape and in particular Port Elizabeth were, during the 1980s, the prime focus and target of the state security police. I lived through that time, and participated in the anti-apartheid struggle. I have always felt that there has been a critical need for an in-depth history of that time to be written by somebody who lived in our city, knew the activists and what was going on, and had an understanding of what took place during a time when the townships of Port Elizabeth and Uitenhage were literally on fire. Now, at last, Rory Riordan has written a book that, importantly, will fill that big gap in the political and "struggle" history of South Africa. I hope it will be widely read.'
– *Judy Chalmers, Black Sash chairperson in the 1980s, ANC Member of Parliament from 1994 to 2015*

'I joined the ANC in 1954 when I returned to Port Elizabeth from Healdtown. I was immediately plunged into assembling demands for the Freedom Charter, and into enacting the M-Plan.

'Since then every day of my life has been in the service of the struggle – serving uMkhonto we Sizwe in the underground; in the sabotage campaign of the early 1960s; then arrest and fourteen years on Robben Island; thereafter banned and house-arrested for another five; then five more years in jail, this time as a state of emergency detainee in both states of emergency in the 1980s.

'With the unbanning of the ANC in 1990 I became its first regional chairperson (for Port Elizabeth and Uitenhage) and in 1994 I became a member of parliament in Cape Town, for nearly twenty years. I became Mayor of Nelson Mandela Municipality in 2013.

'Through my recent years I have encouraged participants in the struggle to write down their experiences, lest it all be forgotten. I am working on my autobiography now.

'It is with delight that I have read Rory's manuscript – for the first time we have a well-researched and comprehensive account of those difficult, terrible and yet wonderful years of the struggle.

'I await its publication with excitement and hope – I couldn't recommend it more enthusiastically.'
– *Nkosinathi Benson Fihla, ANC and struggle veteran*

'I welcome the manuscript of the history of our area, put together so painstakingly and so factually by Rory, with open arms.

'Starting from the earliest of times, and moving forward to the war of the 1980s, he has put it all together in a continuous story that is very readable and very informative.

'I wish Rory's document had been available when I was a lecturer, and I hope a publisher will make it widely available now, for teachers and students both to use.'
– *Danny Jordaan, President of the South African Football Association, ANC Member of Parliament from 1994, former senior lecturer in History at Dower Teachers Training College*

'A meticulous account of the "Struggle" bringing to the surface many of the forgotten faces and many of the forgotten facts. In reading it I became convinced that "truth telling" is the key to any hopeful future for RSA.'
– *Bishop George Irvine, Methodist Bishop of Port Elizabeth and surrounds, 1976 to 1996*

'A riveting account of the hope and horror of a decisive decade. Moving forward, this will be regarded as an indispensable text for our understanding of that turbulent period.'
– *Etienne van Heerden, Emeritus Professor: University of Cape Town, editor of litnet.co.za, novelist and writer*

'There have been over a thousand books written about the 1899–1902 Boer War, and every year sees another number added to this oeuvre.

'By comparison, while there are a good few works on aspects of South Africa's period of insurrection to end apartheid, the 1980s, there are inexcusably few books that approach this period in a comprehensive way. And of this few, still fewer approach this period through the lens of the township revolt that was, in fact, the engine of this period of insurrection. And again, of these very few, I am unaware of any that concentrate on the Eastern Cape townships, the most contested terrain, over this period.

'That was until Riordan's work. Riordan's *Apartheid's Stalingrad* is, to my knowledge, the first comprehensive work detailing South Africa's 1980s period of revolt focusing on the townships of the Eastern Cape. For that alone it deserves a special place in the literature of the apartheid period. But it is more too – for it is a determinedly easy-flowing read, lively and enjoyable, while also well researched with much original material from the archives of Port Elizabeth's Human Rights Trust and its magazine *Monitor*.

'This is a valuable volume in a very limited literature on a massively important period of history.'
– *Deon Pretorius, Nelson Mandela University*

APARTHEID'S STALINGRAD

How the townships of the Eastern Cape
defied the apartheid war machine

RORY RIORDAN

With 18 portraits by David Goldblatt

First published by Jacana Media (Pty) Ltd in 2022

10 Orange Street
Sunnyside
Auckland Park 2092
South Africa
+2711 628 3200
www.jacana.co.za

© Rory Riordan, 2022
© Goldblatt portraits: David Goldblatt.
These portraits are included in the book with the kind permission of the Goldblatt family
© Cover photograph: Alf Kumalo/Africa Media Online
© Endpaper photograph: Peter Auf der Heyde
The crowd Nelson Mandela addressed in Motherwell, Port Elizabeth, 1 April 1990

All rights reserved.

ISBN 978-1-4314-3280-6

Also available as an ebook.

Cover design by Aimèe Armstrong
Editing by John Young
Proofreading by Russell Martin
Indexing by Rita Sephton
Set in Ehrhardt MT Std 10,5pt/14pt
Printed and bound by ABC Press, Cape Town
Job no. 003957

See a complete list of Jacana titles at www.jacana.co.za

Contents

PART THREE
APARTHEID COMES TUMBLING DOWN

Acknowledgements

Many, many years ago, when I was a tall, thin pre-teen, we lived in a world with no computers, no cellphones, no internet and no television. But we had books.

My mother, the most important and trustworthy companion I have had in a long life filled with many marvellous people, used to take my brother Denis and myself once a month to Main Street (now that part of Govan Mbeki Street between the City Hall and Russell Road) where she would do her 'monthly shop'. To effect this exercise with two hyperactive pre-teens she needed a cool head and a plan. She had both.

She would walk us to the sea-side of Main Street, where there was a flight of stairs going down, to below street level. Down we would go, my brother and I now beset with energy and enthusiasm, like two puppies seeing the Boss picking up their leads.

The stairs came out at Basil Fogarty's Bookshop, for us a treasure trove beyond imagining. After a few whispered words with Basil, Mother would pat us on our heads, and depart to do the shopping. Denis and I would sit on Basil's floor at the back of his house of delights (there was a globe in a glass case and maps on the walls!), and Basil would feed us with books to read and inspect. There was not a squeak from either of us until Mother returned.

Basil has long gone, but his wonderful shop continues even in our digital age. It is now owned and run by Resa, Basil's daughter, who has, over the years, taken sizable chunks of my salary cheques (remember them?) in exchange for the stock I still have, which stock made *Apartheid's Stalingrad* possible.

Basil's other daughter, Bridget, is now Jacana Media, and is the publisher of this book. Direct and unfussed by the need for over-politeness, she took on this book within half an hour of receiving my email asking for her help, and has been an invaluable guide through the tortuous rapids of my first book. Thank you, Bridget – when it is all over, I hope you will still talk to me.

There is another debt that I owe Bridget, for she returned John Young into my life, not as the longstanding friend that he is, but now as my editor.

John has toiled heroically to bring order and punctuation to my chaotic text, and I have come to believe that if it has any good points, the credit is his. The failings, of course, (including the too liberal and regular use of the phrase 'of course') are clearly mine alone.

I owe Basil and his daughters much, and hopefully will continue to add to that debt in Resa's shop and in Bridget's publishing business, until time draws a veil over memory, and reading and writing are no longer possible.

Rhodes University in Grahamstown was where my education began. Was it Bernard Shaw who wrote 'My education was temporarily interrupted by my schooling'? In the Philosophy Department, to be precise, where we were given essay topics and, when we asked for a reading list, were pointed to the library across the road. Books, bloody books. Why do so many educators still believe that rote memorising is education?

Here I formed some of the most important friendships of my life: John de Reuck, Chuck Volpe, Jan Raath and Bennie van Rensburg, and, of course, Zoe Lambiris, who was so foolish as to marry me. Three remarkable sons later (Dominic, now in Vienna, and Jonathan and Tristam, both now in Dublin), these friendships are now more solid than they were during the times of massive turbulence for our country and for this human rights worker.

The year 1977 was a turning point for me. It was the year that Andrew Savage invited me to join his campaign team, to attempt to get him elected as MP for Walmer in that year's general election. In this team was Flip Potgieter and hovering around in the background was George Irvine, too absorbed in his church duties and the requirement for neutrality they demanded to join a campaign he nevertheless encouraged.

These three men became the backbone of my life. Andrew and I founded the Human Rights Trust in 1986 after his running mate, Molly Blackburn, had so tragically died. We worked together through those intense times until he left us while still so young, in 1990. Flip Potgieter and I made personal contact possibly daily for over 40 years, until he too went on in 2018. And, wonderfully, George is still with us, a beacon of morality and a friend to thousands. His advice and counselling have moved hundreds of people to a better life – only his overwhelming humility and selflessness prevent him from being overtaken by pride in a lifetime dedicated to others.

Thus was formed my link with South Africa's insurrectionist politics and its many fantastic people.

While Andrew, Flip and George were my bedrock, so many others entered my life as our country became overwhelmed by the failures of apartheid, providing thousands with the energy to rebel, each in his or her own way, against a clearly monstrous political dispensation.

Van Zyl Slabbert and Helen Suzman both became friends whose advice and opinions I was privileged to share. Khusta Jack, Michael Xego, Ivy Gcina, Ernest Malgas, Phil Goduka, Gugile Nkwinti, Mtwabo Ndube, Sandy Stewart, Raymond Mhlaba, Govan Mbeki and Judy Chalmers were also both hugely admired and closely befriended. If friendships with fine people are a measure of wealth, nobody could match my riches.

Then there were the incredible people who made the Human Rights Trust what it was. After Andrew as Chairman came Thole Majodina and then George Irvine. Also as Trustees were Peter Vale, Danny Jordaan, Gavin Blackburn, Nonkosi Mhlantla (now a Judge on the Constitutional Court), Dayalin Chetty, Errol Moorcroft and Ian Macdonald from Grahamstown, Doug Walters and Flip Potgieter. Who can boast such a group of fellow soldiers?

The staff were such a team: Sithile Zondani, my deputy, so calm and thorough; Lesley Frescura, Amber Cummins, Xoliswa Kani, Friday France, Juliette Opperman, David Melunsky and many others over the about 15 years the Trust endured, including the amazing Shaan Curtis, who typed every word I wrote for *Monitor* magazine and for the *Herald* newspaper, and who covered my back through much turmoil.

These were the people of my years up to the end of the *Apartheid's Stalingrad* story.

Since then more riches have come my way.

In 1999 I married Melissa, and now Simon and Michael/Amy complete my second family. They are now the treasures of my every day. Fortunately, we still live under one roof, and, surprisingly, we still enjoy that arrangement and the company. Melissa did not come alone, for her parents, Dad Prof. André Lemmer, now sadly no longer with us, and Mom Isobel, the daughter of Alfred Porter, once the Chief Librarian of Port Elizabeth's library service, live down the road in the wonderful village of Schoenmakerskop. Books thus seem to follow me everywhere and this one would not have been completed had Isobel not provided us with an inverter to remove the vicissitudes of Eskom from my writing schedule.

My commitment to recording the apartheid past has one final foundation – the Red Location Museum and Cultural Precinct.

The idea for this precinct came from Ernest Malgas, whom you will discover more about as you page through *Apartheid's Stalingrad*. It fell on us, the first ANC councillors of Port Elizabeth, to make it happen. In this exercise I met Jo Noero, an architect of unmatched genius, who won the architectural competition to design the precinct. Jo quickly became a close friend and we have walked the years of the Red Location together, and, my heavens, these years have had their ups and downs. Jo's and Albie Sachs's company on this journey has been fundamental in keeping me sane, so dramatic has been the Red Location journey.

This all has been the underlying dynamic, the personal relationships and the political experience that have made *Apartheid's Stalingrad* possible. I thank them, one and all, for putting up with me over the many years that this book has been in process. I admire their patience, and hope the book will be better company than I have been.

One final 'thank you'.

Every writer, I'm sure, knows those midnight awakenings, when a perfect phrase has presented itself, or (more likely) the understanding dawns that the afternoon's writing includes a paragraph so turgid as to need immediate excision.

Up you get, abandoning a warm and comfortable bed for the cold of the dining room, where the laptop is to be opened and the necessary adjustments to the text are to be carried out.

I had many such moments in the writing of *Apartheid's Stalingrad* and, through all that discomfort, I had one companion. For Max, the black-and-white cat, would also decamp from the warm bed, and spring onto the dining room table, there to sit on my keypad, sleep on my notes and knock over my piles of reference books before falling back into sleep on the cold wood of the table.

Max, thank you for putting my company above your comfort. I have no idea why you did so, but it is greatly appreciated. Now you can sit on a completed book, surely a just reward for such faithfulness.

A photographic genius
and a great friend

W e'd just finished the second edition of *Monitor* magazine, and I was in Cape Town. I had lunch with Dene Smuts, and she praised our efforts, but noted that what *Monitor* needed was decent photographs.

I couldn't have agreed more. Dene then suggested that I phone David Goldblatt.

David already enjoyed an international reputation – his photographs were in galleries all over the world. And he had recently done many extraordinary portraits for *Leadership* magazine. It was inconceivable that we could afford David, which I told Dene.

She replied that David didn't think like that – I should just phone him.

I did.

And so began one of the great experiences of my life.

We did many interviews together – I asking the questions, David wandering around the room, putting on and turning off lights – 'Don't notice me – pretend I'm not here' – opening and closing curtains and clicking away.

The next day the pics would be developed (yes, all film then) and David would say, 'This is your portrait.' When he had made up his mind, I quickly learned that the subject was closed.

When all the political activists were freed from state of emergency detention in 1990, I phoned David and asked if he would come to Port Elizabeth and take a series of portraits for use at some future date in *Monitor*. He came, spent a week here, and the result is in this book. They are, in my opinion, infinitely more valuable than my text.

Thank you, David, for these spectacular portraits. And thank you to the David Goldblatt Trust, comprising mostly David's family, for permission to use them.

David was not just one of South Africa's greatest artists, he was also one of the most principled men I have ever met and one of the most interesting companions I have ever spent time with.

Thanks for the grand times, David, and the moral example you set. You were a genius and your portraits bring to life these personalities in a way my words can't. Live forever, Friend.

Introduction

On 10 October 1979 the Zwide and KwaZakhele Residents' Associations agreed to amalgamate, which they did under the name Port Elizabeth Black Civic Organisation (PEBCO). Thozamile Botha was elected as its chairperson. It then began South Africa's first mass mobilisation of the modern era.

Exactly three months later, on 10 January 1980, Botha and his executive were detained and banned. Botha ended up selling potatoes on the side of the road as he (and his colleagues) were prohibited from entering the premises of formal employment. Unable to earn enough to feed himself, he fled South Africa and joined the African National Congress (ANC) in exile. PEBCO fell dormant.

Three months was all the space the 'system' allowed black mobilisation at the end of 1979. Just ten years later, in February 1990, the ANC, the Communist Party of South Africa (SACP), the Pan Africanist Congress (PAC) and other mass-based black organisations were unbanned. Mandela and his Rivonia colleagues were unconditionally freed and South Africa was irrevocably set on the road to universal franchise and an agreed democratic political dispensation.

What had happened in the ten years of the 1980s that caused this massive, unimaginable change?

That is what this writing hopes to set out.

The underlying theme is that the security juggernaut of the apartheid regime, Africa's most advanced and equipped military force at the time, was fought to a standstill in the black townships of Port Elizabeth and Uitenhage in 1985 and 1986. Certainly it was not destroyed then, and it rose up to inflict its many horrors for many more years, but it was never again going to be able to subdue those communities into quiescence.

The black townships of Port Elizabeth and Uitenhage were apartheid's Stalingrad.

Yes, after the battle of Stalingrad the Nazi armies could and did fight on for another three years, but up until Stalingrad these armies had won almost every engagement they had entered into. After Stalingrad, they endured only years of sapping defeats. So it was with the apartheid security juggernaut – up until the 1985 and 1986 Port Elizabeth and Uitenhage black township war, the apartheid war machine had subdued all attempts to overwhelm it. From 1986 on, it also endured only sapping defeats, until stalemate became obvious and negotiations had to happen.[1]

The story does not begin or end in the apparent stalemate at the end of 1986.

In writing about massive historical events, any writer stands on the shoulders of many predecessors – that's how every successive generation of commentators learns to see further and is able to write a fuller account. In this latticework of evolving stories that go back and back, where does one find a beginning?

In truth there is no first story. Stephen Hawking has written that the universe began with infinite heat being compacted to infinite density, causing the 'Big Bang' – where then did 'infinite heat' come from?

To find my 'beginning', I have taken the advice of a reliable friend, 'start at the very beginning, and tell the first bits quickly'. This I have done.

The book is divided into three parts.

The first part begins, as I have promised, as close to the beginning as makes sense.

During the Second World War, in 1942, as part of the now burgeoning Xhosa-speaking population of Algoa Bay, a 22-year-old lad arrived, with his father, looking for work. His name was Raymond Mhlaba, and, from shortly after his arrival, the settled and uneventful politics of this time and this place were to change irreversibly and massively.

Six years later, in the whites-only election of 1948, another tsunami engulfed us. The party of formal apartheid, the Herenigde Nasionale Party, pushed aside the geriatric and complacent United Party of the legendary Jan Smuts and became the government in South Africa. Trouble was ahead.

Great structural and political changes now happened in government as the National Party cemented in apartheid as best they could. Similar changes were going on in Ray Mhlaba's African National Congress, which rapidly learned new and more dramatic techniques of confrontation.

The Defiance Campaign of 1952 brought a new approach to fighting injustice, with Ray Mhlaba, Wilton Mkwayi and Dr James Njongwe's teams in Port Elizabeth showing South Africans how to accept suffering in the cause of freedom as they were jailed in greater numbers here than elsewhere in the country.

In 1955 Govan Mbeki arrived in Port Elizabeth to re-energise both the ANC and the burnt-out Ray Mhlaba, and the area became mobilised and active on an on-going basis.

In 1960 the Pan Africanist Congress, having broken from the ANC, had its first mobilisation – an anti-pass laws set of protests that ended in the disaster that was the massacre at Sharpeville – and South Africa cracked open. A state of emergency saw mass detentions and the ANC, the PAC, and the SACP were banned. Returning from detention, the ANC leadership went underground and then turned to armed revolt. The military wing, kept at arm's length from the ANC, was called Umkhonto we Sizwe.

Sabotage campaigns now began. The gloves were off.

Mhlaba, Mkwayi and Mbeki were now joined by an extraordinary character, Harold Strachan the bomb-maker. Together they made and set more explosive devices in Port Elizabeth than anywhere else in the country. This, however, came at a terrible price and the three-man central command of Umkhonto we Sizwe in Port Elizabeth. Vuyisile Mini, Wilson Khayinga and Zinakile Mkaba, were arrested, tried and executed. The security police were now rampant, and arrests and deaths in detention were everyday occurrences.

Then came the arrests at Lilliesleaf Farm and the Rivonia Trial. The core energy of the Port Elizabeth ANC, Govan Mbeki and Ray Mhlaba, was arrested and sent to Robben Island, seemingly forever. Mhlaba had taken over as head of Umkhonto from Mandela, and on Mhlaba's arrest the poisoned chalice was passed to Wilton Mkwayi. He too was then arrested, and at the end of a trial now called 'Little Rivonia', he also went to Robben Island for 'life'.

A quiet now settled in, as Oliver Tambo structured an exile existence for the ANC and the men of apartheid armed and prepared. In Port Elizabeth the wonderful and lively South End, a large and long-standing mixed-race suburb, was razed and most ANC leaders, national and local, were in jail.

Then came 1976, a political explosion that showed that quiescence was never to last and, despite the brutal murder campaign by the Port Elizabeth security police – including the murder of the brilliant and charismatic Steve Biko – that followed the student uprising, the white electorate was unfazed and gave the National Party its biggest-ever majority in parliament after the 1977 election.

They needed it, for the next challenge was soon on the horizon. The young Thozamile Botha, in a deft and exciting set of manoeuvres, set up the Port Elizabeth Black Civic Organisation in 1979. Alas, it was immediately put to the sword and lasted only three months but it was to prove to be only the first iteration of this organisation. It would later be a full battalion in the army that eventually defeated apartheid.

So ends Part One.

Now for Part Two.

Part Two covers only ten years, the decade of the 1980s. It is divided into five periods: 1980–84; 1985; 1986; 1987 and 1988; and 1989.

The earliest period, 1980–84, was the period of the government's first strategy in the pursuit of sharing power while not losing any: the strategy was 'Reform', to accommodate what was described as the 'legitimate political expectations of moderate blacks', while at the same time 'Repression' was for all blacks who would not become 'moderate blacks'.

The tricameral parliament, along with labour reforms, was imposed on the country. On the other side of the fence, the creation of the United Democratic Front as the principal organisation in opposition to this parliament happened, almost spontaneously. In Port Elizabeth and Uitenhage UDF-affiliated organisations mushroomed and PEBCO was joined by the Port Elizabeth and Uitenhage Youth Congresses (PEYCO and UYCO), two women's congresses and a Uitenhage PEBCO look-alike, URECO. A supervising and coordinating body, the UDF East Cape, was also elected, with Edgar Ngoyi as President, Henry Fazzie as his deputy, and a wide range of other executives: Derrick Swartz, Ernest Malgas, Mtwabo Ndube, Mkhuseli Jack, Stone Sizani, Matthew Goniwe and others.

Initially the fights were two: the UDF against the tricameral parliament and the UDF against the local Black Councils in Port Elizabeth (Kayamnandi Council) and in Uitenhage (KwaNobuhle Council). In late 1984, however, the storm clouds began to form and a determined, broad-based insurrection began in the Vaal Triangle and Uitenhage simultaneously.

The second period of Part Two covers 1985 in Port Elizabeth and Uitenhage. This was the most horrific and blood-soaked year in the history of this metropole and possibly of any metropole in South Africa. It is also the period which saw the beginning of the end of apartheid.

Many terrible events happened, from the Langa massacre (21 March) and the ensuing brutal necklacing of the family of the last KwaNobuhle councillor, Benjamin Kinikini; the state-orchestrated AZAPO–UDF clashes, with all their horror; the detention, torture and brutal killing of the PEBCO executives Hashe, Galela and Godolozi; the UDF's extraordinarily successful consumer boycott; the detention and brutal murder of Matthew

Goniwe and his three colleagues; their enormous funeral; the first state of emergency and the brutalisation of detainees until the Wendy Orr interdict stopped that; the disinvestment of the Ford Motor Company; and the slow inversion of power, from the state to the UDF, as negotiations relating to the consumer boycott began; the Black Council, now the Ibhayi Town Council, was slowly disappearing into oblivion; and the introduction of an alternative type of local government in the townships was underway.

Nationally, disaster also followed disaster, with regional destabilisation particularly of Angola and Mozambique being exposed for the hypocritical fraud that it was, which left apartheid's last international allies speechless. Then PW Botha delivered the Rubicon speech, which left apartheid's last allies infuriated. The end result was that sanctions were piling up.

1985 ended for the UDF with a triumph (the founding of COSATU) and a disaster (the death of Molly Blackburn).

1986 was a less bloody but equally contested year, and is the subject of Period Three of Part Two.

The Commonwealth sent an Eminent Persons Group to South Africa with the express intention of somehow getting the state and the ANC to begin talking. It began well, with PW Botha calling off the state of emergency and access to Nelson Mandela was allowed. However, it ended in disaster, with the South African airforce bombing our neighbouring countries, claiming they were bombing ANC bases, something PW Botha said clearly he would continue to do.

Then the government embarked on two back-to-back massive forced removals, of the Crossroads community in Cape Town and the Langa community in Uitenhage.

These were the first indications of the government's new strategy – its second strategy – based on the theories of an American counter-revolutionary expert, Colonel John McCuen. McCuen believed that a five-stage process was necessary to win a war against a revolutionary opponent: first, the revolution must be crushed, at whatever cost and however messy; second, the damaged institutions of government must be rebuilt; third, service delivery on a massive scale must be effected; fourth, this must be accompanied by a convincing propaganda campaign; and finally, difficult areas must be destabilised, and then brought under control.

Defence Minister Magnus Malan and PW Botha repeatedly came to Port Elizabeth to push this new philosophy along. A second state of emergency was called and now white activists were also detained. McCuen's strategy was given massive resources, but it just never worked in this community.

At the end of 1986 government was stumped. They could subdue the townships of Port Elizabeth, yes, but they couldn't change their ANC–UDF loyalty, they couldn't rebuild the black local authorities and the next flare-up was just one issue away. The game was up, for all the horror they had thrown at it.

For the government there were only two cards left to play, or rather another new strategy, now their third strategy: negotiate with the enemy while you destabilise them undercover.

The years 1987 to 1989, the fourth and fifth section of Part Two, cover this period.

Negotiations began with Nelson Mandela, a willing negotiator, and continued both within South Africa and outside. In both cases, the ANC wiped the floor with the men of apartheid.

Our story covers all of this, as it threads its way through the last three years of the 1980s, and through the last two wars of apartheid: the Namibian War of Independence, fought to another defeat for the men of apartheid, this time in the Angolan bush in 1988; and finally the 'War of Endless Massacres', the war fought in the Inkatha-dominant lands of Natal and around the Inkatha hostels in the Transvaal, in which collusion between the South African security forces and Inkatha saw about 15 000 civilians massacred, particularly between 1990 and 1994. This cascade of civilian blood only slowed when Judge Goldstone published the story of the collaboration between Inkatha and the South African security forces in 1994. This was the war to destabilise the ANC. It also failed miserably.

By then apartheid was moribund and a month later the elections of 1994 finished it off.

Part Three is short and is, of all things, a happy ending.

For it starts with the release of Nelson Mandela and the overwhelming reception South Africans gave him. The Mandela Years were still four intense and blood-soaked years away, but now we could see the finishing flag. And, of course, we got there in 1994. And we had five years of Mandela's magic presidency.

Isn't that a happy ending?

That is the story of the story on which you are now to embark.

When you finish reading, I hope that you, the reader, can come to know and respect the immensely courageous people whose fortitude and capacity to absorb suffering have been the bedrock upon which our current democracy and freedom are built.

Part One

FROM EARLY TIMES TO 1979

I

The ANC gets onto its feet
in Port Elizabeth

The second decade of the twentieth century saw great turbulence in Europe, with the continent's major countries entering a massive war, now called the First World War.

South Africa had only been unified into a single country for four years when this war broke out and the then white government of Prime Minister General Louis Botha quickly joined Britain's side, diverting many of South Africa's very limited resources and many of our young men's lives to this far-away conflict.

These world-shaking events did not penetrate all of the new country of South Africa, and in the little village of Mazoka, between the headwaters of the Tyhume and Koonap rivers in what is now the district of Fort Beaufort in the ancestral land of King Maqoma, a young man whose name was Mxokozeli (I will give you his full name after a few suspenseful moments) did what young men have always done – he fell in love. His beloved, Dinah Mnyazi, was, however, from a wealthy home and when the Mxokozeli family delegation approached Dinah's father to ask him to consent to the marriage of Mxokozeli and Dinah, Dinah's father sent them away empty-handed. They were, for him, too poor.

Mxokozeli was not one to give up easily and he persisted until Dinah's father eventually consented. As part of his wedding present Dinah's father gave the young couple a horse, so that if his daughter tired of this unequal marriage, could ride back to her father. For his part, and as a sign of his commitment, Mxokozeli went off to the mines of Kimberley and Johannesburg to earn his lobola money. The wages proved disappointing, so in 1916 Mxokozeli joined the police force and worked as a policeman for 24 years until 1940.

Mxokozeli and Dinah had eight children. Horrifyingly, five of these died in infancy. Only the last three survived, the eldest being a boy, whom they named Raymond Mphakamisi, and of course he took his father's name, Mhlaba.

Raymond Mhlaba was born in Mazoka on 12 February 1920. He was to become one of South Africa's great heroes and to out-live the cruelties of the apartheid years which he fought with all of his considerable energy and at immense personal cost.

'I spent my early life in Mazoka village. Like many boys of my age, I learned to work in the family fields as a herd boy', Mhlaba recorded in his memoirs.[2] His father was rarely home, for, as a policeman, he was posted all over the Transkei to a variety of rural police stations. Raymond and his mother formed a bond of great affection, and, unlike the common gender-defined roles of the time, he was happy to be with her, working in the kitchen if that was what was required to be near her.

At the age of nine he entered the Mazoka mission school, but three years later he fell ill. As all of his elder siblings had died in their early years, his parents were deeply concerned and decided that the family should move to Balfour where his father was then posted, to be together. Thus young Raymond entered the Balfour Mission School and passed everything, year by year, until he finished Standard 5.

His health had recovered by then and his parents were comfortable to send him to Healdtown Practising School, a boarding school. There he obtained his Standard 6 certificate and his father then sent him to initiation, a 30-day process.

He was back at Healdtown, and says that 'it was at this point in my life that the seeds of my political consciousness were sown ... it was a Mr Sigila, a teacher at Mxhelo, a village almost halfway between Fort Beaufort and Alice, who first introduced me to political concerns'.

Sigala recruited students from the educational institutions of Healdtown, Lovedale and Fort Hare. They formed the Mayibuye Students Association, where they all, as members, undertook to educate their families on particularly the land dispossession issues and other grievances the African community endured. 'Our membership was not big, not more than twenty members', and the Association did not survive their dispersion into the wider world. But it was Raymond's political blooding.

When Raymond was 20, in 1940, his father retired from the police force after 24 years of service. All the elder Mhlaba's pension money was spent buying a plot of land to enable him to farm and thereby support his family.

It did not work and the elder Mhlaba again left his family in search of a paying job, this time journeying to Port Elizabeth. There he found employment as a security guard at the Shell Oil Company. 'However, the wages he earned were so meagre that the following year he decided that I should come and find work in PE.'

Thus, in 1942, began Raymond Mhlaba's years in Port Elizabeth.

The two Mhlabas, father and son, found a flat in Hart Street, Sidwell, which they rented together. Port Elizabeth was then under a liberal City Council, which rejected and refused to apply the pass laws, curfews and compulsory registration. It was seen as a relatively benign place for Africans to live. As the war effort had drawn many young white workers off to military service, there were even jobs for Africans.

'I was employed at the Nannucci Drycleaning and Launderers within a week of arriving at PE,' remembers Mhlaba. 'The workforce at Nannucci was made up predominantly of coloured women' and they immediately recruited the 22-year-old Raymond into the Non-European Laundry Workers Union (LWU).

'I did not have prior knowledge of labour politics and union activities. I did not have a theoretical or practical framework of how the labour movement operated. I knew absolutely nothing about the workers' strikes. I had no experience of confrontations between employees and employers. I had not learned these matters at school nor from my father ... My father did not join any of the workers' unions. My father was almost indifferent to my interest in the union movement. I merely followed my intuition that I was doing the right thing to join the LWU.'

Now Mhlaba's political education began in earnest, as did his circle of political comrades. He began attending union meetings regularly at the offices of the Council of Non-European Trade Unions (CNETU) in Queen Street. There he met and worked with a circle of African unionists including Gladstone Tshume, Clifford Dladla, Reuben Mfecane, Sam Ntunja and Adam Mati. These comrades were to become the hard core of his political circle, his right and left hands, in his emerging years in the Communist Party and later the ANC.

But first a period of human behaviour. After a year at Nannucci's,

Raymond's mother, fearing for her husband's health, insisted that Raymond's father return home to rest. In the absence of paternal discipline, Raymond met, courted, won and married Joyce Meke, also from Mazoka but now working as a domestic worker in Port Elizabeth. They married quietly at the new law courts in 1943. This was a mistake, for his beloved mother was heartbroken. She had for years looked forward to planning her only son's wedding – now that was never to happen. It took years for the relationship to repair.

In that same year, Raymond's regular attendance at union meetings earned him the executive position as a recruiting officer for the LWU.

In early 1943 Clifford Dladla invited Raymond to a meeting of the Communist Party of South Africa (CPSA). Their regular Sunday morning meetings were Raymond's first experience of non-racialism as the CPSA drew members from all races, who openly and on equal terms discussed the affairs of the day. 'This impressed me profoundly and in 1943, on Mayday, I joined the Party officially.' He soon found that all of his close comrades were also in the CPSA.

'It was at the Party meetings that I heard about the African National Congress, a political organisation that was non-racial … I realised that I ought to be a member of that organisation … I believed that a true African communist ought to belong to the ANC … other party comrades encouraged me to join the ANC and I did so in 1944.'

He found that he had joined an organisation in disarray. 'The ANC at national level was moribund during the early 1940s … there was even less political activity at provincial and local levels,' he remembers.

In Port Elizabeth the ANC only got into action once a year, to send a delegation to the organisation's 16 December national conference. They would take the hat around to a small number of white liberal households to raise the money to send a small delegation to the conference. They had no fundraising projects, no bank account and no money. Worse still, the ANC provincial conference was traditionally opened with a speech from the (white) mayor, whose speeches 'sounded patronising and insincere'. To cap it all, the most effective method of mobilising, the mass protestation of grievances, was unused. Raymond Mhlaba was not going to live with this inactivity for long.

One man can do a lot, but a well-motivated team can do so much more. Mhlaba was soon surrounded in the ANC by his comrades from the unions and the CPSA – Gladstone Tshume, Clifford Dladla, Reuben Mfecane, Sam Ntunja, Adam Mati, Caleb Mayekiso, Vuyisile Mini and Wilton Mkwayi. Together they took over the ANC and breathed new life into it. They were joined by comrades from all racial groups – Lilian Diedericks, Mohammed Desai, Dr Yusuf Dadoo and even a small number of white activists, including Gus Coe and Arnold Latti.

By April 1945 the *Guardian* could run an article on the new blood that had brought the ANC in Port Elizabeth to the status of a mass representative movement. What Mhlaba was later to call a 'pattern of overlapping membership' operated now as a 'task force', giving the ANC energy and an intellectual underpinning. 'We came from diverse backgrounds – rich and poor, educated and illiterate … there was even a joke that we were umvubu, a "mixed bag".'

What was needed to really get things moving was a protestable issue, and this the Port Elizabeth City Council handed them in 1945 with an unreasonable rent increase in McNamee village.

The CNETU initiated the setting up the McNamee Anti-Increase Rental Action Committee and a mass protest meeting was called in New Brighton. Nine speakers, from a wide range of organisations, gave solidarity to the McNamee residents.

Soon the protests spread to the Coloured areas of Schauderville and Korsten. And the issues started to grow in numbers, appalling living conditions and much else.

'The rent issue dragged on for more than a year … eventually the PECC finally dropped the idea of increasing the rent in McNamee … the ANC, African People's Organisation, Cape Indian Congress, CPSA, the New Brighton Civic Organisation and the trade unions all worked together to support the McNamee community. This joint effort signalled the beginning of a culture of militancy and popular support for the political struggles against injustices that the white government – local, provincial and national – imposed on the people … it signalled the beginning of racial cooperation and collective mass protest action in Port Elizabeth,' remembers Raymond Mhlaba. He had arrived in South African politics.

'My active involvement in the rent protest impressed upon my fellow comrades my commitment to the freedom struggle. I graduated into leadership positions. In 1946 I was nominated as district secretary of the Party. The ANC's New Brighton branch elected me as chairperson in 1947. The Laundry Workers Union expected me to carry on with my responsibility of organising workers. One of the challenges I dealt with immediately, as a leader, was the British royal visit in March 1947.'

The extended visit to South Africa by the British royal family was to present the emerging ANC with their second campaign after the McNamee rental issues. It was to be nothing like as successful.

The royal family was to visit Port Elizabeth, and the Port Elizabeth City Council intended to spare nothing in making their stay memorable. New Brighton was to form part of the itinerary. A special road was built, to be called the King's Road, to bring the royal family there. In New Brighton the royals were to see the home of Limba, which was, by township standards, a mansion, and a cow was to be slaughtered as celebration. Local performers were to sing and dance for the royal party.

Both the Communist Party and the New Brighton ANC, with Raymond Mhlaba on both executives, considered this visit carefully. Both decided to ask the residents of New Brighton to boycott the food and the performances as they believed that the royal family lived in Britain with excessive privileges in a society torn apart by class divisions. Furthermore, the royal visit to New Brighton was obviously avoiding the areas where black people lived in abject conditions – the Red and White locations and the hostels. 'The South African government and the Port Elizabeth City Council were presenting a false picture to the royal family regarding race relations in South Africa,' Mhlaba remembers.

This campaign was not universally supported. Older residents did not want to disrespect the royals and many walked out of the ANC's meetings because of this.

In the end the boycott just held, but it became clear that mobilisation on issues remote from the day-to-day suffering of the African people should be approached with caution.

The Second World War was now over, and South Africa was suffering from food shortages. It rapidly became apparent to the Communist Party and the ANC that in South Africa food provision, like so much else, had a racial bias. White citizens, who controlled the industries and the commercial food outlets, looked after their own communities and the African community was denied an equal share in food supply.

In 1947 the Communist Party called for food rationing, with every family getting an equal supply, and called for public protest in this regard.

Three thousand people marched through Port Elizabeth, ending on the Donkin Reserve. They were led by members of Ray Mhlaba's 'mixed bag': Mohammed Desai, J Johnson, B Hutton, D Dingaan and, of course, Ray himself. They were charged with leading an illegal gathering, but somehow escaped censure.

As Thembeka Orie has written: 'From the procession during the food protest one could sample Communists, ANC members, teachers, Africans, Indians and whites. Such a heterogeneous group represented a foretaste of the coming Congress Alliance.'

Early in 1948 a strike broke out in the laundry industry in Port Elizabeth. Nannucci, Atlas, One-Day Cleaners and other laundries found their workforces demanding better wages and conditions. Mhlaba was, of course, central in organising and supporting the strikers.

The strike dragged on for a month. The laundry owners became desperate, and employed scab labour. 'When we saw smoke from our factory chimneys, we wondered who was working inside, was it the bosses themselves? Could they really do our jobs themselves? We then discovered that it was scab labour and we went inside to get the scabs out. We did not even think of the consequences, we just fought like nobody's business.'

After a month the strike was settled. The workers got their increases, but at a cost. Eighty workers, 'the troublemakers', were not re-employed. Of course this included the young Mhlaba. During the strike he had been offered, and had accepted, the job of a 'baas boy', which was essentially a management spy. He needed the money and took the job, while clearly not intending to do any spying. It did not save him. 'Troublemaker number one' was sacked and arrested with a crowd of comrades, under the Riotous Assemblies Act for the scab-busting event. Fortunately their lawyer did his work and they got suspended sentences.

Now difficulties settled on Ray's young family. He was out of work and desperately took on anything available. He became a waiter, and then a 'public bar boy'. They mostly had to live off his tiny allowance from the LWU. His wife, he laconically remarked years later, 'learned that she was married to a man already married to politics'. Their difficulties were just beginning.

In amongst the hundreds and thousands of comrades Raymond Mhlaba worked with, and mobilised for ANC duties, was a young man who was destined to make a huge mark on the ANC and on South Africa. His name was Zimasile Wilton Mkwayi and he arrived in the Port Elizabeth ANC community in 1946, as a 23-year-old.[3]

Mkwayi had been born in the village of Chwarhu in Middledrift in the Eastern Cape. He came from a typical rural family – neither of his parents had been schooled, he had six siblings (three of each, boys and girls) and the family was poor and further endured long absences from a father who had to seek work in the mines of Kimberley.

At the age of 12 Wilton's father sent him to work for an aging farmer in the Keiskammahoek area. Here Wilton learned to plough, plant and care for livestock. His farmer-employer saw potential in young Wilton, and enrolled him in the only local school for black children, a school run by the Presbyterian Church. Wilton arrived after his 12th birthday, and could stay only until he finished Standard 4. He tended livestock before and after school, and crops whenever possible. It was a busy life, but one Wilton would later look back on with pleasure.

Wilton's first experience of the real world that black South Africans endured happened when he was 17, in 1940.

The Second World War was raging (mostly) in Europe, and, with many young white men enlisting in the armed forces and leaving the country for military duties, the government went on recruitment drives for hands for the factories. The recruitment men requested King Sandile, the head of the Chwarhu community, to assemble young men for offers of employment.

Sandile was apparently unimpressed with the idea of sending his youngsters to fight in another man's war and didn't cooperate as was expected. For this defiance, he and his village were made to pay a heavy price – they were loaded onto government trucks, people and their belongings, and moved off to Zihlahleni. Others from their village were moved elsewhere. The united community was dispersed and Wilton's carefree childhood was ended with a white supremacist bang.

As a result of this enormous disruption to their lives and in an angry response to it, Wilton's father joined the ANC and also bought Wilton an ANC card. Not yet political, Wilton was not sure what to do with this membership, but time certainly provided the answer.

In 1943 Wilton relocated to Cape Town in search of work. He found work in Saldanha Bay as a construction labourer and thereafter moved to the dynamite factory at Somerset West as a store clerk. He was, in fact, the only black worker inside this plant.

Now his political education was to surge forward, for there was here an active group of young communists who ran classes in lifeskills and political education. Wilton learned about socialist theories of education, housing, trade unions and political rights and freedoms. It all made a lot of sense to a young, hugely intelligent black lad who had already tasted apartheid's boot, and had seen, in Cape Town, the vast lifestyle discrepancies between black and white.

In 1945 Wilton returned home, for his mother had died and his father had quit the mines. Here he met Thembeka Mosi and they fell in love. Regrettably, her parents were not impressed with an unemployed young politico and Wilton was pushed away by her family.

That resulted in him arriving in Port Elizabeth in 1946. Again he found work, firstly in a company called Locko, where he offloaded coal trucks. From there he moved to the docks as a sorter. This gave him much opportunity for overtime pay and he rapidly acquired a taste for fancy clothes and, of course, for girls. Somehow this led to a nickname that lasted all his life – 'Bri-Bri'.

He searched out discussion groups such as he had enjoyed in Cape Town, and here he met Raymond Mhlaba. No bright young African ever entered Mhlaba's company without soon becoming involved in political activity, and young Mkwayi was soon caught up in ANC and CPSA work and structures.

In later years, he stated from the dock in the trial that was to send him to Robben Island 'for life', that he first became politically active in Port Elizabeth in a rent campaign and bus boycotts,[4] and in an ANC Youth League one-day strike on 1 May 1950.

1950 saw Mkwayi leave his employment at the docks for a job at the big Metal Box factory as a store clerk working the night shift. He was not there long when the black staff called a strike. One of their comrades had, apparently, left his job to drink alcohol. He had been fired on his return to duty. While Wilton had not been there, he had no sympathy for the dismissed staff member who had repeatedly been warned by his comrades to leave alcohol out of work. Wilton was, ironically, one of over 100 workers dismissed for striking.

By now he was working with the unions and he was employed as a trade union organising secretary at the African Textile Workers' Union. He was also appointed in the run-up to the Defiance Campaign as Volunteer-in-Chief for the Eastern Cape under Raymond Mhlaba, who was the head of the Action Committee for the Eastern Cape. Both fell under Nelson Mandela, who was both Volunteer-in Chief for the country and chair of the National Action Committee.[5]

The Port Elizabeth way of doing things, joint membership of unions, CPSA and ANC, was again honoured. Mhlaba and Mkwayi now had a great task ahead.

Thus was the ANC in Port Elizabeth quickly coming to its feet. Strong leadership, overlapping with the unions and the CPSA, energetic mobilisation on issues inevitably presented by the white minority government, a willingness to confront whatever the consequences might be, and a more careful choice of the issues around which to mobilise, saw the Port Elizabeth ANC becoming a local and, for the ANC, a national force.

2

The party of apartheid
comes to power in 1948

While the ANC was finding its feet in Port Elizabeth, the national
political ground was to shake under it in 1948.

Since Union in 1910, South Africa had been governed by
a white parliament with three white Prime Ministers: Louis Botha of the
South African Party from 1910 to Botha's death in 1919; Jan Smuts from
then until he and his South African Party were unseated in the 1924 election;
JBM Hertzog of the National Party from 1924 until a coalition was formed
between the National Party and Smuts' South African Party in 1934 –
this coalition was called the United Party (UP), with Hertzog still Prime
Minister and Smuts now his deputy; then, in 1939 when Britain declared
war on Nazi Germany, the coalition broke, with the bulk of the United Party
caucus in parliament wanting to enter the war on Britain's side, following
Smuts' lead in that respect, and Hertzog, and many Afrikaans-speaking
South Africans, believing that South Africa should remain neutral, resigned
as Prime Minister and headed up an opposition minority in parliament.

Smuts was thus again Prime Minister from 1939 through the Second
World War and he was in this position when he called for a (whites-only)
election in 1948.

The two major parties in contestation for power in the 1948 election
were the United Party, led by Smuts, and the Herenigde Nasionale Party

(Reunited National Party, HNP) now lead by Dr Daniël François Malan, a minister in the Dutch Reformed Church.

Smuts was the preeminent South African in the international world in the first half of the 20th century, to be matched only by Nelson Mandela later in the century.

From his earliest to his last years, his achievements were unimaginable.

Born in 1870 on his father's farm near Malmesbury in the Cape Colony, he was destined not to be schooled, as the custom of the time in his world was that only the eldest son was to be formally educated, and Jan, as the second son, was to work on the farm. However, his older brother died early and so Jan entered school at the age of 12.

Within four years he had completed his schooling and earned a place at Victoria College in Stellenbosch, the forerunner of Stellenbosch University. Five years later he graduated with double first-class honours in Literature and Science and won the Ebden scholarship to Christ's College, Cambridge in England, where he again graduated with a double first. One of his tutors, Professor Maitland, described him as the best student he had ever taught and Lord Todd, the Master of Christ's College, later said that his college had produced three truly outstanding members in its 500 years: John Milton, Charles Darwin and Jan Smuts.

He then passed his barrister examinations at the Middle Temple in London in 1891, four years before a friend and foe of his later life did the same, Mohandas Gandhi.

Returning to the Cape Colony, Smuts briefly fell under the spell of Cecil John Rhodes. The Jameson Raid of 1895 ended that and he left for the South African Republic and service as Paul Kruger's State Attorney.

Then came the Second Boer War (1899-1902) and, after seeing Kruger safely off to Europe, Smuts became a soldier in the Boer army, eventually becoming a general who led a daring raid deep into the Cape Colony. He was a negotiator at the Peace of Vereeniging that ended the war, and went on, with another Boer general, Louis Botha, to first negotiate self-government for the Transvaal and then unification for South Africa. Botha was to become united South Africa's first Prime Minister, with Smuts holding multiple cabinet portfolios.

Smuts was South Africa's Defence Minister throughout the First World War (1914-1918) and personally led the troops into East Africa. In that war he became a general in the British Army, a member of the Imperial War Cabinet and was a negotiator at the Paris Peace Conference that concluded the Treaty of Versailles which ended the war. He and the legendary British economist John Maynard Keynes both opposed the punitive conditions that were to be imposed on Germany, but lost that argument.

Smuts promoted the concept of the League of Nations and signed its founding document, as he did the Treaty of Versailles, when it was created.

In 1919 Botha died and Smuts became Prime Minister for the first time. However, his heavy-handed handling of the Rand Rebellion and of the trade unions cost him vital support and his South African Party lost the 1924 election. Smuts ventured into opposition and wrote his book *Holism*. In 1934 he returned as Deputy Prime Minister with a coalition government to combat the overwhelming difficulties of the Great Depression. The coalition broke on the issue of entering the Second World War, and Smuts became Prime Minister for the second time in 1939.

During the Second World War Smuts became a Field Marshal in the British army, a confidant of Winston Churchill, and was mooted as the person to take over the Prime Ministership of Great Britain were Churchill to be incapacitated.

At the end of the war, he was a signatory of the United Nations Charter, the first paragraphs of which he had written. He was the only person to sign both the Treaty of Versailles and the United Nations Charter.

In 1948 he was elected to the Chancellorship of the University of Cambridge, the first and (still) only non-Brit to receive that honour. He was 78 at the time, and facing an election at home.

Daniël François Malan was only four years younger than Smuts, having been born in 1874 in Riebeek-West, near Smuts' birthplace in the wheat and wine lands of the Cape Colony. In fact, Smuts was briefly his Sunday School teacher. Malan also went to Victoria College in Stellenbosch, graduating with a BA degree in music and science. Thereafter he entered the Stellenbosch seminary, graduating with an MA in Philosophy, and became a dominee in the Dutch Reformed Church.

He then went to Utrecht University in the Netherlands where he graduated with a Doctorate in Divinity in 1905.

When the National Party was formed in 1914, Malan was asked to found and edit a supportive newspaper, initially called *De Burger*, later *Die Burger*. He accepted the job of founder editor, and, four years later, in 1918, became a member of parliament. Thereafter he was a career politician, becoming a Minister under Hertzog. However, in 1934 he and 19 other members of Hertzog's party broke away when Hertzog formed a coalition government with Smuts. Naming their new party the Herenigde Nasionale Party, they were the biggest opposition party when Smuts called the 1948 election.

One of the best of the many splendid books written about South Africa and South Africans is undoubtedly Alan Paton's wonderful biography of Jan

Frederick Hendrik Hofmeyr, entitled simply *Hofmeyr.*[6] We will hear more about Hofmeyr shortly, but the following is a clear statement from Paton of the time of the 1948 election.

> When Parliament rose on 24 March 1948 Smuts appeared to be in an invulnerable position. In a House of 153, he held 89 seats. Malan held 49, (Havenga's Afrikaner Party 13), Labour 6, the Stallardites 3, the Independents 3 and three were held by the Natives' Representatives, Margaret Ballinger, Donald Molteno, and Douglas Buchanan. Thus Smuts on his own commanded an absolute majority, and on most issues could count on the support of the other fifteen non-Nationalists. Malan and his ally Havenga of the Afrikaner Party would have to win 28 seats to command a majority. Such a swing would have been unparalleled in Union history.[7]

Smuts should have been less confident, for 18 months earlier there had been an augury of future disaster. There had been a by-election in the Hottentots Holland seat in the winelands of the Cape in January 1947. This was safe United Party territory. In 1943 the United Party had put up someone who was, in Smuts' eyes, a 'first class candidate', young Sir De Villiers Graaff, a scion of the extremely wealthy family that had founded Imperial Cold Storage and made their fortune bringing in meat for the British troops in the Boer War. Young Graaff had been captured at Tobruk in North Africa in the Second World War and missed the nomination. Now he was back, a war hero, handsome, eloquent and wealthy. The seat was impossible to lose.

But they lost it. The United Party win in 1943, with a lesser candidate than Graaff, was by 637 votes. Now they lost by 1 228 votes. For Smuts it was 'rather a bad defeat'.[8]

There was a lesson that this by-election should have brought home. National Party personnel believed that a speech made by Hofmeyr on Graaff's platform on the eve of the election had turned the election. Hofmeyr had said that he foresaw the day when Indians and Natives would have representatives of their own colour in parliament. This was, for the Nationalists, dynamite. Smuts missed it, however, for a year later he made Hofmeyr his Deputy Prime Minister. 'He had delivered himself into the hands of his enemies,' Hancock, Smuts' official biographer, later wrote.[9]

This by-election began a sustained and energetic campaign for Malan's team which was to last 18 months until the 1948 election. Smuts' United Party, confident of victory, only began their campaign on nomination day, 26 April 1948, a month before polling day, 26 May 1948. Sometimes the spoils of the fight go not to the bigger dog, but to the dog which works harder.

The HNP did many things right in their campaign: a well-negotiated pact with Havenga's Afrikaner Party gave the pact 11 uncontested seats, leaving personnel and finances available for marginal seats.

During and after the war, there had been a stream of farm labourers leaving the land for city jobs, which paid four times higher wages. Farmers complained loudly – they couldn't farm without labour. Smuts had let this stream happen, for war production in towns needed the labourers. His Secretary of Native Affairs said that the exodus was because farmers paid too little. The HNP promised, and were believed, that they would intensify the pass laws, to end the exodus. And they would support agricultural marketing boards. These were key moves in what turned out to be a vital swing community of voters.

Urbanising Afrikaners were under increasing pressure to find jobs and in competition with Africans. Then Smuts unleashed another challenge to the under-educated white urban worker. He proposed to bring in thousands of British immigrants to satisfy the need for skilled labour. This was threatening and unpopular with Afrikaner workers. Malan promised to slow this tide of immigration.

To attract English-speaking voters, Malan dropped his long-held call for a republic, and to attract right-wing Afrikaners, Malan allowed BJ Vorster, an Ossewabrandwag general whom Smuts had interned in the war, to stand as a candidate. He promised ex-servicemen a better deal than Smuts was willing to finance. Generally, Malan was more flexible and nimble in addressing voter fears and needs.

This all added up in Malan's favour. But there were two further issues that, between them, provided the death blow for Smuts and his United Party.

These issues were the existing undemocratic system of constituency demarcation and the crude presentation by the HNP of a 'solution' to the 'colour problem' in South Africa.

On the demarcation issue Smuts had only himself to blame, for he had already once been unseated by it. And he would not change it.

At the time, South Africa's constituencies were demarcated by a demarcation board, established by the 1909 constitution to which Smuts had been a signatory. The formula allowed for rural constituencies to be demarcated with 15% fewer voters than the norm (which was the number created by dividing the entire voting population by the number of constituencies) and urban constituencies could be created with a voting population 15% greater than the norm.

The end product of this system had seen Smuts lose the 1924 election.

Before this election Hertzog and the NP had 44 seats in parliament, won by receiving 38.2% of the votes cast. Smuts and the UP had 77 seats, won by accumulating 49% of the vote.

Then in the 1924 election the Hertzogites got 35.3% of the vote and 63 seats. Smuts and the UP got 47% of the vote and only 53 seats. The demarcation formula had been used, cleverly or unwittingly we do not know, to make a rural vote worth 1.6 urban votes, hardly democracy as we now know it.

The same formula was to be applied in the 1948 election. Smuts' advisors had repeatedly requested him to change it. He refused, saying he had been a signatory to the constitution that had created this formula, and he saw it as breaking his word to change it now. This was to have devastating consequences for millions of South Africans over the decades after 1948.

Racism arrived in South Africa in 1652, on board three little ships belonging to the Dutch East India Company. These ships dropped off a small group of Hollanders at the Cape, under Table Mountain. They were the vanguard of what was to become South Africa's white community.

Shortly after disembarking, the leader of this group, Jan van Riebeeck, planted an almond hedge to secure the boundary between his community and the locals. It was apartheid's first trial run, although at the time the word 'apartheid' was nearly three centuries in the future.

The term 'apartheid' was first used in the Cape HNP newspaper, *Die Burger*, in 1943 in the run-up to the 1948 election. DF Malan was the first parliamentarian to use the term in January 1944. He was at the time the Leader of the Opposition.[10]

Malan later elaborated on the meaning of the term: 'I do not use the term "segregation" because it has been interpreted as a fencing off (afhok), but rather "apartheid", which will give the various races the opportunity of uplifting themselves on the basis of what is their own.'

So it was proposed: a South Africa made safe for the white race and, at the same time, the development of the 'non-white' race, according to their own aptitudes and abilities.

Where did this idea come from? Sure, the ideas had been around since Van Riebeeck built his almond hedge to keep the Khoi out, but this new iteration of total separation – whose idea was this?

Allister Sparks suggests an answer: 'It was in the Broederbond where all these ideas and influences were synthesized into the ideology of apartheid … for more than half a century no major new idea in Afrikaner politics was expressed in public without first being pondered, analysed, and intensely debated within this "band of brothers".'[11]

This by-invitation-only group of Super Afrikaners included Nico Diederichs, a Professor of Economics at the time, with a doctorate in economics from the University of Leiden; Piet Meyer, with a Unisa PhD and then running a publishing business; Hendrik Verwoerd, previously a Professor of Psychology at Stellenbosch University and now editing the HNP-supporting newspaper, *Die Transvaler*; and Geoff Cronje, a Professor of Sociology at Pretoria University.

It was Cronje who first published a comprehensive draft of the apartheid ideology in his 1943 book, *'n Tuiste vir die Nageslag*, A Home for Posterity.

It is a terrible document, clearly outlining the intensity with which the apartheid project was to be approached and giving a sense of the ruthless determination that would accompany its implementation.

The primary goal of the proposed political system, Cronje wrote, was to guarantee a national home for the Afrikaner 'nation', its prosperity and its untainted bloodline.

This, he wrote, could only be done through complete racial partition. The choice lay between segregation and total separation. Segregation could only ever offer temporary solutions – total separation could solve the problem for all time. The country would have to be divided into separate racial 'nation-states' alongside a large white zone that would have all the harbours 'for the sake of international trade', alongside three or four ethnically grouped 'nation-states' that should include what was then Swaziland, Basutoland and Bechuanaland.

A 'Coloured nation' would also be necessary, with its own 'Coloured government' under the trusteeship of the white community. Indians would be repatriated to India – it had never been the intention that they should stay permanently in South Africa.

Two issues Cronje repeatedly emphasised: the white government should act with justice towards black communities, and there should be no '*bloedvermenging*' (blood mixing), which could only create 'throwbacks' and the bastardisation of the white race. The main point of government was, he wrote, not the maintenance of gold production, but 'it is over time to keep the white race's blood pure'.

This project was expected to take time, Cronje wrote. In the meantime an interim programme for the immediate enforcement of racial segregation in all areas, transport services and public amenities would be necessary. Whole categories of employment should be reserved for whites and no white worker was to be subordinate to a black supervisor. Inter-racial sex should be prohibited, Coloured voters were to be removed from the voters' roll, and all Coloured and black residential 'spots' were to be removed.

So it was that the Broederbond put out their project for the entire separation of the races, which was quickly called apartheid. *Die Burger* seeded the idea in the minds of the public and Malan brought it into parliament.

It was to be the clarion call, the leitmotif, of the 1948 election campaign.

WK Hancock writes that the HNP conducted their election in 1948 around a slogan and two bogeymen. 'Apartheid' was to become the HNP slogan for the election, and Jan Hofmeyr and communism were to be the bogeymen.[12]

First Hofmeyr.

Jan Hendrik Hofmeyr was born in Cape Town in 1894. His father died when he was three, and he spent the rest of his 54-year life living with his mother Deborah, with whom he formed an unbreakable bond. When he was two years old he contracted hydrocephaly. His illness and his mother's endless care strengthened their lifelong bond.

He went to the famous South African College School (SACS) at the age of six and matriculated four years later. He graduated with a first-class BA Honours at 15 and won a Rhodes Scholarship to Oxford. His mother, however, would not let him take it up until he was 18, so in the meanwhile he took another BA in Science and an MA in Classics. He then wrote a biography of his famous uncle, 'Onze Jan' Hofmeyr, in English and translated it into Dutch.

All of this was behind him at the age of 18, when he enrolled at Balliol College at Oxford. When he graduated, he was first in Classical Moderations and Greats.

Many positions came the way of this prodigy. When he returned to South Africa, he first lectured at the South African College and then became a Professor of Classics at the South African School of Mines (soon renamed the University of the Witwatersrand).

Thereafter he accepted the principalship of the South African School of Mines, which he soon had renamed as the University of the Witwatersrand.

After that he was appointed by Prime Minister Smuts to the position of Administrator of the Transvaal, after Smuts had twice, unsuccessfully, tried to get him to take on the job of Chief Organising Secretary of the South African Party. He was now in the Smuts tradition of politics, with his goal being to unite the English- and Afrikaans-speaking white communities, in loyalty to the British crown.

He was finally persuaded by Smuts to join the South African Party and entered parliament in 1929 as the member for Johannesburg North.

Hofmeyr soon acquired the reputation of being the vanguard of liberalism in parliament. He opposed most of the discriminatory bills that were now a regular feature of the day. Whether the target of this discrimination was Africans or Indian South Africans, and there were by now many bills that affected both communities, he and Mrs Ballinger were the only reliable voices of conscience and principled rejection.

Hofmeyr was at Smuts' side when they negotiated the coalition government that was to govern South Africa from 1934 to the outbreak of the Second World War. In 1934 they together came into government, Smuts as Deputy Prime Minister and Hofmeyr as Minister with three portfolios, Education, Interior and Public Health.

For Hofmeyr this was not an easy time. While Smuts tolerated Hertzog's many racially aggressive bills, Hofmeyr was often lonely in opposition. When Hertzog began moves to remove the Cape's black franchise, Hofmeyr held out in opposition. Finally he had had too much – Hertzog appointed APJ Fourie to the Senate as a minister 'acquainted with the reasonable wants and wishes of the Coloured people'. Hofmeyr resigned from the Cabinet, claiming that Fourie had no such qualities. Hofmeyr also left the United Party caucus in protest at a bill that had as its intent the restriction of the areas where Indian South Africans could buy land.

It appeared that he was about to leave politics when the United Party split on the issue of South Africa entering what was to become the Second World War. Hertzog resigned, Smuts again became Prime Minister and entreated Hofmeyr to join his Cabinet. Hofmeyr readily accepted.

What followed was nine years of endless overload for Hofmeyr as he became Smuts' confidant and workhorse. He began the period as both Minister of Finance and Education. At times three or four additional portfolios were placed on his shoulders. As international duties often drew Smuts out of the country – he was out of South Africa for between two and three months in each year of 1942–45 and much more in 1946 – Hofmeyr had also to deputise for him at home. This intense workload took a terrible toll on Hofmeyr and his health began to deteriorate.

The war ended and Hofmeyr continued as Minister of Finance in the very difficult time of national reconstruction and with the impossible task of providing thousands of returning servicemen with employment and housing.

If these tasks were not enough, the United Party government had to confront a world where the suppression of indigenous peoples was rapidly becoming unacceptable and the emergence of the African National Congress at home was determinedly bringing the issue of universal franchise into the public domain.

As we have seen, Smuts was a signatory to the founding charter of the United Nations, and working on its establishment was the main reason he was out of South Africa for so much of 1946. He proudly participated in some of its first sessions and quickly learned that a new world was emerging. Newly independent India would not accept the inferior civil status imposed on Indian citizens in South Africa, and Smuts was roasted on this issue in the very chambers of the United Nations that he had worked so hard to build.

Things were to be no easier for him in reckoning with organisations representing Africans at home in South Africa.

There were two organisations he had to deal with in this regard: the African National Congress, which in 1945 had issued a Declaration of Rights demanding immediate and total equality between Africans and Europeans in terms of law, politics and society; and the Natives Representative Council, a statutory body established by Hertzog with Smuts' support, in 1935, as a quid pro quo for the restriction of the African franchise.

The second body was the one Smuts was determined to work with. It had been established by government to perform two functions: to consider and report on any proposed legislation sent to it for consideration by the Minister of Native Affairs or other relevant sources; and to recommend to parliament or the provincial councils such legislation that it considered necessary in the interests of the African (then called "Native") community.

Its composition was to comprise of six government officials, including as chairperson the Secretary of the Native Affairs Department; six 'natives' as nominated by the Governor-General; and 12 'natives' elected indirectly by electoral colleges.

Crudely described, it was a talk shop for conservative 'natives'.

Despite government's best attempts, it grew closer and closer to the ANC with time, and in fact had some ANC officials as members.

In 1944 it carried a resolution calling for the repeal of the pass laws and the scrapping of segregation.

Two years later the HNP-controlled Pretoria City Council refused them the use of the City Hall for their Council meetings. They ended up at the Department of Labour building, where the toilets were 'whites only'.

It was at this meeting that the Council blew up. One councillor, a medical doctor from the Orange Free State named Dr James Moroka who had been elected to the Council in 1942 on a ticket to expose its hypocrisies, proposed a belligerent motion that was carried:

> This Council, having since its inception brought to the notice of the government the reactionary character of Union Native policy of segregation in all its ramifications, deprecates the Government's post-war continuation of a policy of Fascism which is the antithesis

and negation of the letter and the spirit of the Atlantic Charter and the United Nations Charter. The Council therefore in protest against this breach of faith towards the African people in particular and the cause of world freedom in general, resolves to adjourn this session, and calls upon the government forthwith to abolish all discriminatory legislation affecting non-Europeans in this country.[13]

Hofmeyr immediately reminded Smuts that this motion had brought the Natives Representative Council into step with the ANC. No longer was there a sweetheart government body to merely talk with and thereafter ignore.

What was Smuts to do? The election was looming, the HNP had a clear policy towards African South Africans (apartheid), and Smuts was in a mess of indecision.

He did two things. He met with six members of the Natives Representative Council, including the redoubtable Prof. ZK Matthews. Secondly, he appointed Judge Henry Fagan to report on future policy on the position of Africans in urban areas and the possible recognition of African trade unions. This team included a young lecturer in Economic History at the University of the Witwatersrand, Helen Suzman.

Smuts' discussion with Prof. Matthews and his colleagues went nowhere. He was not prepared to extend parliamentary representation to Africans, and they were not prepared to accept anything less.[14]

The Fagan Report arrived at the end of March 1948, with the election due only two months in the future.

Fagan and his team declared territorial segregation to be a self-deceiving dream. Black South Africans should rather be accepted as a permanent part of urban South Africa and labour laws should reflect this as a reality. The goal that every working black was somehow a migratory labourer was the dream of an obsolete system. The pass laws should be rationalised and relaxed, but not done away with. In many respects, they advocated that more accommodating labour systems, including labour bureaus, should be set up.

Smuts, desperately needing a 'native policy' to present to the electorate at this late hour, immediately accepted this report on behalf of the United Party.

If there was a guiding philosophy in this report, it was muddy. Nowhere was the black franchise issue addressed and Smuts would not countenance an equal franchise. Thus the ANC's, and now also the Natives Representative Council's, clear demand was not met. Rather, in synch with the Fagan Report, which was a prescription to adjust political reality on the march, Smuts accepted a 'muddle-through' position. The United Party would treat

South Africa's racial issues as and when they presented themselves, flexible to the point of flaccidity.

The HNP was by now on full attack.

Die Kruithoring, the HNP internal newspaper, decided to use the ultra-liberal Hofmeyr as their target. They put out a series of 14 questions that they demanded him to reply to. They were:

1. If natives had the ability, should they be trained as skilled workmen, with the same pay and conditions as whites?
2. Should educated natives have the right to supervise the work of white girls?
3. Should native workmen have the right to found their own trade unions?
4. Should natives enjoy the same academic and social rights at white universities as whites?
5. Should a native be allowed to become, for example, the Chancellor of the University of South Africa?
6. Should natives enjoy the same conditions of work and pay as whites in the public service?
7. Should qualified natives, immediately or eventually, enjoy the same voting rights as whites?
8. Should such voting rights be extended to native women?
9. Should the pre-1936 vote be restored?
10. Should such rights be extended to the northern provinces?
11. Should natives be allowed to sit in parliament?
12. Apply to municipal and divisional elections?
13. Should native farm workers be entitled to wages on the basis of 'equal pay for equal work'?
14. Should the highest posts in agriculture, education and the professions be open to natives?

To all these questions *Die Kruithoring* answered a resounding 'NO'. But, according to the editor, Hofmeyr would answer 'Yes'. Could he, Hofmeyr, please address himself to these questions?[15]

Hofmeyr, of course, refused to reply.

On 29 March 1948, with two months to go to the election, DF Malan set out the HNP's 'Colour Policy' in *Die Burger*.[16] It was straight from the Broederbond's document as written by Cronje.

For Malan, the best route to achieve the happiness of all South Africans was to maintain and protect the white race, and this was the root and foundation of HNP policy. This could only be achieved by residential, social, industrial and political separation. Each separate group would then have their national pride and self-respect.

Coloured voters would be placed on a separate roll, to elect white representatives to a white parliament. Mixed marriages would be forbidden. 'The native reserves should become the fatherland of the native', and all services, particularly education, would be provided there, not in the towns as at present. 'The native in our urban areas must be regarded as a visitor.' Their movement was to be vigorously controlled by pass laws. Native education was to be Christian-National and would be funded from native contributions to the national income. Indians were to be repatriated as much as possible.

Hofmeyr wrote in Afrikaans at the bottom of the Malan statement: 'No longer a policy of uplift but one of oppression.' How right this was to prove to be.

Much has been made of crude racism in the HNP's campaign. 'Die kaffer op sy plek, en die coolie uit die land' was a slogan that appeared at this time. Hermann Giliomee, the excellent Afrikaner historian, believes that there were never any such slogans.[17] Possibly we can concede that they were not part of official HNP campaigning, but much else that was racist was. And Hofmeyr was the bogeyman.

The HNP had three mouthpieces: *Die Burger* in Cape Town, *Die Transvaler* on the Witwatersrand and its in-house magazine, *Die Kruithoring*. All spent months attacking Hofmeyr. Smuts was presented as an old man who should be expected to hand over the Prime Ministership quickly to his deputy, Hofmeyr. Between January and May 1948 *Die Burger* ran 22 leading articles attacking Hofmeyr. He was presented as a man of principle, whose principles would be the end of the white man in South Africa. His liberalism would lead straight to a communist South Africa. Smuts' wartime association with Stalin was all that was needed to 'prove' this. 'Obliterate the red hordes', *Die Kruithoring* demanded. 'A vote for Smuts is a vote for Joe Stalin.' *Die Transvaler* depicted Hofmeyr as a two-headed jackal, the one head saying 'Away with the colour bar', and the other 'I am for Christian trusteeship'.

There was of course much worse doing the rounds, like the above slogans, outside the apparent boundaries of the official campaign.

As Paton records:[18]

A story was being circulated by canvassers that Hofmeyr had an African mistress and that was why he resisted all attempts to ensure that marriage, adultery and prostitution were made illegal activities. There was another story ... that Hofmeyr had got into trouble at a boys' camp, and that only the intervention of Smuts had saved him

25

from public exposure. There was a story about Smuts too, that he was in fact a Jew, and that one only needed to study his portraits to see that this was true. Both these men, it was said, desired only one thing with all their hearts, and that was 'to plough under the Afrikaner'. If the United Party was returned to power, black men would take away jobs from white men, black men would supervise white girls, black doctors would give orders to white nurses.

The United Party sailed on, in confident comfort. The day before the election, *The Forum* published its forecast: United Party 74, HNP 58, Afrikaner Party five, Labour Party four, Independents one, and the other eight doubtful. Hofmeyr pencilled over these figures: UP 86, HNP 53, Afrikaner Party four, Labour Party five, Independent one.

Polling was on 26 May 1948. There were 1 337 534 registered voters and an 80% poll of 1 073 364 voters was achieved.

The results were announced the next day, and they were stunning.

The Assembly comprised 150 seats, all contested on a first-past-the-post system, with rural seats having up to 15% of voters below the average number of voters and urban seats up to 15% above the average.

The HNP swept the Transvaal, Cape and Free State rural seats, rising from 15 Transvaal seats to 32, from 21 Cape seats to 26, and, with their coalition partners, the Afrikaner Party, took all but one of the Free State seats. The HNP ended with 70 seats and the Afrikaner Party nine, together securing a full majority in the House.

Smuts' United Party fell from 44 Transvaal seats to 26 and from 34 Cape seats to 27; in total, from 89 seats to 65. Even with Labour's six seats, and the three Native Representatives, they only totalled 74 seats, not enough to govern. The HNP had 'driven the United Party out of virtually every Afrikaans-speaking constituency in the country', wrote Paton.

This extraordinary result was in direct contradiction to the number of votes won: the UP had won 524 000 votes to the HNP's 402 000. The rural loading of constituencies, which Smuts had refused to change on principle, had worked its poison.

Smuts was out. Not only was the UP now in opposition, but Smuts lost his Standerton seat, which had originally been Louis Botha's seat. The Age of the Generals was truly over. Malan became the first South African Prime Minister who had not been a Boer War general.

'Smuts was almost beside himself,' Paton wrote, and Hofmeyr was little better.[19]

In HNP circles, things were predictably different. Pretoria's Church

Square hosted an enormous, roaring crowd. All Afrikaner centres exploded with celebration: Stellenbosch, Worcester, Bloemfontein, Potchefstroom and, of course, Smuts' constituency Standerton. Honking motor cars, the singing of Afrikaner anthems and songs, and prayers, prayers, prayers. For Afrikaners, it was a new dawn.

'On the day the results of the 1948 elections were announced, Oliver Tambo was walking towards his office in Charter House, on the corner of Rissik and Anderson Streets in Johannesburg's city centre. He was immaculately dressed in suit and tie. Suddenly a white man accosted him, his face twisted with hatred. He worked his mouth and then – without a word – spat in Tambo's face. Tambo walked away. He wiped off the spit with a snowy silk handkerchief. Forty years later he still had the kerchief in his possession.'[20]

Nelson Mandela remembers Tambo from a few hours earlier. 'On election day I attended a meeting with Oliver Tambo and several others. We barely discussed the question of a Nationalist government as we did not expect one. The meeting went on all night, and we emerged at dawn and found a newspaper vendor selling the *Rand Daily Mail*: the Nationalists had triumphed. I was stunned and dismayed, but Oliver took a more considered line. "I like this," he said. "I like this." I could not imagine why. He explained, "Now we will know exactly who our enemies are and where we stand."'[21]

Chief Albert Luthuli gave another opinion on this election result: 'For most of us Africans, the election seemed largely irrelevant. We had endured Botha, Hertzog and Smuts. It did not seem of much importance whether the whites gave us more Smuts or switched to Malan. Our lot had grown steadily harder, and no election seemed likely to alter the direction in which we were being forced.'[22]

Smuts had recently been elected as Chancellor of Cambridge University and immediately after the election was to fly there on his first duty as Chancellor.

'Smuts had flown to England after sending a sad message to the nation, "If there is blame for the present failure, let it be mine – as no doubt the heavy punishment will be." It was left to Hofmeyr to welcome the new cabinet in the Prime Minister's office ... it was the first Cabinet in the history of the Union without any English-speaking Ministers ... Malan was deeply affected. He had entered Parliament thirty-three years before and now he was about to enter the promised land. Before he entered the room he prayed silently that he might prove worthy of his great office. Again one is moved to honour him, again one is repelled, remembering the laws that he had already planned, so callously indifferent to the sufferings of persons, especially those who were voiceless and powerless,' wrote Paton.[23]

3

The Defiance Campaign

I t was not only the white electorate that was moving towards great change. Within the African National Congress, new policies and a new action plan were being created.

On 14 August 1941 the President of the United States and the Prime Minister of Great Britain met in Newfoundland in Canada and signed what became known as The Atlantic Charter. This outlined a set of principles that these two countries saw as guiding the international order after the Second World War. South Africa's Prime Minister, Field Marshal Smuts, was an enthusiastic supporter of this document.

Prelude to the Defiance Campaign

One of the clauses of the Atlantic Charter immediately sparked the interest of the ANC President-General, Dr AB Xuma. This clause read, 'They respect the rights of all peoples to choose the form of government under which they will live; and they wish to see sovereign rights and self-government restored to those who have been forcibly deprived of them.'

Dr Xuma in December 1943 assembled 26 of the 'best brains' in the ANC to inspect this document, and to advise the ANC on how it should react to it. This included five medical doctors, six lecturers and teachers, and many of the ANC's National Executive. One of the 26, being given his first senior role in the ANC, was Mr GA Mbeki, BA, BCom, Trade Secretary, Federation of Organised Bodies, Transkei.

This team wrote a seminal document, 'Africans' Claims in South Africa, including The Atlantic Charter from the Standpoint of Africans within the Union of South Africa'.[24]

Included in 'Africans' Claims' (as the ANC document rapidly became known) were two dramatic developments in ANC thinking.

Firstly, the ANC now abandoned its long-held policy on franchise rights. Previously the ANC had stood for 'Equal rights for all civilised men' but it now moved unequivocally to the universal franchise. 'Africans' Claims' made clear, 'We believe that the acid test of the Charter is its application to the African continent ... in parts of Africa where there are the peculiar circumstances of a politically entrenched European minority ruling a majority European population the demands of the Africans for full citizenship rights and direct participation in all the councils of the state should be recognised. THIS IS MOST URGENT IN THE UNION OF SOUTH AFRICA.'

Secondly, 'Africans' Claims' includes South Africa's first Bill of Rights proposal. This begins: 'We demand the abolition of political discrimination based on race ... and the extension to all adults, regardless of race, of the right to vote and be elected to parliament, provincial councils and other representative institutions.' Eleven other clauses follow, all of which foreshadow the clauses adopted by the South African parliament over fifty years later.

In two days Xuma's committee agreed and drafted the 14-page document, and three days later, on 16 December 1943, the National Conference of the ANC adopted it unanimously. It immediately became the ANC's basic policy statement.

NOW ARMED WITH POLICY certainty, the ANC had to find the determination and the process whereby confrontation with the white government could finally start to bring meaningful results.

We have mentioned some of the highly educated luminaries of Afrikaner nationalism who were, at this time, meeting in secret venues of the Broederbond to plan their 'ultimate solution' for South Africa's race problems – apartheid.

One evening in 1943 in a house in Orlando West in Johannesburg, an equally talented and determined group of six young African nationalists met for the first time. They were to create the institution that was to begin the process of determined African resistance, for the first time outside of Port Elizabeth.

Three of these young men need introduction, the other three hardly do.

Of those needing introduction, the first is the then 34-year-old Anton Lembede.

'Anton Lembede was the principal architect of South Africa's first fully-fledged ideology of African nationalism,' wrote Gail Gerhart in her seminal work, *Black Power in South Africa*.[25]

Simply put, African nationalism defines South Africa as belonging to Africans and only Africans by two rights: by right of first possession, with Africans having occupied South Africa before whites arrived; and by right of numbers, the majority of the population being African. Whites are guests in South Africa, and can only remain here on terms set down by the African community.

Lembede was born in 1914 on a farm in rural Natal. Lembede's father was a farm labourer and his mother a teacher. He nevertheless spent his short life striving for more and more education. When he died in 1947, aged only 33 years, he had a BA, an LLB, an MA and was on his way to a PhD.

This was just part of his extraordinary achievements, for he was first a teacher, then he became a partner in Pixley ka Seme's legal practice, and he was also the principal thinker and energy behind the 10 September 1944 launch of the ANC Youth League. He was the Youth League's inaugural general president, heading an executive that included, amongst others, Walter Sisulu, Oliver Tambo, Nelson Mandela, Ellen Kuzwayo, AP Mda and Dan Tloome.

These firebrands wanted to reform the ANC, which they described as 'a body of gentlemen with clean hands'. They mostly succeeded because under their influence the ANC moved from an organisation that lobbied patiently for change to an organisation committed to civil disobedience in the pursuit of disrupting the state until real change became possible.

Lembede personally created the Youth League's manifesto, from which flowed the Programme of Action adopted by the ANC at its conference in 1949, two years after Lembede's death. This committed the ANC to civil disobedience and led to the 1952 Defiance Campaign. The Programme's final clause declared that 'Congress realises that ultimately the people will be brought together by inspired leadership, under the banner of African Nationalism with courage and determination,' but it never defined the content of that nationalism.

The second person to be introduced is Ashley Peter Solomzi (AP) Mda.

Two years younger than Lembede, he had arrived in Johannesburg in 1937, and was thus the earliest of the six to relocate to the Transvaal. He had been born in Herschel in the Eastern Cape. His father was a tribal headman and his mother a schoolteacher. He attended Catholic schools, graduating with a teacher training diploma. Then he enrolled at UNISA, from where he graduated with a BA in 1946. He eventually studied law and became an attorney in 1960.

His first job was in Orlando, where he taught at a Catholic elementary school. At this time he became an organiser for the ANC. By 1944 he was deputy speaker of the ANC in the Transvaal, which put him on the National Executive.

The third young man was the 27-year-old Jordan Kush Ngubane, from Ladysmith in Natal, the son of a policeman. He entered Adams College in 1933 where he met and befriended Anton Lembede.

His first job was as assistant editor of John L Dube's newspaper *Ilanga lase Natal*. This was the beginning of a long career in journalism. His next post took him to Johannesburg where he worked for Selope Thema's *Bantu World*. Soon he had re-met Lembede, and through him met Mda.

The other three at our meeting need no introductions: Walter Sisulu, then 31, whose house they met in, Oliver Tambo (26) and Nelson Mandela (25). They assembled that night to discuss their political frustrations with the unsuccessful methods of the ANC to wring change out of the white government.

These six men, with many other comrades along the way, were to prove to be as determined in their African nationalism as the Broederbond was in its Afrikaner nationalism, and even more willing to accept massive sacrifices in their determination to remake South Africa in their model – in their case, as a democracy.

From the energies and the vision of these six young men emerged the ANC Youth League.

At this meeting at Sisulu's house, the six agreed to extend their discussions of a Youth League far and wide. This they did, eventually meeting with Dr Xuma to request his support. This they got, and at the 1943 ANC conference Dr Xuma proposed the idea, and the formation of a youth league was authorised.

Lembede, Ngubane and Mda then drafted a proposed Youth League manifesto and constitution, which, in February 1944, a delegation of Youth Leaguers presented to Dr Xuma at his home in Sophiatown.

Xuma was appalled. These youngsters had, in his opinion, tried to usurp the powers of the ANC's National Executive. He had assumed that it was to be his office that had the responsibility to do what these youngsters had done clandestinely. Their document appeared to him to create a separate and independent organisation, something he did not believe the ANC wanted it to be.

It took the youngsters all of their considerable debating skills to save the day. Eventually, given the assurance that all Youth Leaguers over the age of 17 would pay for full ANC membership as well as Youth League membership, Xuma grudgingly let the youngsters convene their inaugural conference.

This they did on Easter Sunday 1944, at the Bantu Men's Social Club. Two hundred attendees elected Lembede as president, Victor Mbobo as his deputy, Oliver Tambo as secretary and Walter Sisulu as treasurer. Mda was also on the executive. They then set out with the clear mission to steer the ANC to a more confrontational and militant course of action.

Deputations and petitions were to be shunned. Lembede tragically died of a heart attack in 1947. The National Executive of the Youth League, including Walter Sisulu, Mandela, Tambo, Mda, Dr James Njongwe and David Bopape, soon drafted a two-page document entitled 'Programme of Action', and circulated it widely.[26]

The document was up for discussion at the 1948 ANC National Conference. To say the least, it was controversial, with the ANC's older guard wanting nothing to do with it. A motion for its adoption was brought up, with Dr Xuma temporarily absent from the conference. In his absence the chairperson, AWG Champion, tried to close the conference early to avoid its adoption. Xuma returned and agreed that it should be held over until 1949 for further discussion.

A year of intensive internal debate followed.

The clause that gave the most concern was clause three, which called for 'the appointment of a council of action ... to carry into effect, vigorously and with the utmost determination, the programme of action. It should be competent for the council of action to implement our resolve to work for: (a) the abolition of all differential political institutions the boycotting of which we accept and to undertake a campaign to educate our people on this issue and, in addition, to employ the following weapons: immediate and active boycott, strike, civil disobedience, non-cooperation and such other means as may bring about the accomplishment and realisation of our aspirations.'[27]

While the debate on this document was underway at local and provincial levels in the ANC, in November 1949, with the next ANC National Conference only a month away, Sisulu, Mandela and Tambo visited Dr Xuma again at his home in Sophiatown to solicit his support for the Programme.

The youngsters couched their argument undiplomatically. They made it clear that, in their opinion, the days when the choice of ANC leader was dependent on the candidate being a doctor or lawyer were gone. Now what was needed was the ability of a leader to mobilise the masses of the people. They said that they would support Xuma if he supported the Programme and that the ANC was now to enter a new age, one of mass action and courting arrest.

Xuma exploded, 'You come to lecture me here!' He said that he had no intention of jeopardising his large medical practice by going to prison. The

ANC should rather build its structures and its managerial efficiencies. He would not be bribed or blackmailed. He would not support their Programme and they could keep their votes. He then dismissed them, at 11 pm, leaving them without transport stranded on his pavement.[28]

The Youth League were, however, resolute. They would only support as President General a person who supported the Programme of Action.

They then approached Prof. ZK Matthews. No chance. For him, the Youth Leaguers were 'naïve firebrands who would mellow with age'. The Programme of Action was not for him.

The Youth Leaguers then took a long shot and approached Dr James Moroka, the medical doctor who had brought the Natives Representative Council down earlier. Dr Moroka was not even at the time a member of the ANC, but he supported the Programme of Action and he had the stature to take on Dr Xuma.

Prior to the ANC's December 1949 National Conference, the Youth League held its own conference. This was very well attended and it was agreed that the Youth League would only support for ANC President General a candidate who supported the Programme of Action.

The ANC Conference analysed the Programme of Action clause by clause, and adopted it unanimously with minor amendments. Dr Moroka was elected as President General in what was said to be a Youth League coup. Walter Sisulu was elected Secretary General. Sisulu became the ANC's first full-time Secretary-General, with a salary of five pounds a month, paid very irregularly as and when funds allowed. Tambo was also elected to the ANC's executive, as were the following Youth Leaguers: AP Mda, Dan Tloome, James Njongwe, Victor Mbobo, Godfrey Pitje and Joseph Mokoena. Mandela was appointed later.

Clearly the African National Congress was anticipating bitter battles with the new National Party government, elected a year earlier in 1948.

These would not be easy battles, as Sisulu immediately discovered that the organisation he was to run had all of one rented office, £400 in the bank, a clerk and a typist. Hardly the arsenal with which to take on a functioning state.

Apartheid starts hitting the statute books

Despite the double difficulty of having an initially wary, even hostile, bureaucracy appointed by the party now in opposition, and secondly little experience in ramming legislation through parliament, the newly elected National Party was soon on its feet, and making into law their cherished vision of apartheid.

In a clear statement of where the core of their prejudice lay, the first two major acts to become the bedrock of apartheid were the Prohibition of Mixed Marriages Act No 55 of 1949, and the Immorality Amendment Act No 21 of 1950.[29] Sexual intercourse between whites and Africans had been legally proscribed as early as 1927, and this legislation now prohibited sexual intercourse between 'Europeans' and 'Non-Europeans' and prohibited marriage between whites and members of other racial groups.

Then came the act that was apartheid's foundation, the Population Registration Act No 30 of 1950. This act pulled together the considerable body of existing racially motivated legislation, and classified all South Africans rigidly as 'White', 'Asian', 'Native' (later 'Bantu') or 'Coloured'. Subsequent legislation subdivided 'Coloureds' into five sub-classes, and 'Africans' into eight. Provision was made for a humiliating and public process of challenging one's 'racial group'.

In the same year, the Group Areas Act No 41 of 1950 was enacted, which allocated specific residential and trading areas in cities, towns and other places to the various population groups. This control was imposed over the entire country with the exception of the African townships, African reserves and the Coloured mission stations and reserves. People now living outside their designated racial group areas were at the mercy of the state as to when and where they were to be moved.

Three years later the Reservation of Separate Amenities Act No 49 of 1953 entrenched this geographical separation. This act allowed, in fact instructed, any individual who had control of any public premise or even a public vehicle, which included all land, building, halls, offices, transport vehicles, etc, to reserve this place or vehicle for the exclusive use of persons belonging to a particular race.

Then the existing Cape franchise arrangements, which were somewhat non-racial, were to be removed. The Separate Representation of Voters Act No 46 of 1951 began the process of removing the Coloured and Indian voters from the Cape roll, and the Promotion of Bantu Self-Government Act No 46 of 1959 removed from parliament the white members who had represented African citizens since 1936.

The Suppression of Communism Act No 44 of 1950 redefined 'communism' to incorporate many kinds of political opponents, and a number of unionists and politicians were quickly removed from public office.

The Native Labour (Settlement of Disputes) Act No 48 of 1953 redefined the term 'employee' to exclude Africans, who, on the enactment of this act, could no longer be members of unions, and it prohibited strikes by African workers.

Amongst this selection of ruthless and destructive acts of parliament, possibly the most damaging was the Bantu Education Act No 47 of 1953, which centralised 'Bantu Education' under a central department, reduced the state funding of mission schools from 100% of teachers' salaries in 1955 to nil in 1958 and redesigned 'Bantu Education' to, as Verwoerd said in the Senate, 'no longer produce pupils who were trained in European ideas'. Per capita spending on pupils changed from 6.3 times as much spent on white pupils as on Africans in 1949, to 16.6 times as much in 1969/70.

With the Bantu Authorities Act No 68 of 1951 the development of the homelands began in earnest. Homeland authorities were to gain additional powers as they gained experience, with full 'independence' to be ultimately granted to the homelands.

The Bantu (Abolition of Passes and Co-ordination of Documents) Act No 67 of 1952 did exactly the opposite of abolishing the dreaded passbooks. From then on every African over the age of 16 was obliged to carry a passbook at all times and present it on demand. Possibly 17 million Africans were prosecuted under this measure over time.

There was much else that helped to construct the edifice of apartheid, but these kernel laws, all passed within five years of the 1948 election, codified this disgraceful and destructive body of racially defined suppressive acts.

How was the ANC to respond to all this?

The ANC's response

The years 1950 to 1952 were fundamental in the history of the African National Congress. They began with the December 1949 adoption of the Programme of Action and ended with the December 1952 election of Albert Luthuli as President-General.

In between these seminal dates, the Youth Leaguers consolidated their hold on the levers of power in the ANC, and petition and deputation were abandoned as the means of attempting to force change. The period began with a wave of fierce African nationalism pushing communists and individuals from minority, non-African communities aside, while the organisation committed itself to non-violent civil disobedience, with strikes, boycotts and the breaking of racist laws to force incarceration being the tactics of choice. At the end of these two short years, the Defiance Campaign was effected, the largest non-violent protest to date in South Africa, run on non-racial lines by Africans and South Africans of Indian descent.

In the Transvaal, the Youth League, while still small in numbers and without a branch structure, had, by sheer force of personality, impacted enormously on its mother body in terms of policy, programmes and personnel. This was effected by a small number of key youth league activists (particularly Mandela, Sisulu and Tambo) fighting against communist and South African Indian Congress leadership in programmes and protests.

In Port Elizabeth the Youth League took another route. Raymond Mhlaba recalls joining the Youth League in 1944, and this completed his full-hand of memberships – the unions, the Communist Party, the ANC and the Youth League. As we have noted, in Port Elizabeth these organisations had overlapping memberships, and all programmes and projects were worked out before implementation.

The Port Elizabeth 'mixed bag' had been supplemented by the arrival in town, in 1948, of a 29-year-old medical doctor, who had already risen high in the ANC.

Dr James Lowell Zwelinzima Njongwe had been born in Qumbu in the Transkei on 12 January 1919. Both of his parents, Dad Mayeza and Mom Jessie, were teachers. They sent him to Chulunta Primary School, where he proceeded to fail Sub B magnificently.[30]

But he persevered, and matriculated at Healdtown before graduating BSc (Hygiene) at Fort Hare University in 1940.

In the summer of 1941 he was at home in Qumbu when two white policemen on horseback arrived.

They gave him clear instructions, 'Be at the University of the Witwatersrand in two days.' He and Siyaluyalu Hermanus had been awarded Transkei Bunga bursaries to study medicine at Wits. They were to become the University of the Witwatersrand's first two African medical doctors. Njongwe graduated in 1946.

While at Wits he met Nelson Mandela, Oliver Tambo and Walter Sisulu and the four became lifelong friends. He joined the ANC Youth League and then went off to do his internship in Durban at the McCord Zulu Hospital.

When that was over, the young Dr Njongwe opened a practice in Port Elizabeth in 1948 as the first African doctor to practise in Port Elizabeth. He set up his home in Ncaphayi Street in New Brighton, not far from the Red Location and his practice in Commercial Road in Sidwell. He married a nurse, Nonzi, who was working with Dora Nginza at the New Brighton Clinic. They had three children, Zwelinzima (born 1950), Patiswa (1952) and Nkukule (1956).

Soon after he arrived in Port Elizabeth, Raymond Mhlaba called to get him to join the New Brighton branch of the ANC. Later in 1949 he joined the ANC's national executive and also the provincial executive. In 1951–1953 he replaced Prof. ZK Matthews as provincial leader when the good Prof. went to the USA for two years. He was in Port Elizabeth when preparations for the Defiance Campaign fell into place. In fact, Thabo Mbeki said that he first became interested in the ANC when, in Queenstown, a car publicising the Defiance Campaign came past him, driven by Dr Njongwe.[31]

Much has been made of apparent differences between Dr Njongwe and the 'mixed bag' in Port Elizabeth. These differences clearly existed and Walter Sisulu has confirmed them. However, they never disrupted the ongoing flow of protest and uprising and they didn't prevent Dr Njongwe from supporting his wife as she became a defier. Differences there may have been, but discipline there also was.

One of the first campaigns Dr Njongwe got caught up in was the bus boycott of 1949.

The bus and train services between the townships and town were run by the South African Railways, who employed only white drivers, conductors and people in other occupations. The service was unsympathetic and irregular. On 1 April 1949, without any warning, the fare of threepence to town was raised to fourpence. The community had been informed that they should expect a seven and a half per cent increase. This increase, of a full third, was as dramatic as it was unexpected. From within the ANC came a call for a bus boycott.

A mass meeting was called for Sunday 17 April, and it mandated a 'broad action committee' of 28 people from the ANC, the Youth League, the Communist Party and the Unity Movement to resolve the fare issue. Raymond Mhlaba led this committee, which also included Dr Njongwe.

As Mhlaba remembers, this strategy worked wonders because members of the various structures committed themselves to the boycott. This strategy also prevented the emergence of armchair critics. Most importantly, it consolidated mass action against the South African Railways.[32]

This umbrella structure held the community together for nearly four months (from 19 April to the first week of August). Committed walking to work eventually extracted concessions. In fact, a few years later a private company took over the buses and started employing black staff.

In the Transvaal the dynamics were very different.

The election of Dr Moroka at the ANC's Conference in December 1949 was to have divisive consequences.

The new National Executive Committee (NEC) had its first meeting in January 1950. Dr Xuma remarked at this meeting that 'with Moroka as President General all the affairs of the ANC would be known to the police', and he repeated this in a letter to the NEC. When confronted and asked for evidence, he refused to retract and instead resigned from the NEC and told *Bantu World* that he had resigned because of 'bribery and corruption' by the

Youth League in Moroka's election. This controversy ran on for months in the newspaper.

With Xuma's place on the NEC now unoccupied, Sisulu organised Mandela to be co-opted in his place. This cemented the friendships between Sisulu, Tambo and Mandela, which, despite all the years of exile and jail, formed the solid base of the ANC until democracy.

More difficulties followed.

Shortly after the NEC meeting, Sam Kahn, a white communist lawyer who was a 'native representative' in parliament, was banned.

Four organisations came together to coordinate a response: the Transvaal ANC, the Johannesburg district of the Communist Party, the Transvaal Indian Congress, and the African People's Organisation. They proposed a Defend Free Speech Convention.

This was vigorously opposed by the Youth League, in particular by Mandela. The principal reason was that the ANC had not originated the convention. The organisers were stealing the ANC's thunder and undermining its Programme of Action.

Meanwhile Dr Moroka had agreed to preside over the Convention, Sisulu had sent a message of encouragement, and both had indicated their willingness to attend.

Walter was immediately under fire from his comrades. Mandela and others accused him of undermining the Programme of Action, and he relented. He left town on the day of the Convention, for 'an unavoidable prior engagement'. But Dr Moroka did not and was fêted by a crowd of 10 000 at a most successful convention.

The Convention proposed a follow-up: a one-day strike on May Day. Again the Youth League opposed the event and Mandela and other Youth Leaguers went so far as to disrupt the programme leading up to the strike and heckled the speakers at planning meetings.

The strike was, like the Convention before it, well supported and it is estimated that half of Johannesburg's African workforce stayed at home on 1 May 1950, despite police banning meetings on the day. Police fired at a crowd, and 19 people were killed. Dr Moroka was again admired at the funeral as he trenchantly criticised the police.

Immediately following the Convention and the killings, the now renamed National Party brought forward the Unlawful Organisations Bill. This was a direct attack on their bogeyman, the Communist Party, which the bill sought to ban and make it an offence to belong to, or to further its aims. This was now to be punishable by a maximum of 10 years' imprisonment.

Sisulu saw this bill as a major step to the National Party banning more and more of its opposition, including, at some stage, the ANC. It must be opposed, with all possible energy. He recommended the formation of a Port Elizabeth-style coalition of affected parties.

Mandela and AP Mda were not keen to work with the communists as they felt that the programme would be hijacked by the Party. Sisulu felt otherwise, and for once his arguments prevailed over the firebrands. They reluctantly agreed to Sisulu bringing together an emergency conference of fraternal organisations on 14 May 1950.

To satisfy the Youth Leaguers, Dr Moroka was to preside. In attendance were to be the ANC, the Communist Party, the Youth League, the South African Indian Congress, the African People's Organisation, the Non-European Unity Movement and the Transvaal Council of Trade Unions. The Unity Movement declined the invitation.

The meeting was a great success. Rusty Bernstein, in his memoir, *Memory against Forgetting*, notes: 'For the first time a unified council of war was set up to run a joint campaign – something the movement had been previously unable to do ... the foundation stone was laid for the ANC coalition that would come to dominate the next decades of South African liberation politics.'[33]

On 11 June Dr Moroka announced that 26 June 1950 was to be called a National Day of Protest and Mourning, and it was to be a day of stayaway from work. This was a very tight schedule, with little more than two weeks from announcement to implementation date.[34]

When the Communist Party took the grave decision to close down, which Sam Kahn announced in parliament on 20 June, the government appointed an ominously named 'liquidator' to assemble lists of persons to be prohibited from teaching, addressing crowds, attending gatherings and more. The gloves were coming off ...

Sisulu was now travelling the country to make the proposed 26 June strike effective. He travelled to Durban, where not much was happening.

Then Port Elizabeth – and a crowd of 15 000 people, the biggest crowd at a political gathering ever in Port Elizabeth. They were, he believed, 'highly organised'.

Then East London, and a long meeting with the ANC executive saw the executive try to avoid commitment to the strike as there had not been enough time to organise it.

In Johannesburg old tensions surfaced and a fight broke out at a meeting between a trade unionist and a political activist. When 26 June arrived, very few people stayed at home. '95% a Flop', wrote the *Rand Daily Mail*.

Eventually the strike was only really successful in Port Elizabeth, where the stayaway was huge. This did not surprise Sisulu, who had grown to admire Port Elizabeth organisation. 'I remember that PE's support for the National Day of Protest was recorded as the best in the whole of South Africa,' Mhlaba remembers.

Nevertheless, Sisulu felt he could characterise the strike as a great success, given that it was organised in two short weeks under intense police intimidation.

The Defiance Campaign

The Defiance Campaign was to be the next programme after the somewhat successful 26 June 1950 strike.

The Defiance Campaign was conceived of, organised and executed by the ANC as a campaign that followed from the Programme of Action. The ANC took in a partner, the South African Indian Congress, to both dampen anti-Indian sentiment and to build on this community's rich resistance history. It was the first planned and executed protest by black South Africans against the newly elected National Party's determined imposition of apartheid on South Africa. It was the conclusion of the ANC's move from moderation to militancy. It was thus very important that it should succeed.

In June 1951 Pixley ka Isaka Seme, one of the founders of the ANC, died in Johannesburg. After his funeral, the NEC took the opportunity of having so many of its number assembled together and met to propose progress on the Programme of Action.

As Tom Lodge has written: 'It was the former Africanist, Walter Sisulu, who was the first to elaborate a civil disobedience strategy.'[35]

According to Sisulu's plan, which he had previously seeded through Mandela and others informally, selected volunteers from all racial groups would deliberately court imprisonment by defying certain racist laws.

Mandela was enthusiastic, but argued that the campaign should be exclusively African, and expressed, again, his reservations about working with 'Indians'. Sisulu emphasised that the proposed campaign was not inconsistent with Africanist strategy: mobilisation was to be on community lines, and only in exceptional cases would 'mixed' volunteer units be accepted.

Behind Sisulu's proposal lay two strategies: firstly, to create chaos in the ruling authorities by filling to overflowing the courts and the prisons; and secondly, to mobilise a committed mass following for the ANC. As Lodge has noted, it is unlikely that many subscribed to the Gandhian notion that the suffering of those punished for disobeying plainly immoral laws could 'activate the inherent goodness of the rulers'.[36]

The NEC meeting called a joint conference of the national executive of the ANC and the South African Indian Congress and the African People's Organisation, which, on 29 July 1951 approved the idea of a 'systematic and organised campaign of civil disobedience based on the principles of peaceful resistance'.[37]

To take the project forward the conference appointed a joint planning council made up of Dr Moroka as chairman, Sisulu and JB Marks from the ANC's NEC, and Yusuf Dadoo and Yusuf Cachalia from the SAIC. This council took a few months to put together a draft plan which Sisulu, Marks, Dadoo and Cachalia took to Dr Moroka at Thaba Nchu for his perusal and agreement, which it got.

After a trip proposing the plan to the ANC's regions, Sisulu put the Defiance Campaign as the main item on the agenda for the ANC's annual December conference, held in Bloemfontein from 15 to 17 December. Sisulu presented the plan, as well as a booklet outlining the proposals.

It was enthusiastically supported. Mandela raised his by-now normal objection to working with the SAIC and Chief Luthuli, who ha1 recently wrested the Natal leadership from AWG Champion, noted that he did not believe that the Natal region, emerging from internal battles, could handle it yet.

The Eastern Cape had another problem.

'At one stage I left the Conference, and found Walter Sisulu wandering around outside,' remembers Raymond Mhlaba, possibly the most determined of the campaign's many supporters.[38] 'He said, "Man, there's a problem inside here. These fellows from the Cape, Prof. Matthews and Dr Njongwe, are against the Defiance Campaign. They claim people will be shot, how can we defend ourselves?"

'Because the Cape was as strong as it was, without its approval the Campaign would not have worked.

'I suggested to Walter that I should talk to Dr Njongwe that evening, which I did. I was heated up, and said: "Man, you are causing trouble – I will expose you!" I was Chairman of New Brighton, and he was our Treasurer. He laughed, and that solved the problem. After that everything went well.'

As this strategy was coming together, Mandela was made the National Volunteer-in-Chief. His responsibility was to ensure that structures and volunteers in numbers were in place all over the country.

In January 1952 the ANC fired its first shot. Dr Moroka and Sisulu, as the President General and the Secretary General, signed an ultimatum calling on the government for direct representation of Africans 'in the councils of state' and to repeal six 'unjust and racially discriminatory laws' by 29 February

1952, failing which 'mass action' would be taken. The specified laws included the pass laws, the newly adopted Group Areas Act, stock limitation and the Bantu Authorities Act, as well as the Separate Representation of Voters Act and the Suppression of Communism Act. The letter emphasised that 'the struggle which our people are about to begin is not directed against any race or national group, but against these unjust laws'.[39]

The Prime Minister did not reply. Instead, his secretary replied on 29 January. The government had no intention, he said, of repealing the long-existing laws differentiating between Europeans and Bantu, which were largely measures for the latter's protection. 'Should you adhere to your expressed intention of embarking on a campaign of defiance and disobedience to the government,' the Prime Minister's secretary wrote, 'and should you in the implementation thereof incite the Bantu population to defy law and order, the government will make full use of the machinery at its disposal to quell any disturbances, and, thereafter, deal adequately with those responsible for initiating subversive activities.' He further noted that the ANC's letter should have gone to the Minister of Bantu Administration, not the Prime Minister.

Dr Moroka and Sisulu responded on 11 February. They regretted that the Prime Minister had rejected 'our genuine offer of cooperation on the basis of equality'. The Defiance Campaign would go ahead.

It was preceded by a National Day of Pledge and Prayer, called to coincide with the government-sponsored celebrations to mark the tercentenary of Jan van Riebeeck's arrival at the Cape on 6 April 1652. The ANC called for mass rallies on this day. Again, the largest were held in Port Elizabeth, where 30 000 people listened to Prof. ZK Matthews, JB Marks and Ida Mntwana. Matthews called for support for the forthcoming campaign, saying that no critic had offered an alternative proposal and that 'it is obvious that in our unarmed state it would be suicidal for us to think of an armed struggle'.[40]

With regard to the government celebrating 300 years since Van Riebeeck, Chief Albert Luthuli put it best: 'To put it simply, while they celebrated three hundred years of white domination, we looked back over three hundred years of black subjection. While the whites were jubilant over what they said God had given them, we contemplated what they had taken from us, and the land which they refuse to share with us though they cannot work it without us.'[41]

The government could see trouble ahead and attempted to head it off by banning, in May, five leaders under the Suppression of Communism Act: Moses Kotane, JB Marks, DW Bopape, JN Ngwevela and Dr Dadoo. They followed this by banning the newspaper *The Guardian* (which closed and immediately reappeared as *The Clarion*); removed Sam Kahn and Fred

Carneson from their positions as 'native' representatives and also banned Solly Sachs (Albie's father) and Michael Harmel. It was immediately announced that those banned would defy their bans and become the first defiers. They were, as they broke their bans, duly arrested.

It didn't help. On 31 May the national executives of the ANC and the SAIC met in Port Elizabeth and decided to open the Defiance Campaign officially on the second anniversary of the 1950 'Day of Protest', on 26 June 1952. This, despite the fact that the ANC was in a financial crisis at the time and that its Natal and Transvaal leadership was in tatters, and that it had only roughly 7 000 members in about 65 branches across the country

Preparations were thorough and went ahead in all major centres. A national volunteer board was established with Mandela as Volunteer-in-Chief.

'The primary launch of the Defiance Campaign was held at Mloteni Square in New Brighton, Port Elizabeth … where a vigorous campaign was being upheld by grassroots support … Oliver Tambo and other representatives of the NEC were on the platform,' writes Luli Callinicos in her biography of Tambo.[42]

One of the outcomes of this launch was the excitement of much international interest. 'We had calls from all over, we had everybody,' recalled Ismail Meer. 'We had the BBC, *The New York Times*, and all of them for the first time. So the BBC was Robert Stimpson. He had covered the transition from British rule to independence (in India) and he had come down here.' For Tambo, this was his first taste of the power of the international media.[43]

A Day of the Volunteers was called for Sunday 22 June. The meetings began with prayers and volunteers were asked to sign a pledge:

> I, the undersigned, Volunteer of the National Volunteer Corps, do hereby solemnly pledge and bind myself to serve my country and my people in accordance with the directives of the National Volunteer Corps and to participate fully and without reservations to the best of my ability in the Campaign for the Defiance of Unjust Laws. I shall obey the orders of my leader under whom I shall be placed and strictly abide by the rules and regulations of the National Volunteer Corps framed from time to time. It shall be my duty to keep myself physically, mentally and morally fit.[44]

Residents were asked to stay at home and pray and fast. Manyanos (women in church-based welfare groups) wore their uniforms and sang hymns at the mass meetings. Speakers extolled the virtues of non-violence and taking on suffering.

On the first day of the campaign, 26 June, Raymond Mhlaba remembers, 'We prayed the whole night at the civic centre in New Brighton. From the civic centre we left for the New Brighton station in the early hours of the morning on 26 June. By five o'clock that morning we found sergeants, not even ordinary policemen, waiting for us. All the people from the Red Location came to witness the event.

'The sergeant in charge asked me to deal with the crowd after watching the volunteers. I assured him that our people were well aware of the procedure of the campaign. I addressed the people and told them to go home or to work after watching the volunteers defying unjust laws. Those who wanted to join the volunteers were to go and register for the Defiance Campaign in our ANC offices.

'I led the very first group and we entered the "Europeans Only" section of the New Brighton station. By half past six we were already in police vans on our way to jail. It turned out that my party was the first to defy unjust laws in the whole of South Africa. Little did we know that we were making history … people of Port Elizabeth gave me the name "Vulindlela" as I opened the way for others to defy an unjust system.

'Nompi Njongwe, the wife of Dr Njongwe, led the first batch of twenty-one women. Dideka Heliso, who was later to become my wife after my first wife died, was part of this group. These women were arrested at the New Brighton Railway Station …'[45]

It was not to be this efficient elsewhere.

The Transvaal campaign was due to start with a group of volunteers courting arrest by entering a township near Boksburg. They were to be led by Nana Sita, president of the Transvaal Indian Congress and a veteran Gandhian disciple, and the Reverend Tantsi, acting president of the Transvaal ANC.

Tantsi did not arrive on time and later phoned the volunteer office to call in ill. Later still, he confessed to Sisulu that he had not been ill, but just could not see the responsibility through. Mandela, the head of volunteers, sent Sisulu in Tantsi's place.

A huge crowd saw them off on their campaign. They found the location gates locked, but waited patiently for the police to open them and then flooded through to court their arrest.

That night 52 men, including Mandela and Cachalia, broke the curfew in central Johannesburg.

And so it spread over the country. In the end 146 volunteers were arrested in June, in July 1 504, in August 2 015, and in September 2 058. By mid-December an additional 2 334 had been arrested, bringing the national total to just over 8 000.

Tom Lodge has done the most comprehensive regional breakdown of resister arrests.[46] In total he believes that over the period June to December 1952, there were 8 326 resister arrests over the country. Of these 5 941 (71%) were in the Eastern Cape, 1 578 (19%) in the Transvaal, 490 (6%) in the Western Cape, 125 (2%) in the Orange Free State and 192 (2%) in Natal.

Only in the Eastern Cape did the rural areas present some resisters. In the Free State and Natal all resisters were arrested in either Bloemfontein or Durban.

Port Elizabeth (2 007) and Uitenhage (600) together provided 31% of all arrests, five times the number of the entire Western Cape and five times the number of Johannesburg.

Resisters were predominantly Africans with a small number of Coloured and Indian South Africans subjecting themselves to arrest. Seven whites resisted in Germiston and four in Cape Town. It had been an African campaign of suffering.

On 30 July, with arrests beginning to happen in numbers, the police went for the leaders.

Mandela was at his law firm, HM Basner, when the police arrived to charge him under the Suppression of Communism Act. They simultaneously raided offices and homes in some 16 centres, entering and confiscating papers. Two weeks later they arrested 20 national and provincial leaders. In September they arrested 15 leaders in the Eastern Cape.

'My arrest and those of the others culminated in a trial in September in Johannesburg of twenty-one accused, including the presidents and the general secretaries of the ANC, the Youth League, the SAIC and the Transvaal Indian Congress. Among the twenty-one on trial in Johannesburg were Dr Moroka, Walter Sisulu, JB Marks, Mandela, Dan Tloome, Nana Sita, Dr Dadoo, Yusuf Cachalia and Ahmed Kathrada,' wrote Mandela in his autobiography.[47] They were granted bail of £100.

On trial in Port Elizabeth were, amongst others, Dr Njongwe, Joseph Matthews, son of Prof. Matthews, and Tsepo Letlaka. They too were granted bail.

The Johannesburg Trial drew huge crowds. 'The court had never been deluged with such crowds before,' Mandela wrote.[48]

'The trial should have been an occasion of resolve and solidarity, but it was sullied by a breach of faith by Dr Moroka ... the President General of the ANC and the figurehead of the campaign,' recalled Mandela. Dr Moroka employed his own attorneys and resisted the rest of the group's entreaty to join their defence. Worse still, he explained this as a refusal to be associated with men who were communists, an issue he claimed he had never been comfortable with.

Even worse was to follow, when he tendered a humiliating plea in mitigation. When asked whether there should be equality between black and white, he replied that there would never be such a thing. When asked by his own lawyer whether there were communists among the other defendants, he pointed out some, including Dr Dadoo and Walter Sisulu. Remarkably, and to cap his humiliation, Judge Rumpff told him to desist as that was not necessary.

In this sorry process Moroka destroyed his future candidature for another spell as President General.

Both the Johannesburg and Port Elizabeth trials ended with the defendants being found guilty of statutory communism, but both courts noted that the defendants had gone out of their way to avoid violence. All were sentenced to nine months' imprisonment, suspended for two years. Probably not what the police had wanted.

The intention of the campaign was for units of volunteers to commit technical offences such as contravention of pass laws, general apartheid regulations at stations and post offices and other such regulations. The volunteers would not defend themselves in court, nor would they pay fines. They would accept imprisonment in Gandhian style.

In Port Elizabeth initially the sentences that the magistrates imposed were light, £2, or 30 days. Quickly this was raised. In September a number of adults, including ladies, were sentenced to £15 fines, or 90 days, and juveniles to four cuts with a light cane.

As the prisons filled, magistrates became more extreme. A 'seizure clause' was implemented. If an offender was carrying money this could be seized and used to pay the fine incurred. Defiers stopped carrying money. And, incredibly, sometimes the courts helped. In Port Elizabeth in July, 19 African defiers were acquitted of entering the European side of the Post Office because there were no European customers there at the time. As they had been charged with 'obstructing the business of the Post Office', this obviously could not have happened, the magistrate ruled!

The campaign of disobedience rolled on, and eventually 2 007 resisters were arrested in Port Elizabeth and 600 in Uitenhage – over 30% of the entire national total. An organisation with 7 000 members across South Africa got 8 300 people to accept imprisonment in its first campaign. This was no mean achievement.

Tragedy was to follow in Port Elizabeth. In the words of the veteran reporter Jimmy Matyu:[49]

On 18 October 1952 'paint riots', which left 11 dead, seven of them blacks, 27 injured and eight buildings, including the plush Rio

47

Cinema, wrecked, ensued in what was regarded by the media as a night of murder, arson and mob violence.

I still remember this newspaper [*The Herald*] with a front page headline on Monday 20 October screaming: 'Armed police quell bloody riot at New Brighton township'.

For the sake of space I will try to reconstruct briefly what I witnessed on that fateful day.

It was on the afternoon of Saturday 18 October 1952 when New Brighton exploded in flames. It all started at the New Brighton Station when a railway policeman tried to arrest two men who were alleged to have stolen a gallon of paint at North End Station and then boarded a train to New Brighton.

The two men resisted and a scuffle ensued. Other passengers, joined by people from the Red Location, came to the assistance of the men. They threw missiles and the constable, perched on the whites-only side of the railway bridge, opened fire. In flight from the police shooting, the enraged mob made its way deeper into the location and the first victim to die was WM Laas, a white man, who had given black fellow workers a lift home.

Shops managed by whites were attacked.

On that Saturday the Rio bioscope was showing a western movie, *The Gunfighter*, starring Gregory Peck. It had packed the house for a week.

Just before the mob, armed with a variety of missiles, arrived at the Rio, some sympathetic people warned the bioscope manager, Rudolf Brandt, his wife Edith, and their assistants to leave, but Brandt refused, saying the Africans were his people and would not harm him. Only the assistant manager, George Thomas, successfully fled in his car which came under a hail of stones.

The café in the foyer was looted and Brandt's car was torched. He, his wife, a technician Gerald Leppan, his assistant, Karl Bernhardt, and Leppan's 15-year-old son Brian, found themselves trapped in the projection room when the building was set on fire.

Later the five appeared with Brandt giving the ANC's 'Mayibuye Africa' salute – right hand with clenched fist and the thumb pointing backwards – in an attempt to exit via the fire escape, but even that demonstration of allegiance to the ANC did not deter the mob from immediately dragging, attacking and callously stabbing them.

Brian managed to escape with minor injuries and sought refuge under a bed in the Grattan Street home of a headman. From there he was whisked out of the township by the late Reverend Douglas Mbopa to safety.

While Brandt lay on the ground and still shouting 'Mayibuye Africa', he was murdered. His wife was dragged across the concrete road, brutally gang-raped and assaulted. She was saved from death by the arrival of a police kwela truck, which was greeted with a hail of stones, and the police retaliated by opening fire on the crowd, which fled.

The next morning an eerie calm prevailed, with some people returning to the wrecked bioscope in search of what they could salvage, possibly money.

Three weeks later another atrocity happened, this time in Duncan village, East London.

Mary Quinlan had been born in Ireland in 1914. A bright and observant young girl, she had taken vows and become a Catholic nun, in the process acquiring the name Sister Aidan.

In the 1930s she had been posted to the Zweleni Convent, 10 kilometres outside of King William's Town in the Eastern Cape. Acknowledging her intellect, her superiors had enrolled her at the University of the Witwatersrand to study medicine. She was in fact in the same class as Dr James Njongwe. They graduated together and were friends.[50]

For years Sr Aidan was a familiar face in Eastern Cape townships, and it was the subject of humour as to how many babies she had helped into the world. She loved her work and her communities loved her.

On 8 November there had been another massacre, this time in Duncan village. Police had raided an evening prayer meeting and had told the congregation that they believed it to be a political meeting, and was thus banned. This was vigorously protested. The police drew their weapons and soon nine of the congregation were dead.

The next day Sr Aidan was answering a call from Duncan village. She was stopped by the police at the entrance to the township, but convinced them that she would be in no danger as she was well known there. She drove five kilometres into Duncan village where a mob stopped her. She was killed and her car and her body were burnt.

The ANC's response to both of these atrocities was horror.

Raymond Mhlaba records how he had been in King William's Town, organising defiers in the rural areas, when he was phoned to return immediately to Port Elizabeth as 'a person had been accused of stealing paint at a station, and there was fighting with the police. Stones were thrown, people were shot, and people were killed by mobs. It was very ugly...'[51]

The organisation immediately placed a statement on the front page of the morning newspaper, *The Herald*. This appeared on 20 October, the Monday after the Saturday riots. It included:

> The recent happenings, in which there was needless loss of human lives, have greatly shocked the South African people.
>
> The ANC, whilst dissociating itself and condemning the unwarranted use of firearms and useless destruction of property, wishes to express the sincerest sympathy of the African people towards the families, both Black and White, who have suffered the loss of their loved ones through this unfortunate, reckless, ill-considered return to jungle law.
>
> The ANC calls upon the African people to cease forthwith from participating in any violent action. They must rally to the call of the ANC, which is conducting a non-violent struggle against racially discriminatory, unjust laws.[52]

At this stage we need to introduce a new face into this story, Albert John Luthuli.

Luthuli has left us a wonderful autobiography, which I sincerely recommend.[53] It tells the story of a deeply Christian man, who spent 17 years as a traditional leader and who only came to politics when he was around 50.

He was born in, of all places, Southern Rhodesia, late in the 19th century. His parents were both Zulu-speaking South Africans (although there was no South Africa then). His father had gone to Rhodesia to serve in the Rhodesian forces in the Matabele Rebellion and had remained there as an evangelist.

Young Albert's father died when he was an infant and his mother sent him back to the family's traditional home in Groutville, Natal, where he lived for a while with his uncle, Martin Luthuli. He did his schooling there and completed a teachers' course at Edenvale near Pietermaritzburg. While teaching at a small primary school in the Natal uplands, he was confirmed as a Methodist and became a lay preacher and a profoundly religious man.

At the age of 22 he received a government bursary to attend Adams College, where he did a higher teachers' course, and thereafter joined the staff. ZK Matthews was at this time the head of Adams, and Luthuli spent 15 years on the staff.

Then he was pressured into taking over the chieftaincy of his Groutville reserve and he did this from 1935 until 1952.

When John Dube died in 1946, Luthuli decided to lend a hand to strengthen the Natal ANC, then a weak body riven with factionalism. He contested the by-election on the Natives Representative Council that had been Dube's seat, and beat off Selby Msimang to join this controversial body.

In 1951 he narrowly beat AWG Champion to become provincial leader of the ANC, and was immediately plunged into the Defiance Campaign. As provincial leader he was 'staff officer' in the campaign, which meant that he did not court imprisonment but rather organised the programme. This did not help. The National Party government sent him to Pretoria to explain how he could be campaigning against the government when, as a chief, he was part of that government. As a result, in the midst of the Defiance Campaign, he was dismissed from the chieftaincy on 12 November.

Luthuli responded with a devastating public statement entitled 'The Road to Freedom is via the Cross'. It contained the remarkable line, 'who will deny that thirty years of my life have been spent, knocking in vain, patiently, moderately and modestly at a closed and barred door?'[54]

'The notoriety gained by his dismissal, his eloquence, his unimpeachable character, and his demonstrated loyalty to the ANC all made Luthuli a natural candidate to succeed Dr Moroka as president general.'[55] And this he did. One month after being stripped of his chieftaincy, Albert Luthuli was, in December 1952 at the ANC's National Conference, elected as President General by a large majority. He was almost immediately banned.

His first problem was what to do with the Defiance Campaign, which was collapsing under greatly increased police suppression.

After the riots in Port Elizabeth, the City Council imposed a curfew and a ban on all political meetings for three months. This infuriated the ANC, who were of course in the middle of the Defiance Campaign.

The ANC called an emergency regional conference in Cradock. This conference agreed on a general strike and a protest demonstration.

Each home was to pray and fast for a day and the next day children were to return to school. All adults were to stay at home indefinitely, 'or until God Almighty changed the hearts of the City Councillors'.[56]

This caused a rift in the ANC hierarchy.

Dr Njongwe, who was not at Cradock, did not believe in an indefinite strike which would, he said, inevitably fail. Walter Sisulu was called and he sped to Port Elizabeth.

Ray Mhlaba had got the city councillors to reduce the period of the curfew and Sisulu agreed with Dr Njongwe. The strike was reduced to one day and was successful.

At this stage, the Defiance Campaign's working committee took stock. Confrontations with the police had resulted in deaths in four parts of the country. The government was being increasingly draconian; on 7 November 52 leaders of the Campaign in the Eastern Cape were banned. This heavy-handed attempt to reassert control would undoubtedly lead to more confrontation and more bloodshed. The philosophy of the campaign – peaceful resistance – was unlikely to hold.

The Defiance Campaign was petering out and something should be done. It was up to the newly installed President General to take action.

'Shortly after the National Conference, I was asked by the Youth League to address a meeting at Alexandria Township, just outside Johannesburg. It was intended that the meeting would precede the sending of batches of volunteers into defiance. After I had spoken, somebody on the platform began a long and rambling speech calling for volunteers, but at the time those who had offered themselves had melted away. The response this time was one old man, and he was tipsy,' wrote Chief Luthuli.[57]

The Defiance Campaign was over. 'Shortly after [the Alexandria meeting] we brought the Campaign to an official end, albeit belatedly. Its back had been broken well before this, by the skill with which the riots were engineered, and by the blatant exploitation of the riots thereafter,' wrote Luthuli.[58]

In Port Elizabeth the end of the Defiance Campaign was followed by a huge loss to the ANC.

Dr James Njongwe, a professional man with independent means, was rumoured to be willing to contest the position of President General at the 1952 National Conference. Somehow he appears not to have, leaving the race open for Albert Luthuli to sweep past Dr Moroka, which duly happened.

Then in June 1954 he contested and won the provincial presidentship of the Cape, taking the position from Prof. ZK Matthews.

But now the strains of his dual life – medicine and politics – took their toll and his health began to weaken. He was simultaneously beset by financial difficulties. He considered returning to the Transkei to establish a new life, his daughter has written, when the government banned him from being a member of the ANC and from attending meetings for two years.

He took his family to Matatiele where he established a practice. He was to live there for the rest of his life. He continued to endure occasional banning restrictions and was jailed during the 1960 state of emergency. He was lost forever to the turmoil of Port Elizabeth's ANC politics.

There are two issues that need inspecting before we close the chapter on the Defiance Campaign:

Firstly, what accounts for the remarkable success of the campaign in the Port Elizabeth and Uitenhage area?

Secondly, was the Defiance Campaign a success?

Why the Eastern Cape, and, particularly, why Port Elizabeth and Uitenhage?

Tom Lodge has written a very valuable book entitled *Black Politics in South Africa since 1945*. It is about 350 pages long, and 10 of those pages are devoted to explaining the remarkable success of the Defiance Campaign in Port Elizabeth.[59] His analysis addresses two areas: socio-economic issues and political issues.

On socio-economic matters he outlines how, in the 1940s, the African population of Port Elizabeth was growing quickly, driven principally by two causes, the poverty of the communities in the Transkei hinterland and the desperate need of these citizens for the opportunities of a big city and the apparent availability of industrial employment in Port Elizabeth caused by a surge of wartime manufacturing.

This caused in-migration at a record rate.

And what did the in-migrating folk find? They joined the poorest African community in a major city in South Africa, and, because of the large numbers arriving, they also found a housing market overwhelmed and unable to provide this basic need. And they found that the manufacturing jobs were not available in the numbers hoped for. The new arrivals had to accept much lower-paid employment in the services sector. Thus the socio-economic environment was ripe for protest.

Now the political environment. Here there were a number of factors in play.

Firstly, the local City Council was, by white South African standards, comparatively liberal. There was no compulsory carrying of passes. There was little job reservation. There was no group areas enforcement (as we have seen, Raymond Mhlaba and his father rented a flat in what became a white area). For Africans, this was not, at the beginning of the 1940s, a bad deal.

Secondly, 'with the wartime expansion of the African industrial workforce came the first serious efforts at trade unionism since the collapse of the ICU fifteen years before'.[60] AZ Tshiwula got a union for African railway workers on its feet in 1943. And the energetic Max Gordon, sent to Port Elizabeth by the Institute of Race Relations in 1941, organised seven African unions in the cement, soft drinks, food and canning, engineering, leather and distribution industries. By 1945 'the nineteen Port Elizabeth affiliates of the Council for Non-European Trade Unions (CNETU) claimed 40000 members ... it was nevertheless evident that trade union membership amongst Port Elizabeth's African workers was unusually high'.

We have noted the overlapping membership of the unions, the Communist Party and the ANC in Port Elizabeth, and how this (in Lodge's wonderful word) interpenetration led to massive community involvement in protests and uprisings in the 1940s. Rent protests, food protests, bus boycotts, the royal visit – these were the issues presented to the community. The overlapping executive memberships, headed up by activists like Mhlaba, motivated the community with minimum dissent and massive protests became the stuff of this collegial arrangement. Where in Johannesburg tensions readily emerged between Youth Leaguers and the Indian Congress and others, in Port Elizabeth all of this was contained and the protesting community was united and wasted no energy fighting amongst themselves. It was a formula that would take until the years of the UDF to return, and it was the stuff of success.

By the time the Defiance Campaign came around in 1952, the ANC in Port Elizabeth had had seven years of protests and action from the McNamee village rent strike of 1945 and on through many others. By 1952 the 'mixed bag' leadership was seasoned in protest and the community was experienced in taking on suffering in a good cause.

This was, surely, the main reason for the success of the Defiance Campaign in Port Elizabeth. They'd done it before. Many times. They were honed in protest and were now ready for a bigger play on a bigger stage.

Finally, was the Defiance Campaign a success?

Tom Lodge believes that the Defiance Campaign 'was to be the most sustained and – in terms of numbers of participants – the most successful organised resistance the ANC was ever to initiate'.[61]

Certainly there were unfulfilled objectives: none of the six laws that were in the Moroka–Sisulu correspondence were repealed. 'We never had any illusion that they would be,' wrote Mandela in his autobiography.[62] The government went no way to meet the bottom line demand of the ANC, a universal franchise. Instead it intensified the number and detail of the apartheid laws it was determined to effect. And it doubled up on both security responses and on the use of the courts to smother the ANC and its ideals. Bannings were now daily things, and activists like Luthuli, Tambo, Sisulu, Mandela and Mhlaba went from one period of banning to the next, almost seamlessly. By 1955, 42 ANC leaders had been banned.[63] And a treason trial was being planned to neutralise the ANC leadership. This began in 1956 and lasted until 1961, with the numbers of defendants whittled down from 156 to 30. All defendants were eventually found not guilty, having spent years in court.

Also on the downside, there were, limited white, Coloured and Indian numbers amongst the defiers. And, apart from the Eastern Cape, total numbers of defiers were lower than early predictions. The riots, which caused the end of the campaign, and which both Mandela and Luthuli believed were provoked by agents provocateurs, certainly caused the white community and its newspapers to pull away from the ANC.

Those were the disappointments. In total, they do not make up half of the story, though.

Firstly, there was the international spotlight, which now began to fall on apartheid and its patent injustices. At the United Nations, South Africa had been under two spotlights. Firstly, as the UN entered the world, India had begun lodging complaints as to South Africa's treatment of its large Indian population; and secondly, South Africa's mandate to govern South West Africa was also challenged. The Defiance Campaign chalked up a big win here, for Asian and Arab delegates asked for the inclusion of an apartheid item. In 1952, with the Defiance Campaign in full swing, the General Assembly voted (with the Western countries abstaining) to set up a UN Commission on the Racial Situation in the Union of South Africa, thereby beginning what was to become a strong political and moral support system for the anti-apartheid forces in South Africa.

Secondly, while white participation was limited, there were two significant developments in the white community.

Late in September 1952 a group of 22 distinguished whites issued a statement which stated that the persons leading the Campaign were 'acknowledged leaders' and called for the revival of the liberal tradition of the 19th-century Cape Colony, which meant the qualified franchise for all 'civilized people'. They stopped short of calling for universal franchise and called for restraint and patience in the African community. This was signed by, amongst others, Margaret Ballinger, Alan Paton, Trevor Huddleston and Ambrose Reeves.

More helpfully, the national action committee called a meeting in November in Johannesburg. Possibly 200 whites attended, some of whom, in 1953, formed themselves into the Congress of Democrats, essentially a 'white wing' of the ANC.

Thirdly, the Campaign saw the ANC's following shoot upwards. At the beginning of the Campaign the ANC had about 7 000 members. Six months later this had risen considerably. Both Mandela and Luthuli estimate that the number crossed 100 000. Karis and Carter report that, at the ANC's national conference in December 1953, the number of paid-up members was 28 900, of whom 16 000 were in the Cape Province, 11 000 in the Transvaal, 1 300 in Natal and 600 in the Free State. Whatever the figure, the number of persons mobilised by the Campaign was undoubtedly massively higher than 7 000. As Mandela has written: 'The ANC emerged as a truly mass-based organisation with an impressive corps of experienced activists who had braved the police, the courts and the jails. The stigma usually associated with imprisonment had been removed ... from the Defiance campaign onwards, going to prison became a badge of honour amongst Africans.'[64]

Finally, the opinions of four of the leaders of the time:

Walter Sisulu: 'Nothing has raised the political consciousness of the masses so high up until that time. Nothing had been more effective in fostering a growing discipline and militancy. Volunteers looked upon themselves as a paramilitary force. Efficiency had increased within the movement, as well as determination.'[65]

Raymond Mhlaba: 'We regarded the Defiance Campaign as political activity of a higher level than we had previously been involved in. This new method involved everybody – the whole family is affected. It was much more than going to jail – it involved the whole community ... It released an enormous amount of energy – it really caused our organisation to grow.'[66]

Nelson Mandela: 'I nevertheless felt a great sense of accomplishment and satisfaction. I had been engaged in a just cause and had the strength to fight for it and win. The campaign freed me from any lingering feeling of doubt or inferiority I might still have felt; it liberated me from the feeling of being overwhelmed by the power and seeming invincibility of the white man and his institutions. But now the white man had felt the power of my punches and I could walk upright like a man, and look everyone in the eye with the dignity that comes from not having succumbed to oppression and fear. I had come of age as a freedom fighter.'[67]

Albert Luthuli: 'So ended a year that changed the political complexities of South Africa. The whites took several more strides towards authoritarianism. Among Africans and Indians, and to a smaller extent amongst Coloureds, the spirit of active opposition came alive, consent to still be governed exclusively by the whites and for the whites was withdrawn, goals became clear. I do not think the outside world saw the full significance of what had happened – it took the Treason Trial to arouse their interest. But, when the history of these troubled times comes to be written, I think it will be seen that, on both sides, 1952 was a turning point in the struggle.'[68]

4

Mbeki, Mhlaba and Mkwayi together in Port Elizabeth

As the Defiance Campaign was stumbling to its end in late 1952, the Minister of Justice, Charles Robberts Swart, had a personally signed letter delivered to 'Raymond Mhlaba, native male'. The letter read that, in terms of the powers conferred on Swart by the Suppression of Communism Act of 1950, 'I do hereby prohibit you from attending, during a period of six months as from the date that this notice is delivered or tendered to you, any gathering in any place within the Union of South Africa.'[69]

At the end of May 1953, six months later, Albert Luthuli was banned from attending public meetings, and prohibited from entering 21 cities and towns for one year, effectively house arrest. By the end of 1954, the ANC could list, in an annexure to its annual report, the names of 95 members of the ANC or allied organisations who were under some kind of ban: 36 Africans, 19 Indians, 38 whites and three Coloureds.[70]

This was just the beginning of the State's fight-back.

The aftermath of the Defiance Campaign

In early 1953 the Prime Minister, Dr DF Malan, called a general election (whites-only, of course) for 15 April 1953.

Much had changed in white politics since 1948. Both Jan Smuts and Hofmeyr had died, and Smuts' United Party was now led by one of the most indecisive of white politics' many nondescript opposition leaders, Jacobus Gideon Nel Strauss. The HNP had meanwhile amalgamated with the Afrikaner Party to form the National Party. Malan had South West Africa demarcated into six constituencies, and voters there participated in the election (no surprise that they all returned National Party members).

Just prior to the election, parliament had a short sitting.

Short it may have been, but it was long enough to pass two bills designed to deal with the 'black peril'.

The first, the Criminal Law Amendment Act, essentially aimed at making another Defiance Campaign impossible. Now, any person committing any offence 'by way of protest or in support of any campaign against the law' (long-hand for 'Defiance Campaign') could be sentenced to a ten-stroke whipping, a £300 fine or three years in jail, or a combination of any two of these delights. Second offenders were to be either whipped or imprisoned and fined. For a person 'whose words or actions were calculated to cause another person to commit an offence by way of a protest', these penalties were increased by an additional fine of £200, or two more years' imprisonment.

Secondly, parliament passed the Public Safety Act. This allowed for the declaration of a state of emergency if the cabinet thought that public order was seriously threatened. Should such a state of emergency be in place, individuals could be summarily arrested and detained, as long as government submitted their names to parliament after 30 days. A state of emergency would last a year and could then be renewed.

This all was sweet music to a white electorate concerned by the Defiance Campaign, and terrified by the riots that ensued. The National Party won a majority of votes cast (598 718 to the United Party's 576 474), and ended with 94 seats in a 156-seat house, a full majority without a coalition being necessary. If there ever was to have been an opportunity to 'dis-elect' the National Party, this election was it – and the electorate failed, miserably.

What was the ANC now to do?

Prof. ZK Matthews had gone to the USA to do a year's lecturing. He wanted to stay on, but the government would not provide an extension to his passport.

On arriving home on 16 May 1953, 'he found African political activity at a lull'.[71] A one-day strike had been called but had not happened. Nothing had been organised for 26 June. If anything was to happen, Chief Luthuli requested it to happen at members' homes.

Ray Mhlaba notes that the Communist Party had been banned for two years at this stage. He had had meetings with other executives and they had agreed to meet 'underground'. 'I had the privilege of being invited to the subsequent illegal conferences of the Party before it regrouped. The secrecy we operated under was incredible. We communicated in codes. We used books to decode messages. We met at secret venues that I did not know and cannot tell you even today … I was present when the new South African Communist Party (SACP) was formally launched in 1953.'[72]

Plainly, there was a lesson for the ANC to learn here. If bannings and repression made above-ground activity impossible, other ways of working had to be devised.

'Along with many others, I had become convinced that the government intended to declare the ANC and the SAIC illegal organisations, just as it had done with the Communist Party,' wrote Mandela. 'With this in mind, I approached the National Executive with the idea that we must come up with a contingency plan for just such an eventuality … They instructed me to draw up a plan that would enable the organisation to operate from underground. This strategy became known as the Mandela-Plan, or, simply, the M-Plan.'

Mandela worked on this issue for months. He wanted a system that enabled leaders to take decisions, even if banned, and for these decisions to get around the full organisation without calling a meeting. The system had to allow contact between the membership and the underground leadership.

He eventually came up with a pyramid system: communities would be divided into cells, or a grouping of about 10 houses. In charge of each cell would be a cell steward. A group of cells formed a zone, which would be directed by a chief steward who reported to the local branch of the ANC. This person reported to the branch executive and they in turn reported to the provincial secretariat. Cell stewards were the eyes and ears of the system. They had to know everyone in their area and be trusted by these folk. They called meetings, if possible, and ran programmes.

Ray Mhlaba was central to implementing the M-Plan in Port Elizabeth. 'When the M-Plan was introduced, we immediately implemented it in PE. I participated in zoning New Brighton into twenty-one zones … Each street had a steward, whose job it was to introduce members to the ANC … they had to know everything that happened on their street. Social events, weddings, funerals, etc … The M-Plan worked effectively in PE.'[73]

It was not so everywhere else.

'The M-Plan was conceived with the best intentions, but it was introduced with only modest success and its adoption was never widespread. The most impressive results were once again in the eastern Cape and Port Elizabeth. The spirit of the Defiance Campaign continued in the eastern Cape long after it vanished elsewhere …,' wrote Mandela.[74]

Under these conditions of banishment, suppression and the inability to organise public meetings (the Port Elizabeth City Council had banned these after the riots), Ray Mhlaba and his team, having put the M-Plan into place, knew that more action was needed to keep the ANC alive in what Prof. Matthews had called 'a lull'.

Firstly they organised 'Let the People Speak' public meetings, called by this new surrogate organisation to allow ANC speakers to reach the ANC audience without the ANC being, apparently, involved. And secondly, they organised a boycott of a small chain of butcheries which had, apparently, been selling low-grade meat to black customers.

But it was not enough. More was needed to keep the ANC moving. And that held for the ANC nationally just as much as it did for the ANC in Port Elizabeth.

The answer came from the Cape Provincial leader of the ANC, Prof. Matthews, in his presidential address at the Cape Provincial Conference of the ANC on 15 August 1953.

Prof. Matthews proposed that the ANC organise a multi-racial 'Congress of the People' campaign, so that 'all groups' could consider the national problems on an all-inclusive basis. This 'Congress of the People', Prof. Matthews said, would represent 'all the people of the country irrespective of race and colour' and it would draw up a 'Freedom Charter for the Democratic South Africa of the Future'.[75]

The Provincial Conference adopted this proposal, which was then put to the December 1953 national conference of the ANC. There it was accepted in principle. The Congress of the People was underway.

Within two months of Prof. Matthews' proposal, two new organisations were formed: the South African Coloured People's Organisation (SACPO) was formed on 12 September in Cape Town and the South African Congress of Democrats (COD) was formed in Johannesburg on 10 October 1953. The COD was formed mostly of left-wing whites.

Thus the symbol of the Congress of the People was a wheel with four spokes: the ANC, the SAIC, the SACPO and the COD.

That year both Prof. Matthews and Walter Sisulu came to Port Elizabeth to talk about this project. Prof. Matthews emphasised that people from all walks of life must be encouraged to submit their ideas. Sisulu stressed that the Congress of the People would be a unity of the four components and as such would be non-racial and democratic.

'We were excited to hear about the formation of the COP. We were enthusiastic about the idea of the Freedom Charter. Through the M-Plan it was easy for the branches of the ANC to spread the message of the Freedom Charter to all the residents in our communities,' remembers Raymond Mhlaba, who personally solicited contributions in New Brighton.[76]

As helpful as this programme was, it could not lift Ray Mhlaba's spirits for long.

Mandela has written: 'Banning not only confines one physically, it imprisons one's spirit. It produces a kind of psychological claustrophobia that makes one yearn not only for freedom of movement but spiritual escape … The insidious effect of bans was that at a certain point one began to think that the oppressor was not without but within.'[77]

For Mhlaba, a breaking point was nearing: 'By now it was abundantly clear to us that the government was determined to crush our organisations. The political atmosphere was intensely frustrating. It felt unbearable for us in PE. We believed we could not remain passive indefinitely…,' he remembered.[78]

Ray Mhlaba turned to the shebeens. In his first sign of weakness, he started drinking. Was this to be the way he would go? Dr Njongwe, burnt out and left town, Ray Mhlaba burnt out and drinking. Had the 'system' won?

Govan Mbeki's life prior to arriving in Port Elizabeth

Sometimes one gets lucky. Ray Mhlaba did. A guardian angel arrived. His name was Govan Archibald Mvunyelwa Mbeki. He was not only to save Ray Mhlaba from the shebeens, he was also to make a dramatic impact on Port Elizabeth's politics.

Govan Mbeki was 10 years older than Ray, having been born in his family home in Nyili village in Nqamakwe in the Transkei on 8 July 1910. South Africa had been united for all of six weeks on his birthday.

Govan's mother, Johanna Mabula, was 40 years younger than Govan's father, Skelewu Mbeki, who had been a widower when he had married Johanna. She nevertheless bore him five children, three daughters and two sons, of whom Govan was the youngest. His first wife left Skelewu with three children, making Govan the *laatlammetjie* of a large brood.

Govan's father was of 'modest wealth', Govan's biographer, Colin Bundy, wrote.[79] They lived in a home Skelewu had had built for his family in stone, the first stone house owned by an African in the district. Their furniture was 'some of the most beautiful furniture I ever saw', Govan told Bundy.

Skelewu owned and farmed about 30 acres of fenced land, where he grew crops and kept chickens and livestock. Further, Skelewu had a transport-riding business, the source of his early wealth.

All of Skelewu's eight children went to high school, for their father believed in education. Govan first attended school in 1918, at a Methodist school six miles from the family home. Then on to Healdtown, another Methodist school, from where he achieved a Junior Certificate pass of such a quality that he was awarded a Bunga scholarship from the Transkeian Territories General Council to proceed to the South African Native College, as Fort Hare University was then formally known.

He entered Fort Hare in 1931 to study for his matriculation. He carried on there, commencing a BA degree in 1934.

He majored in Psychology and Political Studies and he and McLeod Mabude were Fort Hare's first political science majors.

Mbeki loved his years at Fort Hare: 'Fort Hare shaped Govan Mbeki profoundly, intellectually and politically. His years there gave him the formal skills that fuelled his output as journalist and author; they also politicised him deeply and dually.'[80]

At Fort Hare he met two people who helped the development of his political awareness. Neither were members of staff at the university.

The first was the eccentric Eddie Roux, a PhD botanist who was a member of the Communist Party and who came through the Transkei with a new bride, a donkey and a tent. The second was the even more bizarre Max Yergan, an Afro-American who was, at the time, also a communist, although he later repented of this and became a proponent of apartheid and the philosophy 'black people have it good in South Africa'. Both moved the young Govan towards his life-long commitment to communism.

In 1936 Mbeki joined the ANC while at Fort Hare. His thinking, at this stage socialist, made him one of a very small number thinking this way. He did not join the party until a number of years later, in 1953, when he joined the underground South African Communist Party. What delayed his joining was his lifelong determination to mobilise in rural Transkei. The SACP believed in mobilising in urban areas; Mbeki believed that urbanising Africans should have been 'reached' by that time.

'Latin poetry and the Little Lenin library. Wordsworth on Westminster Bridge and SEK Mqhayi on his hill top. Secretary of the rugby club and in the same year a new member of the ANC. These were just some of the experiences that constituted Govan's experience of Fort Hare. He was representative of a new strain in Fort Hare's politics. He and others sought to reconcile their education and their aspirations with their frustration and their Africanism ... Calling upon an African national identity ... was another, indispensable component [of their nationalism].'[81]

In 1937 Govan graduated with a BA from Fort Hare. He then did two things: firstly, he enrolled with UNISA for a BCom in economics, which he got in 1941; and secondly he took on a teaching post at the Taylor Street Secondary School in Durban.

There he met the 22-year-old Epainette Moerane, whom he married in January 1940. They were to have four children between 1941 and 1948: Linda, Thabo (later President of South Africa), Moeletsi and Jama. Both Govan and 'Piny' were activists. 'It [the relationship] just came naturally because we were both interested in bettering things,' Piny said.[82]

The next year Govan moved to Adams College, the premier African school in Natal. Edgar Brookes was Principal, and Govan taught Latin. He did not last long, for late in the year he received a telegram inviting him to join the staff of the Clarkebury School in Engcobo in the Transkei.

His arrival at Clarkebury in 1939 started badly: 'When I arrived at Clarkebury the manager, before he had offered me a seat, said, "Have you abandoned your communist tendencies?" Now, when he invited me to teach there, he knew who I was. I suppose he was thinking "Well, he left his job behind, he just can't take his bags and go now." He was rude, and I have not forgotten it.'[83]

He lasted 18 months at Clarkebury before the manager fired him.

By 1936, Govan Mbeki had begun writing, the second of his three callings, the others being teaching and political organising.

'I then got down to writing and I put together a manuscript on conditions in the Transkei. By 1937 it was finished (called 'Transkei in the Making'), and I took it to a Durban-based liberal magazine owned by Dr Edgar Brookes and others. They ran it as a serial.

'Then two chaps from the Transkei who jobbed as printers wanted to start a publication to advertise their main work which was printing. They saw these serials and approached me, saying: "Look, take that manuscript out of the hands of that magazine and we will try to have it published as a booklet. Then we want to start a paper. We will give you all the freedom to express your ideas – all we are interested in is that the paper should be there, and that it advertises our services."

'That's how *The Territorial Magazine* started,' said Mbeki.[84]

By June 1938 Mbeki was listed as editor, and 'In the forties the newspaper was renamed *Inkundla ya Bantu*, and I stopped editing it in 1944.'[85] According to Bundy, *Inkundla* remained, until its demise in 1952, the only significant newspaper owned and run by Africans.[86]

Mbeki found other outlets for his prodigious writings. 'There was what I call the Guardian family of newspapers, which was established in 1938 by Bertie Sachs, the wife of Dr Sachs, both members of the Communist Party. *The Guardian* was not officially a paper of the CP, but it was largely people who were thinking in that direction who ran it. It was banned under the Suppression of Communism Act and it was then followed by a succession of other newspapers which is why I call them the Guardian family of newspapers: *Advance*, *The Clarion*, *The New Age*, and finally *Spark*.[87] Mbeki was listed as a member of the editorial board of *The Guardian* and frequently wrote for it.

By now he was becoming recognised in the ANC as a young man of great potential. As we have noted, in 1942 Dr Xuma called together 28 of the ANC's 'best brains' to draft a response to the document 'Atlantic Charter', which had described the proposed world that would emerge from the Second World War. Signed by Churchill and Roosevelt, it clearly implied the withdrawal of the great powers from colonies, which would then be run by the indigenous community. Smuts had agreed to this, in theory, and the ANC saw an opportunity to thrust South Africa into this debate. Mbeki was in this team, which set two new policy platforms for the ANC: universal franchise and a Bill of Rights, both of which were proposed in the ANC response, 'Africans' Claims in South Africa'.

When *Inkundla* ceased publishing in 1944, Mbeki decided to enter formal politics.

He 'chose to work within existing local organisations rather than try to create new Congress branches'.[88] In 1943 he joined the Bunga, a Transkeian advisory and deliberative council set up to 'oversee' the Transkei. He rapidly realised the folly of this institution: 'This is a toy telephone ... You can say what you like, but you would have no effect because the wires are not connected to the exchange.'[89] He was also elected as Secretary of the Transkeian African Voters Association, a body with an extensive network throughout the Transkei. This was in October 1941 and lasted until 1948 when he was voted out.

His philosophy, of working within an existing organisation and patiently converting it to the ANC, just did not work.

And his family life was in chaos.

Finances were always a problem. The little trading store he started had supplied some income, but just not enough. Epainette's own life was lost in the daily slog of parenting. Govan was seldom home and when he was, he was too busy to pay attention to the household and the children. 'I pushed them to their mother,' he notes.[90] Epainette finally confronted him. It was agreed that he leave for a teaching position offered him in Ladysmith and she would keep the store, such as it was, and the children. In 1953 Govan headed off to Ladysmith.

Here he was much loved as a teacher but his other commitment, to political organisation, led him to busily assemble grievances and demands for onward referral to the team assembling the Freedom Charter in Johannesburg. The authorities were not charmed. In April 1955 he received a letter banning him from teaching. Again.

Luckily Fred Carneson and Ivan Schermbrucker, both members of the Communist Party, were negotiating with him at that time for Govan to become local editor and office manager of the Port Elizabeth office of the *New Age* newspaper. *New Age* was a successor to the banned *Guardian* and Govan was delighted to take on this challenge. He set off for Port Elizabeth.

Govan Mbeki's early years in Port Elizabeth

In July 1955 Govan Mbeki arrived in Port Elizabeth to set up the local presence of the *New Age* newspaper. And much else…

At this stage, both Mbeki and Mhlaba were rising in prominence in the ANC. In 1953 Mhlaba had been elected to the Cape Executive and shortly thereafter Mbeki became National Chairman. The organisation they were prominent in was growing in numbers of members (from about 7 000 before the Defiance Campaign to about 28 900 at the 1953 conference. Of these about 16 00 were from the Cape Province). Although numbers were growing, the money was not. Dr Conco, acting as treasurer in Dr Molema's absence in May 1955, wrote to Oliver Tambo: 'You may perhaps be surprised to learn that since conference last year, there have been no monies coming into this office at all. The bank balance in the national office is – NIL. Shortly after Conference in January, I sent directives re all Congress funds and subscriptions to all the provinces and I have had no response …'[91]

The parlous state of the ANC was a small problem compared to the environment they now had to operate in.

The Defiance Campaign had set the government off in pursuit of ANC leaders. Of the Port Elizabeth ANC leadership, 13 had been charged under the Suppression of Communism Act. Many more were banned. The City Council had prohibited the ANC from holding meetings in New Brighton, and in March 1956 the government made it an offence to hold or address any gathering of 10 or more Africans in the districts of Port Elizabeth and Humansdorp.

Mbeki instilled new methods of activity. 'Now it was during this time, 1956 to 1960, that we perfected methods of working underground.'[92]

'Govan's key contribution to mobilisation in Port Elizabeth was essentially one of political education – he mounted a programme of political education without equal in any South African city in the 1950s. He wrote, cyclostyled and distributed a booklet of about 50 pages, in Xhosa, called *Isikhokhelo ngesimo nenkqubo ye ANC*, outlining the history, aims and policies of the movement. The booklet was used by study groups of ten people at a time. There were eventually scores of such groups …,' wrote Bundy.[93]

Attending this political education programme was a 24-year-old who was to become one of Mbeki's right-hand men. His name was Nkosinathi Benson Fihla.[94]

Fihla had been born in the village of Cildara in the Middledrift area on 13 June 1932. His father was working as a waiter at hotels in Cape Town, his mother was a domestic worker and he had two sisters. So proud was his father of his newly born son that he insisted that the infant Nkosinathi live with him in Cape Town for the first five years of his life. Thereafter the youngster returned to Middledrift, where he schooled until Standard 5.

In 1945 the entire Fihla family moved to Port Elizabeth and Nkosinathi attended Standard 6 at a church school before doing forms one, two and three at Newell High. In 1952 he was off to Lovedale, where he did a teachers' diploma. Here he first discovered politics as there were vigorous debating groups which included students from Fort Hare, Lovedale and Healdtown.

Young Fihla was a keen and accomplished sportsman and played cricket and baseball at a high standard. This saw him drawn to Healdtown in 1953, where the sport was excellent. Regrettably the food was not. Young Nkosinathi got drawn into a food boycott which saw him expelled just before year-end exams. Thus ended his formal schooling.

Back in Port Elizabeth, Nkosinathi found a militant and energetic ANC operating under the leadership of Ray Mhlaba and others. In 1954 he joined the ANC Youth League and the next year he found himself plunged into the business of assembling demands for the Freedom Charter and mobilising M-Plan structures. Most of this work was performed by what the ANC called the Volunteer Movement, which young Fihla was happy to join. He joined a group of 10, the maximum the restrictions then allowed, to study political developments, Govan Mbeki's course.

The Congress of the People came and went. Neither Mhlaba (banned) nor Mbeki (finishing up in Natal) could attend although they were electrified by the result, the Freedom Charter. Miraculously neither was accused in the Treason Trial that ran from 1956 to 1961, draining so many senior comrades from ANC work. A total of 156 activists were originally charged.

One who was not to be spared the tasks of assembling input for the future Freedom Charter and who had the good fortune to be present at the Congress of the People was Ray Mhlaba's Volunteer-in-Chief of the Eastern Cape, Wilton Mkwayi.

Mkwayi had, as a volunteer assistant, an energetic and endlessly hard-working young man from New Brighton, John Nangosa Jebe.

On the night of Friday 23 March 1956, Jebe was in a church group walking down Mendi Road to Embizweni Square in New Brighton. A police lorry caught up with the crowd, passed it and a group of African constables jumped off the lorry, which then moved on, and spun around to block the passage of the walking group. Their offence was, most probably, congregating in a group of more than 10 people, which a recently promulgated municipal ordinance had forbidden.

Suddenly the group panicked and ran off in many different directions. A shot was fired and Jebe fell down dead. He died in his volunteer uniform and army boots.

New Age ran this story, combined with a later story about Jebe's funeral, on Friday 30 March. Both stories were written by Govan Mbeki, the newspaper's Port Elizabeth correspondent.[95]

'At the greatest funeral ever known in these parts, over 30 000 people gathered in New Brighton last Friday to honour the memory of John Nangosa Jebe, who was shot during the clash with the police on March 23. "He lived and died for a noble purpose," said Mr Gladstone Tshume, speaking at the funeral.'[96]

Wilton Mkwayi also spoke and praised Jebe. Mbeki's article concludes thus: 'the most impressive sight took place at the entrance to the cemetery as thousands of volunteers and pioneers, giving the Afrika salute and singing *Senzenina*, lined up on either side of the road. Mkwayi returned the salute ... As the bier was lowered into the grave the Congress flag was furled and again the song in honour of the volunteers went into the air from thousands of dedicated freedom fighters ... That day the ANC ruled New Brighton.'[97]

Mbeki had come to Port Elizabeth to run the Port Elizabeth office of *New Age*, and that took up his working day and more. He contributed many stories and analytical articles to this journal, and also to Ruth First's magazine *Fighting Talk* and Michael Harmel's *Liberation*.

In 1958 and 1959 he began the book that many believe was his best, *The Peasants' Revolt*. Ruth First describes the ordeal of its writing:

> This book had a painful birth. Govan Mbeki is recognised widely in South Africa as an expert on the Transkei and on rural and agrarian problems. But not for him the seclusion of a study or library, the facilities for patient interviews and field work. This manuscript was written in fits and starts on deal tables in the kitchens of several African homes in Port Elizabeth townships; its progress was frequently interrupted by police raids when the sheets of paper had to be hurriedly secreted, or moved away from where the writer lived and worked, for his and their safe-keeping. A great slice of this book was written on rolls of toilet paper when Mbeki served a two-month

spell of solitary confinement, awaiting trial on a charge of making explosives. Mbeki was acquitted after those court proceedings; the manuscript was smuggled out of the cell to a typist who pored over the faint pencil writing on the thin paper, by candlelight and in the privacy of her township room. Some final portions were written from Govan's last hiding place in Johannesburg after he had moved from Port Elizabeth after he was drafted by the ANC National Executive to direct ANC campaigns from underground.[98]

Mbeki was a man of boundless energy. Not only was he cyclostyling training booklets and running educational groups, and writing stories and columns for magazines and writing books, by 1960 he was also producing a monthly broadsheet called *Izwe Lomzi* (The Voice of the People) for his beloved rural groups.

This was printed in a safe house in Walmer, in the heart of white Port Elizabeth. 'Under a table soundproofed with mattresses, two Gestetner cyclostyle printers ran non-stop, week after week, producing broadsheets ... which were then distributed by car – at a certain mileage along a certain road would appear an uncertain motor car with uncertain number plates ... its boot open ... at ten pm precisely ... to this day, as far as I know, nobody ever found out where the broadsheets were coming from, and we had the paper going for more than six months,' wrote one of Mbeki's accomplices, Harold Strachan. We will shortly hear more of him.[99]

By now the tensions in the ANC that followed from the clear non-racialism of the Freedom Charter had caused a break: in April 1959 Robert Sobukwe and other ex-ANC comrades launched the Pan Africanist Congress at the Orlando Community Hall in Soweto. Suspicious of white and 'communist Indian' influence in the ANC, they would not accept the shift in philosophy from the nationalist Programme of Action to the non-racialism of the Freedom Charter. They decided that their first campaign was to be against the hated pass laws and this was to happen on 21 March 1960.

'We in the ANC were planning on having a big occasion on which we were going to burn our passes. The PAC decided to get in just before our date and they chose (amongst others) Sharpeville at which they were going to lodge their protest. Our date was known publicly and they decided to move in just a little ahead of us. Then of course the people were shot.

'We decided in the ANC that this was not the time to start condemning them, but it was the time to show our condolences. And that is how we responded, and that is really how we felt,' said Raymond Mhlaba many years later.[100]

At this moment tragedy befell the Mhlaba family: Raymond's wife Joyce died in a motor accident.

'The support I received from comrades in the region was incredible. We buried Joyce in Fort Beaufort, our place of origin. A big and beautiful funeral was arranged. People such as Govan Mbeki, Themba Mqotha, George Pemba, Ma Baard and many others consoled me. I felt I was not alone. My sisters also helped me a lot to raise my young children. From then onwards my children became theirs, and I moved on with my political life,' Mhlaba remembers.[101]

By now Mhlaba had had enough of passive resistance. He began to talk openly of taking on the 'boers' militarily. 'I remember suggesting to Mandela that we could fight the boers.' Events that now unfolded made this move inevitable.

Just a few days after the Sharpeville massacre, the government declared a state of emergency.

The 1960 state of emergency lasted from 24 March to 31 August. In all, 11 503 people were detained. Robert Sobukwe was jailed for three years for burning his passbook. In the most decisive and authoritarian step, on 8 April 1960 the government banned both the ANC and the PAC. Democratic options to effect change in South Africa were no longer possible. The armed struggle was all that was left.

In the sweeping up of activists that characterised this state of emergency, both Raymond Mhlaba and Govan Mbeki were detained.

'I spent five months in detention, right here in Rooi Hel (North End Prison, Port Elizabeth). Rooi Hel was packed, packed, packed! You couldn't lie on your bed, you had to lie on your side, and if you lay on your back you were taking up space that others needed. At night one had to tread carefully to find one's way to the toilet.

'Some of those prison experiences were in fact very unpleasant. One can certainly remember the jail lice. A jail lice is long and big and when you crush it, as tough as it is, it goes "gedoef!" When we complained to the jail authorities, they said we had to go outside one morning after breakfast: "Take off your clothes, everything, strip."

'We stripped and they took all of our clothes off and boiled them. They took our blankets and sprayed them with DDT.

'They left us standing there for the entire day in the yard naked. Amongst us were reverend gentlemen like Rev Canon AJ Calata. There were two old chaps, both around 80 years. They stood there naked the whole day. Well, one doesn't easily forget that.[102]

The turn to the armed struggle

In late 1961 the paths of Ray and Govan split, for a while anyway.

The continued pursuit of non-military solutions was no longer an option and in October 1961 Ray Mhlaba received 'a coded message from the central committee of the Party that I was to leave for military training. The day after receiving the message I took a train to Johannesburg without saying a word to my family...'[103]

From Johannesburg Ray and Andrew Mlangeni were driven by John Nkadimeng to Lobatse, and from there they flew to Tanganyika, then to Ghana, to the Soviet Union and to China. He spent 10 months in northern China and two months in the south, learning about guerrilla warfare and the manufacture of explosives. He returned to South Africa in December 1962.

Mbeki remained in Port Elizabeth. In December 1960 he led an ANC national delegation that attempted to reconcile with the PAC. It did not succeed.

Now the pace towards a decision to enter what became known as the 'armed struggle' was quickening. Possibly the best description of the agonising within the ANC on making this fateful decision came out in Mandela's speech from the dock later in the Rivonia trial:

> In describing the popular mood of May 1961, Nelson Mandela, speaking from the dock three years later, said: 'It may not be easy for this court to understand, but it is a fact that for a long time the people have been talking of violence – of the day they would fight the White man and win back their country' ... ANC leaders had always prevailed upon them to avoid violence, but from the beginning of 1961 criticism of non-violence had grown among loyal members of the ANC – they were developing 'disturbing ideas of terrorism'. Towards the end of May Mandela had learned that small groups that had come into existence in urban areas were spontaneously planning to implement those ideas.
>
> At the beginning of June 1961, 'after a long and anxious assessment', Mandela and 'some colleagues' abandoned the ANC's policy of non-violence. They could not escape the conclusion, he said in his 1964 courtroom speech, that 'fifty years of non-violence had brought the African people nothing but more and more repressive legislation'. By 1961, he said, 'all channels of peaceful protest had been barred to us'. The government had deliberately created 'the atmosphere for civil war and revolution' ... 'Only two choices were left – submit or fight.'[104]

At the time, the ANC recognised four forms of violence – sabotage, guerrilla warfare, terrorism and open warfare. 'Sabotage was adopted, and, after assuming careful and rational control, no further decision on tactics was to be made until that method had been tested exhaustively.'

Govan Mbeki amplifies this position: 'Our choice of sabotage shows the concern of the ANC to avoid bloodshed as far as possible. It was our policy to hit non-personnel targets ... in South Africa we had had two previous situations of a similar sort – in both the First and Second World Wars some Afrikaners embarked on sabotage, when they had the franchise ... but they resorted to throwing bombs. How much more reason the ANC had to embark on such activities! We had no vote, and nowhere to express our views. What else was left to us?'[105]

It was time for many to make a commitment and in 1961 Nkosinathi Benson Fihla did. He joined both the SACP and MK. Quickly he found himself swept up in underground politics. As the ANC was banned, it became more and more difficult for 'the big names' to operate. Fihla found himself, with Silas Mtongana and Kopo, on the 'Caretaker Committee' of senior operatives tasked with keeping the ANC operating underground. Fihla was chosen because, at this time, he was little known. He was a polished ballroom dancer, sportsman and did other 'normal' things. He asked Govan Mbeki if he should give them up and concentrate on ANC activity. Mbeki was emphatic – 'NO' – all this 'normal stuff' provided a good cover for the necessary political work.

The beginnings of sabotage and the arrival of Harold Strachan

With Ray Mhlaba now in China, it fell on Govan Mbeki to prepare some 'sabotage events' to happen to coincide with the ANC's planned public launch of its 'armed struggle'. As help here, he enlisted a most extraordinary character, Harold Strachan.[106]

Strachan was born in Pretoria in 1925. His father was a Scot who had worked in the Newcastle shipyards before emigrating to South Africa. His mother was an Afrikaner teacher. The marriage fell apart when Strachan was three, when his mother ran off with another Scot, Jimmy Brown. Three years later Brown died, and Harold's mother moved her two daughters and Harold to Pietermaritzburg, where Harold was schooled. Here the young Harold began to develop his individuality. Maritzburg College was, for him, brutal and racist, designed to produce a white master race. He wondered at the school's ornaments, mementoes of the 1879 Anglo-Zulu war.

As he finished school, Strachan joined the South African Air Force, ending up as a bomber pilot. After the war he did a Fine Art degree at the Natal University College in Pietermaritzburg – his work is remarkable, and some of it is today in the collection of the Durban Art Gallery. In 1950 he won a scholarship to the Camberwell School of Arts and Crafts in London and followed that with a course in painting restoration at the State Academy of Fine Arts in Stuttgart.

Ever restless, Strachan became a security guard in London, then joined his brother-in-law's decorating business in (then) Northern Rhodesia, and finally returned to South Africa.

Obviously a fine athlete, he apparently trained for the Comrades Marathon (a road race about 90 kilometres in length between Pietermaritzburg and Durban) in 1954 by 'drinking gin and vermouth with his wife'. Incredibly, he finished eighth, and won a gold medal.

He was a lecturer and teacher between 1955 and 1960, during which time he and his first wife, Jean Middleton, were divorced. He married a student of his, Maggie von Lier, in 1959.

Politically he was beginning to take a stand by now. He was a founder member of the Liberal Party with Alan Paton and Peter Brown, but left them for the Congress of Democrats in 1957.

Then came 1960, the Sharpeville massacre and the resultant state of emergency. Strachan was in Durban.

'Strachan and his wife, Maggie, followed the tide of Africans who streamed out of the Cato Manor area of Durban to demand the release of their political leaders. The security forces used Saracen armed vehicles to try to block their advance. When this did not work, the shooting began.

'In Syringa Avenue, Strachan saw a young African, hurrying home from market with a packet of apples, shot dead: today Strachan's painting of the scene holds pride of place in Durban Art Gallery. When the police warned that they would shoot the crowd if it did not disperse, the Strachans, gambling that they would not shoot white people, stood in front of the guns to the fury of the police, who judged the situation too explosive to manhandle them away.

'Realising that the police would not take lightly to being thwarted, and that a warrant was out for them, the couple fled to Swaziland, then home to many refugees from South Africa's white left.

'It was a turning point for Strachan, who could not abide the white communists from Johannesburg who ruled the roost. "They set up a politburo right away, began arrogating power to themselves and disciplining others. They were clearly just compensating for deficiencies in their own personalities" was Strachan's verdict.

'He and Maggie decided to slip back to South Africa and go to Port Elizabeth, well known as the African National Congress's best organised bastion. "That was the volcano," he recalled. "Everyone knew that Govan Mbeki and Raymond Mhlaba ran one hell-of-a-show. We were keen to work with them, but not with the Joburg lot."'[107]

He and Govan hit it off immediately. He began working with Govan by printing and distributing *Izwe Lomzi*, and, after joining the Communist Party in 1961, he helped edit *New Age*.

Then came the decision to begin preparations for sabotage.

Govan asked Strachan to build explosive devices: 'This was our job, devices and explosives. So I said, for God's sake, why me? And they said, no well, you were a bomber pilot in the war, you see, so you must know how to make bombs. I said, but for Christ's sake, Govan, we didn't make our own bombs. And they said, but you know about these things, and I said, no, bombs were made in bloody factories, I didn't know. So he said, anyway, you're appointed. We did a good job, actually.'[108]

Strachan was to work with photographer Joseph Jack, who was selected on account of his knowledge of photographic chemicals. 'So we go off and drink a certain amount of booze and have faith like anything and set to work with the chemicals,' Strachan said.

Finally a demonstration explosion – at a deserted beach at Schoenmakerskop, a tiny seaside village to the south of Port Elizabeth. There they blew a public toilet sky-high. One of the witnesses said, 'Comrade, if we are going to conquer all South Africa one shithouse at a time, we'll all be in the grave before liberation.' This was Umkhonto's first explosion.

Joe Slovo was apparently there and was impressed. He 'shouted slogans and gave the clenched fist salute when the remnants fell into the sea'. He wanted the manufacturing details for the bomb.

Strachan did not trust him. 'The agreement was no killing, but it was clear even then that Slovo was a man utterly without compassion or scruple. If we'd given him that, there'd soon have been killings, so we just gave him the formula for the incendiary bomb instead,' said Strachan, who claims that later bombings, with civilian targets, confirmed his initial judgement.[109]

On 16 December 1961 the ANC was willing to announce the birth of Umkhonto we Sizwe and the beginning of the armed struggle. Ironically, this was just a few days after Chief Luthuli, the ANC's President General, had received the Nobel Peace Prize.

Some 200 sabotage hits followed all over South Africa in the few months after the announcement of the formation of MK. Of these, 58 were in or around Port Elizabeth.[110]

An electrical sub-station in New Brighton was bombed; a telephone booth in town was blown up; attempts were made to set two wool stores alight; a chemical factory was damaged in a blast; many telephone and telegram wires were cut; Kaiser Matanzima's Port Elizabeth representative's house was burned down; a quarry's office was burgled for dynamite; Detective Gazo's house was burned; and an iron clamp was fitted to a railway line in an attempt to derail a train in Perseverance.[111]

By now MK in Port Elizabeth had structured itself for sabotage: the apex structure was the High Command (we will inspect this in the next section); next came the Sabotage Task Team or Technical Team, whose members were Mbeki, Harold Strachan, Joseph Jack and Nkosinathi Fihla – their job was to make the explosives; and the third tier was the many cells, whose members planted and detonated the bombs.[112]

How this worked was expounded two years later in the cross-examination of Sikumbuso Njikelane in the Rivonia Trial (more later).[113]

He outlined how, on Christmas Day in 1961, with MK having announced its existence only nine days earlier, Nkosinathi Fihla and Joseph Jack arrived at his house in New Brighton township at 7 o'clock in the morning, asking for his assistance, and particularly for his car. He then drove Mbeki, Fihla, and Jack to Court Chambers, an office building across the road from the Port Elizabeth court structure. Mbeki got out, entered Court Chambers, and returned immediately with two 'shopping bags'.

They then drove to Jack's house and left the bags there.

He then had to take them 'for a drive' on the Uitenhage Road for five or six miles, returning to New Brighton and the end of stage one of this mission. He went home to sleep, having agreed to return to them at 2 pm.

He overslept, and was awoken by Fihla at 3:15 pm. Fihla now directed him to Wilson Khayinga's house in KwaZakhele, from which Khayinga and another unknown man emerged, carrying two potato pockets, both empty.

Off to New Brighton beach, where Khayinga and the other man remained while the driver and Fihla went to Jack's house and picked up Jack. They then went to Mbeki's house, then back to the beach where they picked up Khayinga and the other man with the two bags, now filled with sand. Khayinga and the other man were dropped off at Khayinga's house and he then drove Fihla to Jack's house, where Fihla went inside with the bags. After a while he returned, with Jack and the bags. Njikelane was now suspicious and demanded to know what was going on. He was told that the bags were now bombs.

He was aghast and refused to drive on. After some wrangling, and a warning that Mbeki would be angry if Fihla, Jack and the bags were not 'in

New Brighton' by 6 pm, he surrendered the driving seat to Jack and they went to KwaZakhele to Khayinga's house, where he dropped his cargo. He, alone now, went back to Mbeki's home where he received payment for the use of his car.

And so it went on, for some of 1962.

Then came disaster.

Govan Mbeki remembers:

Harold Strachan and Joseph Jack were the technical committee of MK in Port Elizabeth. Harold at the time taught at the Tech.

Two young chaps came down from the Transkei to learn how to make bombs and incendiary devices. They received their training in Central in Port Elizabeth in a couple of garages, from Harold and Joseph. When they had completed their training, they were sent to my offices in Court Chambers in Main Street. I told them that they should wait somewhere along the road near Novoboard and that somebody would pick them up and take them back to East London.

They then went back to the Transkei and planted an incendiary bomb in the offices of the Engcobo magistrates' court.

They made a technical mistake that resulted in everything being uncovered. They bought a plastic bottle and filled it with petrol at the petrol station. Instead of leaving a small gap between the top of the liquid and the top of the bottle as was their instructions, they filled the bottle to the very top. This meant that when the fuse went off it fell into the liquid and in fact got drowned in the petrol. There was meant instead to have been a small gap at the top of the petrol where gas would form and that would have resulted in the entire device igniting. As such the bomb did not go off and it was found by the police.

They then went to the various petrol stations and asked who had bought petrol in that container. They were put onto these young guys and they were arrested. They in turn fed information back to the police as to where Harold had trained them, and how they had been trained.

Harold and Joseph were arrested and so was I for my part in finding them a lift back to East London. At the trial I got off on what might be called a technical detail. One of the two young state witnesses left the country at the request of the ANC. The other one then said that when they had come to my offices he had not heard anything that I had said, because I had made my statement to the second person – the one who had left the country. On that ground alone the case against me fell away.[114]

While in custody Mbeki smuggled a message to Fihla: Fihla was to discourage the two Transkeians from giving witness (Fihla got the one to leave the country and join the ANC in exile – the other could not be so persuaded), and he was to 'organise a bombing in the white town'. This was even more challenging.

Fihla realised that the operatives who were to plant the bomb could not run away after planting it, as this would attract undue attention. So he organised a bomb with a 30-minute time switch. This was attached to the bomb which was planted at the Donkin Street Post Office just off Main Street. The bomb was, in Fihla's words, 'sensational – it shocked the government'.

Back at court, Mbeki was found 'not guilty' but Harold and Jack were not as lucky. Harold was found guilty of sabotage on 8 May 1962 and was sentenced to six years in prison, three of which were suspended. His first 13 months in Pretoria Central Prison were in solitary confinement.

One day he woke up with a dreadful toothache. He requested to have his teeth 'looked at' and was thus in the queue for the District Surgeon the next morning. What follows here is from the records of the Truth and Reconciliation Commission:[115]

I stand in this great queue in the hospital yard, long queue, all these blokes waiting for the dentist. It is the only queue I have ever been in where you can jump position towards the front any time because everyone wants to be at the back. Because they know what is going to happen.

And as we get closer and closer, I met there a guy called Tokkie Waters, who was with me in this cell in Port Elizabeth and as we get close to the District Surgeon we could hear the sound of plonk, plonk and we didn't know what it was and when Tokkie looked around and there he could see the District Surgeon in a long white apron, plastic apron covered in blood and he is a rugby player, Lock van Druten, and he's got this guy's head in a sort of one-man scrum and he is pulling this guy's teeth out and chucking them into a bucket held by a bandiet there with his corduroy jacket.

He is looking into this guy's mouth to see all these teeth coming out, they don't fill teeth in prison, that is what they do. And Tokkie said OK, I said Tokkie just do it and shoved him in. And it was my turn next and the guy pulled out twelve teeth in a quarter of an hour and I passed out on tooth six.

He picked up my head again, got it in the scrum again and pulled out the other six. Five years later bits of bone were coming out in my gums...

Strachan was released in May 1965. Now he met the *Rand Daily Mail* journalist Benjamin Pogrund. Pogrund was interested in prison conditions and Strachan gave him plenty to publish. This Pogrund did in June and July 1965.

Both Pogrund and Strachan were charged under the Prisons Act, and Strachan was sentenced to another two and a half years in jail. An appeal and an amnesty got him out after a year but the authorities were not going to settle for that. He was both banned and placed under house arrest for a decade. No matter. Govan and Ray were in jail, and Harold's interests turned to painting, writing, running and fishing for shad. He later wrote a satirical column for *Noseweek*. Activist politics were behind him.

Many years later, with the unbanning of the ANC, Strachan, now a deeply committed political agnostic, was encouraged to attend the ANC's first conference back in South Africa, in Durban in 1991. Govan Mbeki was there and, when he heard that Strachan was also present, he sought him out. They were delighted to see each other.

'You know, Govan, we were quite brave,' Strachan suggested. 'My God,' said Mbeki, 'We were fucking brave, we really were.' Both men wept. And hadn't they been brave!

Harold Strachan lived to the age of 94 and died in a care home in Durban in 2020. His paintings are now revered, his books admired. His courage remains an example to all of us, and his strong individuality saw a final statement – he demanded that he was to have no funeral.

So it was to be, for a man who saw himself as of no importance.

5

Four devastating trials

So it was for the men who made the bombs – what happened to the men who planted them?

1963 was to be a very hard year.

The MK high command in Port Elizabeth is arrested, tried and executed

A youth who was endeavouring to leave the country to join the ANC was captured in a train at Addo just outside Port Elizabeth. He implicated Ndwayi, a senior ANC operative, for organising his departure. Ndwayi was arrested, isolated and tortured until he broke. He implicated 26 ANC operatives, including Nkosinathi Fihla, who was working as a messenger at Barclays Bank at the time.

They were picked up and some were taken to the security police headquarters in the Sanlam Building. Fihla was taken first to the Walmer Police Station, from where he and a number of his co-arrested were taken to corrugated iron buildings in the Thornhill Forest, which they called the 'Fridge' on account of its coldness. There they were interrogated and tortured. Then, mostly on the information supplied by Ndwayi, they were sent to trial.

Fihla was sent to trial in the Port Alfred courts, where he and others were tried by a judge and two assessors, well away from friends and family.

By now there were a large number of similar trials underway, and Fihla's case was not given the same priority as the Rivonia trial, the Malgas–Fazzie trial, or the Vuyisile Mini trial. Their lawyer was, for Fihla, 'weak'. He valiantly conducted much of his own defence. The state had got a date wrong in his charge sheet and he proved that he was at a dancing competition at the time. He also discredited the fingerprint evidence on the bottle that the state was relying on.

It did not help. The judge said that he personally would have released Fihla but his assessors did not agree. In the end Fihla got 10 years for sabotage, and 14 years, to run concurrently, for possessing the dynamite he had organised to be stolen from quarries in Thornhill.

On 15 January 1964 Nkosinathi Benson Fihla entered Robben Island for 14 years, to emerge on 14 January 1978 as a free man. He was then banned from 14 January 1978 to 31 January 1983, restricted to his home at 1 Masupa Street in New Brighton.

So it was with many of his colleagues. However, an altogether more dreadful fate was to go the way of the Port Elizabeth MK High Command.

Here one of the great horrors of our apartheid past played out.

On 10 May 1963 the security police made another three arrests in Port Elizabeth. The security police and the state prosecution put together a watertight case. More than 70 witnesses were called to a special trial of the Eastern Cape Supreme Court, held in Port Alfred to escape the huge Port Elizabeth crowds. The State vs Zinakile Mkaba, Vuyisile Mini and Wilson Khayinga ran until Judge O'Hagan delivered judgment on 16 March 1964. It was these arrests and this trial that devastated Umkhonto we Sizwe in Port Elizabeth.[116]

In Judge O'Hagan's judgment, the newly formed organisation Umkhonto we Sizwe was controlled by a National Executive Committee called the National High Command, operating out of Johannesburg.

The day-to-day affairs of MK were run by regional committees, called 'the Region'. All acts of MK, including all sabotage acts, happened only with the express authority of this committee. The National High Command provided this committee with financial help, advice, directions and instructions on making bombs. The regional committee devised and executed all programmes, be they sabotage or whatever else, including the manufacture of the explosives to be used. The regional committee was the nerve centre of MK.

In Port Elizabeth this regional committee from its inception comprised three persons: Zinakile Mkaba, Robert Mbanjwa and Wilson Khayinga. For security reasons, Mbeki and Mhlaba were kept at arm's length – they were too well-known, too easily watched. Late in 1962 Mbanjwa left the country. He was replaced, in October 1962, by Vuyisile Mini. Thus this trial was a trial of the central executive of MK in Port Elizabeth.

Vuyisile Mini had been born in Tsomo in rural Transkei. His father had moved to Port Elizabeth at a young age and had become involved in community struggles. This inspired the young Vuyisile, in his teen years, to get involved in Ray Mhlaba's bus and rent increase campaigns. His first taste of prison was when he was a volunteer in the Defiance Campaign. At the time he was a packer at a battery factory and a budding unionist. Of course he lost his job then.

On release from prison he rose quickly in the ranks of the ANC, becoming secretary of the Cape Region. In 1956 he and 155 others were swept up in the arrests for the Treason Trial. The state's case against Mini collapsed and he was acquitted in April 1959. Not long after, he was detained in terms of the 1960 state of emergency. That did not stop him becoming one of MK's first recruits, in 1961, and quickly rising to the position of a member of the regional committee, or, as MK would term it, the High Command.

There was another side to Mini, for he was a gifted singer, poet, dancer and composer of freedom songs. His song from the 1950s, *Pasopa nantsi ndodemnyama we Verwoerd* (Look out Verwoerd, here are the black people) is still a favourite. He had a wonderful bass voice.

The three accused faced 17 counts of sabotage (eight for burning down houses, eight for cutting telephone wires and one for the unlawful possession of incendiary bombs); one count of breaking into and entering an explosives magazine and theft therefrom (they stole dynamite and detonators from Frazer's Quarries); six counts under the Suppression of Communism Act; and, most dangerously, one count of murder.

It turned out that all of the acts of arson had happened before Mini had joined the regional leadership, so he was found not guilty of these. (The arson attacks had happened between 18 September and 2 October 1962, thereafter the National Command Council had instructed that the organisation turn rather to cutting telecommunications.)

The real disaster was the assassination of Sipho Mange, an MK operative who had turned state witness and was to testify in a sabotage trial in early 1963. In the early hours of 12 January 1963 four men had stormed into his home and killed him with a weapon apparently supplied by Khayinga.

The 70 witnesses the state called included a number of members of MK who earned immunity from prosecution by supplying incriminating evidence. Further there were taxi drivers, who claimed to have driven the accused and many others around, sometimes unwillingly. One of these we have already met.

It all added up to a devastating indictment, and all three were found guilty of a number of offences, but most particularly murder with no extenuating circumstances. For such a crime there was no punishment possible in law at the time but the death penalty, which the three got in March 1964. The judge praised the police for their extensive and tidy work and noted that since the three accused had been arrested 10 months before, there had no longer been any acts of sabotage. MK had really been hammered.

The three were to be hanged on 6 November 1964. International pleas for clemency fell on deaf ears. An offer by the police to Mini to provide them with information, which, they said, would lead to his execution being abandoned, was rejected by Mini.

All executions in South Africa were carried out in Pretoria Central Prison. This macabre place was also where white male political prisoners were incarcerated. At this time Ben Turok was there, serving a three-year sentence for MK activities. He wrote thus of the three's last minutes:

> The last evening was devastatingly sad as the heroic occupants of the death cells communicated to the prison in gentle melancholic song that their end was near… It was late at night when the singing ceased, and the prison fell into an uneasy silence. I was already awake when the singing began again in the early morning. Once again the excruciatingly beautiful music floated through the barred windows, echoing around the brick exercise yard, losing itself in the vast prison yards. And then, unexpectedly, the voice of Vuyisile Mini came roaring down the hushed passages. Evidently standing on a stool, with his face reaching up to the barred vent in his cell, his unmistakeable bass voice was enunciating his final message in Xhosa to the world he was leaving. In a voice charged with emotion but stubbornly defiant he spoke of the struggle waged by the African National Congress and of his absolute conviction of the victory to come. And then it was Khayinga's turn, followed by Mkaba, as they too defied all prison rules to shout out their valedictions. Soon after, I heard the doors of their cells being opened. Murmuring voices reached my straining ears, and then the three martyrs broke into a final poignant melody which seemed to fill the whole prison with sound and then gradually faded away into the distant depths of the condemned section.[117]

Ernest Malgas, Henry Fazzie: Exile, training, capture

After the riots in Port Elizabeth that closed off the Defiance Campaign, the police searched for those they believed were involved. In the Red Location they picked up a 15-year-old youth mistakenly; they were in fact looking for his neighbour. He was dragged off and spent six weeks in cells. Thus began the political education of Ernest Malgas. His arrest turned out to be a massive mistake, because Malgas was later to prove that there was no suffering that he could not endure in the fight for freedom.

Ernest Malgas was born in Korsten, Port Elizabeth in 1937.[118]

His young life was one of massive hardship. In fact, his whole life was to be one of massive hardship.

Some of his earliest memories were of him standing naked begging from passing trains as soldiers headed to and from the Second World War. He had learned that to be naked brought better results. '"Bread please, or a penny please, I'm hungry," that's how I started. The soldiers would start throwing food and that was something very good for my family, although I was not encouraged to do that but when the food comes to the house, it will be acceptable.'

The young Malgas was asthmatic and escaped the rigours and the pleasures of schooling entirely. When he was 12 his father, who was a labourer on the railways, was crushed while offloading a truck. He survived but was boarded. Then, 'One Friday my mother was working, my father was back from hospital, I was playing with other kids outside. This man started coughing and he called me – the amount of blood that came through his nose. I was then young and still useless, looking at him dying. So when he died it was my mother, myself, my two younger brothers and my sister.'

Malgas' next survival behaviour was to search for lead from scrapheaps, melt it down and re-sell it. But it could never be enough. The young family was moved from house to house, always unable to pay the rent.

Then came his 1952 detention and new, political friends.

The ANC was now in the process of creating the Freedom Charter which was eventually approved at Kliptown in 1955. The Charter was controversial. Robert Sobukwe headed up a group within the ANC that resented the replacement of the 1949 Programme of Action with the Freedom Charter. They did not approve of the non-racial line of the Freedom Charter, believing that it was abandoning the ANC's long-standing Africanist thrust. Further they had concerns about the Communist Party and its influence on the ANC.

The tensions led to this grouping withdrawing from the ANC and, in April 1959, they constituted themselves as the Pan Africanist Congress.

Within a year the PAC began its first campaign.

Incredibly, at the time over 365 000 Africans were prosecuted annually for pass law offences. The PAC saw this as an obvious first campaign. On 18 March 1960 Robert Sobukwe, at a press conference, announced that the PAC would begin a campaign to have the pass laws abolished. The campaign would begin on 21 March.

On that date a crowd estimated by the *Rand Daily Mail* at 10 000 gathered at the Evaton Police Station demanding to be arrested as they were not carrying their passbooks. The police refused. Military aircraft flew low overhead and the crowd dispersed.

Another crowd, estimated at between 3 000 and 4 000, demanded arrest at the Vanderbijlpark police station. The aircraft did not work here, nor did nine canisters of tear gas. The crowd was finally dispersed by a baton charge and deadly fire. Two men were shot dead.

On to the Sharpeville police station. Here, a protest was attended by about 10 000 protesters, demanding to be arrested. The police contingent of roughly 20 officers called for reinforcements. Four Saracen armoured vehicles with 130 reserves arrived. Again, airforce jets flew overhead to scatter the crowd.

This all had the opposite effect. The crowd continued to grow and stones were thrown. In the early afternoon two white policemen opened fire without authority. About 50 others then followed suit, using service revolvers, rifles and Sten guns. Sixty-nine protesters were killed and 180 others, including eight women and 10 children, were injured. Thirty shots had entered the wounded or the dead from the front, and 155 from the back.

Years later, at the Truth and Reconciliation Commission, it was agreed that the shooting was more than 'inexperienced officers losing their nerve'.

The fury was everywhere. Nine days later a PAC leader, the 23-year-old Philip Kgosana led a march of approximately 30 000 protesters from Langa township into the centre of Cape Town. Protests were everywhere. Even the United Nations passed Resolution 134, condemning the shooting of unarmed protesters in South Africa.

The National Party government reacted, for the first but certainly not the last time, with a draconian crack-down. A state of emergency was called on 30 March and the Unlawful Organisations Act of 7 April banned the ANC and the PAC. Some 18 000 activists were detained, including Mandela and Sobukwe.

The one who wasn't detained was Oliver Tambo.

As early as April 1958, Oliver Tambo had come home to his wife Adelaide and their infant son to tell her that the ANC wished for them to leave South Africa to establish a Mission-in-Exile. Neither of them could see how they could do it. As time went on, the call became stronger. With the Sharpeville massacre it became clear – Tambo had to leave the country immediately.

But how? Here a friend, whom Tambo didn't know well enough to trust fully, made an offer. He was Ronald Segal, the editor of the liberal journal *Africa South*. He would drive Tambo to the Bechuanaland Protectorate (Botswana). Tambo agreed. Everyone else was in chaos, running around destroying records, making plans for the coming storm.

There was another surprise. Segal said that to drive his own car was suicide, as he was closely watched. However, his mother had not only a car, but also a chauffeur. Tambo could don the chauffeur's kit, drive, and Segal could be 'die baas' in the back.

The deal was agreed. Tambo, ever meticulous, worked through the night closing off files in their office (Mandela was his partner in their legal practice, and late the next day they were off, arriving in Bechuanaland on 28 March 1960. The ANC had a Mission-in-Exile, albeit one man and his suitcase.

Nearly 30 years later Hugh Murray, the editor and proprietor of *Leadership* magazine, travelled to Lusaka to meet the ANC-in-exile. Ever bombastic, he was later quoted as saying that 'the ANC couldn't run a bath, let alone a country'.

In fact, what Oliver Tambo achieved between 1960 and 1990 is nothing short of a miracle. From standing alone in Bechuanaland in 1960, he assembled the resources and the finances to run an enormous organisation, with offices and missions in many countries, military training camps, hundreds of cadres in universities around the world, and a significant underground network in South Africa.

This they accomplished despite enormous difficulties. Their mail was repeatedly intercepted, their money stolen and their offices bombed or destroyed. All of the following figures are for the 1980s alone. Offices bombed: London headquarters March 1982, Botswana June 1985, Lusaka July 1985, Harare May 1986 and May 1987, Stockholm 1986. Senior personnel assassinated: Joe Gqabi 1981, Jabu and Petrus Nzima 1982, Z Mbali 1982, Ruth First 1982, Keith MacFadden and Zwelakhe Nyanda, 1983, Jeanette Schoon 1984, Vernon Nkadimeng 1985, Cassius Make and Paul Dikeledi 1987, Jacob Molokoane 1988, Sipho Ngema 1988, Dulcie September 1988, Mazizi Maqekeza 1988. Members of the National Executive survived assassination attempts: Chris Hani 1981, Nat Serache 1985, Reddy Mazimba 1987, Thomas Nkobi and Alfred Nzo 1988, and Albie Sachs 1988. In addition, many raids, commando attacks and bombings destroyed property and killed personnel. In 34 such attacks in the 1980s, 190 ANC cadres were killed.[119]

All of this Tambo's teams endured while developing, in 30 years, from a standing start with nothing but one man and his suitcase, to a massive organisation that won the diplomatic war against the South African government, while training hundreds through university and many more through military camps.

Tambo's problems were quick to arrive in the early 1960s. In 1961 the

ANC, now banned, abandoned polite diplomacy and took on the armed struggle. Umkhonto we Sizwe was formed in late 1961 and this led to a rush of young cadres jumping the borders of South Africa, determined to become soldiers capable of taking the fight to 'the Boers'. Somehow Tambo and his team had to accommodate, clothe, feed and train this huge contingent.

One of the first to arrive was Henry Mutile Fazzie from Site and Service, Port Elizabeth. It is not certain whether Fazzie crossed the border in 1960 or 1961, but he was trained and ready to receive a small group of youngsters in Dar es Salaam in 1961. This group included Matthews Makhalima, also from Site and Service in Port Elizabeth, and Jack Ndzuzo, Alfred Khonza and, of course, Ernest Malgas, all three from New Brighton.

Malgas explained his presence: 'In 1961 somebody came to me and said, "I was going to come and tell you, you are to go to other countries and go for military training, then you must come and fight against the government."'[120]

To this Malgas later laconically remarked, 'I didn't have in mind any reason to say no.'

Off to Jo'burg, where Joe Modise met them at Park Station. Four weeks there, then across the border to Bechuanaland, and, while carefully avoiding the British South African police (for all South Africa's neighbours then had historical agreements with South Africa to return undocumented arrivals), they went from vehicle to bus to train for 12 days, until the young group was in Dar es Salaam to meet with the man who was to become their commander in Umkhonto, Henry Fazzie.

One day in Dar es Salaam a man, well known to these recruits by reputation, visited them.

'He was wearing a military shirt, a khaki one, and battle-dress trousers and a military belt. He had a pistol with him, a beret – you could see he was a soldier. We all greeted him, and were honoured to shake the hand of this man, Mandela. The youth were crazy about this man ... He told us he was coming from Ethiopia, and had just completed three months' military training. He said he was going home now – "I don't want to go to prison, neither do we want to die, but we are prepared to go through this so that our people can taste the fruit of freedom".'

Malgas was overwhelmed. 'It was the first time that I had heard Mandela talking, and it was the first time that I had seen this man, but I think he is one of the greatest people I have ever met.'

In early 1963 the above group, led by Fazzie, began the tortuous return journey to South Africa. On 26 January 1963 they all – there were nine of them – alighted from a train at Bulawayo Station and fell straight into the arms of the British South African Police, acting on a tip-off. These police confiscated their documents, bagged and sealed them, and handed the nine activists and these documents over to the South African Police, who brought them through to Pretoria.

There they were kept in custody in various police cells and were brought before a regional court magistrate on 1 and 2 April, charged with leaving the Republic without being in possession of valid passports. Unrepresented, they faced a maximum sentence of two years' imprisonment. This they got, along with some homespun wisdom from the magistrate:[121]

I would be making a ridicule of the law if I treated your crime in this instance leniently. The whole country is riddled with this kind of thing. One is only to look in the press to see confirmation of this. I conceive it the duty of the court to punish with severity occurrences such as these, which ought not to take place. If you choose to continue in this fashion then you must not complain when the law steps in and treats you harshly. Each of you two years' imprisonment.

They were returned to prison, believing that this was to be their full punishment.

On 11 July the police raided the Lilliesleaf Farm in Rivonia, a semi-rural suburb of Johannesburg, arresting most of the Umkhonto leaders. Whether this emboldened the system or not we will never know, but our grouping, now of seven, was brought to a magistrate's court on 3 September and told that they were to be tried for 'wrongfully and unlawfully undergoing training of a military nature which could be of use in furthering the achievement of the objects of the African National Congress, an organisation which has been declared to be unlawful'. The trial was to commence in the Supreme Court on 23 September. Two of their group of nine had accepted an indemnity offer and had turned state witnesses. Later in September Looksmart Ngudle, a trade unionist rumoured to be an Umkhonto leader in the Western Cape, died in a Pretoria jail cell after 17 days of detention, South Africa's first death in detention of a political activist. Things could not have looked worse.

But they got worse. On returning to prison, our group of seven prisoners applied to four firms of attorneys, requesting representation. They received no replies. Not even from the normally reliable Defence and Aid Fund. They returned to court on 23 September to find no attorneys, nor any counsel. Judge Theron was unsympathetic and directed the trial to proceed forthwith. Which it did, and quickly. By 1 October 24 state witnesses, including the two turncoats from their group, had given evidence. Judge Theron immediately gave judgment. All seven guilty. On that same afternoon he pronounced sentence. It was as quick and as terse as the trial had been:

> The crime of which you have been found guilty is considered a most serious crime, meriting a very severe sentence. I have considered in your case whether the appropriate sentence would be the death sentence. I have come to the conclusion that it is not. The reason I have come to that conclusion is that the evidence clearly that you people were recruited by leaders of your organisation. You were herded together where mass psychology misled you, and you were misguided by your leaders, but it is obvious that you went out to seek training to return to this country, to do damage to the security and the safety of the state. By applying and practising the knowledge you obtained there and the military training you acquired there, would be dynamite to the security and safety of the state, and the safety of the public in general. For that reason your crime that you committed merits a very severe sentence.
>
> The sentence of the Court is that you shall be imprisoned for TWENTY (20) YEARS.
>
> The Court adjourns.

Meanwhile the cadre Fazzie and Malgas had met in Dar es Salaam, Nelson Mandela, had returned to South Africa. Within three weeks of his return he had gone to Natal to brief Chief Luthuli. Apparently his whereabouts was provided to the South African police by the CIA and he was arrested at a roadblock near Howick in August 1962. He was also sentenced for leaving the country without documents, and, by incredible coincidence, was held in Pretoria's 'New Look Prison' with the Fazzie group.

On hearing of the plight of the seven, Mandela organised for their appeal. Fortunately Defence and Aid now kicked in, and the celebrated attorney Joel Joffe, who was also part of the Rivonia team, was briefed. (Shortly after the Rivonia Trial ended, Joffe emigrated to the UK where he had a most distinguished career, ending up as a Labour Party-nominated member of the House of Lords.) An appeal to the Supreme Court of South Africa, Appellate Division, followed, and this appeal court on 24 September 1964 reduced their sentence to 12 years. The two years for leaving the country without documents remained, so Fazzie and Malgas went to Robben Island for 14 years. There Fazzie had a further seven years added for sabotage. So Henry Fazzie (21 years) and Ernest Malgas (14 years) were put into cold storage until a later phase of the struggle.

In November 1963, between the Supreme Court sentencing and the successful appeal, Ernest Malgas wrote to 'My dearest Mother'. As we have noted, he was entirely illiterate (his court documents are all signed with a cross), so much of this letter must have come from a helpful official. But it has the ring of Ernest about it:

> You will probably have read in the newspapers that I got a further charge under the Sabotage Law, that my sentence has now been increased to 22 years.
>
> (In prison) I have the privilege to buy some toilet requisites once a month, and I am also privileged to write (and receive) one letter in six months. Life is difficult in prison, but I am trying my best to bear it and I wish you and the rest of the family do not worry yourselves too much about me. How are my brothers and sister getting on? I think about them very much and I do hope that they are in good health and that they are happy.
>
> How is my young son? He must be steadily growing into a man. I am eager that he should go to school as soon as he reaches the right age.
>
> I shall always make it my duty to keep in touch with you even if the privilege is given once after six months. But I shall give you the smallest news about myself so that you should not remain anxious. I do hope that you will give me as much news about yourself when you do write.
>
> I am your devoted son, Ernest.

In Ernest Malgas' 14 years on Robben Island he did not receive one visitor, family or lawyers, nor did he receive one letter. Nor did he receive one cent in gift money. He served every day of his sentence, with no remission.

The state clamps down

We are now in a period in which the ANC is being pushed backwards, rolling under the punches.

In June 1962 Albert Luthuli used the *New Age* to exhort black South Africans to 'draw inspiration from the great battles of Tshaka and Moshesh, of Gandhi and Hintsa'. Six months earlier he had been awarded the Nobel Peace Prize, but this did not spare him from the men of apartheid. This *New Age* communication was to be his last legal public statement within South Africa, as from now on the Sabotage Act was used to prohibit the reproduction of any statement made by anyone banned from attending meetings. In this way, on 30 June 1962 another 102 persons, half of whom were white, were banned from public communication.

On 30 November 1962 *New Age* was finally banned. At the time it had a circulation of 20 000, 90 percent of whom were black South Africans. It was immediately replaced by *Spark*, but this did not survive the attentions of the state. This time they banned many members of staff, and on 28 March 1963 it too closed down.

On 14 September 1962 the Congress of Democrats was banned. Laws were tightened up. 'Sabotage' could now be almost any anti-government protest. House arrest orders were made in large numbers, including those of Helen Joseph, Walter Sisulu and Govan Mbeki. Many so restricted left South Africa on one-way passports.

By early June 1963, 126 people had been convicted under the Sabotage Act, the lightest sentence being eight years, and another 511 were awaiting trial.

On 1 May 1963 John Vorster, the 'Justice' Minister, pushed the General Law Amendment Act through parliament, with one dissenting vote, Helen Suzman's. This act enabled the authorities to hold anyone for 90 days, which could be repeated, without a warrant and on the flimsy grounds of 'suspicion'. People so held could be held without access to a lawyer. On that day, commentators described South Africa as having become a police state.

Ray Mhlaba returned from China in late 1962 and was immediately taken to a farm in Rivonia north of Johannesburg that Arthur Goldreich had bought as a hide-away headquarters for the ANC, MK and the Communist Party. Called Lilliesleaf Farm, it was now humming with underground activity.

When Mhlaba got there, he discovered that Mandela had recently been arrested near Howick in Natal after clandestinely briefing Luthuli. He had just returned to South Africa after a period in Africa drumming up support for the ANC.

Mandela had been chief commander of Umkhonto we Sizwe, and this job now fell onto Mhlaba's shoulders. He was hardly in it when he was instructed to accompany Joe Modise out of the country. Both Modise and Mhlaba were, naturally, on the run from the police. They were driven into Basutoland and journeyed on to Tanganyika, Algeria, Morocco and Czechoslovakia. They successfully encouraged all of these countries to pledge support to the ANC.

Mhlaba was expected to return to South Africa by the end of June and crossed the border from Bechuanaland on 1 July 1963. There he had had to bribe a terrified truck driver to take him through the police gauntlet, and this happened safely. He was dropped in Potgietersrus and caught the train to Johannesburg. He found his way to a house in Soweto that had previously accommodated him. No chance now – the police were everywhere, and the owners would not take the risk. He phoned Duma Nokwe's wife. She fetched him and took him to Lilliesleaf Farm. There he found the ANC's political leadership, preparing to move to Travallyn Agricultural Holdings, newly bought by the movement as Lilliesleaf was 'too hot' by now. They were to have 'one last, final meeting' at Lilliesleaf on 11 July 1963. Then it was to be abandoned.

Govan Mbeki was under intense state scrutiny also. He was very active now, but it was proving increasingly difficult. He had been detained for five months in the state of emergency that followed Sharpeville. In 1961 he was arrested on charges of furthering the objectives of a banned organisation. In 1962 he was detained for a few months when he and Harold Strachan and Joseph Jack were arrested under the Explosives Act. When acquitted, he was put under house arrest.

Despite all of this, he had been on the National Executive of the ANC before it was banned, and on the National Action Committee (its underground leadership structure) after the banning. He had been an early advocate of the armed struggle, and became a founder member of the High Command of Umkhonto. His sabotage campaign, begun in Port Elizabeth after the launch of Umkhonto, was the biggest and most successful in the country. On receiving his house arrest orders, he disappeared, going fully underground. In fact, he was living on Lilliesleaf farm, dressed in tired overalls to appear to be a gardener. In July 1963 he and the rest of the underground leadership moved to Travallyn for security reasons. He returned to Lilliesleaf on 11 July 1963, for the 'very last, final meeting', on this farm.

'The last meeting of the High Command at Lilliesleaf was one too many. It took place because Rusty Bernstein ... who represented the Communist Party on the High Command, was subject to a house arrest order. He had to report to the police between 12 and 1pm every day and be at home at 6pm on weekdays and by 1pm on weekends. At the previous meeting on a Saturday they could not agree on another venue. Rusty had to leave or face imprisonment for not being home in time. As a last resort they agreed to meet at Lilliesleaf one last time,' Denis Goldberg writes in his autobiography.[122]

Lilliesleaf Farm and the Rivonia Trial

The agenda of the 'very last, final meeting' at Lilliesleaf farm was the consideration by the High Command of MK of a plan for guerrilla warfare in South Africa, entitled 'Operation Mayibuye'.[123]

With the inestimable advantage of hindsight, this plan appears somewhat naïve.

Initially, four groups of 30 armed and properly equipped guerrillas would be simultaneously landed in South Africa with enough equipment and ammunition to last at least a month. They would join up with 7 000 armed and trained guerrilla forces inside South Africa. On landing they would attack pre-selected targets … creating the maximum impact on the populace, 'creating as much chaos and confusion for the enemy as possible'. The initial area would have a shadow political authority in place which would 'supervise the struggle' and 'in due course of time, develop into a Provisional Revolutionary Government'. The strength of the apartheid state, which is 'powerfully armed with tremendous industrial resources', was counterbalanced by 'the almost unlimited assistance which we can obtain from friendly governments'.

This document was apparently drafted by Govan Mbeki and Joe Slovo, and they and Ray Mhlaba and Wilton Mkwayi argued passionately that it had been agreed to by both the ANC and Umkhonto. According to Denis Goldberg, Slovo claimed that he had already begun arrangements to secure the external support needed.[124]

Mandela, who was at this time a prisoner on Robben Island, later argued differently. 'As far as I was concerned, Operation Mayibuye was a draft document that was not only not approved, but was entirely unrealistic in its goals and plans. I did not believe that guerrilla warfare was a viable option for South Africa … [it] had not been approved by the ANC executive or even seen by Chief Luthuli.'[125]

At this meeting on 11 July, while this debate was raging, Joe Slovo had to leave. This left Lionel Bernstein, Arthur Goldreich, Bob Hepple, Abdulhay Jassat, Ahmed Kathrada, Govan Mbeki, Raymond Mhlaba, Andrew Mlangeni, Moosa Moolla, Elias Motsoaledi, Walter Sisulu, Harold Wolpe and Denis Goldberg on the farm (Sisulu was there for a friendly dentist to fill a noticeable gap in his front teeth, and Denis Goldberg was not in the meeting but was reading a book in the main house).

In the afternoon, a dry cleaner's van entered the premises and began to make its way up the long drive. A young African guard stopped it, and out of it dozens of armed security policemen emerged, with a number of police dogs.

The game was up.

The meeting was being held in a thatched outbuilding and, as the police entered, the draft document of Operation Mayibuye was open on the table the High Command was sitting around. There were also tonnes of other documents, many in the handwriting of the accused, including a handwritten diary of Mandela's. A total of 106 maps were found, many identifying targets including police stations, the homes of African policemen, power stations and the like. The police could not contain their delight. The High Command of Umkhonto and its library, in one afternoon's work. As a prominent exile said when he was told, 'This is the death knell of amateurism.'[126]

After arrest the comrades were separated and taken off to different prisons. Sisulu, Mbeki, Mhlaba, Bernstein and Goldberg were taken to the Johannesburg Fort; Hepple, Wolpe, Goldreich, Moosa and Jassat were taken to the Marshall Square Police Station, as were the domestic workers and staff from Rivonia. Others were taken elsewhere. The Sisulu group was later taken to the Pretoria Prison. Initially they were detained in terms of the '90 Day' clause, while the prosecution got the case together. Through this period they had no contact with lawyers, family or the outside world.

A month after arrest, on 11 August, Wolpe, Goldreich, Moosa and Jassat escaped from Marshall Square, having bribed a young guard. All four managed to escape South Africa, much to the fury of the security police, who plainly believed that Goldreich was the brains behind everything. This fell in with the belief of the Minister of Justice, John Vorster, that behind every black activist was a white agitator.[127] Racism clouding judgement, for sure.

This left the state with just nine accused. In their fury at the escape, the police arrested James Kantor, Wolpe's brother-in-law and partner in their firm of attorneys. He endured long months of detention and the collapse of the law firm before being freed at the end of the prosecution's case – no case to answer. As Denis Goldberg believed, he had been arrested out of spite alone.

Then came the big shock.

Nelson Mandela was on Robben Island, serving a five-year sentence for his missions out of the country. One evening he was told to pack his belongings. The next morning he was taken back to Pretoria local prison and put into solitary confinement. There he helped Henry Fazzie and Ernest Malgas, also prisoners, to get defence counsel.

He suggested that they contact Harold Wolpe. Then he heard that Wolpe was in police detention. 'That was my first intimation that something had gone wrong,' he later wrote. Then he saw Andrew Mlangeni in the prison. Then the Lilliesleaf staff. This could mean only one thing, 'the authorities had discovered Rivonia'.[128]

A day or two later he was summoned to the prison office and there he found Sisulu, Mbeki, Mhlaba, Kathrada, Mlangeni, Hepple, Goldberg, Motsoaledi, Bernstein and Kantor. His worst fears were confirmed. They were all to appear in a magistrate's court the next day to be charged with sabotage. He believed that the charge was not treason because the burden of proof was more complex for the crime of treason, and both sabotage and treason carried the death penalty anyway. A charge of 'sabotage' was the shortcut to the gallows.

Govan Mbeki believed that Mandela was unlucky to be charged with them. 'Nelson would probably not have been involved in the trial anyway, but, Nelson had, call it a weakness, and that is that he always jotted his thoughts down on paper, and he always kept a diary. I suppose that this was a result of his training as a lawyer, that he always kept this diary. Now one could ask what is the use of a diary for someone who is in hiding? But to Nelson it just seemed a way of doing something properly.

'They also found that he had been reading a book by a Chinese person entitled "How to be a good Communist". He had taken down notes from this that were interpreted by the police and the prosecution as notes that he was writing in preparation to giving lectures to other people. Speak as he might, and he certainly argued about it, he couldn't wriggle out of this, and could not explain it to them. And so he joined us.'[129]

They faced four charges:

- recruiting persons for training in the preparation and use of explosives and in guerrilla warfare for the purpose of violent revolution and committing acts of sabotage;
- conspiring to commit the aforementioned acts and to aid foreign military units when they invaded the Republic;
- acting in these ways to further the objectives of communism; and
- soliciting and receiving money for these purposes from sympathisers in Uganda, Algeria, Ethiopia, Nigeria, Liberia, Tunisia and elsewhere.

The judge was to be the Judge President of the Transvaal, Judge Quartus de Wet. Judge De Wet had been appointed as a judge by the United Party when they were in government many years before. This was seen as a good point, as he was not a National Party lackey.

The prosecutor was Dr Percy Yutar, the Deputy Attorney General of the Transvaal. Yutar was noted for his dogged and persistent cross-examination, and for his ability to continue cross-examination ad nauseam or until he elicited admissions. He was clearly to be feared.

The accused now needed a legal team.

'Well, firstly we had to assemble a team of lawyers. Some people suggested that we should get Issy Maisels, who at the time had a world reputation as an outstanding lawyer. Ultimately the view amongst us prevailed that we should get political lawyers. So Bram Fischer came in as leader of the team and others who came in with him included of course George Bizos, and the young Arthur Chaskalson. Chaskalson was then a junior, but what a brilliant junior Arthur was. There was comment that "This is going to be the second Maisels of South Africa".

'Then we also used Harold Hanson who came in to plead mitigation and that was a brilliant piece of work,' said Govan Mbeki years later.[130]

Bram Fischer was taking a great risk by accepting this brief, for he too was on the High Command of MK, and had not yet been uncovered. When the Lilliesleaf staff were cross-examined, he was absent from the court for fear of an accidental recognition.

Joel Joffe was the briefing attorney.

It was clear to the other accused that Kantor had in no way been involved in the activities of the MK High Command, and it was agreed that he should have a separate team of lawyers.

And so South Africa's most famous trial, 'The State vs Nelson Mandela and Nine Others', began on 9 October 1963 at the Palace of Justice in Pretoria.

Yutar presented his indictment. Fisher immediately challenged its validity. The accused, instead of being charged individually, were charged as 'The High Command', and anyway the defence had not had sight of the indictment. Judge De Wet agreed, and quashed the indictment. Round one to the defendants, who then tried, and failed, to leave the court as free men.

The indictment returned in early December and was equally defective. Judge De Wet, however, wanted progress, and allowed it. At this stage Yutar dropped a bomb – Bob Hepple had agreed to turn state witness. He had written a statement to the police, requesting to turn state witness. They had refused it as too unspecific. He then wrote for 48 hours, and this was detailed enough for the police to accept him as a state witness. He was discharged from prison on 30 October 1963.

Then the most unexpected thing happened. Bram Fischer visited Hepple secretly and convinced him to leave the country. And he helped with the arrangements for Hepple to escape, which he did in November. Hepple fled to Britain, where he became a prominent lawyer and ended up as 'Sir Bob'. He made a public statement that this had always been his intention, to escape and not testify. Some of his co-accused did not believe him. Denis Goldberg received a Christmas card from Hepple, but told his wife to tell Hepple that he wished to have nothing more to do with him.[131]

In the first three months of proceedings, the state presented 173 witnesses and introduced thousands of documents and photographs into the record.

Their star witness was Bruno Mtolo, who had been a leader in the Natal region of MK. He had conducted a number of acts of sabotage, had visited Lilliesleaf Farm and had met Mandela. His testimony was wide-ranging and very detailed. The judge found him reliable and believable as he outlined acts of sabotage, the making of bombs and the underground workings of MK. When he finished, Mandela believed: 'His evidence concerning me in particular made me realize that the state would certainly be able to convict me.'[132]

The key document of the state's case was the document on Operation Mayibuye that had been on the table at Lilliesleaf when the police had raided. That, and so much else presented, made it clear that the accused had very little hope of a 'not guilty' judgment. In fact, the call to guerrilla warfare in the Operation Mayibuye document was so damaging that George Bizos warned that the accused had to convince the judge that they had not decided on guerrilla warfare, otherwise he would certainly impose the death penalty.[133]

The state's case closed on 29 February 1964. James Kantor was released, all charges dropped.

Now the accused had little over a month to assemble a defence.

They immediately agreed that their main objective was to use the trial to strengthen the cause for which they were struggling, and in which they so believed. The very unlikely 'not guilty' verdict came second to that. While they had all pleaded 'not guilty', they would now not deny that a core group of them had been responsible for acts of sabotage, and they would concede that this group had turned away from non-violence. 'We would readily admit what was known by the state to be true, but refuse to give away any information we thought might implicate others,' wrote Mandela.[134]

To counter 'Operation Mayibuye', they would admit that they were making contingency plans for guerrilla warfare if sabotage failed, but they would claim that it had not yet failed because it had not been sufficiently attempted. They would deny the claims the state had made of murder and injury to innocent bystanders and they would deny that they had called for the intervention of foreign military forces.

The accused then took the decision to get Mandela to make a statement from the dock, rather than be called as a witness. It was agreed that his diary and the document 'How to be a Good Communist' in his handwriting would be impossible to slip past in Yutar's cross-examination. If he was a witness, he would be cross-examined, but if he made a statement from the dock, this would not happen. Thereafter Sisulu and Mbeki could be witnesses and take the blows of cross-examination.

Mandela spent two weeks crafting his address, which he then read to his fellow accused. They approved of it and he then passed it to Bram Fischer.[135]

Fischer immediately saw the address as a wonderful document, but the last paragraph gave him grave concern. This read:

> During my lifetime I have dedicated myself to this struggle of the
> African people. I have fought against white domination, and I have

fought against black domination. I have cherished the ideal of a democratic and free society in which all persons live together in harmony and with equal opportunities. It is an ideal which I hope to live for and to achieve. It is an ideal for which I am prepared to die.

Mandela then describes Fischer's response: 'Bram became concerned after reading it and referred it to a respected advocate named Harold Hanson. Hanson told Bram, "If Mandela reads this in court they will take him straight out to the back of the courthouse and string him up." That confirmed Bram's anxieties, and he came to me the next day and urged me to modify the speech ... Bram begged me not to read the final paragraph, but I was adamant.'[136]

On Monday 20 April the accused were brought back to the Palace of Justice to begin their defence.

Fischer began the defence. He said that parts of the state's argument would be conceded by the defence, but not all of its arguments. He noted that the defence would rebut, amongst other issues, the assertion that MK was a wing of the ANC; that the ANC took orders from the Communist Party; and, particularly, that MK had already adopted the document 'Operation Mayibuye' and that, in fact, MK had not embarked on preparations for guerrilla warfare.

'That will be denied?' asked Judge De Wet incredulously.

'That will be denied,' replied Fischer.[137]

Fischer continued. The defence case would begin with a statement from the dock by accused No 1.

Yutar was startled. He had relished the possibility of cross-examining Mandela. 'My Lord, a statement from the dock does not carry the same weight as evidence under oath.' Judge De Wet was curt. 'I think, Dr Yutar, that counsel for the defence has sufficient experience to advise their clients without your assistance.'

Nelson Mandela then spent four hours in the dock, reading his statement. It is one of South Africa's most famous speeches, and for good reason. It is a tour de force, a staggeringly well-put statement of the sufferings of black South Africans, of the history of the ANC, of its years of petitioning, the endless ratcheting up of suppression, then the belief felt by some that there were no options left but armed struggle, and how South Africa had got to where it was. The independence of the ANC from the Communist Party and of MK was outlined, and Mandela denied that he was a communist.

'I had been reading my speech, and at this point I placed my papers on the defence table, and turned to face the judge. The courtroom became extremely quiet. I did not take my eyes off Justice de Wet as I spoke from memory the final words.'[138]

Then Mandela spoke the final paragraph, the section that had caused Fischer and Hanson such concern. He got to the last line but changed it to, 'But if needs be, it is an ideal for which I am prepared to die.' A brief but significant adjustment had been made. Would it prove to be enough to save them from the gallows?

'At the end of the address I simply sat down … it was the last time that Justice De Wet ever looked me in the eye.'[139]

Mandela was banned, and could not be quoted in print. That did not stop that incredible newspaper, the *Rand Daily Mail*, from printing his address the next morning, 'virtually word for word'.

Mandela and his comrades had pulled off a major coup, but would it be enough to save them?

Walter Sisulu was the first into the witness box. He was a controversial choice. As his name was mentioned, a court official approached one of the defence lawyers and warned that Sisulu was unsuitable for the enormous task. He was a man who was 'not even properly dressed'. (At the time he was in an ill-fitted jacket borrowed from his son Max, and had on a carelessly knotted tie.)[140]

Yuter was nevertheless not taking any chances. He had instructed the police that Walter was to be kept isolated throughout the long days (and nights) that Yutar kept him in the witness box. Even at lunch breaks he was not to be with his co-accused.

Yutar's cross-examination was endless, and he would repeatedly ask similar questions, trying to get Sisulu to incriminate others. In this he was assisted by the Judge, who also interjected repeatedly.

But it did not work.

Joel Joffe thought that Walter was one of the finest witnesses he had ever seen. 'We felt that Walter in the witness box had been a triumph … the whole court had been impressed by this small man of meagre education but of tremendous sincerity, calm, conviction and certainty … his colleagues who had persuaded us beforehand that he would be more than a match for Yutar had understood him well.'[141]

Next it was Port Elizabeth's turn in the dock.

Firstly Govan Mbeki.

'Govan Mbeki admits to being a member of the National High Command of Umkhonto; to membership of the African National Congress and the Communist Party. Perhaps "admits" is not the word; rather he declares proudly that he has played a substantial role in these organisations.

"'As you have answered in the affirmative to questions or actions concerning all four counts against you, why did you not plead guilty to all four counts?"

"'First, I felt that I should come and explain under oath some of the reasons that led me to join these organisations. There was a sense of moral duty attached to it. Secondly, for the simple reason that to plead guilty would to my mind indicate a sense of moral guilt. I do not accept that there is moral guilt attached to my actions."

'Something in Govan's quiet and courteous way of speaking arouses in Yutar a greater antagonism than he has yet displayed to the accused... He returns again and again to questions of identities, places, names, which Govan refuses to answer.

'Although Govan's admissions make it unnecessary for Yutar to press his cross-examination of Govan – there is no question of the verdict in his case – he continues to question him for three more days, interspersing questions about documents with the questions that seek information. He is like an angry fly hitting himself again and again against a pane of glass; because the glass is transparent he believes he only has to hit hard enough and he will reach the other side. Govan steadfastly refused to answer any questions which might incriminate anyone else.'[142]

Later came Raymond Mhlaba and another great act of courage.

Mhlaba was presented with evidence supplied by one of the taxi drivers whose evidence had been used in the trial of Mkaba, Mini and Khayinga. This driver, Kholisile Mdwayi, alleged that Mhlaba had got into his taxi, accompanied by two comrades from the Transkei.

'He claimed that I had commanded them to go and sabotage two places. He reported that as we were moving in the taxi I had said things like "Oh very good my boy, you have done a good job."

'I was in China at this time. Throughout the period they claimed I was guilty of sabotage, I was out of the country.'[143]

Francis Meli, in his *History of the ANC*,[144] notes that Mhlaba was out of South Africa when MK was launched and the sabotage acts happened. When he was captured at Lilliesleaf Farm the police could find no evidence to charge him other than that he was caught at Lilliesleaf. So they cooked up evidence, in the hope that he would release information when defending himself.

'In the trial Mhlaba denied he was guilty of the charges against him. Yutar demanded that Mhlaba reveal then where he had been at the time of the alleged crimes. Mhlaba's answer to Yutar's relentless pressure was his infectious high-pitched laugh and firm retort, "I am not going to tell you that." This all was later confirmed by Mhlaba.'[145]

And so the Rivonia Trial slowly ground to its conclusion.

20 May 1964 was the day of final argument.

It began with Yutar's distribution of a dozen blue leather-bound copies of his final speech. It was a flop.

The day was to belong to Judge De Wet, who four times startled the court.

Firstly, when Yutar was in full flight in his final speech, Judge De Wet interrupted him, 'Mr Yutar, you do concede that you failed to prove guerrilla warfare was ever decided upon, do you not?'[146]

'Yutar was stunned … he haltingly told the court that preparations for guerrilla warfare were indeed made.'

'Yes, I know that,' De Wet replied impatiently, 'the defence concedes that. But they say that prior to their arrest they took no decision to engage in guerrilla warfare. I take it that you have no evidence contradicting that and that you accept it?'

'As Your Worship wishes,' said Yutar in a strangled voice.'

Secondly, Arthur Chaskalson, in his concluding arguments, noted that other organisations had committed acts of sabotage for which the accused had been blamed. Judge De Wet again interrupted and said that he had already accepted that as a fact.

Thirdly, when Bram Fischer argued that no decision had been taken to begin guerrilla warfare, Judge De Wet again interrupted: 'I thought that I had made my attitude clear. I accept that no decision or date had been fixed upon for the beginning of guerrilla warfare.'

And fourthly, Fischer again argued that MK and the ANC were separate organisations – De Wet again interrupted to say that he had accepted that too.

'We were jubilant … Court was adjourned for three weeks while de Wet considered the verdict.'[147]

On 11 June the accused were brought back to the Palace of Justice.

Judge De Wet was quick and to the point.

Rusty Bernstein was found not guilty and discharged. Ahmed Kathrada was found guilty on only one count, the second count, of conspiracy. The other eight were found guilty on all four charges.

Judge De Wet set sentencing down for the following morning, and suggested that the defence team might wish then to bring argument in mitigation. He then adjourned the court.

That night Mandela, Mbeki and Sisulu decided that they would not appeal, even if the sentence was the death penalty. They passed this on to a stunned defence team. The accused remained resolute. They would not water down the moral case they had made by begging for mercy.

On Friday 12 June 1964 they returned to court.

Harold Hanson and Alan Paton delivered pleas in mitigation. Mandela believes that Judge De Wet did not listen to either of them. 'He had obviously already decided,' wrote Mandela 30 years later.[148] The judge appeared nervous. It must be the death penalty, Mandela reasoned. He is normally so calm.

Mandela was, of course, splendidly wrong.

All of the accused got life imprisonment.

There was a gasp of relief in the court. Denis Goldberg's wife could not hear the judge. She shouted to her husband, 'Denis, what is it?'

His reply is historic, 'Life! Life! To live!'

Denis was immediately bundled off to Pretoria Local, where he was to spend the next 23 years.

At midnight the others were pulled from their cells, handcuffed, and driven to a military airport. There they were loaded onto a Dakota aircraft that had seen better days. Later that day they landed on an airstrip on Robben Island. This, and a few other prisons, were to be their homes for the next many years.

The 'little Rivonia' trial

By mid-1953 Prof. ZK Matthews had returned from the United States and was again teaching at Fort Hare University. Frustrated by the 'lull' in political activity at the time, he convened a small group of activists at his home in Alice. This group included his wife, Frieda, their sons and Dr James Njongwe who had deputised as provincial president of the ANC when Prof. Matthews had been in the USA. Also present was Robert Matji, Cape secretary of the ANC.

Together they created the idea of aiming for a series of public meetings to which everyone, including the National and United parties, would be invited. The meetings would culminate in a national convention at which an agreed manifesto, a set of aspirational goals for South Africa, would be adopted. 'Thus originated the idea of a Congress of the People and a Freedom Charter.'[149]

Prof. Matthews seeded this idea through the Cape provincial congress of the ANC in August 1953, and the idea was thereafter adopted by the ANC's national conference in December 1953. It was to be different from the ANC's 'Africa Claims' document in that it would not be drafted by a team of intellectuals, but would rather reflect the visions and aspirations of the broader population, as assembled through thousands of solicited 'demands'.

To get this highly ambitious objective to happen, the ANC decided to coordinate its four racially separate congresses, the African National Congress, the South African Indian Congress, the Congress of Democrats and the South African Coloured People's Congress, as the 'Congress Alliance'.

Two hundred organisations attended a planning conference called by the Congress Alliance at Tongaat near Durban on 21 March 1954. The National and United parties were invited but did not attend. The Liberal Party did attend, albeit nervously. A National Action Committee was set up at Tongaat to run the campaign. It was chaired by Chief Luthuli, with Walter Sisulu as secretary. When he was banned, Oliver Tambo deputised for him.

By the end of 1954 the National Action Committee claimed that 10 000 Freedom Volunteers were at work, assembling demands.

In Port Elizabeth Ray Mhlaba and Wilton Mkwayi were respectively head of the National Action Committee for the Eastern Cape and Volunteer-in-Chief. Their task was made easy by the existence of a functioning M-Plan structure, and thousands of demands were assembled.

Nationally all demands were studied and drafted into the Freedom Charter by a small committee of the National Action Committee and this draft was agreed by the ANC's National Executive Committee on 22 June.

And so the days of 25 and 26 June 1955 arrived with thousands of delegates arriving at a sportsfield at Kliptown, 20 km from Johannesburg, for the Congress of the People. Tragically, Chief Luthuli could not attend, as he was both banned and had suffered a stroke in early 1955, which caused him to spend two months in the McCord Zulu Hospital recovering. He nevertheless deposed a recorded speech, calling the Freedom Charter the Magna Carta of South Africa, a document that would lead South Africa to a place where everyone would have a vote.

The agreed draft of the Freedom Charter was put to the Congress of the People, with 2 884 delegates,[150] and read clause by clause. Eventually, section by section, it was adopted by 'acclamation, with a show of hands and shouts of "Afrika"'.[151]

With two sections remaining to be approved, a large contingent of police arrived and invaded the sportsfield that the Congress of the People was using as a venue. All documents were seized, cameras and rolls of film confiscated and nobody was allowed to leave until their names and contact details had been recorded. All papers held by delegates were confiscated and stored in individual envelopes, with names written on them. This all concluded well after dark; the police had brought tables and hurricane lamps. They were well prepared, and made it plain that they believed that treason was being committed.

And 'treason' it was to be.

Further mass raids on 27 September 1955 yielded even more documentation and the Minister of Justice, Charles Swart, announced in parliament on 30 April 1956 that 'Everything still has to be correlated, but it is expected that about 200 people will be charged.'[152]

There were 156 to be exact. And they were scooped up from 5 December 1956 onwards, for a trial, now called the Treason Trial, that began on 19 December 1956 in the Old Drill Hall in Johannesburg.

And what a fiasco it turned out to be.

A year into the trial, on 17 December 1957, charges were dropped against 65 of the accused, but not against Mandela, Sisulu, ZK Matthews and Wilton Mkwayi. A new indictment was prepared against the remaining 91 accused and the next phase of the trial began in August 1958 in a new venue, an old synagogue in Pretoria. The accused were divided into batches of about 30 and they would be tried one group after the other, beginning with the group against whom the prosecution felt that the evidence was strongest. The first group included Mandela, Sisulu and Mkwayi.

Then came the Sharpeville massacre, and the resultant state of emergency. Both the ANC and the PAC were banned. And Oliver Tambo left the country, to set up the ANC in exile.

Again the trial was postponed.

At this time Wilton received a terse instruction that he was to leave the country for 'training'. He, and all the other Treason Trial accused, were out on bail, and he decided to move immediately. He entered Lesotho in the company of a football team and in September 1960 he began a series of flights that took him to Accra in Ghana, then London, then Prague to the headquarters of the World Federation of Trade Unions. Here he was joined by another South African, Nanda 'Steve' Naidoo. Together they flew to Moscow and then on to China in August or September 1961.

Meanwhile at home, on 29 March 1961, the first group of Treason Trial defendants was acquitted, and this included Wilton. Charges against the remaining 61 were withdrawn. The Treason Trial, possibly the longest trial South Africa has experienced, was over, after four and a half years, with nobody convicted of anything.

In late 1961 Abel Mthembu arrived to join Wilton and Steve, and he was soon followed by Joe Gqabi. Three more weeks passed, and Ray Mhlaba and Andrew Mlangeni arrived. This core group of six comrades was the first group of South Africans to leave South Africa to receive military training abroad; in fact, Umkhonto we Sizwe was only announced to the world in December 1961, well after these six activists were out of the country and in China.

They spent five and a half months in training, Steve and Andrew in northern China learning about communications (how to make and modify radios, how to use Morse code, etc.), and the other four went south where they learned how to make Molotov cocktails and home-made hand grenades and the like.

The Chinese believed they needed to know how to make war using readily available resources: cow dung explosives, and how to use small guns, not artillery pieces.

They met Mao Tse-tung, who advised them that the topography of South Africa was different from China and that they should be ever vigilant, and learn from their own environment.

After training, there followed two months touring China. Thereafter they returned to South Africa. Wilton came home with Mhlaba, Gqabi and Mthembu, through Dar es Salaam (where Oliver Tambo was astonished to find that ANC personnel had gone on military training without his knowing of it). They were picked up in a car by Joe Modise in Bechuanaland, and made it safely home in the first week of 1963. They were taken straight to Rivonia.[153]

At Rivonia they were debriefed by Walter Sisulu and Joe Slovo and informed about the founding and aims of Umkhonto. It was clear that the ANC was on the run. The police were hounding activists, and all senior personnel were now underground and in hiding.

After a few weeks at Rivonia, Mkwayi and Mhlaba made their way home to the Eastern Cape. There they began to train activists in methods of sabotage and helped set up routes for comrades to leave the country.

Back at Rivonia, in May 1963 Umkhonto set up a 'Logistics Committee' to control and provide the necessary weaponry and associated training. Denis Goldberg was on this committee, with Arthur Goldreich, David Kitson, Dr H Feinstein, Lionel Gay, Mhlaba and Mkwayi.

At this time, Mkwayi met and courted Irene Mhlongo, a nurse who moonlighted for the ANC. Their relationship was to sustain Mkwayi through the difficult times ahead.

As we have seen, on 11 July the police raided the Rivonia farm, arrested almost the entire Umkhonto High Command and seized their documents and records. Mkwayi was miraculously not there at the time, and returned that afternoon. Sensing trouble, he quickly crossed the road and pretended to be herding the cattle there. He got away and was advised to go to a safe house in Soweto.[154]

On 9 October 1963 the Rivonia Trial began, and on 26 November Mkwayi was made the head of the New National Command of Umkhonto. On this New National Command was David Kitson, Lionel Gay and Laloo Chiba. Despite the terrifying working conditions they now had to endure, including the constant use of disguises, they raised the membership of Umkhonto from 100 in late 1963 to 500 in early 1964. Possibly more importantly, they suspended the sabotage campaign for fear that its continuance would endanger the Rivonia defendants. Mkwayi and Mac Maharaj nevertheless continued to make and store pipe bombs.[155]

Mkwayi managed to avoid arrest for nearly another year, during which he continued to help activists leave the country and he continued to make bombs. Mac Maharaj was arrested in July 1964. Wilton now knew that the net was getting closer all the time.

At this stage he made a bad mistake.

He had met and was working with Bartholomew Tlhapane, a veteran of the ANC, the SACP (where he was on the Central Committee) and detention. Tlhapane was a source of money which Mkwayi used to help activists leave the country and he was often interested in the details of Mkwayi's life. He managed to convince Mkwayi to take him to Irene Mhlongo's house, and, against his better judgement, Mkwayi did so.

In late September 1964 Mkwayi got shot in his thigh. Whether this was from someone else's or from Mkwayi's own gun, Wilton was not sure. But he made his way to Irene's home where she cleaned and dressed the wound. Wilton returned to his work.

Later that day he became exhausted, and returned to Irene's home, requesting to sleep there. She agreed.

In the middle of the night the police arrived carrying a photo of Wilton, and dragged him off. It was 1 October 1964, and Wilton was to spend the next 24 years in jail, having been sold out, he believed, by Tlhapane.[156]

It took the state all of six weeks to bring Mkwayi to trial, in a trial immediately known as 'Little Rivonia'.

It was 'little' in every respect.

Firstly, there were only five accused: Wilton (number 1), David Kitson, Laloo Chiba, John Edwards Matthews and Mac Maharaj. Then there were only 33 witnesses: all for the prosecution, as the defence called none. And a short list of charges: Wilton faced 12, but they were essentially sabotage and treason. There were a handful of lawyers: Joel Joffe was the briefing attorney for the defence and the ubiquitous George Bizos their advocate (although Chiba had his own counsel). But most particularly, 'Little Rivonia' was little in that it began on 18 November and judgment was given by Justice Boshoff on 15 December 1964.[157] The state had plainly learned many lessons since the Treason Trial.

What made it quick and easy for the prosecution was the appearance of two key witnesses: Abel Patrick Mthembu, who had accompanied Wilton in China and who thus established incontrovertibly for the state that Wilton had received military training in China, and had been making bombs on his return; and Lionel Gay, who could in turn establish that Wilton had been originally on Umkhonto's Logistics Committee and later on the New National High Command. As the defence called no witnesses, the testimony of these two turncoats was uncontested, and the accused were in for the high jump.

Thus, at the age of 41, Zimasile Wilton Mkwayi was sent to jail for life because the judge felt that he should get the same sentence as the 'Big Rivonia' accused. Having sampled the pleasures of Pretoria Central, then Leeuwkop, then Aucamp No 4, he finally landed on Robben Island in about June 1965. His four co-accused received prison sentences of between 12 and 20 years. He was 66 years old when he, at last, could walk on a pavement unhindered. Between trials, scurrying around in the underground and his years in jail, Wilton Mkwayi spent half of his entire life.

Political doldrums

The townships of Port Elizabeth and Uitenhage, for 20 years the central volcano in African resistance against white domination, were s ashed by late 1964.

Ray Mhlaba, for 22 years the engine and the energy of the local insurrection, was on Robben Island serving a life sentence.

Govan Mbeki, who had added so much after his arrival in 1955, was also on Robben Island, also for life.

Wilton Mkwayi, Mhaba's right-hand man from 1946 to 1956, was in jail for life.

The MK High Command in Port Elizabeth, Zinakile Mkaba, Vuyisile Mini and Wilson Khayinga, had been caught, tried and executed.

Dr James Ndjongwe had burned out, been banned and left town.

Benson Fihla had been arrested and jailed on Robben Island.

Henry Fazzie and Ernest Malgas had also been arrested and jailed on the Island.

The ANC, the Communist Party, the Pan Africanist Congress and Umkhonto we Sizwe were all banned.

The police, particularly the security police, were much better resourced, motivated and trained.

This was the beginning of 12 years of political doldrums for the area, as it was for South Africa.

6

The destruction of South End

As we previously noted, Port Elizabeth and Uitenhage grew on the back of one removal of black communities after another. The two biggest of these removals were the removal of Korsten in the 1950s and the removal of South End in the 1960s.

The first major removal was the removal of Korsten. This was performed by the 'liberal' Port Elizabeth municipality under the guise of 'slum clearance'.

This municipality constituted a 'Slum Elimination Committee' which decreed that in Korsten there were '8 000 to 10 000 African families living there in slum hovels which are totally unfit for human habitation'.[158]

To resettle this huge community KwaZakhele was laid out, to become about 12 000 serviced sites with time.

By June 1957, 3 589 homes in Korsten had been demolished, and 21 000 Africans rehoused in KwaZakhele. A year later this clearance was nearly over, with 40 000 Africans having been moved. The last 1 059 families were due to be moved in June 1958.

By means of these removals, Port Elizabeth became racially stratified. By 1960, 84% of all Port Elizabeth's Africans had been dumped into what were to become 'African Group Areas'.

The National Party by now had proclaimed the Group Areas Act and they were not to leave it to rust on the statute book. The Act had a number of potential uses, but, for the National Party, the vital one was to clear inner-city areas that had, over time, become inhabited by 'mixed' communities.

Heartened by the 'success' of the destruction of Sophiatown in Johannesburg, where on 9 February 1955, 2 000 policemen had begun the removal of about 60 000 residents, 90% of whom were Africans (this was not a Group Areas removal, but in terms of the Native Resettlement Act of 1954), the government then turned on Cato Manor in Durban in 1958, where about 60 000 residents, mostly Africans and Indian South Africans, were driven out, this time in terms of the Group Areas Act.

Then it became Port Elizabeth's turn.

By 1960 white and African Port Elizabethans were mostly living in their designated group areas. The weight of the Group Areas Act was thus to fall on the Coloured community. The affected communities were to be Fairview, to the west of Walmer, and South End, a central community just to the south of central Port Elizabeth, an established and settled mixed suburb.[159]

South End goes back almost as far as the early little settlements of Algoa Bay. The biggest portion of what was to become South End was a land grant by the governor Lord Charles Somerset in 1820 to one Gerhardus Oosthuizen. His heirs divided this into plots, which sold very slowly.

In synch with the rest of Algoa Bay in these early years, nothing much happened.

The non-racial nature of South End began with the early purchase of plots there by people from the Malay community. This community had arrived in Algoa Bay in 1846 at the end of a frontier war in which they had been conscripted, and settled between what was then Main Street and Strand Street. A mosque was built in Grace Street shortly after this community arrived.

This Malay community was, of course, pushed out when expansions of the white community absorbed their land and they were granted land south of the Baakens River, which soon became known as 'South End'. They were followed by many other groupings, including Indians, Chinese, St Helenians, Portuguese, Greeks, Khoikhoi, Mfengu and Xhosa.

Soon South End was surrounded by 'white' communities in Humerail, Humewood, Central and Walmer. With the National Party becoming the government, trouble lay ahead.

By the 1960s South End was a bustling non-racial community. By 1965 the population included 6 350 persons classified as 'non-white', which included 4 950 'Malays and Coloureds', 1 255 Indians and 155 Chinese. They occupied 539 properties, 398 of which were occupied by Coloured people.

There was so much more: eight Christian churches of seven different denominations; two temples and two mosques; 13 schools including South End High and St Thomas's; four hotels; a cinema; a few factories including the Lions Clothing Factory, and many shops and traders. It was a noisy, busy world, full of kids and energy and sports clubs, and dancing studios and life.

None of which was to save it from apartheid's bulldozers.

In the year that group areas were put in place in Port Elizabeth, in 1961, South End was declared a 'white' group area. Even the Port Elizabeth Council, which had so shamefacedly pretended to be liberal and concerned for the community in South End while working with government to remove them, called for South End to be zoned 'Coloured', and that its settled population be allowed to remain. This made no difference.

The South End community kicked up a storm in protest, wrote many letters to the *Herald*, formed an 'Anti-Coloured Affairs Department' Group and a 'Group Areas Action Committee', went to court, made submission after submission to the government's appointed 'Group Areas Board'. Nothing changed the inevitable.

To convert the already converted, and to present their endless good intentions to whoever might still be sceptical, government presented a 'Transformation Plan' for South End, and had a model built, of skyscrapers galore, buildings bridging newly created boulevards and all sorts of other wonders.

The transformation plan presented a total 'scrape-away-and-rebuild', with the existing South End buildings, parks, roads and infrastructure almost totally destroyed. A newly redesigned 'white world' was to rise from the ashes, all leading off a newly created 'Walmer Boulevard'.

This plan was enough to turn the flip-flop Council into acolytes. A minute of a joint meeting, Council with State, reprinted in Agherdien, George and Hendricks' book, shows Councillor Ralph Hancock, who two years later stood for the Progressive Party for parliament, effusing: 'the opportunity presented to Port Elizabeth should be "grasped" in the broad sense. He said that the clock should be put back 150 years and that South End should now be envisaged as a hill with nothing on it, and that consideration should be given to transforming the hill into something worthwhile.'

Even the *Herald* was half-in and half-out of this nonsense. On 1 May 1965 it ran a headline, 'Port Elizabeth's 125-year old South End will be rebuilt. A far reaching scheme announced by the government last night will entail moving 8 742 people of all races to other areas of the city, demolishing hundreds of slum dwellings [sic], rebuilding streets and designing new developments.'

The white residents would be mostly unaffected. Coloureds would be moved to Bethelsdorp and Gelvandale, Indians to Woolhope (now Malabar) and Chinese to an area in the vicinity of Kabega Park, all areas far distant from South End, with its proximity to the harbour and to the city centre.

On 10 May 1965 the first residents received their expropriation notices from the Group Areas Development Board. Occupants were given three months to vacate.

In parliament, predictably, only Mrs Helen Suzman attacked this horror. She blamed this all on Afrikaner people wanting land that Coloureds had occupied for a century.

Agherdien, George and Hendricks conclude this nauseating business appropriately: 'And when the day came, the people moved. After years of discussion, protest, letters and petitions, the government got its way and the people moved. When the last non-white family had moved out, when the laughter and the cries of the children had slowly died; when the excited gossip had trickled to a halt; when the calls of the fishermen and the other hawkers were finally silent – the bulldozers moved in and levelled the area. 125 years of history bit the dust. Within a short time, houses, shops, schools, churches and various businesses lay in a pathetic heap – just so much rubble. The life went out of South End.'

At one time, the South End Museum displayed a moving exhibition item of the bulldozers coming into South End. It was a Sunday, but apartheid was now in a hurry and demolition had to be hurried. In the Catholic church, the priest was saying Mass when the bulldozers started destroying his church hall. In horror the priest screamed, 'Can't they even wait for me to serve communion before they destroy everything?' They couldn't, and didn't.

This all was over by 1972 and Councillor Ralph Hancock got his 'empty hill'.

This terrible business, which has left an open wound in the body of Port Elizabeth's Coloured community, was followed by Fairview and Willowdene also being razed.

In total population figures, 1% of white Port Elizabethans, 40+% of Coloured Port Elizabethans, and all of the Indian and Chinese community, and an unknown but large percentage of the African community, were moved in terms of the Group Areas Act.

By the mid-1970s segregation was completed in Port Elizabeth and by 1985 only 3.3% of Port Elizabeth's population was housed outside of its group area.

There are four issues to be noted before we leave this tragic business of the demolition of South End.

Firstly, why was the protest at these removals so muted, so law-abiding, when the law had been so twisted, so debased, in order to destroy an entire community? Why did the community settle for letters to the press, petitions, submissions to phoney government bodies that were marching anyway to a predetermined conclusion? Why was there no '*klipgooiery*', no attacks on the vehicles of the perpetrators of this naked aggression?

The answer probably lies in the balance of forces at the time. The ANC had just been crushed, its leaders were mostly all in jail (and no one then did not believe that 'for life' was 'for life'), or in exile, or, worse still, executed or still awaiting trial. The security police at the time had no restraints. Sabotage attacks were no more. The time of protest was not now. South End died with hardly a whimper.

Secondly, the much promised 'urban renewal' never happened. Yes, South End was scraped away, and Walmer Boulevard built. But then? The skyscrapers? The magic new world of Councillor Ralph Hancock? The grand buildings straddling Walmer Boulevard at height?

It was all a lie. This all was to purge the area of 'non-whites' – there was not much beyond that. The land, this precious heritage of so many families and their churches, schools, parks, halls, businesses – that was all scraped away, to be replaced by hundreds and hundreds of middle-class townhouses for 'whites only', monotonous in the extreme. The developers queued up for the land, made a quick buck, and left a world of many little dwellings with no schools, shops, parks, sports facilities, churches, or community. The mosques remain, as did the two temples, as lonely testimony of an earlier time.

Thirdly, the most bizarre twist of fate.

Twenty-three years after the last bulldozers had left a demolished South End, the first fully democratic local government election was held across South Africa, including Port Elizabeth, in 1995.

The Coloured community in Port Elizabeth had now been consolidated into the 'Northern Areas', which was demarcated into seven wards. These wards had the lowest average turnout in the then Port Elizabeth (45%), and, incredibly, 40% of all who voted here, voted for the National Party, the political organisation that had, 23 years earlier, bulldozed South End.

Fourthly, and lastly on bulldozed South End, tribute should be paid to the next community that was to be confronted by apartheid's bulldozers.

In 1964 the Department of Community Development set up a commission to investigate the re-planning of the 'slum' of District Six in Cape Town. In June 1965, all property sales in this area were frozen. On 11 February 1966 District Six, some of the best-situated land in South Africa, was decreed to be for 'whites only'. Here we go again.

In 1968 the removals in District Six began. By 1982, 60 000 people, predominantly Coloured folk, had been moved 25 kilometres east to the Cape Flats, to conditions so different from their memories of the inner-city District Six that they had been driven out of.

There were many other removals around South Africa over that time, but this is not the topic of this book. Just to note – as a result of the removals mentioned here, Sophiatown, Cato Manor, South End and District Six, nearly 200 000 people were displaced. The population of Bloemfontein in 1968 was 175 000.

7

1976

The 12 years from the Rivonia Trial until 1976 were relatively, by South African standards, quiet, or, should we say, in a world where blood was regularly and brutally spilled, comparatively bloodless, except for the Group Areas removals.

The National Party went on their merry way over these years and the few preceding years. South Africa left the Commonwealth and became a republic. Black South Africans were stripped of their South African citizenship by the Bantu Homelands Citizenship Act, and their citizenship rights were instead now to be effected in the bantustans. These, in turn, were moved forward with Transkei, Bophuthatswana, Ciskei, Lebowa, Venda and Gazankulu becoming 'self-governing' and, in 1976, the Transkei became 'independent'. The new Terrorism Act allowed for indefinite detention without trial. Bram Fischer was caught and suffered the same fate as the Rivonia accused but, as he was white, not on Robben Island. Wilton Mkwayi, who had taken over the leadership of Umkhonto, was taken a few months later. At this stage John Vorster, then Minister of Justice, said, 'We have broken the back of the ANC.' Southern Rhodesia declared UDI from Britain and South African security forces upped their numbers as guerrilla activity in South West Africa scaled up.

The ANC in turn made progress: Chief Luthuli was awarded the Nobel Peace Prize in 1961; a mission-in-exile was opened in Tanzania; and the ANC's first consultative conference was held in Morogoro; Mozambique and

Angola expelled Portuguese rule, became independent in 1975, and South Africa lost an important piece of its cordon sanitaire; ANC structures inside South Africa were carefully re-seeded and the international ANC acquired resources and allies. Steve Biko led a breakaway from the liberal student body NUSAS, and called it the South African Students' Organisation. Umkhonto guerrillas began operating in Rhodesia. And strikes in Durban in 1973 were the first evidence of a resurgence of mass-based protest and the beginning of independent unions.

There were also, of course, terrible events. For the National Party, Prime Minister Verwoerd was assassinated in parliament. For the ANC, the station bomber John Harris was hanged; Ahmed Timol was killed while in police detention; and James Tyitya became the first Port Elizabeth activist to die in police detention – official explanation, 'suicide by hanging'. Four years later another Port Elizabethan, Caleb Mayekiso, also died in detention.

The build-up to 1976

Generally however, by South African standards, the 12 years from 1964 to 1976 were quiet years.

In 1974 the ANC sent one of their key men back into South Africa, to test the water.

'I crossed from Botswana, I was alone, round about six in the evening, and there was that thrilling experience as I jumped the fence, and I landed on the other side, in South Africa,' said Chris Hani in a 1990 interview with *Monitor* magazine.[160]

'Then I walked through the evening. I made no contact with anyone, I was just walking alone. I was not quite sure of my position – I had never been in that part of the country – I was using stars to guide me deeper and deeper into the country. That part of the country is full of farms, white farms. I had to change course because of dogs.

'I walked through the night and the following day until 3 pm, resting for 30 minutes, and then trudging on until I reached this town, Zeerust.

'I went to the station to buy a ticket to Joburg, and for the first time in my life I went through the experience of calling this fellow who was selling the tickets "baas" in my broken Afrikaans! I thought he would rather accept a Bantu who was trying to speak Afrikaans than someone who looks smart and was speaking English. He was excited about that! I think he thought I was a good kaffir!

'The following morning I was in Joburg. I remained in Joburg for four months. I had some friends there. I discussed the situation inside – the underground structures had collapsed, there was just nothing in 1974!

'It was, however very dangerous, even the people who were keeping us were very uncomfortable. You got a feeling that they had a duty to look after me, but at the same time you got a sense that you were endangering their position and the position of their family. To compound the problem some people had come back and, when arrested, had broken down and had implicated a number of people. The confidence in us, in our capacity to remain strong under interrogation, that confidence had been dampened. The police were very ruthless, very, very ruthless. At that time people had been tortured, a few had died, not only guerrillas but also those who had harboured them.

'There was a feeling of helplessness. This was the time of the strikes of some workers in Durban, but on the whole one would characterise this period as one of a relative lull in terms of mass political activity. After four months I left for Lesotho.'

Port Elizabeth and Uitenhage

And in Port Elizabeth?[161]

Barney Pityana, banned and living in Port Elizabeth from February 1973, felt as did Hani. 'I wasn't approached by the ANC underground during the five years I was in Port Elizabeth – I don't think there was any substantial ANC underground, as far as I know.' His wife Dimsa was involved with a South African Institute of Race Relations project, involving fewer than 50 people, and yet she was the subject of massive harassment at the time.

Thozamile Botha, who in the second half of 1976 was teaching at KwaZakhele High School, also recalls that the ANC was very quiet then, and he certainly had no contact with them.

Saki Macozoma recalls the mood of the time: 'People wouldn't even talk of the ANC – they would say, for instance, if somebody had been arrested, that so-and-so's father had been arrested during the "big thing" – meaning, the events of the early 60s! ... I recall trying to set up a branch of the South African Students Movement at KwaZakhele High in 1975 [he was then in Std 9 at the school] but it was very, very difficult to set it up, and there were very, very few people who were willing to identify with that sort of thing.'

One who was willing to join was Macozoma's classmate, Mike Xego. 'I first came across SASM in 1975 at KwaZakhele High – they did have a structure at the school, but a very shaky structure that I was very reluctant to join as I feared arrest.'

Mkhuseli Jack, in Std 7 at Cowan High in 1976, recalls that 'we feared the ANC because to talk about it was such a big crime', and that his first political contact was a pamphlet he received in 1975 at a rugby stadium. The pamphlet was distributed by PAC stalwart Moki Cekisani, and called him to his first political meeting, to commemorate Sharpeville, in 1975.

Thus was the political atmosphere in Port Elizabeth's townships in 1976 – state power brutally applied, political suppression and fear of exposure.

Then came 16 June 1976 and South Africa, and Port Elizabeth, would never be the same again.

The explosion – Soweto 1976

School education in South Africa has always been massively, disgustingly, biased against black schoolkids. By the mid-1970s the state was spending R644 per year educating a white kid, and R42 educating a black one. Classrooms in black schools regularly had to accommodate around 60 kids. As Jonathan Jansen has said (albeit about other South African schools in another time), teaching was more about crowd control than educating.

In Soweto, Johannesburg, the National Party government then made two mistakes.

Firstly, between 1962 and 1972 they had built no high schools in Soweto. Black kids were supposed to get their education in the bantustans. Then they made their next mistake; they conceded, and from 1972 until 1976 built 40 schools in Soweto. The number of secondary school pupils rose from 12 500 to 34 500. Black kids came out of roving social gangs into classrooms, where they could accept leadership and be mobilised. Big mistake by the system.

Secondly, the Department of Bantu Education in 1974 passed an 'Afrikaans Language Medium Directive'. From 1975 in high schools, mathematics, arithmetic and social studies had to be taught in Afrikaans. The Deputy Minister of Bantu Education, Punt Janson, was quoted as saying, 'A black man may be trained to work on a farm or in a factory. He may work for an employer who is either English speaking or Afrikaans speaking and the man who has to give him instructions may be either English speaking or Afrikaans speaking. Why should we now start quarrelling about the medium of instruction amongst the Black people as well? No, I have not consulted them, and I'm not going to consult them. I have consulted the constitution of the Republic of South Africa.' Another mistake.

The matter became a flashpoint. On 30 April 1976 the pupils of the Orlando West Primary School went on strike and refused to go to school. This strike spread. Tsietsi Mashinini of the Morris Isaacson High School called a meeting of school committees. An Action Committee was formed and it called a mass rally at the Orlando Stadium for 16 June 1976. Mashinini was the only identifiable student leader. He was head prefect at Morris Isaacson and president of the Soweto Students Representative Council. He was in and out of hiding. The police offered R500 for information leading to his arrest, which later drove him further underground and finally to the ANC in exile.

The children were to move from school to school, gathering numbers, and then move on to the stadium. On the day, they found their path blocked by police barricades. They found alternative routes. Desperate police tried to block these. Teargas was fired and all hell broke loose. The police fired and fired. Hastings Ndlovu, aged 15, was the first killed. Then, at Orlando West High School, Hector Pieterson, aged 13, was gunned down. The photographer Sam Nzima was there and his photo of Mbuyisa Makhubu running while carrying Hector's body, with Hector's sister alongside him, was instantly transformed into an icon of the struggle.

By nightfall somewhere between 176 and 700 children had been shot. Doctors at emergency units were informed to keep the names of those treated for gunshot wounds. They refused. Bottlestores, beerhalls and 23 buildings of the municipality were burned down that day. Dr Melville Edelstein, a humanitarian social worker who had dedicated his life to the Soweto community, was stoned to death. Soweto was on fire, and South Africa followed.

Chris Hani describes these events thus: 'We were not responsible for these events. They were a spontaneous outbreak of anger and resentment, which had been building up in African schools against the system of bantu education, and against the compulsory use of Afrikaans and the inferior facilities generally. This anger had welled up and had reached a point where the students in a number of schools, especially in the Transvaal, decided that enough was enough and they were going to demonstrate.[162]

'As usual in our country if the police had not overreacted, that revolt would not have shaken the world, but the response of the police to, really a peaceful demonstration by students, the violent response spread to other parts of the country and impacted on the world. This was a turning point in terms of the militant struggle in our country.

'From then there was no turning back. We latched on. For the first time we had conditions where the young people were angry, and where they had experienced the brutality and atrocities that had been perpetrated against them by the police, and they were ready to join Umkhonto we Sizwe. Recruiting began to spread at a real pace now and we received more recruits in that year than we had in all the years when I had been there. Then the structures that we had built inside the country began to spread rapidly and we stepped up recruiting, especially from the Eastern Cape. There had been no cadres from the Eastern Cape going out because of the distances, but now they began to flood Lesotho, coming from the Eastern Cape, from the Free State, everywhere.

'We were ready to receive them. We had established military camps in Tanzania, the Soviet Union, the German Democratic Republic, Cuba – they were all ready to receive and train us, so we were in a better position than the PAC. And the quality of the training improved all the time.'

How Port Elizabeth's and Uitenhage's townships responded

How were the youngsters in Port Elizabeth's townships to respond?

As we have noted, there was little organised political activity at the time. But there was some. SASM had a presence at KwaZakhele High and at Newell and Cowan.

Mkhuseli (Khusta) Jack has written an excellent autobiography.[163] In it he notes, 'I gathered that the SASM leaders in Port Elizabeth were caught off-guard by the student outburst in Soweto.' These leaders nevertheless 'identified two crowd-pulling events'. The first was a boxing tournament to be held at the Centenary Hall on Saturday night, 7 August, between Nkosana 'Happy Boy' Mgxaji, the local hero, and Norman 'The Pangaman' Sekgapane from Soweto.

Khusta and other students whose political consciousness was being formed were to have their political blooding:

> The command given to us was straightforward: we were to confront the riot police. Government-associated properties were to be burned to the ground. Liquor stores, Bantu Affairs buildings and any vehicles belonging to or associated with the government were to be razed. Our operational leaders were spot-on in their prediction that this boxing match was the best opportunity to start the uprising in Port Elizabeth.

There were 7 000 people inside and outside the hall by the time the supporting bout ended. This huge crowd presented them with a 'now or never' opportunity.

The riot police had been stationed at the New Brighton Police Station 300 metres down the road, and would only intercede if the police at the hall called them. Between rounds three and five, eruptions began. The crowd outside the hall torched a police van and then another police van was lifted and thrown onto the burning van. The ordinary cops fled and the riot police charged. Chaos. A riot policeman hurled a canister of tear gas into the hall as round six began. Panic. Stampede to the door. More tear gas.

The SASM leaders were pleased – they had wanted a police overreaction, and had got it. Solidarity with Soweto had been shown.

Khusta Jack went home, to his uncle's house. 'I went to bed that evening feeling very good. I had participated in the struggle for the first time.'

Khusta was in unusual company. The four Watson brothers, Gavin, Ronnie, Valence and Cheeky, who that year had begun to coach the Kwaru rugby team in the townships, had been asked to get involved in this boxing event and they also were in Centenary Hall that evening. As Cheeky Watson later said, 'Teargas was used, a riot ensued! The promoter rushed up to me and thrust a couple of thousand rand at me. "Please look after this." That made a deep impression on me – they trusted me with a lot of money. Then I realised how totally they had accepted us … they really wanted to get on with whites. I was deeply moved.' This boxing match was also the brothers' first taste of the rough side of South Africa's politics.[164]

Mono Badela had invited the Watsons to coach Kwaru, knowing and hoping that this could lead to them playing for this township team. What a step forward this could be for non-racial sport. And he got his wish. On 2 October 1976, Cheeky and Valence, having lain on the floor of a township taxi to avoid the roadblocks set up to apprehend them and prevent them from playing, ran onto the field for Kwaru for the first time. Cheeky had been promised a place in the Springbok trials if he quit this township stuff – he politely refused. A delegation from their 'white' club, Crusaders, had likewise pleaded with them and been turned away. Cheeky and Valence were arrested and convicted for being in a 'proscribed area'. But play they did.

Shortly thereafter they began providing information to the ANC, an unimaginably brave thing for white folk to do in 1978. And they paid the price for that. In 1979 Gavin and Valence were in their Commercial Road shop when four men ran in, pretending to be in a scuffle. Gavin interceded and was stabbed in the chest. He was rushed to hospital and died twice in the operating theatre. He recovered. That night, at 11 pm, security police arrived. Fortunately Ronnie was at Gavin's bedside. They left. They had wanted to 'take a statement'. Security police, investigating an attempted murder. The assailant 'escaped from police custody' only to be rearrested for another crime. He eventually got 10 years for attempting to kill Gavin. He was obviously a hitman.

Kwazakhele High School, September 1976

The months of August and September 1976 in Port Elizabeth saw 89 buses stoned, 39 police vehicles and 21 Bantu Affairs vehicles damaged, arson attacks on 20 black schools, five bottlestores and 12 shops and much other damage done to government buildings. The total damage, according to Colonel Goosen of the security police, was R1.4 million. Tragically also, the Colonel reported 34 people killed, 27 of them by the police.[165]

The focus of the riots was, according to the Colonel, the result of a series of unlawful meetings convened by pupils of the KwaZakhele High School, which began on 16 August, and ended in an extraordinary event on 9 September 1976. This event is worth dwelling on in some detail.

There were two tensions operating at KwaZakhele High in mid-1976.[166]

The first was between pupils and teachers. There were many manifestations. Mncedisi Siswana, in matric that year, notes that this tension resulted from 'the general attitude of the teachers – some kind of arrogance, of condescension', and the students had now 'found a small space to express themselves freely'.

Thozamile Botha, who taught maths and physical science in the second half of 1976 and on until the middle of 1978 at KwaZakhele High, notes that at the time the principals of the four township high schools formed what they called a 'high command' and issued statements throughout 1976, criticising the students for being on strike, calling them irresponsible and saying that what was happening in Soweto had nothing to do with Port Elizabeth and calling on the kids to come back to school.

Then Mr Mesatywa, the matric maths and science teacher, resigned without an obvious replacement being available. He was the only teacher qualified to teach these subjects at matric level. The pupils were incensed at his desertion, particularly as he was going to a job in the Ciskei.

The second range of tensions were the political ones – how to respond appropriately to the Soweto uprising.

There was a series of disruptions to classes as the kids met out of the classroom to discuss these issues. The security police would come and be handed a petition. They then used tear gas in a heavy-handed response, and all hell would break loose.

This was all ad hoc, and not seen to be an adequate response.

The school had electricity and most pupils' homes did not. Senior students would often stay at school into the night to study. The deputy headboy, Mbulelo Hewana, and some others had keys to make this possible. Hewana was extremely bright and went on to become a doctor. However, he was seen by many students as being too close to the teachers, which was to cast one's loyalty to the other side of the fence. Most of the more political students would have not asked for, nor accepted, prefectship as it was not elected but rather appointed by the teachers. To compensate for his lukewarm acceptance, Hewana would occasionally scribble political slogans on the blackboards anonymously, as this was seen to be highly daring.

On 9 September 1976, word went around the two matric classes that the boys would remain behind after school to plot a structured response to the Soweto uprising. That night 43 KwaZakhele High School pupils met at the school. Between them they hatched out a rather wild plot to do the following.

They would remain at the school that night, painting posters and debating. The next morning, when the balance of the school arrived, they would divide the school into 43 groups each led by one of the matrics. These groups would make their way into the Mayor's Garden in the centre of white Port Elizabeth, all by different routes, some by bus, some by train, some by taxi, to prevent apprehension. There they would present their grievances to the attention of white Port Elizabethans.

Now the plot becomes more challenging, for the youngsters were to carry petrol bombs and bombs made from the chemicals in the science laboratory (essentially sodium and calcium). To make their exit possible in an anticipated rush of police, they would torch a few shops as a distraction.

Through the night they plotted, painted, sang and slept. At 5 am with the dawn came security policemen Wilken, Nieuwoudt and others, supported by the riot police. Whether they had been tipped off, or had followed up on clues from midnight calls on some students' houses (which had happened), we don't know. What we do know is that 43 frightened and surprised matric students were bundled off to Algoa Park Police Station and rough justice.

In the end, 10 of the 43 became state witnesses, including Mbulelo Hewana, who was the prize performer for the state in a specially convened court in Grahamstown in the recess of the Supreme Court, in January 1977. Judge President Cloete heard the case himself, wherein another new name emerged, Brigadier Lothar Paul Neethling of the police's forensic laboratory.

Neethling, a German orphan from the Second World War, had been adopted by an Afrikaner family, and already had two doctorates in chemistry. He presented to the court a devastating description of Port Elizabeth's city centre aflame, with white women trapped in lifts in flaming tower buildings. According to one 19-year-old awaiting his fate, Michael Xego, 'when he had finished, we knew we were in for it'. Small matter that the petrol and chemical bombs never existed except as schoolboy theories, it was a frightening time of revolt and Neethling had the court's ear.

On 21 January 1977 Judge President Cloete sent 33 youngsters to Robben Island for five years each. This extraordinary group included future AZAPO members Mbu Dukumbana and Lulamile Mati; future ANC MP and then international businessperson Saki Macozoma; future ANC luminaries Mpumi Odolo, Mike Xego, Alex Rala, Boy Mkaliphi, Smally Maqungo and

Prince Msutu; future Municipal Workers Union general secretary Fezile Mavuso, and others.

The night after sentencing, these youngsters were dumped into a truck at Grahamstown jail and driven to Cape Town harbour without a stop, whereupon they were put into a ferry and, on 22 January 1977, they arrived on Robben Island.

When, 14 years earlier, Henry Fazzie and Ernest Malgas arrived on Robben Island, there were 200 prisoners there, about 150 PAC and about 50 ANC. By 1977 Robben Island held 500 prisoners, with the vast number of novices being the 1976 intake, who were mostly what can be described as loosely Black Consciousness in orientation.

Most of these youngsters knew little of the ANC and non-racialism. What pamphlets had done the rounds were BC, and Biko was then the big name. Xego describes being put in a cell with 32 others, including Saths Cooper, Strini Moodley and Terror Lekota. All were BC stalwarts and 1976 veterans. Young Xego found them massively politicised and overwhelming. If they were BC, so would he be.

The story of the conversion of most of the 1976 youngsters from BC to the Congress tradition merits a study of its own. Suffice it to say that many of the ANC veterans played a significant role. Pata Madalane, on the Island for trying to leave the country, was a hard BC man and worked with Vuyisile Thole in taking the food trolleys from the kitchen to the various blocks. The youngsters were in E Block, the Rivonia men in B Block. The trolleys became one of the means of moving notes around.

'Read the Freedom Charter, clause 5, it reflects on the debate you are having,' would be on a note from the omniscient in Block B. Govan Mbeki's notes, later published, came through also. And, finally, Harry Gwala was put into E Block.

Then things started changing. A vital signal to the youngsters was when Terror Lekota left BC for the Congress tradition. That was in 1978 and many followed him. Quickly tensions rose, and Lulamile Mati, who came off Robben Island still BC, reported physical fights and considerable tension.

8

The state's murderous response in the Eastern Cape

B ack in the Eastern Cape the security police, determined to drown out the unrest that continued to manifest itself, employed ever more ruthless methods.[167]

The murders of Mapetla Mohapi and George Botha

Mapetla Mohapi, the regional secretary for the Eastern Cape of SASO, was detained on 15 July 1976. On 5 August 1976 his body was found, with his jeans around his neck, hanging from the bars in a cell at the Kei Road police station. A 'suicide note' alongside his body was proved to be a forgery. The magistrate at the subsequent inquest could find no wrong in the police behaviour.

A few months later George Botha, a young teacher at Paterson High School in Port Elizabeth, was taken into custody by the security police. Five days later he 'jumped' to his death down the six floors of the stairwell at the Sanlam building, the Port Elizabeth security police headquarters. In a predictable repeat of the Mohapi inquest, the magistrate found nobody culpable. This despite the fact that the government-appointed senior pathologist, Dr Knoebel, found skin abrasions on Botha's shoulder, upper chest, upper right arm and armpit, which were from wounds that had been inflicted two to six hours before his death. This was confirmed by

Dr B Tucker, the district surgeon. The magistrate ignored this. The police witnesses were credible, he found. Nobody was culpable.

The unrest kept rolling on. In the middle of June 1977 Ndyebo Mali, a teacher in KwaNobuhle in Uitenhage, who was a member of SASO, and who was organising a June 16 commemoration, was arrested and handcuffed in front of his students at his school. The now normal circumstances unfolded: student protest, police overreact crudely, an uprising ensues. Two government liquor outlets, the Langa community hall, schools, shops and a funeral parlour were torched. The riot police arrived – 10 people were killed, eight shot by police. A magistrate subsequently exonerated the police of illegal action.[168]

The murder of Steve Biko

If the security police were looking for an opportunity to stamp out the ongoing protests, they were given it on 18 August 1977 when they stopped a car at a roadblock just outside Grahamstown, and discovered Steve Biko and Peter Jones inside.[169]

Steve Biko was tall, big, strong and very good-looking. Furthermore, he was charming, personable and easily liked. Then, to top it all, he was brilliant and marvellously articulate. Steve Biko had everything. Including a banning order. Which he was plainly breaking on 18 August 1977.

Biko was the most prominent member of the newly emerged Black Consciousness movement.

The Black Consciousness movement began, of all places, in the white-dominated National Union of South African Students, NUSAS.

NUSAS was founded in 1924 by Leo Marquard, who also founded the Liberal Party. It was a grouping of elected representatives from student bodies at South African universities. Within 10 years of NUSAS's founding, the Afrikaans-language universities had withdrawn, leaving the core of NUSAS to come from the universities of Cape Town, the Witwatersrand, Rhodes and Natal. In 1945 NUSAS, determinedly non-racial, invited the Fort Hare student body to join, which they did.

After the banning of the ANC and the PAC and the state of emergency in 1960–61, African students, frustrated by the lack of political outlets, increasingly turned to NUSAS, which had developed a profoundly anti-government culture and stance, much more so than any of the white political parties. After flirting briefly with revolutionary prospects under their president Jonty Driver in 1964, NUSAS pulled back in 1964.

This conservative tranquillity was to last two years, until a 19-year-old enrolled to study medicine at the Natal University medical school for black students, known as Wentworth, in 1966. In that year he was elected onto the Students Representative Council and in July 1966 he was invited to attend the NUSAS annual conference as an observer. His name was Steve Biko.

Biko was never one to hold back, but at his first NUSAS conference he listened, and 'increasingly began to question the value of what he saw as the artificial integration of student politics. As in South African politics generally, Africans were hanging back, resentful but reticent, hiding behind white spokesmen who had shouldered the job of defining black grievances and goals. For liberal whites, verbal protest and symbolic racial mixing were seen as the outer limits of action. Apartheid was defined as the enemy, and non-racialism prescribed as the antidote. Repeated over and over in words and symbols, this liberal approach, and in fact the entire liberal analysis, had to Biko's way of thinking become not an inspiration to constructive action, but a sterile dogma disguising an unconscious attachment to the status quo.'[170]

These suspicions came to a head at the next NUSAS annual conference, in July 1967, at Rhodes University in Grahamstown. Again Steve attended, this time as a full delegate of Wentworth.

Before the congress began, the issue of the sincerity of the white NUSAS students' commitment to genuine non-racialism was immediately thrown into the fire, as Rhodes University had provided separate accommodation, eating facilities and even social facilities for the black delegates. While the white NUSAS executive complained, concerns about their sincerity were exposed. The black NUSAS delegates were to be put up at a church. Biko immediately canvassed white delegates to join them. Robert Schrire, then vice-chairman of NUSAS, saw this not as a genuine issue, but as an attack on NUSAS.

The next morning the congress started.

Biko rose to make a point of order – and spoke in Xhosa. Many white students protested that they could not understand. Biko replied that they now knew how it felt not to be heard. From within 'white' NUSAS, a motion was put condemning the university for the segregated arrangements, and calling for a 24-hour hunger strike in protest. It was carried. Biko moved a second motion: he condemned NUSAS for not handling the accommodation issue adequately. The NUSAS executive must have known about the accommodation arrangements, and instead of finding another suitable venue, they had allowed the conference to go ahead at Rhodes. He proposed that the conference be suspended. The issue was debated from midnight to 5 am, and Biko's motion was defeated. He left the conference, 'a broken and disappointed man'.[171]

Biko did not let his disappointment hold him back for long. After much thought, discussion and advice, he decided to put his medical studies on hold while he canvassed the launching of a new student movement, this time an all-black organisation.

In December 1968 he gathered 30 students from the student representative councils of black universities at Mariannhill, the Catholic boarding school in Natal at which he had matriculated. He quickly got agreement that an exclusively black student movement should be formed. Thus was born the South African Students' Organisation, SASO, the first of a slew of new Black Consciousness organisations. It held its inaugural conference at Turfloop in July 1969, which saw Biko elected as president. Its executive included Barney Pityana, Strini Moodley and Aubrey Mokoape.

Searching for a coherent ideology, Barney Pityana, in the September 1971 SASO newsletter, wrote:

> Nyerere's 1967 Arusha Declaration rings true when it says 'We have been oppressed a great deal, we have been disregarded a great deal. It is our weakness that has resulted in our being oppressed, exploited and disregarded. Now we want a revolution – a revolution that brings to an end our weakness, so that we are never again exploited, oppressed or humiliated. The message is simple. BLACK MAN YOU ARE ON YOUR OWN.' Like Nyerere we must minimise reliance on external aid. No one in a position of power and prosperity can offer such aid as would threaten his own security.[172]

Biko was a prolific writer. At the first general students council of SASO in July 1970 he stepped down as SASO president (Barney Pityana took on that role) and was elected as chairman of SASO publications. He immediately began a SASO newsletter, with a column entitled 'I write what I like' written by Biko himself. Many of these columns were, after his death, collected and published by Father Aelred Stubbs, and make fascinating reading.

With SASO becoming a coherent organisation, the Black People's Convention followed. Announced in January 1972, and formally launched in July of that year, the BPC had its first congress in December 1972. In planning the BPC, Biko had envisaged a cultural movement, but the demands of the day drove it in a political direction, something Biko accepted and eventually voted for. He did not make himself available for leadership. He had many reasons, one of which certainly was to encourage a broad spread of leadership talent, to try to avoid the inevitable collapse of an organisation when repression happened. Which for Steve Biko was March 1973, when he was banned, restricted to King William's Town and prevented from holding any 'political' office.

Biko had been careful to remain behind the first tier of leadership in these organisations. He had, however, not confused the security police. They knew he was a big fish. Hence his 1973 banning order; he couldn't leave King William's Town, he could not be quoted in the press, he couldn't work, nor could he be in a meeting of more than two people. The police wanted him absolutely out of circulation and out of influence.

Now they had him at a roadblock, contravening his banning order. What had he been doing? This the security police determined to find out.

They took him to the Walmer Police Station in Port Elizabeth. Here they kept him naked with his legs in shackles for 19 days. Then on 6 September he was transferred to room 619, Sanlam building, there to be met by 10 security policemen including Major Harold Snyman, Gideon Nieuwoudt (of whom we will hear much later), Ruben Marx, Daantjie Siebert and Johan Beneke.

What followed was one of the most disgusting episodes in the brutal history of our country.

Firstly he was interrogated for 22 straight hours, naked, in handcuffs and leg irons and chained to a grille.

The beatings that he endured resulted in three brain lesions and a massive brain haemorrhage. He nevertheless was forced to remain standing and was shackled throughout.

His behaviour became less coherent so the security policemen called in Dr Laing, the district surgeon. He could find nothing physically of concern and signed a certificate stating this.

Biko's behaviour became more and more irregular. A specialist physician was called in, who was informed that in a previous detention Biko had shammed injury. The physician found that Biko was suffering from echolalia, a condition where the patient repeats a word or sentence addressed to him. Further, he displayed an exterior plantar reflex, indicating a lesion in the brain. A lumbar puncture was performed to check for brain damage. The result of this was to find a significant number of red blood cells, indicating brain damage. A neurosurgeon was consulted on the phone who recommended that Biko be admitted to hospital for observation. This the security police refused to allow.

Biko's condition worsened, and it was agreed to send him to a prison hospital in Pretoria. He was then dumped in the back of a Land Rover, naked and manacled, and driven non-stop the 1 100 kilometres to Pretoria. He died in a cell in Pretoria a few days later.

When Khusta Jack heard of Biko's death in detention he said, 'I had never heard of Steve Biko before'. He was nevertheless horrified and furious. That was certainly not an unusual response.[173]

One who had heard of him, however, was Biko's friend Donald Woods, the editor of the *Daily Dispatch*, the major newspaper in East London. In a blind fury Woods ran this terrible story over his front page. From there it went around the world like wildfire.

At the end of the inquest into Biko's death, Magistrate Prins concluded that Biko had died of brain injury which led to renal failure. The head injuries 'were probably sustained on 7 September in a scuffle in the Security Police offices in Port Elizabeth ... The death cannot be attributed to any act or omission amounting to a criminal offence on the part of any person.' (Sounds familiar?).

Biko's death was the 46th such death to occur during interrogation by the security police. His funeral attracted 20 000 mourners and lasted five hours. He had become an international celebrity.

The murders of Mzukisi Nobadula and Lungile Tabalaza
The security police were hardly chastened by these events.[174]

Mzukisi Nobadula died in a Port Elizabeth prison in December of that year. He was awaiting trial on a charge of perjury, having retracted a confession that had been tortured out of him in an effort to convict a political activist.

And Lungile Tabalaza 'jumped' out of a fifth-floor window at the Sanlam building on 10 July 1978 while under interrogation. Jumped?

The whites-only election of 1977
Nor was the white electorate disapproving of all of this. Biko died on 12 September 1977. Eight days later, on 20 September, Prime Minister Vorster announced that he was bringing the date of the next scheduled white general election forward by eighteen months. It would now be held on 30 November. The results were stunning. The National Party won 135 of the 165 possible seats, or 82% of the House. This was the highest proportion ever gained by one political party in South Africa's history. The Progressive Federal Party became the official opposition with as few as 17 seats. The Soweto uprising and the murder of Steve Biko had effectively turned the white electorate into a consolidated reactionary unit.

Robert Sobukwe's funeral in Graaff-Reinet, 1978
In February 1978 Robert Sobukwe died in Kimberley. He had been banished to Galeshewe township there since being released from Robben Island in May 1969. His family decided to bury him in Graaff-Reinet, the dusty Karoo town of his birth.

The funeral arrangements were put together by Sobukwe's family, and included a number of persons who were in 'the system' that Sobukwe had fought with all his energy for all of his 54 years.

On 10 March Khusta Jack was on the last bus from Embizweni Square in New Brighton to attend the funeral.[175]

On arriving in Graaff-Reinet, he was asked to speak to the assembling comrades to raise their spirits. He was given a pointer also: Chief Buthelezi was due to attend, and the comrades thought that that was not as things should be. After all, he was running a homeland government, against the wishes of the ANC.

Khusta revved the crowd up with stories of how hard life was for poor blacks (many of these stories were from his own experience) and finished off by finishing off Buthelezi.

Then a group of old PAC notables, supported by youth from Soweto and Khusta's comrades in Port Elizabeth, confronted the organising committee and demanded that the list of notables be redrawn to exclude those of the 'system' from the list of official mourners.

Their demands, delivered with a ferocity that could not be ignored, saw Sonny Leon of the Labour Party, Tsepo Letlaka, an old PAC comrade but now a Transkeian Cabinet Minister, and Professor Njisane, now Transkei's ambassador to Pretoria, all withdrawn. Lastly, and most dangerously, off the list came Chief Mangosuthu Buthelezi.

A huge procession accompanied the casket from Sobukwe's early home to the showgrounds, the only venue large enough to accommodate the size of crowd now assembled. There they found Buthelezi, who had been at Fort Hare with Sobukwe and who was not the type to fade away quietly.

The youth overran the coffin and the wreaths to get at him. All pleas by the officiating clergy, in whose ranks was the beloved and respected Bishop Tutu, fell on deaf ears as the youngsters, spitting at Buthelezi and throwing silver coins at him, demanded his withdrawal.

It was only the intercession of the ministers of religion and Buthelezi's bodyguards that stopped the Chief from being physically ejected. 'Let Gatsha go like a dog. He is a boer and a bantu. He is not of Azania.' Buthelezi left defiant and furious. This was his first such humiliation, and he was not the sort of man to forget such an affront. As Tom Lodge wrote: 'That day Graaff-Reinet belonged to the youth, but the price to be paid by their generation for the humbling of the chief would be a heavy one.'[176]

Khusta Jack felt differently: 'I left Graaff-Reinet feeling rejuvenated. I felt that Sobukwe's funeral was my graduation to a proper life of comradeship.'

9

PEBCO: Its founding
and first three months

The next phase in Port Elizabeth's struggle was about to emerge. For the maths and science teacher at KwaZakhele High, who had left town when the matric class had gone to Robben Island, returned to Port Elizabeth in early 1979, and now had a job at the Ford Motor Company. PEBCO, MACWUSA and the political career of Thozamile Botha were about to begin.[177]

Thozamile Botha obtained his schooling in conditions that can scarcely be believed.

At six years of age he suffered a back injury and spent a year in the Walton Orthopaedic Hospital. Thereafter he left Port Elizabeth to live with his grandparents in Alexandria, doing Sub A and B there. He would rise at 5 am to get to school by 9 am because he and his grandparents lived on a farm and he had work to do in the fields before school. After Sub B he 'escaped' by working on a chicory farm for a month, earning R1.20 or 40 cents per acre picked. With that he bought a ticket to Port Elizabeth, half a loaf of bread and two and a half cents of sugar, and got out of the bus in New Brighton.

He found his way to his grandmother's sister's house and begged her to help him to get schooling. He tried to get into Std 2 but he was quite old, nor did he have Std 1, nor transfer papers from the school in Alexandria. He lied about having his transfer papers, claiming they had been misplaced, and got through Std 2 and on to another school.

The same lies were repeated right up until he passed Std 6 in 1968. He sold ice creams on weekends and was nearly 20 at this stage.

After finishing Std 6 he still did not have a resident's permit. The Labour Department had instructed him to return to Alexandria. However, he followed procedures and got around that one.

He found work making tea, then as a labourer, and saved R90 for trousers and books and, in 1970, returned to school in KwaZakhele. He ran out of money but a teacher found him a bursary and he made it through Std 8. In matric he had to stop and work as his mother was ill until a friendly principal took him into his home, and he passed matric proudly in 1974, aged 26.

On to Fort Hare University. Then came 1976, and expulsion. He returned to KwaZakhele High and taught there when the matric class were sent off to Robben Island.

In September 1977 he was plunged into civic affairs when 474 pupils were arrested and he had to arrange money and defence for them. He put together a 'Save the Children' show at the Rio Cinema. At 3 am the security police picked him up, as well as Monica Vula, the MC for the show. 'During interrogation Colonel Goosen picked up a hosepipe and hit me. All the police standing around took turns to beat me. Within minutes my lips and eyes were swollen, and I was bleeding. This started at about 5 am and lasted until 11 am, non-stop. That was tough interrogation!'

Monica Vula spent two hours in interrogation. 'When she returned, we couldn't recognise her face. She was really, really beaten. I thought that was too much.'

In 1978 Botha left to teach in the Ciskei. That didn't work out and he returned to Port Elizabeth, to a job at the Ford Motor Company, in 1979.

While Botha was in the Ciskei, the government pushed through elections for a 'community council'. The community feared that this council would be merely an extension of the Bantu Affairs Advisory Board, and the election caused no enthusiasm. The poll was 11.2%, but the council was nevertheless instituted.

On returning to Port Elizabeth and before starting at Ford, Botha got a house in Zwide. 'There were no floors, no ceilings, no plaster – just the roof and the walls,' he remembered. Then residents began receiving high water accounts. The residents in the area, particularly the women, came together, and sent a delegation to the area manager at the rent office. They were told that their husbands would be given a hearing by Louis Koch, then Chief Director of the Administration Board. Botha was elected the leader of this delegation, called the Zwide Residents' Association, at a general meeting of the residents of Zwide on a Sunday in early 1979.

Before seeing Koch, the residents met with the (also one-month-old) KwaFord Residents' Association chaired by Mr Z Skosana, a bottlestore owner.

> We went to see Koch and were met with arrogance. We returned home and convened meetings, Wilberforce May and myself, every Sunday at the Dan Qeqe Stadium. We called these meetings through a megaphone early in the morning, while driving around our area.
>
> There was a Council in place, headed by some old and tricky Councillors, Lamani, Yeko, Skosana. And they had a following. They phoned me at Ford, and wanted to meet with us from Zwide. I was working with Dumile Makanda and Dennis Neer – they were not keen that I should see them – my attitude was different. These people had some support and were talking about forming a bigger, Port Elizabeth-wide body. The issues were becoming much broader, and we needed to involve everybody.
>
> So I met with them. It was a risk – if it had gone badly, my executive would have fired me. But I felt that if we went ahead without the support these people had, we would split the township. My interest was to get the people.
>
> My approach with these people (we met in September 1979) was that we wanted to form one municipality for Port Elizabeth – we did not want to replace the community councils. We wanted the total destruction of the councils and thereafter one municipality, and we said we would not work with people in the structures. This was in the constitution of the Zwide Residents' Association.
>
> They said, after much argument, that they were willing to dissolve their committees and give over their membership to us – I said we'd organise a public meeting to do just that.
>
> I met with my executive – they were very happy with this. We realised that we ran a great risk that these experienced politicians would hijack our meeting. So we put the Zwide and KwaFord Residents Associations on the stage, and them in the first row of the Centenary Hall. Otherwise, with their eloquence, they would have all gotten elected. I chaired the meeting, on 10 October 1979, and residents agreed that we should combine our bodies into the Port Elizabeth Black Civic Association (PEBCO). There we elected PEBCO's first interim committee, whose task was to draft a constitution and then dissolve at a public meeting at which the actual PEBCO executive would be elected.

The 10 elected included Botha as chairperson, Mono Badela, Dan Qeqe, Mr Sogoni the lawyer, and Messrs Somyalo, Skosana, Madope, Phalo Tshume, A Yeko and John Kani, the actor.

This committee performed its tasks, met with Koch repeatedly and generated much interest and much publicity. Twenty days later, on 30 October, PEBCO was officially launched with Botha as chairperson at a meeting of between 8 000 and 9 000 residents in Centenary Hall. The mass movement was beginning to emerge.

Events moved quickly for PEBCO. On the day Botha was elected as chairperson of PEBCO, he was fired from Ford for this involvement. This precipitated an immediate strike at Ford, and PEBCO was catapulted into union politics. The existing unions rejected the strike: Fred Sauls called it 'political' and asked his union, the National Union of Motor, Rubber and Allied Workers (NUMWAROSA) to stay out of it. The paid-off workers formed the Ford Cortina Workers Committee, elected Botha as chairperson and Dumile Makanda, Dennis Neer Government Zini and R Tou as its committee. From this group the Motor and Allied Components Workers Union of South Africa (MACWUSA) eventually emerged.

Ford management refused to speak to the Ford Cortina Workers Committee, wanting instead to speak to the union. The union wouldn't represent the strikers, claiming that the strike was political. An impasse thus formed.

PEBCO then took the pressure to Ford with the slogan 'Boycott Ford Products!'

'We also called for a boycott of white-owned shops in town. The idea was to pressurise business to pressurise government, then Ford would give in. So that's where we began to call for boycotts of all sorts!' Botha said.

After forming PEBCO, branches were formed in KwaZakhele, Walmer/ Gqebera and New Brighton. Dr Nthato Motlana of the Soweto Committee of Ten visited in November to offer support. The Uitenhage Black Civic Organisation was formed on 23 October 1979, and steering committees were formed in both Graaff-Reinet and Cradock. The Malabar Ratepayers Association became affiliated. By January 1980 there were 3 000 card-carrying members of PEBCO. A plan was afoot to begin a youth organisation.

On 6 January 1980 a New Brighton PEBCO rally of 3 000 decided to call a one-day stayaway on 14 January to coincide with a proposed tour of Walmer Township by a Deputy Minister. On 9 January Ford reinstated its strikers. Little did they know it at the time, but PEBCO had just reached its high-water mark.

The next day Botha, Phalo Tshume and Mono Badela were detained.

They were held until 27 February and were served with three-year banning orders on release. Botha could not work at a factory in terms of this banning order. He tried to live by selling fruit and vegetables and on 1 May he left South Africa to join the ANC.

From the founding of PEBCO to the banning of Botha was a period of all of three months. That's about as much space as the security police would allow a black political movement at the time. By the time-honoured device of immobilising a new and fragile leadership, PEBCO was put down.

PEBCO's achievements were two-fold: firstly, it put the mass back into Port Elizabeth black politics, albeit briefly; and secondly it showed that mobilisation could be achieved around civic issues. Both were considerable achievements at a time of massive suppression, a lack of political confidence in the townships and a considerable deference to conservative politics, the politics of the elders. PEBCO's actions at Ford asserted the political movement over the trade unions on civic issues, a trend that continued. Further, it revealed the takeover of the political platform by young politicians over inactive elders.

PEBCO fell because it had not strategised around its leadership being taken out, because of the still unprepared nature of ANC underground activity and because of PEBCO's lack of contact with the ANC.

It was spontaneous stuff, the first three months of PEBCO, and the return of mass politics to Port Elizabeth.

Part Two

THE 1980s: ONE OF SOUTH AFRICA'S CIVIL WARS

Period One
The pre-conflict phase, 1980–1984

10

Social and economic conditions
of South Africa in 1980

The 1980s in Port Elizabeth and Uitenhage was the most terrible and blood-soaked decade in the long history of this metropolitan conurbation, and possibly of any major South African urban area.

There are many reasons for this dreadful and unnecessary decade of conflict and killing. Two are unquestionably the belligerent and bullying personality of PW Botha and the racist *kragdadigheid* (brutal force) of the National Party that elected him as their leader, on 28 September 1978.

At the time BJ Vorster resigned as Prime Minister, Botha was Minister of Defence, a position he had held for 12 years. He was chosen to be Prime Minister by the NP caucus over two other contenders, Connie Mulder and Pik Botha. Both were more open to the realities of the day. PW Botha was the hawk, the embodiment of NP intransigence. His election, at that time and over those other two contenders, meant two things – 'reform', best described as NP-led political changes that claimed to accommodate 'the legitimate needs of moderate people of colour' while not disturbing the control over all matters of consequence by the white parliament; and '*kragdadigheid*', best described as the entire destruction of 'communist terrorists', that is SWAPO/PLAN in Namibia and Angola and any black insurrection that was foolish enough to raise its head within South Africa. Military men do not seek compromise and then tolerate uncomfortable agreement; they seek overwhelming victory by any means necessary. We were in for a rough ride, from 28 September 1978, and by heavens we got it.

In 1980 many factors pointed to the impossibility of the continuation of 1970s political circumstance.

Firstly, South Africa's demographics had changed dramatically over the time of NP governance. In the 1951 census, the first after the NP accession to power in 1948, there had been 12.6 million South Africans, of whom 68% were black/Africans and 21% white. As of the 1980 census, South Africa's population had grown to 28 million, of whom 72% were black/Africans and 16% were white. Furthermore, the urban black/African community had grown from 4.8 million to 7.7 million – the homelands were plainly not functioning as points of attraction.

Secondly, South Africa's economy was not riding out the storm.

In 1982 South Africa's gross domestic product shrank by 1%. In 1983 it shrank further, by 3%. The current account on the balance of payments was negative by R3.7 billion in 1981 and by R2.9 billion in 1982. South Africa had to crawl to the IMF for a loan of R1.2 billion in 1982, as foreign reserves had dried up. The IMF's conditions included that South Africa freeze consumer subsidies and increase sales tax, thereby shifting the burden of the loan onto the poor.

Volkskas Bank reported that since 1974 inflation had never been less than 10%. In 1981 it was 15.3%, causing the Reserve Bank to raise the prime overdraft rate to 18%. Foreign investment was also drying up; the first half of 1983 saw an outflow of R1.3 billion. Unemployment was high and rising. Registered unemployment in the white, Coloured and Asian groups rose by 21% between December 1982 and June 1983. And the financial year-end for government saw an unprecedented budget deficit of 2.4% of GDP in 1982.

Much of the above was caused by defence spending, which was, of course, the fiefdom of Minister PW Botha. In 1966, when PW Botha became Minister of Defence, defence spending was 1.6% of the budget. In 1973, as the Namibian War of Independence ratcheted up, it rose by 150%. By 1982 it was 15% of all spending, much more even than education. It subsequently rose to 23%.

A war that had started with Sam Nujoma visiting Namibian refugee camps in Tanzania in 1962 and sending four men back into Namibia to begin recruiting, was by 1975 a full-blown military campaign, with the SADF and its UNITA allies up against forces from the People's Movement for the Liberation of Angola (MPLA), aided by Cuba and Russia. In that year Botha had told parliament that 'the MPLA has the upper hand'. On 25 October he sent 2 500 South African troops, out of uniforms and pretending to be mercenaries, as the beginning of a massive covert operation into Angola. With Botha becoming Prime Minister this situation predictably escalated and escalated. By 1983 Savimbi's National Movement for the Total Independence of Angola (UNITA) had been given control of most of Angola south of Benguela by the South African forces. These forces appeared to be on top of a disorganised and ill-equipped set of opponents.

Thus, at the beginning of the 1980s, Botha could frequently be heard to say that this war was under control, but in truth the cost was unsustainable and the enemies too many and too committed. Wiser men than PW Botha could see that the writing was on the Namibian wall.

Thirdly, sanctions against apartheid South Africa were now a reality.

In 1977 the United Nations agreed to a mandatory arms embargo on South Africa. While South Africa invested enormously in self-manufacture at ARMSCOR, using often excellent technology either stolen or provided by friendly states, plainly it was impossible to keep up with the best technology in particularly aircraft and anti-aircraft missile defences, and South Africa quickly lost the edge.

Also in 1977, American firms which were invested in South Africa got a director of General Motors, the Rev. Leon Sullivan, a long-time human rights activist, to create a code of conduct for these companies that could diminish disinvestment pressures. This only helped for a while. In 1985 the Ford Motor Company withdrew from Port Elizabeth and in 1986 General Motors followed. This was a major disaster for the local economy.

American banks were no longer willing to lend to the South African state, which created the need for the 1982 loan from the IMF. However, the next year the IMF needed the American parliament to vote it an increase in capital. Anti-apartheid congressmen added a rider that the American vote at the IMF, which accounted for 20% of all votes, would never again support a loan to a country that 'practices apartheid'. So that door also closed.

Fourthly, South Africa was losing its cordon sanitaire, and quickly Mozambique and Angola wriggled free of Portuguese control in 1974, and Zimbabwe from Britain in 1980. While plainly these new governments had to act with extreme caution in their relations with South Africa, the new regimes equally plainly saw apartheid South Africa very differently from their previous colonial masters.

An ordinary politician would have seen in the circumstances above the need for pause and consideration – but not so PW Botha. He had the solution – repression for communist agitators and reform to bring the world back in line, and 'moderate blacks' into the fold.

So it was in 1980. Botha had been Prime Minister for two years. The Namibian War appeared to be going well. Botha had been persuaded to relinquish the additional job of Minister of Defence. He had hand-picked his replacement, Magnus Malan, previously head of the Defence Force. For Botha, this was just fine. Repression and reform. It was that simple.

The government's strategies: Repression and reform

I t was to prove not as simple.

Let us consider first the repression side of the coin. Here three atrocities outline the new freedom the security police felt they now enjoyed under a hawkish Prime Minister.

(Again, the murders documented here are those from Port Elizabeth and Uitenhage).

The murder of Griffiths Mxenge

Griffiths Mxenge was an exceptional person. Born in a rural area just outside King William's Town, he finished his schooling at Newell High in Port Elizabeth in 1956. His connections to Port Elizabeth went deep. His brother practised medicine (still practises medicine) in Motherwell, Port Elizabeth. Griffiths finished his undergraduate degree at Fort Hare in 1959 and then enrolled for an LLB at the University of Natal in Durban. He joined the ANC Youth League and worked in ANC campaigns just at the time the ANC was banned.[178]

In 1966 he was detained for 190 days, and then sentenced for 'furthering the aims of the ANC', to two years on Robben Island. On release he was banned, thereby preventing him from returning to a university campus.

He, however, had a friend in the liberal Prof. Tony Mathews, and somehow Matthews helped him to finish his LLB in 1970. Articles followed, under the Natal Indian Congress stalwart Ruhi Bagwandeen, and, despite another banning order, Griffiths opened an attorney's practice in Durban in 1975, just before the Soweto explosion. This kept him very busy.

In 1981 he was called in by the security police for allegedly laundering ANC money through his practice to defend political trialists. The evidence was not enough to get a conviction and Griffiths denied it. Maybe there was a quicker way of dealing with him than the notoriously unreliable courts.

Fast-forward eight years.

Butana Almond Nofomela had made a career in the security police. Possibly that gave him the feeling that he was beyond the sanction of the law, though we don't know. But he made a tragic mistake. While off duty he robbed a farmer. A scuffle ensued and Nofomela killed the farmer. The mistake was that he had killed a white farmer, and such a murder the uniform branch took seriously. He was arrested, tried, found guilty and sentenced to be hanged. The hanging would take place in October 1989.

While on death row he got messages from senior police officers promising to have him freed if he remained silent on his activities in the security police. He agreed, but his freedom never arrived. Three days before he was due to be hanged, a police captain visited him. 'Sorry,' he was told, 'we can't get you out.' The captain ended with a reassuring phrase: 'You will have to take the pain.'

Nofomela decided to try to avoid the pain. A lawyer from Lawyers for Human Rights was called in and the beans were partially spilled. Four weeks later those two fantastic, crazy Afrikaner journalists, Max du Preez and Jacques Pauw, in their well-known but then little-read tabloid newspaper, *Vrye Weekblad*, covered their front page with the headline 'Bloedspoor van die SAP'. Now the beans were truly spilled.

Vrye Weekblad's article relied extensively on interviews conducted with Commander Dirk Coetzee, a highly intelligent but very unstable security policeman who had headed up Unit C10 of the security police, stationed at an isolated farm near Pretoria, called 'Vlakplaas'. The unit comprised security policemen including Nofomela and 'askaris', ANC guerrillas who had been captured and who had been 'turned', doubtless to save them from the cruel deaths they were now expected to deal out to others. Coetzee was later followed as commander of Vlakplaas by one Eugene de Kock, known to the press as 'Prime Evil' and possibly the most murderous and cruel of South Africa's long line of murderous and cruel enforcers of apartheid.

Coetzee's and Nofomela's testimonies are similar in many details. Vlakplaas was a camp of execution, and its staff could at best be described as a 'death squad'.

Griffiths Mxenge was one of the first victims to be dealt with by Vlakplaas operatives. His terrible death is bluntly recorded in the report of the Truth and Reconciliation Commission:

> Coetzee told the Commission that Brigadier van der Hoven, then divisional commander of the Durban security police, approached him and told him to 'make a plan with Mxenge', which Coetzee understood to mean that he was to make arrangements to kill him. He was told that the security police had been unable to bring any charges against Mxenge, who had become a 'thorn in their flesh'. Coetzee said that van der Hoven had told him to make it look like a robbery. (The operatives were told not to use guns, and were given three okapi knives and one hunting knife.)
>
> Coetzee said that he put together a hit squad of four black Vlakplaas operatives including Nofomela. The 'details of the killing were left to the four members of the squad'.
>
> Nofomela told the Commission that the four men intercepted Mxenge on his way home from work on the evening of 20 November 1981. They dragged him out of his car and took him to the nearby Umlazi stadium where they beat and stabbed him repeatedly. Nofomela told the Commission that he resisted his attackers fiercely until he was struck on the head with a wheelspanner. He fell to the ground and the stabbing continued until he was dead. He was stabbed 45 times. They then disembowelled him, slit his throat and cut off his ears. They took his car, wallet and other belongings to make it look like a robbery.

Four years later the security police murdered Mxenge's widow, bludgeoning her to death in front of their children.

The murder of Sizwe Kondile

Coetzee and his Vlakplaas operatives were not finished yet.[179]

Gcinisizwe 'Sizwe' Kondile was a founder member of COSAS and a Port Elizabeth activist. In 1980 he and a few others formed an underground ANC cell in Port Elizabeth. Two of their six members were arrested and the other four (Kondile, Vusi Pikoli, Thozi Majola and Phaki Ximiya) realised that the time was right to get the hell out of Port Elizabeth. They sped to Maseru.

There they met Thozamile Botha and Chris Hani. The four were then trained in Lesotho and were asked to help build the underground in Port Elizabeth and the Eastern Cape. In June 1981 Kondile briefly returned to

South Africa and made it safely back to Lesotho. Later that month Kondile borrowed Hani's yellow Datsun, and drove to a Maseru callbox to phone his girlfriend. During the call he hung up and was never seen again by his Lesotho or South African friends.

The South African police claimed many things relating to Kondile's disappearance, the first of which was that he had been arrested in Port Elizabeth late in June 1981 and released in August. He had been in good health on release, they said.

Then Dirk Coetzee reappeared. He claimed in 1990 that Kondile had been abducted in Lesotho by members of the Vlakplaas unit. He was brought to Port Elizabeth and detained there. He was then taken to Jeffreys Bay police station where he was tortured and sustained a brain haemorrhage. General Nick van Rensburg of the security police, stating that 'we don't need another Biko', asked Coetzee to finish Kondile off. Kondile was then driven to Komatipoort on the Mozambique border, poisoned, shot, and his body burned on a pyre for nine hours while the Vlakplaas team drank beer.

Eventually in 1997, five security policemen made application for amnesty to the Truth and Reconciliation Commission for the murder of Kondile: Generals van Rensburg and Erasmus, Colonel Du Plessis, Sergeant Raath and Coetzee. Van Rensburg now changed his story again. He had persuaded Kondile to turn sides and report on Hani's movements. Thereafter Van Rensburg had intercepted a note from Kondile to the ANC saying that he was pretending to have changed sides. Van Rensburg then realised that he had to be killed as Van Rensburg had given him names of SAP operatives in Lesotho. This childishly improbable story appears not to have been believed by the Commission.

The murders of Simphiwe Mthimkhulu and Topsy Madaka

Then came the third of the new-style killings: the murders of Simphiwe Mthimkhulu and Topsy Madaka.[180]

The following is an edited extract from the report of the Truth and Reconciliation Commission report on this matter:

> Mr Simphiwe Mthimkhulu was a student activist in Port Elizabeth from 1979 until 1982, when he disappeared. He was chairperson of the Loyiso High School Students' Representative Council and an active COSAS member. It is also widely believed that he was an underground member of the then banned ANC.

Mthimkhulu was involved in the COSAS schools boycotts of 1980–81, and a campaign against Republic Day celebrations in 1981, which involved the distribution of ANC pamphlets in Port Elizabeth. Along with other COSAS members, he was detained on 31 May. After being shot while trying to escape detention, he was treated in Livingstone Hospital. He was held at the security branch headquarters in Port Elizabeth, as well as Algoa Park and Jeffreys Bay police stations, and was subjected to extensive interrogation and torture, including suffocation, electric shocks, sleep deprivation and being forced to stand on bricks for many hours.

He was released without charge on 20 October 1981, after five months in detention. He made a statement to his lawyer and instituted a case against the Minister of Police for assault and torture. The day after his release Mthimkhulu complained of pain in his stomach and legs, and was soon unable to walk. Fighting for his life, he was admitted to Livingstone Hospital.

At this critical moment, Mthimkhulu was to receive help from an unexpected source, which is of such a nature as to warrant a brief detour in this narrative.

Edgar 'Buller' Pagden was the founding partner of what was to become, from the 1960s, one of the largest practices of attorneys in Port Elizabeth. This practice still operates and is still called 'Pagdens'. In the days when Buller was senior partner, its clientele was a who's who of Port Elizabeth businesses.

Not only was Pagden a successful attorney, he was also extraordinarily liberal for his time. Historically he was a member of the United Party, but became disenchanted with their policy towards black South Africans. He became a member of the first breakaway group from the United Party that formed the Progressive Party.

Pagden and his first wife Molly had two daughters, both of whom were to become famous for their township-based political activity. The elder was Molly Blackburn and the younger Judy Chalmers.

Molly entered formal politics with a bang when she won a seat on the all-white Cape Provincial Council, a parliamentary body with jurisdiction over what is today both the Western and Eastern Cape Provinces. This was on 29 April 1981, in that year's general election in South Africa (whites-only, of course). Molly stood on a Progressive Federal Party ticket with Andrew Savage, the retired businessman who was the force behind the surge forward of the PFP in Port Elizabeth. Andrew was to go to parliament in Cape Town and Molly to the Provincial Council. Both assemblies had comfortable and long-standing National Party majorities, so their role as opposition politicians was clearly defined. The election of 1981, which saw Savage and Blackburn elected, turned out a similar result to 1977 – the National Party won 131 of 165 seats, the Progressive Federal Party won 26 and remained the official opposition. While the Afrikaner right won no seats in the first-past-the-post system, between the Herstigte Nasionale Party and the new Conservative Party they garnered 17% of the vote, a great increase.

Molly did not confine herself to the governing assemblies. In 1981 Saki Macozoma, accused number two in the KwaZakhele High School matric class of 1976, returned to Port Elizabeth from Robben Island. He was employed by the Eastern Cape Council of Churches as a field worker of the Dependants Conference, which ran the newly formed Detainees Parents' Support Committee. There he and Molly met and he introduced her to the townships. Shelagh Gastrow believes that this led to the 'first structured contact between black and white political groups in the area'. It certainly set Molly off on a fascinating path, combining formal parliamentary politics with township struggle.

One of her first interventions followed from a phone call from the Rev. James Haya, asking her to help Simphiwe Mthimkhulu, who was then at death's door in Livingstone Hospital. Molly and her friends in the Black Sash sprang into action and got Mthimkhulu into the care of Prof. Frances Ames, the neurologist at Groote Schuur Hospital in Cape Town. Ames diagnosed Mthimkhulu as having been poisoned with thallium, an odourless and tasteless poison only available to the state in South Africa.

Back to the report of the Truth and Reconciliation Commission: 'In January 1982 Mthimkhulu returned to Port Elizabeth in a wheelchair. The police claimed that a top-level investigation into his poisoning was being conducted. On 2 April 1982 he instituted a second claim against the Minister of Police, this time for poisoning. Within two weeks, he had disappeared.'

At the time he disappeared, he was being driven around by a COSAS friend, Topsy Madaka, who disappeared with him.

'About a week later Madaka's car was found at Sterkspruit in the Transkei, near the Telle Bridge border crossing with Lesotho. Madaka's passport and Mthimkhulu's wheelchair were inside.'

For eight years Mthimkhulu's disappearance remained a mystery. Until, again, Dirk Coetzee continued singing:

In April 1990 Mr Dirk Coetzee revealed ... that Mthimkhulu had been poisoned, kidnapped and killed and this had been arranged by

Brigadier Jan du Preez of security branch headquarters in Pretoria and Colonel Nick van Rensburg of the Port Elizabeth security police. Coetzee alleged that Brigadier Jan van den Hoven had had the rare poison flown to van Rensburg, who had it administered to Mthimkhulu before his release from detention ...

In January 1997 amnesty applications for the murders of Mthimkhulu and Madaka were received by the TRC from security branch officers Gideon Nieuwoudt, Colonels Nick van Rensburg and Gerrit Erasmus, and Major Barend du Plessis.

At a press conference in Port Elizabeth on 28 January 1997 it was revealed that the bodies of Mthimkhulu and Madaka had been burned and their remains thrown into the Fish River near the disused Post Chalmers police station near Cradock.

Later, things turned out differently. Remains of both Mthimkhulu and Madaka were found at Post Chalmers in the septic tank and reburied in Port Elizabeth in 2009.

Such was the development of state repression under PW Botha's leadership. Previously, black leaders had been arrested, beaten to a pulp both for information and for the amusement of the police, detained for as long as was seen necessary, then dumped back onto the street. Deaths in detention seem to have been mostly unplanned excesses in interrogation. Now murder was moving to the centre of the suppression stage. The dangers for township comrades were multiplying very quickly.

Labour reform
And 'reform'?

The obvious place to start was in the labour relations field.

The first mass action post-Sharpeville was the development of labour unrest mostly around Durban. The statistics: during the 1960s in South Africa about 2 000 workers were involved in industrial action each year. In 1972 this rose to about 5 000 strikers. In 1973, 160 strikes involving 61 000 workers exploded the tranquillity.

Business began to panic. These strikes were brilliantly organised. The strikers refused to elect leadership: the traditional response, 'identify the leaders and arrest them' cannot work when leadership is unnamed and in the middle of thousands. Then the workers stayed around their factories. There, brutality would be too public. More sophisticated responses than repression were called for.

Much was done by business, and urgently. Memoranda were constructed, calling for amelioration in the living conditions of urban Africans. The Urban Foundation was established in 1976 and did much work in improving housing conditions for the urban poor. And calls were made for the acceptance of the permanent status of urban Africans.

Government responded by establishing two commissions – the Wiehahn Commission to look at labour matters and the Riekert Commission to investigate issues around urban Africans.

The Wiehahn Commission, named after its chairman, Prof. Nic Wiehahn, spent nearly a year and a half hearing from 184 witnesses and studying 250 written submissions. Its first report was presented in early 1979.

At the time, the existing Industrial Conciliation Act controlled trade unions tightly, and such rights as existed did not flow to African workers, who were not deemed to be 'employees' in terms of the act. By a slim majority of its 13 commissioners, the commission urged the government to grant all South African workers the right to join trade unions, to also dismantle once and for all the system of job reservation long used to bar African workers from certain jobs, and to allow all unions the right to be incorporated into South Africa's tight, restrictive, labour-relations machinery.

Government was encouraged to accept these recommendations on the grounds that these new unions would be adequately controlled by the existing regulations. It did not work out like that. On accepting many of the Wiehahn recommendations and permitting African trade union activity, government effectively unshackled the black trade union movement and made it possible for this movement to become a vital player in the final push for liberation.

Reform in the conditions of 'urban blacks'
The Riekert proposals were a horse of a different type.

The Commission created a new category of person, 'qualified urban black persons'. There were three ways to qualify: blacks who had lived continuously in the town where they had been born; those who had lived continuously in one town with permission for 15 years; and those who had worked in unbroken registered employment with one employer in one town for 10 years, and various members of their families.

This group would now qualify for housing (the government, wedded to its 'homelands' concept, had frozen the building of houses for blacks in the urban environment in 1968); employers could now own housing for their staff in black areas; and, most importantly, 'qualified urban black persons' could now bring their families to town to live with them if they had housing.

This was not to be state-sponsored largesse: responsible authorities should 'initiate purposeful programmes in order to recover more and more

150

of the cost of services from the black communities themselves'.

This was rapidly seen as a crude attempt to create a class of black/ Africans with too much to lose to become 'agitators'. Sheena Duncan of the Black Sash calculated that possibly one and a half million blacks would benefit, as 'qualified urban black persons', from a black population of around 16 million black/Africans.

There was another brutal catch: it was proposed that it would no longer be an offence for black people to be unregistered in their work. Sounds great? The catch: penalties on employers who employed unregistered blacks would be greatly increased and more strictly enforced. Penalties that would be applied included higher fines, imprisonment, fines to be calculated on the length of time the unregistered person had been employed, and the cost of repatriating such a worker would be recovered from the employer. Again Sheena Duncan: 'If the new measures recommended by Dr Riekert are accepted there will be no jobs at all for unregistered workers.' The whole possible pool of African workers would be the one and a half million 'qualified urban black persons'. Dr Riekert concluded that 'If the recommendations of the Commission are approved, it will be possible to apply influx control more effectively than at present'. Some reform.

Sheena Duncan summarised the Riekert Commission's report succinctly: 'Dr Riekert's report is a very skilled, very clever and highly sophisticated recipe for national disaster. No country can jettison three quarters of its population and survive.'[181]

Both the Wiehahn and Riekert Commissions were entirely silent on the position and political rights of the black/African population. They made no attempt to change anything here. The homelands remained the only hope black persons had for the franchise.

The government's next two attempts at 'reform' played into this critical area. New proposals were forthcoming regarding both local government as it applied to blacks, and constitutional reforms with regard to the franchise in general. We will consider these two issues in turn.

Local government reforms for blacks
Firstly, local government reforms as applied to blacks.

The Black Local Authorities Act was the reform agent in the field of local government. This was described by its sponsors as 'the provision to Black communities of local government structures similar to those operating in white areas'. Councillors were to be elected in regular elections, and the councils they would oversee would have control over the allocation of housing, licences, business sites, student bursaries and much else, as was then in the ambit of the white city councils.

The act was rammed through parliament in 1982 and the first elections were scheduled for December 1983.

As always, there was a catch. No local government in South Africa has ever been able to deliver meaningful services to large communities of poor households unless it had access to redistributing income taxed from commercial and industrial properties. In all South African local governments in 1982, all of these properties were zoned in the area of jurisdiction of the white local authority. Black local authorities had, as their tax base, the entire collection of properties owned by poor South Africans and almost nothing else. They had, in the words of Van Zyl Slabbert, the unique opportunity to 'administer their own misery'. There was no honour in accepting this poisoned chalice, by becoming a councillor. The only possible motivation for taking on this hopeless task was either the wage that went with it (and, in a massive community of poor, this must not be underestimated), or the opportunity to 'make it on the side'. And that is how it worked out.

Reforms with regard to the national franchise

Here a labyrinthine process was undertaken.

Firstly, the National Party put up constitutional proposals in 1977. These were then, as draft legislation, referred to a select committee of both houses of parliament (the Schlebusch Committee, named after its chair, the Minister of the Interior) in March 1979. This committee was then converted to a 24-person commission, comprising five cabinet ministers, 14 members of parliament (seven NP, four PFP, two New Republic Party, one South African Party) and five senators. This commission had the support of all parties, had powers to call for submissions, to accept evidence and generally to encourage public involvement. The main issue was to be a new constitution for South Africa. It was stated that all races would be able to give evidence. It was also, sinisterly, made clear that any recommendations that were contrary to NP policy would be put to NP congresses.

This commission reported on 6 May 1980. Amongst its recommendations were 'the appointment of a President's Council consisting of 60 members of the white, Coloured, Asian and Chinese communities who were recognised by their representative communities as leaders, as well as nationally recognised experts in their respective fields'.

This Council was to advise the State President on any matter, obviously including a new constitution. It was not to include Black Africans, who would later be accommodated in a separate council which would be consulted on matters affecting Africans.

The result was predictable. The official opposition in parliament, the PFP, opposed the legislation at all three stages on account of the exclusion of Africans. So did all the homeland leaders, including Chief Buthelezi, who refused even to attend a meeting of homeland leaders with Prime Minister Botha.

This meeting predictably did not change Botha's determination to continue with this process. He appointed the chairs of the five President's Council sub-committees. Four were previously Cabinet Ministers, the fifth being Denis Worrall, who had been both a Senator and a Member of Parliament for the NP. One could sense where all this was going.

If the above clues were not clear enough, the President's Council adopted several premises and points of departure before considering the evidence it would receive. These included the following: for South Africa, a unitary state in which one-man-one-vote applied was not an option; and a single political system which included Africans on an unqualified majoritarian or consociational basis could not function as a successful democracy in current and foreseeable circumstances. Furthermore, at the opening of the National Party's Federal Congress on 30 July 1982, Botha stated clearly that Africans would have to exercise their political rights through the homelands.

During 1982 the President's Council presented three reports on constitutional reform. Unsurprisingly, these reports followed the National Party's 1977 constitutional proposals. (Please note this process: the NP puts forward constitutional proposals for South Africa in 1977. Parliament then appoints a multi-party committee to make proposals for a new constitution. This is turned into a parliamentary commission, which takes public submissions. This commission then reports that what is needed is a 60-person President's Council, containing many independent experts, to investigate, consult and recommend on this matter. This is formed and it works for years, while the five chairs of its sub-committees are four ex-cabinet ministers and a party hack. The Council eventually reports in 1982: what the NP had agreed in 1977.)

The majority of the President's Council's recommendations were accepted by the National Party in July 1982, and it was clearly expected that in the new year a bill would be presented to parliament that would legalise all of this and put into place a new constitution for South Africa which excluded black South Africans from any position in government and from the franchise. If there was to be a mobilisation against all of this, now was the time.

12

The UDF is born

In the Transvaal, a group calling themselves the Transvaal Anti-South African Indian Council (TASC) was established. This organisation rejected the President's Council's report, and particularly rejected the position of the South African Indian Council which had accepted the proposals. TASC called its first conference on 22 January 1983 in Johannesburg, which was attended by some 2 000 delegates. It was opened by the 77-year-old ANC veteran Helen Joseph.

Speakers included Thozamile Gqweta from the South African Allied Workers Union and Samson Ndou of the General and Allied Workers Union, and there were speakers from the Congress-aligned Natal Indian Congress.

The keynote address was given by Dr Allan Boesak, then President of the World Alliance of Reformed Churches. Boesak condemned the President's Council proposals and the Labour Party for criticising these proposals while at the same time concluding that they would participate in the forthcoming election for the 'Coloured Chamber'.

Boesak ended with an example of the splendid oratory that was his hallmark:

> We say NO to apartheid, racial segregation and economic exploitation of the oppressed masses in South Africa ... This is the politics of refusal, and it is the only dignified response black people can give to this situation. In order to do this we need a united front ... There

155

is no reason why churches, civic associations, trade unions, student organisations and sports bodies should not unite on this issue, pool our resources, inform the people of the fraud which is about to be perpetrated in their name, and on the day of the election expose these plans for what they are.[182]

Emboldened by Boesak's oratory, the conference committed itself to the formation of a united democratic front constituted around an unshakeable conviction in the creation of a non-racial unitary state.

So, in a conference of Charterists coming from small and new civic organisations and trade unions, lit up by Allan Boesak's rousing oratory, the United Democratic Front (UDF) was born.

The tricameral parliament is put forward

Things were moving fast. In May 1983 the Republic of South Africa Constitution Bill was presented to parliament. In July a parliamentary select committee debated the bill and it went to the full parliament in August.

The Bill proposed a state president who would be both head of state and head of government (thereby unifying the existing powers of the ceremonial state president and the executive prime minister), and who would be elected by a college of 50 white, 25 Coloured and 13 Indian members of parliament; three houses of parliament – a white House of Assembly (178 members, 166 directly elected, eight indirectly elected and four nominated), a Coloured House of Representatives (85 members) and an Indian House of Delegates (45 members); and a President's Council of 60 members, 20 elected by the white house, 10 by the Coloured house, five by the Indian house, and 25 appointed by the President. This council was to advise the government on matters of public interest and to resolve disputes that arose among the houses of parliament. All matters to be debated were to be divided into 'general' and 'own' affairs. Only the president could decide which was which, and thereafter send the item to the relevant house.

To its credit, the PFP, led by Van Zyl Slabbert, saw right through this nonsense. In the parliamentary debate they rejected the bill for a host of reasons, including that Africans were totally excluded; all existing discriminatory laws and practices remained in place; the President was given autocratic powers that were framed to be beyond attack from the courts; the proposed constitution reinforced apartheid, undermined the rule of law, marginalised the courts and would undoubtedly raise rather than diminish racial tensions. Sadly, no other party in parliament was interested in this line of argument.

On 31 August, during the parliamentary debate, the government applied the guillotine after only 34 of the 103 clauses had been debated and passed the 41 government-sponsored amendments. The guillotine ensured that the 200 amendments sponsored by the opposition parties would fall away.

On 22 September the State President assented to the Republic of South Africa Constitution Act No 110 of 1983. All that was now needed to bring the 'tricameral parliament' into law was the referendum, which Prime Minister PW Botha had promised for 2 November. The UDF had a very tight time frame to work to.

The UDF in the Eastern Cape puts up leadership

By August the UDF had established a national secretariat, which announced that later in that month the national launch would happen in Cape Town. Huge energy was expended to form as many organisations as possible which could then be affiliated to the body, with as many signed-up members as could be reached in a month.

In and around Port Elizabeth the Congress-aligned groupings rapidly began to pull together. Unlike the uprisings of 1960 and 1976, this was not to be a spontaneous process, held together by a young and inexperienced leadership. For Robben Island had now released a number of veteran ANC personnel, and also many young but now seasoned comrades.

Edgar Dumile Ngoyi returned to his home in Port Elizabeth in 1981 after 17 years on Robben Island. He was 55 years old and had been born in Stutterheim, the son of a peasant farmer. He got as much schooling as a poor black child was ever likely to get in Stutterheim (Std 6), whereafter he began helping his father in the fields. Then to the mines, then back home, and finally off to a job in a factory in Port Elizabeth in 1951.

There he encountered the ANC and he volunteered to be a 'defier' in the Defiance Campaign. He was briefly detained. Out from detention, he joined the ANC Youth League and in 1953 was elected to the ANC's Port Elizabeth executive.

He was then involved in a number of ANC-led boycotts and campaigns and participated in preparations for the Congress of the People, which he attended at Kliptown in 1955 when the Freedom Charter was adopted.

When it became obvious that the government was to act against the ANC, Ngoyi went underground as part of the team to implement the M-Plan, a system of cells and committees that would enable the ANC to operate underground. He was arrested with other activists in 1963, the start of 17 years on the Island.

Henry Fazzie we have met before in this book. Also born in Stutterheim, two years before Ngoyi, his father was a brickmaker and teacher. As with Ngoyi, Stutterheim afforded him little schooling. Thereafter he worked as a gardener and in a hotel. He moved to King William's Town, where he ended up in a cloth manufacturing factory as a foreman and called a successful strike in 1952 during the Defiance Campaign. He was arrested but not jailed.

This got him fired, and he then moved to Port Elizabeth. Again he found work and quickly became a shop steward and executive member of the Food and Canning Workers Union. He was again dismissed, challenged the dismissal, was reinstated and moved on.

He was in 1952 an executive member of the ANC's Korsten branch and worked in various campaigns. He was detained during the 1960 state of emergency, along with Raymond Mhlaba, Govan Mbeki and Vuyisile Mini, and, on release, decided to join the ANC in exile. After many near scrapes with the security forces of South Africa's neighbours, he got to Tanzania. From there the ANC sent him to Ethiopia for military training for a six-month period. He became the leader of a group of 20 guerrillas. They returned to Tanzania, where he was put in charge of a group of nine and instructed to re-infiltrate South Africa. The story of this disastrous mission has already been told.

When on Robben Island, Fazzie was taken back to Port Elizabeth to face trial for the burning down of a township school. He had seven years added to his sentence, and served 21 years on Robben Island, to return to Port Elizabeth on 1 September 1983.

Ernest Malgas we have also met. With Fazzie, he was sent to Robben Island for 14 years in 1964. Unlike Fazzie, that was the full extent of his imprisonment at that stage. He returned to Port Elizabeth in 1978 and was immediately served with a banning order, the equivalent of house arrest, for five years. He thus returned to political duty in 1983.

Stone Sizani was born in 1954 in Alexandria, a farming centre 100 km from Port Elizabeth. He could get junior schooling in Alexandria and achieved a Std 6 pass in 1970. He went to a boarding school in Peddie, but was expelled for his activity in a student strike there. He went on to Loyiso High in Port Elizabeth, and transferred to Healdtown High in 1975.

He had become friends with Mapetla Mohapi (who was killed in police detention in 1976), Malusi Mpumlwana and Barney Pityana. They were all in the Black Consciousness tradition and Stone followed. He became chair of SASM at Healdtown in 1975. A strike against hostel conditions and other matters began in October of that year, and Stone was again expelled. He went into hiding to avoid the security police, who searched for him from October until January 1976.

They caught up with him in January 1976, and he was charged under the Terrorism Act and was sent to Robben Island for five years until his release in September 1981. He passed his matric on Robben Island.

On release he returned to Alexandria, but as the Development Board would not allow him to stay, his parents persuaded him to go to Port Elizabeth to live with an aunt. He began work as a laboratory assistant with a chemical firm in Port Elizabeth in November 1981 and in 1982 joined PEBCO, which still existed but was mostly inactive. He also joined the Port Elizabeth Youth Congress (PEYCO), and, when the UDF Eastern Cape was formed in August 1983, he was elected as treasurer and later became publicity secretary.

Also returned from Robben Island were the 33 matric students from KwaZakhele High who were sent to Robben Island for five years each in 1977. Two were still members of AZAPO, but the balance were now in the Congress tradition and willing to get involved.

Fortunately PEBCO still existed – it just needed to be revived. With Thozamile Botha's move into exile in 1980, Qaqawuli Godolozi, then 25 years old, had taken on the reins as President. Khusta Jack and others in 1982 led an interim executive tasked with the resuscitation of PEBCO. They oversaw elections which resulted in Godolozi remaining President, and he was joined by Sipho Hashe, then 48, who had spent 1962 until 1973 on Robben Island for ANC underground activity. On release Hashe had been under house arrest until 1978 and had been very careful in his activity until joining the PEBCO executive as General Secretary in 1982.

Also elected to this executive was Champion Galela, who came on as organising secretary. The 45-year-old worked for Town Talk Furnishers and was a member of the General Workers Union. He and Godolozi had both avoided Robben Island but, after taking on PEBCO duties, were detained for a number of months in late 1983.

To this new executive was added Edgar Ngoyi as an executive member, as was Ernest Malgas. Then, on 1 October 1983, just one month after being released from Robben Island after 21 years inside, Henry Fazzie was co-opted as Vice-President. PEBCO, a civic organisation that had originally been organised around local grievances, now became a fully fledged member of the Charterist movement.

All of this made for a battle-hardened executive, a blend of long-term Robben Islanders, a PEBCO veteran and some younger blood. They could hardly have foreseen the horrors ahead.

Just preceding Thozamile Botha and PEBCO's 1979 emergence was the emergence of COSAS, the Congress of South African Students, an organisation designed to mobilise high school students and some tertiary education students, but not including university students. This organisation began mobilisation in June 1979 under its first president, Ephraim Mogale, who was from the Northern Transvaal. COSAS's next three presidents were all from Port Elizabeth, Wantu Zenzile, Shepherd Mati and Mlungisi (Lulu) Johnson. Port Elizabeth became the epicentre of the COSAS uprising. As Lulu Johnson later said, 'In the Western Cape we had branches of 12 members, here it was thousands.'

COSAS was different from the UDF in that it was motivated by, and its foundation agreed with, the ANC. As Johnson says, 'We can safely come out in the open now, our comrades were fully behind the formation of COSAS.'

In 1979 COSAS ran two campaigns: firstly, the campaign to prevent the hanging of Solomon Mahlangu (which did not succeed), and secondly, a campaign to commemorate the centenary of the Battle of Isandlwana, when Zulu forces routed the British army in Zululand.

In 1980 COSAS called for an expansion of the schools boycott, and 100 000 scholars came out of school on strike.

In 1982 Oliver Tambo made a call on Radio Freedom for the youth to get organised. COSAS then called a youth conference at which a resolution was passed to form youth congresses in general and the Port Elizabeth Youth Congress in particular. This was to be a big one, to be led by one of the most interesting and important of Port Elizabeth's political personalities, Mkhuseli 'Khusta' Jack.

PEYCO begins

Jack is the only one of the central personalities in this book who has, as yet, written an autobiography – *To Survive and Succeed*. This is an important document not just because of the light it sheds on the major political events of the day, but because it brings into clear focus three other aspects of the horror of apartheid that are often quickly acknowledged and then skipped over.

Firstly, the hardships black people working on others' land had to endure. The endless dispossessions, with the resultant discontinuous schooling for children and repeated cycles of casual employment and no employment at all, for adults. Secondly, the impossible struggle of black South Africans to get a formal education with acknowledged and provable qualifications. Khusta went to and through about 10 schools to get a matric certificate at the age of 24, a man who then sailed through a Bachelor's degree and an honours degree at a British university thereafter, in the normal time frame. This saga is repeated in all of the short biographical notes in this book: including Ernest Malgas, Thozamile Botha, Edgar Ngoyi, Henry Fazzie, Stone Sizani, and is the joint result of the long periods of classroom boycotts coupled with an unresponsive, uncaring and under-resourced Department of Bantu Education. What talent, and with it so many lives, we have wasted through apartheid education. And thirdly, the regular and brutal torture and abuse that political activists had to endure, after taking on the leadership roles that were so necessary for the collapsing of the apartheid system. Khusta's autobiography is an indispensable document to help us understand these often little-acknowledged horrors of apartheid.

Khusta was born on the farm Mauritzkraal in the Gamtoos Valley on about 31 May 1957. He was one of eight children; his mother and her family were desperately poor farm labourers, and were repeatedly moved from farm to farm. He was schooled at a farm school, at an Anglican Junior School, at a school in Jeffreys Bay, and then on to Loyiso, Cowan and Technical high schools in Port Elizabeth. He was headboy and head of the Student Christian Movement at Cowan in 1979. He also spent some time at Wongalethu High in Mdantsane. Eventually, in 1982 he matriculated at the age of 24.

His introduction to politics happened in the 1976 student protests and was confirmed at Robert Sobukwe's funeral. His first of innumerable detentions was in March 1979, after he had organised a Sharpeville Massacre memorial. In the same year he was elected to be a delegate to the launch of COSAS at Wilgespruit in the Transvaal, but did not attend: I got cold feet about it and ran away. I was afraid of the police.'[183]

Running away didn't help. The security police continually found him. His detentions became regular, as did the public platforms he spoke on. The one followed the other. He spent Christmas 1980 in Modderbee prison for his work on the student boycott. He was held for five months. His detentions became harsher and harsher. Possibly his worst was at the hands of the Ciskei security police. His torture there was personally overseen by Charles Sebe. Sebe gave his thugs clear instructions to get information about ANC operatives in Mdantsane from him, 'at all costs'. Their captain, Ngwanya, told him that he would torture him so 'that even if by mistake your freedom is realised, you should be so paralysed that you should not enjoy it'.

Three times he was taken to a deserted beach, bound up with a bag over his head and thrown into the sea to drown. Each time, just before the end, he was pulled out. This went on for three months. The beatings were endless, inflicted by shift after shift of black security policemen. 'Being tortured by black people who, in my view, had nothing to gain by defeating my resolve, baffled me,' he wrote. 'However, I was quick to work out that people are tools of evil…'

Jack was caught up with Black Consciousness until 1981. What made him change was the security police's delight that he was in BC, and thereby divisive in township politics. 'I saw them seeing my role as helpful to them in keeping the ANC and COSAS at bay – my utterances against the ANC or non-racialism were sweet music to them, I could see in interrogation.'

Jack was at the COSAS conference in Cape Town in 1982 which called for the setting up of youth congresses, and came back to Port Elizabeth to do just that. 'The experience of PEBCO and many other organisations that have been wiped out by the enemy was that you can't go out until you have a strong base. The organisation had to grow from within and that is how we started to grow the organisation, starting to bring in small numbers of people, inviting people individually.'

The beginning was a chance meeting in early 1983 that Khusta had with Michael Xego and Mpumi Odolo, two of the matric class of KwaZakhele High from 1976 that went to Robben Island and had come home to Port Elizabeth in 1981. Well, anyway, Khusta believed it was a chance meeting. Xego says that a number of the KwaZakhele High Robben Islanders had met and agreed that Khusta would be the ideal leader of a youth congress and they set out to put the idea into his head. It worked.

PEYCO's first meetings were in the small hall of the Holy Spirit Anglican Church in KwaZakhele. This could accommodate 30 people and was soon too small. Then the library hall at Great Centenary Hall. Also soon too small.

In his autobiography Khusta writes: 'Our youth organisation was the first to be formed and launched in South Africa. We were followed by the Soweto Youth Congress … one of the reasons for PEYCO's strength was that it was joined by almost all of the 31 ex-Robben Islanders from KwaZakhele High. We were also joined by other brilliant and recently released young people such as Stone Sizani, Soto Ndukwana, and Phata Madalane.'

PEYCO was eventually launched in July 1983. Khusta was president, Odolo vice-president, Mthiwabo Ndube secretary and Xego, Alex Rala, Mandla Madwara, Mcebisi Msizi, Monde Mtanga and Africa Maqolo were all roped into sharing responsibility.

From this energetic and trusted core, PEYCO was founded as a mass movement with a consolidated leadership that knew well that they would be targeted by the repressive state. They would have to be flexible and share responsibilities. But the core of it all was Mkhuseli Jack.

Jack had the qualities needed to be a political leader through the revolution of the 1980s. Firstly, he is a top-class orator, using humour, tradition, style and ability to verbalise the grievances of the day. He is good-looking and is naturally a people's person. Even some of the police liked him, a fact that probably saved his life.

Secondly, he had courage. Mike Xego recalls how Jack came across a group of youngsters on their way to burn down someone's house. 'Jack spoke to them as if he had an army, just around the corner, and if they didn't go home they would be in such trouble. They went home. It was just his personality, his presence, that saved the day.'

He lasted as a high-profile leader despite at least 13 periods in detention, all involving extensive torture sessions. He was banned, charged twice but never convicted, shot at and nearly run over. He kept coming back, despite it all.

PEWO is formed

As Janet Cherry has written: 'The leadership of civic organisations – including PEBCO and CRADORA – was almost entirely male.'[184] There was one exception – Ivy Gcina was on the PEBCO executive. There she began to organise a 'women's committee'. Quickly she changed gears. With Buyiswa Siwisa, who later married Henry Fazzie, they revived the idea of a women's organisation. From this the Port Elizabeth Women's Organisation (PEWO) emerged.

Ivy Gcina was born in the now trendy suburb of Richmond Hill in Port Elizabeth in 1937. Soon thereafter her parents divorced. Her mother left the children in the care of their father and he moved his family to Veeplaas. Here the ANC Women's League assisted to get the children into English-language schools, which continued until the newly elected National Party cut the grants and Ivy faced the reality of a township school or, more likely, no schooling at all.

Again the Women's League stepped in. A campaign was started, with Ivy enthusiastically a part of it, to boycott schools under the slogan 'Nobody goes to school until Bantu education is over'. Ivy joined the ANC Youth League and remained a member for 14 years. She was an enthusiastic pamphlet distributor, working in fish and chips in the London Café to stay alive.

At 18 years of age, in 1956, Ivy married. After a brief time in Adelaide, her husband 'took her back to New Brighton'. She got a house there in 1959, which was to be her family's home through the struggle years.

When the schoolchildren rose in revolt in 1976, Ivy was there, distributing pamphlets. 'Black Consciousness was not good. The Freedom Charter was the right route,' Ivy believed.

Meanwhile, with the active encouragement of her husband and his brother recently released from Robben Island after 10 years there, her three sons were becoming politicised. She first records this at the time of Steve Biko's funeral. She was there with her son. When she got home to Port Elizabeth, he was not there. He had fled to Maseru.

Soon the well-informed security police arrived at her home. She claimed no knowledge of his whereabouts. They were not convinced she knew nothing. 'You are going to die in this house,' Major Roelofse told her. A few nights later a petrol bomb exploded in her kitchen. She ran into the street to see the police car pulling off. Fortunately her neighbours helped quell the blaze.

Two weeks later they picked her up from her new place of work, Westering High School, where she was a much-loved cleaner. They took her to the New Brighton police station to find her husband there. 'Where is your son?' They took her 11-year-old son, and beat him 'blue – head everywhere'. Immediately her husband took their remaining two sons to another house. They were told 'you know nothing (about your brother), only about your mother and me'.

Police intimidation became a fact of her life. 'If there were two days I was not picked up, I would think – "what did I miss today? What have I not done today?"'

Her two other sons left in 1980 and 1983. She decided to see them. She and some friends went to Maseru. There she found one of her sons, 'Mom, I'm sorry I didn't tell you. If I die tomorrow you mustn't be worried.'

In December 1983 a man arrived at their home. He was a representative from the ANC. He implored them not to provide any information about their sons.

In August 1984 Ivy was taken to the Sanlam building. She was shown picture after picture of young men. She acknowledged only her son. 'Where is he?' 'In Maseru.' They told her he had returned to South Africa and had been apprehended. 'He is in Barrastoke Cemetery in Aliwal North, in grave 437,' they told her.

Ivy returned home. They got lawyers to apply for her son's details, to find out if and when he had been killed. Nobody replied.

Ivy Gcina and her husband lost their three sons; two killed in combat with the police and one in a dreadful accident outside South Africa.

Ivy gave her life and her sons to the struggle. Now PEWO was to be the vehicle through which she expended this massive commitment and overwhelming suffering.

PEWO was launched in November 1983. Ivy was elected chairperson. One of the first things she did was rent a hall in the townships in which PEWO sewed uniforms as in the ANC Women's League tradition. She ran outreach programmes, attempting to create women's organisations all over the Eastern Cape. PEWO became a significant structure in the UDF insurrection.

Matthew Goniwe and CRADORA

Matthew Goniwe was born in Cradock in 1946. He attended his first school, St James, in Cradock, where he was schooled up to Std 6. Then came the Cradock 'Bantu' Secondary School, where he passed the Junior Certificate, which got him admission to Healdtown to do matric. He passed matric and earned a teacher's diploma as well. When he was 14 his brother skipped the country, joining the ANC. Later his brother was to die in exile and obviously this had a bearing on Matthew's worldview.

Now Matthew was what his parents had dreamed he would become, a teacher, but in the Bantu education system at the Cradock 'Bantu' Secondary School, later renamed the Sam Xhallie Junior Secondary, where he had been schooled. Matthew was truly a son of Cradock.

Not many people can claim to have built a school, but Matthew Goniwe did.

He tired of teaching in Cradock so he and John Hlekani, also a Cradock teacher, left for the Transkei. There Matthew noticed that there were many pupils without schools. Then he noticed a derelict church hall. He gathered some unemployed artisans and together they built the Holomisa Secondary School, which opened in 1973.

Inevitably they attracted the attentions of the security police. Matthew, Dumisa Ntsebeza and three others were arrested for underground work and charged under the Suppression of Communism Act. Matthew got four years in jail. He used his time in prison to good effect and obtained a BA degree in Education and Political Science. He was released in 1981.

Fortunately he was accepted back at the Sam Xhallie Junior Secondary School, where he became deputy principal in 1983.

Now community tensions were very high. A new section of Lingelihle had been built and the rents were out of line compared with the old township. Matthew was asked to take the matter up with Louis Koch, the administrator in charge of a number of Eastern Cape townships: yes, the same Louis Koch who had given Thozamile Botha such problems in the 'old days' of PEBCO.

Matthew's letter was accompanied by a petition signed by 80% of Lingelihle residents. No matter, Koch was never going to listen. Matthew called a public meeting. He suggested that the community elect a body of leaders to fight for their rights. He enlisted the help of Molly Blackburn, who was to become a lifelong friend. Molly suggested a youth organisation and a residents' organisation. The final wording of the constitution of the Cradock Residents' Association was agreed in Molly's Summerstrand house.

And so, on 12 August 1983 a mass meeting in a church hall in Lingelihle brought into being the Cradock Residents' Association. The Cradock Youth Association was likewise formed. In Matthew's speech, on the evening of 12 August, he threw down the gauntlet. The rent increases were simply not acceptable, and members of the community should not serve on any 'dummy bodies'.

Thus was CRADORA born in a meeting recorded by one of the audience. The transcription of this recording was read the next day by Henri Fouche, the head of Cradock's security police. From then on CRADORA could not get access to community hall and the battle lines in Cradock were drawn.

As the August deadline for the national launch of the UDF was fast approaching, there would not be time to put a regional executive into place in Port Elizabeth. When finally agreed and elected, it was to comprise Edgar Ngoyi as president, Henry Fazzie as his deputy, and Derrick Swartz, then a teacher but later the successful vice-chancellor of both the universities of Fort Hare and Nelson Mandela, as general secretary. Stone Sizani was treasurer initially but soon moved to the position of publicity secretary. Mtwabo Ndube was elected recording secretary, and, later, Matthew Goniwe as regional organiser.

Thus were falling into place the organisations and the individual leaders required to carry forward the coming revolution.

PEBCO, now remodelled after the departure of Thozamile Botha, had an executive capable of growing it and making it a social force. Godolozi, Fazzie, Hashe, and Galela were all there, as was Ernest Malgas, the stormtrooper from the Red Location, and Edgar Ngoyi, the Robben Island veteran.

COSAS and PEYCO were structured and effectively manned, with enough executive material to withstand high levels of detention. The KwaZakhele High '31' had infused PEYCO with much political experience and determination, and in Khusta Jack they had found a now seasoned and ready struggle leader.

PEWO under Ivy Gcina was rapidly becoming a township force, and CRADORA had leadership and issues to mobilise around.

Everywhere there was enough leadership to rotate. It was hoped that this would make the organisations impregnable to the detention of some leaders.

The UDF comes to life

In August 1983 all roads led to the Cape Flats outside Cape Town where 575 organisations were represented by about 1 500 delegates who were accompanied by somewhere between 5 000 and 15 000 observers.

They converged on the Rocklands Community Centre in Mitchells Plain for the 20 August launch of the United Democratic Front.

Speakers ranged from ANC elder statespersons (Frances Baard, Archie Gumede, Aubrey Mokoena) to the next generation of ANC notables, Frank Chikane and, of course, Allan Boesak.

Boesak was again the standout orator:[185]

In the meantime, brothers and sisters, let me remind you, as I've done before, of three little words that I think we should hold onto as we continue the struggle, and these three words that express so eloquently our seriousness in this struggle. You didn't have to have a vast vocabulary to understand them. You don't need a philosophical bent to grasp them – they are just three little words.

And the first word is the word ALL! We want all of our rights. Not just some rights, not just a few token handouts here and there that the government sees fit to give – we want all of our rights. And we want all of South Africa's people to have their rights. Not a select few, not just a few so-called 'Coloureds' or 'Indians' after they have been made honorary whites. We want all of our rights for all South African people, including those whose citizenship has already been stripped away by this government.

The second word is HERE! We want all of our rights and we want them here, in a united undivided South Africa. We do not want them in impoverished homelands, we don't want them in our separate little group areas. We want them in this land which one day we shall once again call our own.

And we want them NOW! We want all of our rights, and we want them here and we want them now!

We have arrived at an historic moment. We have now brought together under the aegis of the United Democratic Front the broadest and most significant coalition of groups and organisations struggling against apartheid, racism and injustice in South Africa since the 1950s...

The decisions taken at the conference, that they would fight the new constitutional proposals and the Koornhof Bills, were agreed with acclaim. Organisations affiliated to the UDF would build and strengthen non-racial democratic organisations as an alternative to apartheid itself. If there were to be elections or a referendum to validate the new constitution, the UDF would mobilise to stop all of that. Every organisation committed to these goals was welcome – Christian or Islamic, Communist or Capitalist, liberals or radicals – all were welcome; the enemy was outside, not inside.

In the long (575) list of delegate organisations were a good number of Eastern Cape organisations: COSAS Eastern Cape; Rhodes University NUSAS and Rhodes University Black Student Society; Port Elizabeth Youth Congress (PEYCO); Gelvandale Youth; Uitenhage Youth; MACWUSA Union East Cape; General and Allied Workers Union; Port Elizabeth Black Civic Organisation (PEBCO); Malabar Ratepayers and Tenants Association; Port Elizabeth Women's Organisation (PEWO); and the UDF Interim Committee, Eastern Cape.

Malusi Mpumlwana had said that what the struggle organisations needed was 'critical mass' to take on the vast state machinery. From the evidence on display at Mitchells Plain, it would appear that this 'critical mass' was now assembled, in Port Elizabeth and around the country.

The UDF was founded in August 1983 and was banned 56 months later in February 1988. As Tom Lodge has written: 'The UDF in its brief lifespan presided over the most sustained and massively supported series of civil disobedience campaigns ever witnessed in South Africa, borrowing certainly from the ideology and motif of a mythically evoked perception of the struggles of the 1950s, but expressing them with much greater force and resonance.'[186]

This massive and extraordinary campaign in Port Elizabeth and Uitenhage certainly began with elected and respected leadership. However, their role as leaders became increasingly impossible to execute effectively as time moved on.

For half of the UDF's legal existence, South Africa was governed under two states of emergency. The first lasted from 20 July 1985 until 7 March 1986 and the second began on 12 June 1986 and lasted for two years after the banning of the UDF, until 8 June 1990. Almost everything the UDF did during these periods was rendered illegal by the emergency regulations.

Navigating through these states of emergency was just one of the difficulties this new leadership had to cope with. There were many other difficulties inflicted on them to render them inoperative.

Edgar Ngoyi's house was petrol-bombed on 1 May 1985 and again, with massive destruction, on 7 June of that year. He was arrested for murder on 8 June and held in custody until all charges were dropped on 24 December 1985. He was detained on 12 June 1986 for the duration of the second state of emergency.

Henry Fazzie's home was petrol-bombed on 4 May 1985 and he was detained for the duration of both states of emergency. In between these events

Raymond Mphakamisi Mhlaba

Vuyisile Thole

Ernest Malgas

Mr and Mrs Henry Fazzie

Govan Mbeki

Nkosinathi Benson Fihla

Danny Jordaan

Michael Xego

he was banned in January 1986, only to be freed by the courts that month.

Ernest Malgas's home was petrol-bombed three times – on 19 March 1985, and again on 3 June and 18 June of that year. He escaped detention for a few months in the first state of emergency while in hiding, but was later caught and jailed. He was detained for the duration of the second state of emergency.

Ivy Gcina's home was petrol-bombed on 30 April 1985 and she was detained for the duration of both states of emergency.

Stone Sizani managed to hide successfully for the first state of emergency, but was detained for the second one.

Derrick Swartz received a scholarship from a university in the United Kingdom and left the country for post-graduate studies after a period of detention.

Mkhuseli Jack managed to hide for some months at the beginning of both states of emergency, but was later caught and spent most of both in detention. Like Fazzie, he was banned in January 1986 between the states of emergency, but he also was freed by the courts.

Matthew Goniwe was detained on 30 March 1984 and only released on 17 December. He then became the UDF's rural organiser, and, with his three friends, was picked up by the security police on 27 June 1985. They were all brutally murdered on that day.

Sipho Hashe, Champion Galela and Qaqawuli Godolozi were abducted from the Port Elizabeth Airport on 3 June 1985 and were also brutally murdered.

Thus it was with the Eastern Cape UDF leadership – four were murdered, one (mercifully) obtained a scholarship and left for the UK, and all of the other six spent most of the states of emergency in hiding or in detention.

Through these processes, the UDF was, in the words of Tom Lodge, 'beginning a revolt it would soon not be able to control'. The only time when its leadership was not beset by murderous harassment was the early times, late 1983 and 1984. In these years, with harassment initially low but nevertheless mounting in savageness and frequency, the leaders quickly found that they could no longer lead and the UDF began the process of 'no longer being led from the top, but rather dragged from the bottom'.

We will now consider the times of this change, from an organisation being led by elected leadership to an organisation being driven on by anonymous activists.

The UDF was founded on the campaign premise to oppose the proposed new constitution and the upcoming elections of parliament's three chambers, as well as the proposed new structures for black local authorities. In this regard there was no time to spare.

PW Botha sets the tricameral parliament in motion

With the UDF all of four days old, on 24 August Prime Minister Botha announced that a referendum for white citizens only would be held on 2 November, in which all white persons over the age of 18, not just registered voters, would be asked to answer 'yes' or 'no' to the question: 'Are you in favour of the implementation of the Republic of South Africa Constitution Act, 1983, as approved by parliament?'

As the sponsors of the referendum, the National Party headed up the 'yes' grouping. They had some of the usual supporters: Allan Hendrickse and the Labour Party, Amichand Rajbansi and the South African Indian Council, and Lennox Sebe of the Ciskei Government. Surprisingly they were joined by a broad-based grouping of businesspersons including Gavin Relly, chairman of Anglo American, Raymond Ackerman of Pick n Pay, Sol Kerzner, Dr Frans Cronje, Eric Ellerine, Andreas Wassenaar of Sanlam and many other businesspersons. Also petitioning for a 'yes' vote were about 200 academics from Afrikaans-language universities. Possibly the biggest surprise was the support of a number of traditionally liberal (although some, like *The Citizen*, were conservative) English-language newspapers: the *Sunday Times*, *Daily Dispatch*, *Natal Mercury*, *Financial Mail*, *Finance Week*, *The Friend*, *The Citizen* and, of course, most Afrikaans-language newspapers.

The liberal 'no' grouping was headed up by Dr Frederik van Zyl Slabbert, leading the PFP, and Chief Buthelezi. Five other homeland leaders joined them, including George Matanzima. They were also joined by a small grouping of businesspersons including Harry Oppenheimer and Tony Bloom of the Premier Group. Senior church leaders of the Anglican, Catholic and Methodist churches also urged a 'no' vote, as did the *Rand Daily Mail*, *The Argus*, the *Cape Times*, the *Natal Witness*, the *Pretoria News* and the *Sunday Express*.

The newly formed UDF rejected the entire process leading up to the referendum, and thus refused to advise supporters to vote in either direction, or to abstain. Instead it called a 'People's Weekend' for 29-30 October. Speeches, rallies and all-night prayer vigils were held.

The 'no' grouping had a very unusual bedfellow, the Afrikaner right. Dr Andries Treurnicht of the Conservative Party called the new constitution 'political suicide' as the 'power-sharing' nature of the new constitution would deprive whites of their sovereignty. They were joined by Jaap Marais's Herstigte Nasionale Party, Eugene TerreBlanche's Afrikaner Weerstandsbeweging (AWB) and Prof. Carel Boshoff's South African Bureau of Racial Affairs.

Physical disruptions of the referendum were restricted to five bombs in

Johannesburg and Durban, for which no one claimed responsibility. Apart from that, the referendum went ahead undisturbed.

There were 2 713 300 white South Africans of an age eligible to vote. Of these 2 062 469 (76%) voted. 1 360 223 (66%) voted 'yes' and 691 577 (34%) voted 'no'. The vote was counted in 15 regions, the regions with offices of the Department of Home Affairs. Only one region had a majority of 'no' votes: Pietersburg in the northern Transvaal, with a 52% 'no' majority. For the rest, it was 'yes' everywhere. The new constitution and its tricameral parliament were to go ahead.

Dr Dirk Laurie of the Council for Scientific and Industrial Research later estimated that just under 30% of 'no' voters were PFP supporters, the rest were the right-wing. The PFP voters, Dr Laurie calculated, stayed away (40%) and of those that voted, there were seven 'yes' votes for every five 'no' votes.

Botha and Treurnicht appeared elated by the results, and Slabbert and Buthelezi were dismayed. Buthelezi said that the 'road to a negotiated future was closed'. The UDF dismissed the whole miserable show and saw 'vast and tragic conflict ahead'.

The UDF in Port Elizabeth and Uitenhage takes on the Black Council

Meanwhile Khusta Jack, having been released and banned by the Ciskei security police who had brutalised him so determinedly, had returned to Port Elizabeth. 'I had come a long way ... Now I didn't care whether I died in the struggle.' He found employment as a clerk at a food-processing factory only to be retrenched within a year. One worker retrenched with him felt that his 'misplaced and futile political foolishness' had caused them all to lose their jobs (he was now President of PEYCO).[187]

Despondent, he attended meetings of many organisations, including the Detainees Parents' Support Committee, the same organisation where Molly Blackburn had met Saki Macozoma. 'It was at those meetings that I met Dr Zoe Riordan, a clinical psychologist. She was very kind and listened to my life's vicissitudes and agonies ... Zoe gave me her undivided attention, and wanted to know more about my ambitions ... I told her I was looking for a job to keep me occupied and that I intended to enrol at Wits University to read law the following year ... Zoe told me that her then-husband Rory Riordan was opening a building-material warehouse in North End. She advised me to report the following day. I was lucky to be the first employee on site ... The work was hard and physical but I had no complaints; I was just happy that I had something to do during the day. At night there were political meetings. Rory had two partners: Des Chalmers (Judy's husband and Molly Blackburn's brother-in-law), and Laurie Webb.'[188]

This venture was to prove to be an excellent example of a great idea at the wrong time (October 1983), of which more later.

Next on the horizon were the Black Local Authority elections, slated for a variety of dates between 25 November and 3 December.[189]

The involvement of blacks in local government had previously been governed by the Community Councils Act of 1977, which had created a network of community councils. This election was to be under the new Black Local Authorities Act of 1982, and this act broadened the definition of 'voter' to now include all Africans 18 years old or older (previously the lower limit was 21). Further, to comply with the Riekert Commission recommendations on an improved environment for urban Africans, voters had now to be either SA citizens or citizens of a territory previously a part of South Africa and they had also either to live permanently in the council area, or, if a migrant and a permit holder, be resident in the council area for 12 months prior to the election. Migrants could previously not vote.

Twenty-nine local authorities were due for elections between 25 November and 3 December. The government's intentions were to 'upgrade' another 84 community councils for elections in 1984, and the remainder in two or three years' time. In the first batch, the 1983 grouping, were Kayamnandi (Port Elizabeth), KwaNobuhle (Uitenhage) and Lingelihle (Cradock).

The UDF was part of forming the Anti-Community Councils Election Committee nationally, which included a range of the UDF-affiliated organisations, and, on this issue, it had the support of AZAPO. Meetings and rallies were organised and speakers included the Soweto Civic Association's Dr Nthato Motlana and the UDF's Oscar Mpetha. *UDF News*, a newspaper, appeared three times before the election dates, and half-a-million leaflets were distributed. The UDF's campaign was vigorous.

In Port Elizabeth on 3 November 1983 the *Herald* wrote that the Department of Information magazine *UMSO* had published an article revealing a coat-of-arms for the 'soon-to-be black municipality of Port Elizabeth', now named the 'Kayamnandi Municipality' (Beautiful Home) and that Mr RJ Scholtz, the Chief Executive of the Port Elizabeth Community Council, was to be its town clerk. (Mr Scholtz denied knowledge of this.)

The UDF in Port Elizabeth responded immediately with a public meeting at which, amongst others, Duma Lamani urged the youth to persuade their parents not to vote.

The elections in Port Elizabeth were scheduled for 1 December. Two parties contested them: the Zamukulungisa Party led by Norman Khaulela, previously acting chair of the soon-to-be defunct community council, and the Asinamaki Party. Of the 21 seats, 20 were contested and 43 candidates stood. A miserable 13.7% of registered voters voted, or 14 975 of 109 304 voters, and the Zamukulungisa Party swept all 21 wards.

On 14 December Khaulela was inaugurated as mayor with Thamsanqa Linda as his deputy. With life-sized portraits of Kaiser Matanzima and Lennox Sebe, the leaders of the Transkei and Ciskei homelands, behind him, Khaulela called on the government to give his new council 'real power' and 'subsidies'. 'We had better close shop if we are to depend on rentals,' he said prophetically.

In KwaNobuhle in Uitenhage and Lingelihle in Cradock there were no elections. One candidate stood in each ward and was duly elected unopposed.

Nationally the overall poll was 21%, compared with 30% in community council elections in 1978. In Soweto the average poll was 11%. Of the 27 councils 'elected' only seven had polls higher than in 1978.

The UDF held that the overall voting percentage was much lower, as most Africans had not registered as voters. As an example, in Kagiso the percentage poll was 3% and not 36% as claimed. This was undoubtedly correct. The new black local authorities were in deep water the moment their councillors donned their new robes.

UDF campaigns against the tricameral parliament

After the campaign against the Black Local Authority elections, the UDF plunged immediately into the two remaining issues that flowed from the new constitution: what was to be the UDF's position if Botha called for a referendum or referendums in the Coloured and Asian communities regarding participation in the two new houses of parliament, and what was the UDF to do when elections were called? To get to grips with these issues the UDF called its first national conference in Port Elizabeth on 17–18 December 1983. Port Elizabeth was chosen as it was the 'territory' of Rev. Allan Hendrickse, the leader of the (Coloured) Labour Party, which had of course rejected the proposed constitutional proposals, but had nevertheless declared its willingness to stand in elections for the Coloured house.

Of these two issues, the second one was agreed easily. The UDF decided unanimously that it would not participate in the upcoming elections for these houses. However, the first issue proved more divisive. Some delegates wished to participate in any referendum that might be announced, in order to destroy the legitimacy of these two parliamentary houses with a resounding 'no' vote. Other delegates were clearly committed to a boycott. A commission was formed to break the logjam and a compromise was worked out. The UDF would not participate in the upcoming elections, but would instead run a Million Signature Campaign to destroy the legitimacy of the elections. This campaign kicked off in Soshanguve on 21 January 1984 and eventually collected only 400 000 signatures, mostly at the end of May. The UDF nevertheless felt that the campaign was a success in training and mobilising, and in learning the techniques of door-to-door canvassing. And Botha turned out to be anyway too wily to call referendums which he could have lost.

Matthew Goniwe is 'transferred', Janet Cherry arrives and the 'other' tricameral elections

Meanwhile in the Eastern Cape the security establishment continued with its work.

On 7 December 1983, in an unseasonal thunderstorm in the Karoo, a postman delivered an envelope to the household of Matthew Goniwe. It contained a letter informing him that he was to be transferred to the Ngweba High School in Graaff-Reinet, an hour's drive from Cradock.[190]

After consulting with CRADORA and his comrades, Matthew replied that he refused the transfer. By return of post he got a second letter – by refusing the transfer, he had dismissed himself as of January 1984. Matthew replied – he accepted that he would no longer be acting principal; rather he applied to be reinstated as a teacher in Cradock. This too was refused and immediately 2 000 Lingelihle scholars refused to return to school. They had a set of demands: the reinstatement of Matthew Goniwe and the right to elect student representative councils, as opposed to the system of prefects being appointed by the headmaster. All seven schools in Cradock's African township stood empty. Another schools boycott had started.

This quickly spread, with boycotts breaking out in schools in Port Elizabeth, Uitenhage, Grahamstown, Queenstown and other areas. Each area had a different set of complaints: cramped classes, the age limit law, actions of headmasters, etc. In Port Elizabeth a Crisis in Education Committee was set up, with delegates from pupil, political, youth and parents' associations. This committee soon won a concession when 90 students, previously not admitted to school because of their age, were allowed into school. Pupils then returned to school in Port Elizabeth.

The security police arrived at the Goniwe house at 4 am on 31 March 1984. Matthew and his nephew Mbulelo were taken off, as were Madoda Jacobs and Fort Calata from their homes. Matthew and Mbulelo were taken to Pollsmoor Prison in Tokai in the Cape, and Jacobs and Calata were taken to Diepkloof Prison in Johannesburg. There they were to spend six months, until they were returned to Cradock on 10 October.

At home all meetings of CRADORA were banned, and an application to court to overturn this failed. Fort Calata's wife was dismissed from the Cradock Hospital for wearing a 'Free Mandela' t-shirt. Calata himself was dismissed from his job as a teacher. Sparrow Mkonto was dismissed from the South African Railways for 'unauthorised absence'. Gladwell Makaula, who had taken over from Matthew as acting chair of CRADORA, had his house petrol-bombed. Cradock was now a centre of struggle.

Janet Cherry arrives in Port Elizabeth

In early 1984 Janet Cherry came to live in Port Elizabeth.[191]

Janet was 22 years old at the time. She was from an activist family: her father, Prof. Robin Cherry, was a Professor of Physics and Dean of Science at the University of Cape Town. Janet did a degree in Economic History and Industrial Sociology at UCT, graduating in 1982.

Janet was, and is, and always will be, an extraordinary activist. At UCT she became involved in the Wages Commission, doing support work for independent black trade unions. She was, briefly, detained for the first time, in 1980, when she supported the meat workers in their strike. She worked in adult literacy campaigns in Crossroads and Nyanga townships. In 1980 she was elected to the Arts Students Council and in 1981 to the Student Representative Council.

In 1982 she was recruited into the African National Congress and in 1983, a year after graduating, she was elected as Secretary General of the National Union of South African Students and worked full-time there for a year.

In 1984 a group of township activists, including Lulu Johnson, Shepherd Mati, Khusta Jack and Mandla Madwara, encouraged her to move to Port Elizabeth. On arrival she immediately set up the East Cape Adult Learning Project and began teaching literacy skills to union members and gave activist training for PEYCO and CRADORA, amongst others. She was elected as the chairperson of the Port Elizabeth UDF area committee and was involved in the UDF's Million Signature Programme. When the state of emergency regulations later prohibited her literacy programme, she established a crisis information centre that supported detainees and people on the run.

The 'other' tricameral elections

Shortly after Janet's arrival, Port Elizabeth and Uitenhage were plunged into the concluding episodes of the settling in of the tricameral parliament, the elections for the (Coloured) House of Representatives (22 August) and the (Indian) House of Delegates (28 August).

Minister Heunis noted that there were 1 500 558 Coloured people over the age of 18 in South Africa, and 514 946 South Africans classified as 'Indians' of this age. Of these 1 020 721 and 329 970 respectively had registered to vote.

The UDF anchored the 'don't vote' lobby and they were well supported by the General Secretary of the South African Council of Churches, Bishop Tutu, other Christian leaders, the Islamic Council of South Africa, the Federation of South African Trade Unions, the South African Council on Sport and many other organisations.

In all, 272 854 Coloured votes were cast, and 83 613 'Indian'. This made polls of 18.2% (Coloured) and 16.2% (Indian). Rev. Allan Hendrickse, who led the Labour Party to win 77 of the 80 seats in the House of Representatives, expressed his satisfaction at the poll, while the anti-election groupings felt the same. The tricameral parliament was now ready to go.

At this stage the UDF was a year old. It had battered its way through three campaigns – its first intervention in the white electorate's referendum on the new constitution had changed nothing. This community had voted in its usual numbers and had endorsed this constitution, even ignoring the desperate pleas of the leader of the Opposition, Frederik van Zyl Slabbert. Then came the first elections for the new black local authorities. Here the UDF's call for a boycott was more effective – nationally the poll dropped from 30% (1977) to 21%. The final campaign, for a boycott of the election to the Houses of Representatives and Delegates, was also very effective, with both elections having polls under 20%.

UDF versus the Kayamnandi Council

Now the fight moved from high-level political campaigns to on-the-ground, local government issues.

Here, the new Kayamnandi Town Council gave the UDF and its friends two quick wins.[192]

Firstly, the Council picked a fight with the local taverner industry. In August it declared that it was 'not policy' for Council to legalise the hundreds of shebeens that were buying in bulk from the Development Board's liquor outlets, and bluntly told the petitioning East Cape Taverners' Association that it 'was not feasible to invite you to further discussions on this issue as it was contrary to Council's policy'. Later Council 'declared war on the shebeens', and stated its intention to enlist the police in stamping out 1 000 or so illegal taverns. Council held the view that 'the three licenced on-consumption liquor outlets (the Development Board outlets) were sufficient'.

Four days after Council declared 'war', Louis Koch, the Chief Director of the Development Board (whose liquor outlets supplied the taverners), announced that he had been given the assurance of Council that they were about to begin talks with the taverners with a view to expediting the granting of licences to the taverners. The taverners had made joint representations to Koch, who had 'interceded' as he was troubled by the 'hard line taken by Council'. Koch concluded that his 'faithful and frank discussions' with Council had resulted in Council wanting 'to make sure that the legalisation of shebeens was coordinated in the public interest'. The Council had just lost its first fight with public opinion.

Fresh from its first defeat, Council plunged headlong into a second anti-populist fight when it decided to implement a rise in a wide range of township service charges. From 1 December shack dwellers were to be charged R25 monthly for service charges (against an existing R10) and lodgers' fees were to be upped from R3 per month to R15 for a single-parent family and R25 for a full family. Hostel dwellers were to pay R15 service charge per bed per month (as against R7).

This issue provided an immediate rallying point for the newly formed UDF bodies. PEBCO held a public meeting at which 8 000 people voted to stay away from work on 26 November and called on residents to boycott rent offices as a protest, thereby threatening the existing flow of rent payments to the council. In a recently learned lesson, PEBCO tacked on a demand that the Development Board's liquor outlets be boycotted from 26 to 28 November. This would have stopped Council's entire revenue stream.

Like magic, the council decided not to implement the proposed increases and the Deputy Mayor, Councillor Thamsanqa Linda, noted that this decision was taken 'in the light of objections received'. The Town Clerk noted that these objections were from the 'Redhouse Benevolent Society and the PE Charity Organisation'.

These badly strategised and unpopular campaigns clearly exposed Council's soft underbelly – protest and boycotts could immediately redirect Council's proposed actions. This was not going to be an easy ride for the Kayamnandi Council.

Deputy Mayor Thamsanqa Linda was in late 1984 to emerge as Council's dominant personality. He had been born in Port Elizabeth in 1946. After matriculating he began work as a railway ticket inspector, then worked as a greengrocer. He dabbled in Ciskei politics, but backed the wrong side. He returned to Port Elizabeth and was elected to the Kayamnandi Council in 1983, and immediately became deputy mayor.

In September 1984 it became known that a clique of councillors wished to unseat Mayor Khaulela, who was chairman of the Executive Committee and mayor, and replace him with Linda. Despite denials, this happened in early October (MAYCO) and December (Mayor). From then on the fortunes of the council and its flamboyant mayor were tied inextricably together.

Confident in his rise to power, Linda rose simultaneously in controversy. In August Nkosinathi Mavela, one of nine children of widow Alice Mavela, revealed to the *Herald* that his family was to be evicted from their spacious eight-roomed home in Veeplaas, and re-housed in a four-roomed house. His mother was up to date with her rental payments, he said. The reason for their removal was that Linda wanted their house, as it was big and next door to his shop. Linda and his town clerk, Scholtz, steadfastly refused to comment.

Mrs Mavela claimed that her belongings arrived at the four-roomed house in Zwide on a municipal truck and trailer and 'the labourers told me that Mr Linda had told them to dump them in the yard if I refused to accept them. This they did.'

She then produced a letter written to the Community Council by Linda in 1982, before he became a councillor, requesting to take over 'the house and garden used by Mrs Mavela because I am struggling to look after my shop in the evening since I am staying in New Brighton', and listing five recent burglaries at his shop. Town Clerk Scholtz confirmed that the letter had been written by Linda and stated that the request had been turned down as the house was occupied by Mrs Mavela.

Instantly the council's opponents seized on the issue. PEBCO called a mass public meeting which 'resolved to demand' the return of Mrs Mavela to the house she had been 'evicted from to make way for Mr Linda'. Linda refused to comment on these demands: 'There is no point in saying anything now. This has gone too far.'

Crowds gathered at Linda's shop, demanding a boycott of it until Mrs Mavela was returned to 'her home'. The council decided to auction the house instead.

Before this could happen Mrs Mavela went to court, claiming that she had been illegally evicted from her house by 'fraud, deceit and trickery', and that Linda had moved into her house after she had left it. In a replying affidavit, Scholtz claimed that Mrs Mavela had been moved as the complex including her home was to be sold. Linda also deposed an affidavit, claiming that the legal action had been instigated by the UDF and PEBCO for political reasons, because of their opposition to town councils. The trial was delayed, then settled and the settlement was made an order of court. By this settlement Mrs Mavela was provided with another eight-roomed house in

Maku Street and her previous home was to be sold by auction. Much later, in June 1985, the only tender for the purchase of the home was received from one Thamsanqa Linda.

Two months later it was destroyed by arsonists. When rebuilt, it was returned to Mrs Mavela after Scholtz claimed that Linda had never come forward with the necessary deposit. Mrs Mavela in turn credited her final good fortune to the UDF, which had rallied around her. In Khusta Jack's autobiography he notes that even the security policeman Roelofse agreed with her, Linda's '*gemors*' (mess) had served only to make the activists look '*ordentlik*' (decent and credible).

Jack writes that this seemingly unimportant event had great advantages for the township activists: 'We had moved into top gear and fanned public outrage to the max. The public, already on edge because of pass laws and other urban controls, were horrified by Linda's greedy actions ... The numbers attending our meetings began to swell. There were new faces ... For the first time since I joined the struggle the numbers of adults at our meetings were greater than those of the youth ... Our message was simple: "It was Mrs Mavela today. Are you next?"'[193]

13

The storm gathers strength

We have reached mid-1984, and tensions are beginning to show throughout South African society.

Possibly it is time to take stock. What were South Africans thinking? What were their feelings for the future?

Here we can be guided by two major surveys conducted by the Human Sciences Research Council.[194]

The first was a survey of 1 024 adult (over 18 years of age) urban white South Africans conducted in February–March 1984.

The second was a survey of 1 478 black South Africans, aged 18 and over, and resident in the PWV complex, conducted in June–July 1984. The PWV complex was chosen because it was felt to have a less homogeneous black population than, say, Durban or Port Elizabeth.

The survey of white political opinion showed that 'slightly more than half (50.7%) of the sample (54.3% of the Afrikaans speakers and 44.5% of the English speakers) were "very satisfied" or at least "satisfied" with the current state of affairs in South Africa in general, in contrast to 21.7% who were "dissatisfied" or "very dissatisfied". 52.5% believed that the political situation had "improved over the last few years" – 20% only were of the opinion that it had deteriorated, and 51.9% were of the opinion that the situation would improve over the "next few years"'.

The 'credibility of the SA Defence Force was accepted by the great majority of respondents', and only 13.5% felt that the South African government was spending too much on defence, with almost 80% believing that too little or just enough was being spent here. 90.6% of respondents believed that the 'Government's handling of the issue of combating terrorism was very good or good'.

On the other hand, only 29.3% believed that the government was handling the 'influx of Blacks into the cities' well. However, just over half felt that 'constitutional reform' was being well handled.

The study outlined white opinions on seven 'fundamental apartheid structures', and these were:

Over 60% of white respondents were in favour of the Mixed Marriages Act; the Immorality Act; the Group Areas Act; and Separate Public Amenities.

Over 70% of respondents were in favour of separate schools for whites, the Black Homelands and separate voters' rolls.

Over 40% believed that libraries, public transport and hotels should 'never' be opened to all races, and over 50% believed the same for cemeteries, parks, restaurants, cinemas and health clinics. Over 60% believed thus for public toilets, bars, hospital wards and nursery schools. With regard to public swimming pools, over 70% said they should 'never' be opened to all races.

82% felt that 'white government' was good, with 3% feeling the same for 'Black government' (93.6% felt that this was a bad idea).

This cocoon of comfort for the apartheid world was, predictably, not agreed to by respondents in the black survey.

In this community the greatest acknowledged problems were economic – unemployment, poverty, lack of housing – these were felt to be the 'greatest problems' faced by the community (64% agreed), followed by apartheid measures (influx control, lack of political rights, etc., 21.3%). That these two problems were interrelated was clearly acknowledged by the researchers: 'it is clear that Blacks ascribe these (economic) problems to the political structure … the solutions to the economic problems are thus also seen to be political', and 'can only be achieved through political power'. Thus over 80% of all 'greatest problems' could only be solved by blacks achieving political power.

And who did they trust to wield this political power?

Here we must remember two things: firstly that the ANC was banned and had been for over 20 years and that Nelson Mandela was likewise banned and had not been seen for even longer. To support either Mandela or the ANC publicly was a legal offence. Secondly, the first survey of black political opinion in South Africa was conducted by Theo Hanf of the Bergstrasse Institute in Germany, in 1977. This found that Buthelezi was the most popular leader, with much more support than the ANC.

This survey, by the HSRC, found differently, for on leadership and for organisations,

> Mandela definitely enjoys greater support than any other Black leader. For every one person supporting Buthelezi, there are three Mandela supporters, and this despite the fact that Mandela is a member of a prohibited organisation and that to support him openly is an indictable offence – hence the percentage response in favour of Mandela must be seen as 'conservative'.
>
> Of the respondents that registered a choice, the ANC managed to secure the support of 35,4%, whereas homeland and national leaders received a mere 11,7% support from the same group. Hence, for every supporter of a homeland leader, the ANC has three supporters.

Thus the simple conclusion of these two mid-1984 surveys: the white community was very comfortable in their apartheid world and saw no need for major political compromise and the black community was now on a quick march in step with the Congress tradition. The major issue of South African politics, namely the white community's unwillingness to concede a universal and equal franchise, was nowhere near resolution.

For the white community, a typhoon was about to arrive onshore. For the black community, years of massive suffering and sacrifice lay ahead.

14

The UDF insurrection begins

In late 1984 the typhoon arrived.

The Report of the Truth and Reconciliation Commission states that 'Up until late 1984, there had been no political violence to speak of in Port Elizabeth.'[195] That was to change, in both South Africa (in the Vaal Triangle, an hour's drive south of Johannesburg) and in Uitenhage and Port Elizabeth in early September 1984.

Tom Lodge notes:

On September 3, 1984, two events occurred that symbolized the polarities of South African politics. On that day, the new constitution came into force and was celebrated by PW Botha's government in Cape Town. The new Indian and Coloured parliamentarians were decked out in the strange costume favoured by Afrikaner politicians for important occasions: homburg hats, stiff collars, morning coats and striped trousers. Far to the north, in a cluster of crowded townships in the Vaal Triangle, a different reaction occurred. All day long, angry mobs roamed the streets, burning businesses, government buildings, and cars; throwing stones; battling with the police; and killing several municipal councillors. The longest and most widespread period of sustained black protest against white rule in South Africa's history had begun.[196]

The uprising in the Vaal Triangle townships (Sebokeng, Sharpeville, Zamdela and Boipatong, all under the Lekoa Council) had two precursor grievances. In April 1984 COSAS had called a national schools boycott, because of bad matric results and an unwillingness of the education authorities to readmit older pupils. Quickly over 200 000 children were out of the classroom all over South Africa and these schoolchildren were more than willing to be on the frontline of protest. Secondly, the recent anti–Black Council protests were still fresh in memory. When the Orange Vaal Administration awarded 19 of their 25 liquor licences to councillors, of whom 12 were members of the mayor's family, the anger burst out. Then, on 5 August, amid extensive retrenchments in the local economy, the Lekoa Council announced a massive rent increase (R5.50 per month on a R30 base), and the Vaal Civic Association called for a worker's stay-at-home for 3 September. The match was in the tinder.

Lodge again:

On the morning of Monday, September 3, picket lines of young people stopped the buses from entering the townships. By noon most of the shops and public buildings in Sharpeville had been reduced to ashes. Sixty percent of the township's workers stayed away from work … A week-long state of paralysis set in … thirty-one people were killed, by police or enraged crowds … on September 23, seven thousand soldiers from the South African Defence Force, accompanied by an array of armoured vehicles, entered Sebokeng and checked passes, arresting people whose papers were not in order. Called Operation Palmiet, it was the first time in twenty-five years that the army had been used to suppress civil unrest.[197]

A township uprising began in Uitenhage at the same time. A similar scenario: the KwaNobuhle Town Council, cash strapped as were all black local authorities, decided to raise rents and service charges. On 9 September the councillors called a public meeting to inform the community of these increases. At the meeting Mayor Tini realised that it was not worth his life to announce increases and backed down, announcing instead that the expected increases would not happen. The crowd, angry and ready for action, screamed him down and called him a liar. The councillors escaped through a side door.

This time, the words of Mark Swilling analyse the situation: 'This was the turning point. From this point onwards, the relationship between the local state and the community shifted: it was no longer about a race between different political projects using different means to improve township living, it became an outright violent confrontation.'[198]

Back to the Transvaal.

On 27 October the Transvaal Regional Stay-Away Committee was formed, comprising COSAS, trade unions and youth congresses. The committee called a two-day general strike to begin on 5 November. FOSATU, the UDF-aligned Municipal and General Workers Union, the Soweto Youth Congress and the Release Mandela Committee put out 400 000 pamphlets outlining the reasons for the stayaway. The demands were general and encyclopaedic: no rent increases, reinstatement of workers, release of detainees, withdrawal of soldiers and police from the townships, and more.

Incredibly, over a million workers and students participated. The Labour Monitoring Group called the stayaway 'a new phase in the history of united action amongst organised labour, students and community groups'. The trade unions had been effectively pulled into the community struggles.

Back in the Eastern Cape tensions were escalating.

In Uitenhage a group of men euphemistically calling themselves 'Peacemakers', led by businessman Jimmy Claasens, formed a vigilante group around the councillors and particularly around Councillor Benjamin Kinikini, another local businessman. The Uitenhage Youth Congress called for councillors to resign and, when they did not, called for a boycott of their businesses. The UDF applied for the use of the KwaNobuhle Community Hall, which was controlled by the council. Kinikini, brandishing a firearm, heatedly refused to part with the keys. Quickly young supporters of UYCO began to form themselves into an informal militia called the 'Amabutho'. Thus began the series of violent skirmishes between the Peacemakers and the Amabutho.

'Amabutho' is a name derived from the Xhosa word for warriors who resisted the settler invasion during the frontier wars of the 19th century. The term was now used to describe those youngsters who were the product of the post-1976 social revolution that had swept black townships. Young activists were now positioned in the frontline of the uprising and there was a weakening of the traditional deference of youth for their elders. They were the products of the classroom revolution that had seen the breaking of the traditional disciplinary ties running from old to young. The Amabutho were emerging, emancipated young people, now the frontline of the struggle.

There were no membership cards for the Amabutho and little formal organisation either. They had fashioned their own military structure, bypassing the UDF and its code of non-violence. Instead they declared their loyalty to the ANC and Nelson Mandela. Otherwise their ideology was limited to basic slogans and freedom songs. They were armed with anything they could get their hands on – rocks, guns, knives, tyres and especially petrol bombs. They manned the barricades in the great revolt, making housewives eat soap powder bought in times of consumer boycotts, petrol-bombing trucks and buses moving in times of other boycotts. They ran their own people's courts, often very brutally. They emerged, in the mid-1980s, as the cutting edge of the township war, the foot soldiers of the emerging revolution.

The first experiences of youth taking on this dangerous and brutal role came in two events in the Vaal Triangle and Uitenhage. In Uitenhage their role began after a deadly event. On 3 December the home of Fikile Kobese, a member of the trade union MACWUSA and an executive member of the UDF, was firebombed. His younger brother, Leslie, was burned to death in this conflagration. Activists believed that a sophisticated chemical bomb had been used, pointing to security force involvement. If that was so, and we don't know for sure, then this was South Africa's first death by burning and many believe that it was the precursor of the later 'necklace' horror.

Leslie's vigil on 17 December was broken up by the police, inflaming this terrible situation further. After the funeral, a mob of young people murdered Zamuxolo Mondile, a nephew of the councillor Benjamin Kinikini. Uitenhage was being prepared for a ferocious 1985.

As was Port Elizabeth. Here Mayor Linda was plunging headlong into war with the UDF. Firstly he threatened to ban churches 'who give their halls to political organisations that were part and parcel of irrelevant organisations'. His council would no longer rent halls to such organisations. PEBCO replied by threatening a boycott of both the Development Board's liquor outlets and councillors' businesses. Linda replied that 'All UDF affiliates, particularly PEBCO, are led by non-residents because their leaders do not own homes. They are politically immature people who resort to intimidating people to gain support and who manipulate residents.' He challenged UDF leaders to a public debate. Sipho Hashe called this invitation a 'mockery – Linda is not a politician but a civil servant put there to regulate the lives of township residents'.[199]

But there was no stopping Linda. He called on the Minister of Law and Order to ban the UDF in Kayamnandi: 'We will not allow that rubbish to continue after their meetings to stone buses and houses.'

Linda ended with an unveiled threat to those who joined the workers' unions and civic associations. They would have to approach PEBCO when they wanted houses, as council would not help them.

But possibly the most sinister of the (very veiled) threats came from

Town Clerk Scholtz. On 10 December he announced that council had now approached the appointment of municipal police in terms of the Black Local Authorities Act. Kitskonstabels were on the way, with all the lawless havoc they were to wreak. Port Elizabeth, like Uitenhage, was being prepared for a ferocious 1985.

Period Two
1985

Any person, reviewing 1984, might have been excused for imagining that since things were so bad, they were bound to get better. That same person, reviewing 1985, would have to chide himself for false optimism: things have not only not got better, they have got much worse.

–   Frederik van Zyl Slabbert

15

The story begins in Cradock in 1984

W e have noted that Matthew Goniwe and three friends were detained in early 1984. Immediately this triggered a boycott of school attendance in Cradock. A total of 7 000 students from all seven of Lingelihle's schools pulled out of school, thereby beginning the longest and most universal school boycott in South Africa's history; it lasted 15 months, until April 1985, despite every possible inducement to the students to return to class. A consumer boycott of Cradock's white shops was called for seven days in August 1984 to build further pressure for Goniwe's release. Eventually the Goniwe group was returned from jail to Lingelihle, on 10 October, to a hero's welcome.[200]

Now the community became more resolute. The beerhall was boycotted for four months from December. In January 1985 all of the councillors on the Lingelihle Council resigned and were accepted back into the community. This was South Africa's first total council resignation. A delegation from CRADORA was sent to meet the Deputy Minister of Education and Training, Sam de Beer, but he remained unmoved. Matthew was not to get his teaching post back in Cradock.

The UDF saw this as an opportunity. In its 8 January statement the ANC had called on domestic organisations to 'make South Africa ungovernable'. Matthew was then appointed as the UDF's rural organiser, with responsibility to establish community-based organisations, both civic and youth, in a circle of small towns around Cradock including Fort

Beaufort, Kirkwood, Colesberg, Alexandria, Steytlerville and Noupoort. This he did with his customary energy, introducing the street committee system, creating an activist grid so dense that 'even the family is seen as a structure of the organisation'. This was to become the bedrock of the UDF's concept of 'People's Power'. Ungovernability first, with authority taken from the regime, then people's power, with the people starting to exercise control.

As UDF executive Derrick Swartz later reported:

> We went to our people who have supported us under dangerous circumstances and involved them in democratic organisations and structures, and decision making processes. We said: 'in the streets where you live you must decide what issues affect your lives, and bring up issues that you want your organisation to take up. We are not in a position to remove debris, remove the buckets, clean the streets and so on. But the organisation must deal with these matters through street committees' … from there each area will meet and discuss and coordinate the grievances of a number of streets … we had to form area committees from the street committees.[201]

Street and area committees became the building blocks of the UDF structure, and, while they might not have originated in and around Cradock, Matthew Goniwe certainly created the template that the East Cape UDF took on and used to such effect over time. With this as a communication and mobilisation structure, the boycotts that became the hallmark of the UDF insurrection could be effectively organised. Thus with Matthew's work went school and consumer boycotts, boycotts of beer halls and massive pressures on black local authorities, councillors and township police. Although CRADORA was banned, a decision of its executive was heard through Lingelihle in 30 minutes, thanks to Matthew's system.

Matthew's organisational ability was not missed by the regime. The head of the Cradock security police, Henri Fouche, appeared unable to counter the work of the fast-moving Goniwe. He was replaced by Major Eric Winter, a much tougher and more ruthless customer.

Within days of arriving in Cradock, Winter visited Matthew at his home. He particularly wanted to know what had to be done to end the endless school boycott. Matthew suggested that should he and Fort Calata be reinstated, he believed that the boycott would end. A later meeting requested by Jaap Strydom, head director of the Department of Education and Training, and his deputy, JN Vermaak, with Matthew at the Masonic Hotel, ended with these two officials agreeing with this analysis, and they reported to the minister that they believed that Goniwe should be returned to his job. Regrettably and tragically, in another part of the government's structures, some had another fate planned for Goniwe.

16

The Langa massacre

In Port Elizabeth and Uitenhage two separate processes were now running parallel. These were to come together in late March in a cataclysmic event that would change South Africa's political landscape dramatically.

First, there was a series of delicate negotiations between UDF structures and the labour unions around a proposed 'Black Weekend' of shop boycotts and a work stayaway for 16 to 18 March. Secondly, there was a low-intensity war developing in Uitenhage's townships between all four youth structures associated with the UDF (PEYCO, UYCO, COSAS and the Amabutho) and the security establishment and its vigilantes (the 'Peacemakers') around township police and the community councillors. We will consider these in turn.

Pressure builds

There was pressure to coordinate a stayaway to rival the November stayaway that had been so dramatically supported in the Transvaal. Rumours circulated about this in November 1984, but were denied by PEBCO and MACWUSA. On 9 November there was a successful stayaway in Grahamstown, called by COSAS to accompany the funeral of a 15-year-old killed by the police.

At the end of January PEBCO held a meeting at the Rio Cinema. Here a stayaway was proposed, and PEBCO's leaders were mandated to meet the unions. A few days later, on 3 February, a press leak made the idea public before FOSATU had been consulted. FOSATU immediately rejected the idea. Four days after this, on 7 February, UDF leaders met with the non-UDF unions. The Ford Motor Company, possibly Port Elizabeth's biggest employer, had just announced that they were to merge with the Anglo American-owned AMCAR and that the Port Elizabeth assembly line was to be closed. Assembly would be relocated to the AMCAR plant in the Transvaal. This was dramatic news – a success for the UDF's sanctions and disinvestment campaign, but a pending disaster for Ford workers. The unions undertook to go back and consult with their members, and on 17 February announced that their members did not support the stayaway call. As Khusta Jack has written: 'negotiations with reactionary factions of FOSATU failed to reach an agreement'.[202]

On 17 February PEBCO called a meeting which was attended by about 2 000 people. The unions' opposition to the stayaway was announced and a vote on the process to be followed was taken. It was agreed that the stayaway should go ahead, FOSATU or no FOSATU. A stayaway committee was formed and the unions were invited to send representatives. They refused and PEBCO went ahead without them. Dennis Neer committed MACWUSA to cooperate. The dates were set – Black Weekend, 16-17 March. Stayaway on 18 March. Both were for Port Elizabeth and Uitenhage.

The non-UDF unions made a final attempt to hold off the process. They called a meeting with the UDF and Black Consciousness organisations (who also opposed the stayaway) for 13 March. They argued that the stayaway would cause divisions in the community, with some workers losing three days' pay and others only one; that the Coloured community had been ignored, another source of division; and that jobs would surely be lost. They had no other action to propose and PEBCO simply rejected their calls. All systems go. Even the desperate pleas from the mayors of both Port Elizabeth and Uitenhage and from the business chambers could not stop the unstoppable. And as Khusta Jack notes, 'The street and area committees were running smoothly and were the best means of communicating with the entire community at any time.' Matthew Goniwe's system was in place.

Alongside the negotiations to make the Black Weekend a reality, there was a concurrent and much more deadly social process underway. In Uitenhage's black townships, KwaNobuhle and Langa, the processes driving social change were becoming much more violent. Week by week, and later in 1985, day by day, the uprising was intensifying and becoming more deadly.

In early January the homes of two councillors, Cllrs Mbengo and Mqolomba, were attacked by large groupings of youths. On 11 January a crowd of about 1 000 in Mabandla Street set a bus and two delivery vans on fire. Police responded with birdshot and rubber bullets, and Violet

George and Mthetheleli Makhapi were both killed. The next day a bakery van in Langa was torched. On 16 January police fired on a rowdy crowd in KwaNobuhle. The next day three policemen's homes were burned down. Another crowd was fired on with birdshot, two more policemen's homes were torched. On 21 January Mthetheleli Makalipi's vigil was broken up by police, and a week later vigilantes set upon a group of young men – one died. A deadly rhythm was settling in – attack on police or councillors – police fire and kill – a mass funeral – attack on the police thereafter – more killed.[203]

In February the conflict around education also intensified, particularly in Uitenhage, with Coloured schools now being brought into the stayaway. Immediately secondary schools in Port Elizabeth, Graaff-Reinet, Somerset West, Mossel Bay and Humansdorp, as well as the Dower Training College, boycotted in solidarity with the Uitenhage schools. The Labour Party leader, the Rev. Allan Hendrickse, accused students of trying to embarrass and insult him. The Uitenhage Parents Committee was formed and began negotiations with COSAS.

On 14 February another house in KwaNobuhle was burned down, and police fired on the crowd of 200. Immediately a bus was torched. On 18 February pupils at the Uitenhage Secondary School were beaten by police with quirts.

The pressure on the KwaNobuhle councillors was now unbearable, and four resigned in February. The rest, except Benjamin Kinikini, resigned in early March.

Captain Goosen of the police reported that 'sporadic incidents of unrest and firebombing are the order of the day … the situation has escalated … with more attacks on police patrols taking place'. In mid-February the Minister of Police, Louis le Grange, visited Uitenhage with the national Commissioner of Police, General Johann Coetzee. The Uitenhage police reported to him that 'soft' weaponry for riot control purposes was no longer effective. As Janet Cherry has written: 'The amabutho developed tactics and skills to engage in violent conflict, including the making of petrol bombs and the use of tyre tubing as protection against "soft" ammunition (rubber bullets and birdshot) and urine-soaked cloths, and Vaseline, against teargas.'[204] Wounds were now status symbols.

Whether Le Grange and Coetzee were part of the next decision or not we don't know, but less than a month later, on 15 March, Uitenhage police were no longer issued with tear gas, rubber bullets and birdshot when approaching 'unrest situations'. They now took live ammunition. On 19 March a telex was sent from police headquarters under the hand of General Hendrik de Witt, the Deputy Commissioner of Police (he was later promoted to the position of Commissioner, the top post in the police force), authorising the use of R1 rifles in 'unrest incidents'. The telex concluded, 'wanneer suurbomme en/of petrolbomme na polisie-voertuie, privaatvoertuie en geboue gegooi word moet daar onder alle omstandighede gepoog word om die skuldiges te elimineer' (when acid bombs or petrol bombs are thrown at police vehicles or private vehicles, and buildings, every attempt must be made to eliminate the guilty party).[205]

Thus Lieutenant Colonel Frederik Pretorius, station commander in Uitenhage, issued orders that no more tear gas, rubber bullets or birdshot cartridges were to be issued to township patrols in his area. Instead they were given 7.62mm semi-automatic R1 rifles, and extra-heavy SSG shotgun cartridges (buckshot). A disaster was inevitable.

Meanwhile the rhythm of violence continued: on 3 March two were killed in violence in Langa. Four days later a bus was burned in Rosedale. On 8 March the only library serving all of KwaNobuhle was burned down. On this day a man was killed while he hurled a petrol bomb at the police. Councillor Kinikini's home was again stoned. Another policeman's home was petrol-bombed. Between 8 and 10 March 23 arson attacks and 18 stonings were perpetrated in KwaNobuhle. We were now speeding to the disaster.

Saturday 16 March, the first day of the Black Weekend, arrived. In Port Elizabeth 99.5% of the African workforce in the commercial sector stayed away from work, but there was minimal Coloured community support. On Monday 18 March, 90% of African industrial workers stayed away, and again there was negligible Coloured support. In Uitenhage most African workers were on short time on Saturday, and were not expected at work. Of those meant to come to work on 18 Monday, 36% stayed away.[206]

The *EP Herald* reported that nine people died over this weekend, in New Brighton, Motherwell and Uitenhage. In Langa three petrol bombs were thrown at police vehicles and a 22-year-old man was shot and killed. Two policemen's homes in Langa were burned down.

On Sunday 17 March, Molly Blackburn was asked to help find children allegedly taken by police. She entered the side door of the Uitenhage Police Station to find a youth, Norman Kona, being beaten by police. He had been sjamboked, hit with a broomstick, kicked in the stomach and generally assaulted. Molly, in typically indomitable fashion, ended the assault and saw that charges were laid.

The community had earlier put in place arrangements for the funerals of four youths killed in unrest, and had arranged these funerals for Sunday 17 March, in the middle of the Black Weekend. Captain Goosen immediately applied to prohibit the funerals on this day, using the wording that the funerals rather be allowed 'on any day other than a Saturday, Sunday or a public holiday, or Monday 19 March'. The Chief Magistrate of Uitenhage agreed to this order.

The community then rearranged the funerals for the 21st and called a mass meeting requesting a stayaway on that day, the day commemorating the Sharpeville Massacre. On 20 March Captain Goosen applied again to prohibit the funerals, this time from the 21st, and sought, and got, an order stating that the funerals could only be on a Sunday, which was, of course, a contradiction of his first banning order which still stood. Thus the funerals could only be on a Sunday, yet couldn't be on a Sunday.

As time was at a premium, this new banning order was communicated through loudhailers on the evening of the 20th. However, only one name (of a youth to be buried) was announced, leading to yet more confusion as four were to be buried. It thus appeared that the other three youths could be buried. Further, the loudhailing was only done in KwaNobuhle, leaving the mourners of Langa, about 10 kilometres away, in the dark.

21 March 1985

'March 21, 1985, and a funeral crowd is gathering on Maduna Square in the centre of Langa township, a run-down jumble of old houses and tin shanties adjoining the industrial town of Uitenhage in the eastern Cape. It is the twenty-fifth anniversary of the Sharpeville massacre, and before this fateful day is over there will be another massacre here, not as big as the first one but as horrifying. A generation has passed, but little has changed in the psyche of repression.' So wrote Allister Sparks in *The Mind of South Africa*.[207]

Sparks continues: 'So at about eight o'clock on that brittle-bright autumn morning the people of Langa began arriving in Maduna Square to board busses that would take them to the big sports stadium in KwaNobuhle, on the far side of Uitenhage, where the funeral rally was to be held.'

Then a Casspir armoured troop carrier arrived, captained by Warrant Officer Pentz, and filled with its crew of two and its complement of 12 policemen, armed with shotguns with buckshot, R1 rifles and service pistols. At this stage Pentz estimated the crowd to be about 250 people, led by two men dressed in black gowns girdled at the waist. One of these two took on the role of leading the crowd, and became known throughout the (later) extensive documentation of this tragic event as 'The Rastafarian'. He was never given a name beyond that.[208]

Pentz spoke to the crowd in Afrikaans, and asked what was the nature of the gathering. The Rastafarian responded, also in Afrikaans, that they were going to a funeral. Pentz informed him that the funeral had been banned, to which the Rastafarian allegedly replied, 'I know that, but you will not stop us today.' He then linked arms with about 25 others, forming a front line, and they began walking down the road to Uitenhage centre, through which they would have to walk before turning south on the main road to KwaNobuhle, 10 kilometres distant.

Pentz then guided his Casspir down Maduna Road ahead of, but in the direction taken by, the crowd. He stopped, and again called on the group to turn back. The Rastafarian, according to Pentz, responded with an obscene gesture and carried on, leading a crowd that had now grown, Pentz estimated, to 1 000 or so. Pentz drove on to Uitenhage.

His Casspir reached a junction where 14th and 15th Streets met Maduna Road, from where he radioed to Lieutenant Fouche, who was commanding a second Casspir, and requested his assistance. They quickly arrived, and the two Casspirs parked in an inverted V formation facing the crowd, which they now estimated to be possibly 3 000.

When the crowd was within earshot, Fouche instructed them to turn around and disperse. This order was repeated in Xhosa by one o Fouche's colleagues. The Rastafarian urged the crowd to ignore this, claiming that the police were only trying to scare the mourners. The crowd continued to advance, led by the Rastafarian. Thus far there is general agreement as to the facts outlined. What followed is greatly disputed.

Fouche claimed that when the Rastafarian had come to within 10 metres of his Casspir, he fired a shot into the ground at his feet, to 'bring him to his senses'. The Rastafarian then, according to Fouche, 'reached inside his gown and pulled out a black notebook and a bottle with reddish contents, and held these aloft'. Simultaneously, Fouche said, a 'bare-chested woman, possibly a Coloured', picked up a stone and hurled it at Pentz's Casspir. Fouche, believing that his men and the citizens of Uitenhage just beyond them were at risk, gave the order to fire.

The shooting did not continue for long before Fouche called ceasefire, but the effects were horrifying: 41 shots of SSG buckshot were fired, three R1 rifle shots and an uncounted number of 9mm pistol shots. At least 20 mourners from the crowd lay dead, including five women, nine youths under 16, and one younger than 11. There were 27 more writhing in agony, injured but thankfully not fatally. Of the 47 persons shot, 35 were shot 'broadly speaking, from the rear'. A total of 27 people were taken to hospital for attention. The scene was so blood-soaked the police had to use fire hoses to wash away the blood.

Later that day the Minister of Law and Order, Louis le Grange, released a statement on the massacre. The police, he said, had been 'forced to open fire on a crowd of between 3 000 and 4 000' who had been 'armed with sticks, stones, petrol bombs and bricks'. The commanding officer had 'fired a warning shot into the ground next to the leader', but to no effect. 'The crowd surrounded the police who were pelted with stones, sticks and other missiles, including petrol bombs' and the shooting was clearly in self-defence. Once the shooting commenced, 'the crowd retreated and firing stopped immediately'. Le Grange said that 17 had been killed, and another 19 were wounded. This statement was the first in a cornucopia of crap that poured out of the police on the issue of the massacre.[209]

The Kannemeyer Commission

Realising the disaster the massacre would have on the international image of the sanction-threatened country, President Botha immediately announced a 'Commission of Inquiry into the Incident which occurred on 21 March 1985 at Uitenhage'. It was to be a one-man commission, run by Judge Donald Kannemeyer from the Grahamstown Supreme Court. Judge Kannemeyer had a good reputation for disentangling complex legal issues and was seen to be a competent conservative-liberal judge. His appointment was welcomed by Errol Moorcroft, an opposition Progressive Federal Party parliamentarian from Grahamstown, who organised his party, with of course Molly Blackburn involved, into supporting the commission in every possible way.

More sceptical persons noted the entire failure of one-person commissions into the deaths in detention of Mapetla Mohapi, George Botha and Steve Biko, which had been handled by white Afrikaner magistrates. These inquiries had followed a template – 'ignore difficult evidence incriminating the police, comment on systems unfortunately being unable to fully protect the deceased, and thereafter find that no one person or institution could be held responsible'. The later judgment of history, when the full body of evidence was considered, would clearly show that the detainee had been murdered, but that would be later. For now, the embattled security establishment was to be sternly spoken to, but exonerated.

Would the white, English-speaking judge break the mould and get to the bottom of what the black community was absolutely sure was a massacre?

Kannemeyer ran an efficient commission. Appointed on 25 March, he delivered his report to the State President on 11 June, less than three months later. He heard many witnesses, visited the site of the massacre and accepted witnesses that the PFP team brought forward. But, incredibly, he stated that he could not, and would not, review the pattern of township protests and police reaction which formed the background to the massacre. The community were thus frustrated in their wish to bring forward background information. Yet when he delivered his report, he noted that he considered such background information important. He had thus got it only from the police. An ominous sign.

That Kannemeyer was in many respects critical of police behaviour is undoubtedly true. On the release of his report, *The Star* ran a headline, 'Report a devastating indictment of the police'. Helen Suzman called some of the revelations 'shocking'. These included:

- In banning the funerals, Captain Goosen had 'used Section 46 of the Act for a devious purpose', and the judge was critical of the contradictions in the banning of the funerals, and suggested that without the banning of the funerals there might have been no clash on Maduna Road.
- The change from normal riot control weaponry to the use of deadly ammunition was a 'tragic decision', yet he found nobody accountable for it ('accountability was difficult to discern'). He found that police attempts to minimise the effectiveness of tear gas as a means of crowd control were unpersuasive.
- Kannemeyer found that 'the fact that so many of the injuries came from the rear is disquieting' (an extraordinary use of the word). He found that Fouche's explanation, that after the front row 'had been shot down' the crowd continued to rush the police, and then 'scattered in all directions', was incorrect, or 'there must have been other officers firing from the back'. 'The conclusion must be reached that the majority of the shots fired by the crews of the two Casspirs were fired after the crowd had begun to disperse and run away.'
- Kannemeyer found that remarks made by the police at the square at the beginning of the day were 'particularly disturbing and provocative, and would have been likely to incite the crowd to retaliation and violence. They are the very types of remarks which members of a patrol whose duty it is to maintain law and order should refrain from making and show a serious lack of discipline … It must be accepted that these remarks were made at the square.'
- Kannemeyer further rejected the notion that the crowd had harboured any intention to attack the white community of Uitenhage. There was no evidence of organisation, and the composition of the crowd made it highly unlikely that an attack had been planned, he said.
- The judge also rejected the police's assertion that they had been under fire by sticks, stones and other missiles. He argued that not a single object that the crowd could have used as a projectile was found in either Casspir (Casspirs have no roofs) nor were there any

signs of debris that the crowd might have used as weapons close to the vehicles. Despite coming to this conclusion, he nevertheless had sympathy for the police, who were, to him, clearly in danger.

There were further items where the judge agreed with the police version of events, where in fact this version was as dubious as the positions taken by the police as noted above.

Of vital importance was the judge's conclusion that the crowd did in fact have two petrol bombs. He wrote: 'The evidence that the leader possessed a petrol bomb is also conclusive ... while no petrol bombs were thrown or set alight, it is clear that two were on the scene.'

This conclusion was arrived at from the apparently threatening brandishment by the Rastafarian of 'a bottle, with reddish contents' and secondly, from the discovery, amongst the debris on the site after the crowd had fled, of two broken bottlenecks, one a Fanta bottle and one a milk bottle, both stuffed with paper from the same issue of a newspaper. The police laboratory claimed that there were traces of petrol on these papers and one of them apparently had the Rastafarian's fingerprints on it.

All of this was questionable. The only analysis was from the police laboratory, which was hardly independent. Nowhere were the shards of broken bottles, or evidence of spilled petrol, found. That Rastafarians frequently smoke marijuana from bottlenecks was never considered. The learned judge reached an inappropriate conclusion about the existence of petrol bombs.

Another example of police conspiracy to fabricate evidence came from a dispute as to the existence of a 'boy on a bicycle'. We have inspected the police version of what preceded the shooting – a surging crowd, a warning shot, provocative behaviour and then the shooting. The community had a significantly different version. They claimed that a young boy, riding a bicycle, had come past their column. He had raised his fist in a black power salute as he approached the Casspirs, and, when he was abreast, the shooting started. He was the first victim, blasted backwards with a shot to the head. Every police witness denied this incident. Nothing of the sort had happened, they said.

The inventory of items collected by the police after the shooting contained one bag of stones, three bags of clothing, an umbrella, a piece of wood, an iron rod, and ... a bicycle.

Meanwhile a Mrs Bucwa requested help to bail out her son. He claimed to be the boy on the bicycle, and, when led as a witness to the commission, clearly identified the bicycle as his own. He had hospital records to show that he had been shot in the head but had, miraculously, survived. As all police

205

witnesses had provided the same lie, plainly they were being led and were fabricating evidence. This should have been enough for the judge to see the police submissions in a negative light. Regrettably, Judge Kannemeyer took a different route to his conclusions.

Similarly, there is more than enough evidence to suggest that the police were not pelted with rocks. As we have mentioned, the police inventory of the scene could only find one bag of stones. Police video footage revealed no stones either in the two Casspirs or on the tarmac around them. Police contentions included that every stone had ricocheted 30 paces and that God had miraculously intervened. The judge rejected the police version of a dramatic stone attack – and then accepted that some stones must have been thrown, 'as they often were in township unrest'. As Haysom has written, 'The chairman's explanation … is thin.'[210]

The commission's eventual conclusions included: 'The blame for the deaths of the persons killed in the incident, and for the injuries sustained by others, cannot be attributed to the error of judgment or the human frailty of one person.' Fouche, who gave the order to fire, could not be blamed for giving the order under the circumstances.

This is all eerily reminiscent of the inquests into the deaths of Mohapi, Botha and Biko. The line taken amounts to: 'The system failed, no individual can be held to account.' Plainly the communities of Langa and KwaNobuhle were not going to buy this. They had reached their own conclusions, even before the appointment of the Kannemeyer Commission.

The gruesome deaths of the Kinikini family

'As word of the Langa bloodbath spread, Langa and nearby KwaNobuhle exploded.'[211] On the night of the massacre, the homes of 13 black policemen living in KwaNobuhle and Langa were petrol-bombed and all the policemen living in these townships had to be evacuated immediately. For the next two days the town's black workforce, at rates of 97%, stayed away from work. Langa was in a state of siege, with policemen in every available vehicle mounting roadblocks at every available entrance. The security police banned all meetings in the two townships, warning residents not to assemble in groups of more than four. Despite this, KwaNobuhle was a scene of devastation. 'There was a veil of teargas over the town, houses are burning, helicopters are circling – it's a frightening atmosphere,' one witness told sociologist Martin Murray. Eighteen houses were burned down, the homes of those suspected of collaboration with the security or apartheid establishment. Shops that did not support the hastily organised stayaway were looted and burned. The KwaNobuhle beerhall, which belonged to a department of government, was torched.

'There is a particular type of anger reserved for those who are seen to have warmed their hands at the hearth of the enemy when their nation had been invaded,' Winston Churchill wrote many years earlier.

In KwaNobuhle, the most prominent of such people was Councillor Benjamin Kinikini.

Kinikini had become a wealthy man through business concessions, sometimes provided by the council of which he was now the sole remaining councillor. He was the representative of the council who had refused to hand over the keys to the community hall when a senior official had given permission for the Uitenhage Youth Congress to meet with other organisations to try to resolve the schools boycott. He and Jimmy Claasen spearheaded the vigilante group 'Peacemakers', which harassed UDF leaders (at the funeral of Leslie Kobese, for example), and his home was guarded by the police, while it was rumoured that his Peacemakers were giving information on the activities of the 'comrades' to the police. He told a reporter of the *EP Herald* that 'I will never be dictated to and intimidated by youth' when asked why he was the only councillor not to heed community calls to resign.[212] All of these were sins, certainly, but even in total they didn't remotely justify the terrible punishment he and his family were now to endure.

In the bloodbath and turbulence described above, wise counsel would have suggested to Jimmy Claasen and Benjamin Kinikini to go for cover or, at best, to get-the-hell-out-of-town. Whether they got such counsel or not we don't know. If they did, they didn't heed it. In fact they carried on as if nothing had happened. In the pre-dawn hours of 23 March, a group of Jimmy Claasen's Peacemakers, brandishing guns, abducted four youths from their KwaNobuhle homes. They took them to Kinikini's funeral parlour, known as 'The Barracks' on account of its strong security. There they were held in the coldroom with corpses, until they were taken off to the outskirts of KwaNobuhle and beaten horribly.

As word spread of their abduction, numbers of KwaNobuhle youths began assembling to consider responding. An alert policeman, Lieutenant Kritzinger, saw this and realised that trouble was imminent. He spoke to the group and convinced them to send two leaders with him to try to find the abducted youth. Their first call was 'The Barracks', which Kinikini allowed them to search. The youths were no longer there. They then heard that a police patrol had picked up the beaten youths and had taken them to a temporary police camp. When the leaders reported back to the growing crowd of young people that the four were in police custody, no answer could stop the flood of anger.

First the crowd surged up Mabandla Road and attacked and burned down Jimmy Claasen's supermarket. They rushed on to Kinikini's house. Fortunately the police were still strong enough to load Kinikini's wife, Joyce, and daughters, and whatever they could carry, into police vehicles and speed off out of KwaNobuhle. Looking back, Mrs Kinikini could see flames rising up, engulfing her home. Much worse was to follow.

The mob's third destination was 'The Barracks'. Here Benjamin Kinikini, his sons Stanley and Silumko, his nephews Eric and Qondile, and a relative, Zolisile Pram, were locked in, under siege. The building was torched. The fugitives attempted to escape through a window. They were surrounded. They begged for forgiveness, to no avail. It was demanded that Silumko surrender his gun. He refused. Their fate was sealed.

There are a number of eyewitness accounts of the horror that was to follow, and we will consider just two. Firstly, Kinikini's widow, Joyce, who, although not present at the fire, testified as follows at the Truth and Reconciliation Commission:

> About their deaths I did not witness it, I was told. I was told that he was stabbed by spade on his head, then they stabbed him several times. He was made to drink petrol, they put a tyre over him then they ignited him. During this time my younger son was hiding under the car, some of the petrol got to him and when he was trying to escape somebody saw him. Silumko was hiding in one of the shops at Mboya. He asked one of the businessmen to hide him under the counter, they took him and they ignited him alive in front of the shop. I am telling you as it is. They cut his testicles while he was still alive. Then on Monday at the police station [she was requested to identify the bodies], the doctor said he was going to inject me, at the time I had not seen them yet, when I got in, I will not be able to tell you about the head of my husband.[213]

The ever-present Mono Badela, reporting then for *City Press*, got a call that morning at his home in New Brighton: 'You must come ... things are bad ... come quickly.'[214]

He got to KwaNobuhle at about 10 am. He saw Claasen's supermarket burned down, and then Kinikini's home. He estimated the crowd at about 7 000 by then. He saw the Kinikini group being dragged from the funeral parlour. 'The angry crowd started hacking at their bodies with pangas, beating them with sticks, and then dragging them to the township's main road, Matanzima Street. Tyres were placed over what was left of their bodies, and they were roasted. People danced around the bodies of these people as they burned. To them, they were burning the symbols of oppression … For the next two days, police were unable to enter the township. It was a no-go area. All the police could do is hover around the area in a helicopter, powerless to act. It was a day to remember, the first necklace killings in South Africa.'

So ended one of the many terrible sequences of events of 1985.

The funerals

As a prelude to the burying of the Langa Massacre dead, on 24 March a crowd of about 35 000 attended the funeral of the recent victims of political unrest. The sociologist Martin Murray reported: 'Army and police threw a cordon around Uitenhage … troops and police stood guard impassively along the route of the funeral procession and at strategic points – including the entrances to residential areas and factory gates – in and around Uitenhage. As the crowd converged on KwaNobuhle, government troops made no effort to halt or disrupt it. In KwaNobuhle, the scene after three days of rioting resembled a war zone: streets were blackened by petrol bombs, barricades partially blocked main thoroughfares, and suspected allies of the white majority regime smouldered under a grey winter sky.'[215]

Three weeks later, on Saturday 13 April, about 70 000 people entered the KwaNobuhle stadium under similar conditions of police scrutiny to mourn the deaths of 28 people, the Langa Massacre dead and a few others. Very unstrategically, persons seen as followers of AZAPO and the National Forum were turned away, a gesture that was to inflame township rivalries further.

Local unionist Fikile Kobese chaired the proceedings, which were addressed by Dr Allan Boesak and Bishop Desmond Tutu.

Boesak laid the blame for the tragedy squarely on the doorstep of the government. He asked, 'What makes it possible for police to shoot people and then throw stones next to their bodies – what makes it possible for the police to lie and then hope someone else will be held accountable?'

Bishop Tutu reminded the crowd that the government always blamed unrest on agitation. 'We do not need agitators to tell us that ours is an inferior system of education. We do not need agitators to remind us that we live in ghettos while others live in affluent quarters. The greatest agitator in this country is apartheid.' He went on, weaving the Tutu magic, 'Let us not use the methods of the enemy because only the enemy rejoices when we set our opponents on fire … let us use methods that we will be proud of when we look back after attaining our liberation.'

Regretfully, the great Archbishop was not listened to. Just two weeks later, on the night of 28 April, Aubrey Fuleni, a Uitenhage police officer, was at home with his wife, Nokuzola, when a group of attackers broke in and shot and injured Mr Fuleni.

They were both dragged to a car and driven to a house in Soweto-on-Sea in Port Elizabeth.

Mrs Fuleni later described the horrible scene to the Truth and Reconciliation Commission:

'They took him out of the house. They had black plastics and five litres of petrol and some tyres … then I was made to watch him. I was made to look at him for the last time. During all this time I only had a night-dress on. I was told to stand outside and look as this dog was dying. Then I asked them to burn him with me because I could not endure to listen to his cries. They said that the petrol that they had was only for him. They were going to burn me up tomorrow. They made him drink petrol and he was also crying that he must be burnt with me … They burnt him right in front of me until he died.'[216]

The Langa massacre in perspective

Derek Catsam believes that the Langa Massacre was a catalyst for some of the most tumultuous years in South African history. 'More than perhaps any single event the Langa Massacre set the stage for the tensions of the years from 1985 to 1987 … The Langa Massacre gave the protests their greatest resonance both within the country and on the international stage.' He further argues that the Langa Massacre taught the securocrats in Pretoria that frontal confrontation should no longer be their tactic of choice. The state then 'began stepping up its already extensive reliance upon covert operations by what became known as the "Third Force" and its colleagues in Vlakplaas, Koevoet, the "Hammer Unit" and in other official and quasi-official arms of the security forces … This reliance on terror and lack of accountability that characterised covert operations would in turn be the defining model for a state-imposed reign of terror that would last for nearly a decade after the shots were first fired from police vehicles at Langa on the morning of 21 March 1985.'

How right this was can be seen from events that Port Elizabeth had experienced two days before the Langa Massacre. On this occasion, covert operations had been stepped up to a new level. On 19 March, four petrol bombs were thrown at the home of PEBCO's Sipho Hashe and another one was thrown at Ernest Malgas' home. Then, on 21 March, another was thrown at the home of Ndabuzo Vuyo Mkhalipi, who worked for the South African Council of Churches. The AZAPO–UDF clashes had begun, with all their well-hidden tentacles reaching back into the security establishment.

1_7

The AZAPO–UDF clashes

A
ZAPO was, in 1985, the most prominent organisation in the Black Consciousness movement.

From the inception of the Black Consciousness movement, the relationship between Black Consciousness and the white community, particularly liberal, sympathetic whites, as well as the coloured and Indian communities was fraught with difficulties. The hardline Black Consciousness adherents rejected alliances with white and other groupings, while the non-racial adherents favoured such arrangements. These tensions endured within the ANC until, in 1955, the ANC adopted the Freedom Charter, which clearly announced that South Africa 'belongs to all who live in it, black and white', and the break between the group promoting the non-racial approach and the unchanging black nationalists became inevitable. In 1959 Robert Sobukwe and his black nationalist grouping broke from the ANC to form the PAC. African nationalism had a new home, away from the ANC.

The fate of the PAC we have already covered. As a source of social and political upheaval, it had a very short life, but as a source of intellectual underpinning for the struggle against apartheid, African nationalism continued, this time in the form of the soon-to-emerge Black Consciousness movement.

The impact of South Africa's Black Consciousness movement is not the topic of this book, save to note that it was undoubtedly one of the underpinning issues of the 1976 uprising in Soweto. Thereafter, as we have written, Biko was apprehended at a roadblock near Grahamstown while obviously breaking his banning order. He was handed to Port Elizabeth's security police and murdered. He died on 12 September 1977. A month later, on 19 October 1977, all 17 Black Consciousness organisations that he had conceived of, birthed and nourished were banned, as was *The World* newspaper.

It is possible to ban an organisation, but much more difficult to prevent the ideas that caused its creation from continuing to spread and again be concretised. Six months after the banning of the Black Consciousness organisations, on 28 April 1978 the Azanian People's Organisation (AZAPO) was formed. It in turn had its inaugural conference in September 1979 and elected a national executive with Curtis Nkondo as its first president. Black Consciousness again had a standard-bearer in South Africa.

The first opening for AZAPO in the Eastern Cape was the opportunity to speak at Robert Sobukwe's funeral in 1978. Thereafter AZAPO arrived in the Eastern Cape in 1981, according to Rev. Maqina. In 1983 Mbu Dukumbana became Eastern Cape chairperson, operating from the BAWUSA trade union in Alfin House in Port Elizabeth. (Dukumbana was one of the KwaZakhele High School matric class of 1976 who were bundled off to Robben Island for five years.) They co-existed with the emerging UDF organisations until 1985, when troubles began.

Nationally, tensions between the UDF and AZAPO broke out at the beginning of January 1985, when Edward Kennedy, US Senator from Massachusetts and a brother of the assassinated duo John and Robert Kennedy, visited South Africa.

Kennedy was invited to South Africa by Desmond Tutu, who had been awarded the Nobel Peace Prize in 1984, and Allan Boesak. While Kennedy's invitation was not a UDF project, plainly Tutu and Boesak had UDF pedigree. His visit was to gather information and, for him, to highlight to the world the harshness of apartheid. Plainly this worked, for the next year Kennedy was part of the ushering through Congress of the Comprehensive Anti-Apartheid Act, the toughest set of sanctions yet imposed on South Africa. President Reagan vetoed the Act, but Congress overruled his veto and it became law in the USA.

AZAPO went in another direction. Presenting Kennedy as an 'agent of international capitalism', they dogged his eight-day visit with protests and disruptions. When he arrived at Jan Smuts Airport, 40 AZAPO protesters harassed him. When he was introduced to a housewife in Soweto, she told the press that she had been scared to see him, as 'others will follow him'. Everywhere he had to be protected and his meetings were disrupted. The UDF was not amused.

Shortly after these events, and the souring of relations that went with them, AZAPO in Port Elizabeth came out against COSAS's schools boycott. Then they opposed the Black Weekend that preceded the Langa Massacre. This caused the infuriated comrades to turn AZAPO followers away from the massacre funeral and feelings were dangerously inflamed. Earlier, there had been the petrol bomb attacks on the homes of Hashe, Malgas and Mkhalipi. The townships were on the edge of a war.

While the formal elected structures of AZAPO told one story, in 1985 the power in AZAPO was in the hands of the Reverend Mzwandile Ebenezer Maqina.

Maqina was born in Aberdeen, Eastern Cape, on 2 October 1937. Both of his parents were schoolteachers and at the age of two he and his parents moved to Port Elizabeth. He was schooled in New Brighton and Keiskammahoek and eventually at Lovedale, where he did a teachers' course.

He studied to become a minister of religion as a member of the Anglican Church. He soon became dissatisfied with mission church work and left to join the independent churches. 'We emphasise the need to look at our own religion, which is not necessarily Christianity. It is the religion of the people of Africa. We won't exclude Christianity – I was born Christian – but we are aware of the dichotomy. The system wants you to have Christian names, go to Christian churches. I am somebody searching for religion for my people. I am not shutting out Christianity. Christ has a role in Africa. I minister, but not in a Christian way. Rather experimentally, in a searching way. Some Christians would not approve of us – but we are looking at ourselves.'

In the 1970s Maqina became a leader in the African Independent Churches Association, which had a membership of 480 churches. This association decided with other community-based organisations to form an over-arching cultural organisation and met in Pietermaritzburg to do this. Maqina describes this meeting as having been 'hijacked by the SASO people'. SASO wanted a political organisation and Maqina found their ideas 'quite refreshing'. Thus the Black People's Convention (BPC) began, as did the friendship between Maqina and SASO's Steve Biko.

Biko and the BPC needed offices. Maqina had rented a floor of offices in Alice, some of which were then sublet to the BPC. He encouraged the students at the independent churches' seminary to join SASO. Against Biko's advice, Maqina led his churches out of the Christian Institute, which Maqina saw as a 'white' movement. Biko, despite being 'very much for black power', nevertheless felt that the time for the break was not right as the black organisations were struggling for money.

Then came 1976, the Soweto uprising, the murder of Biko and the banning of the 17 Black Consciousness organisations. Maqina was not spared. In 1974 he had written and performed three 'protest and socio-political plays'. Now they were banned. In 1977 came a bigger sanction – he was banned for five years, effectively put under house arrest in his home in Grattan Street, New Brighton, until 1983. During this time he established the Roots Cultural Group. He was repeatedly requested by the newly formed AZAPO to assist with the establishment of an AZAPO branch in Port Elizabeth. Initially he resisted as he was banned. Later he helped through Roots. 'The Roots Cultural Group initiated the establishment of a branch in PE and of course I was the founder of this group ... (thus) I was looked upon as the founder of AZAPO in the Eastern Cape.'

In 1984, with his banning behind him, Maqina somehow got involved with the Education Crisis Committee (ECC) and began attending their meetings. He resisted the 'tendency' to call the ECC a UDF affiliate. Then late in 1984 'the students decided to boycott classes ... We stood firmly against it. But all the UDF affiliates were encouraging the students. The conflict then started [in Port Elizabeth].'

Matters intensified when AZAPO in Uitenhage refused to support March's Black Weekend, which led to the Langa massacre. As we have noted, known AZAPO activists were barred from the funeral of the massacre victims.

Then came a funeral of a youth associated with AZAPO, Patata Kani, on 6 April 1985. At this funeral Maqina said that his life had been threatened by a COSAS youth. This was, he later said, the beginning of the war that was to engulf the UDF and AZAPO.

At this time – between the Langa massacre (21 March) and the funeral of its victims (13 April) – tensions were extremely high in and around the townships of Port Elizabeth and Uitenhage. On 29 April the Deputy Minister of Foreign Affairs, Louis Nel, made the first public attempt to tie UDF's activity to the ANC and, of course, the SACP. He claimed that there was 'incontrovertible evidence of an orchestrated attempt by forces from beyond our border, joined by radical elements inside the country, to make the country ungovernable and to bring about a revolutionary situation'. Two days later, on 1 April, the Deputy Minister of Law and Order confirmed that, also for the first time, 'the South African Defence Force is in South African townships.'

'Senior members of the UDF advised all leaders to be extra cautious as the Black Weekend approached,' wrote Khusta Jack in his autobiography.

The hunt was on for the UDF leadership ... In the early hours of 19 March the police petrol-bombed the house of Sipho Hashe, the

ex-Robben Islander and a PEBCO leader. The same day a petrol
bomb was also tossed at the home of Boy Mkhalipi, one of the former
KwaZakhele High Robben Islanders ... When my comrades' homes
were petrol bombed, I jumped walls and fences to make my way back
to my uncle's home in Zwide, where I was staying at the time... I
was told that my uncle Ndumiso Mpendu had not been seen since
being 'fetched' on the Saturday afternoon of the Black Weekend by
unknown men aligned to Thamsanqa Linda, the puppet leader and
so-called Mayor of Ibhayi... On Wednesday 20 March I heard the
sad news of the death of our senior comrade, Sthembele Xhathasi.
The news of his death and the manner in which he had been killed by
state vigilantes shocked me... [Jack decided to search for his uncle]...
accompanied by family members, I set out to go to all the police
stations to check whether my uncle had been detained ... a policeman
advised us to go to the mortuary, saying that many 'trouble-makers'
had been killed that weekend... The mortuary was the ugliest sight I
ever had to contend with. Mortuary staff pulled out trays of mutilated,
bloodied and bullet-riddled bodies. Every corpse had a number and
a tag with the words 'swart man', and 'onbekend'. Some of the trays
were stacked with three corpses, one on top of the other. After looking
at ten bodies we found my uncle. His body was in the same state as all
the other victims, riddled with more than fifteen bullet wounds. We
left the mortuary with broken hearts.[217]

On 27 April, just two weeks after the funeral of the victims of the Langa
massacre, 35 000 mourners attended the funeral in Zwide in what was called
in the *Rand Daily Mail* 'the largest funeral in Port Elizabeth's memory'.
Fifteen victims of vigilante and police killings, including Khusta's uncle,
were buried. The coffins were draped with ANC flags. After the funeral
there were the inevitable clashes with the police.[218]

The hideous rhythm of funeral, clash with police, shootings, followed by
another funeral, was now in place, to be repeated time and again. Another
funeral, this time for four youths, killed in unrest, was held in the same
cemetery the next weekend.

The cycles of unrest and violence were now becoming uncontrollable.
Youngsters were more and more to the fore, attacking police, councillors
and anyone thought to be an impimpi. Police response became less and
less controlled.

In such a context the exertion of leadership, control and discipline was
next to impossible: as the UDF's secretarial report conceded at the national

conference on 5 April: 'In many areas the organisation trails behind the masses thus making it more difficult for a disciplined mass action to take place. More often there is a spontaneity of action in the townships.'

Three days after the funeral of the 15, on 30 April, an attack was made on the home of Ivy Gcina, the president of PEWO. Mrs Gcina says that Mr Nguna, Mr Klaas and Mr Majongosi, all AZAPO leaders known to her, entered her home, to be repulsed by the youth guard that had volunteered to guard her home (and the homes of all other UDF leaders). Rev. Mzwandile Maqina, also known to Mrs Gcina, appeared and fired shots into the ground. She confronted him, and she, together with her daughter and the youth guard, eventually expelled them from her property.

The next day, 1 May, the *EP Herald* reported that 'A simmering confrontation between affiliates of the UDF and AZAPO in Port Elizabeth has broken into the open'. That night the home of Edgar Ngoyi, the regional chair of the UDF, was petrol-bombed. His front door was hacked, so he pushed a couch against it to keep it closed. He was hit on the head with an iron rod. Three petrol bombs didn't penetrate the fine-mesh burglar proofing on his windows, he said.

Two days later, in Maqina's words, 'Op 3 May 1985 het alle hel losgebars op Njoli Plein, waar UDF, and AZAPO mekaar aanhoudend aangeval het'. That day 100 AZAPO youth moved into Maqina's home in Grattan Street, New Brighton. Maqina estimates that there were possibly 200 AZAPO youths in Port Elizabeth at that stage, the majority of whom sought the protection of his home.

The next night, 4 May, the home of UDF leader Henry Fazzie was attacked. His front door was hacked and petrol bombs exploded on his premises. His daughter saw Maqina amongst the attackers.

That same night, Mono Badela, the local reporter for *City Press* and the sports administrator who had encouraged the Watson brothers to play their rugby in the townships, was at home.[219]

I was asleep expecting nothing when I heard some bricks coming through the windows and banging on the door. They were AZAPO people … my daughter was on the executive of COSAS, and I thought they were coming for her. But no, they wanted me. I was taken from the house and put on an open truck and taken to their headquarters and beaten up. They used knives, so my head was full of wounds. I was told to tell the UDF leaders that they must stop misusing AZAPO. Apparently one of the trade union leaders had attacked AZAPO at the funeral. I was also given a month to resign from *City Press*, which they reckoned was a UDF publication.

I was nearly necklaced, you know. I was put in a small truck. There was a tyre there ... but they fought amongst themselves. They couldn't agree. The AZAPO chairman said no, we didn't take this guy to kill him. We had a specific reason for abducting him, he said: to tell the UDF to stop fighting AZAPO. The Rev Maqina and a group of them said I must be killed. Maqina said after I had been interrogated I should be taken to the truck.

I could hear that there were some differences amongst them. The chairman of AZAPO said: 'Come inside.' There I found three youths with white sheets over them. The AZAPO people said that these youths had tried to attack Maqina's house and had been caught. They said they were sent by me. Around five o'clock in the morning they put me in a small truck. Two people guarded met. There was a tyre at my back. They argued over me for about an hour until the group that said I must not be killed won the day. It was daylight and people were already going to work. It was difficult for them to kill me now as it was daytime. They took me back inside and beat me up again. Then they said 'Okay, we are taking you home'. They drove me to a certain spot and said I must walk home ... My family had taken me for dead. Then the feud spread. It became furious ... Fazzie's house was totally destroyed ... every time people went to Maqina's home to attack it, it was well protected. There were three army hippos standing there. You couldn't get close. That's how this black-on-black violence was.

Badela refused to resign from *City Press* so they came back to his house, almost exactly a month later, on 5 June. Again he was assaulted and this time his house was gutted. 'It was only my car that was left. Fortunately I had parked it on the opposite side of the street ... So we used the car and went to the home of the Watson brothers. We spent two nights there before leaving for Johannesburg,' and years away from Port Elizabeth.

18

Trojan horses and assassinations

While this crude and murderous thuggery was being effected by non-police vigilantes, the security establishment had other plans underway. Their first plan was novel, the first South African adaptation of the 'Trojan horse' assassination exercise, and the second was the return of the death squads. We will consider each in turn.

On 18 April 1985, the Truth and Reconciliation Commission later reported: 'A municipal truck loaded with branches drove past the Nomathamsanqa Higher Primary School in Despatch (then a separate village between Port Elizabeth and Uitenhage). Scholars were on boycott at the time and were playing games in the streets. The truck was stopped by youth in the streets. The driver got out and fired a gun into the air, at which police officers emerged from under the branches and opened fire on the group of youths, hitting six people. Four later died…'[220]

Two weeks later, on 2 May, another Trojan horse ambush led to killings, this time in Mabandla Street, KwaNobuhle. Seventeen-year-old COSAS activist Khayalethu Swartbooi was killed. His mother told the TRC:

On 2 May a hippo (police troop carrier) had collided on Mabandla Street, Uitenhage at about 11h00, damaging a door. Khaya and another comrade left to go and see this accident. While travelling up Mabandla Street, a municipal truck loaded with cardboard boxes passed by. Police came out of hiding under the boxes and shot Khaya who fell. The truck stopped and they picked Khaya up and put stones in his hands and put him in a plastic bag and loaded the bag before they drove off.

The TRC report notes that: 'The so-called 'Trojan Horse incident that took place in Athlone, Cape Town, on 15 October 1985 is well-known ... three youths were killed. Similar tactics were tried in the Eastern Cape twice before the Cape Town incident...'

Death squads reappear

The second escalation, the return of the death squads, marked a clear and determined attempt by the state to bring the unrest under control at any cost.

PEBCO, like all institutions, required fundraising efforts if it was to meet its financial obligations. The PEBCO leadership approached the British Embassy, amongst others, for grant funding. On 7 May Sipho Hashe received a phone call at his home. A man with an English accent stated that he was from the British Embassy, and requested that a PEBCO delegation meet him at the Port Elizabeth airport on the next evening, as he had a cash donation from the embassy for PEBCO.

The PEBCO executive conferred. Given the importance of both the donation and relationships with the British Embassy, PEBCO decided to send a significant delegation. Henry Fazzie, the vice-president, had another appointment. So it was agreed that Qaqawuli Godolozi, the PEBCO president, Sipho Hashe, the secretary, and Champion Galela, the organising secretary, would meet the embassy official.

They set off for the airport on the evening of 8 May. Thereafter nothing was heard from them. They disappeared. No, the embassy had not sent anyone to Port Elizabeth. Airport baggage handlers felt that they might have seen them, but it was not conclusive.

Twice the families approached the Supreme Court to have the police produce them. Nothing. A security policeman is said to have shown a Cradock detainee a hand in a bottle, and said it was Galela's. But nothing could be proved, no evidence could be found. Often security police told detainees that, if they did not cooperate, they would go the way of the 'PEBCO Three'. Always later denied.

It took twelve and a half years for the truth, or rather for three versions of the truth, about the PEBCO Three to come out. With the struggle over, democracy having come, the Truth and Reconciliation Commission was instituted and begun its work – only then did the appalling and cruel facts of the end of the PEBCO Three emerge.

On 11 November 1997, while applying for amnesty at the TRC for various murders, Gideon Nieuwoudt finally began the truth-telling. [221] He was joined in his amnesty application for the murder of the PEBCO Three by four other security policemen – Herman du Plessis, Harold Snyman, Sakkie van Zyl, and Gerhardus Lotz – and two askaris from Vlakplaas, the security police's assassination centre near Pretoria, Peter Mogoai and Johannes Koole, and a white security policeman also from Vlakplaas, Gerhardus Beeslaar. Another askari, Joe Mamasela, was also involved but he refused to apply for amnesty, although he gave lurid testimony.

Firstly, the uncontested facts in these applications.

Nieuwoudt had organised a paid police informant to pose as the official from the British Embassy and phone Hashe and ask him to bring a senior team from PEBCO to the airport on 8 May. This having been organised, Vlakplaas was brought in and a team of three askaris was brought down. As Van Zyl testified: 'We decided to make use of the askaris. Captain Venter was in charge of the askaris, because they weren't known in the area, and because their vehicle wasn't known, that they should carry out the abduction and that would then mean that no member of the security branch would be implicated in the abduction.'

When the PEBCO team arrived at the airport, they were abducted in their car at the carpark by the askaris, who were quickly joined by the white security police.

They were handcuffed and manacled and driven to a disused police station called 'Post Chalmers' (the building has a large and gaudy sign on it, 'Post Chalmers Holiday Farm') near Cradock. Here they were held and interrogated and eventually murdered.

All this is agreed between the applicants for amnesty. That is all that was agreed. For there are now three different submissions as to how the PEBCO team was treated at Post Chalmers. These are:

Gideon Nieuwoudt, with the other white security policemen concurring, submitted that the three detainees were housed in a garage, and were taken out, one by one. Van Zyl had a .22 pistol, and Hashe was brought out first. Van Zyl shot and killed him. Then it was Godolozi's turn. The pistol was passed to Nieuwoudt, and he shot and killed Godolozi. Then Galela. This time Lotz pulled the trigger, and he was killed. At no stage were the PEBCO Three tortured or even interrogated, Nieuwoudt said in his testimony, which was affirmed by his security police team.

Then a large pyre was set up, and it was soaked in diesel. The bodies were put on top of the pyre, they in turn were soaked in diesel, and the pyre was set alight by Nieuwoudt. This all was 'totaal uitgebrandt', over six to eight hours.

Van Zyl gave Nieuwoudt instructions to destroy all evidence and the next morning Nieuwoudt scraped together all the ash, put it into a black bag, and took it to the Fish River 'just before Cradock', and emptied the bag into the river. Thereafter he drove back to Port Elizabeth.

The two black askaris, Mogoai and Koole, told a different story, a story containing gruesome details of assault and torture.

Hashe was interrogated first. He obviously understood that he was to be killed, and told his interrogators to kill him as he had nothing to tell them. He was then dreadfully beaten, with fists and kicking, by all of the interrogating party. Still he was uncooperative. He was returned to the garage, to again be interrogated the next morning, when he was brought outside 'onto the stoep'. Again he was brutalised, 'only worse'. He pleaded, 'Please stop, I'll lead you to some AK47s.' He said that they were hidden at his sister's house, and he would take them there.

The assault paused. He was left alone with Koole. He told Koole that he had lied, there were no guns, he was just trying to stop the beatings. That proved to be a terrible mistake. The 'white people' then 'rushed at him with violence'. They were 'really emotional'. Everybody kicked him until he fainted. When he regained consciousness he was taken back to the garage and again tied up. His interrogators had been 'really angry, really frightening'.

Then Godolozi was fetched and brought to 'the stoep'. He was handcuffed, and his face was covered. He screamed, 'I will tell you nothing.' They then covered his head with a bag and tightened it at the neck. He was suffocated. The bag was removed. 'Now talk.' 'No, there is nothing I will say. Kill me.' They were now 'more angry'. He was taken to the garage, the door was closed. Koole recalls a piercing scream …

And so it went on. Beatings, kicking, suffocation, finally death. They were, according to Koole and Mogoai, eventually shot. And the story of the pyre is agreed.

Joe Mamasela had another story to tell. Similar to the above but, if it is possible to imagine, worse.

Mamasela is a self-confessed multi-murderer. He had been part of Vlakplaas teams that had killed Griffiths Mxenge and '30 to 35' others including the Mamelodi 10, a group of youngsters he convinced to join the ANC. When they agreed, he and colleagues murdered all 10 of them. He is still a free man.

Mamasela confirms most of what Mogoai and Koole had submitted, but with some lurid additions. Hashe had promised to find some guns, and had later admitted they didn't exist. Then Koole, described by Mamasela as a 'vicious bull terrier', jumped on Hashe's chest, knees first, and strangled him to death.

Godolozi tried to tell his captors that he worked for the National Intelligence Service, Mamasela said. This saved him for 24 hours and he had to sleep alongside the bodies of his PEBCO colleagues. The next morning a man in a smart suit arrived, who 'looked like a gentleman'. He was apparently from NIS, and said that Godolozi had provided them with no worthwhile information. Godolozi was then beaten to death.

If it is imaginable, the torture inflicted on Galela was even worse. He endured a prolonged beating with a stick and steel pipe, alongside the kicking and punching. At one stage Beeslaar squeezed his testicles 'until they were the size of golf balls', and then punched them with his fist. 'This was the most brutal thing I've ever witnessed. It was a dehumanising experience.' Galela died from his injuries.

In 1999 the TRC came to its conclusions on all of this. All of the security policemen and the askari Koole were refused amnesty, for many reasons, but certainly including their lack of willingness to admit the assaults, which plainly the TRC believed did happen. Ironically, Harold Snyman was granted amnesty, but he had died. Mogoai was also granted amnesty.

A few years later (2007) the National Prosecuting Authority's Missing Persons Task Team did excavations and inspections at Post Chalmers. They found 'a large quantity of burnt human bone fragments' in the septic tank. They concluded that 'indications are that the burnt remains were thrown into the septic tank and not the Fish River'. The security police's story had obviously again been sanitised, and these grotesque details removed.

So this dreadful business was driven to a conclusion, however appalling. This was 14 years from 1985, a period that must have seemed an eternity to the families and to the victims' surviving comrades in PEBCO. Incredibly, on 8 May 1985, the night the PEBCO Three were abducted, Sipho Hashe's house, occupied by his wife Elizabeth, was attacked. And, about a month later, on 3 June, a petrol bomb was thrown at Godolozi's house. His wife believed she saw Maqina in the crowd. Plainly, information got just so far in the system.

19

More AZAPO–UDF violence

Things were now moving very fast. The battle between the uprising and the state's counterinsurgency was coming to a head.

Two days after the PEBCO Three were abducted, on 10 May, Khusta Jack got many phone calls at work. There was a standoff at Grattan Street, alongside Maqina's house. Four young comrades had been abducted by the large group of AZAPO youth living at Maqina's house and were being held in this house. About 2 000 young comrades had assembled nearby, determined to free them. 'The problem was that getting to the Reverend's house was rendered impossible by a large barricade of SADF soldiers plus regular cops and railway police... State helicopters chopped the air loudly and menacingly above...,' Khusta wrote in his autobiography.[222] The security forces had drawn a line in the road. Any comrade to cross it would be shot.

Khusta got there at 4:30 pm, and spent the next six and a half hours negotiating between the comrades and the security forces. Eventually at 11 pm Khusta and three comrades accepted an 'enemy escort' to enter the house and negotiate the release of the four hostages.

He got inside and had to negotiate with Maqina, who said that the four had been sent to blow up his house on the instructions of Mono Badela. The four told a different story. They had not received any instructions, but had attacked the house because 'people who had attacked the homes of UDF leaders had beaten a hasty retreat to his [Maqina's] house.

Three of the four were released to Khusta and the fourth to the child's

225

parents. Khusta had saved the day, and in the process provided his enemies with the opportunity to describe him as 'too soft'.

At this point the ministers of religion from the townships stepped in. Co-ordinated by the highly respected Rev. De Villiers Soga, the next day (11 May) a meeting was held between Khusta Jack and Maqina, under the supervision of members of the Interdenominational Ministers' Association, including Rev. Soga and Rev. Mvume Dandala. It was agreed that UDF and AZAPO supporters would not engage in violent attacks on each other.

Three days later an AZAPO youth was apprehended with a petrol bomb at Ivy Gcina's house. He told her he was sent by Maqina. Five days later UDF executive Sicelo Apleni was shot in his hand – his assailant escaped.

Plainly the peace plans were on the edge of collapse just days after agreement. Rev. Soga, desperate to keep them on track, invited all parties, including Maqina and AZAPO, to an interdenominational prayer service at the massive open-air Dan Qeqe Stadium in Zwide at the end of May.

It was a disaster. The crowd turned on Maqina, who just escaped with his life. 'The Dan Qeqe Stadium was packed to capacity. The vast majority of people wanted to see an end to the conflict, while a small but very vociferous and determined minority wanted to annihilate AZAPO members,' wrote Khusta.

The local chairperson of AZAPO, Mbuzeli Dukumbana (the KwaZakhele High School matric pupil who had been sent to Robben Island for five years in 1977), was abducted by these vociferous comrades but was fortunately later freed. Maqina claimed that this prayer meeting was a trick and the UDF executive was deeply embarrassed.

Three days later (3 June) a petrol bomb was thrown at Godolozi's home, despite the fact that he had disappeared nearly a month earlier. Two days later the attack on Mono Badela's house happened, which saw it gutted and Badela and his family leave for Johannesburg.

Two days after this (7 June) the President of the UDF, Edgar Ngoyi, had his house burned to the ground in a petrol-bomb attack. Maqina said that he was 'investigating the incident' and warned the UDF to halt attacks on AZAPO homes.

The next day (8 June) a further tragedy occurred. Phakamisa Nogwaza, a 24-year-old, was brought by his mother to Ngoyi's wrecked house to deny his involvement in AZAPO and to obtain Ngoyi's blessing. While they were conversing Ngoyi, whose telephone had been destroyed in his burnt house, was called down the road to take a call. In his absence the young guard at his house murdered Nogwaza, having accused him of the burning of Ngoyi's house.[223]

This horror had a further disastrous outcome, for Ngoyi, his wife and seven others were arrested for murder. This allowed the state to keep Ngoyi in custody until the end of 1985, thereby denying the UDF the leadership of their president at this vital and gruesome time.

The complexity of the relationships between violence, township youth and the UDF is brought out in the trial record of this tragic event.

Two days after the murder, one of the accused, Lulamile Cyril Mkalipi, made the following statement to the police. He subsequently claimed that he was assaulted and had made the statement under duress. After a trial-within-a-trial, his statement was found to be admissible:

On Friday night, the evening before the death of Phakamisa Nogwaza, I was at the house of Edgar Ngoyi who is also known as Pres. We call him Pres because he is the President of the UDF of the Eastern Cape. We were singing freedom songs. This was between 19h00 and 20h00. There were many of us at the house. It was already dark. There were some other comrades in the street in front of Pres's house. I heard a noise out on the street. I heard some people shout 'catch him!' A lot of us then ran out into the street and I saw a lot of other comrades running after someone. I saw that they were chasing someone into a house owned by a man I know as 'Peti'. At this point I realized that it was Peti they were after. At first I did not know who they were chasing. We also joined the first group at Peti's house. The comrades searched Peti's house, but could not find him. I stood in the street, while the search was conducted. There were already a lot of comrades in the house, searching and I did not even attempt to go inside.

Peti was not found, so we all returned to Pres's house.

Who are the comrades?

The comrades I refer to are young people, who are predominantly members of the organisations COSAS and PEYCO.

What is PEYCO?

Port Elizabeth Youth Congress. These organisations all fall under the UDF. I am a member of COSAS. We are all known in the townships as the comrades.

On our return to Pres's house, we continued to sing our freedom songs. Throughout the night, we sang freedom songs, until early the next morning, the Saturday.

At about 6h00 or 7h00, I went home to have breakfast. While at home I heard a shout outside. We all ran out of the house to see what was going on outside. I could hear the shouting coming from up the street. I saw a lot of people in the street. The person who was crying

227

was Sindiswa. At this point the people came out of the houses all around us. The crowd up the street threw stones at us and told us not to watch them. I dodged the stones. I went into Kindile's yard and watched what was happening.

I saw that the people were attacking a man, I know as Peti, Phakamisa Nogwaza. I saw that he was full of blood. I saw him fall. The people who were attacking him were the comrades. The same people who were at Ngoyi's house the previous evening. Of the people I saw attacking the deceased, I recognised the following:

Walk-Tall, I don't know his real name. He was hitting the deceased with some kind of object.

Mtutu, he had a sword. He was hitting the deceased with the sword.

Lunga Petros, he had a sword. He was hitting the deceased with this sword.

Break-Dance, also known as Boy-Boy, surname unknown. He had a small knife. He was stabbing the deceased.

Xolisile, the one who I was arrested with, who was also there. I could not see what he had in his hand. He did however have an object in his hand. I saw him hitting the deceased.

There were others as well who took part in assaulting the deceased, whom I know, but I cannot put a name to. I only know them by sight.

At this point it became obvious that the deceased would not be getting up again. The comrades then left. We also went into one house and I had breakfast.

After a while I came outside and saw that the police had arrived. I then saw that a tyre had been placed on the deceased.

The reason why they killed Peti was because they suspected him of being a member of AZAPO. This was also the reason the comrades had chased him the previous evening as well.

I am one of the leaders of the comrades. I normally give instructions to the comrades at Ngoyi's house, who do ground duty there. The comrades themselves appointed me as their leader. The comrades carry out all my instructions. The comrades have special times when to meet at Ngoyi's place. Then they gather there. Should there be a reason for them to meet, besides at the appointed times, I normally get them together by blowing a whistle. When this happens, they gather at Ngoyi's place.

The picture created in this statement is one of an amorphous group of uncontrolled and uncontrollable youngsters, whose leader did not know the names of his 'followers', and they in turn did not acknowledge the authority of his leadership. Their loyalty to the UDF leadership appeared to be total, and the leader of the group claimed to be a member of a UDF affiliate. Their politics appeared to be the politics of freedom songs and slogans. The overwhelming tensions of the time had turned them into a group that could immediately bypass the UDF's code of non-violence. Township conditions of siege, warfare and alienation obviously required strong organisational cement to contain outbursts of violence.

Ngoyi was charged, with eight others, for this murder. This, with the wisdom of hindsight, was obviously the police seizing an opportunity to incarcerate a UDF leader and 'dirty-up' his name, which state of emergency detention did not provide.

He was nevertheless not convicted as he was obviously not involved in the murder. He willingly made a statement to the police about the event. Henry Fazzie, another UDF leader, willingly became a state witness. Neither of their evidence implicated anyone, as neither party had been a witness to the crime. Both claimed to be deeply shocked and saddened by the event.

The pattern of tit-for-tat petrol bombings nevertheless continued. On 12 June the South African Council of Churches executive, Mkhalipi, had his home petrol-bombed. That night two AZAPO members' homes suffered the same fate. Four days later (16 June) Zamile Mazantsana, an Umkhonto guerrilla, hurled two hand grenades, one at Maqina's home, one at his car. Maqina survived.

Two days later (18 June) the UDF's Ernest Malgas' home was petrol-bombed. He had a large youth guard, many of whom were burned. This was the third attack in a few weeks on Malgas' home, and this time the consequences were tragic. His son, the object of his loving letter on his earlier incarceration, was burned to death.

Another petrol-bomb attack occurred on that night, this time on MACWUSA's Themba Duze's house, but fortunately it had no tragic consequences.

According to the report of the Truth and Reconciliation Commission, by the end of July, 80 to 90 homes of UDF members had been burnt down, and 55 houses belonging to AZAPO members. This all had happened in four months.

20

The Port Elizabeth consumer boycott

A midst all of this horror, with three colleagues missing and assumed murdered; the UDF President in custody on unconvincing charges; UDF leaders' homes, families and their persons continually under threat of murderous assault; all of which could be expected from any or all of the vigilantes attached to the local Black Council (as happened to Khusta's uncle); AZAPO youth left unchallenged, even sponsored, by the police (as happened to the homes of Ngoyi, Fazzie, Hashe, Malgas, Gcina ond others); by the traditional police (as had happened to Ngoyi); and, of course, by the most ruthless of all, that new combination of security police and Vlakplaas death teams (the fate of Mthimkhulu, Godolozi, Hashe, Galela): amid all of this chaos, mayhem and murder, the UDF executive in Port Elizabeth put together plans for a civil disobedience strategy that was to go down as one of the masterstrokes of non-violent rebellion in human history – the Port Elizabeth Consumer Boycott.[224]

This boycott, which was the refusal by the black/African community to shop in 'white' shops, possibly had its beginnings in the few first meetings between PEBCO (a delegation headed by Godolozi, Hashe and Galela) and the Port Elizabeth Chamber of Commerce around the time of the Black Weekend and its one-day stayaway (16-18 March). These unminuted meetings, clearly requested by business leaders to head off continual work stayaways, could well have planted the seeds of an idea in the PEBCO team – the business community was willing to negotiate. How far they would go nobody could

231

tell, but economic pressure could secure negotiations around political issues.

Then there was the Port Alfred boycott, started in May 1985. Nineteen youths had been taken into custody after a township funeral turned violent. The Port Alfred Civic Association called the boycott, stapling a number of social and political issues onto the demand for the release of the youth. Immediately the boycott bit, negotiations began, resulting (in August) in the business community supporting the idea of a single, non-racial municipality for Port Alfred.

Such were the precursors – now came the push. 'The idea of the boycott originated in a group of amazing women in KwaZakhele. They came up with a plan to withhold their buying power in order to draw the attention of white people to the hardships that ordinary black people were experiencing every day,' wrote Khusta Jack, later to become the spokesperson for the Consumer Boycott Committee.

This Committee was formed in mid-June and consisted of representatives of the UDF regional committee, PEBCO, PEYCO, COSAS, the Dance Association and the two UDF union affiliates, the Motor Assembly and Components Workers Union (MACWUSA) and the General Workers Union (GWUSA). As before, the local members of the FOSATU unions did not initially join, but did later, at the end of the month.

'The logic of the Port Elizabeth Committee was to use the boycott as a platform to talk directly to the white electorate for the first time,' wrote Jack, and that was certainly part of its extraordinary success. The UDF and its predecessors had exhausted themselves in the slow and unrewarding business of petitioning the authorities; they were plainly not going to get the ear of PW Botha or his structures, which were more likely to order their deaths than order government personnel to negotiate with them. The early days of PEBCO under Thozamile Botha had shown them the limited time frame the state would allow their insurrection to continue. It was now or never, and they had to hit, not the state and its security establishment, as it was obvious that would not work at this stage, but rather to hit the business community and local government to make them take the pain, to move them to break open the granite state and cause it to begin discussions with the UDF and its affiliates. By targeting business, the consumer boycott created a middle layer in the crisis – now it was not just the UDF taking on the all-powerful state, but, if correctly handled, the business community and local government could also carry their demands to government.

Under conditions of ongoing harassment as outlined above, the Boycott Committee put together the plans for the boycott. 'The preparation and planning of the consumer boycott was one of the most detailed and successful campaigns that I have ever been involved in,' wrote Jack. He was not alone in this assessment. The South African Institute of Race Relations wrote at the time, 'The boycotts, occurring as they did on an unprecedented scale, were indeed one of the most important political developments in 1985 ... The longest and most effective was the Port Elizabeth boycott.'

The Committee began by phrasing demands. These included an official explanation for the disappearance of the PEBCO Three; the release from detention of community leaders; the removal of an alleged racist superintendent at a local hospital; proper medical treatment for township residents and the non-interference of the police in hospitals; the withdrawal of troops from the townships; the opening of the central business district to all races and the removal of discrimination in trading; the scrapping of the black local authorities; the establishment of democratic constitutions for student representative councils so that pupils could return to school; and the equalisation of racially discriminatory state pension payments. Later in the year, specifically political demands of a national character were added, including the release of Nelson Mandela and other political leaders and the unbanning of the ANC and COSAS (which had been banned on 26 August).

Then another horrific disaster struck. Matthew Goniwe and his three comrades were abducted and murdered on 27 June. Their burnt-out car and their four bodies were found much later because the bodies had been deliberately separated and hidden. As this information became public, townships were again convulsed with anger. Another demand was added to the already-long list, the demand for justice for this new, particularly cruel set of murders, and, on 15 July, the Port Elizabeth Consumer Boycott was declared.

In the first month of the boycott, 32 of 43 retailers interviewed by the Progressive Federal Party said that their turnovers had dropped by 80-100%. Two of these businesses closed during this month. The whole of the Boycott Committee was either detained or went into hiding. Very quickly, advanced social, economic and political processes began.

In the townships, the boycott had significant motivational and educational effects. Many of its effects were clearly visible – white businesses were closing down and the desperation of businessmen which was evidenced in the media and in personal interactions with their staff, all this was reported that this new strategy was working. As the boycott progressed in Grahamstown, Rhodes University researchers found that 89% of township residents saw the lifting of the state of emergency as important or very important; 86% saw the resignation of the Rini Town Council as important; 94% saw the withdrawal of the SADF and the SAP from the townships as important or very important. There is no reason to assume that attitudes in Port

Elizabeth's townships were any different. The coercion of the community, which all admit did happen, was seen as less important than the need for political changes by 88% of respondents.

A second area in which the boycott helped the emergent UDF affiliates was the impetus that the boycott gave to the formation and development of the street and area committees. These structures provided low-profile leadership that not only kept the uprising going when high-profile leadership was detained, but they also were effective channels of information and communication and a means of keeping some level of control over the youth.

When the boycott began the committee had considered that the white business community and the white council had two options – to fight it, or to reinstate the negotiations that had begun around the Black Weekend period.

In Colesberg the consumer boycott brought a quick response. The state forced township shops to close and water supply to the townships was shut off.

In Port Elizabeth the Boycott Committee had judged that the other option would be followed: negotiations would begin and the 'middle layer' between the township communities and the repressive state, which was, of course, the business community, would be quickly involved.

They were right. When negotiations became impossible because of detentions and harassment of black leaders, the Port Elizabeth Chamber of Commerce issued a manifesto calling for, inter alia, a common citizenship for all, the inclusion of Africans in the government decision-making process, the removal of discriminatory legislation and the participation by blacks in the private enterprise system. The boycott was working.

21

The murder of the Cradock Four and the first state of emergency

To return to the late June murder of Matthew Goniwe and his three comrades.[225]

In late May, Goniwe met with Jaap Strydom, Head Director of the Department of Education and Training, and his deputy, JN Vermaak, at the Masonic Hotel in Cradock. We have noted that they reported back to their Minister that the answer to the schools boycott was the reinstatement of Goniwe to the Cradock teaching post he wanted.

It took a month. On 24 June a delighted Molly Blackburn phoned to say that Matthew was in fact reinstated and that the official paperwork should be expected.

Two days later Matthew was due to attend a UDF meeting in Port Elizabeth. He put it off for a day, partly to accommodate some comrades, Fort Calata, Sparrow Mkonto and Sicelo Mhlauli, who wanted a lift to Port Elizabeth. Fort was an activist in Cradock and Sicelo in Oudtshoorn. Sparrow was a friend wanting a lift. The four set off on Thursday morning 27 June, in Matthew's blue Honda Ballade. Matthew assured his wife, Nyameka, that on the return journey that night they would stop for nothing except police roadblocks.

En route they stopped in Cookhouse and Somerset East, arriving in Port Elizabeth at about 3:15 pm.

The UDF meeting Matthew was to attend would normally have been held in the UDF offices in Court Chambers, across the road from the Magistrates' Courts in Port Elizabeth's North End. Now they had been asked to redirect the meeting as, incredibly, across the corridor from the UDF offices in Court Chambers was the AZAPO office. Tensions were high, with Maqina and his group storming into the UDF offices on occasion. The meeting was now to be held at Michael Coetzee's house in Gelvandale. They arrived there at about 6 pm. Michael's wife prepared and served soft drinks and snacks. Derrick Swartz arrived at 7 pm, and the discussions ended at around 9:30 pm. Matthew, Fort, Sicelo and Sparrow then left for Cradock at about that hour.

They were never seen alive again.

That night the four's families slept little if at all, with rising levels of terror as the night wore on and the four did not return. At 5:30 am Nyameka Goniwe could no longer handle her terrors alone so she woke up Alex Goniwe, Matthew's brother. Gladwell Makhaula, who had acted as CRADORA's chairperson when Matthew was in detention, phoned from Port Elizabeth – was Matthew back home? Nyameka phoned Molly Blackburn – she had last seen him as he went off to Michael's house. At 9 am Nyameka phoned Derrick Swartz. He said that the four had left for home at 9:30 pm the night before. Now the terror really set in.

It was agreed that Gladwell would leave from Port Elizabeth on the Cradock road, in an attempt to find them. And Alex Goniwe, Madoda Jacobs and Nyameka would drive from Cradock the other way, down towards Port Elizabeth.

The Cradock car stopped at Cookhouse, where the police denied detaining the four. Also at Adelaide and Somerset East. Further down the road to Port Elizabeth they met Gladwell coming up. They conferred. Nothing. There was no option but to return to Cradock and wait.

They did not have long to wait, for at about noon on that day, a *makweta* whose name was Zitambele Ngalo, dressed in a palm leaf skirt, taking a walk from the grass hut he shared with other initiates, found a corpse in the bush just off a dirt track which led from the N2, near Markman Industrial Township just north of Bluewater Bay in Port Elizabeth. This corpse was distinctive in that large areas of the body were burned, including the face and hands. Zitambele alerted a passing Casspir, and Warrant Officer Fanie Els of the Murder and Robbery Squad in Port Elizabeth was sent to inspect the murder scene and the body.

Els discovered a place about 15 metres from the body where there was a patch of blood and two .22 cartridge cases. He stored the cartridge cases in evidence bags and also samples of the bloodstained soil. He recorded the body burns and noted three knife wounds in the chest and three on the back. There were also two bullet wounds to the head. He summoned a police photographer and the mortuary van. His work on site then complete, he returned to police headquarters in Port Elizabeth, the soon-to-be notorious Louis le Grange Square.

He was not there for long. He received a phone call from a Sergeant Basson of the uniform branch of the SAP. Basson had found a burnt-out Honda Ballade near the Aldo Scribante Racetrack, also just off the N2 in north Port Elizabeth, which was the road to Cradock. The vehicle was off the road, as if it had been hidden. The radiotape was on the front passenger seat. The fact that it had not been taken made Basson believe that this was not a robbery. Because he suspected foul play, he called the Murder and Robbery Squad.

Els arrived at 3:45 pm, and found a number plate in the burnt-out grass around the vehicle. It was the plate of a Cradock car, CAT 8479. In the grass in front of the vehicle he found a second number plate. This time it was a Port Elizabeth plate, CB 10627. How could one car have two different number plates? The vehicle had no documentation and no contents.

Back at Louis le Grange Square, Els found out that the CAT registration plate belonged to a Honda Ballade owned by a Matthew Goniwe and that the Port Elizabeth number plate was from a Datsun owned by a Mr A Mzima of New Brighton township, Port Elizabeth. It turned out that this vehicle had been scrapped sometime before.

Then Els rang the home of Matthew Goniwe. He spoke to Matthew's nephew, Thembani, who was alone at the home. Els left the message that a burnt-out Honda Ballade had been discovered just north of Bluewater Bay, and that this vehicle belonged to Matthew Goniwe. It is easy to imagine the terror this message evoked when passed on.

The next day, Saturday 29 June, a fisherman who refused to give his name phoned Louis le Grange Square to report that there was a partially burnt body on the coastal dunes just north of the Swartkops River in Bluewater Bay. Again this murder was assigned to Warrant Officer Els, who went to the crime scene that morning.

The body was partially burnt, particularly the upper part of the body and the face. The throat had been slashed, and there were 25 stab wounds in the chest and seven in his back. This time the right hand had been cut off and was nowhere to be found. The faint footprints found here were identical to those Els had noticed at the burnt-out vehicle. Furthermore, there was R9 in cash lying under the body. Like the Honda Ballade case, Els noted, robbery could be ruled out.

That day UDF activist Gillie Skweyiya visited the Port Elizabeth morgue and positively identified the bodies as those of Sparrow Mkonto and Sicelo Mhlauli.

In Cradock there was deep sorrow, mourning and huge anger. Elsewhere in the country there was fury and a demand for the authorities to find Goniwe and Calata, hopefully alive.

Realising that a police enquiry would lead nowhere, Molly Blackburn and Judy Chalmers believed that an independent forensic investigator was required. On Sunday 30 June they called Dr David Klatzow in Johannesburg. He came immediately, flying to Port Elizabeth that same day, and starting his investigation that afternoon. He took blood samples from the two murder sites and inspected and photographed the car.

On consideration of his investigations, Klatzow concluded that there was no evidence of the Honda having been in a collision or having had a breakdown and that the vehicle must have been stopped by its driver, for whatever reason. There was no fault in the Honda's fuel system, so the car had been deliberately set on fire. There was no evidence of blood in the vehicle, so Klatzow concluded that the two were murdered outside of the vehicle. He believed that they were probably murdered at the sites where their bodies had been incinerated, given the amount of blood there. There was much petrol around one of the sites but he could not identify the petrol. Plainly the murderers had been determined to disfigure the bodies beyond recognition.

Two days later, on Tuesday 2 July, the Murder and Robbery Squad organised a search party with the help of 35 Defence Force members, to search for the two other bodies. It took only an hour for these bodies to be found, this time in a small clearing adjacent to the Bluewater Bay beach. Again the bodies had been partially burnt and both had been stabbed many times. The body that was to prove to be Goniwe had a crushed skull. A metal car spring was there also, which possibly accounted for this injury. He also had nine stab wounds, including one straight through the heart. The body that was Fort Calata had had hair pulled out and his fingers had been cut off. There were three stab wounds that had reached his heart, and four on his back.

In total on the four bodies there were 55 stab wounds, two bullet wounds, extensive burns, the mutilation of fingers and the severing of a hand. After death, the bodies had all been placed on their backs and petrol poured onto, particularly, their faces, and then lit, clearly to prevent identification. A more brutal set of murders is difficult to imagine.

Alex Goniwe, Gillie Skweyiya and other Lingelihle residents took a taxi to Port Elizabeth for the grim task of identifying the bodies. They endured distasteful comments from the police at the mortuary as they did this horrible task. Yes, it was Matthew and Fort. The disappearances had been resolved – now, the murders needed to be.

The official culprit was to be 'black-on-black violence', with the Deputy Minister of Foreign Affairs, Louis Nel, immediately saying that 'the alarming statistics of blacks killed during violent unrest in recent months is indicative of a deliberate campaign of terror by Black radical organisations directed specifically against moderates and those prepared to negotiate' (i.e. the UDF killed Goniwe). Lieutenant-Colonel Eric Strydom, head of the Eastern Cape Murder and Robbery Squad, stated that the warfare between the UDF and AZAPO had by no means halted. Two leads, both pointing back to AZAPO and Maqina, one investigated by Errol Moorcroft, the PFP Member of Parliament for Albany, and the other by Warrant Officer Els, led nowhere.

South African law states that for the administration of justice to be complete and to instil confidence, it is necessary for an official investigation to happen in every case of death by unnatural causes. In this case, as with the deaths of Mohapi, Botha, Biko and the Langa Massacre, a formal inquest was to happen. Incredibly, it took three and a half years for it to begin. Would it, like the others mentioned, again conclude that no individual or individuals could be blamed?

Alex Goniwe, Matthew's elder brother, asked Kobus Pienaar, a young attorney then employed by the Legal Resources Centre in Port Elizabeth, to represent the family. Kobus was an engaging and serious young man, given to great thoroughness and very long working hours. To his personal credit he realised that the job of advocate leading the family's interests was for a bigger desk than his, and he obtained the services of the National Director of the Legal Resources Centres, Arthur Chaskalson SC, to fill that role.

The inquest opened on 15 February 1989 in the New Brighton Magistrates' Court building, with Magistrate E de Beer presiding.

Warrant Officer Els testified that he had had the bullets and their cartridge casings assessed by the police forensic department, and they were from a Gevarm rifle, and that he had searched to find one that matched the cartridges, but to no avail. He further testified that the false number plate CB 10627 had been on a car that had been written off in an accident eighteen months before the four murders, and had then been scrapped by the insurance company and the wreck sold to Heine and Strydom, a firm that scraps vehicles that have been extensively damaged. There it had been crushed and sold to a steel manufacturer.

Prof. Gideon Knobel, a pathologist from Cape Town, confirmed the dreadful injuries as outlined above.

One of the youngsters whose statement had pointed back to AZAPO and Maqina, Msonezi Ndyawe, denied everything under cross-examination and nothing would follow from his earlier statement incriminating Maqina.

Maqina himself was interrogated and he also denied everything, including that he was, or ever had been, a member of AZAPO. Under Chaskalson's cross-examination he nevertheless conceded that he had issued statements on behalf of AZAPO and had been expelled by this organisation.

No other witnesses were called, and it was then up to Chaskalson to summarise the facts. This he did in an extraordinary example of logic, mental organisation and attention to detail.

Firstly, he argued that 'from the circumstances of the killing, it must have been a political murder'. Plainly it was not a robbery, for the car was not stolen, nor was its radio or even the money under Mr Mkonto's body. 'Casual robbers bent upon stealing property for gain could hardly be expected to separate bodies which they have robbed, and take them to different parts of Port Elizabeth.' And Goniwe, Calata and Mkonto had high political profiles. Goniwe's 'phone was tapped, his car was regularly followed and he himself had been detained and interrogated a number of times'. Likewise, Calata and Mkonto. Sadly for Mr Mhlauli, who had hardly any political profile, 'once one or more of them were to be killed, none could be allowed to go free'. There could be no witnesses left alive.

Secondly, this was a 'well-coordinated and skilful killing'. The bodies were removed considerable distances from the car. One was 1.7 km away, two were between four and five km away, and one 14 km away. The intention could only be that the bodies, if found, would not be linked to the car, or to each other. Furthermore, the bodies were burned in a way to hide their identities. All four were laid on their backs, petrol was then poured over their faces, and then set on fire. The intention could only be to hide their identities. Add to this the fact that the Honda's number plates were removed, and another plate substituted for them, and it is clear that the murderers were determined to conceal the identity of the car as well as the identities of the murdered four. Their mistake was, in the darkness and the turmoil of the killings, to have misplaced and left behind one of the car's real number plates, which gave the whole game away. The killers came prepared not just with the tools of killing, but also with the number plate and petrol needed to lay a false trail, and hide, possibly forever, the identities of those killed. Except they misplaced a genuine number plate.

So who could they be, these 'well coordinated and skilful killers'? Chaskalson described them as a 'strong and well organised group', who could stop Goniwe's car without doing it any damage despite the fact that the group of four had said they would stop for no one except law enforcement. This group was sufficiently strong and numerous to overpower and subdue the four and were equipped with guns and knives, petrol and false number plates. They had transport that could take their prisoners to remote places and the killers knew the territory sufficiently well to be able to go off-road on bush tracks for considerable distances, and knew the area and the routes they wanted to take. All of this in the dead of night. The group had planned all of this, as well as how to leave false trails.

This was a 'group of people who knew who they were looking for, knew the route that they would take and the road they would be on'. The group had intelligence possibly gleaned from intercepted phone calls; had vehicles, numbers, knives, petrol, stolen number plates and, particularly, a gun that had not before been used in criminal activity. And they had developed a plan to stop, overpower, abduct and kill the four in a way that suggested township-style violence. Then they would be able to transport the bodies to remote and inaccessible places in the dead of night and burn off their distinguishing features, all the while leaving false trails. This was surely to ensure that there would be no funeral and no martyrs.

Certainly, Chaskalson argued, this was not AZAPO. The evidence linking Maqina to the killing 'has been discredited and is of no real value. The modus operandi of the killers was far better resourced than AZAPO was, and the killings were not of the terror and counter-terror type. No, AZAPO was not in it. Instead this group of killers 'constituted themselves into an illegal group which can only be described as having lain in wait for the Cradock Four, constituted themselves as it were into a death squad, stopping, killing them and seeking to make them disappear.'

This was a masterful summary, spectacularly insightful in its ordering of the available facts. It clearly established that Goniwe and his three comrades had been murdered by a death squad, and that the resources they brought to the crime were such that only the South African security establishment could muster.

Despite Chaskalson's remarkable efforts, there was not enough evidence to assign responsibility to any individual or group, and he conceded that. Magistrate De Beer delivered his findings: 'There is absolutely no acceptable evidence before me that any member of the Force had anything whatsoever to do with the killings ... The only findings I can make in this regard is that the deaths were brought about by a person or persons unknown.'

Again, as George Bizos entitled his autobiography, there was no one to blame.

It took three and a quarter years for the next lead to emerge.

On 14 May 1992 the front page of the *New Nation* newspaper was devoted to the presentation of the following document, stolen from the records of the Eastern Province Joint Management Committee in Port Elizabeth, dated 7 June 1985, and translated from Afrikaans:

> Personal for General Van Rensburg.
> 1-Telephone conversation Gen Van Rensburg/ Brig Van der Westhuizen of 7 June 85 refers.
> 2-Names as follows:
> Matthew Goniwe
> Mbulelo Goniwe (brother or nephew of above)
> Fort Calata
> 3-It is proposed that the above-mentioned persons, as a matter of urgency, be permanently removed from society
> 4-Wide reaction can be expected locally as well as nationally as a result of the importance of these persons, especially the first-mentioned, for the enemy e.g.
> a-Interdicts as recently with the disappearance of Godolozi, Hashe and Galela (Pebco officials)
> b-Reaction from leftist politicians such as Molly Blackburn
> c-Protest as in the case of Oscar Mpetha in sympathy.

This note, in military parlance a 'signal', had been sent by Brigadier Van der Westhuizen, the head of the military unit Eastern Province Command in Port Elizabeth, to General Van Rensburg, who served in the Strategy Department of the State Security Council in Pretoria. The State Security Council was a body comprising South Africa's highest-ranking politicians (including the State President and the Ministers of Defence, Law and Order, Foreign Affairs and Justice) and top bureaucrats (the Director General of the National Intelligence Service, the Chief of the Defence Force, the Commissioner of Police and the secretaries of Justice and Foreign Affairs). The signal was handwritten by Commandant Lourens du Plessis, who was Senior Staff Officer of Information at Eastern Province Command and the secretary of the Eastern Province Joint Management Centre.

The release of this document was, of course, devastating. Not only because it was possibly concrete proof of state-sponsored murder, but also because, as a State Security Council document, it pulled both the military and politicians at the very top of South Africa into the business of assassination.

That the signal ever emerged was the end result of a number of events.

Commandant Du Plessis had taken early retirement from the military in 1990, as democracy in South Africa appeared to be unavoidable. On leaving, he signed an undertaking that he had not removed any confidential documents. But he had – a briefcase full, including the Goniwe signal. He had buried them in his garden, and, when he lost a lot of money on a failed fast-food business in Alice, the small town where Fort Hare University is centred, and needed a fill-up of cash, he offered his documents, at a price, to the *Weekly Mail*, who refused to pay for them.

In March 1992 he received a phone call from General Bantu Holomisa, then head of the military junta that ruled the Transkei, but also a man clearly on the rise in the by-now unbanned ANC. They were distant friends, and Du Plessis asked Holomisa if he, the general, had any employment opportunities for Du Plessis. The general was unhelpful until Du Plessis said he had some sensational documents the general and the ANC might wish to see. That certainly grabbed the general's attention.

On 21 April 1992 Du Plessis met Holomisa, Joe Nhlanhla, the head of security in the ANC, and Zwelakhe Sisulu, the editor of the *New Nation*, and Zwelakhe's political correspondent, Enoch Sithole, at a hotel in Johannesburg. He handed over the Goniwe signal to this group and the result was predictable.

Immediately then President FW de Klerk ordered the reopening of the inquest into the deaths of the Cradock Four in a terse note that also specifically and clearly denied any Cabinet or State Security Council involvement in 'murder or any crime at any stage'.

The reopened inquest started before Mr Justice Neville Zietsman, Judge President of the Eastern Cape, on 1 March 1993. It was to last a year and two months, and attracted some of South Africa's finest legal talent.

Sadly, Arthur Chaskalson was immersed in the CODESA negotiations, drafting South Africa's new constitution, and he couldn't make it. In his place, and on his recommendation, the Goniwe and other families were represented by Chaskalson's old friend, George Bizos SC, the greatly experienced human rights lawyer. The South African Defence Force appointed Anton Mostert SC, who had been a judge previously and who had headed up a commission on exchange control regulations. While chairing this commission Mostert had become aware of the abuse of public funds when the Department of Information had laundered state money into Louis Luyt's businesses to start a pro-National Party newspaper, *The Citizen*. This Mostert personally exposed, causing the 'retirement' of BJ Vorster, then State President, and chaos in National Party ranks. Two years later Mostert had been granted permission to leave the bench and return to the bar. The reasons were never made public for this, a most unusual occurrence.

The South African Police appointed Dup de Bruyn, a very eminent Port

Elizabeth SC. To this hugely talented group was added, mid-enquiry, the young and very nimble Advocate Glenn Goosen, brought in to represent Commandant Du Plessis when the state eventually refused him counsel.

With lawyers of this calibre, affidavits aplenty, many witnesses to be cross-examined and no time restrictions, the record of the inquest is enormous. It is not the purpose of this book to summarise it all, but rather to bring out the germane issues. These include:

- The security police kept Matthew Goniwe under strict surveillance. Colonel Winter, a Koevoet veteran chosen to run Cradock's security police during this time, confirmed that he had obtained ministerial permission to tap Goniwe's phone from 8 June 1985 to 7 December of that year (presumably the other time periods were without permission). Transcripts were immediately made and the tapes then erased and reused.

- The security police had planted a 'tomato' listening device in Goniwe's home, sensitive enough to discern almost any conversation.

- The security police were in possession of a transcript of a telephone conversation between Matthew and Derrick Swartz wherein it was set out that Matthew and his comrades would not come to Port Elizabeth on Wednesday 26th as was their regular habit, but would instead be there the next day.

- Under cross-examination Colonel Winter admitted that the Cradock police possessed all that was necessary to have performed the murders, and that two of Winter's old Koevoet colleagues, Sakkie van Zyl and Gert Lotz, were in the security police unit in Cradock, and another Koevoet veteran Sakkie du Plessis was with the Murder and Robbery squad in Port Elizabeth.

- Winter left work early with two security police officers on the day that Goniwe and his comrades were killed, and one of his black phone-tappers reported that the day after the murders, and before the bodies were found, Winter had hung around the phone-tappers, desperately seeking any information of activity on the Goniwe line.

- Just prior to Goniwe's death, surveillance had been stepped up and his car was tailed by the security police. How then could the murders have happened without security police knowledge?

- Between when CB 10627 was scrapped and the murders, a vehicle bearing that number plate had received five parking tickets in Victoria Quay and Strand Street, within walking distance of the Sanlam Building where the Port Elizabeth security police had their offices.

Despite their remarkable skills at cross-examination, neither Bizos nor Mostert could secure an admission that could lead to a charge of culpability sticking to any of those cross-examined. This was mostly because of evasive answering. As Mostert said to Colonel Winter late in his cross-examination, 'you have said "I don't remember" no fewer than 135 times; 19 times you have said "I do not have knowledge" which amounts to the same thing; and 83 times you have evasively stated "I don't know" or "no comment"'.

The granite wall, which turned out to be a wall built from well-rehearsed falsehoods, would not break down. A three-month recess was agreed, and the legal teams went off to sharpen their cases.

Now an excerpt from George Bizos' autobiography, *No One to Blame? In Pursuit of Justice in South Africa*:

> We returned on 14 June after a three-month postponement, ready to start du Plessis's evidence … There was an air of anticipation and excitement in court. Mostert, whom one would have expected to be nervous in the face of testimony incriminating his client, seemed to have regained his composure. I knew why. He had invited me to his home. He could be friendly and charming in private if he thought his or his client's interests would be better served. He informed me that he had hard evidence that the police had killed Goniwe and not the defence force, whom he represented. He swore me to secrecy until he had made the evidence available in open court. In his study he set up a video screen and projected tests carried out by military experts which proved that the 1989 killing of three policemen and an informer had been carried out by the police, not the ANC; they had been killed to prevent a leak that the police had planned the execution of Goniwe. He asked for my cooperation and support for his application to pursue what the judge might consider irrelevant to the issue. Never before had there been such a split between army and police. I readily agreed.[226]

The event Mostert was referring to was an apparently inexplicable murder of three black security policemen, Mgoduka, Faku and Mapipa, and an informant, Charles Jack. They had been travelling in a white Jetta on a little-used road that left the N2 just on the Port Elizabeth side of the bridge over the Sundays River, and went from there to Uitenhage. The vehicle had been provided to them by Lieutenant Nieuwoudt, who had sent them on their mission, after telling them not to use their normal vehicles as they were well known in Motherwell, where they were to arrest an MK operative. Late on the night of 14 December 1989, possibly 100 metres from the N2 the

Jetta had been blown to smithereens and all four occupants were killed. An Eastern bloc VZD3M detonator was found on the scene, suggesting ANC involvement. Incredibly, when the explosion and the identities of those killed were made known, the ANC accepted responsibility.

When the Zietsman inquiry was concluded, further investigations revealed that Mostert was in fact right. Nieuwoudt, an explosive expert who had attended every day of the Zietsman inquiry on behalf of the security police, was charged and convicted of the murders of the four occupants of the Jetta. It was said that the murders had been caused by the black security policemen stealing funds from left-wing organisations, and not sharing them as agreed. It was clear later that information about the Goniwe murders was, in fact, the real issue. Nieuwoudt died of cancer while his appeal was pending.

When Mostert began the deposition that would bring all this out, Judge Zietsman queried how this was to relate to the military signal that had caused the reopening of the inquest. Mostert asked for, and got, permission to drop his bomb anyway, which he then did.

The inquiry went on for many more months, with Bizos and Glenn Goosen battling valiantly to elicit the phrase or two that would break open the case against the Defence Force and, ultimately, expose the well-hidden path from the murderers all the way up to the State Security Council.

Glenn presented the enquiry with another of Commandant Du Plessis's well-hidden treasures, documents that set out a half-baked and half-executed military project, put together by Van der Westhuizen (of signal fame) to topple Lennox Sebe's regime in the Ciskei and thereafter to create some kind of a superstructure incorporating the Transkei, Ciskei and the Eastern Cape, to form an anti-UDF bulwark. (This nonsense, called Operation Katzen, will be dealt with in a later section.) The documents clearly envisaged bloodshed, murder and mayhem, and, as Goosen set out, showed that Van der Westhuizen was willing to incorporate death into his anti-UDF plans.

When the submissions and the cross-examination ended, the families of the deceased and their lawyers hoped that they had opened enough trails for Judge Zietsman to apportion culpability.

Judge Zietsman delivered his findings in an 82-page report on 28 May 1994, less than a month after Nelson Mandela had become South Africa's first democratically elected president. The event turned out to be hardly as exciting as the inauguration of South Africa's first black president.

Zietsman found that much of the evidence led was not of the standard required to establish a prima facie case.

- The totality of the evidence linking the security police to the murder 'raises a suspicion' that Colonels Snyman and Winter knew that Goniwe and his comrades were to be murdered, but that 'The acceptable evidence however falls short of establishing a prima facie case against them...'

- However, the documents on Operation Katzen constitute 'prima facie evidence that Van der Westhuizen was party to a plan that included as a possibility the killing of Lennox Sebe and others...'
- 'It has been proved prima facie in my opinion that [the signal] was a recommendation that Matthew Goniwe (et al.) should be killed...'
- Zietsman found that there was no justification for the proposition that the signal was sent to higher authority (in the State Security Council bureaucracy) and then acted upon. 'There is no evidence that the persons who murdered Matthew Goniwe and the others knew of the signal. Evidence to link the signal to the murders is lacking...'
- Zietsman concluded, 'In my opinion, there is prima facie proof that it was members of the security forces that carried out the murders ... and a case of suspicion has been made out [against named security policemen and defence force personnel], but suspicion does not constitute prima facie proof.'

So there it was. Again, 'no one to blame'. At least this time Judge Zietsman had opened the possibility for the sorrowing and frustrated families of the deceased to sue the state. Something, for sure, but hardly justice for the Cradock Four.

Another two years and eight months had passed when on 28 January 1997, Dr Alex Boraine, the co-chair of the Truth and Reconciliation Commission, issued a statement to the press that the TRC had received amnesty applications from a number of former policemen who had admitted responsibility for the killing of Biko, Mthimkhulu, the PEBCO Three and the Cradock Four.[227]

In the case of the Cradock Four, there were six initial applicants: Eric Alexander Taylor, Gerhardus Johannes Lotz, Nicolaas Jacobus Janse van Rensburg, Harold Snyman, Hermanus du Plessis and Johan Martin 'Sakkie' van Zyl. Later two other applicants applied for amnesty for other offences, which included issues pertinent to the Cradock Four: these were Eugene de Kock and Jaap van Jaarsveld.

Anton Mostert had been spot-on. This was a security police operation, even without the murderous assistance of Vlakplaas operatives. He was right on a second issue: included in the death squad were two black security policemen, Faku and Mgoduka, and the informant Sakati. All three had been blown to bits by Nieuwoudt in the car bomb on the road to Motherwell in 1989. It was all tied up, as Mostert had pronounced four years earlier. And he was also right when he asked Colonel Winter who his Koevoet colleagues were, now in the Eastern Cape. They were Sakkie van Zyl, Gert Louw and Herman du Plessis. This was a death squad supreme, as Arthur Chaskalson had concluded eight long years before. Now it was all out in the open.

Colonel Snyman stated that he had been called to a security briefing in Cradock on 14 February 1985. There he found the Minister of Law and Order, Louis le Grange, the Commissioner of Police, General Johann Coetzee, the Minister of Co-operation and Development, Barend du Plessis, and the Divisional Commissioner of Police for the Eastern Cape, Brigadier CA Swart.

Snyman reported that he did not think that law and order could be restored unless Goniwe and his comrades were 'dealt with'. Le Grange had told him that he had to 'make a plan with these activists'.

The plan was then created by Nick van Rensburg, Herman du Plessis and Sakkie van Zyl. The murderous event was to be staged to simulate a robbery or a vigilante attack, to throw a false trail.

Of the hideous events of that evening we have only one story, for, unlike the killing of the PEBCO Three, in this instance no one from the death squad of white security policemen gave a different, second story. Those with more lurid details had already been accounted for in a white Jetta eight years earlier.

Initially they claimed that the team was only Van Zyl, Taylor and Lotz. They were informed of the travel arrangements of the Cradock Four, and awaited them, in two vehicles, near the Olifantshoek Pass on the Port Elizabeth to Cradock road. When the Honda passed them, at about 11 o'clock that night, they overtook it and pulled it off the road. They pulled the four from their vehicle and handcuffed them. Van Zyl then took Sparrow Mkonto and Sicelo Mhlauli and Lotz took Goniwe and Calata. Taylor took Goniwe's car.

The convoy returned to St George's Strand Beach in Bluewater Bay. Lotz and Van Zyl took the Honda off to near the Aldo Scribante Racetrack and poured petrol over it and burned it.

Then Van Zyl drove off with Sparrow Mkonto to find a deserted place to kill him. The intention was first to knock him unconscious with a rubber truncheon and then to stab him to death with a knife. Mkonto however grabbed Van Zyl from behind. Van Zyl pulled a .22 rifle from under his seat, and shot him. He then pulled Mkonto from the vehicle and again shot him, this time in the head.

When Van Zyl was sure Mkonto was dead, he drove to a meeting place in New Brighton where he picked up Faku, Mgoduka and Sakati. They returned to Mkonto's body and Faku stabbed it repeatedly, despite Mkonto obviously being dead. They turned the corpse on its back, poured petrol over it, ignited the petrol and returned to Taylor and Lotz and the other three abductees.

Van Zyl, Faku and Mgoduka then took Mhlauli a kilometre or so away. Faku beat him unconscious with the truncheon and Faku and Mgoduka then stabbed him repeatedly. The three then returned to Taylor and Lotz and Goniwe and Calata.

Next it was Calata's turn. He was led off and the same fate was inflicted on him.

Finally, Matthew. Despite putting up as good a fight as he could, he too was knocked unconscious by Taylor and repeatedly stabbed by Faku and Mgoduka.

Thereafter Van Zyl gave the instructions that the handcuffs were to be removed from the corpses, and they were then laid on their backs, petrol poured over them and they were set alight. Faku claimed to his fellow murderers that he had had to cut off Mhlauli's hand to remove the cuffs. They alleged that it too was burned on the site of the killings.

The murderers all claimed to be ignorant of Commandant Du Plessis' signal, and instead had acted on orders from superiors in the security police.

All that was left for the grieving families of the Cradock Four was to sue the state for the loss of their breadwinners, the opening that followed from Judge Zietsman's findings. At a time when apartheid South Africa's chief spy Dr Niël Barnard was given a golden handshake of R1 million to complement his (very adequate) state pension, Mrs Goniwe got R380 446, Mrs Calata R433 863, Mrs Mkonto R74 560 and Mrs Mhlauli R174 257.

Thus was the curtain drawn on this dreadful event.

The Cradock Four funeral and the 1985 state of emergency

'If you were actively determined to free yourself and South Africa of apartheid, there was only one place you had to be on 20 July 1985: at the mass funeral of the Cradock Four. All roads led to Lingelihle township', wrote Khusta Jack.[228] And were those roads busy. The largest funeral the platteland had ever witnessed saw a crowd of somewhere between 40 000 and 60 000 arrive. This included diplomats from France, Norway, Canada, Australia and Sweden, and messages of sympathy were read from the governments of the United States, the United Kingdom and the Netherlands.

Clergy arrived from all over, in great numbers. From Port Elizabeth came the local heads of the 'big three churches': Bishops Patrick Coleman and Michael Murphy of the Catholic Church; Bishop Bruce Evans and Canon Mcebisi Xundu of the Church of the Province; and Rev. George Irvine, head of the Methodist Church. The biggest roars were reserved for Rev. Allan Boesak and the hero of dissident Afrikaners, Rev. Beyers Naudé, both of whom were carried shoulder-high.

Whether these clergy were comfortable or not, showing their final respects under enormous banners of the South African Communist Party and the African National Congress, we do not know but they stuck it out, and were loved and admired for it. 'This huge banner [of the South African Communist Party] … flew above the dusty melee. In the context of the regime's extreme phobia about the South African Communist Party, this was the most outright act of defiance. This was freedom then and there. You heard it in the belly-roar of the crowd and you felt it in your bones,' wrote Jack. Mkonto's and Mhlauli's coffins were draped in ANC colours, and Goniwe's and Calata's in red velvet. There was to be no restraint in the showing of political loyalty on 20 July 1985.

Boesak was at his oratorical best: 'The people know and I know who murdered them. I say to you it was the death squads of the South African police. The people are being oppressed by the children of Adolf Hitler.'

Jan van Eck, a Member of Parliament for the Progressive Federal Party, wrote in depth about the funeral:

It was clear that the funeral was much more than a funeral for four loved and respected leaders; this was a rallying occasion for thousands of the oppressed, an opportunity to rededicate their commitment to liberation and an opportunity for people to mobilise and broaden the commitment in South Africa, forge stronger links and strengthen their political organisation … When the Rev. Allan Boesak, a UDF patron, and Dr Beyers Naude, the then President of the South African Council of Churches, arrived, pandemonium broke out. To roars of 'Boesak, Boesak' both speakers were carried shoulder high to the platform … Although the speeches, sermons and prayers coming from the platform were powerful and emotional, reflecting the feelings and often the anger of the communities, it was the crowd, to me, that was the most impressive of the whole ceremony: their completely disciplined behaviour, yet their frequent outbursts of anger and hatred; their shouts and laughter, but most of all their passionate singing and dancing … How can I ever forget the clear voice of a six-year-old boy, standing right next to me on a trestle table, singing the verses of *Nkosi Sikele' iAfrica*, and *We are the soldiers of Mandela* with a dedication and passion that sent a shiver of hope and fear up my spine.

One of the final speakers was attorney Victoria Mxenge, widow of the brutally murdered Griffiths Mxenge. From her deep experience of the pain the system could still inflict, she reminded the crowd of Canon Calata, who refused to divorce Christianity from the liberation struggle. Scarcely two weeks later, she in turn would be shot multiple times, and then hacked to death. The system had not given up yet.

And certainly the system was not giving up on the day of the funeral of the Cradock Four.

That afternoon it was made known that the State President, PW Botha, would make an announcement on state television that evening. During this announcement he declared a state of emergency in 36 magisterial districts in terms of the Public Safety Act of 1953. These magisterial districts of course included Port Elizabeth, Uitenhage, Cradock and fifteen others in the Eastern Cape.

The Act allowed the State President to 'make such regulations as appear to him to be necessary or expedient for providing for the safety of the public', and, in his wisdom, PW Botha took this very widely. Now any member of 'the force' (i.e. the South African Police, the South African Defence Force, the South African Railways Police and the officials of the Prisons Service) could, without a warrant, arrest any person for a period not exceeding 14 days (unless the period was extended by the Minister of Law and Order) and interrogate any person detained, and, at any time, search any person or place and seize any article that was deemed to be relevant or suspected to be related to the possible commission of an offence.

These actions were now beyond the control of the courts as 'no civil or criminal proceedings could be brought against the state', and also beyond publication, as now the filming, photographing or recording of any 'public disturbance, disorder, riot, public violence, strike or boycott' was prohibited.

No further funerals could be held outdoors and only a minister of religion could address a funeral. He 'could not attack, criticise, propagate or discuss any form of government', or even 'discuss the existence of a state of emergency'.

A total of 35 372 SADF personnel were flooded into the townships to supplement the SAP, and Eastern Province Command was given 34 townships in the Eastern Cape to patrol. Earlier, at the end of March, the Minister of Law and Order had banned all meetings of the UDF in 18 magisterial districts, 16 of which were in the Eastern Cape. By August 45 of

251

the 80 executive members of the UDF, nationally and regionally, were either in detention, awaiting trial or had been assassinated. Detentions reached new record numbers for South Africa. Detentions under the Internal Security Act numbered 4 389 in South Africa and the 'independent homelands' for 1985, and 7 361 people were detained under the emergency regulations from 21 July to 27 December. This made a total of 11 750 detainees, more than after Sharpeville (11 500) and the 1976 uprising (2 430 detainees). The Detainees Parents' Support Committee estimated that 60% of all detainees were from the Eastern Cape, with Port Elizabeth providing by far the biggest number.

Two 'Treason Trials' were also begun, with the 'Pietermaritzburg Treason Trial' having 19 accused, including Albertina Sisulu, Frank Chikane, Aubrey Mokoena, Archie Gumede and others. The second such trial, the 'Delmas Treason Trial', had another 22 accused, including Terror Lekota, Popo Molefe and Moss Chikane. Both trials dragged on throughout the year. The Delmas Trial seemed to drag on forever after. The defendants were freed on appeal in 1989. Plainly these trials were used to tie up the UDF leadership.

In Port Elizabeth on the morning of 21 July the regime set out its intentions clearly. 'At dawn I awoke to the sounds of military vehicles rumbling in and taking up strategic positions to blockade every township entry and exit point … Overnight our streets were turned into a military zone. As the day progressed, the news of security police raids on political activists ripped through the township communications network,' wrote Khusta Jack.[229]

He was one of only three of the UDF executive that missed immediate detention, along with Henry Fazzie and Stone Sizani. The rest were all 'inside' by the evening of 21 July.

With the consumer boycott continuing at full intensity, the detaining authorities took the position that they could beat a cessation of the boycott out of the leaders they had caught. And for that they particularly wanted Jack.

And they got him, on 2 August, hiding in a home in New Brighton.

Dr Wendy Orr

Jack knew to expect no mercy, and he was right. The following is from an affidavit he later deposed in court, in an application for a restraining order on the police:[230]

On the following day, that is 3 August 1985, two security policemen W/O Nieuwoudt and Bezuidenhout came to fetch me [from the cell he was being kept in at Swartkops Police Station]. They took me to Louis le Grange Square. I was taken to W/O Coetzee's office. Coetzee was alone in his office. He took out a pair of handcuffs and said: 'Ons het jou gekry en vandag sal ons al die politiek uit jou kop slaan. Jy wil mos nie hoor nie.'

He took out a towel and tied towelling around each of my wrists and placed the handcuffs over the towelling. He screwed the handcuffs tight. I was told to sit on the floor and place my handcuffed arms over my legs. A stick was then inserted below my knees and above my forearms locking me into a permanent crouch. Nieuwoudt entered the room and assisted Coetzee to push the stick through. Both men then lifted me up by means of the stick and suspended me between two tables.

This form of torture is known as 'the helicopter'. Apart from being quite helpless and exposed, one hangs upside down with all one's weight being taken on one's knees and forearms. It is extremely uncomfortable, the blood rushes to one's head and there is the constant strain of permanently bending one's neck to see what is happening and to avoid the throbbing.

Coetzee sat at one of the tables with documents that I assumed were documents taken from my file. He asked me questions and the answers were recorded by him. After a while I began to cry out because of the severe pain resulting from the suspension alone. I began to plead with Coetzee but to no avail. I remember him saying 'Toemaar – you are going to talk the truth. This is the room of truth.'

At some stage Sgt Ndiyane, Lt Strydom, W/O Nieuwoudt and Bezuidenhout came into the office. Bezuidenhout and Nieuwoudt took me off the two tables and removed the stick between my legs and replaced it with what looked like a thick broomstick. They suspended me again between the two tables but this time the tables were drawn closer to each other. Ndiyane rocked me so as to expose my buttocks above the level of the two tables. Bezuidenhout struck me with a sjambok, accusing me of calling the Port Elizabeth police 'gestapo' at a meeting I had addressed in Cape Town.

When Bezuidenhout stopped hitting me he put the sjambok on the table and Strydom picked it up and took a turn hitting me on the buttocks. At some stage Nieuwoudt hit me with an object that looked like a hosepipe. While each blow was not inflicted with full force, the overall effect of the blows to the head and to the buttocks, together with the rocking motion, was so painful and disorientating that I still have nightmares about the incident...

Much interrogation followed, including Jack being taken to a toilet and police pouring a bucket of dirty water, including an irritant, over him.

I was again taken to W/O Coetzee's office where my questioning continued. Coetzee and Nieuwoudt were in the room. Coetzee asked me what business it was of Molly Blackburn's to value herself with blacks and my organisation particularly. When I replied that Mrs Blackburn understood the hardships that blacks suffered, Nieuwoudt stopped writing and took up his sjambok, hitting me several times shouting 'You lie, all Mrs Blackburn wants is a violent overthrow of the state and one-man-one-vote!'

I was thereafter taken to Algoa Park Police Station by Nieuwoudt. On the way there he warned me not to lay any complaints of assault against the police. He said that if I did, I would disappear like Godolozi, Hashe and Galela, or that my body would be found burnt like Goniwe and others...

That afternoon members of the reaction unit at Algoa Park took me to St Alban's Prison. A Sgt Kumm and another prison warder took down our particulars. I told Sgt Kumm that I had been assaulted by the police and he wrote that down. I was then, with other detainees, stripped naked. When the other detainees saw my body, particularly my swollen left buttock, they exclaimed and expressed shock. Sgt Kumm too saw my injuries and invited other prison warders to come and look at me saying: 'Hy is goed gebliksem'. I was then locked in the same section as Henry Fazzie and Elijah Jokazi, and others, who also saw my injuries.

I complained to the prison medical orderly when he did his rounds the following day that I had pains all over my body and a severe headache. I told him that I had been assaulted by the police and showed him the injuries. On Monday 5 August I was taken before a young male doctor. I told him that I had been assaulted by the police. He told me to strip and examined the swelling and the marks caused by the beating. He made entries on what I suppose is a medical file and prescribed some medicine.

On Wednesday 7 August I was again taken to Louis le Grange Square by two black security policemen, Sgt Nani and Const Gqamane. I was taken to the office of Major Du Plessis. He told me to telephone the newspapers and tell the journalists that the consumer boycott had been called off. When I told him that I could not do so because the people themselves wanted the boycott, he accused me of lying and said that I was responsible for it. He told me that I must think very seriously about ending the boycott. He said that he had wide powers and that he would deal with me personally. He told me that Godolozi, Hashe and Galela had all been warned but they had been stubborn … This day I was not assaulted, and was later returned to St Alban's.

And so it went on – security policemen, bound by no statutes of behaviour, left to do what they did best: brutalise suspects, for the enjoyment of it, with a bit of interrogation thrown in.

Ivy Gcina, then 47 years old, the mother of five children and the chairperson of the Port Elizabeth Women's Organisation, had a similar story to tell, which she also did in an affidavit:

In the morning of 30 July 1985, I was taken from North End Prison to Louis le Grange Square police station. I was taken to W/O Coetzee's office. Coetzee, W/O Van Wyk and a Smith questioned me at length about speeches I had made, and the activities of the Port Elizabeth Women's Organisation. Whenever they were unhappy with my answers Smith and Coetzee swore at me, calling me a 'liar', a 'bitch', a 'rubbish' and other abusive terms. They threatened me that they would call a certain policeman whom they said was renowned for hitting women. One said: 'Ek wonder hoekom hy so laat is vandag. Hy slaan die vrouens so lekker.' I thought they were just frightening me.

A short while later, Sgt Ndiyani entered the office and commenced to interrogate me. I was standing when one of the white policemen told me to keep my feet together. Quite suddenly I was hit behind the knees, causing me to fall. As I got up, Ndiyane hit me very hard with an open hand on the side of my face. I took off my spectacles to see if they were broken, when Ndiyane hit me again with his open hand. The white policeman standing behind me would hit me on the back of my neck. I tried to remain dignified and not call out or cry, but this only seemed to provoke them further. Van Wyk suggested that they should use teargas. One of the white policemen, he was taller than the others, grabbed me and pushed me into a nearby toilet. He sprayed me with teargas. I suffocated but I managed to prevent him from locking me in the toilet. I stood in the passage and coughed until the effect of the gas wore off.

I was then taken by a white policewoman to her office. I sensed that she had taken me into her office to protect me from further assaults.

When she heard voices in the passage she pretended to hit me. The white policeman who had sprayed me with teargas came in and chided her for not hitting me. He took the baton from her and started to hit me on my arms and my shoulders. The policewoman left immediately.

The tall policeman again sprayed me with teargas. This was done directly into my face. I immediately began to suffocate and to cough. I could hardly breathe. I rushed into the passage for air ... A black policeman came down the stairway and told Coetzee not to use teargas since some of it was going up to the upper floors.

Coetzee told me that I would be assaulted every day unless I 'told the truth'. I was then taken back to North End prison.

On returning to North End prison, Ivy complained to the prison staff of great pain. A female warder offered to get her medicine. She was taken back to her cell, in extreme pain, and, as night came on, could not sleep.

The same night I saw a light and my cell was opened.

I did not know who was opening my cell. I did not look at the person.

She said to me: 'Ivy, it is me. I am Sgt Crouse. I have fetched your medicine.'

She rubbed me. She made me take my medicine. I told her I could not even hold anything, but I could try. I told her I was going to try by all means. She said: 'It is fine. Do not worry yourself. I will help you.'

So she made me take the medicine, and then she massaged me. Then after that I could at least try to sleep.

Ten years later, at the Truth and Reconciliation Commission, the Commission reunited Ivy, now a Member of Parliament, with Sgt Crouse, who was by then 37 years old.

'I thought you would never remember me,' said Sgt Crouse. Both women were delighted to again see each other. Ivy replied, 'Could you ever forget someone like that?' Sgt Crouse replied, 'I was only doing my duty.'

If Ivy Gcina found her personal angel in Sgt Crouse of the prison service, the whole consort of security detainees was now to be extraordinarily fortunate in finding their own guardian angel. Her name was Wendy Orr, and she was all of 24 years old in 1985.

Wendy Orr was born in Port Elizabeth in 1961. Her father was the much-loved and long-serving Presbyterian minister of the Hill Street Presbyterian church, one of the beautiful historic stone churches of Port Elizabeth's

Central area. Her mother was a social worker.

Wendy graduated MBChB at the University of Cape Town medical school in 1983 at the age of 22. She then took up employment as a medical officer in the District Surgeon's Office of the Department of Health in Port Elizabeth. Her duties consisted in 'conducting autopsies at the police mortuary in New Brighton, and providing clinical services to sentenced and awaiting trial prisoners in two prisons – St Alban's and North End'.

She was in this position, and performing those duties, when, in July 1985, PW Botha declared the state of emergency. Immediately her responsibilities changed significantly. 'Within days dozens of people had been detained in Port Elizabeth, and over the next few days that number rose to hundreds. Although political detainees were usually kept in police cells, the sheer number of people being detained in this state of emergency meant they had to be sent to prisons – white and female detainees to North End prison, and black men to St Alban's. This meant that, as part of my daily prison sick parades, I started to see state of emergency detainees as well.

'From the onset it was evident that very many of the detainees showed signs of having been assaulted … when I asked them how the injuries had been sustained, they said the police had assaulted them.'

These assaults, Dr Orr quickly realised, came from two circumstances: firstly on initial arrest, many were beaten and whipped immediately. 'While the detainees were in the police station precinct, [they were] randomly assaulted, beaten and brutalized.'

The second set of circumstances was detainees in prison, who would then be taken out to police headquarters for interrogation. 'During this interrogation they would be tortured. So, on admission [to jail] they would be injury-free, but at some stage during their detention they would be brought to me with complaints, and, very often, horrific injuries.'

One such torture victim was Ernest Malgas, whom Dr Orr describes thus:

> I had not examined him on admission. However, according to the prison's record, he did not have any complaint on his admission. When I saw him, he was severely injured. His injuries included large areas of severe and deep bruising on the lower back and buttocks. The bruising was not merely sub-epidermal, but intra-muscular. The muscles were very swollen and tender. The bruises were predominantly purple and red, consistent with a particularly violent assault with a blunt instrument. His condition was such that I was unable to take a history from him. I asked the nursing sister, a Sister Prins, whether she knew what had happened to the man … she

257

told me that the South African police had taken the detainee to the Louis Le Grange Square for interrogation the previous day. Upon his return he was severely injured and complained that he had been assaulted by the police.

In the first Truth and Reconciliation Commission hearings, in 1996, Mr Malgas gave evidence that he had been subject to 'helicopter torture' the day before I saw him. He said that he had had the inner tube of a tyre wrapped around his face to suffocate him. He was then handcuffed with his hands in front of him and a stick was passed over his left wrist, behind his knees and over his right wrist. The stick was then lifted, thus suspending Mr Malgas upside-down. Hanging by his wrists and the tender spot behind the knees, he was balanced between two tables. In this hanging position, he was hit with a baton across his lower back and buttocks.

Later Dr Orr noted: 'I recalled what happened when Mr Malgas was brought to see me ... when he was brought in for me to examine him, a number of prison officials came in to look at him because he was so severely injured. One of the warders commented that "Hy het dit seker nodig gehad" (He certainly must have needed that). The others agreed. No one suggested that anything be done about the fact that this man had obviously been very seriously assaulted by the police.'

If nobody else had either the courage or the willingness to act, that was their decision – but the 24-year-old Dr Orr was no longer willing to tolerate this situation:

By late August I simply could not contemplate the thought of continuing to see the daily litany of pain and injury and do nothing about it. I had advised my superiors at the District Surgeon's Office in Port Elizabeth of what was happening (and indeed they themselves had conducted sick parades in the prisons, so they were fully aware of the situation); their response was simply that I should record the injuries and prescribe appropriate treatment. There was no acknowledgement on their part that our roles as physicians went beyond this blinkered and narrow approach. It was therefore apparent that if any action was to be taken, I would have to act independently and outside of the usual 'escalation' procedures.

'Through a remarkable confluence of events', Dr Orr was contacted by Halton Cheadle, the senior partner of the renowned Johannesburg firm of attorneys that specialised in labour law and human rights issues, Cheadle Thompson & Haysom. She decided to go public.

By the time Cheadle and his team had worked their magic, there were 661 pages of affidavits. Dr Orr's affidavit was of course the foundation of the case, and was 40 pages of brutal information. She was backed by affidavits from the 'Golden Two', Bishop Bruce Evans and Rev. George Irvine. Thereafter followed 140 affidavits by detainees, their families and friends and people detained at later dates. This included the sections by Mkhuseli Jack and Ivy Gcina referred to here.

The documentation hit the Eastern Cape Division of the Supreme Court on 25 September 1985, in the form of an application for an interim order restraining the police from assaulting detainees in Port Elizabeth prisons. Dr Orr concluded her founding affidavit thus: 'It ultimately became clear to me that, unless I made a stand and did something about the plight of the detainees, I would be compromising my moral beliefs and my perception of my moral responsibility. My conscience told me that I could no longer stand by and do nothing ... I respectfully submit that this application is very urgent. The police are apparently engaged in a pattern of daily assaults on detainees. For every day that goes by those apparently unrestrained assaults continue.'

The interdict was granted by Mr Justice Eksteen, the Deputy Judge President, and was all over every news medium around the world the next day. The assaults immediately dropped to a trickle.

The matter was put down for reply and argument. The police's replying affidavits were 74 in number, covering 1 246 pages. They in turn were replied to by the applicants with a further 93 affidavits covering 445 pages. The matter was set down for trial on a date in 1986, but by this date the state of emergency was over, and the matter disappeared.

No policeman was in any way sanctioned. The Judge President of the Eastern Cape, Mr Justice Cloete, the judge who had sent the KwaZakhele High School matric class to Robben Island in 1977, on 27 September told the press that judges in his division had seen hundreds of detainees and he personally had received only one complaint of assault.

On 3 October Dr Orr was told to stop seeing detainees by her superior, Dr Ivor Lang, the doctor who had so scandalously not treated Steve Biko eight years earlier. She was moved to duties in old age homes. Her colleagues would no longer talk to her. She resigned from her job late in 1985.

Apart from the enormous relief that the detainees felt, there was one further gratifying result of the brave stand taken by Dr Orr.

In November 1984 six doctors had approached the Transvaal High Court to attempt to get the court to order the South African Medical and Dental Council to hold an inquiry into the conduct of two of Port Elizabeth's district surgeons, Dr Ivor Lang and Dr Benjamin Tucker, for their neglect of Steve Biko when the security police were in the process of murdering him. Mr Justice Boshoff had ruled in January that there was prima facie evidence of improper and disgraceful conduct by these two, and they had been put before a five-man disciplinary committee of the Medical and Dental Council.

Dr Tucker was found guilty of disgraceful and improper conduct, and, incredibly, was given only a three-month suspension from the medical roll, and this was in turn suspended for two years. Dr Lang was also found guilty of improper conduct and failing to keep adequate records and for filing misleading reports on Biko's condition. He was reprimanded and cautioned.

The lightness of these sentences caused consternation, and then along came Dr Orr and her affidavit. Three weeks later the Medical and Dental Council had a re-think, and Dr Tucker was struck off the roll. A minor ricochet from the Wendy Orr bullet, maybe, but another necessary step towards justice.

22

South Africa's regional destabilisation

Van Zyl Slabbert became a Progressive Party Member of Parliament in 1974. The Prog numbers were then tiny, so everybody was given tasks. He was immediately made defence spokesperson.

'One of my first duties as defence spokesperson for the Progressive Party in parliament was to visit the so-called "operational area" with an all-party group of parliamentarians … in 1975. None of us, including members of the ruling National Party, had the faintest idea of South Africa's involvement in South West Africa (Namibia), Angola, Rhodesia or Mozambique, which was, in any case, repeatedly denied by John Vorster, then prime minister.

'In the study of the commissioner-general of Ovamboland, Jannie de Wet, General Magnus Malan, then head of the SADF, told General Constand Viljoen, then head of the army, to explain South Africa's military involvement. Viljoen pinned a little square map on the wall and told us that South African troops were a hundred and twenty kilometres away from Luanda, and the idea was to secure Angola militarily so that a government of national unity could be formed and it was imperative that Savimbi, as head of Unita, should be part of it. We all just sat there, speechless and stunned. Some of the Nationalist MPs were slightly grey in the face. How were they going to explain this to their constituents?

'After Viljoen's presentation, we had a dinner reception at Jannie de Wet's house. PW Botha was also present. He was slightly tipsy … he grabbed hold of my arm and said, "If it was not for the fucking Americans, we could take

Luanda and Windhoek tomorrow. In fact we could take the whole of Africa."
This was the first time that I realised that he was an extremely limited and
dangerous individual.'[231]

Thirteen years earlier, in March 1962, Sam Nujoma, the head of the
South West Africa People's Organisation (SWAPO), had visited camps in
Tanzania built to house refugee Namibians. He instructed two exiles to
return to South West Africa to begin the infiltration of small groups of exiles,
as the start of a guerrilla war designed to eventually win independence for
Namibia from South Africa.

The guerrilla war began well for SWAPO. Counter-insurgency was
then the responsibility of the South West African police force. They were
quickly pushed onto the back foot by the numbers and the determination
of the insurgents. Pretoria started to adopt new tactics. On 26 August 1966
South African paratroopers attacked a camp of SWAPO insurgents at
Omugulugwombashe in Angola. A number of guerrillas were killed, and this
action is today seen as the start of SWAPO's revolutionary armed struggle.

SWAPO began getting more support, more recruits and more and better
weapons all the time. By 26 January 1973 their confidence had risen to the
point where 50 insurgents, now from SWAPO's armed wing PLAN, attacked
a police station in Singalamwe, with considerable success.

This caused the SADF to take over counter-insurgency control from the
South West African police, which happened on 1 April 1974. Some 15 000
SADF recruits were put into South West Africa, the SADF budget increased
150% from 1973 to 1974, and the SADF cleared a 5-km strip on the banks
of the Kunene, to be called 'The Cutline'. The war was beginning in earnest.

Twenty four days later, on 24 April 1974, Portugal's Caetano government,
the Estado Novo, which had ruled Portugal since 1933, and was Europe's
longest existing dictatorship, was ousted in the Carnation Revolution. Later
that year Portugal's new government announced that it was to give both
Angola and Mozambique independence. Realising that this would require
the different groupings in Angola to somehow coalesce, Portugal worked
for, and got, the ALVOR agreement of cooperation between these three
groupings: the People's Movement for the Liberation of Angola (MPLA);
the National Union for the Total Independence of Angola (UNITA); and the
National Liberation Front of Angola (FNLA).

Of these three, the MPLA had Soviet backing and was a Marxist
organisation. This was enough for the South African government of John
Vorster, advised by his Intelligence Chief, Hendrik van den Bergh, to
decide to take steps to prevent it from becoming the sole governing party
in Angola. Immediately they began funnelling arms and money to the other

two organisations, particularly UNITA. The Central Intelligence Agency of the United States government, the CIA, did likewise.

Realising that this was happening, and on request from the MPLA, the Soviet Union supplied weapons and advisers to the MPLA's armed wing, the People's Armed Forces of the Liberation of Angola (FAPLA), and Cuba sent 200 advisers. This helped FAPLA to drive both UNITA and the FNLA out of Luanda, and South Africa's Defence Minister, PW Botha, stated that 'The MPLA could now, for all intents and purposes, be considered the presumptive ultimate rulers of Angola.'

South Africa had funded a dam on the Kunene River (the Angola–South West Africa border) at Ruacana and a hydroelectric station at Calueque in Angola, which would have supplied all of South West Africa's needs when completed. It was not yet commissioned. Using this as a ruse, Botha committed 1 000 SADF troops to Calueque in August 1975, apparently to guard this investment.

Portugal had announced that 11 November 1975 was to be the date of independence for Angola, and, as the MPLA had sole control of the capital, Luanda, they were to become the government of Angola. Botha would have none of this and the invasion that Van Zyl Slabbert spoke of began.

By early November the South African troops were over 500 kilometres into Angola, causing the Soviet Union to begin a massive arms airlift into Luanda. Thousands of Cuban troops also arrived after South African troops attacked a FAPLA base and killed a number of Cuban advisers there. Castro immediately said that he would do 'whatever is required' to beat back the South African troops.

They did just enough, and independence was granted on 11 November to the MPLA government, who then controlled Luanda and not much else. When press reports, including photographs of white troops dressed as mercenaries, clearly identified the South African involvement, the American Congress forbade any further clandestine CIA involvement. Other African countries, including Nigeria and Tanzania, previously undecided, now fell in behind the MPLA.

The game was up and the South African troops, shorn of their American aid, returned to South West Africa, leaving the FNLA to be wiped out and UNITA to retreat to their southern Angola stronghold.

About 30 South African troops were killed, about 100 wounded, and seven were paraded as prisoners by the Cubans. The white South African public, deliberately kept in the dark until now, was both startled and unhappy.

This was the first South African military incursion into Angola, and had been termed 'Operation Savannah' by the SADF.

South Africa was invested in Angola and South West Africa for another thirteen years, from 1975 until 1988. Its strategy was threefold: firstly and most prominently, it waged intense war on SWAPO and its armed wing PLAN, both against guerrillas who infiltrated South West Africa, and also against SWAPO bases in Angola. On occasion they fought against FAPLA, the Angolan government and its Cuban and Soviet advisers within Angola. Secondly, it initiated and conducted secret negotiations with representatives of the Angolan government, beginning almost as Operation Savannah was concluded and continuing, albeit in a low-key manner, until South Africa abandoned its occupation of Namibia. Thirdly, it pushed forward with cosmetic attempts at 'democratic government' in South West Africa in a futile attempt to outflank SWAPO. We will consider these three strategies in turn, beginning with the attempt to construct a 'democratic government' in Windhoek but, of course, without SWAPO.

The South African occupation of South West Africa was, from the onset, overlain by international legalities. South Africa had been handed a 'mandate' to administer South West Africa after World War I (during which South African troops had subdued the German occupying force there). With time this mandate had grown more and more controversial, until, in 1971, the International Court of Justice in The Hague had ruled South Africa's occupation 'illegal'. The next year, the United Nations, to South Africa's fury, ruled that SWAPO was in fact 'the sole representative of the South West African people', and six years later, in 1978, the United Nations passed Resolution 435, calling for an immediate cease-fire in South West Africa–Angola, and for UN-controlled elections in the country, to determine a democratically elected government. South Africa pretended to accept 435, but immediately made its implementation impossible by continually attacking SWAPO bases on Angolan soil.

Determined to create an alternative scenario, South Africa put into place in Windhoek a political 'arrangement', the Democratic Turnhalle Alliance (DTA), which immediately formed the Turnhalle Constitutional Conference, to establish constitutional proposals for South West Africa, and to form an interim government for two years from early 1977. On 5 November 1977 this body elected Dirk Mudge, a local white politician with roots back into South Africa's National Party, as Chairperson and Clemens Kapuuo, an Herero chief, as President. Kapuuo was assassinated in 1978 in an as yet unexplained event. Mudge then drove the process on and in December 1978 an 'election' was held, without SWAPO or any political parties. All representation was by ethnically based 'tribes': it was, as a critic described it, a 'confederation of bantustans'. The DTA won 41 of the 50 seats. Mudge became Chairman of the Council of Ministers of an assembly inaugurated by South Africa. No other country recognised this nonsense.

Constitutional principles were negotiated and accepted in 1982 and in 1985 another interim government, the Transitional Government of National Unity, was created, without SWAPO's involvement. This charade persisted until 1989, when events overtook it and democratic elections at last happened.

If Pretoria's political shenanigans in Windhoek have an unreal, fairy-tale appearance, this was definitely not so with the military operations that filled the thirteen years from Operation Savannah to the end of the battles of Cuito Cuanavale. These were well-organised and utterly deadly.

In this time the SADF invaded Angola 43 times, often with devastating effect.[232]

In the first period of the war, from Operation Savannah in 1975 until Operation Askari in late 1983, there were three other major invasions:

Operation Reindeer (4–10 May 1978) was aimed at SWAPO bases in Chetequera, Dombondola and Cassinga, about 250 kilometres inside Angola. It involved carpet bombing by South Africa's aging Canberra and Buccaneer bombers, who at this stage encountered no sophisticated anti-aircraft batteries. They dropped many fragmentation bombs on these camps and the attack was followed up by a botched paratroop drop at Cassinga, the biggest of the camps. 624 SWAPO personnel were killed, and another 611 injured. Of these 167 were women and 298 teenagers. SWAPO termed the camps refugee camps; South Africa of course styled them 'military bases'. Three SADF soldiers were killed.

Operation Protea (23 August – 4 September 1981) saw 5 000 SADF soldiers enter Angola to attack SWAPO 'command centres' at Xangongo and two other sites. This time 831 guerrillas were killed and 25 captured. Ten SADF troops were killed and 64 wounded. Despite these being termed SWAPO camps, 13 Russians were also amongst the dead.

Operation Askari was the lengthiest of the four operations (9 December 1983 – 5 January 1984). Again, South Africa had control of the air and its goals were to overwhelm the SWAPO and FAPLA bases at Lubango, Cahama, Mulondo and Cuvelai, and drive the newly arriving SAM anti-aircraft missile bases away from the South West African border. FAPLA bases were also to be attacked, as South Africa believed that SWAPO guerrillas took refuge in FAPLA bases and that the SAM missile bases were there.

Askari was aborted in early January without success, with the SADF having failed to dislodge FAPLA soldiers from their bases. The SADF, however, seized much equipment, including some SAM missiles and their launchers. In total 426 FAPLA soldiers were killed, as were 45 PLAN guerrillas, five Cubans and 25 South Africans.

Meanwhile, apart from the bloodshed that followed from this hopelessly unequal war, South Africa was engaging simultaneously in a series of top-secret negotiations with the Angolan government on a variety of issues of mutual concern. These talks were never publicised, and only recently came to light when South Africa's Department of International Relations and Cooperation in Pretoria made its archives public in the late years of the first decade of the 20th century. Christopher Saunders inspected the records, and published a paper on them.[233]

Saunders shows that these negotiations began in April 1976 and eight meetings had happened by June 1980. Initially the topic was the inauguration of the Ruacana hydro-electric scheme, designed to supply all the power South West Africa needed. This project was underway but was not complete at the time of Angolan independence.

Angola, for its part, wanted a demilitarised zone on the Angola–South West Africa border, to be monitored by joint helicopter flights. However, as South Africa would not end its raids into Angola, the Angolan authorities stopped the sluices and immobilised the hydro-electric scheme.

Later meetings of the negotiating teams were always bedevilled by South African military raids. A meeting in 1980, attended by Magnus Malan, was again poisoned by a raid. It was only in 1982, when a team of South Africans, including Foreign Minister Pik Botha, Minister of Defence Magnus Malan, and the Director General of Foreign Affairs met a high-level Angolan team at Ihla do Sal, an island off Africa's west coast, that South Africa offered to withdraw from Angola if SWAPO withdrew far north of the border, and the Cuban forces even further north.

Again, a battle between UNITA forces and FAPLA at Cangamba in August 1983 saw a UNITA victory, and the Angolans declared that they had 'no interest in continuing dialogue with the South Africans'.

Then came Operation Askari, and on 5 January 1984 Sam Nujoma approached the United Nations Secretary General, Javier Pérez de Cuéllar, and requested him to arrange a ceasefire. Pérez de Cuéllar involved Dr Chester Crocker, President Reagan's newly appointed Assistant Secretary of State for Africa. Crocker was an academic, whose writings on Africa had caused Reagan to appoint him as his African point man.

Crocker immediately moved American policy on South Africa from the strident criticism and escalating anti-apartheid actions of the Jimmy Carter presidency, to 'constructive engagement', with a loosening of the arms embargo from the USA to South Africa and a strengthening of diplomatic relations with South Africa.

Despite initial failure and deep suspicion from African leaders, Crocker persisted. Eventually he brought President Kenneth Kaunda to Washington to meet Reagan, and from this and much more diplomatic pushing and pulling, the Lusaka Accords flowed.

These events caused an intensification of the meetings between South Africa and Angola. The Angolan head of negotiations, 'Kito' Rodrigues, who later became Angola's ambassador to the newly democratic South Africa, met with Crocker and Pik Botha, but without SWAPO, the Russians and the Cubans.

Together Pérez de Cuéllar and Crocker laboured on, and by 31 January 1984 they had got South Africa and Angola to, reluctantly and with deep suspicions, agree to a ceasefire.

The ceasefire was concretised in the Lusaka Accords, signed by South Africa and Angola in 1984. These called for the withdrawal of South African troops from Angola, and Angola agreed to keep an area 120 kilometres wide, from the Angola–South West Africa border north, free of SWAPO. Post-signature, General Geldenhuys demanded that there be a phased Cuban withdrawal and the removal of SWAPO camps from Angola, but this was not conceded. Angola demanded that South Africa desist from supporting UNITA and this was also not agreed. A Joint Monitoring Commission was established to survey the implementation of the agreement. Russia and Cuba, both of whom had not been consulted in the process of these accords, were aghast. Russia immediately stepped up its military aid to FAPLA, as did Cuba.

On 18 April 1985 a small ceremony was held on the border as the last South African troops left Angola, leaving about 60 men at the pump station at Ruacana. Constant Viljoen said that he 'hoped there would never again be a reason for South African troops to enter Angola', and on 1 May Pik Botha wrote to Rodrigues that he was 'pleased that we can now renew discussions'.[234]

PW Botha, now South Africa's President, basked in the glow of his peacemaking attempts, which were again on show in this year in Mozambique. Was peace really to come to the sub-continent?

South Africa, in the mid-1980s, was destabilising, to one degree or another, all of its neighbours. We will return to SWAPO and Angola shortly. Now we turn to Mozambique.

FRELIMO began an insurgency against Portuguese colonial government in the 1960s, and also provided a hospitable launch-pad for liberation movements from Rhodesia and South Africa. It paid a massive price for this courageous generosity.

First to attack Mozambique was the UDI regime from Rhodesia.

In 1963, two years before Ian Smith declared UDI, Rhodesia's Prime Minister, Winston Field, approached the Deputy Commissioner of the British South African Police in Salisbury, Ken Flower, and requested Flower to set up Rhodesia's secret police, to be called the Central Intelligence Organisation (CIO). This Flower agreed to do.

One of Flower's first fact-finding missions was to Angola to meet Dr Sâo José Lopes, the head of the Portuguese security police. Dr Lopes had introduced into Angola a unit of the security police called 'Flechas', or 'Arrows'. These were local Angolans, recruited from either disaffected members of the liberation movements, or 'turned' guerrillas. They were, in Flower's words, 'encouraged to do their own thing' (i.e. operate without any statutory restraints) and in Angola they 'accounted for 60% of all terrorist kills'. Flower immediately saw the potential of this model.[235]

In the early 1970s Flower began such an organisation, which he describes as 'a small-scale pseudo-operation', which he set into operation in Mozambique to counter the insurgency quartered there, which was infiltrating into Rhodesia by the Zimbabwe African National Liberation Army (ZANLA). He describes this as 'protecting our borders from beyond our borders'. The CIO began to 'recruit Mozambicans who were encouraged to do their own thing in Mozambique without having to rely on support from Rhodesia'.[236]

This was named the Mozambique Resistance Movement (MNR or later RENAMO), which Flower kept 'small and clandestinely manageable during the first five years, whilst it could provide the eyes and ears of our Intelligence in Mozambique'.[237]

The decision by the Portuguese government to give Mozambique independence on 25 June 1975 was preceded by a prior decision, in September 1974, that FRELIMO was to be the sole representative of the Mozambican people, and would be the entire government thereafter. This caused the splintering off of smaller movements, grist for Flower's mill, and they were quickly incorporated into the MNR. Heavy-handed behaviour by FRELIMO after independence and the purging of their ranks, with many guerrillas being put into 're-education camps', caused more splits. In 1975 the Rhodesians freed Andre Matsangaissa from one such camp and he became the first leader of the MNR, now rapidly growing into a large movement.

In 1977 the Mozambican Civil War began, with RENAMO and FRELIMO now irreconcilable. Matsangaissa was killed in 1979 and Afonso Dhlakama became RENAMO's head, running a brutal and merciless war, with RENAMO roving the countryside, moving from one atrocity to another, and FRELIMO desperately trying to control the urban space, with fortified villages being created to house peasants, often against their will.

Into this difficult situation was thrown the rapidly escalating Rhodesian war, with the Rhodesians conducting a number of cross-border raids, the most prominent of which, the 9 August 1976 raid on the camp at Nyadzonya, saw about 1 000 Zimbabweans massacred by a team of Selous Scouts in FRELIMO uniforms driving vehicles with Mozambique number plates.

The Rhodesian situation quickly unravelled and in 1979 negotiations began between the Smith regime and the various liberation movements. White minority government was on its last legs.

In South Africa the Vorster regime had been overwhelmed by the Information Scandal, and PW Botha had become Prime Minister in 1978. He immediately took the 'Rhodesian matter' away from Vorster's most trusted aide, General Van Den Bergh, and handed it to the Military Intelligence Directorate (MID), which fell under the Defence Force, which was under his control as Minister of Defence.

By mid-1979 the MID was already supplying weapons to RENAMO and already over $1 million of South Africa's clandestine military budget had been spent on the rebels.[238]

As the Smith regime became increasingly powerless to stop the flood towards democracy, Magnus Malan, the head of the SADF, and his Rhodesian counterpart, General Peter Walls, cut a deal that in the event of the collapse of 'white' Rhodesia, the groups in the Rhodesian defence forces that would have been 'compromised' would be integrated into the South African army.

Robert Mugabe's ZANU won the first democratic election in 1980 and white minority government was over, forever. Flower's CIO was forced to close down its RENAMO operations and the rebels were offered the choice of continuing to operate as RENAMO under South African control or to reintegrate into civilian life in Mozambique. Most chose the South African option.

They were loaded into Lockheed C130s and flown to the Northern Transvaal. This included their radio station 'Radio Voz da Africa Livre' and all RENAMO personnel. Those wishing for a return to Mozambique were regrouped at a base in the Sitatonga mountains in Mozambique.[239]

'After the transfer to South Africa, RENAMO's situation was, nevertheless, precarious initially. In June 1980, the Mozambique Armed Forces captured Sitatonga base and shattered the last concentration of rebels in Mozambique. With no base and no supplies, the remaining groups dispersed. They survived by pursuing a career of uncoordinated armed banditry ... From Maputo's perspective, the threat was over.'[240]

Maputo should not have been so sanguine.

The South Africans moved quickly. A camp was set up at Walmerstad, a farm 50 kilometres out of Pretoria. There RENAMO's radio station and its leadership were quartered. Military training facilities were established at Zoabastad and Phalaborwa and by the end of 1980 the first batch of trained insurgents were airlifted into central Mozambique. By early 1981 6 000 or 7 000 rebels were in operation in Mozambique, a much higher number than when RENAMO had been under Rhodesian control. By the end of 1981 there were RENAMO insurgents in every Mozambican province.

Thus began one of Africa's most ruthless and bloody insurgencies. RENAMO, from 1980 to 1988, all the time under South African control and reliant entirely on South Africa for weapons and ammunition, communications and transport, and medical and other supplies, was responsible for a terrorist campaign that saw nearly a million citizens either killed or starved to death, and nearly five million displaced.[241] Some 1 800 schools, 720 health units, 900 shops, and 1 300 trucks and buses were 'rendered inoperative'.[242]

RENAMO's modus operandi was exposed when the Mozambique Armed Forces overran a RENAMO base in Garagua in Manica Province on 5 December 1981. Documents that had been hastily stuffed down a toilet were retrieved and showed that RENAMO's 'handlers', the South African military, had given RENAMO the mandate to 'turn Mozambique into a destabilized buffer zone' and to curb ANC infiltration into South Africa.[243]

Not everything was left to RENAMO, and tensions between South Africa and FRELIMO escalated as FRELIMO allowed the ANC to operate from Mozambique. South Africa's response was cross-border raids, the first of which happened in 1981. In 1983 South African aircraft bombed the Beira fuel depot. For months, neither Mozambique nor Zimbabwe had fuel.

All of this caused much disquiet in the major democracies. With the arrival of Chester Crocker as President Reagan's Assistant Secretary of State for African Affairs, increasing pressure was put on Pretoria to negotiate with Maputo and to end this brutality. South Africa thus began talks with the Mozambican government in late 1983 (the Mbabane talks), and this led on to what PW Botha felt was his next successful peace initiative, the Nkomati Accords.

On 16 March 1984 Mozambican President Samora Machel signed the Nkomati Accords with PW Botha, in a great show at Komatipoort in South Africa.

Khusta Jack wrote of this: 'The apartheid government scored a sensational psychological coup ... our very own hero, President Samora

Machel, and the repulsive apartheid state president and belligerent dictator, PW Botha ... signed a non-aggression pact ... My nightmare was capped by a picture showing PW Botha and Foreign Affairs Minister Pik Botha posing with Samora and his wife Graça.'[244]

This agreement stated that South Africa would no longer support RENAMO and the Mozambican government would expel the ANC from its territory. It reduced the ANC delegation in Maputo to ten people. The balance of the ANC personnel were told to either enter UN refugee camps, or leave the country. Only the top four ANC personnel, including Oliver Tambo, would retain their mobility in Mozambique. All training camps, bases, accommodation and transit facilities were to be shut down. Joe Slovo left Mozambique in July.

The ANC inside South Africa was quick to retaliate in response to this set-back, and a series of bomb blasts followed. On 3 April a car-bomb exploded on the Esplanade in Durban, killing three people. On 5 April a bomb destroyed the Transkei Consulate's information centre in Bloemfontein. Then another bomb in Durban – this time on 12 May on the 25th floor of the Trust Bank Building.

On 13 May ANC guerrillas launched an audacious rocket attack on Durban's oil refinery, which saw seven people killed. Their escaping car was caught by police and all four occupants of the getaway car were killed. Three were from Port Elizabeth – Clifford Bruiners, who had been detained when he was in matric in 1977 and thereafter left South Africa, and Vuyisile de Vos and Vuyisile Matroos, both from KwaZakhele, who had both left South Africa in the late 1970s. De Vos and Matroos were buried in Port Elizabeth on 11 June, and a crowd of 5 000 defied the tight restrictions imposed by a magistrate on the funeral. PEBCO, PEYCO, COSAS and the Release Mandela Committee were all represented. At the funeral Aubrey Mokoena of the Release Mandela Committee declared both guerrillas as 'saints'. The police meanwhile held that this group were responsible for all the recent Durban bombings.

And so 1984 was the year of Pretoria making peace. Both Angola (Lusaka Accords) and Mozambique (Nkomati Accords) were now expecting to get on with rebuilding their shattered countries, with no further South African destabilisation. PW Botha was rewarded by Mrs Thatcher, who organised a trip for him to meet various European heads of state, and he was received with much praise there and in the press.

It did not take long for the first cracks to show.

By May 1984 RENAMO had clearly not been reined in, and Maputo called for a first high-level meeting with the South Africans. Dossiers of evidence of South African resupply of RENAMO were presented by the Mozambicans and denied by the South Africans.

What followed was another of Pretoria's elaborate charades, as Foreign Minister Pik Botha convened meeting after meeting with FRELIMO and RENAMO, sometimes apart, sometimes together. Conditions for a unified government were thrashed out, agreed, abandoned, insults thrown, positions changed overnight, until eventually, in October 1984, RENAMO withdrew. Further heroic attempts by Pik Botha to resurrect the talks failed.

In fact, the South African government had no intention whatsoever of slowing the destabilisation of either Angola or Mozambique. Now it was to be done in an underhand way, underground.

Firstly, Angola.

In 1985 nearly 90% of the foreign exchange that the government of Angola earned flowed from the sale of oil into the world market. Almost all of this came from oilfields in the disputed Angolan province of Cabinda, an enclave of land just north of mainland Angola and separated from the bulk of Angola by a sliver of the Republic of the Congo and the Congo River. To add complexity to the issue, the only refinery in Cabinda was owned by Gulf Oil, an American company.

Operation Argon was South Africa's answer.[245] This was a frolic so extraordinary that only a country run by PW Botha could have conceived of it. And so dangerous that it had to be hidden from the Reagan administration for even they, despite their desperate and ruthless determination to rid Africa of Cubans and Soviets, would have prevented it.

The macroplan was simple – destroy the foreign exchange earning potential of the Angolan government, and they will rush to return the Cuban troops to Cuba. (How the second part of the sentence was automatically to follow from the first, nobody had bothered to think out.) The fact that millions of Angolans would then be trapped without medicine, food, vehicles and other goods was of no concern – the nebulous conclusion that the Cuban troops would then leave, that was all that mattered.

This was to be effected by destroying the oil tanks at Cabinda, thereby crippling Angola's main industry. The refinery, with its American ownership, could not be touched, but the tanks, owned by the Angolan Government, could be destroyed, and that would have the same effect on the Angolan economy.

How could this be effected?

An aerial bombardment was out of the question, as the Americans could then easily establish who was responsible, and anyway it could certainly not be assured that the aeroplanes involved could return safely given the anti-aircraft missile banks and the MIG fighters stationed in Angola.

Hence the plan of Operation Argon. On 7 May 1985 the submarine SAS *Johanna van der Merwe* left Simonstown and stopped over in Saldanha to load two inflatable boats, fuel, weapons and ammunition for nine operatives, other equipment as required and enough explosives to blow up the Cabinda oil tanks, with camouflage explosives that would suggest UNITA operatives had effected the operation. The submarine then headed off towards Cabinda over 100 nautical miles out to sea.

On 12 May 'the required authority to execute Operation Argon was signed' and the next day, at 8pm on 13 May, the strike craft SAS *Jim Fouché* left Saldanha with a nine-person raiding team from 4 Reconnaissance Regiment (Recces) headed by Capt Wynand du Toit, two doctors and other support operatives on board.

On 17 May the strike craft and the submarine made their rendezvous, about 100 nautical miles to sea west of Cabinda, and the nine Recces and their support team were transferred to the submarine.

Two days before the raid was to happen, the submarine conducted a 'periscope recce' of the proposed landing beach from 12 nautical miles out, and ascertained that all was OK. The next day a trial landing was made at Ponta de Malembo, the proposed landing point. The team identified emergency evacuation points and returned safely to the submarine.

On 20 May 1985, twelve days after Godolozi, Hashe and Galela were abducted and murdered, Operation Argon went ahead.

The submarine surfaced at 7:45 pm and a periscope sighting of a small fishing boat meant they had to go further offshore. The inflatable boats were launched at 8:30 pm, nearly an hour late and 16 nautical miles offshore. They arrived at the beach at 10:30 pm, to discover a fisherman in a makorro and two men at a fire on the beach. The team had to again wait and only landed at 11:30 pm. Capt Du Toit was concerned that, should they withdraw and return the next night, they might well not have enough fuel for the inflatable boats stored in the cramped submarine to make the second trip. He thus decided to press on and he and his team set off immediately.

Due to the delays the recce group now had to lay up for the night. Then they discovered a camp of FAPLA soldiers that their reconnaissance had not detected, and the next morning they saw a small team of FAPLA soldiers following their tracks. The trackers then withdrew, and a large unit of troops then returned on their tracks.

The recces were weighed down by their cargo of explosives and thus had limited ammunition for the firefight that ensued. Two were quickly wounded and Capt Du Toit and two others decided to move ahead to draw the soldiers away from the rest of the group. This they did at great personal cost. Both Capt Du Toit's colleagues were killed and he was immobilised by gunshot wounds and was captured. The other four, however, were not pursued and made it back to the submarine and eventually home.

The Angolan troops seem to have believed that the group were mercenaries (certainly they were not in uniform) and Du Toit was shot in the neck after capture. He nevertheless was transferred to hospital and recovered, and was, much later, swapped in a prisoner swap and returned to South Africa.

When news of the disastrous mission emerged, Magnus Malan, the South African Minister of Defence, said that this was a reconnaissance force sent to find ANC and SWAPO training camps.

Capt Du Toit however revealed the whole sorry story of the mission to his Angolan captors and they then revealed it all to the international news media.

Later, on 27 September, Malan explained this mission again, this time as follows: 'What we may or may not have been doing in other parts of Angola, whether we may or may not have been gathering intelligence, has absolutely nothing to do with the [Lusaka Accords].'[246]

The results were predictable. On 30 May the Minister of Foreign Affairs, Pik Botha, said that the Angolan government had broken off all negotiations with South Africa. And the Americans, dumbfounded by this development, withdrew their ambassador, Mr Herman Nickel.

The Lusaka Accords were the only things that were blown up in Operation Argon.

And then there was Mozambique.

After Nkomati, the FRELIMO forces were on the front foot and in August 1985 they overran the RENAMO central base in Gorongosa. There they found many abandoned documents, including the diaries of Francisco Vaz, a RENAMO National Council member and adjunct to the RENAMO president, Afonso Dhlakama. These diaries covered the period from December 1983 to September 1984 and provide a unique insight into the relationship of the South African government and RENAMO over the period just before and after the Nkomati Accord.

An entry in these diaries from 16 January 1984 notes that 'because of the commitment that the South Africans will make to Machel, the resupply for the first six months of 1984 will all be delivered in the first few months'.[247]

On 11 February the diaries note that '1 730 AK-47s and 4 279 boxes of AK-47 ammunition' were air-dropped in nine areas, spread over Mozambique, and on 13 February '900 AK-47s and 500 boxes of AK-47 ammunition' were dropped in Zambezia province. A great way to prepare for peace.

The South African Military Intelligence contact person was Colonel Charles van Niekerk, who spoke Portuguese and some Mozambican African languages. He was clearly trusted: 'Colonel Charlie guarantees to RENAMO that even if an agreement is signed with Machel, they will still continue to send airplanes now and then.'[248]

A copy of a letter was also found. Written on 16 June 1984, it was from RENAMO President Dhlakama to 'Friend Commander Charles'. It noted that 'we no longer have war material ... so we want to remind our friends of the pledge they gave us of keeping up supply to us clandestinely'. In July Van Niekerk replied that he had arranged a drop of 26 tons beginning 1 August, in 'the drop zone to the east of Inhaminga'.

The diaries further note that a RENAMO delegation was taken by sea to South Africa on 9 August 1984. They met with Defence Minister Magnus Malan, Military Intelligence Chief Van der Westhuizen, Colonel Van Niekerk and other officers. The South Africans said that 14 air deliveries had been made from May to July, but there were now problems. They could no longer use airforce planes, and they couldn't use the Navy 'because the information might leak'. So civilian aircraft were to be used, the first six drops from which happened between 31 August and 25 October 1984.

Later, South African parliamentarians obtained copies of these diaries and they demanded to be informed of their authenticity. Minister Pik Botha replied that 'the information tallies with the flights undertaken by the air force'. He had never been informed of these acts, and this is corroborated by the diaries.

23

The Rubicon speech

So much for the political fallout from Operation Argon and Mozambiquan destabilisation. There was, however, an economic tsunami building up, which was to follow the declaration of the state of emergency on 21 July 1985.

By mid-1985 certain positive trends were evident in the South African economy. In 1984 the whole economy had grown by 4%, a reasonable achievement. By June 1985 excess demand in the economy had begun to drop, a large surplus on the current account of the balance of payments had built up, and the rand appeared to have stabilised at around 50 American cents. These trends were seen to be helpful and the Minister of Finance, Barend du Plessis, was confident that things could now improve.

Then came the state of emergency.

Three days later (24 July) the French Prime Minister Mr Laurent Fabius withdrew indefinitely his country's ambassador to South Africa, Mr Pierre Boyer, and suspended all new French investment in South Africa. This he attributed to a 'new and serious deterioration in South Africa's internal situation'.

France was not alone in condemning the recently imposed state of emergency: the European Economic Community condemned it and demanded that Botha release all of South Africa's political prisoners. Even President Reagan, while initially silent, eventually publicly stated that PW Botha should lift the state of emergency.

At the time South Africa had about R60 billion in foreign debt, of which about R34 billion was short-term (i.e. could be recalled overnight). Of this short-term debt, R16 billion was owed by South Africa's banks, R11 billion by private companies, R4 billion by government and government corporations, and R3 billion by the Reserve Bank. This debt had arisen because of the policy of the South African Reserve Bank, which raised interest rates to over 20% in a misguided belief that this could lower the dangerously high rate of consumer inflation at the time, which was 18.4% for 1985. With interest rates at these levels, many banks, businesses and government bodies borrowed offshore, where rates were much lower, causing the rise in foreign debt. When this debt fell due for repayment, the collapse of the rand that followed the declaration of the state of emergency resulted in rand repayments for dollar borrowings being impossible to meet.

On the declaration of the state of emergency, word got around that a group of banks, led by the American bank Chase Manhattan, had decided that they were to call up all maturing loans made to South African borrowers. On 31 July the chairperson of Chase Manhattan, Willard Butcher, met his chief executive, Thomas Labrecque, in New York and this dramatic decision was taken. Four other banks, including the Bank of America, then followed Chase. This would have left the South African Reserve Bank in a position where its dollar stock would have been more than depleted.

Thus a double disaster: with the rand beginning to slide against the dollar (it fell nearly 25% against the dollar in 1985), South African borrowers were being massively penalised when they attempted to repay dollar debt from rand earnings. The Reserve Bank had also not anticipated this run on dollars and couldn't supply enough dollars. In August 1985 foreign banks extracted $400 million out of South Africa and the Reserve Bank seized up.

Pik Botha recalled: 'I will never forget the night of 31 July when [Minister of Finance] Barend du Plessis phoned me. I still perspire when I think of it. He said, "Pik, I must tell you that the country is facing inevitable bankruptcy ... The process has started".'[249]

There was only one possible opportunity to save the situation. President PW Botha was to make a speech on 15 August at the National Party Congress in Durban. If only that speech could somehow reassure the international community.

There was to be a day-long session of senior National Party ministers and office-bearers to prepare for the congress, and this was scheduled for 2 August.

This meeting was to be held at a secret Military Intelligence complex at the Astronomical Observatory at Fort Klapperkop in Pretoria, attended by 33 NP ministers and chaired by PW Botha himself. The meeting has become known as the 'Sterrewag' meeting, named after its strange venue. Its main purpose was to tweak NP policy for presentation to the 15 August congress. It was now or never for the reformers in the Cabinet as aggrieved banks grew in number, and as 15 August, the date for PW Botha's speech, approached.

At the time, the minister on whose shoulders the responsibility for legislative changes with regard to blacks in politics rested was the Minister of Constitutional Development and Planning, who was also the chair of the all-important State Security Council, Minister Chris Heunis.

Late in July PW Botha requested Heunis to prepare proposals for the upcoming Sterrewag meeting, and Heunis delivered these to Botha on 31 July for the 2 August meeting.

Heading up the Chief Directorate in Heunis's department at the time was Dr Fanie Cloete, who went on to have a respected academic career. Recently Dr Cloete, now an academic, was referred to documents held in the Archive for Contemporary Affairs at the University of the Free State in Bloemfontein, which include a previously unknown 133-page transcript of the Sterrewag proceedings, including PW Botha's handwritten notations. When Cloete enquired of other participants at the Sterrewag meeting, none had any knowledge of the transcription, nor that the meeting had been recorded. Cloete believed that Botha had secretly had the proceedings taped and transcribed, something he had done on other occasions also (one secret transcription he used to embarrass Van Zyl Slabbert at another time, and his famous meeting with Nelson Mandela was also recorded).

There are other reconstructions of the Sterrewag proceedings, but we will use Dr Cloete's article.[250]

The issues under discussion at Sterrewag were the issues the world wanted to hear the South African government's intentions on, particularly the two issues of the incorporation of legitimate black voices into mainstream South African politics, and also developments with the release from prison of Nelson Mandela and other black political prisoners.

PW Botha both chaired the Sterrewag proceedings and led the debate.

Cloete noted that 'the views expressed by PW Botha reflect very conservative perspectives that did not leave any room for major policy changes'. Botha stated that he was not in favour of a unitary state model, or a federation or a fourth chamber of parliament. The 'independent homelands' had to be retained, and, while every population group should be managing their own 'own affairs', in the case of blacks outside the then existing 'self-governing' and 'independent' homelands (Botha used the term 'states' to refer to the homelands) their 'own affairs' should be managed at local government level in a way that linked them to the homelands.

As usual Botha expressed himself forcefully, and 'no minister took a contrary stance to these forcefully expressed views during the rest of the proceedings … knowing how short PW Botha's fuse was'. 'During the rest of the proceedings, none of the speakers gave any indication that they were prepared to relinquish final white control over the country. On the contrary, there were explicit calls by more conservative as well as more progressive ministers for the protection of "civilised Western values" by retaining white political control in South Africa.' These calls came from, amongst others, Pik Botha and Gerrit Viljoen.

It was clear from his introductory remarks that PW Botha was not planning to introduce fundamental changes to government policy at this time. Cloete describes the situation charmingly: 'It is now clear that by 1985 PW Botha had reached the ceiling of his transformative potential.'

Heunis nevertheless did his best. He tried to bring in his proposals regarding power-sharing among all races at executive level in a Council of Cabinets. His proposals included representation on this Council for blacks living outside of the homelands. His cabinet colleagues politely ignored these proposals. 'The only generally accepted principle of legislative powers for black South African citizens that was acceptable to the meeting was that the black self-governing homelands and the black independent homelands should have full legislative powers in their own parliaments. In addition, those parliaments could have legislative control over black municipalities,' Dr Cloete writes from his study of the transcription of the meeting.

On the issue of the freeing of Mandela, there was no substantive discussion.

PW Botha, as was his custom, concluded the session.

He did not summarise the proceedings, nor did he call for motions. He requested Heunis, Pik Botha and Barend du Plessis to provide guidelines for his speech, taking into account the day's proceedings. Through this procedure he left himself with maximum flexibility in his future drafting.

Given the conservative and unimaginative opinions that were the meat of the Sterrewag day, what followed was an extraordinary set of events.

Firstly PW Botha wrote identical letters to German Chancellor Helmut Kohl and British Prime Minister Margaret Thatcher, informing them that his party had made breakthrough proposals to him, and that 'I am at present giving serious consideration to these proposals, and intend to make an announcement on my government's decision in the near future'.

He then conveyed a similar message to President Reagan and instructed the Minister of Foreign Affairs, Pik Botha, to meet with Western diplomats, to inform them of what was ahead.

Pik Botha spent 9 and 10 August in Vienna with, amongst others, Reagan's security advisor Robert McFarlane, Thatcher's chosen diplomat Ewen Fergusson, and officials from Germany and elsewhere. One of the American group, still stinging from Operation Argon, said afterwards, 'From bitter experience we know that South African officials will talk about their plans, then return home and back away at the last moment because of second thoughts or fear.' (Spot-on, as things went.)

Pik Botha's press secretary also briefed both *Newsweek* and *Time* magazines. *Time* reported, just before the speech, that 'the country should be prepared for the most important announcement since Dutch settlers arrived at the Cape 300 years ago'.

Then something happened.

Stemmet and Barnard, two staff from the Department of History at the University of the Free State, believe that PW Botha got wind of Pik Botha's briefing of Saatchi and Saatchi, the London advertising agency, to get them to maximise the impact of the upcoming speech and PW Botha then pulled back.

Minister Heunis believed that it was Pik's leaks to the English-language press that caused the change of tone.

Whatever it was, when Heunis drove to Groote Schuur to hand-deliver his requested inputs, on 10 August, he noticed an *Argus* billboard: 'Exclusive on PW's speech'. PW Botha met him at the door, and was distinctly cold. Heunis was, unusually, not invited in. His text was received in this unfriendly environment and he left.

That night he got a telephone call, 'I will not deliver that Prog speech,' PW famously said (for 'Prog' read Progressive Federal Party, shorthand for a speech attempting to address black demands).

Heunis frantically prepared a watered-down five-pager, and had it delivered on 13 August.

His reward was to be invited, along with the entire cabinet and Rev. Allan Hendrickse and Mr Amichand Rajbansi, the chairs of the ministers' councils in the Houses of Representatives and Delegates respectively, on Wednesday 14 August, to PW's office, where they were treated to 45 minutes of PW Botha reading the full text of the speech to be delivered the next day. This was not in an atmosphere where changes could be suggested by ministers wanting to still be alive at dinnertime.

The speech was, for sure, now PW's own.

If Operation Argon was an own goal by the National Party government, the Rubicon speech was another own goal, this time in extra time.

The Durban City Hall was packed to the rafters on the evening of 15 August 1985. This included news teams from 33 different country networks.

Possibly 200 million people watched PW deliver his Rubicon speech, including Ronald Reagan, Margaret Thatcher, Oliver Tambo and almost every citizen of South Africa.

PW's third and fourth paragraphs were:

> Most of the media in South Africa have already informed you on what I am going to say tonight, or what I ought to say, according to their superior judgment.
>
> Of all the tragedies in the world I think the greatest is the fact that our electorate refrained so far to elect some of these gentlemen as their government. They have all the answers to all the problems. And these answers differ from day to day and from Sunday to Sunday.

Any speech beginning thus is unlikely to later transport its audience into the heavens of enlightened political reform, and PW's Rubicon speech didn't bother to try. No new formula to include black South Africans into government. No new initiatives to free Mandela.

> Reasonable South Africans will not accept one-man-one-vote in a unitary system ... consequently I reject it as a solution ... Destroy white South Africans and our influence, and this country will drift into faction, strife, chaos and poverty ... Don't push us too far in your own interests, I tell you ... We have never given in to outside demands and we will not do so now.

There's more where this came from, but I sense you've had enough for now.

Dave Steward, FW de Klerk's communications adviser, has described this as 'the worst political communication by any country at any time'.[251]

When the baying boere had left the Durban City Hall, South Africa waited in fear of what was next.

First from Germany. Helmut Kohl responded to Botha's earlier letter: 'I am firmly convinced that the complete elimination of apartheid has to be the nucleus of any political and social system in South Africa.'

Mrs Thatcher was also instructive: 'It seems to me that you will need an eye to the international repercussions of the timing and the presentation of your decisions. What was eventually said in your speech ... did not match the expectations which had been created nor indeed the reality of the decisions that you were then considering. I would like to see you present the sort of proposals you mentioned to me.'

In September President Reagan reluctantly agreed to limited sanctions against South Africa. He said he had authorised this in response to the current situation in South Africa. 'The pace of reform in South Africa has not fulfilled the expectations of the world community nor the people of South Africa. Recent government actions regarding negotiations on the participation of all South Africans in the government of that country have not sufficiently diffused tensions and may have indeed exacerbated the situation ... The recent declaration of a state of emergency in 36 magisterial districts by the government of South Africa, the mass arrests and detentions, and the ensuing financial crisis are of direct concern to the foreign policy and economy of the United States.'

The economic consequences were less diplomatically put.

Chase Manhattan immediately announced their position on their South African book and other banks joined in.

On 28 August the South African Stock Exchange had to be suspended for three days as the rand plunged to 34 US cents, its lowest point in history.

The repayment of US dollar loans in dollars for rand-earning companies and banks became impossibly costly, and anyway the Reserve Bank didn't have the dollars.

On 2 September the South African authorities introduced a four-month standstill on certain foreign debt repayments. Desperately the Reserve Bank reintroduced the dual commercial and financial rand system, which had been abandoned only two years earlier.

The Governor of the South African Reserve Bank, Dr Gerhard de Kock, flew to Europe and the USA and pleaded with bankers there and at the International Monetary Fund in Washington. Returning to South Africa, Dr De Kock said that foreign bankers had told him that, judged purely on economic grounds, South Africa's standstill would be the 'easiest on record to handle, but for political reasons it would be difficult to negotiate a solution'. This carried a 'clear and unmistakable message for South Africa'.

On 18 September Minister of Finance Barend du Plessis announced the establishment of a standstill co-ordinating committee, chaired by the Director-General of Finance, Dr Chris Stals.

On 24 October the committee, with its recently appointed Swiss mediator Dr Fritz Leutwiler, met with South Africa's creditors and reported back that there was little hope of a quick settlement. Dr Leutwiler said that South Africa should speed up its political reforms and the standstill was extended for another three months.

Disinvestment and the Ford Motor Company

Meanwhile the broader economy was deteriorating very quickly.

After the first six months of the year, it was felt that moderate economic growth for the year was possible. The state of emergency put paid to that and the economy contracted by 1% in 1985.

The downturn of the economy led to a reduction in consumer imports, which eventually led to a surplus of R7.1 billion on the current account of the balance of payments. This was more than completely offset by the withdrawal of foreign capital on the capital account, which had had to be stopped when it reached R10.5 billion.

Inflation surged to the highest consumer price index (CPI) increase in 66 years, at 18.4%, and interest rates remained foolishly high.

The motor manufacturing industry had a terrible year, with Alfa Romeo, Peugeot and Renault closing their manufacturing plants in South Africa.

For Port Elizabeth, the worst economic catastrophe in its history was about to hit.

Disinvestment, or the withdrawal of foreign ownership and technology from existing, foreign-owned South African businesses, was always going to affect different areas of South Africa differently.

The great mines of the Transvaal and the Orange Free State were mostly locally owned, and anyway a mine cannot be moved as a factory can be. Farms likewise stay put, as do tourist attractions and so much else that forms the building blocks of the economy.

Businesses that are candidates for disruption should disinvestment happen are factories that are wholly owned by foreign corporations and multi-nationals.

And that was the basis of the Port Elizabeth and Uitenhage economy, for the Ford Motor Company, Port Elizabeth's oldest and biggest manufacturing plant, General Motors South Africa, Volkswagen, Goodyear, Continental Tyres and many other plants in the area were wholly foreign-owned. They could disinvest, and some did.

Of course, it was not just political pressure from foreign governments that drove the disinvestment bus, economic realities did too.

In 1981 301 000 vehicles were sold in South Africa. Driven by massive cost increases caused by historic levels of inflation, much higher import costs fuelled by a collapsing rand and other challenges, new vehicle prices doubled between October 1983 and September 1985. Sales collapsed to 176 500 units in 1986. The big assemblers suffered combined losses totalling R700 million in 1986. Investment in new plant simply stopped, and clearly a crisis was underway.

In 1984 Port Elizabeth's Ford Motor Company had begun secret negotiations with the Anglo American motor assembler, AMCAR, whose assembly line was near Pretoria. Both Ford and AMCAR had excess capacity on their lines, and both were losing lots of money.[252]

In January 1985, having consistently denied rumours of a merger, Ford and AMCAR came clean – they were to merge, as the South African Motor Corporation (SAMCOR), and Anglo would take up 58% of the equity in the new company; Ford would hold 42%. In the course of 1985 Ford closed its Port Elizabeth assembly lines (with the exception of an engine manufacturing plant) and nearly 4 000 hourly paid workers in Port Elizabeth lost their jobs. In all motor industry plants in South Africa, employment dropped from about 50 000 jobs in 1982, to 29 000 in 1986. This was the greatest economic blow Port Elizabeth has ever sustained, but unfortunately it did not prove to be the last.

24

A massive conflagration on Park Drive

‘ "Old Port Elizabeth" (the Port Elizabeth the English settled in the early 1820s) was built on a row of hills with kloofs in between, now turned into roads. There were really several villages with their own schools and churches and shops: South End, the Hill with the town centre below, Hospital Hill/St Paul's Hill and North End.' So wrote the wonderful Margaret Harradine, for many years the librarian in charge of the South African and Port Elizabeth collection in Port Elizabeth's Main Library, in her monograph *Hills Covered with Cottages*.

The town centre was a strip of coastal land between the Hill and the harbour, and it was the centre of the emerging Port Elizabeth economy, which of course got most of its life from the harbour immediately adjacent to this 'Main Street' commercial and industrial area.

Behind this rose sharply the Hill, today mostly the Donkin Reserve, named after Sir Rufane Donkin, who was acting governor of the Cape Colony in 1820, and who named Port Elizabeth after his wife, Elizabeth, and built her a memorial, a pyramid, on this Donkin Reserve.

Behind the crest of the Hill was a flat area, which was soon to include a large park, named St George's Park. The park was almost oval, with Park Drive, a major road, anchoring its outer boundary. Inside the park was to develop the grounds of the first cricket club in South Africa, on whose field was to be played the first cricket test match in South Africa, South Africa vs England, March 1889. Much else developed in this park over time – a

287

second cricket and rugby ground, an Olympic-size swimming pool, an art gallery, a tennis club, a cemetery and park and playlands. A hundred and forty years later it is still the premier park of Port Elizabeth.

On the other side of the road named Park Drive large plots for large homes were developed. These sites were much larger than the plots of Cora Terrace or Donkin Hill, and were soon taken up by the newly rich and successful of Port Elizabeth society. In the late 1800s a number of splendid homes were built looking onto St George's Park, of which, sadly, only a very small number survive today.

One such home later became the family home of the Brinkman family. This was a large house built on an even larger Park Drive site, two properties away from the St Joseph's Catholic Hospital.

The materfamilias of the Brinkman family was Gertruida Brinkman, one of the earliest female architects in Port Elizabeth, who has left Port Elizabeth a trove of fine buildings that she designed and built. While she did not build her Park Drive home, she understood its history, and cherished it while it was hers.

The Brinkmans sold this wonderful home, number 34 Park Drive, and, on the night of 19 October 1985 it was consumed by a massive explosion and a conflagration that was dramatic and quick. This splendid home was reduced to cinders and a little rubble in what seemed like only a few minutes.

The Brinkman home had been bought by the Watson family, the family of the four rugby-playing brothers and their elderly parents, who had lived in it a few short years. The Watson seniors, and Ronnie and Valence and their wives and children, lived there at the time of the conflagration and they had all been away for the weekend of the fire.

Guarding the house for the weekend had been two of the Watson brothers' most trusted friends, Archie Velile Mkele and Poni Geoffrey Nocanda. Their tight friendships had been held together by a shared commitment to rugby and Christianity, and by the fact that Archie and Geoffrey worked in the Watsons' chain of clothing stores.

Both Archie and Geoffrey subsequently drafted statements that told a terrifying story. They had been asleep at the house on the night of 19 October. They had been attacked as they slept, and, as they were pulling themselves together, a massive explosion and fire engulfed the world around them.

They were both badly burned (Archie suffered 40% burns). Disorientated, they fled the conflagration on the valley side of the house and stumbled their way down the valley to Essexvale, a tiny suburb in the Baakens Valley. There a passing motorist picked them up, and took them to the nearby Provincial Hospital.

Initially refused treatment (it was then a 'white' hospital), they were stabilised by cutting off their clothes and by applying a white paste to their extensive burns. They were then, naked but covered in this paste, put in an ambulance and sent off to Livingstone Hospital (the 'black' hospital). As Archie says, 'We were in terrible pain.'

By now the police had been alerted to their whereabouts and their condition. The ambulance was diverted to Louis le Grange Square, police headquarters. They spent three hours there, in the ambulance but with the door wide open in the freezing night, being cross-examined by more than five policemen. Captain Prinsloo, of the uniform branch, who was later to head up the enquiry into the burning down of the home, was there. Despite their condition, they were bombarded with questions, demanding to know 'why did you burn down the house?' Their guilt had, for the police, already been established.

'I can't remember Livingstone Hospital at all that night. I became properly conscious only two days later, and even then my eyes were so swollen that I couldn't see,' reported Archie in a statement taken down by the Human Rights Trust later. They each had two guards in hospital, uniform branch, and no visitors were granted access to them. Captain Prinsloo visited them twice, requesting to take down a statement. Archie replied that he would, when recovered sufficiently, make a statement to his lawyer. Ronnie Watson got access to them on the Monday and his visit was taped secretly and later used in court. Slowly Archie and Geoffrey recovered, and they were released from hospital to their homes. They then made statements to Leon Schubart, an attorney at Rushmere Noach. Both statements repeated the description above, and neither implicated themselves or the Watsons.

At the end of May 1986 Geoffrey was detained, and the security police detained Archie at the Watson shop in Main Street on 30 July. He was apparently detained in terms of the security legislation that flowed from the second state of emergency. 'Jy hoef hom niks te sê, vat die man,' a security policeman said as Warrant Officer Van Wyk hauled Archie off.

He spent that night sleeping on a bench under guard at the Algoa Park police station. The next day he was transferred to the Swartkops station. Both police stations were crammed with emergency detainees, and at Swartkops he shared a cell with 30 detainees.

The next day, Friday 1 August 1986, was to be Archie Mkele's day in hell.[253]

At 7:50 am two black policemen came for him. They signed him out, and, in the car park alongside their police van, tied his wrists together behind his back with a rope, put a thick cloth bag (thicker even than a bank bag), over his head and twisted it and tied it behind his neck. Thus blindfolded, he was put in the back of the van which headed off on an unspecified journey. Archie kept his wits about him, and concluded after the 20-minute journey that they were at Louis le Grange Square.

At the destination he was led, as a blind man, into a building until they entered a room where he was put down on some blankets on a cement floor. At this stage the bag was lifted to above his nose to allow him unhindered breathing, but still below his eyes.

The policeman who had brought him here then questioned him for about 20 minutes. The questions varied from membership of PEBCO (Archie denied this), to a visit to Lesotho (Archie admitted this, but said it was for personal reasons), and, of course, to the fire at the Watson home (Archie stuck to his statement as taken down by Rushmere's attorneys).

During this interrogation Archie was told that Geoffrey, who had been detained two months earlier, had eventually 'told the truth'.

The uniform branch policeman did not get the answers that he sought. He left. Archie had not been assaulted.

Ten minutes later 'some white men entered, speaking English with Afrikaans accents'. Archie had been passed from the uniform branch to the security police. His hell was about to begin.

The interrogation began on the fire at the house. After Archie had given the same answers possibly 10 times, the topic changed to a trip the Watsons had taken to Lesotho. Archie claimed he had not accompanied them, and anyway it was a business trip. Then the questioning moved to a cousin of his that the police claimed the Watsons had helped to leave this country (again Archie professed to know nothing), and on to other matters.

Eventually the questioning returned to the fire at the Watsons' home. Five times, again, Archie repeated the story as in his statement. Eventually, inevitably, the security police lost patience.

His bag was now pulled to below his nose. 'They then tied a blanket around my legs, and over this they tied a rope to secure my legs together. Presumably the blanket was to prevent the rope from making detectable marks on my flesh … They then put on a machine that makes an incredibly loud sound, a ZWEEEE sound, like a Boeing taking off. The machine was put right in front of me, and then the interrogators left, and I heard the door close … The sound was overwhelming – I started sweating, and felt like vomiting. My head was splitting in two. My ears were bursting, I was shivering. After about thirty minutes the interrogators returned and switched off the machine.'

Plainly the torturers were operating in the post-Wendy Orr period, with the security police now experimenting with 'non-bruising' tortures that left no visible evidence behind. This one didn't work. Archie continued to repeat his statement.

The threats got more and more extreme. Not only would they kill Archie, easily and with no consequences, but they would also kill his family. Still Archie resisted.

> At this stage they started pouring water over the bag on my head. The bag itself smells like excrement, and when wet begins to cling to your face, obstructing my breathing. After the bag was wet, they smeared a chemical liquid over the facial part of the bag. This liquid smells very strongly of soap ... Thereafter they started tightening up the bag from behind and I began to suffocate. It became incredibly difficult to get a gasp of air. They also beat and kicked me, being careful not to hit me over my burn wounds.
>
> After a while I collapsed. They would then release the tension at my neck, I would get a short breath, and they would tighten the bag again, and start again. This went on for what seemed like hours.
>
> I began to believe their earlier threats to kill me. I simply could not hold out against this. I agreed to sign whatever they wanted me to. They were happy with this – they said that they wanted to see the Watsons crawl like snakes. They got someone to fetch a tape recorder, told me what to say, and made me repeat it over and over. They then recorded it, and got me to listen to it many times.
>
> When I agreed to make the statement, they again lifted the bag to above my nose. They loosened my hands for me to eat, but before I could lift the bag, I heard one say – 'My friend, we'll kill you.' After food the bag was lowered, my hands tightened, and the same black policeman took me back to Swartkops Police Station. I was now put into my own cell, and from this day to my release (five months later) I was left alone, in solitary confinement.

In this time of solitary confinement with its enforced loneliness, and deeply concerned not only for his personal safety and for the consequences that his 'confession' would have on the case that had been put together against the Watsons (Valence, Ronnie and Cheeky had now been charged with arson, fraud and attempted murder – of Archie and Geoffrey - and were in North End jail as they were denied bail), Archie contrived to deliver a series of notes to his wife Carol. These notes outlined clearly his torture and the duress he had endured in making a statement he now said was false. Carol approached the Supreme Court to restrain the police from further assaults on Archie.

One of the police respondents was Major CJ Roelofse of the security police. His description of Archie's interrogation deserves recording here. My translation from the original Afrikaans:

> On 1 August I had Archie [he did not use Archie's full names] fetched from Swartkops Police Station to the Louis le Grange offices … I questioned him re his political involvement … after I had asked him about this, I began to speak generally with him about the fire at the Watsons and in more detail over the issue of his burn wounds. After the issue of his burn wounds was discussed, Archie burst into tears and so the story came out, which implicated the Watsons. I was not however convinced that this was the whole story and I requested Archie to return to the Swartkops Police Station and to then think about what he had said.

Gentle reader, there you have a second version of Archie in interrogation. Please come to your own conclusions as to which to believe.

Archie was, on the release of his scribbled, smuggled notes, abandoned by the police as a possible state witness. But he was to be punished for his lack of cooperation – he was left to languish in a cell at Swartkops Police Station until the trial began five months later, and only then was he released. 'I thus spent five months in cells, denied my liberty, for no reason,' he noted in the statement taken by the Human Rights Trust.

In August 1985 Valence, Ronnie and Cheeky were arrested, denied bail and held in North End jail.

'Wow, that place … The conditions were so cramped that Ronnie had to stop a guy washing his eating utensils in the toilet. The cell was so small that my feet would meet Cheeky's head and we would completely fill the cell when lying down. The porridge had worms in it and was the best food of the day … there were no fresh vegetables or fruit … there was something called dehydrate. We were denied running water in the cell … In our group of thirty prisoners we had thirty minutes a day to exercise, wash our clothes and shower – under a trickle of water! And even this was a 'privilege' which was often taken away,' said Valence in a *Monitor* magazine interview in 1988.[254]

'When we started spreading the word of God, the guys would come to us however they could … They wouldn't let us speak to the blacks in isiXhosa, only English or Afrikaans.

'Then you get hardened criminals in with others, and guys get sodomised or even killed. Before we got admitted, in the Awaiting Trial Cell the inmates had tried to hang one of their co-inmates. The warders had just cut him down in time. There was a hunger strike there – they teargassed those guys who locked themselves in a cell, and brought warders in from St Alban's and set dogs on those guys, and really beat them up. Then they put them into single cells, and when they came out, they walked with dragging footsteps,' Cheeky added in the same interview.

The first court appearance of the three brothers was in January 1987, in the Regional Court, in Port Elizabeth's 'new' law courts. The trial was presided over by the President of the Regional Court, Chief Magistrate Gert Steyn.

The Watsons were charged with arson, fraud and attempted murder. The state made the case that the fire was a conspiracy between these three brothers and their two staff members to destroy the house for the insurance payout.

It was argued that their business had been in difficulties, which it was. Controversially, the Watson shops had not been exempted from the consumer boycott, despite their pleas. The boycott committee had decided that any exemptions would lead to others, that this would make the 'policing' of the boycott too complex, and the breaking of the boycott too easy and too widespread. Their difficulties began and quickly they became huge. Because of these difficulties the brothers had decided to burn down their home for the insurance payout, the state argued.

The trial was, in the words of a much-later book *The Bosasa Billions*, by James-Brent Styan and Paul Vecchiatto, 'unlike anything the Eastern Cape had ever seen. The public galleries were always packed with black supporters of the Watson brothers.' When they were now granted bail, 'the brothers were carried out of court and down the street on the shoulders of their supporters'.

'The only so-called evidence they had against us was their witness Geoffrey [Nocanda, the other Watson staffer who had been burned in the conflagration]. Now Geoffrey made a statement to attorneys saying we didn't do it, then got taken by the security police and while in custody said we had done it, then let out that he was being tortured to make the statement, then came out and said "Yes, I was tortured to say that they did it, but it's true, they did it". And Nieuwoudt of the security police was every day in court, just watching him! And on that witness only they found Valence guilty in the Regional Court!' said Ronnie in the *Monitor* interview.

Magistrate Steyn could find no direct evidence linking Ronnie or Cheeky to the instructions to set the fire, but concluded that 'the totality of the evidence leads only to one inescapable inference' – there was a conspiracy to burn down the house and file an insurance claim to pay the Watsons' creditors.

He found only Valence guilty.

In his judgment, Magistrate Steyn said: 'I must at this stage say that if

Geoffrey was assaulted, and the possibilities are clearly that this happened, this happened before he was handed to Captain Prinsloo (of the uniform branch). I cannot express my disapproval of this assault, if perpetrated, in strong enough terms. I am also perturbed that nothing up to the time of Captain Prinsloo's testimony has been done about investigating these claims. I am not impressed by the reasons given for this failure, and I expect the allegations to be investigated without delay.'

Nearly a year later, a newspaper enquiry resulted in the admission that this matter 'was still under investigation'. It must still be, as no one has ever been charged.

From Magistrate Steyn's court the matter went on appeal to the Supreme Court in Grahamstown. Here the judge found that the 'cornerstone of the state's case was the testimony of Geoffrey Nocanda' and that he believed that the house had been set alight by Archie and Geoffrey, but that it was not proven that this had happened on Valence's instructions. Furthermore, accepting the testimony of a witness who had convincingly contended that he had been tortured into making his statement was unacceptable.

Not guilty. Valence walked out a free man to join his brothers and Archie. By now their businesses were bankrupt, and they all had to start their business lives anew.

Unlike many other murders and arson cases, the burning of the Watson home did not lead to any Truth and Reconciliation Commission admissions, and as such is still the subject of speculation.

There are three questions that need to be faced:

- Why would the Watson brothers decide to burn down their home to pay their debts, and in the process lose their furnishings, mementos and precious possessions, when they could have sold it instead?
- Have there been other buildings burned down that can be attributed to the security forces of the time? Answer, yes, quite a few, including Cosatu House and Khotso House.
- Would anyone in the security establishment at the time have felt that it was a good day's work, should the Watsons' home be burnt down and the brothers convicted of causing this conflagration?

25

The attack on Builder's Market

At this time, 'In Port Elizabeth a series of strange events took place,' wrote Christopher Nicholson in *Permanent Removal*.[255]

'The investigations by Molly Blackburn and her sister Judy Chalmers into the deaths [of the Cradock Four] were not doing them much good. Judy's husband Des ran a hardware business in Port Elizabeth under the name Builder's Market.'

The following is taken from Nicholson's book:

Des and his partner Rory Riordan employed PEYCO President Mkhuseli Jack and Sandy Stewart, who was prominent in the End Conscription Campaign, an organisation aiming to end Whites-only conscription into the apartheid army.

Once thriving with contacts all over town, Builder's Market found business gradually tailing off until no clients entered the shop or placed orders. Des and Rory were mystified. The business soon went into liquidation leaving Rory to pay R100 000 to creditors. Des asked his erstwhile clients why they had ceased to do business with the firm but no one would give any reasons. On one occasion Rory was deep in discussion in the office of a former client, trying to fathom the sudden boycott of his business, when the businessman was called away from his office. Rory glanced at the papers on the untidy desk. The heading on one caught his attention: 'Why we don't buy at Builder's Market'. Rory snatched up the document, folded it and put it into his pocket. When the man returned, Rory excused himself and left the shop. Once out on the street he dug out the paper:

'Did you know that Des Chalmers and Rory Riordan of Builder's Market have cosy little connections in the Department of Education and Training? This explains why Builder's Market supplies the materials for rebuilding schools and Mkhuseli Jack burns them down. The consumer boycott chairman, Mkhuseli Jack, is "employed" at Builder's Market along with his lackey and partner in crime, Mike Xego. They plan to use the consumer boycott to "intensify mass political action and ungovernability in the townships, and to allow the working class to win control of the means of production". Straight communism. Builder's Market still does a roaring trade in black areas due to Jack's influence. This is one reason he has bought a new car, helped by his bosses. Another reason is that he steals the money from his people.

'Jack's white girlfriend Sandy Stewart also works at Builder's Market. She is a member of the End Conscription Campaign, which has recently built a crèche in the Walmer Township under the banner "Troops out now". Builder's Market supplied the building materials for free, but provided a receipt so that the ECC could pocket the cash (R1 000) donated by Goodyear. The "committee of ten", with Gavin Watson and Dennis Creighton (regional manager of SA Perm) – who push support for the ANC – have approached Chalmers and co for support. But Jack is not amused because Watson rightly argues that Jack is not a true representative of the people. With all those misguided political adventurers making a name for Builder's Market, we white and black businessmen should show our solidarity against the forces of disorder, corruption and socialism. UNITE TO BOYCOTT BUILDER'S MARKET.'

Rory rushed home and called Des and Sandy to show them the pamphlet. So this was the reason their business had collapsed!

But who had done this?

It was years later that the question was answered.

During the second Goniwe inquest, Advocate Glenn Goosen brought Commandant Du Plessis into the witness box. He had handwritten the 'signal' for Matthew Goniwe's 'permanent removal'.

It turned out that there were more things he could explain. 'We [Military

Intelligence] also destroyed the business of Des Chalmers and Rory Riordan because they employed an activist named Mkhuseli Jack, by issuing a pamphlet called "Why we don't buy at Builder's Market" in which we alleged all sorts of things that weren't true. There were many such campaigns.'[256]

26

1985 moves to an end

By now 1985 was moving to its end.

The consumer boycott, which had begun on 15 July, was continuing without interruption. The state of emergency, called six days after the consumer boycott was begun, was also still underway, and by now all the senior UDF leaders were in detention. Khusta Jack was the latest arrest, having evaded the security police until 2 August.

On 8 August the UDF nationally called on all centres to follow Port Elizabeth's example and institute consumer boycotts. By then 10 more Eastern Cape centres had boycotts underway: East London, King William's Town, Stutterheim, Queenstown, Grahamstown, Cradock, Fort Beaufort, Alexandria, Bedford and Somerset East.

In September the townships of Johannesburg and Pretoria also began boycotts. Here the organisation did not live up to the Port Elizabeth model, and quickly unionists were questioning the popular mandate of the boycotts. Storekeepers had not been warned to stock up and coercion by gangs of youths quickly got out of hand. The UDF structures could not restrain these youths and wholesalers' trucks were attacked. Prices rapidly rose as price controls had not been agreed. These boycotts spluttered on, to be called off in January.

Negotiations on the consumer boycott begin

Port Alfred, which had begun its boycott even before Port Elizabeth, rapidly moved to an outcome that can only be seen as a great success for the township folk. Here businessmen agreed to call for a single, non-racial municipality for Port Alfred and rent arrears were scrapped, along with the creation of discounts for pensioners on the cost of municipal services. Even police behaviour was improved. By the end of August the Port Alfred boycott was suspended and joint committees were instituted, town and township, to address public works expenditure.

In Port Elizabeth, much activity emerged from the business community. The Chamber of Commerce had a young and energetic director, Tony Gilson, who met with whatever township leadership was out of jail and available in a frequent series of negotiations. On 24 August he called for black participation in local government, common citizenship, political rights for blacks and an end to discriminatory legislation – government's response was to ban COSAS two days later. Further meetings were also held between the white mayor, Councillor Ivan Krige, and UDF personnel, possibly six meetings in all, but these were informal and were halted by the detention of UDF leaders.

It was in early November that Khusta Jack created the breakthrough that really got the negotiation process moving.

Jack was in St Alban's Prison, a very unhappy detainee. At this time he was transported by the prison officials to court because he had been accused of some minor offence. The magistrate was unimpressed with the court papers and the prosecutor agreed to withdraw charges. Jack was left alone in the court, a free man as far as the magistrate was concerned.

Jack realised that his freedom would be very short-lived, and that if he escaped and was apprehended he, alone, would be under intense pressure to call off the boycott. He thus came up with a plan.

He phoned Tony Gilson, and asked for a lift back to St Alban's to fetch his belongings. Gilson was only too happy to oblige, as the trip would give him an hour or so to talk to Jack.

On arriving at St Alban's Jack spoke to the warder in isiXhosa, and said he should be re-detained as he had been mistakenly released. He was thus re-detained in Gilson's company.

Gilson was horrified that his chance to get the boycott lifted had been lost, as Jack had hinted that this was a possibility if his fellow UDF executives were released with him. He rushed back to the Chamber and informed them that all that was standing between them and the end of the boycott was the release of the UDF leadership.

The Chamber pressured government, and, *mirabile dictu*, in a few days the leaders were released and, on 15 November, the boycott was suspended until April 1986, which various Commonwealth countries had set as a deadline for the imposition of sanctions.

On 22 November, again in terms of the agreement between the Chamber and the government, all security forces were withdrawn from the townships, and, on 1 December, at a public meeting attended by about 50 000 township citizens, it was unanimously agreed to suspend the boycott.

The UDF, through its consumer boycott, had made massive gains.

The Ibhayi Town Council continues to wobble

As year-end approached, there were other victories to add to the tally.[257]

The Kayamnandi Town Council, renamed the Ibhayi Town Council in August, began to fall apart.

After the Langa massacre and the brutal murder of Benjamin Kinikini in nearby KwaNobuhle, eight councillors in Ibhayi resigned, including the Deputy Mayor Bacela and ex-Mayor Khaulela. Many councillors had their homes attacked by groups of youths.

This in turn caused the Ibhayi Council to speed up the establishment of a municipal police force.

This force had been approved by council in December 1984, in terms of the Bantu Local Authorities Act. In May 1985 the Chief Director of the Development Board, Mr Louis Koch, announced that the first 70 recruits would begin training on 1 June, and that their training would be conducted in Board premises, where previously inspectors had been trained. Their training would be stringent, Mr Koch said, 'covering all the relevant aspects laid down by the SA Police'. All recruits had matric, he said, and had passed (unspecified) aptitude tests.

Their training was all of 16 weeks in duration, and somehow the cash-strapped council had assembled enough funding for another 100 recruits, to begin training immediately after the first batch.

By now, Council's fortunes rose or fell in an inverse ratio to those of the UDF. And the Council's fortunes were personalised with those of its mayor, Cllr Thamsanqa Linda.

In August the house he had occupied when Mrs Mavela was removed was gutted in an arson attack. He claimed that he had lost possessions worth R250 000 and was not insured. 'I am not going to remove my family from the townships because I belong here,' he said, 'and I will not change my policy because of this incident because I know where I am leading my people.'

He then moved his family into the Summerstrand Holiday Inn, which was as far from the townships as one can get in Port Elizabeth.

He now appears to have fallen out with his fellow councillors, who passed a motion to remove him from his chairmanship of the executive committee of council. He was saved by a technicality – the recent resignation of councillors meant that council could no longer muster a quorum of 14 councillors. The Town Clerk, Mr Scholtz, went to see Minister Heunis on how to break this particular logjam.

Linda then accused Scholtz of undermining him and checked out of the Holiday Inn, leaving an unpaid bill of R11 000. This was for a third room Linda had booked for a police guard. The bill was never paid as Council repudiated it.

Plainly the UDF was now dominant and the Ibhayi Council was in tatters. Local businessmen dealt directly with the UDF to resolve their township issues, bypassing the Ibhayi Council. Carl Coetzee of PE Tramways kept his buses rolling by this method. Tony Gilson dealt directly with Mkhuseli Jack about consumer boycott issues.

It was time for Linda to go, and he did. In January he was disrobed as Mayor and as chairperson of the executive committee, as he had disqualified himself by missing four successive council meetings. He moved to the Transkei.

Further victories for the UDF in Port Elizabeth and Uitenhage

On 24 December the UDF chalked up another two victories. The trumped-up murder charge against Edgar Ngoyi was dropped and he returned to the townships in triumph. He immediately met Rev. Maqina, and they agreed to a ceasefire. The 100 AZAPO youths holed up at Maqina's home returned to their own homes and immediately expelled Maqina. He said he did not care as he had never been a member anyway, and the youths were just protecting themselves. Thus the AZAPO–UDF conflict came off the stove.

On the national front, much else had been going well for the comrades.

In the world of sport, white cricket had had its last international tour as long ago as 1970. White Springbok rugby received twin blows in 1985, with the All Blacks cancelling their 1985 tour in July. The British Lions followed suit in December 1985, calling off their 1986 tour.

While the UDF was gaining credibility on the ground, with many business and other organisations negotiating directly with them, the African National Congress in exile was beginning also to receive new groupings of visitors, with Gavin Relly, the Chairman of Anglo American, leading a business delegation to Lusaka in September 1985, and Frederik van Zyl

Slabbert bringing the Progressive Federal Party executive in October. A delegation of South African clergymen led by Bishop Philip Russell, the head of the Church of the Province, then also arrived, as did representatives from the student representative council of the University of Stellenbosch.

The launch of COSATU: A great triumph

The event of late 1985 that gave the greatest cheer was an event that took place over two days, 30 November and 1 December.

Since the Durban strikes of 1973 there had been a resurgence of black worker activism in South Africa. The Metal and Allied Workers Union was formed in 1973, followed by the Chemical Workers Industrial Union and the Transport and General Workers Union in 1974.

All of this was pulled together into an umbrella federation of unions, the Federation of South Africa Trade Unions (FOSATU) in 1979. Initially FOSATU was wary of committing itself to community (political) issues, opting instead to build its structures in the workplace.

FOSATU was not the only federation of unions. CUSA, with Black Consciousness origins, and TUCSA, from predominantly Coloured factories, were also mobilising.

Plainly there were gains to be made by coming together and unity talks began in 1981. Further rounds were held in 1982 and 1983.

Then came the founding of the UDF, and seven unions immediately pledged their loyalty there. CUSA was unhappy with the non-racial ethos of the UDF and would not join up. CUSA's biggest union, which was in fact a start-up union which rapidly became bigger than all other CUSA unions put together, the National Union of Mineworkers, was more adventurous.

NUM's general secretary, a young lawyer named Cyril Ramaphosa, was asked to chair a final unity summit on 8 and 9 June 1985. Gently he moved NUM from CUSA to the proposed super-federation, to be called the Congress of South African Trade Unions (COSATU), the founding congress of which he chaired. This was on 30 November and 1 December 1985 at the University of Natal. 760 delegates attended, from 33 trade unions.

FOSATU folded its entire structure into COSATU, and NUM also joined. This was enough to make it South Africa's biggest union federation from day one, with 500 000 signed up and 450 000 paid-up members.

Five fundamental principles were agreed at the congress: non–racialism; one union one industry; worker control; representation on the basis of paid-up membership; and cooperation between affiliates at national level.

This founding congress elected Elijah Barayi as president (he was vice-president of NUM), and Jay Naidoo as general secretary (he was general secretary of the Sweet, Food and Allied Workers Union).

The resolutions passed at this founding congress gave embattled township activists great cheer: the withdrawal of the South African Defence Force from the townships; the unconditional release of all detainees; rejection of the homelands; federalism rejected as a 'total fraud'; and the way forward for South Africa was to be a unitary state based on one person one vote, amongst many like-minded resolutions.

Shortly hereafter Jay Naidoo travelled to Lusaka, and the beginning of a relationship between the ANC and organised black workers was set. Yes, this did cause tensions in the new movement, because workers had many different political loyalties, but the core of the COSATU executive were Congress-tradition activists, and they quickly moved the new movement in that direction.

It is impossible to overestimate the importance of the founding of COSATU at this time and in this place. In any struggle against an overwhelmingly powerful oppressor, to have a set of your supporters relatively immune from arbitrary persecution (for black workers would have, as a vital ally, white management of business) is a major advance. And to have these supporters now willing to put their considerable muscle behind the UDF's programmes and goals was fantastic. This the besieged UDF had acquired.

Thus was developed a third front – the UDF and white business (because of the consumer boycotts) were now joined by organised black workers.

December had started on a great note.

A final disaster to end a frightful year
December was, however, to end with another disaster.[258]

Our story of 1985 is to end on a national road somewhere between Oudtshoorn and Humansdorp, on the night of 28 December 1985. Molly Blackburn, her sister Judy Chalmers and her colleague in the Provincial Council Di Bishop, and Di's husband Brian, were returning to Port Elizabeth from a township meeting at which they had (yet again) been requested to take statements of police brutality.

By the time the Port Elizabeth car began its return journey, night had fallen. The journey began silently. Brian Bishop was driving.

Some distance out of Oudtshoorn Brian suddenly screamed. An oncoming car was upon them, and only when it was within unavoidable distance did its lights come on. Brian could not have seen it, and hadn't.

The crash was head-on and deadly. Molly and Brian were both killed. Di had a leg fractured in a number of places, and was to spend a year in recovery.

Judy, miraculously, was uninjured but endured the horror of experiencing her sister die on her lap.

The driver of the other car also died. He was a teetotal lad, but on this occasion he had a high level of alcohol in his blood. This fact, and the endless dirty tricks outlined in this book, still leave some believing that there could be more to this accident than pure bad fortune.

The funeral that followed on 1 January 1986 would have been exactly as Molly would have wanted it. Rev. George Irvine was requested to preside in St John's Methodist Church in Port Elizabeth Central. Typical of his way of doing things, George suggested to the grieving family that Molly was bigger than any one denomination, and requested that he include in the service the heads of the Catholic Church and the Church of the Province. This was agreed and Michael Coleman and Bruce Evans co-presided with George. Allan Boesak was welcomed as an unexpected mourner.

St John's was then a very long-established church with a traditionally white-dominated congregation. The funeral was scheduled for midday. From 7 o'clock that morning, bus after bus of township mourners began arriving. Eventually there must have been 30 000 UDF-supporting township folk outside St John's, for they were respectful of the church's traditional congregation and did not take up the inside seating.

It was a funeral unlike any other Port Elizabeth had ever experienced. It was the first and is still the biggest non-racial gathering ever to happen in old 'white' Port Elizabeth and it remains clearly etched on many minds – including the mind of Andy Augustyn, the municipal official in charge of the traffic police and crowd control. He later told Rev. Irvine, 'When I saw this crowd arriving, George, I nearly shat myself.'

Period Three
1986

As we move into 1986, we need first to consider four issues of national politics before returning to the townships of Port Elizabeth and Uitenhage:

- The issues covered by President Botha in his opening of parliament at the end of January
- The inauguration of the Joint Management Centres and the National Security Management System at the end of 1985
- The ending of the 1985/86 state of emergency and
- The visits of the Commonwealth Eminent Persons Group from February to May 1986.

27

PW Botha opens parliament

On 31 January 1986, President PW Botha opened the parliamentary session with a typical PW speech – belligerent and arrogant, he again told the world and South Africa how far 'he' (for there was seldom a reference to a team coming from PW) would go.

He certainly announced some meaningful concessions, however: Africans would now have freehold property rights; all South Africans would now have a uniform identity document; and black South Africans who lived permanently within South Africa, but who had had their rights removed from them when some bantustans had gained 'independence', would be restored to full citizenship. 'We have outgrown the outdated colonial system of paternalism as well as the outdated system of apartheid,' he declared.[259] And, again, he promised to free Mandela if Mandela renounced violence.

Then came the (almost) surprise: he intended to negotiate with African leaders for the establishment of a national council, to meet under his chairmanship. This council would advise him on matters of common concern to all communities in South Africa prior to the creation of constitutional structures for Africans, to be agreed on jointly.

Later the details of this proposed council were released by the Minister of Constitutional Development, Minister Chris Heunis. Heunis made it clear that the council was to serve as an instrument for the negotiation of a new constitution. A flawed process, certainly (for no black leaders with genuine constituencies had been involved in the conceptualisation of this council), it, at first sight, appeared to have some potential.

Then came the details, and all four wheels fell off.

The council would be composed of the chief ministers of the six non-independent homelands; 10 'representatives of Africans permanently resident in the white-designated areas appointed by the state president from nominations submitted to him'; such members of the cabinet as the state president saw fit to appoint; the presidents of the three ministers' councils; and 'not more than ten persons nominated by the state president'. The council would be chaired by the state president, who would decide when and where it met.

Dead before born.

In late August Heunis announced that the bill to support this all would not be introduced in parliament in 1986 because 'delicate negotiations were in progress'. The government had held 190 discussions with African leaders, and 120 memoranda had been received. Nevertheless 'distrust and intimidation' had hampered negotiations, he said. He was, however, proud to announce that Mr Thamsanqa Linda and Bishop Isaac Mokoena would be willing to join the body.

As Van Zyl Slabbert had said: the government was determined to find a formula whereby 'they could share power without losing any', a mighty task indeed.

A week after PW's speech, the debate on it was still underway, with the Leader of the Opposition, Dr Van Zyl Slabbert, due to reply to the debate in the afternoon. 'I joined Helen Suzman's lunch party', wrote Ken Owen, serial editor of many of South Africa's English-language newspapers, and veteran polemicist.[260]

> She was her usual gracious self, but excused herself from the table early. Half an hour later, she was on the front bench beside Slabbert, face carved in stone and body turned slightly away from him in an attitude of rejection. From the press gallery she looked very angry as Slabbert rose to reply to the week's debate. He spoke elegantly, as usual, but with more contempt for the governing party than I had ever heard from him.
>
> At the end of his speech, he announced his resignation [from parliament].
>
> To state that the announcement was a political shock is to understate the effect. In her memoirs Mrs Suzman called it a 'shattering blow' and Colin Eglin said that, although Slabbert had prewarned both of them, he had 'never seen Helen so angry'.

Why had Slabbert done this?

Owen believed: 'He was completely disillusioned with the increasingly impotent Tricameral Parliament, dominated and manipulated by the security establishment, lied to, deceived and serving mainly to sustain a pretence of democracy. As he was to say later, he thought that the PFP had been reduced to helpless spectators, overwhelmed by the contradictions of their position.'

The militarisation of South African society

While Slabbert's decision was devastating to the PFP, it was soon to be clear that he was right. For, in this session of parliament, in answer to a question from MP PA Myburgh of the PFP, the Minister of Defence, Magnus Malan, revealed that, as of 31 December 1985, 12 Joint Management Centres (JMCs) had been established, each to coincide with, and be housed in, a command headquarters of the South African Defence Force. One of these was in Port Elizabeth.

Sub-JMCs had also been established, roughly one in each of the 57 Regional Services Councils. And about 350 Mini-Management Centres were also established, one in each town in South Africa.[261]

What was this all about?

There is a history to the creation of these structures that needs telling.

For the first 15 years of National Party government, from 1948 to 1963, the Special Branch of the police was tasked with controlling internal insurrection. Then, when BJ Vorster was Minister of Justice, in 1963 the security police came into being under General Van den Bergh and was given this task. Military Intelligence also existed in the SADF, and this was consolidated into a Directorate of Military Intelligence in 1964.

On the assassination of Prime Minister HF Verwoerd in 1966, BJ Vorster was elected as Prime Minister and immediately made PW Botha Minister of Defence. Tensions rapidly emerged between the security police and Military Intelligence. Vorster attempted to resolve these by creating the Bureau for State Security (BOSS) under General Van den Bergh, a long-time confidant of Vorster's. Thereby all information gathering on opponents of the state was consolidated in this Bureau.

But, instead of consolidating this function, it instead now ended up split three ways – the security police, Military Intelligence and BOSS, with personal rivalries and gamesmanship going in all directions.

Vorster then appointed Judge HJ Potgieter to head a commission of inquiry, and he recommended the creation of a State Security Council (SSC). This came into effect in 1972 and appeared to limit the influence of Van den Bergh, and widen the scope of PW Botha's turf.

By now Vorster and Botha were on different tracks.

Vorster believed in attempting to create a better image for apartheid by winning over press and news sources, and this led to the catastrophe of the Information Scandal and the end of Vorster, Connie Mulder, Louis Luyt and the Rhoodie brothers.

Botha, on the other hand, began to believe, with his top generals, particularly the Head of the Defence Force, General Magnus Malan, that South Africa was facing a 'Total Onslaught' which could only be countered by a 'Total Response'. Buying good publicity was just not going to cut it.

The 'total onslaught' thinking came to South Africa from the writings of a French anti-guerrilla strategist, General André Beaufre, who had honed his thinking in the French response to the liberation struggle the guerrillas of Algeria had waged.

Beaufre put forward the thesis that, in a conflict where one side has the control of the state, including established police forces and armies, and the other side has only the limited resources of the guerrilla, the guerrillas have to create an attack at many different levels: psychological, political, economic, diplomatic, social, religious and, as best they can, military. Thus the guerrilla response is a 'total onslaught', which has to be countered by a 'total strategy'. Such a strategy should bring together the state's military, economic, political and all other capabilities, under the overall guidance of the military. Hence a creeping, determined, undercover taking of control of all aspects of the state by military thinking and authority.

PW Botha has his many critics, and this writer is surely one – but on one ground we have to concede. He was enormously energetic in the pursuit of his vision. And that vision was to save South Africa from the communist thrust that was determined to push aside white Christian South Africa, and remake his beloved country as a black-run, godless communist state. In other words he had to save South Africa from the Total Onslaught masterminded from Moscow, and run through Moscow's local surrogates, SWAPO, the ANC and the SACP.

About three weeks before Botha was made John Vorster's Defence Minister, just before Verwoerd's assassination, the South African Defence Force and the South West Africa Liberation Army (SWALA, as Sam Nujoma's guerrilla army was first styled) met in battle for the first time in South West Africa.

Botha immediately concluded on the future path.

He remained Defence Minister for 14 years, from 1966 to 1980. During that time defence spending rose from 1.6% of South Africa's budget to nearly 20%. South Africa's tiny 'Armaments Procurement Board' grew into, from 1968 onwards, the 'Armaments Board of South Africa', the procurement division of the Defence Force, and the 'Armaments Development and Production Corporation of South Africa', ARMSCOR, which developed to become the eighth-largest exporter of weaponry in the world.

In 1977 Botha began South Africa's nuclear programme, designed to make South Africa a member of that very restricted club, those countries that made and had available, nuclear weapons.

Thus began what Sampie Terreblanche, that loveable dissident Stellenbosch University economist, called the 'Military Industrial Complex', with huge manufacturing contracts becoming available for the manufacture of weaponry and components. This in turn drew into Botha's orbit big business, traditionally English South African in ownership, and English-language voters, of whom, eventually, Botha was to claim a majority.

By 1975 Botha had plunged South Africa into military incursions into Angola and other neighbouring countries, and this activity continued until late in the 1980s.

By this time Botha had become Prime Minister (from 1978 to 1984) and, when the traditional role of ceremonial State President was swapped for an Executive President in the tricameral system, he took on this position, which he held until 1989. By then he had been in effective charge of South Africa's war effort for 23 years.

On becoming Prime Minister, Botha in 1978 rapidly discovered that the efficiencies he and others had built into the war machine did not exist in government generally. He commissioned a white paper on the Rationalisation of the Public Service and Related Institutions. This reported in 1980: the existing decision-making structures of the state 'make it difficult for the central executive machinery to act swiftly and effectively to solve problems and crises'. By 'restructuring state decision making structures', this report argued, 'a more manageable machinery of government to meet new challenges and crises' should be created.[262]

What followed has been described by Van Zyl Slabbert: 'The period 1979-87 saw the militarisation of South African society on an unprecedented scale.'[263]

Firstly, the 'Office of the State President became the epicentre of state power. No major macro-policy decision was taken without the President's personal approval or direct involvement in its formulation.'[264]

The Office of the State President involved a large number of committees, advisers, secretariats and ministries dealing with every possible function of government. The most important included the National Priorities Committee (which essentially directed all government spending, and thereby directed the budget); the Commission for Administration, which gave the President models for restructuring the administration and could issue instructions that ministers were obliged to carry out; the National Intelligence Service, with 5 000 employees under Director General Dr Niël Barnard, which gathered 'sensitive' information, analysed it, and made recommendations on action to the President; the Ministry for Information, which disseminated propaganda and linked into the communication committees of the Joint Management Centres, to ensure a seamless approach to information dissemination; and the Economic Advisory Council, which Botha inherited, then gutted of officials and academics to make it a meeting place for himself and big business.

Through all of this, 'the Office of the State President emerged as the lynchpin of key strategic thinking and action … it had become the most decisive decision-maker in the state'. And one guess who was controlling all of this.[265]

In addition, Botha reduced the number of cabinet committees and co-ordinated their agendas. The State Security Council (SSC) was now elevated to a position of special prominence. Botha chaired this committee and it adopted the National Security Management System (NSMS) on 16 August 1979. Here the Total Strategy responding to the Total Onslaught found its home.

The SSC had a secretariat of about 100 civil servants drawn from Foreign Affairs (11%); Prison Services (1%); Security Police (11%); Railway Police (5%); SADF (16%); and National Intelligence Service (56%). Thus this frightening structure, designed to turn the whole of South Africa's society around to face the Total Onslaught, was 89% drawn from security establishments.[266]

This thinking, and this style of organisation, cascaded down from the national level to the regional level (where we have seen that 12 Joint Management Centres opened, one in each of the SADF's 12 command centres), and on to the local level, where 60 Sub-Management Centres coincided with the Regional Services Councils; and to the local level, where 350 Mini-Management Centres covered most of South Africa's towns. At this local level civilians become involved in the Total Strategy, for local leaders were co-opted onto the JMCs, and they would be involved in the Total Response.

In the words of General Piet van der Westhuizen, then Secretary General of the SSC, 'the JMCs are the eyes and the ears of the NSMS as they monitor the implementation of total strategies … Their prime objective is the lowering of the revolutionary climate; the prevention/diffusion of unrest, and combatting terrorism and other revolutionary actions'.[267]

Thus, as Slabbert writes: 'PW Botha, by defining the security interests of the South African state, has given it a coherence and a unity of purpose which it had not had before ... every state structure, including Parliament, homeland governments, "independent states" and neighbouring countries, are subservient to the goals and logic of the Total Strategy ... Constitutionally the response has been a massive and sustained erosion of accountable politics in favour of co-optive decision making.'[268]

PW Botha ends the first state of emergency

The first state of emergency, called on 21 July 1985, lasted for about seven and a half months.

It began in earnest.

David Webster, a lecturer in Anthropology at Wits University and stalwart of the detainee monitoring group the Detainees Parents' Support Committee (DPSC), believed that in the period 21 July to 31 December 1985, 7 367 persons were detained, at a rate of 46 per day. In the last two and a bit months, from 1 January 1986 to the end of the emergency, 7 March 1986, 631 people were detained, at an average of 10 per day.[269]

In all, the South African Institute of Race Relations believed that, in 1985, the busy period of the Emergency, 1 953 people were detained in the 'independent homelands'; another 2 436 were detained in terms of the regularly used security legislation, namely the Internal Security Act; and another 7 361 were detained in terms of the Emergency Regulations, from 21 July until 27 December 1985, making the total detained in 1985 of 11 750. This would put the total detained in terms of the 1985/86 state of emergency at about 12 300.[270]

Max Coleman and David Webster believed that over 60% of all detainees were from the Eastern Cape, with Port Elizabeth providing 51% and Uitenhage 15%.[271]

Coleman and Webster show that 12 of the 16 members of the UDF's national executive were detained, as well as 50 of 80 members of the many regional executives The state of emergency was, unquestionably, a very determined attempt to put down the UDF.

The South African Institute of Race Relations quotes the Minister of Law and Order, in replying to a question in parliament, as saying that between 1 September 1984 and 24 January 1986, 955 people died in 'unrest related activities'. Of these 628 were killed by state actors and 321 by their own communities. Twenty-five security force members were killed. This tallies with the Institute's own records; of 879 deaths in 1985 unrest, and 247 in the 1986 balance of the state of emergency.[272]

The state of emergency did taper off: the initial 36 magisterial districts covered by the state of emergency were reduced to 24 by 7 March 1986, and Pottinger notes that when the state of emergency was eventually ended, there were only 241 detainees left to free.

And so this state of emergency limped to its conclusion.

On 4 March 1986 PW Botha told a joint sitting of parliament that he was satisfied that the situation had improved sufficiently for him to lift the state of emergency then operating in a restricted number (24) of magisterial districts in South Africa. Initially the state of emergency had been declared over 36 magisterial districts. On 25 October another eight, all in the Western Cape, were added, and six of the original 36 were dropped. On 3 December the state of emergency was lifted in another eight magisterial districts, and on 7 February in another six. In the Eastern Cape, the last remaining magisterial districts were Albany, Cradock, Fort Beaufort, Port Elizabeth and Uitenhage.

On 7 March he did this, although, as his biographer Brian Pottinger writes, it was ' bitterly opposed by the security chiefs'.[273]

Pottinger believes that there were three reasons for this action.

Firstly, he had reluctantly agreed to allow the Commonwealth Eminent Persons Group to come to South Africa and to carry on with their agenda, as unhappy as he was with this venture. They were now in South Africa, and sanctions and disinvestment were snowballing realities. He was playing into this dynamic, Pottinger believes.

Secondly, he had devised new legal remedies, for he was pushing ahead with a new system of legislation whereby the Minister of Law and Order could proclaim 'mini-states of emergency' in restricted areas, thereby eliminating the need for a national state of emergency and all the international outcry which it created.

Thirdly, with the Joint Management Centres now up and running, he now had a co-ordinated vehicle to oppose the uprisings as they happened, in a comprehensive manner. They were, said Magnus Malan, 'the government's early warning system for internal threats to state security, and were a highly mobile mechanism to defuse revolutionary unrest'. The JMCs reported to Lieutenant-General Pieter van der Westhuizen, in a further militarisation of South African society.

In other words, PW was readying himself for a totally different response to insurrection.

As Pottinger has noted: 'The first round between Botha and the forces for radical change had ended indecisively – or so it appeared to the outside. The revolutionary drift had certainly not been checked in the townships – quite the reverse. Neither had the state institutions for blacks been rehabilitated.'[274]

Not a stalemate, but a defeat for the system.

28

The beginning of negotiations

The first attempt to co-opt Mandela into hopelessly unequal negotiations happened in 1976 when Jimmy Kruger, then Minister of Justice, Police and Prisons, arrived on Robben Island to visit Mandela.

Mandela used the visit to sum Kruger up – he found a minister of government who did not know that the ANC was older than the National Party, and who had never heard of the Freedom Charter. Short on knowledge, short on smarts, but long on arrogance, Kruger did not impress the wily Mandela.

Kruger's offer was crudely put: if Mandela was willing to recognise the legitimacy of Kaiser Matanzima's newly independent Transkei, and if Mandela was willing to move there, Kruger could dramatically reduce his sentence.[275]

Mandela bluntly declined the offer. No matter, for Kruger returned with it again, a month later. 'No' a second time. Subject closed.

Kruger went off to chair the Senate and then to an early retirement. In October 1980 a much more polished minister took on the joint portfolios of Justice and Prisons, which by this time also gave the incumbent a seat on the State Security Council. His name was Hendrik Jacobus (Kobie) Coetsee.

Kobie Coetsee had been born in Ladybrand in the Orange Free State in 1931, of working-class National Party parents. He had made his way to the University of the Free State, and had graduated both BA and LLB,

317

and practised as an attorney in Bloemfontein. At university he had enjoyed the Classics, and could quote many of the heroes of Greek antiquity from memory.

In 1972 JJ (Jim) Fouché, the Member of Parliament for Bloemfontein West, become State President, and thus had to resign from parliament. Coetsee won his seat. He helped clean up the mess that followed the Information Scandal, and caught the eye of the new Prime Minister, PW Botha. Thus the joint portfolios of Justice and Prisons became his from 1980 until 1993, the years of the township revolt.

Throughout these years Coetsee had both the polish and the integrity necessary to attain the respect of the ANC, who supported his later election to become President of the Senate in 1994. He retired in 1998.

In the year 2000 a historian at the University of the Free State, Jan-Ad Stemmet, phoned Coetsee and requested an appointment to interview the retired minister. This was agreed, and Stemmet met Coetsee at Coetsee's home. Coetsee obviously took a liking to the young historian and promised that he would open his extensive archive to Stemmet, and that, thereafter, 'bombs will blow up, atomic bombs'.[276]

Somewhat shell-shocked, the young historian had hardly recovered his breath when, two days later, he turned on the television news to find out that Coetsee had just died of a massive heart attack. Project over.

But Stemmet's luck held, and 13 years later Huibre Lombard, the Head of the Archive for Contemporary Affairs at the University of the Free State, sent him a note – the Archive had received a new collection which they were organising, but meanwhile there was some of it that might interest Stemmet. He made his way over to find the entire Kobie Coetsee archive, recently donated by his widow. It contained the most complete record of Mandela's prison years, there waiting for him.

In conjunction with his friend Riaan de Villiers, a journalist with decades of experience, Stemmet organised the publication of a fraction of the archive, covering the Mandela years as prisoner 913, and related issues. Now published by Tafelberg, when read with Niël Barnard's memoirs and of course Mandela's autobiography, it makes a fascinating chronicle of the prisoner Mandela and his interaction with government.

The post-Jimmy Kruger action began in April 1982, when the commanding officer of the prison at Robben Island called on Mandela in his cell – 'Pack up, we are transferring you.'[277]

No explanation, or even a destination, was given. The same orders went to Walter Sisulu, Raymond Mhlaba and Andrew Mlangeni. All four found themselves on the ferry to Cape Town, and thereafter in the back of a windowless truck. After an hour's journey the truck came to a halt and they were hustled in the dark into what was clearly another security facility. A sympathetic guard told Mandela that they were now in Pollsmoor Prison.

Conditions here were incomparable to the Island. They now had beds, no longer mats on the concrete floor; the food included dinners of meat and vegetables, not the interminable 'pap'; and their quarters they called 'The Penthouse', for it was a three-bedroomed flat on the top of the prison, including a balcony, a lounge and a selection of showers.

Why were they now in Pollsmoor?

They agreed that this was a divide-and-rule strategy, 'cutting off the head of the ANC on Robben Island by removing its leadership'.[278] This seems the most likely reason, for a few days later Ahmed Kathrada and a young attorney who had just been jailed for treason, Patrick Maqubela, also arrived. Nothing approaching negotiations followed at this stage from their move, although they were now allowed news material and were provided with a radio. Mandela was allowed contact meetings with Winnie and their children in 1984.

We have to wait until 1984 for developments in negotiations.

On 3 December 1984 the State Security Council (SSC) decided to request a subcommittee of the SSC to 'work out a strategy for the release, from a position of strength, of certain security prisoners from the right and the left before Christmas, and that the Minister of Justice (Kobie Coetsee) was to submit a strategy in this regard to the SSC on 14 December 1984'. The subcommittee consisted of Ministers (Pik) Botha, De Klerk, Le Grange, Viljoen and Coetsee.[279]

On 13 December this grouping saw Coetsee put forward a report which gave a number of possibilities.

In Mandela's case, there were six options tabled:

Options 1 to 3 would have seen Mandela end up in the Transkei, under a range of conditions. Minister Coetsee, the author of the report, did not recommend these as 'feasible'.

Option 4 would see Mandela released in South Africa, after negotiations with him. 'The subject is to undertake that he will do nothing to warrant re-arrest' (would not in any way promote violence as a political strategy). Coetsee did not believe that Mandela would sign this, so he also regarded this option as 'not feasible'.

Option 6 was the equivalent of 'parole' – Mandela would be released on strict conditions, such as daily reporting to a police station. Again, Coetsee did not see this option as 'feasible'.

Option 5 was Coetsee's favoured option. Here Mandela would be released in South Africa unconditionally, and this would be justified on the grounds of his age (he was 66), and that he had served 20 years in jail, and that several black leaders, including Buthelezi and Matanzima, had requested his release. But he would only be released after Govan Mbeki had been, 'and that Mbeki's release had provided proof that Mandela's release would not lead to unrest'.[280]

In its own clumsy way, the SSC appears to have kept its options open between 4 and 5, and used a convenient stratagem to reach its final choice. As it happened, a prominent UK politician would be the catalyst. A Conservative Party peer with a particular interest in prison issues, Lord Nicholas Bethell, had repeatedly applied to see Mandela in Pollsmoor in order to interview him for a newspaper article.[281]

Now the government agreed to Bethell's request. He was briefed by Coetsee both before and after the interview. Bethell was known for his anti-communist attitudes, and the government wished to use his interview in their decision making as to whether they could risk Mandela's unconditional release. If Bethell emerged from the interview with Mandela refusing to back down on the armed struggle, Bethell's article would be all the ammunition they needed to refuse to release him.

Thus an astonished Bethell got permission to be the first foreigner to meet Mandela since his incarceration, and the first person in 22 years to be able to print an interview with the world's most famous prisoner.

Of course it went as expected. Mandela neither could, nor would, renounce the armed struggle. This was all over the *Mail on Sunday* in London on 27 January 1985, and six days later, in parliament in Cape Town, PW Botha announced that 'Mandela can leave prison if he renounces violence … from now let it be clear, it is not the South African government that is keeping Mandela in jail, it is he himself'. Botha took one question before leaving the chamber: Mrs Helen Suzman requested to know if Botha's offer (of freedom if a renunciation of violence was made) applied to all political prisoners. Botha replied, 'Yes, on those conditions.'

Botha, confident that he had now exposed both the ANC and Mandela as unwilling to abandon violence, relaxed in the glow of positive publicity that his 'offer' had generated. Britain backed Botha's proposal; both Van Zyl Slabbert and Helen Suzman saw no problem with it; and the *Sunday Times* proposed that Mandela accept.[282]

Botha's 'offer' was delivered to Mandela within hours. A 40-minute consultation with his 'Penthouse Pals' saw Mandela write a reply that was smuggled out of Pollsmoor and read at a huge rally at the Jabulani Stadium three weeks later. The event was to celebrate the awarding of the Nobel

Peace Prize to Bishop Tutu, and a huge crowd heard Zindzi Mandela read the speech now known as 'My Father Says'.[283]

Zindzi was wearing a yellow UDF t-shirt, and was ushered through the crowd by Desmond Tutu and Allan Boesak, with the crowd lifting her shoulder-high onto the stage.

And her father said: 'Only free men can negotiate. Prisoners cannot enter into contracts ... I cannot and will not give any undertakings at a time when you and I, the people, are not free. Your freedom and mine cannot be separated. I will return. Amandla!'[284]

Mandela had won that one, without doubt. As Kobie Coetsee had foreseen, Mandela and his Rivonia team would only accept unconditional release. Botha had merely dug a trench in the negotiations field.

Seven months followed, with no contact between the ANC group at Pollsmoor and the government. Then, in September 1985, shortly after the Rubicon speech, Mandela was admitted to Volks Hospital in Cape Town for prostate surgery. He recalled:

In 1985 after a routine medical examination from the prison doctor, I was referred to a urologist, who diagnosed an enlarged prostate gland and recommended surgery. He said the procedure was routine. I consulted with my family and decided to go ahead with the operation. I was taken to Volks Hospital in Cape Town under heavy security. Winnie flew down and was able to see me prior to the surgery. But I had another visitor, a surprising and unexpected one: Kobie Coetsee, the minister of justice ... He dropped by the hospital unannounced, as if he was visiting an old friend who was laid up for a few days. He was altogether gracious and cordial, and for the most part we just made pleasantries. Though I acted as though this was the most normal thing in the world, I was amazed. The government, in a slow and tentative way, was reckoning that they had to come to some accommodation with the ANC. Coetsee's visit was an olive branch.[285]

Mandela believed that there was now space for ANC–Government negotiations.

When Mandela had finished his recuperation at the hospital, to his surprise he was taken out of the hospital by the Commanding Officer of Pollsmoor, Brigadier Munro. Munro told Mandela that he had instructions 'from head office' that Mandela was now to be held alone, in a set of rooms on the ground floor of Pollsmoor. Munro gave no explanation, other than it was an order from his superiors. The rooms proved to be spacious, but damp and musty and without natural light.

After a few days alone in these circumstances, Mandela 'came to a realisation about my new circumstances. The change, I decided, was not a liability but an opportunity ... my solitude gave me a certain liberty, and I resolved to use it to do something I had been pondering for a long while: begin discussions with the government. I had concluded that the time had come when the struggle could best be pushed forward through negotiations ... My solitude would give me an opportunity to take the first steps in that direction, without the kind of scrutiny that would destroy such efforts.

'We had been fighting against white minority rule for three-quarters of a century. We had been engaged in the armed struggle for more than two decades. Many people on both sides had already died. The enemy was strong and resolute. Yet even with all their bombers and tanks, they must have sensed that they were on the wrong side of history. We had right on our sides, but not yet might. It was clear to me that a military victory was a distant if not impossible dream. It simply did not make sense for both sides to lose thousands if not millions of lives in a conflict that was unnecessary. They must have known this as well. It was time to talk.'[286]

Again, it took months for the next contact to happen.

This time a very large stage was set, for the intervention was at the behest of the Commonwealth Heads of Government.

In October 1985 the heads of government in the 49 member states of the Commonwealth met in Nassau in the Bahamas. The issue they all believed would dominate the agenda was an item about a country that had, in fact, left the Commonwealth 24 years earlier – South Africa.

By now, South Africa had been described as 'the polecat of the world'. It had almost no friends. 'Almost' because the apartheid government of South Africa had two friends, and they were in massively strategic positions. Ronald Reagan was President of the United States and Margaret Thatcher was Prime Minister of the United Kingdom.

Both were at the time in very strong positions in their home countries.

Reagan had first been elected President in the 1980 American election, beating the incumbent President Jimmy Carter by 489 electoral college votes to 49, a landslide. The 1984 election was even more convincing – Reagan beat the Democratic Party candidate, Walter Mondale, by 525 electoral delegates to 13. In fact, Reagan carried 49 of the 50 states, with Mondale carrying only his home state, Minnesota, by a razor thin 0.18% margin. The American electorate was behind the 'Gipper', for sure.

Mrs Thatcher was not as well supported, but was nevertheless way out in front of the Labour Party opposition in her first two elections. In the 1979 election her Conservatives won 339 seats to James Callaghan's Labour's 269. In 1983, with the Falklands War pushing her popularity, the Tories won 397 seats to Michael Foot's Labour's 209 – Mrs Thatcher had an unassailable majority of 144 seats in the House.

Thus, both of apartheid's friends had no domestic challenges to be concerned about.

However, at the Commonwealth Heads of Government, it was another matter. For here, on the issue of sanctions against apartheid South Africa, the result of a vote could readily be predicted: 48 to 1. The Commonwealth against Maggie Thatcher.

And so it was.

In 1985 Britain's trade with South Africa had amounted to $5.9 billion, the same amount of money Britain earned from North Sea oil. British investment was 40% of all investment in South Africa. Mrs Thatcher was not the type to throw this all away. No, she would not go along with any more sanctions. Fullstop.

Without Britain's commitment, sanctions from the other Commonwealth countries would add up to an insignificant amount. No Britain, no significant sanctions.

A compromise was sought at the meeting in the Bahamas, and found.

The Commonwealth would send a small group of 'Eminent Persons' to South Africa, to try to create a 'possible negotiating concept'. This would be an attempt to get agreement from the Botha government to end apartheid, lift the state of emergency, remove the SADF from the townships, end arbitrary arrests, release Nelson Mandela and other political prisoners, legalise the ANC and other banned organisations, and 'establish the conditions for meaningful dialogue'. As a quid pro quo, the black political organisations would suspend violence.

This group was headed by three luminaries: Malcolm Fraser, previously Prime Minister of Australia; Olusegun Obasanjo, a military ruler of Nigeria who had turned his country over to civilian rule; and Mrs Thatcher's appointee, Lord Barber, previously Chancellor of the Exchequer and now chairman of Standard Bank, a British bank with an extensive presence in South Africa. There were four other members.

The group appear, to have limited their mission to a more realistic set of requests: they wished to meet Nelson Mandela to ascertain whether he and the ANC were willing to enter meaningful negotiations with the Botha government; and to attempt to set up such negotiations if they believed that there was some prospect of success.

Initially things went swimmingly: the Minister of Foreign Affairs,

Pik Botha, welcomed the initiative with open arms; General Obasanjo's assessment of Mandela (whom he met three times at Pollsmoor) was that he was a remarkable man, and more than willing to request his organisation's commitment to negotiations; and they were told that 'the authorities would negotiate on this basis'.

General Obasanjo concluded on their first visit to South Africa, 'Well, I became hopeful.'[287]

The second visit to South Africa was in May, and now things moved at a blistering pace.

On 15 May PW Botha told parliament that he was prepared to negotiate with citizens of South Africa, provided that 'they did not resort to violence as a means of attaining their political goals' and that 'negotiation of necessity implies that participants should accept that not all their requirements were likely to be met'.[288]

On Friday 16 May the group met Mandela at Pollsmoor Prison. Included in the group was Botha's State Law Advisor, Jan Heunis, the son of the Minister of Constitutional Development.[289]

Barber informed Mandela that the group had put together a 'negotiating concept' that they were hopeful could form the basis for talks between the government and the ANC.[290] He provided Mandela with a written copy, and went through it.

> The guts of the matter is first the release of prisoners like yourself as well as detainees. Secondly the unbanning of the ANC and the PAC, and thirdly, the opportunity to have free discussions and meetings and the abolition of detention without trial. On the other side, we would ask the ANC and others to do two things, namely to enter into negotiations with an open agenda, and that the black community should be represented by people of their own choosing. They would also have to agree to suspend violence.[291]

Mandela responded that 'As far as I am concerned, I have no problem with this document', but noted that it had to be seen by Oliver Tambo and the ANC's National Executive Committee in Lusaka. Young Heunis committed to try to get government also to accept the proposals.[292]

Then things started to unravel.

At the EPG's next meeting with the government team, a new demand hit the table: the ANC and other black organisations must not just 'suspend violence', but 'renounce it'. Obasanjo noted a different mood now: he later told the *New York Times'* Joseph Lelyveld that 'obviously something had snapped'.[293]

The next day, Saturday 17 May, the group flew to Lusaka to meet Oliver Tambo. He stated that, so long as the initiative was in line with the Nassau Accord, 'it would command the support of the ANC'.[294]

Pottinger writes that the US State Department (unofficially) described this situation as 'the pig in the slaughterhouse syndrome', 'a sudden awakening by the security forces to the fact that face-to-face negotiations with the ANC were around the corner with a possible incalculable effect on security force morale and white confidence'.[295]

Was this when the second state of emergency was finally decided?

On Monday 19 May, the SADF launched three cross-border raids into Botswana, Zambia and Zimbabwe. 'The following targets were attacked: the operational centre at 16 Angwa Street in the centre of Harare; a terrorist transit facility at 19 Eve's Crescent, Ashdown Park, Harare; and a terrorist transit facility at Mogoditshane outside Gaborone…'

PW Botha said that 'South Africa would continue to strike ANC targets in other countries in accordance with our legal rights… We have only delivered the first instalment, and if necessary we will strike again… South Africa has the will and the capacity to break the ANC'.[296]

At the time these raids became public, the EPG was addressing the SA Cabinet's Constitutional Committee in South Africa. The meeting stopped halfway and the EPG members packed their bags and returned home.

In early August the Commonwealth agreed to some sanctions, but with minimal British support. Of 59 eligible states, 32 withdrew from the Commonwealth Games later in 1986 on this issue.

As a response to Botha's intransigence, the Thatcher government had its first meeting with the ANC when, on 25 June, Minister Lynda Chalker met Oliver Tambo in a ground-breaking meeting.

Pik Botha, apartheid's Minister of Foreign Affairs, was left to try to pick up the shattered pieces of this debacle – incredibly, he had not been informed of the raids before they happened. Neither had Magnus Malan, the Minister of Defence, who had been in hospital. PW Botha had ordered the strikes personally.

Mandela was discouraged by the collapse of this initiative, but he was now committed to negotiations, and within a month of the departure of the EPG he wrote to the Commissioner of Prisons, who then came to see him.

He requested the Commissioner to arrange a meeting with Minister Coetsee. To Mandela's surprise, the Commissioner rang Coetsee in Mandela's presence. Coetsee was in town and the meeting happened that day, Sunday 20 July 1986. Mandela was driven immediately to Coetsee's house. This all 'greatly encouraged' Mandela.

Mandela told Coetsee that while he had previously been 'an opponent', now he wished to make a 'positive contribution'. He wished to meet with both Botha and leaders in his own organisation.

Coetsee repeated, often, the demand that Mandela renounce violence to get the process started. Mandela nevertheless said he was working on a manifesto for Botha that he believed could break the logjam. This manifesto would later include concessions that were outside the ANC's current positions: he offered the suspension of violence if the government did likewise, to be followed immediately by a conference, ANC–Government, that would involve real negotiations.[297]

They parted amicably, with Coetsee's commitment to do what he could.

Coetsee recorded the meeting in detail and immediately passed the note over to Botha. It included the observation that '913 [Mandela's prison number] was not as confident as previously – he appears to be trying to regain lost ground after the Eminent Persons Group'.[298]

Botha had just called another state of emergency and he replied in this mood: Mandela was to have no more foreign visitors; Botha couldn't meet with him while he was a prisoner; and Mandela should renounce violence to get out of prison to make a meeting possible.

Plainly, nothing was to be conceded at this stage. The rest of 1986 was fruitless.

29

Port Elizabeth and Uitenhage in 1986

'The first five months of 1986 will go down in recent history as the most exhilarating and exciting period of struggle in the Eastern Cape, as the structures of "people's power" were built up and consolidated,' wrote that extremely energetic academic commentator, Mark Swilling.[299] There were other reasons to help one be exhilarated with developments in Port Elizabeth and Uitenhage politics in early 1986.

The creation of alternative organs of government
From the November 1985 release from detention of the UDF leadership, 'the activists began their tireless efforts to reorganise the townships'.[300] By mid-year, most streets had street committees, and area committees, comprising about 20 delegates, one from every street in the area, were also mostly in place. Each area had an Area Committee Council, comprising two delegates from each area committee. This structure was accompanied by the Forum, a political organisation comprising representatives from PEBCO, PEYCO, PEWO and PESCO (a local students' council). Thus were political organisations melded into the geographic street and area committees body.

The Forum was the main policy-making body. However, major decisions needed the support of both the Area Committee Council and the Forum.

Thus were the townships of Port Elizabeth and Uitenhage organised. By mid-year this had mostly been accomplished, and provided not only a political command structure, but also an extremely efficient communication network.

The Ibhayi Council continues to disintegrate

The council that in theory 'controlled' the core black suburbs of Port Elizabeth had begun life in December 1983 as the 'Kayamnandi Town Council'. This name changed in August 1985 to 'Ibhayi Town Council', and again in mid-1986 to 'Ibhayi City Council' (ICC).

The Goon Show that was the ICC continued its shenanigans in early 1986.[301]

In January, Thamsanqa Linda was disrobed as Mayor and as chairman of the Executive Committee. His one-year term as Mayor had expired, and by missing four successive Executive Committee meetings, he was disqualified from that post. Linda was living in the Transkei and did not comment at the time. Later he said that other councillors had sided with Town Clerk Scholtz to get rid of him because he was a 'strong man' and because they wanted his job.

James Nako, an insurance salesman, was inaugurated as the new mayor and Reuben Ntsini as his deputy. Because of resignations of councillors, and Linda's AWOL, the council lacked a quorum. Ministerial approval was requested and received for the (illegal) 'appointment' of two new councillors, despite the law clearly stating that councillors had to be elected. These co-options were a 'temporary measure' until elections could be held, but these were 'inadvisable in the present climate in the townships', said George Reynolds of the Department of Constitutional Development and Planning.

Fresh from the chaos and controversy of the eviction of Mrs Mavela, Council now proved that often lessons are not learned, and mistakes readily repeated.

A house in Ntshekisa Road, allocated to the Ciskei Government in 1982 as it was close to the New Brighton Police Station, was returned to the ICC with a letter from the Ciskei Government saying that it was now let to Mrs Florence Mgwatyu, a single parent with five children. The ICC, however, had other ideas. A councillor, Mrs Nonqaba Petela, was holed up in a hotel in town, and the ICC decided to evict Mrs Mgwatyu and install Councillor Petela.

This they did, on 12 February. Mrs Mgwatyu refused to accept this bullying, and immediately restored her belongings and her family. Cllr Petela fled. Town Clerk Scholtz then wrote to Mrs Mgwatyu, insisting that she vacate the house. She did not and the ICC found another house for Cllr Petela.

Again the ICC had lost a fight, and its authority was even further diminished.

With the ICC slipping away into oblivion, and the UDF leaders clearly representing a constituency growing larger by the day, organisations with issues that needed township endorsement or even just help began approaching the UDF leadership, looking for solutions.

The first contact between the Port Elizabeth Chamber of Commerce and PEBCO was around the 1985 Black Weekend. The PEBCO delegation was headed by Godolozi, Hashe and Galela, whose dreadful demise we have described.

From then until 15 July 1985, many meetings happened as business tried to head off the 15 July Consumer Boycott. The community demands outlined to the businessmen by PEBCO for the calling off of this boycott included demands far beyond the PECOC's capability to influence (for example, the freeing of Mandela, and the unbanning of the ANC) and the boycott was instituted on 15 July. The publicity head of the Consumer Boycott, Khusta Jack, stated that the boycott would not be endless or even lengthy. However, the institution of the first state of emergency on 21 July 1985 led to the detention of the boycott leadership, and the boycott dragged on until the Gilson–Jack meeting in November and the 11 November temporary suspension. It was clearly stated that if the community demands were not met, the boycott would be reinstated in April 1986.

Further negotiation ensued, including six meetings with Mayor Ivan Krige, which concluded at the end of 1985. The discussions had been about non-racial local government.

In January 1986 PEBCO leaders and the Midland Chamber of Industries met and came forward with a concrete proposal for a non-racial municipality based on England's Greater London Council. When the Town Clerk of the Port Elizabeth City Council was asked to support this, he replied that he had no mandate to negotiate on such issues. Pressed further, the Town Clerk agreed that a negotiating committee should be formed to enter into negotiations with the Consumer Boycott Committee. However, as the letter was to be delivered, the next state of emergency had been declared and the Consumer Boycott Committee was either in jail or in hiding.

In July 1986, the exasperated Town Clerk made a speech in Queenstown calling for non-racial local government.

On 7 April 1986 the consumer boycott was reinstated, and now great pressure was exerted by business on government at all levels to solve these issues.

On 4 June 1986 a historic meeting was held at the offices of Mr Phil Gutsche, the chairman and principal shareholder in the enormous SA Bottling empire, which was then Africa's biggest bottler of Coca-Cola. Attending were Dr Scheepers, Deputy Director General of the Department of Constitutional Development and Planning, three Port Elizabeth and

Uitenhage National Party Members of Parliament, Messrs Dawid le Roux, Sakkie Louw and Gert van der Linde, and a full representation from the UDF's Eastern Cape Executive.

The issues under negotiation included a government allocation of R200 million for township upgrading; the establishment of a task force to carry on negotiations; the acceptance of the UDF organisations as the representatives of the township communities; and the necessity of genuine negotiations to carry forward political and institutional developments.

The meeting ended on an enthusiastic note, and another was scheduled for 23 June. The second state of emergency however, was called on 12 June and all of this was put in abeyance.

There was a second set of negotiations underway, about the retention and upgrading of the old Langa township in Uitenhage. They also quickly developed into a significant forum.

The Supreme Court lends some unexpected cheer

In early 1986 the Catholic Bishops of Belgium, acting through Father Smangaliso Mkhatshwa in South Africa, invited the 27-year-old Mkhuseli Jack to Belgium, the Netherlands and the United Kingdom on a speaking tour. Jack willingly accepted and used the opportunity to call for the intensification of disinvestment, sanctions and isolation for the apartheid regime.

Retribution was swift, and after a month home, Jack was served with a five-year banning order under sections 19 and 20 of the Internal Security Act, as was PEBCO's Henry Fazzie at the same time.[302]

The Minister of Law and Order had signed two notices.

The first notice confined Khusta to his house, except between 6 am and 7 pm on any day not a Saturday, Sunday or public holiday. It also prohibited him from being in any black area except New Brighton, any Coloured or Asiatic area, any factory, any printing or publishing establishment, the premises of any organisation that attacked or criticised the state, any trade union premises or any educational institution.

He was also banned from preparing, publishing or disseminating any publication defined in the Internal Security Act, or communicating with any person whose name appeared in the consolidated list referred to in the Act.

The second notice prohibited Khusta from attending any gathering at which the state or government policy was criticised, protest meetings, demonstrations or student gatherings.

The Minister signed these notices on 26 February, and they were served on Khusta on 11 March.

The Minister justified this in his order by merely stating that he was 'satisfied that Mkhuseli John Jack promotes activities that endanger law and order' and that the information which led the Minister to this conclusion could not be disclosed without detriment to the public interest.

But the world moved on, just a little, nine days later, on Thursday 20 March.

A series of cases had found their way through the Natal Division of the Supreme Court, called, in combination, *Nkondo and Gumede v Minister of Law and Order*, had reached the Appellate Division in Bloemfontein, then South Africa's apex court, and judgment came down on that day.

The Appellate Division ruled that if 'the Minister merely reiterates one of the statutory grounds for detaining (or banning) a person and has not given that person reasons within the meaning of the Act and that general and vague statements (such as that a detainee has "promoted activity that endangers law and order") do not constitute proper reasons for ministerial action. Since the court found that as the Minister had not compiled with his statutory obligations to provide the detainee with reasons, the court held that the detention orders were invalid'.[303]

Khusta decided to test the courts, and he was represented by staff from Port Elizabeth's newly opened Legal Resources Centre. Advocate Jeremy Pickering didn't have to argue the issues when Justice Van Rensburg heard it on Saturday 22 March 1986. In a telex the Minister conceded the new judgment, and ominously noted that he would have to redraft some of the regulations. But for today Khusta was a free man, as were Henry Fazzie and a number of other banned people, including Rowley Arenstein, who had been banned for 33 years.

A great victory!

Khusta tore his banning order up on the steps of the Supreme Court, noting that his five-year banning order had lasted 11 days!

Much was going very well indeed.

The Women's March

This murderous rhythm of 1985 continued into early 1986.

With his attempt to ban Khusta Jack and Henry Fazzie in tatters, six days after the Supreme Court pronounced his banning order null and void, Minister Louis le Grange prohibited all public outdoor gatherings in terms of the Internal Security Act.

This ruling met its first challenge the next weekend, on 5 April, when the Centenary Hall was booked for a funeral of eight people killed by the police while they allegedly were raiding township bottlestores.

About 4 000 people arrived at Centenary Hall, to be confronted by 'Police

Casspirs and SADF Buffels surrounded the Centenary Great Hall at New Brighton in the heat of the day on Saturday – rifles were cocked, and some police carried orange sjamboks,' wrote Lloyd Coutts and other reporters in Monday's *Herald*.[304]

> The hall pulsed with shouts of 'Amandla–Ngawetu' in response to highly charged addresses from African community and church leaders.
>
> At the entrance a group danced the 'toyi-toyi' and gave power salutes.
>
> From a Casspir, police filmed the events and a helicopter circled the area.
>
> Teargas was fired at mourners approaching the venue on foot and shots were fired at crowds massing outside the hall.
>
> When a young girl was carried into the hall, allegedly the victim of birdshot, the atmosphere became more volatile.
>
> A second victim carried inside resulted in a delegation of leaders approaching the police with an appeal to stop taking action against the crowds.
>
> The 'toyi-toyi' dancers were still stamping the dust…
>
> At about noon police ordered people trying to get into the hall to disperse. A clergy delegation explained to the lieutenant that there were coffins outside, waiting to be carried inside.
>
> Clergymen, led by the Rev. De Villiers Soga, ushered people inside. The lieutenant used a bullhorn to tell television crews to leave the area, but they disappeared into the building.
>
> Mourners shut the windows and the temperature soared. An emotional charge from Mkhuseli Jack raised the mercury a little higher.
>
> A police quirt was held aloft and carried to the front of the hall, and the crowd erupted, cheering loudly.
>
> A speaker inside said: 'We must dig trenches in the townships, comrades. We must fill these trenches with landmines, and the buffels will fall into them…'.
>
> Moments later the police ordered the meeting to be disbanded and mourners were given two minutes to disperse. A surge of people poured over the outside walls and from the doors, only to be confronted by police bearing weapons.
>
> Following a line of cars to the graveside in Zwide, a Buffel careened by on the right hand side of the road, swerved across to the left hand

pavement and fired tearsmoke canisters into the road.

About 10 metres down the road, another tearsmoke canister was fired into a garden.

At the graveside an angry mob of mourners and about eight SADF buffels confronted one another. The atmosphere was tense.

More township activists were killed, and the community braced itself for another weekend of confrontation a fortnight later on 20–21 April. Four unrest victims were to be buried from the Church of Christ in Avenue A, New Brighton. The rhythm looked like continuing.

Then Ivy Gcina, the chairperson of the Port Elizabeth Women's Congress (PEWO), and her executive had a brilliant idea.

The police justified the numbers of youths killed by their on-duty officers by claiming that their personnel and vehicles were constantly under attack from '*klipgooiers*' (stone-throwers) and lawless youths who frequented funerals and stoked confrontation continually during and after the funeral.

Why then not have a women's-only funeral, and see if and how the violence begins?

As Virginia Ngalo, a member of Ivy's PEWO executive, said: 'Women are playing a leading role because they are tired of collecting the bodies of their children from the mortuaries. Women must now take the unusual step of organising and conducting a funeral because they wanted to prove the truth about who provoked incidents in the townships between the "so-called stone-throwers" and the police … When our sons are killed, it is always said that they were throwing stones and petrol-bombs at the armed police.'[305]

After exhaustive consultation ('We mobilised all the church women, all, all the churches of Port Elizabeth,' says Gcina), it was agreed that the planned funeral from the Avenue A church on 20 April would be preceded by a march to the church, then the funeral service within the church and then a march to the graveside.

And all participants would be women. Black Sash agreed to participate, adding a non-racial dimension.

And so it was to be.

The march to the church was 'extremely well organised, with thousands of church members participating, and a group of white Black Sash leaders … the march was dispersed by the security forces with excessive shooting of tear-gas canisters and the use of a sneeze machine … women of all races and ages were caught in the clouds of gas, trampling each other as they attempted to run for cover … women were taken into the houses of residents who assisted them in obtaining relief'.[306]

On entering the church things hardly improved: 'The packed church was tear-gassed, suffocating those inside and causing them to dowse themselves with water from the baptismal font'. Nevertheless Gcina and others managed to speak, including a white speaker from the End Conscription Campaign.

The journey to the graveside and the ceremony there were likewise disrupted with tear-gas and, now, also birdshot: 'When we arrived at the graveside, the police were there, the tear-gas was like smoke, we couldn't see each other, we couldn't see but we managed to come home, no one knows how, because they were shooting now,' said Gcina.[307]

Some mourners were injured, and one was killed when he fell from a bakkie.

But no one was killed from police action, as extreme as it had been.

No one was killed but the source of the provocation was clearly identified. The PEWO women and their friends must have felt that a good day's work had been done.

Umkhonto steps up its activity

What was not tapering off was the scope of the Umkhonto insurgency.

Tom Lodge notes that, following the 1985 ANC Kabwe Conference, there was a 'striking increase in guerrilla activity'.[308]

1985 had seen 48 attacks in the first half of the year and 88 in the second half, making an annual total of 136.

1986 saw 228 attacks, 'towards the middle of the year almost daily'. The biggest category was attacks on police and state witnesses (68), followed by grenade or limpet mine attacks in built-up areas (52), attacks on community councillors (23) and attacks on municipal police (10).

There was also a new front of attack in the planting of landmines in agricultural areas near South Africa's borders.

30

The end of April 1986:
An assessment

By the end of April 1986 the UDF and its supporters in Port Elizabeth and Uitenhage had much to give them cheer:

- The state of emergency was over, and arbitrary detentions had dropped significantly in number.
- The Port Elizabeth and Uitenhage townships were divided into street and area committees, and these were keyed into the UDF leadership for quick and efficient communication.
- The brutal, destabilising war with AZAPO was over, for the time being anyway.
- Van Zyl Slabbert had left parliament, confirming the UDF's position that parliament had been made irrelevant by the extra-parliamentary street battles and the surge to military rule in PW Botha's time.
- The Joint Management Centres were in place, but their programmes had not yet been felt.
- The Commonwealth Eminent Persons Group and the international sanctions and disinvestment campaigns were furthering the isolation of PW Botha's government and damaging the South African economy.
- International support for the UDF institutions was evidenced

daily in visits from foreign embassy staff and other eminent foreign visitors to the UDF leaders.

- The UDF was enjoying huge amounts of good publicity in both foreign and domestic media, except, of course, state-owned media in South Africa.
- The consumer boycott was again underway.
- The Wendy Orr interdict had reduced security police brutalisation considerably.
- The Ibhayi City Council was clearly in a death spiral.
- Many significant organisations in the white community were now negotiating with the UDF structures and not the official government bodies, and these negotiations were both exhilarating and making meaningful progress.
- The Supreme Court had, with both the declaration that Khusta Jack's banning (and later Henry Fazzie's) was illegal and by granting the Wendy Orr interdict, come to the assistance of the comrades in their long and brutal war with the system.
- The Women's March, and the brutal handing of it by police, had confirmed the source of the ongoing township unrest.
- Umkhonto had upped its game, and more heartening attacks were happening.

It thus appeared, to the forces of the township struggle, that great progress had been made, even if at a murderous cost in lives and homes destroyed in the horror of 1985. That progress showed no sign of abating, as of the end of April 1986.

But was it really so?

At this critical moment, three things happened that suggested that PW was not yet finished.

Firstly, the government announced an amnesty for all non-political prisoners in South Africa's jails, cutting their sentences by six months, ostensibly to coincide with the anniversary of the Republic. Why did the government want many cleared and available jail beds?

Secondly, PW Botha had, on the basis of a decision he had taken without any consultation in the political world around him, instructed cross-border raids against 'ANC bases' (which were not ANC bases) in order to end the Eminent Persons Group initiative, just when it seemed it had established a playing field for negotiations between the government and the ANC. As General Obasanjo said, 'Something had snapped.' What? And what were the further implications of this rupture?

And thirdly, on 18 May, the day before the cross-border raids, the government fired the starting pistol on the most extensive and cruel assault on a poor community when it sanctioned Johnson Ngxobongwana and his 'witdoeke' in their destruction of the Crossroads squatter communities in Cape Town. This appears to have been the first Joint Management Centre 'project', and certainly a most brutal and merciless 'project' it was. Was this the beginning of a National Party fightback?

31

The destruction of Crossroads and Langa

The night of 17 May 1986 was a cold winter's night in Cape Town, and even colder to the city's east, on the Cape Flats.[309]

As dark settled in, men ran from house to house in Old Crossroads, which is situated across the national road from Cape Town's airport. They called the men of Old Crossroads out, to bring with them any weapons they had – clubs, pangas, knives, swords – any weapons. Some of the mobilising party had the most desired of weapons, guns. Many had the weapon of the mob, petrol bombs, for fire was the tool to clear shacklands.

They were also to wear an item of clothing that would be easy to identify: a white panel of material, ideally worn as a scarf or a headdress – a *doek*, in Afrikaans, a 'witdoek'. Then they could identify their own group in this dark night.

Just to the west of Old Crossroads were three squatter camps, Portland Cement, Nyanga Bush and Nyanga Extension. These were tonight's targets. They were to be cleared of 'comrades', the youngsters who were doing the UDF's bidding and who were disrupting the authority that the men of Old Crossroads were trying to establish. And, as 'comrades' were now indistinguishable from other residents, the men of Crossroads were to clear the entire area.

The attacks began around midnight. The first camp attacked was

Portland Cement. The sleeping community had no chance. Fight back they did, but it got them nowhere. The next morning was a Sunday, and Sunday newspapers were finalised too early to report the horrors. By Monday, when the press first carried the story, the three camps had essentially been razed. Possibly 30 000 refugees had been instantly created.

There was then a four-week lull, as a devastated community and an astonished world tried to get to grips with what had happened. On 9 June it happened again. In another attack that showed military precision, 'witdoeke' assembled in the early morning at the Administration Board offices and began a similar attack on the Zolani Centre, and then turned on the huge KTC camp.

This time it took two days and the resistance had stiffened. But the result was the same. At the end of this operation there were an incredible 60 000 refugees who had lost everything that they could not carry in their hands. Hundreds died.

The story of the razing of the satellite camps of Crossroads has been extensively told and is anyway not in the ambit of this book, but there are some important characteristics of the Crossroads destruction carried over to the mass removal of Langa in Uitenhage, which followed immediately after the Crossroads horror, that should be considered.

Firstly, the courts can provide some temporary protection, but a determined rogue state can always get past the law.

The Western Cape had traditionally, in the madness of South Africa's omnipresent racial segregation, been a 'Coloured Labour Preference Area'. This caused a persecution of Africans, who alone had to carry passes, and who had to concede preference in employment opportunities to 'Coloured' South Africans, and for whom the state provided housing inadequately. Some Africans were tolerated, and Guguletu and Nyanga were developed to house these insiders, for business needed labour, but 'surplus and undesirable blacks' were to be clustered in squatter camps pending their repatriation to areas such as the Transkei and the Ciskei.

In synch with this perverted world view, the Cape Divisional Council in February 1976 created Crossroads as a transit camp. Quickly the adjacent squatter camps sprang up, now occupied by anybody who wished to avoid repatriation. Thus in June 1976 the Divisional Council approached the Supreme Court and applied for permission to demolish the area.

The Supreme Court took a different view, and instead declared Cross-roads as a 'Legal Emergency Camp' in terms of section 6 of the Illegal Squatting Act, and instructed the Divisional Council to desist from demolishing, and to instead provide the community with rudimentary services.

Then an elaborate 'dance of development' began, with the recently created Urban Foundation (created by the business community to help deliver reasonable living conditions for the urban black community) working with firstly local Crossroads leaders – this group of leaders was, from 1978 on, spearheaded by Johnson Ngxobongwana – and government, led, on the political level, by Minister Piet Koornhof, and on the administrative level, by Timo Bezuidenhout, recently lauded by *Leadership* magazine as 'The Cape Doctor', having put in place the 'most significant reformist achievements by any government official in recent years',[310] and Ulrich Schelhase, a career township bureaucrat, who from April 1986 was the Town Clerk of Crossroads. Plans aplenty proliferated, and things began to look promising. Upgrades of the squatter camps were considered, and extended occupation rights were on the table.

1983 was a watershed year. Johnson Ngxobongwana had become the first chair of the Western Cape Civic Association (WCCA) and was flirting with the emerging civics movement. The UDF was formed that year and the government decided to develop Khayelitsha, far in the east of the Cape Flats, as an African area and as a place to resettle the Crossroads people. Also in this year, Crossroads elders, known before as 'Fathers', now began to occasionally wear identifying 'witdoeke'.

The people of the squatter camps refused adamantly to consider far-away Khayelitsha as a possible solution to their demands and stuck to the previously promised upgrade of Crossroads. The mood intensified, and the squatter camps were now led by 'comrades', youth loyal to the UDF structures. Ngxobongwana was still, at this stage, within the UDF structures.

In January 1985 members of the Cape Youth Congress (CAYCO) and the United Women's Organisation (UWO), both now affiliates of the United Democratic Front and neither with branches in Old Crossroads, organised a campaign against the perceived high rentals in New Crossroads. Tensions from many issues spilt out, some of which were caused by campaign leadership being from outside Crossroads. When police arrested a number of the women, CAYCO and UWO activists began searching for 'sell-outs'. Much violence and the burning of property ensued.

Eleven people were arrested, including Ngxobongwana, who was only released on bail in late April. Shortly after his release he was acquitted in the Regional Court in Paarl and immediately announced that he was cutting his ties with the UDF. His reasons were their lack of support of him when he was in custody (the fact that the government had effected this custody and he was now courting them he did not explain), and the fact that, while he was in jail, the UDF had organised in Crossroads and had 'caused divisions', which had certainly happened.

By early 1986 the state believed it was under attack from the ANC's 'Total Onslaught", fought through the United Democratic Front. Guided by the ruthlessness, determination and energy of PW Botha, it believed it had an answer. This answer lay in two operations: firstly the theory of an American military theorist, who had honed his ideas in the Vietnam War, and secondly, the militarisation of South African society that the newly created Joint Management Centres provided.

Firstly, the theories of Lieutenant Colonel John J McCuen, as set out in his book, *The Art of Counter-Revolutionary War*.[311]

This work, coming as it did from another war in another world, nevertheless proved immensely influential in the securocrat world that was rapidly emerging in South Africa.

McCuen proposed a two-pronged response to a popular insurrection: firstly, one needed to crush and destroy, as quickly as possible, the revolutionary organisation; and thereafter to replace it with an efficient restructured bureaucracy/government that would 'Win the Hearts and Minds' (WHAM) of the populace, by attending to the material needs of the community.

'The decisive element in any revolutionary war is that the great majority of the population is normally neutral and initially uncommitted to either side ... The objective must be to mobilize this majority so that it supports the governing power.'[312]

McCuen acknowledged that the first step, the crushing of the revolutionary organisation, could be cruel and messy, so he advocated that it be effected quickly and not in a long-drawn-out fashion. This process should be accompanied by the development of swiftly trained militias, whose methods did not have to comply with the professionalism of the official armed forces. They would be fundamental in the maintenance of law and order – this the South African government effected with the creation of 'kitskonstabels' ('instant police') which we will discover later.

Then society should be rebuilt: social society must be realigned and clubs, churches, associations etc. refocused away from the rebellion. And the needs of the people must be addressed: water, roads, schools, etc., all must be seen to be provided.

All this must be accompanied by an all-out propaganda campaign, designed to emphasise the new developments as much as to discredit the revolution.

Plainly this could not all be accomplished immediately wherever the revolution was underway – hence McCuen's final stroke of genius, the 'oilspot' ('oliekol' to the Afrikaans securocrats) strategy. This envisaged specific smaller areas, most noticeably under the influence of the revolutionaries, to be 'pacified' first. When under control, the government and its development works could spread outwards, like a drop of oil on a piece of paper, and put neighbouring areas under control later.

With a fervency of belief that was breathtaking, PW Botha and his securocrats set to work in 1986: firstly, to crush the revolution, a second state of emergency, much better planned and more ruthless, was to be effected; then 1 800 urban renewal projects were launched in 200 townships; and finally, 34 'oilspots' were identified for special and immediate attention, including many in Uitenhage and Port Elizabeth, New Brighton and most particularly the Red Location in Port Elizabeth, and Langa township in Uitenhage. Langa was to endure the same fate as the citizens of the Crossroads squatter camps.

Crossroads was to be the first 'oliekol' project, and the first JMC-run WHAM 'experiment'. In early 1986 its fate was sealed in the chambers of the Western Province Joint Management Centre. The chairman of the JMC's Social, Economic and Welfare Committee was Ulrich Schelhase, the Town Clerk of Crossroads, and this 'mini-JMC 'operated from his office in Crossroads'.

Schelhase gave evidence to the Truth and Reconciliation Commission on 11 June 1997. He was apparently honest. The following is an excerpt from his questioning by Dr Ramashala, of the TRC:[313]

Would you say that it was in the interests of the Development Board for the attacks on the satellite camps to occur?

Yes, Ma'am.

Was the State Security Council keeping abreast with the developments amongst the 'witdoeke'?

Yes.

Your interests, the interests of the security forces and the witdoeke merged in a sense?

Yes, yes.

For the security forces, to clear the area of comrades – for the witdoeke, to get rid of the UDF related allies?

Yes Ma'am.

Therefore it is not surprising Sir that the reports that have been given that when the witdoeke gathered in numbers at the Development Board building that in fact that Casspirs and security forces were accompanying the witdoeke to make sure that they proceed from one area of destruction to another?

It would probably be, Ma'am – it was necessary for me not to stop [the violence] although I didn't agree with it necessarily but that's beside the point – it was an oilspot, and we had to get development, so that it could spill over to other areas, for progress.

Plans for the destruction of the squatter camps were put in place in March 1986. General Wandrag of the SAP issued guidelines that included: 'Efforts must be made to get the residents of the black areas motivated to resist the revolutionaries as follows: contra-mobilization must be small scale and implemented at regional level. Positive resistance movements must be encouraged. This must be done clandestinely.'[314]

By 14 April the JMCs had concluded their final plans, which were presented to the State Security Council on this day. At the meeting were President PW Botha, and ministers Magnus Malan, Adriaan Vlok and Roelf Meyer. Also in attendance were Niël Barnard of the National Intelligence Service (NIS) and the Commissioner of Police, General Johann Coetzee.

The plans included: 'Goal: To remove the influence of the Comrades and other activists on the community. Tasks: To support well-disposed moderate blacks. Actions: Covert organising of adult law abiding black men (fathers) to go against the Comrades in their terror campaign against the residents of black areas.'[315]

One month later, on 19 May, the first attacks happened, as we have recorded, on Portland Cement, Nyanga Bush and Nyanga Extension. The day's horrors were watched from a distance by large numbers of SAP and SADF troops. Thirty-eight people were killed on that day, and 30 000 were rendered homeless – not one 'witdoek' was arrested. With the community driven out and their homes razed, the troops now found their energy and encircled the area with razor wire to prevent members of the community from returning.

After this first period of destruction, and with the 'witdoeke' clearly preparing for an attack on KFC, the community enlisted the help of the Legal Resources Centre and lodged an urgent application with the Supreme Court on 26 May. The relief requested was restraining orders on the SAP, the SADF, Ngxobongwana and his lieutenant, Sam Ndima, from unlawfully entering KTC and destroying the camp. An interim order was granted on that day, with the state being given the return date of 13 June to present its case. Was it a coincidence that KFC was razed three days before this return date?

The KTC community then enlisted the Legal Resources Centre to sue the Minister of Law and Order for damages sustained in this attack. The

Minister and all defence witnesses denied police collusion in the attacks, including Generals Johann Coetzee and Wandrag, who had both been part of framing the plan for the attacks. Evidence requested from the SAP by the Legal Resources Centre was barred in terms of the Internal Security Act, which allowed a Minister, on his own judgement, to prevent such disclosure. The case ran on and on, and was settled out of court in February 1990 with R2.5 million being disbursed to the client community, mostly to build community facilities.

The law had proved helpless in the face of a determined and ruthless state. While the state had not destroyed the camps with state staff and state bulldozers, they had found and used alternative and even more ruthless techniques. Others had done the killing and the razing for the state. The courts were helpless spectators. There were lessons here that the community of Langa in Uitenhage would have been wise to pay attention to.

The destruction of Langa in Uitenhage

Langa/Kabah township, later referred to as just 'Langa', had been established in 1844, and was to remain the biggest township for black persons in Uitenhage until the development of KwaNobuhle from 1967 on. By 1920 three other, smaller residential areas for black persons were also occupied: Doornhoek, Gubbs and Oatlands.[316]

The high cost of administering four distinct and distant 'locations', and the difficulties of preventing racial mixing which had, by now, become prohibited by the Urban Areas Act, caused the authority of the time, the Uitenhage Municipality, to decide to demolish the three smaller locations and move their residents to Kabah. Kabah was not only the biggest of the four locations, it also had the best water supply, superior streets and street lighting. So, in the late 1930s, the fate of Doornhoek, Gubbs and Oatlands was sealed.

Thus the pattern that had been followed in Port Elizabeth played itself out here also. Initial black 'locations' were established on the periphery of the developing white town. As this town expanded, the 'locations' were engulfed, demolished, and their inhabitants moved to a further remote location. And, as in Port Elizabeth, they were unwilling to undergo this move.

To make the reluctant inhabitants move in the time before bulldozers and witdoeke, other incentives were employed. Firstly, married children of residents of the three doomed locations would no longer be allowed to reside with their parents 'but be settled in Kabah with their new families'.[317] The further taking in of lodgers in the three locations was prohibited. Repairs to damaged homes were forbidden. In addition, building materials were offered on attractive hire-purchase terms – but only in Kabah.

As usual this all was presented in glowing terms: 'In fact,' wrote the Town Clerk of Uitenhage, 'the hut-holder in Oatlands Location is moving from what is an unhealthy and badly laid out slum to what the Council hopes to shortly make into a model location.'[318]

This consolidation of the four locations having been effected, the Medical Officer of Health, the acting Town Engineer and the Location Superintendent of Uitenhage changed their opinion of the 'model location'. In 1945 they claimed that 90% of the houses in Kabah were unhygienic; the land available for extension was insufficient, and – of course – the location was too close to the white areas, thereby diminishing the value of neighbouring white properties and blocking further expansion of the white town. Kabah had to go.

An eminent town planner was employed to provide a general plan for the future development of Uitenhage. TB Floyd also concluded that Langa/ Kabah must be moved and he decided that the farm Sandfontein to the east of the town was a good area to move it to. His motivation was twofold: in Kabah, Coloured and black residents were now intermingled, and black workers had to walk through the white town to get to work in the factories.

Incredibly, the white Council, dominated by councillors from Smuts' United Party, refused the proposed move. Dr MS Ofsowitz, a local doctor and councillor, argued that only 10 years earlier, the Council had moved the residents of the smaller locations into Kabah, all the while promising them improved amenities. This had not happened – the proposed amenities 'had not been adequately provided and 95% of the homes occupied by the residents of Kabah were unfit for human habitation'.

'Having moved the natives at considerable expense to Council and much inconvenience to the persons concerned, and having said that Kabah was now to be their "home", it is manifestly inconvenient and unfair to the Natives concerned to decide to move them again.'[319] By a vote of 10 to 5, Council agreed and refused Floyd's recommendation to move Kabah.

Two years later the Smuts government, not knowing that it only had a year left in control of South Africa, voted £99 390 to construct 320 pairs of brick semi-detached units, thereby expanding Kabah into McNaughton Village. This was to be the high point of Kabah's existence, as the next year the National Party took over the reins of governance in South Africa, and Kabah was in for it.

It took the NP nine years to instruct the Uitenhage Municipality that it would get no housing loans until it had cleared 500-yard buffer strips between Kabah and white and Coloured Uitenhage. Why not just move

Kabah, the Chief Native Commissioner for the Eastern Cape, Mr Brownlee, suggested? Again, Council said this was impracticable.

But now there was no more wiggle room available. Louis Smuts, the Under-Secretary of the Bantu Affairs Department offered to pay the relocation costs if Kabah was moved, which government demanded should happen. Kabah was to be moved to the farms Boshoogte and Naros, he insisted. Naros is the current site of KwaNobuhle.

In January 1961 the Uitenhage Council agreed to remove Kabah, a vote that now had only one dissenting councillor. The period of a white council standing up for black rights had ended. Black people were only to retain what property rights they could in Kabah, from now on, through their own struggle. The period 1961 to 1985 was a period of quiet struggle for property rights in Kabah. As Glenn Adler has written: 'For nearly two decades Kabah could not be emptied. The removals orchestrated by the Administration Board came more and more to resemble a man trying to transfer water with a fork: with the lure of industrial employment, the relaxation of influx controls, declining rural conditions and the refusal of the state to build new housing, thousands of people flocked to the old location, so that by 1985 there were as many residents in Langa as there had been when the removals began in 1968.'[320]

KwaNobuhle was now developing, albeit slowly. The first extensions were created as follows:[321]

	Number of Plots	Date Developed
Extension 1	2 500	1967
Extension 2	2 000	1974–75
Extension 3	1 815	1980–81
Extension 4	3714	1984–85
Extension 5	187	1984–85

As the Kabah squatters were scattered, like crows they circled and returned. In 1985 the population of Kabah was as it had been in 1968. By quiet struggle black people were trying to keep their property rights in Langa/Kabah.

This quiet was destroyed by the explosion of gunfire on 21 March 1985. The Langa Massacre ended the quiet struggle for Kabah.

Less than two months after the Massacre, the Mayor of Uitenhage circulated a petition amongst the residents of Levydale, a white suburb within the proverbial 'stone's throw' from Langa. The result was predictable. All 350 white households signed the petition that called for the removal of the Langa squatters. The Mayor handed the petition to the Deputy Minister of Cooperation and Development.

After press reports of the 'white petition' became public, a meeting was called in Langa of about 1 800 people to discuss the possible removal. The meeting elected a delegation to meet with the KwaNobuhle Town Council (KTC) to find out what was envisaged. The delegation was to be led by B Haas from the Uitenhage Youth Congress (UYCO) and comprised Weza Made (also UYCO), B Sandi, P Speelman, G Nojilama and S Nxusa (all from Langa's area committees) and S Mandabana from the union MACWUSA.

By now, following the Massacre, the KTC had no councillors, all of whom had resigned. It fell to its white Town Clerk, Eddie Coetzee, to meet the delegation. At the meeting of 11 June 1985 he was accompanied by P Veldtman, S Somtsewu and RD Basson from the KTC.

And so Langa's 'Dance of Development' began.[322]

The KTC team was supplemented by the appointment of Barry Erasmus as Administrator on 13 September 1985. Erasmus had recently retired as Town Clerk from the Uitenhage Municipality and it took the Deputy Minister three months to get him to agree to take on this frightening post, for there were no councillors or political figures of any sort, and a community in open revolt. Eddie Coetzee, KwaNobuhle's Town Clerk, was his right-hand man.

The Langa team was restructured from the above individuals and became known as the Langa Coordinating Committee (LCC) on its inception on 8 October 1985. It then comprised Freddy Magugu and ME Antoni (from FOSATU), Weza Made, TE Makoka and Z Mge (from different structures of UYCO), Sipho Mandabana (MACWUSA), Nelson Teyise (representing the street committees of Langa) and the Reverends Bashman and Alec Diko (later to be the Methodist Bishop), representing the clergy. What was surprising was the successful inclusion of delegates from both MACWUSA and FOSATU, as these unions had had a tense relationship in Uitenhage.

Pressure from the Uitenhage Municipality forced the KTC's hand and eviction notices for the 426 households of Langa squatters were delivered in October. This got the LCC into action, and they wisely understood that more than emotional argument was needed. They had met two PLANACT staffers, PLANACT being a support service of Johannesburg and Durban academics including a number of town planners, and they requested their help. PLANACT sent two staffers, including Mark Swilling, who quickly came up with a document entitled 'Proposed Steps for Developing Langa'. This was expanded by Dr Mike Sutcliffe, a Durban-based urban planner, who on 26 October, after a lightning visit, compiled a memorandum entitled

'Feasibility Study of the Prospects for Upgrading Kabah, Uitenhage'. The case for upgrade was now on the table.

This document was handed to the KTC at a meeting on 28 October. This did not work. KTC staff dismissed the Sutcliffe document, not least because he had not consulted them on his visit to Uitenhage. And the LCC were not convinced by the KTC's offered incentives to entice the Langa community to move to KwaNobuhle, which was still the KTC's position. Stalemate.

This stalemate was broken in dramatic fashion by the KTC serving notices on the 426 families of squatters on 8 November. The affected families had 14 days to indicate whether they would respond, and a further 14 days to file responding affidavits. The KTC case was thorough, with 78 pages of supporting argument, including an affidavit from Major Theron, head of the police riot control unit, who decried the lack of streets and facilities, all of which made policing in Langa impossible, he argued.

Response was required. The LCC decided that they were going nowhere with the KTC and they rather somehow approach the government's Task Team, a team set up by Minister Heunis that saw the possibility of upgrade.

To get to the elusive 'Task Team', the LCC called in another actor, the Urban Foundation (UF), which had an office in Port Elizabeth, headed by an inventive and open-minded engineer, Roger Matlock. Matlock was initially sceptical of working with the 'comrades', but rapidly converted into a trusting, trusted and determined resource for the Langa community.

The first meeting with the UF was on 10 November, with the ink on the notices delivered to the squatters still wet. The UF agreed to support upgrade as opposed to removal, and an important ally was obtained for the Langa cause. And the UF agreed to handle the costs of the looming court case, which was due to begin on 25 March 1986.

This was interrupted by the formation of the Uitenhage Residents Congress (URECO) in December 1985. At its founding meeting, URECO attempted to take over the issues of the Langa removal, and included none of the LCC activists on its executive. Later, to placate the uproar that followed this exclusion, URECO brought Weza Made onto the executive.

The PLANACT team completed a more detailed strategy document, entitled 'Langa: The Case for Upgrade', and presented this at a large press conference on 19 March 1986. The KTC did not pitch. Plainly more pressure was needed to get the upgrade idea accepted. Two days later, on 21 March, the anniversary of the Massacre, a work stayaway was 99% successful, and 60 000 people packed the KwaNobuhle Stadium. The removal was discussed and rejected.

This too was not sufficient to get the KTC to move. 25 March was the beginning of the court case. Incredibly on the morning of the 25th, Minister Heunis sent a message to the KTC's lawyers, urging them to settle. These lawyers then put forward a proposal: if the 426 families of squatters agreed to move to KwaNobuhle, the rest of Langa would be upgraded. The LCC turned this down, pending consultations. Judgment was reserved. Unbeknown to the township activists, they had just turned down the state's final offer.

The KTC had another string to its bow, for the issue of the removal of the Kamesh Road squatters came to court on 15 April. The judge issued a removal order, to be effected on 30 April if the squatters had not moved by then.

By now the Midland Chamber of Industries (MCI), the coordinating body for industry (as opposed to commerce, and, with Volkswagen, Goodyear and others in Uitenhage, Uitenhage was an industrial town), had become involved and convinced the KTC to stay the removal of the Kamesh Road squatters while the MCI negotiated with the LCC.

A flurry of meetings between the MCI and the LCC followed, and, after associated community consultations, the negotiators agreed on 14 June to the following six key points, which the MCI undertook to lobby support for:

- Kabah/Langa will indefinitely remain an area zoned for black residents;
- Kabah/Langa will be upgraded and, if necessary, extended on the northern side, to accommodate the existing residents;
- All income groups, including squatters, will be accommodated;
- Local labour will be used in the upgrading projects;
- PLANACT will be used by the Municipality of Uitenhage to provide a Master Plan for the upgrading of Kabah/Langa, which will define the future of Kamesh Road;
- If the authorities agree to the above, the squatters will voluntarily move.

A further and broader meeting was hosted by Phil Gutsche, the Chairman of SA Bottling, at his business. This meeting, and a few others, brought the UDF executive, National Party members of parliament, government bureaucrats, chambers of business and the KTC into the upgrade fold, and such a broad meeting on 20 June 1986 saw agreement on the six key points enunciated at the meeting of 14 June.

The LCC activists were overjoyed. Langa was not to be removed, but upgraded. All relevant bodies had accepted this. A further meeting to iron out detail was set for 23 June.

But it was not to be. The second state of emergency had been imposed on 12 June, and before the meeting of 23 June all the Langa activists were in prison cells. All trust was broken and this frantic merry-go-round of meetings, community conferences, professionals drafting proposals and good people negotiating in good faith came to nothing. Langa was, like Crossroads just two months earlier, to be razed.

Mark Swilling believes that the decision to remove the Langa community and then resettle the demoralised remnants in KwaNobuhle was taken on 11 July 1986 at a meeting between officials from the KTC and the South African Police, the local member of parliament and senior government officials. The meeting, he states, agreed on three points: (i) to immediately establish a police station in Langa as the nerve centre of the removal (this was in place by 5pm on that day); (ii) to prevent any further building of shacks in Langa; and (iii) 'to intensify the process of persuasion of shack dwellers to move to KwaNobuhle'.[323]

The destruction of Crossroads was accompanied by the lie that the state was not involved, and that the security forces were impartial. This lie the quoted testimony of Ulrich Schelhase at the Truth and Reconciliation Commission has destroyed. The destruction of Langa was to have its own lie – that the removal was not forced but voluntary, hence the wording of (iii) above. What follows will show this to be similarly false.[324]

By 13 July the first shacks in Langa were 'dismantled' and their inhabitants and their belongings were removed to KwaNobuhle. Immediately four Langa residents approached the Supreme Court requesting an interdict to restrain the KTC from 'demolishing or threatening to demolish or ordering the demolition' of various homes in Langa.

Barry Erasmus replied:

> In the applicants' affidavits a picture is presented of the respondent and its employees acting harshly and indiscriminately; breaking down people's structures and dwellings; doing this against their will; forcing them to remove their belongings and move to KwaNobuhle and, generally, acting in an uncaring and inhumane manner.
>
> I object in the strongest terms to this false picture. For the reasons set out hereunder I deny that any of the applicants or other people were forced to break down their own structures or dwellings, or forced to move from the area in dispute. I personally abhor forced removals and am fully aware of the fact that the situation surrounding the removal of people from the disputed area is a delicate one which has featured prominently in the press as well. I think the record of the respondent, as it appears from the steps taken in the previous application under Case No. 2966/85 speaks for itself and shows

that the Respondent has throughout this unfortunate episode, acted circumspectly and reasonably.[325]

The replying affidavits included this one, from M Mantewu, previously of Langa but now removed to KwaNobuhle, and deposed on 23 July 1986:

I resided in a two-room corrugated sheet shack at 1500 5th Ave, Kabah, and am employed at Farm Fare (Pty) Ltd, Kruisrivier, Uitenhage. I erected my residence myself during June 1985.

On a certain day, I cannot remember the day and date, at about midnight I was awakened by a knock at the door of my shack, and when I opened I was confronted by a white Police Officer dressed in camouflage uniform. This officer did not introduce himself so I do not know his name. He handed me a piece of paper and explained to me that it was a notice stating that I would be required to move from my house to KwaNobuhle as this area is a health hazard, due to the lack of sewerage facilities. I was also informed that I would be called to the E. Cape Development Board in due course to be formally informed about the eviction date. The Police Officer then left and I saw him walking to the house next door. I also noticed two 'Hippo' police vehicles outside. I was also informed that no. 1500 has been allocated to my house.

The following day I heard that all the residents in the area have received similar notices from the police, and people were talking about it. I heard that some of the people have gone to the offices of the E. Cape Development Board to be informed of their eviction date. They were told to remain in the area pending the outcome of a Court decision.

I did not hear anything about this incident until Monday 21 July after work when I was again approached by a police officer at my house and was instructed that I would be moved to KwaNobuhle that day and was instructed to prepare my belongings to be loaded later. There were a lot of policemen present and I saw one Hippo vehicle. There were also trucks from the Development Board onto which some of the people's belongings were being loaded. These people were unhappy about the removal and were protesting as they were being moved against their will.

When being instructed by the police to get my things ready for removal I told him that I did not want to move and I was told that I was the only person objecting against removal as the other people had agreed to move, so I had no option but to comply with the instruction. The police left my house and I moved my belongings out of the house and then demolished the house. I did this because of fear of being assaulted if I did not comply. The water supply to the taps in the area had also been cut off.

At 13h05 a truck from the Development Board stopped at my place and four Black Police Officers, dressed in camouflage uniform, took my belongings and loaded it onto the truck. They did not say anything to me. The material that I had used to build the shack was also loaded. Then I was instructed to board another truck with my family. There were other families also on the truck. We were then taken to the offices of the Development Board and upon arrival taken into an office. A white clerk placed a form in front of me and instructed me to sign it. The contents of the document were not explained to me so I refused to sign my name ... We were then instructed to again board the truck to be driven to KwaNobuhle.

At KwaNobuhle the truck stopped at a site where a lot of army tents had been erected and I was allocated a tent where all my belongings were offloaded. The tent was divided into two sections. One section is used to store my belongings and the other section serves as living quarters for me and my family.

I wish to object to the removal in the strongest terms as I have forcefully been removed. I did not give my consent for the removal. Physical force was not used on me.

M Mantewu's affidavit outlines some of the modus operandi of the removal: the midnight visit by police and officials who instructed the shack dweller to visit the temporary police station where the shack dweller was coerced into signing a form that was not explained to him/her; this form stated that the shack dweller wished for transport to KwaNobuhle and that he/she was moving voluntarily; later, when the initial chaos was settling, the shack dwellers (after Mr Mantewu) were given a green card with a stamp on it, two bags of nails, 500g each of salt, sugar beans and samp, 200g of mielie rice and a tin of canned fruit. The move then happened as outlined by Mr Mantewu, and on arrival in KwaNobuhle the shack dweller had to produce his card to the police, and then got allocated a 'site' (to prepare for the influx, a Uitenhage hill was mechanically scraped to remove the vegetation, then some areas were scraped a second time – they were to be the roads) and tent (the 'two-roomed' tents were soon used up – most then got a small plastic tent with no groundsheet to keep the mud out), and the shack dweller was on his/her own, to somehow, from his pile of material, rebuild his/her home and his/her life.

Through this process the second biggest 'state of emergency' forced removal (after Crossroads) was effected. The following are the statistics the Minister of Constitutional Development released to the PFP's and the Human Rights Trust's Andrew Savage.

A total of 7 226 families, comprising 48 870 people, were forced from Langa and the smaller Despatch shack community to the new and yet-to-be established shackland in KwaNobuhle, in 1986.

What conditions did they move into?

Three months after the removals had begun, on 18 October 1986, the Human Rights Trust took a group of professional people, including four medical professionals, to inspect the tent/shack settlement. This now numbered 43 000 people, some of whom had been there for the three months. The following accounts come from their notes.[326]

According to Dr Zoe Riordan, clinical psychologist:

On Saturday afternoon, 18 October, our party visited the tent town, known as Tjoksville to the local inhabitants, to get an idea of conditions there.

The weather was fine after days of heavy rain, and there was considerable activity by men working on the construction of wood and tin shanties, to replace the accommodation provided by small green tents. Piles of rubble, from which these dwellings were being constructed, lay on the ground alongside the tents.

One noticed numerous black rubber containers, some with roofs, some open. The open ones were water containers; the closed ones were latrines. Four or five 'houses', at the very least (probably ten or more) shared each latrine, and each water tank probably served even more family units.

Of the numerous persons, male and female, of all ages, that I personally spoke to, not a single one said that he/she wanted to come to this area and were indeed extremely unhappy to be there. They were unanimous in their desire to return to Despatch should the opportunity arise, citing as reasons for their unhappiness, the lack of water, appalling sanitation, and high transport costs.

Despite considerable anger at having been moved – and, indeed, everyone we saw was most determined that he/she had been moved against his/her will – no attempts to organise the people (who are no longer a 'community' in any sense) were apparent. Clearly the sheer effort involved in such basic tasks as getting enough water, or keeping dry, makes any further work beyond the capacity of those we saw. If the intention was to quash community organisation, this has succeeded magnificently. Despair characterised the conversations; neglect and deprivation characterised the physical appearance of the dwellers.

In summary: the following points can be made:

1. The physical terrain, as it is now, is hostile and uninviting being on an exposed hill slope, with rudimentary clearing and road construction.

2. There is no electricity and totally inadequate provision of water, sanitation and housing.

3. Medical facilities are non-existent, as are basic social amenities such as schools, shops, etc.

4. Privacy is entirely lacking; whole families are forced to live in a tent or a small shack.

5. Stable, well-established communities have been arbitrarily 'lifted' out of their context, and dumped apparently haphazardly in a place kilometres away.

6. The geographical isolation of the township presents enormous problems for school children, workers, work-seekers, small business entrepreneurs, as well as the unemployed.'

In the words of Dr Luke Krige, specialist physician who later became the doyen of the medical profession in Port Elizabeth:

Prophylactic situation: the situation here is a disaster. No hygiene is possible. Unclean communal toilets have their contents either buried or 'dumped over the hill'. People are excreting 'in the bush'. There are no bathing or showering facilities.

Medical care facilities are non-existent. I met one man building his home who should have been in hospital. My colleague, Dr Noel Blott, found another man who should have been in hospital – but he claimed there was no ambulance, he had no car and couldn't walk the distance. In all probability he could die there.

I repeat – there are NO medical facilities where we visited.

Dr Lindsay Pillay, specialist gynaecologist, said: 'I feel the whole situation is medically hopeless.'

When confronted with these realities, the KTC's response was to obfuscate and to be downright dishonest. As a submission to the Legal Resources Centre made clear:

> At a meeting on 22 October attended by Messrs Erasmus and Coetzee of the KTC and Messrs Andrew Savage and Rory Riordan of the Human Rights Trust, Coetzee said that there were ± 6 000 sites allocated for the ex-Kabah/Despatch residents, and that 2 100 were fully serviced, a tender for a further 2 300 had been awarded, and that a tender for the remaining 2 300 sites was to go out within a month.
>
> The Human Rights Trust did three surveys of the Tjoksville residents, and residents vigorously disputed this. A further meeting of the above four, now also attended by Dr D Evans of the Uitenhage Municipality Health Department, saw Coetzee change the above to: now, 1 000 sites had services, but the sewerage service was still to be connected; an 11-month contract had been signed on 13 November for an additional 3 000 serviced sites; and another tender, for an additional 2 000 serviced sites, was to close in 'January/February'. This revealed that there was no waterborne or any other sanitation in the area prior to the removal.

With regard water provision, Coetzee said that six tankers delivered 720 000 litres a day, which, despite the apparent herculean efforts of the drivers, working around the clock to make the 720 000-litre deliveries, if this was in fact happening, still only amounted to 18 litres of water per person per day. This, as the Human Rights Trust's surveys had shown, was (if it was happening) clearly inadequate.[327]

With regard to bucket toilets, Coetzee said there were two sanitation lorries which worked three days a week in this community, servicing 6 000 toilets, and cleaned all of these 6 000 toilets on each of these three days. This, again a herculean effort, would mean that each lorry would service a bucket every ten seconds: plainly the residents' survey data, which suggests that 78% of the toilets were serviced once a week or less, was more credible.

Dr Evans attended because Savage had demanded independent monitoring of the services: this Erasmus had refused, as he claimed that this was the agreed responsibility of the Uitenhage municipality, and Dr Evans was the member of staff responsible.

Evans admitted that he had only one trained black health worker, whose job was to monitor water deliveries and toilets over the entire Uitenhage black area. One man was catering for the needs of a black population of 130 000. He further admitted that he did not agree with the KTC's statistics for water provision and toilet services in the new areas.

This all seems to confirm the concluding remarks of Tim Douglas-Jones in his contribution to the Human Rights Trust report: 'My overwhelming impression was that the welfare of these people could not have been further from the minds of the people who ordered the removals. People were dumped in the middle of the veld and left to fend for themselves.'

We end with a personal cameo: I supervised and in some instances was part of the Human Rights Trust's team doing the fieldwork in their three surveys, and record my experiences on the evening of 27 October:

> Worked for three hours in rain to do the pilot study.
>
> Indescribable misery of the tent town in the rain – found one home at 19h30 in the dark and wind and rain where the shack was two-thirds up and really offered no protection. The desperate couple were sitting on chairs on the mud floor at the back with a radio trying to help, and a pathetic fire in a galvanised drum being the only sign of any cheer.
>
> Their tent had collapsed. Nelson Teyise of URECO was with me and I tried to right it, when he got me to look inside. It was flooded, a wet sodden mess (no tents here have any groundsheets – the people live in mud).
>
> Their position was hopeless. We got into our car and left.[328]

And so another tragedy reaches its painful conclusion.

As with the residents of Crossroads, the citizens of Langa had been creative and energetic in the pursuit of their dream – an upgraded Langa.

In both Crossroads and Langa, the community negotiators had done so much to make this possible – they had involved experts, who had created models proving it was all possible; they had involved business, the press, the courts; and all the while had kept their own community fully informed, and had regularly taken democratic mandates. All had been done in good faith, despite great misgivings as to the integrity of the government negotiators. The 'dance of development' had been thoroughly and honourably seen to its conclusion.

In both communities an outcome had finally been negotiated that both sides could live with. Textbook stuff – compromise, then finally agreement.

What had not been anticipated was the undercover securitisation of government, and the JMC takeover with the decision to head to a second state of emergency. That was the end of it all. Crossroads and Langa were seen as unchangeable breeding grounds for 'comrades'. They had to go, their communities had to be destabilised to the point where political involvement could no longer be managed – simple survival to replace political mobilisation.

And so both Crossroads and Langa were razed.

Barry Erasmus undoubtedly took his pension, supplemented significantly by his earnings as 'Administrator' of KwaNobuhle and later also as 'Administrator' of the Ibhayi City Council. Eddie Coetzee had neatly circumvented all tender procedures in the purchase of the tents, toilets and water tanks, and a merchant grew fat on the deals – R13.5 million was in fact spent, a not-so-small fortune at the time – fat enough for the merchant to fund the purchase by Coetzee of a Mercedes-Benz. Coetzee was charged with corruption, and anyway, with the dawn of democracy beginning to glow on the horizon, in 1993 he resigned as Town Clerk of KwaNobuhle. It seems that the charges disappeared as democracy became inevitable.

But for the nearly 50 000 newly-arrived residents of KwaNobuhle, only misery and difficulties were ahead. It was years before even rudimentary services arrived in Tjoksville, but well before that, state-supported vigilantes were to again ravage this world.

32

The second state of emergency

*S*outh African Review was an excellent series of books that came out
almost annually in the 1980s. Edited by Glenn Moss and Ingrid
Obery, the series contains three thorough essays on the two states
of emergency and allied issues: 'Repression and Detentions in South
Africa' by Max Coleman and David Webster, *South African Review 3*,
Ravan Press 1986; 'Repression and the State of Emergency' by David
Webster, *South African Review 4*, 1987; and 'Repression and the State
of Emergency: June 1987 – March 1989' by David Webster and Maggie
Friedman, *South African Review 5*, 1989. The common denominator here
was Dr David Webster, who paid with his life to make this information
available for those interested. I pay my most sincere respects to Dr Webster
for this fantastic work.

South Africa in the mid-1980s had two items of legislation whereby
security personnel could detain individuals.[329]

The Internal Security Act of 1982 contained four sections providing for
detention of persons deemed to be a danger to state security: Section 28
allows indefinite preventative detention, to remove activists from society;
Section 29 allows a policeman of the rank of lieutenant colonel or above
to detain a person indefinitely, if the police officer believes the person to
be a 'threat to state security'; Section 31 allows for the detention of an
individual deemed to be a potential state witness; and Section 50 allows a
low-ranking police officer to detain a person deemed 'instrumental in an

unrest situation' to be detained initially for 14 days, and thereafter, with the agreement of a magistrate, indefinitely.

The Public Safety Act of 1953 empowered states of emergency, and allows any security officer, including members of the military, to detain an individual for 14 days, and thereafter, with the permission of the Minister of Law and Order, indefinitely. Under this act, visitors are almost never allowed, and 'insubordinate' behaviour was punishable.

When the first state of emergency ended on 7 March 1986, the security establishment released the few hundred remaining detainees and seamlessly moved onto new detentions in terms of the Internal Security Act. In 1986 there were 3 989 Internal Security Act detainees, almost twice the number of 1985. Every month, 639 people were detained in the period between the states of emergency, all under the Internal Security Act – 88% of them under section 50.

Then came the second state of emergency, called on 12 June 1986.

As David Webster wrote: 'The new emergency showed signs of lengthy and careful planning. On the night before it was declared, security forces swept through black communities detaining thousands. By June 1987, 26 000 people had been detained. In the first eight months of this emergency, security police detained as many people as the total held under previous emergencies and security legislation for the previous 26 years. Internationally, South Africa was now second to none on an index of repression.'[330]

The night before the state of emergency was announced, security forces rushed through black areas, detaining activists wholesale. As there was no state of emergency at this stage, they were held under Section 50 of the Internal Security Act. The next day they were switched to the emergency regulations. There was to be no escaping this time.

While the first state of emergency was declared over a restricted geography, this one was declared over the entire country, and, while this was not known at the time, the government had set no time limits. This state of emergency would last until well into 1990, over four years, renewed annually.

The numbers detained were astonishing. In total, Webster and Friedman believe over 32 000 people were detained over the years of this state of emergency. Initially huge numbers were caught in apartheid's dragnet, but were freed within months.[331]

The core of the UDF leadership was not so lucky, and in Port Elizabeth Khusta Jack and the senior leadership would only be released in May 1989, just a month short of three years in jail. Jack had eluded the security police for just over a month in the beginning, and had finally been caught in New Brighton on 25 August 1986. Nieuwoudt was to make him pay for

Mkhuseli 'Khusta' Jack

Mzimase Mangcotchwa

Mthiwabo Ndube

Max Mamase

Janet Cherry

Pata Madalane

Judy Chalmers

Lulu Johnson

Mpumi Odolo

Dan Qeqe

his elusiveness. He was 'chucked like a sack of potatoes into the boot of a small Toyota sedan. They'd pulled a bag over my head so at the time I didn't know where they were taking me. I learned at the TRC hearings that it was Willowdene near Fairview ... There I was tortured for hours before being thrown into the boot and driven to a place called Fort Brown'.[332]

There Khusta, with his hands and legs both cuffed, was kept in a windowless dungeon of an 1835 Frontier War fort which was now a historic add-on to a rural police station, in isolation. Nieuwoudt told the duty sergeant that 'Hy moet daar vrot' (He must rot there). And rot he did, for five long weeks, until less vengeful police had him moved to St Alban's, where the UDF leadership 'enjoyed' an entire section to themselves, 40+ to a cell, with the detained 'rank and file' being held at Kirkwood prison.

Again, as always, the Eastern Cape was the most affected: of those detained in 1986, fully a third came from the Eastern Cape. As Tom Lodge has written: 'In the Eastern Cape, so many people were taken into detention in the first few days of the emergency that the police had to use cold-storage facilities normally used for beer as holding centres.'[333]

There was another change from the first state of emergency. Now the focus of detention was firmly on the UDF leadership, but also, and most particularly, young people. David Webster: 'In 1982, only eight people under the age of 18 were detained; in 1984 nine were held. The 1985 emergency changed all of that. Approximately 2 875 children under the age of 18 were held – 25% of the total – of whom 2 000 were under 16. In the 1986 emergency, the Detainees Parents' Support Committee calculates that about 10 000 aged 18 and under have been detained – 40% of the total. If one adds to this the youth (age 25 and younger), the figure for detained youth and children totals 79% of all detainees, or 18 750. Some detained children are as young as 11 and 12.'

Of course it was the UDF that the state went for: 70% of detainees were members of local UDF affiliates. By August 1986, 50 national and regional UDF leaders had been arrested. And their detention was not just by the powers of the emergency regulations: Terror Lekota, Popo Molefe, Moss Chikane and 19 others were arrested on 16 October 1985 on charges of treason. This trial, the Delmas Treason Trial, tied the three up until 15 December 1989, in jail all the time, until their convictions were quashed. Similarly, 58 political trials were underway in June 1988, with clear indications that a similar fate awaited the UDF top team in Port Elizabeth.

By February 1988, even this was not seen to be sufficient by the state: on 24 February 1988, 17 organisations, including the UDF, CRADORA and PEBCO were banned from 'carrying on any activity or acts whatsoever' in terms of the state of emergency. Unlike banning under the Internal Security Act, the minister had no responsibility to provide reasons for a state of emergency banning – nor did he bother to. PEYCO joined this grouping in November of that year.

Later in the state of emergency, detainees were released in terms of banning orders: in the first state of emergency 68 released detainees were banned; in the second state of emergency this number rose to 580. Over 400 of these were in 1989, when the senior UDF executives were released.

The media did not escape this horror. In 1986 the police issued nine orders restricting press coverage of detention, detainees and 'unrest' activities. The editor of *New Nation*, Zwelakhe Sisulu, was detained twice in 1986, the second time for several months. In Port Elizabeth two journalists, Mike Loewe and Brian Sokutu, were detained. In December 1986 newspapers were barred from publishing non-governmental accounts of police or army activity.

There was another novelty in the second state of emergency. In Port Elizabeth and Grahamstown, for the first time the state now moved against white people in numbers.

33

Whites against apartheid

The white community of Port Elizabeth and Uitenhage in the 1980s was changing over time, and by the mid-1980s it was dominated by a conservative populace and institutions that reflected their attitudes and opinions. These attitudes were, at best, quietly accepting of apartheid and its mindset and its cruelties, and, at worst, openly and enthusiastically accepting of white racial domination.

As incredible as it now seems, what is now the Nelson Mandela Metropolitan municipal area, in the early 1980s, had nine separate local authorities operating in it: the Port Elizabeth Municipality, the City Council of Ibhayi, the Town Council of Motherwell, the Development areas of KwaDwesi and KwaMagxaki, the two Management Committees of the Coloured Group Area and the Indian Group Area, the Uitenhage Municipality, the Despatch Municipality and the KwaNobuhle Town Council. Not one of these institutions lifted a finger to oppose apartheid, ever.

In 1988, however, municipal elections in Port Elizabeth saw the election of a number of liberal councillors – Flip Potgieter, Ivan Krige, Angelo Dashwood, Bobby Stevenson and Graham Richards joined the long-standing liberal, Graham Young. They were much more confrontational of apartheid but never enjoyed a majority on council.

Then there were four chambers of business: the Uitenhage Chamber of Commerce, the Afrikaanse Sakekamer, the Midlands Chamber of Industry and the Port Elizabeth Chamber of Commerce. Only the Port Elizabeth

Chamber of Commerce, whose members were hard hit by consumer boycotts, ever risked an opposition position.

The judiciary, the Afrikaans-language press, the charismatic churches, the University of Port Elizabeth (in the decade of the 1980s this university awarded ten honorary doctorates – nine to white Afrikaans-speaking males, and one to an Afrikaans-speaking female – all safely tucked up in apartheid's bed, for sure) ... and so on. At best, quiet on politics. We all knew what that meant.

But these institutions no longer represented a monolithic white community; there were a number of 'opposition' institutions and bodies, if by 'opposition' we mean institutions that believed that apartheid was a cruel disaster, both immoral and destructive of the opportunities of people of colour, and that it should be replaced by a non-racial society with enshrined human rights and (for some of those who opposed apartheid) a universal and equal franchise for all South Africans.

The institutions mentioned here all came to believe in such a society at different times and through different processes. What they did collectively was to bring these opposition values to our society. And, in their own, maybe tiny way, they all helped to enable the township war of the 1980s to reach the conclusion it eventually did.

The Eastern Province Herald *and* Evening Post

Continuously in print since 1845, the *Eastern Province Herald* is a veteran of the South African newspaper scene. And it was never apartheid's puppet, unlike its Afrikaans-language cousins.

By the 1980s, it had had a recent series of liberal editors, including Mac Pollock, who dropped dead in the *Herald* offices in 1969 (father of cricketers Peter and Graeme), Harry O'Connor (ex-*Rand Daily Mail*), Koos Viviers and Derek Smith (also ex-*Rand Daily Mail*). The *Herald* held a liberal line, thanks mostly to its deputy editor of the time, Robert Ball, and its parliamentary/political correspondent, Patrick Cull. A series of reporters, including Jimmy Matyu, Mono Badela, Edyth Bulbring, Peter Dickson, Dawn Barkhuizen, Lloyd Coutts, Kin Bentley, Adrian Cloete and Barbara Orpen, all found ways to get things published despite state of emergency restrictions.

Things were the same with the *Evening Post* under editors John Sutherland and Trevor Bisseker. They held the line. Even their most determined critics from the left nevertheless watched the 'papers' for 'their story'.

Today these newspapers provide a significant record of the struggle years. At the time of the struggle they gave opposition activists cover and credibility.

The Black Sash

'In 1955 six White women in Johannesburg said "enough is enough" when the government enacted a law to disfranchise "Coloured" South Africans, rescinding their right to vote. Along with a wave of other women my mother, Peggy Levey, joined this group. Their formal name was the Women's Defence of the Constitution League, but everyone called them the Black Sash. We lived in Port Elizabeth in the Eastern Cape Province ... Soon she was elected regional chair,' so begins Susan Collin Marks' memoir, *My Mother against Apartheid*.[334]

This was the beginning of Port Elizabeth's most long-standing human rights organisation, the Black Sash, with its 'Cape Eastern region' being founded in 1955 in Port Elizabeth. Di Davis, whose name still identifies the first crèche in Gqeberha Township, hosted the first meeting in her lounge.[335]

It did not take long for apartheid's bullies to get to work on the Sashers, and in 1964 Peggy Levey was 'warned' in terms of the Suppression of Communism Act and her passport was removed. Three members of the regional council were warned two years later, and two resigned from Sash. Mary Burton believes that the Cape Eastern region closed in 1978 'due to security police harassment', although other Sashers have disputed this.[336]

It really came back to life in 1981, when the two Pagden sisters, Judy Chalmers and Molly Blackburn, joined.

Judy joined first, while Molly, recently elected as the Member of the Provincial Council for Walmer, settled into her new job. Molly visited her friend Di Bishop's Sash project in Cape Town, an advice office for disfranchised and impoverished citizens, and became convinced that this was something Port Elizabeth needed. When her profile in Port Elizabeth's black townships skyrocketed, and long queues of people started forming at the Progressive Federal Party's offices in Port Elizabeth, Molly said she would join Sash if they opened an advice office. This was done, and she too joined.[337]

In the 1980s Sash played a considerable role, considering that it was a volunteer organisation with a tiny budget. It ran advice and crisis offices in Port Elizabeth (run by the stalwart Shelagh Hurley) and Uitenhage (run by the equally resolute Eurelia Banda), conducted endless protests in the long-standing tradition, and recorded and publicised many township horrors.

One of the Sash interventions was the support they provided the Langa Uitenhage community after the massacre of March 1985. Molly Blackburn and Judy Chalmers were instrumental in drawing Errol Moorcroft, the Progressive Federal Party MP from Albany in, to help pull together the full picture. Arriving here also was a young, recently admitted attorney, Vanessa Brereton, brought in by Molly as a much-needed professional to take statements and, if necessary, assemble cases for the courts. Vanessa's real motivation was, tragically, not this. 21 March 1985 was her first day as both a human rights lawyer and an apartheid spy.

Judy Chalmers was at the centre of much of the Sash activity, and was for years the chairperson but she was not alone. Long-standing members Bobbie Melunsky and Peggy Levey, Presidents Zoe Riordan and Isobel Douglas-Jones, members Baa Thompson, Debbie Mattheus and advice office stalwarts Shelagh Hurley and Eurelia Banda, Cathy Binnell, Val Hunt, June Crichton, Cate Turner, Therese Boulle, Leslie Greensmith, Lindsay Woods, Sandy Stewart, Janet Cherry and Vicky Proudlock – and more – were dedicated human rights workers, delivering a quality of work that was exceptional.

The Progressive Federal Party

The Progressive Party was begun in 1959 when a group splintered away from the official opposition of the time, the United Party. Amongst this first group of breakaways was EB Pagden, a prominent Port Elizabeth attorney and the father of Judy Chalmers and Molly Blackburn. Its early years were tough, and in the general elections of 1961, 1966 and 1970, 'the Progs' returned only one member of parliament, the redoubtable Mrs Helen Suzman.

From this tiny start, the Progs, which was, with the Liberal Party, the most progressive white party of the time, grew by absorbing other small breakaways from the moribund United Party and moving on under new names: in 1975 it became the Progressive Reform Party and in 1977 the Progressive Federal Party (PFP), with Colin Eglin as leader. In the whites-only election of this year, the party jumped from six members of the House of Assembly to 17, with a new shadow leader in the wings. A palace coup was organised by Gordon Waddell, Harry Oppenheimer's son-in-law, and it resulted in Frederik van Zyl Slabbert, the brilliant intellectual Member for Rondebosch, becoming the leader of the party in 1979. This was the year after an internal party commission, chaired by Slabbert, had committed the party to the universal franchise.

While the centrepiece of South Africa's politics in the 1980s was undoubtedly the township war, formal 'white' politics was also a busy place. There were 'white' general elections in 1977, 1981, 1987 and 1989, as well as a referendum on the tricameral parliament (1983). In all of this, the Progressive Federal Party was a determined player (it became the Democratic Party in 1989, in time to fight the 1989 election under this banner).[338]

A quick survey of the national trends in white politics over this period shows the following:

The white ultra-right began in formal politics with the Herstigte

Nasionale Party contesting the 1970 election; they won 3.5% of the vote, but no seats in parliament thanks to the first-past-the-post system of constituency representation. They repeated this template of dismal failure in the 1974 and 1977 elections, winning about 3% of the vote but no seats. The 1978 resignation of Prime Minister John Vorster and PW Botha's accession to the prime ministership saw the HNP grow to 15% of the electorate in the 1981 election, but, again, no seats resulted.

Then came the much more successful Conservative Party, formed in 1982/83, and using the referendum for the tricameral parliament as a rallying issue. Again, the white ultra-right took about 16% of the vote in this referendum, but there was no doubt that it was the Conservative Party that had won this.

The 1987 election saw the Conservatives winning 27% of the vote, and 22 seats in parliament, thereby deposing the PFP as the official opposition. In the 1989 election the CP took 34% of all votes. In the process it rose from no representatives in parliament to 39 in 1989.

On the other side of the political spectrum, the PFP went up, then down, then up again.

Initially this was from a series of voter donations by the rapidly dying United Party and its successor, the New Republic Party. In 1970 the United Party polled 38% of the total vote and won 29% of all seats. By 1989 it, and the New Republic Party which represented a conservative splinter within the UP, had disappeared. The National Party had been gifted 23% of all voters, and the PFP/DP 15%. For every 100 United Party voters in 1970, 60 voted for the NP in 1989, and 40 for the PFP/DP.

The 1977 election was kind to the PFP, but in a limited way. It rose from 5% of the electorate in 1974 to 14%, and had 17 members of the House, enough to be the official opposition to the enormous National Party of BJ Vorster, which had 135 parliamentary representatives and total control over South Africa.

But a second, less noted, event had been part of the 1977 election – in Port Elizabeth, a remarkable person had set his seal on PFP politics, as Andrew Savage left his enormous construction business, Savage and Lovemore, to be the PFP's candidate in the Walmer constituency.

He did not at first succeed. He lost to Theo Aronson, the ex-United Party sitting member in the 1977 election, but in the process he assembled a determined team that breathed new life into the PFP. Lindy Pagden, the attorney EB Pagden's second wife, ran the campaign, accompanied by a long list of PFP notables.

Savage was an exceptional man. A decorated hero of the Second World

War (which he had entered by bluffing his way through the medical exam – he only had one functioning eye and was also underage), he had his superiors use his insomnia creatively. He was sent out, night after night, alone, to survey the land ahead during the Italian campaign. On his reports they then made their progress safely. He was awarded for his leadership in taking out a machine-gun establishment on foot at night.

When the war ended, Savage and his friend David Lovemore pooled their demobilisation pay and bought two second-hand army trucks. From this, the civil engineering giant Savage and Lovemore grew, making both Savage and Lovemore wealthy and hugely respected.

Then came the crisis of 1976 and its disastrous fallout. Savage decided there was no future in 'counting his beans', and he set his sights on parliament, where, or so he believed, logic and argument had to eventually win.

After the 1977 failure, he returned as a candidate in the 1981 election. This time he had a brainwave, and it came in the form of Molly Blackburn as his running-mate – he for parliament, and she for the Provincial Council. They beat the National Party's Theo Aronson and Sheila Linton and in Port Elizabeth Central John Malcomess and Eddie Trent also had success. In total the PFP won 18 224 votes in Port Elizabeth – 1 747 in Algoa Park, 4 488 in Newton Park, 5 903 in Port Elizabeth Central, and Savage polled 6 146 in Walmer.

Now the PFP had public representatives in Port Elizabeth, and with Savage skewering the NP in parliament and Molly showing us all that for every white citizen, Port Elizabeth had four of colour, liberalism had a new set of champions. A great age seemed to be possible. This was well supported by the new director of the party in Port Elizabeth, Bobby Stevenson.

When Molly died, Savage realised that the remarkable work she had been doing could not be allowed to fade away. By now, foreign governments were putting considerable resources into organisations working for democracy in South Africa, and, to leverage this, he conceptualised an organisation independent of the PFP (which could not, by law, take foreign funding), and so Operation Real South Africa, later the Human Rights Trust, arrived. For this he called in myself, a veteran of his two campaigns, and a man known in the townships. Nobody could replace Molly, or do things as she had done, but that option no longer existed, and a new way had to be begun.

The next white election, 1987, was to be a disaster for the PFP. Slabbert had abandoned parliament in 1986, and, with the townships in full revolt, security issues, always the biggest challenge the PFP faced with an increasingly tense white electorate, proved unhelpful. The PFP share of the national vote dropped from 19% in 1981 to 16.3% in 1987, with its parliamentary representation dropping from 27 to 19.

In the Eastern Cape the PFP took two dramatic reverses: Savage had decided to abandon his Walmer seat, and instead stood in conservative Humansdorp, leaving Walmer to his cousin, Paddy Ball. This proved to be a bad reading of the options. Both Ball and Savage lost, as did Errol Moorcraft in Albany. The PFP went down to one representative in Port Elizabeth, Malcomess in PE Central. In total the PFP dropped 2 000 votes, to 16 229.

In the 1989 election it was the National Party's turn to take a bath – they dropped nationally, from 120 seats at the dissolution of parliament to 93. The CP rose from 22 to 39, and the DP from 19 to 33. Still not the official opposition, but in Port Elizabeth the reconstituted Democratic Party was back to holding Walmer (General Bob Rogers) and Central (Eddie Trent), and won, in total, just over 19 000 votes.[339]

Of the white, 'non-apartheid' organisations, the PFP was undoubtedly the most supported, and from this large body of support flowed many people who could, and did, support other organisations that needed resources and volunteers.

The citizens of Port Elizabeth owe Andrew Savage and Molly Blackburn a great deal of gratitude. Opposition political parties throw up ideas, criticise and expose government's mistakes, and keep their supporters in the political and legal system. Andrew and Molly did that and much more – they helped enormously to open up racial contact in a closed society, and to allow decency to flow through the cracks they bravely prised open. They added so much to the society they served.

Other supportive organisations within the white community

The war in the townships in the 1980s created an energy that in turn saw a number of creative interventions emerging in the white community. Most of these interventions saw white and black South Africans working together, and with time they became increasingly staffed and supported by black activists. But they started as initiatives from white South Africans, and we will brand them as such. The institutions that follow all had a presence in Port Elizabeth in the 1980s.

IDASA

When Dr Slabbert resigned from parliament at the beginning of 1986, he was joined by another prominent PFP parliamentarian, Dr Alex Boraine, in the creation of an institute to promote dialogue and a democratic culture in South Africa. This they named the Institute for a Democratic Alternative in South Africa (IDASA), and they purposefully chose Port Elizabeth as the site of IDASA's first branch, which opened in December 1986. IDASA's national launch happened in Port Elizabeth on 8–9 May 1987. Its first staffers were Max Mamase (later to be an MEC in the Eastern Cape Province's first cabinet) and Wayne Mitchell, a PFP youth leader, both from Port Elizabeth.

IDASA hit the headlines two months after this launch when Slabbert and Boraine led a group of nearly 40 (mostly) white Afrikaans-speaking South Africans to Senegal in July 1987, known as the Dakar Initiative. Slabbert was determined to present it not as IDASA's one-trick pony, but as just one of 'at least six other such meetings'.[340] It dominated the headlines for a considerable time. IDASA coordinated many conferences, focus groups, and discussion opportunities over the years to democracy, and thereafter.

Detainees Parents' Support Committee

Founded in Johannesburg in 1981 as a vehicle to support detainees and their families, it soon opened in Port Elizabeth at the instigation of the Black Sash, and was a useful vehicle for much non-racial activity. It was at a DPSC meeting that Molly Blackburn first met Saki Macozoma, in what Shelagh Gastrow has described as the first cross-racial political contact of the new era. Much of the energy of the DPSC in Port Elizabeth came from a committed Methodist priest, Rev. Paul Verryn, who sadly was moved from the Eastern Cape to Johannesburg in 1984.

The Urban Foundation

Originally established by Harry Oppenheimer and Anton Rupert in the wake of the 1976 revolt, the Urban Foundation made a number of interventions in the living conditions of South Africa's urban blacks, and then, most particularly, the housing conditions of this large grouping.

Soon an Urban Foundation established a presence in Port Elizabeth, initially headed up by Prof. Bill Davies. It was when Davies handed the reins over to Roger Matlock that the Urban Foundation really got moving. Matlock, an engineer who never accepted the traditional way of doing things, soon established a large non-racial staff, including Ernie Bergins, Mbulelo Cagwe, Bheki Sibiya, Noel Staples and many others, and embarked on what was then a world-leading *in situ* upgrading of the enormous Soweto-on-Sea informal 'town'. Community centres were established in KwaZakhele,

Walmer Township/Gqeberha and KwaNobuhle, and technical assistance was provided to many communities who needed help in upgrading projects.

Port Elizabeth Chamber of Commerce

Initially galvanised into action by the 1985 Consumer Boycott of many of its members' businesses, the Chamber had as its Chief Executive Tony Gilson, who rapidly acquired a taste for township politics, and, backed by members wishing to ensure no repetition of the Consumer Boycott, Gilson became a loud and determined advocate of a new, non-racial political dispensation.

The Watsons

Ronnie, Valence and Cheeky spent most of 1986 in jail, having been refused bail for the destruction by fire of their Park Drive home, for which they were eventually found not guilty. Here we can just note that, at this time, they created a Concerned Citizens movement, to offer white citizens a UDF-type alternative, and later they created a chamber of business that was ahead of its time.

The Bishops

Here we find four remarkably brave and principled people: Bishops George Irvine (Methodist Church), Bruce Evans (Church of the Province) and Michael Coleman and John Murphy (Catholic Church).

These church leaders dragged their churches forward, criticising apartheid for the crime it was, demanding progress on human rights issues, allowing their church properties to be used for meetings that they dared not inspect the agendas of, signing petitions, providing, as best they could, protection for anti-apartheid activists of any organisations, and leading marches, thereby trying to keep the cops at a distance.

Their churches lost white members to the charismatic churches that allowed no discussion or criticism of apartheid and, in some instances, ran campaigns funded by state money to vilify black political movements. All this the bishops fought with all their energy, and were absolutely resolute in their stance.

They provided the strongest possible moral leadership, and received much criticism from often-terrified constituents. But they never wavered, despite their vehicles being sprayed with graffiti, their children being vilified and their persons being attacked and insulted.

Legal Resources Centre

The idea of a legal resources centre in South Africa began with the work of Felicia Kentridge. She was herself an advocate and married to one of South Africa's most prominent advocates, Sydney Kentridge. After exposure to the provision of free legal services to the poor in the United States, she began the first law clinic in South Africa at the University of the Witwatersrand. Modifying her thinking as she went on, in conjunction with Geoff Budlender, from Port Elizabeth but then practising as an attorney in Johannesburg, she convinced Arthur Chaskalson to accept the leadership of the proposed organisation, and Budlender to be its first staffer.[341]

Thus Legal Resources Centre (LRC) began operations in Johannesburg in January 1979. It was exceptionally well run, attracted much foreign sponsorship, and, as the terrible 1985 strife engulfed Port Elizabeth, was in a position to open in the city.

Opening in Port Elizabeth in early 1986, the LRC appointed outstanding staff. The first director was Fikile Bam, a long-time Robben Islander who was also an advocate and who was later to be the President of the Land Claims Court. Then there was Jeremy Pickering, later a judge in both Mthatha and Makhanda. Two further appointments, to fill out the initial staff, were Vas Soni and David Mias. It was a formidable team, and immediately they stamped their authority on the local legal world by having Khusta Jack's banning overturned.

The LRC regretfully only lasted six years in Port Elizabeth, but they were the six most difficult years of 1986 to 1992. It was a very valued, if brief, intervention.

Human Rights Trust

Initially conceived of by Andrew Savage, who saw that there was clearly need for organisations that could create interaction with the warring township communities, the Human Rights Trust (HRT) was another of the organisations that were spawned in the war of the mid-1980s. There was foreign money available, Savage reasoned, and so he put the idea to me, and in October 1986 the HRT was begun.

For the rest of the 1980s, it worked for detainees and their rights and conditions, and to provide exposure of the horrors and abuses of the time. It published a magazine, *Monitor*, which in turn earned a reputation for in-depth reporting of the complexities of South Africa's transition.

After the 1980s, the HRT worked in local government negotiations and change, and its Sithile Zondani became a legend for his work on prison conditions. After Savage's death in 1990, Thole Majodina and then George

Irvine chaired the Trust, which included Dr Gavin Blackburn, Prof. Peter Vale, Ms Nonkosi Mhlantla (later a judge on the Constitutional Court), Danny Jordaan, Dayalin Chetty, Flip Potgieter, Bishop Dwane, Errol Moorcroft, Prof. Ian Macdonald and Zandile Jakavula. Staff included Shaan Curtis, Lesley Frescura, Xoliswa Kani, Amber Cummins, Phumla Dlotu, Lynn Foster and Friday France.

Janet Cherry and the End Conscription Campaign (ECC)

All of the above organisations had relevance and value and did much important work. However, none of them got under apartheid's skin anywhere nearly as effectively as did the ECC. Of all the white organisations in the anti-apartheid business, it was the ECC and its chairperson in Port Elizabeth, Janet Cherry, that took the full heat of the apartheid fire.[342]

The ECC had the courage to tackle the state in a sensitive and vulnerable area – the reluctance of white male school-leavers to postpone for two years their dreams of making their future while they instead took on the dangerous lifestyle of being a rookie soldier, being bullied by uneducated junior officers for the purpose of fighting in a far-away war they had not commissioned, nor, in reality, could see the point of.

The ECC was promoting a campaign of disobedience which threatened the South African Defence Force's manpower requirements, while the ECC as an organisation had no significant umbrella of protection. It was both brave and dangerous, and, inevitably, many ECC personnel paid a high price in terms of imprisonment, political detention and crude, brutal harassment.

The ECC came about because of several events: in the late 1970s four young men, including Port Elizabeth's Anton Eberhardt, claiming religious reasons, refused to enter the SA military, and were each given jail terms. At the time compulsory military service was extended from one to two years, and a series of lengthy annual camps was added to the burden.

The first two clearly 'political' objectors, Billy Paddock and Pete Hathorn, refused to do service in the early 1980s – they were each sentenced to two years in prison. And Port Elizabeth's Brett Myrdal left the country, on advice from friends, to avoid being jailed for refusing the call-up.

In 1983 the Black Sash, at its annual conference, called for an end to conscription. This was not illegal, whereas attempting to persuade young men not to do their service was. The newly formed Conscientious Objectors Support Group (COSG) then had a conference, at which the concept of the End Conscription Campaign was presented and agreed. It knew to tread carefully.

After a year of branch building, the ECC was publicly launched at the

Claremont Civic Centre in October 1984. Soon there were 13 branches all over the country and Janet Cherry and Gavin Evans, the son of Bishop Bruce Evans, moved from Cape Town to Port Elizabeth, to set it up.

In Port Elizabeth they found a 'tiny handful of white activists', including Dominique Souchon (from the Catholic Church's Justice and Peace Programme) and Sandy Stewart (working in the Detainees Parents' Support Committee), who were willing to join the cause.[343] They carefully solicited further support – Molly Blackburn and Black Sash came on board, as did a variety of church leaders from the established churches. On 21 March 1985, which was the night of the Langa Massacre (unknown to anyone planning the launch), they launched Port Elizabeth's End Conscription Campaign branch at the Cathedral of St Mary in Central.

Quickly the ECC went forward with a series of highly creative and brilliantly strategised programmes.

The first was a gift from PW Botha, for in September 1984, with the townships in open revolt, the government sent the army into these townships, to support the overstretched police. Suddenly conscription no longer sent youngsters to a highly glamorised war, far away, that was to keep the godless communists from overwhelming Christian South Africa; now conscripts were in the township down the road, exchanging bullets for rocks with the children of the township, maybe even, sometimes, with the children of people one knew. South Africa's second war was manna from heaven for the ECC.

'Troops out of the Townships' was a campaign launched by the ECC on 17 September 1985 in Port Elizabeth in St Augustine's Catholic Cathedral. Church services, 'Fasting for Peace' and vigils, eventually even a debate between Ken Owen, senior editor of South African Associated Newspapers and the ECC's Janet Cherry, all attracted publicity while at the same time, it touched the raw nerves of the securocrats.

These ECC campaigns fell on eager ears. In answer to questions in parliament, the government admitted that, of the January 1984 call-up, 1 594 youngsters had not pitched up. For the same call-up in early 1985, the number had risen to 7 589.[344] Thereafter the government refused to answer such questions, a sure indication that this trend was on the up.

The second and third ECC campaigns in Port Elizabeth were done simultaneously: Working for a Just Peace, and support for a local conscientious objector, Philip Wilkinson.

Working for a Just Peace was conceptualised to demonstrate that there were better things for white youth to do than exchange bullets for stones in the townships.

The ECC spent plenty of time in negotiating with elders in Walmer

Township on a suitable project. It was agreed that the ECC, with township youth in tow, would renovate the Di Davis crèche in the township in early April 1986.

This was duly done, after a press conference and a religious service conducted by Bishop Evans. Tim Hoffman, a young botanist from the University of Port Elizabeth, found an olive tree and took it to the crèche on his scooter, for a commemorative planting.

Pictures of the project became as widespread as they were heartening: pictures of Dominique Souchon, hammer in hand, reassuring a Buffel of young *troepies* that it was in fact safe to be white in a township if your intentions were good; and of Sandy Stewart, her clothes more painted than the wall she was so amateurishly splashing, getting it done, eventually.

Philip Wilkinson had little in common with most other conscientious objectors at the time. They were often English-speaking young men, pulling in very superior marks at English-language universities and heading for professional careers. Philip's education had stopped at Standard 8, and he worked in a butchery. He had done his basic military training, but in his workplace his friends were the young black staff who took him to watch township football matches. He became unable to take a gun and patrol their townships, and he refused his call-up for the endless annual camps that young men like him were liable for.

On 24 April 1986 he agreed to speak on an ECC platform in Grahamstown. After that he went to an ECC rally in Johannesburg, where he was arrested. The ECC got into top gear and even Archbishop Tutu called for his release. He was released on bail on 6 May, pending trial on 23 May. His prosecution dragged on and on, and it was a full year before he was convicted, fined and released. In the meanwhile, he had been in state of emergency detention for a very long time.

The first state of emergency (called in July 1985) had not seen mass detentions of white activists in Port Elizabeth. In Grahamstown Roland White, Sue Lund and the spy Olivia Forsyth were detained. Forsyth notes that this was in the 'time honoured strategy to cement my leadership' of the many left movements she had infiltrated at Rhodes University.[345]

In Port Elizabeth only Janet had been detained, but earlier, at the end of June. Her detention was in terms of section 29 of the Internal Security Act, in connection with pamphlets she had typed for an MK member for use in the education boycott.[346] She was held in solitary confinement for three weeks.[347]

The first state of emergency had been a triumph not only for the UDF but also for the ECC, for their 'Troops out of the Townships' had been, with the consumer boycott, instrumental in ensuring that, at the end of November

1985, the SADF had in fact been called out of the townships.

Detention was not the only abuse the ECCers now had to face.

The early conscientious objector, Pete Hathorn, had come to Port Elizabeth to help the ECC's fledgling structures survive. He was accompanied by his partner, Barbara Orpen, who became a reporter on the *Herald*, who immediately began to make an impact with her reporting.

Pete was attacked by five white youths in front of a church and Barbara was whipped by masked attackers as she returned to their flat one evening. Sandy Stewart had her phone number advertised in a prostitutes column in the *Herald*, and her car was vandalised. Janet and Sandy had a tear gas canister fired through the rear window of their car. The number and intensity of these attacks mounted. An edition of the Aida Parker newsletter alleged the ECC was a puppet of the Soviets, and their members were druggies, homosexuals and corruptors of the youth. The Media Council found all of these claims to be false and scurrilous.[348]

Janet was, of course, the principal target of these harassments. She had a cat nailed to the wall of her house and the tyres of her car were slashed time and again (as were Barbara Orpen's). In March 1986, as she was to leave for Paris to represent the ECC at the SOS Racisme conference, she and her housemate, Dominique, were raided at their home and mandrax uncovered by the narcotics squad in an outside bathroom. Fortunately, the uniform branch of the police saw through this, and they never faced charges.[349] Her office was repeatedly burgled. On one occasion all her files, and no valuables, were removed.

As 1986 wore on, it became clear that the government was again about to crack down. Around midnight on 11 June 1986 Janet got a call from Mike Evans in Cape Town – 'run and hide'. She and Dominique immediately moved into the flat of a friend as the mass detention of 12 June happened. UDF activists by the thousand were detained and over a hundred ECC activists were also arrested and detained.

ECC activists in Port Elizabeth called an informal, secret information meeting at a Catholic church in Newton Park. Lawyers were invited to explain what was still possible, and what kinds of actions were now prohibited.

The meeting had hardly opened when a large cohort of security police arrived, and, for the first time, a number of white activists were simultaneously detained. Dominique Souchon was to spend five months in detention, as was Philip Wilkinson. Sandy Stewart, a single parent of two young boys, was held for three months. Mike Loewe, whose stinging reports in the *Weekly Mail* were a beacon of the times, was held in solitary, and 'suffered severe ill-health'. Tim Hoffman, Barry Eason and Anneline Bester, none of whom were in the 'organising circle' of the ECC, were held for three weeks, 'presumably to frighten them off', Janet believes.[350]

Even Simon Whitehouse, a young man who had recently begun lodging in the same house as Philip, was scooped up and detained. He was overwhelmed by this, and broke down and confessed that he was a planted spy and was nonplussed that he had been detained. He apologised to Philip, and, at the soonest possible moment, left the country.

In Grahamstown the same pattern was underway. Here the ringmaster was a security policeman named Lloyd Edwards, whose elder brother, Karl, was coordinating the Port Elizabeth detentions. Both were the sons of Kurt Edwards, an employee of General Motors whose infamy came from the flood of letters he poured into the *Herald*, outlining the wonders of apartheid and the endless shortcomings of its critics. Both Karl and Lloyd had allowed their father's fanaticism to dictate their futures. They joined the security police and entered English-language universities where they were paid to 'send information home'.

Karl was quickly busted, and younger brother Lloyd, then on the Rhodes campus, was immediately neutralised. Lloyd was left with the only option being to 'go public', so he joined the security police in Grahamstown as a desk officer. His spy colleague, Olivia Forsyth, said of him: 'Some of the worst agents I knew turned out to be fellow members of the security branch. One of the aforementioned was Lloyd Edwards … I think he was of more use [in the role of desk officer].'[351]

Lloyd was nevertheless allowed free rein to choose and detain. This he did with relish – Ann Burroughs, his ex-girlfriend, Melissa de Villiers, Bridget Hilton-Barber, Louise Vale, Karen Thorne and André Roux, a brilliant young lecturer at Rhodes with master's degrees in both mathematics and economics. This time Olivia was not in the net, as she has left Grahamstown many months earlier, still masked, to attempt a hare-brained scheme to infiltrate the ANC in Lusaka that could have cost her her life had the ANC been more ruthless, and certainly ended her career as a spy.

All of this was in terms of a security police campaign called Operation Crocus, an activity aimed exclusively at the white left.[352]

Operation Crocus appears to have begun in December 1984 at a party in Port Elizabeth. There Karl Edwards spotted a young (26-year-old), recently admitted attorney, Vanessa Brereton.

Vanessa was from an impeccable liberal family in Port Elizabeth. Her father was a well-respected general practitioner, and she had been schooled at the Holy Rosary Convent.

However, she had a congenital hip defect that had merited six months in hospital at the age of 11. She emerged from hospital with one leg shorter than the other, a pronounced limp and very limited self-confidence.

In fact, perfect prey for Karl Edwards.

He picked her up at the party, swept her away, and became her first lover. He had quickly garnered a spectacularly successful agent, both as a prominent and trusted member of the white left, and as an attorney with a growing practice of detainees to represent, with files and files of information. The fact that, two months after meeting, he admitted to Vanessa that he was married did not deter her a bit. He was her man, and, like Olivia, she noted that the money was not much, but both had the perk of a handler to bonk, and that was enough to give the Security Branch two remarkably useful spies, neither of whom was uncovered until years later.

On her 'first day on the job', heading for the Langa massacre site, Edwards briefed her: 'The left is radicals and liberals. The radicals are devoted to communism ... liberals are being used by commies. Molly lib, Janet commie. I should try to get in with the commie grouping but the libs are also useful in that they can help me gain access to the radical groups.'[353] Such was the simple formula of the security police.

It was Janet they most wanted, but she had had the foresight not to attend that information meeting in Newton Park and had missed the first scoop. She remained on the run for two months, first in Port Elizabeth, then to a secret ECC national meeting in Natal, then to Cape Town, where she was apprehended in August 1986. Off to Rooi Hel. An application to the Supreme Court for her release in June 1987 failed – Port Elizabeth was not Cape Town or Johannesburg. She was to spend nearly a year in Rooi Hel, being released in July 1987, with a restriction order keeping her from both the ECC and the UDF. She had meanwhile been an Amnesty International Prisoner of the Month in November 1986, and won a Reebok Human Rights Award in December 1988. Possibly Janet's greatest compliment came from an unexpected quarter, Olivia Forsyth, who said of Janet: 'A seriously committed activist for whom I had the greatest respect.'[354]

On her release, IDASA, now well established, employed her in Port Elizabeth as a researcher. Slowly normality began to seep back into her eventful and hard life, albeit normality under a state of emergency.

Under such conditions of harassment and disruption, one would think the ECC would have gone dormant. Incredibly, it did not. In 1987 the ECC ran a 'War is not Compulsory – let's choose a just peace' campaign, and in 1988 a 'Know your rights campaign'.

In 1987 23 youngsters, including Port Elizabeth's Glenn Goosen, announced that they were not willing to obey their call-up.

On 3 August 1988 this number swelled to 143 who would not go, now including both Glenn and Kobus Pienaar, a young attorney who had joined the Legal Resources Centre in Port Elizabeth. Objectors were now treated savagely: in March 1988 Ivan Toms was sentenced to 21 months' imprisonment; in July David Bruce to six years; in December Charles Bester also got six years. Nothing, however, stopped the flood of resisters.

This all was too much for the state; on 22 August 1988 the ECC was banned.

It hardly changed anything. By September 1989 the number of conscripts refusing to submit had grown to 771, and the end of the Namibian war and the extraordinary politics of the early 1990s effectively destroyed conscription. In 1993 Kobie Coetsee, then Minister of Defence, faced the reality of almost no-show on admission dates, and announced that the July 1993 intake would be the last. Conscription was dead, and one of the first acts of the ANC in government was to halt the prosecution of the last defiers, on 28 August 1994.

At that stage, the ECC 'claimed victory and disbanded'.[355]

There is something so special in winning a hopelessly unequal fight, one in which you had no chance of victory. As the youngsters flooding out of school from 1994 on should have realised, they owed those few who had fought for their right not to waste precious years in the deadly pursuit of war a huge 'thank-you'. As is so often the case in politics, however, I doubt they paused a second to express gratitude.

34

Sanctions and disinvestment

A partheid was a moral and political abomination. It was also an economic disaster.

For many economists, the seeds of apartheid could be seen growing shoots of a vine that was clearly going to strangle the entire state, as its needs grew and grew.[356]

The cost of imposing influx control, and of maintaining South Africa as a white state, which necessitated the endless duplication of 'black states, separate and equal', was mounting inexorably.

Job reservation, possibly manageable in the 1960s when mining was the bedrock of the economy, was proving more and more a handicap as manufacturing took over the role as leading economic activity in the 1970s, and the apartheid state, with its deliberately weakened black education system, could no longer deliver skilled workers in the number, and at the skills level, that were needed.

This derelict 'Bantu Education' system, which saw no black schools built in the cities and towns, was running too few schools. These schools were also inadequately staffed. To supplement these schools in the numbers required, and at the level of staffing required, was by 1980 financially impossible.

The administration costs of the apartheid state, with its duplication of administration along racial lines, and again in the homelands, and with its enormous security and military needs, were overwhelming the fiscus.

Industrial decentralisation, another of apartheid's bedrocks, was aimed at creating meaningful economies in the homelands in order to draw blacks from the urban areas to the homelands. This began with the state subsidising labour costs in these areas. This, of course, proved inadequate, and capital subsidies, then transport subsidies, then every possible type of subsidy, were added. Subsidy dependence and subsidy corruption immediately set in.

Import substitution, the subsidisation of essential industry in times of threatened isolation, added yet another cost. While it effectively engendered many industries initially, it rapidly had the effect of causing higher domestic prices for subsidised, inefficient manufacturers.

All of these structural weaknesses were built into the apartheid economy and caused many commentators to clearly announce that this was unsustainable. Change was urgently needed before the roof fell in on the South African economy.

And the indicators suggested that they were right: South African GDP, and GDP per capita, were collapsing. Between 1960 and 1969, GDP changed by 5.8% and GDP per capita by 3%. By the 1980s, this was 1.3% and -1.1% GDP per capita.[357]

And unemployment was surging: Dr Ronnie Bethlehem, a prominent economist, believed that 25% of the economically active population was unemployed in 1960. By 1985 this had risen to 37%, or 4.5 million people.[358]

The 1980s added three new challenges that together were to help speed up the demise of the apartheid economy.

Firstly, and probably most effectively, capital flight.

We have seen how capital flight began with the Chase Manhattan bank and a number of other American banks, just after the imposition of the first state of emergency on 21 July 1985, refusing to roll over overdue loans to the South African state and its banks. This was exacerbated by PW Botha's belligerent and retrogressive Rubicon speech on 15 August.

In the four years from 1985 to 1988, South Africa underwent a sustained and uninterrupted period of capital flight, with, in total, about R25 billion leaving the country. This was accompanied by a collapse in the value of the South African rand vis-à-vis the US dollar, which in turn caused exports to surge, and over these years the balance of payments showed a total surplus of R22.2 billion. But this surplus was not enough to counteract the capital exodus, and gold and foreign reserves held by the South African Reserve Bank dropped by R1.7 billion to R6.5 billion, a worryingly low level.[359]

This in turn led to lower Gross Domestic Fixed Investment, dropping from 7.7% between 1960 and 1969 to -4% in the 1980s.

And so a very unvirtuous circle was formed: capital flight led to lower levels of fixed investment, which led to a lowered economic performance (lower

GDP per capita), which in turn led to higher unemployment and poverty.

Dr Fred du Plessis, the Chairman of Sanlam, said in 1987 that 'South Africans were poorer now than in 1974', and Aubrey Dickman, the chief economist of the Anglo American Corporation, noted that other developing countries were showing better real increases in per capita income than South Africa – Brazil, Greece, Portugal, Chile, Spain, Hong Kong, Singapore, Korea, Mexico and Malaysia.[360]

After capital flight came sanctions and disinvestment. This was the most worrying problem for apartheid.

In truth, South Africa had had long experience with sanctions and disinvestment by 1986. Arms boycotts had been the most publicised, but other financial and sanction weapons were by now being developed and tried. And, as we have seen, the biggest American company in South Africa, the Ford Motor Company, had closed its Port Elizabeth assembly lines in 1985. They had effectively disinvested.

1986 was to be a historic year for United States sanctions against apartheid.

In 1985 a Democratic Party-sponsored Anti-Apartheid Act failed in the Senate – President Reagan was entirely unsupportive, and the Republican senators, obedient to his wishes, filibustered it away.

In 1986 the Democrats had more luck and more support from the other side of Congress. After haggling, a number of Republicans agreed to support a weaker package of sanctions, and the Democrats jumped at this offer. Unexpectedly, this weaker package was passed in the House of Representatives, and in August 1986 also in the Senate by a massive 84 to 14 vote.

As expected, Reagan vetoed the bill on 26 September and frantically worked with Senate Republicans on a weaker-still set of sanctions to prevent the Senate overriding his veto. He even, amazingly, enlisted the South African Foreign Minister, Pik Botha, to contact wavering Republicans.

If there was a hero in this process, it was the Republican Senator Richard Luger, then chair of the Foreign Relations Committee. His support was steadfast. 'We are against tyranny, and tyranny is in South Africa,' he declared on the Senate floor. Reagan's veto was overridden by Congress (313 votes to 83) and the Senate (78 to 21) on 2 October.

The Comprehensive Anti-Apartheid Act was now law.

The Act had 68 sections, which we will not detail here. Most important was the impact of the process. For the first time, President Reagan endured the humiliation of both the House and the Senate overriding his veto. This sent a clear message to the apartheid government. Trouble and more trouble lay ahead.

And a first example immediately followed the passing of the act. Again, in Port Elizabeth.

The Comprehensive Anti-Apartheid Act forbade, amongst much else, American companies operating in South Africa from making new investments in their South African subsidiaries after November 1986. The General Motors plant in Port Elizabeth was somewhat run-down and plainly needed investment. It was also debt-burdened and unprofitable. GM America was looking for an out, and the Act provided a time frame (November 1986) that caused them to act.

GM's chairman, Roger Smith, announced that GM was to 'review their presence' in South Africa. The National Automobile and Allied Workers Union (NAAWU) demanded clarity. GM said Smith had been 'misquoted'. A week later GM announced that their South African subsidiary was to be sold. A confrontation with the union was immediate, caused by a belligerent letter from a GM director that was leaked to the press.

A strike followed, which GM crushed with the help of the security forces. 570 strikers were fired.

GM announced during the strike that the company was to be sold to executives within the company. GM would liquidate the company's debt before the deadline set by the Comprehensive Anti-Apartheid Act. The new company was to be renamed Delta Motors, and further reductions to the staff complement were effected. The GM decision that the company would no longer sell vehicles to the government was overturned. American GM, and Japan's Isuzu, continued to provide technical cooperation.[361]

The largest remaining American company in South Africa had disinvested.

'World opinion counts,' said Sir Timothy Bevan, the chairman of Barclays Bank in the United Kingdom. 'It affects business, and world opinion has changed quite a lot this year.'[362]

On 25 November 1986 his company sold its South African subsidiary to the Anglo American Corporation, thereby disinvesting from South Africa. Bevan's bank was the largest British company operating in South Africa at the time.

In 1988 the United Nations identified 520 multinational companies which had sold all their equity in their South African or Namibian subsidiaries. A further 80 were in some such process. Of these companies, their origins were Australia (17), Canada (21), Germany (10), United Kingdom (92), and the United States (350). Companies from nine other countries had also left.[363]

A trickle became a stream, and thereafter a flood.

There is much argument as to the efficacy or otherwise of sanctions and disinvestment in bringing apartheid to its grisly end. Philip Levy of Yale, with the benefit of 10 years of hindsight,[364] believes that the marginal cost to South Africa of the mid-1980s trade sanctions was US$354 million annually, or 0.5% of South Africa's GNP. This is a not inconsiderable sum. Undoubtedly sanctions and disinvestment played both a financial and a psychological role in ending apartheid.

35

The last kick of apartheid's dying donkey

A s we have noted, late in 1985 the South African government had
been overtaken by a new conception: that of a para-military state,
with political decision-making having been replaced by political
institutions that were co-opted into a new, securocrat-led set of arrangements
called the National Security Management System.

Behind all this was the writing of a colonel in the United States army,
whose experiences in Vietnam had led him to write *The Art of Counter-
Revolutionary War* – Colonel John McCuen.[365]

That this was by now the guiding philosophy of the apartheid government was set out by Ulrich Schelhase, the ex-Town Clerk of Crossroads,
in his submission to the Truth and Reconciliation Commission, for it was
in Crossroads that the first traceable 'oliekol' project was undertaken.
Undoubtedly the Langa removal was the next one.

Emboldened by these two 'successes', the government moved on to an
enormously ambitious 'oliekol' – New Brighton township in Port Elizabeth.

New Brighton was no small challenge: at the time it had an estimated
population of 87 482,[366] occupying 8 575 households, spread over seven
suburbs – Boastville, Elundini, Fordville, KwaFord, McNamee, White
Location and the Red Location. Plainly, a target this big needed significant
resources to 'subdue'.

As a first measure, as the second state of emergency was declared, New

Brighton was entirely surrounded by razor wire. Only three entrances were maintained, all manned 24 hours a day. All vehicles entering or exiting New Brighton were searched.

Security forces began distributing a new and unique identity document, without which entrance to and from New Brighton was to be denied. These cards bore the crest and the name of the Ibhayi Town Council, and had space for an 'official stamp of the South African Police', who said that the cards were part and parcel of the security operations in the area.

Then came two high-level official visits: firstly on 22 August 1986, with the state of emergency just over a month old, the Minister of Defence, General Magnus Malan, accompanied by the head of the Police Counter-Insurgency and Security Units, Major-General Bert Wandrag, and a host of local defence force officers arrived to meet with the Ibhayi Town Council and its mayor, Mr Jimmy Nako. Secondly on 2 October, the State President, PW Botha, accompanied by General Malan and Ministers Heunis and Du Plessis also arrived. They also inspected the razor wire barricade, and spent time with the Ibhayi Town Council and its new Town Clerk, Mr EI Pullen, who had recently replaced Mr Scholtz.

Both visits were held close to apartheid's chest: after the first, Mr Pullen mentioned that matters under discussion were 'matters of common concern'. After the Botha visit, no statement was released, as this visit was not intended 'as a publicity stunt'.[367]

The secret of Oliekol New Brighton was later let out by Mr Pullen in a moment of unguarded honesty.

On 17 November, with a removal of the residents of the Red Location to Motherwell imminent, Andrew Savage and Rory Riordan met with Mr Pullen at his office on the perimeter of New Brighton.[368] His candour was astonishing.

The intention of the security forces in the Port Elizabeth townships was to adopt an 'oliekol' approach, he said, 'You drop a drop of oil here, and you spread it out.'

Initially, 'they' (presumably the Ibhayi Council and the security forces) would tackle New Brighton by applying the security fence and roadblocks. They would 'stabilise and neutralise' New Brighton until it became a 'sterilised area'. Then 'they' would move on to the next area.

The Red Location, for Mr Pullen, had two qualities: firstly 'it is a dangerous, unhygienic place', and secondly, 'it is difficult to control' so it had to be done first. 'They' couldn't do the whole township of New Brighton at once, so the Red Location was, in true McCuen fashion, to be done as a first phase. The whole township was too big, so it had to be 'stabilised' in phases.

After the Red Location and New Brighton were 'stabilised and neutralised', the forces would then move on to Soweto-by-the-Sea, which was the next area scheduled for the bladed wire and 'stabilisation and neutralisation'. Just the previous week, Mr Pullen noted, the security forces had detained '150 genuine, acknowledged, diagnosed extremists' there.

The role of the army was to 'eliminate the bad elements'. The decision to deploy the army came from 'government level', Mr Pullen said.

So there we have it – textbook McCuen counter-revolutionary war.

First you crush the revolution, however messy this proves to be, and you use 'a swiftly trained militia, whose methods are not the professionalism of the armed forces'.

Then you rebuild the institutions of government and society, however besieged and overwhelmed they might have been in the revolution.

Then you provide services, quick, quick. As the Roman poet Juvenal wrote two thousand years earlier, 'Two things only the people anxiously desire – bread and circuses.' The politics of distraction. Distract them from the quest for political rights with the swift provision of schools, and services.

All of this was to be accompanied by a massive propaganda campaign, emphasising the delivery of services and the advantages of the new dispensation.

And, finally, areas of determined opposition must be destabilised, as were Crossroads and Langa.

So it was envisaged for Oliekol New Brighton.

But how did it work out?

Stage one: The revolution must be crushed

The first stage of the state's action was, of course, mass detention.

In the first year of this second state of emergency, 26 000 people were detained. A further 6 000 were later added, making approximately 32 000 detainees in all. Many detentions now were short term. A year into the state of emergency, Webster and Friedman estimated that only about 3 000 people were still in detention. This number diminished slowly over the remaining years of the state of emergency, until, after three years, only about 2 000 were still in jail. Most of the senior UDF leadership were in this 'cell veteran' group.

The Eastern Cape bore the initial brunt of these detentions, and in 1986, again in Webster and Friedman's calculations, a third of all detentions were in the Eastern Cape. In the townships of Port Elizabeth and Uitenhage, about 1% of the entire African population, man, woman and child, experienced state of emergency detention in the second state of emergency, as opposed to 0.0001% of the white community.[369]

Another remarkable feature of this emergency was the change in age of the detainees: in the first state of emergency, possibly 25% of detainees were under 18 years of age – in the second state of emergency, nearly four times the number of under-18s were detained, and, if the cohort of under 25 is added, about three of every four detainees now fitted into this enlarged group of youth. These youngsters were detained, abused and soon released.

Conditions in the cells were horrifying. The jails were now so overcrowded that detainees universally slept on the floor, and shoulder to shoulder. There was no turning over in one's sleep.

Detention was the dominant form of crushing the revolution, but it was not the only one. Killing, torture and severe ill-treatment were also prevalent.

Torture now evolved into a different process. Probably stung by the Wendy Orr interdict and the massive wave of critical publicity that accompanied it, the security police sought out, and found, a new method of torture, one that left less physical evidence (bruises, cuts, broken bones) for an inspector to uncover. Suffocation torture became the norm.

The Human Rights Trust took a series of 37 statements of this type of torture and compiled it into a document.[370] 10 of those who made statements were under 20 years of age, and another 19 were under 25, making youth 78% of this group.

The following is just some of this gruesome evidence that these statements document. Ernest Nzwanana recalls:

The next week Jambo and one other black security policeman picked me up at Bethelsdorp Police Station where I was being held in detention. They took me out to a white bakkie with canopy outside, put me in the back, tied my hands behind me with a 3-inch bandage, sat me on the floor of the bakkie, and pulled a bag over my head. The bag was made of a tent-like substance, and was white. Then they said: 'Today you are going to tell us.' They then got in the front of the bakkie and we drove off.

We then drove a long distance and, obviously, I couldn't see where we were. When we stopped, I was taken out, inside a building, and made to sit on a cushion. There were lots of men in this building – I recognised Nieuwoudt's voice, and he questioned me in Xhosa and Afrikaans.

They then opened the bag at the neck, and, with a hand, splashed water over my face. They then smeared soap over my face, and pulled the bag tight behind my head. They would then pull a rubber tube over the bag, and pull it tight on my face.

For four hours I was suffocated, revived and questioned. The bag was tightened up four times. I couldn't breathe. Once I passed out, and fell over. Somebody kicked me in the mouth. Three of my top right teeth were broken in this kick. Soap was re-applied to my face four times. I urinated in my pants, and fainted once.

I gave them no answers ... after four hours I was taken back to the bakkie, and driven back to Bethelsdorp ... There Jambo said to me 'If you lodge a case against us for assault, we'll charge you under the state of emergency and you'll spend years in jail.'

My mouth was bleeding from the broken teeth, and I was taken to Warrant Officer Visagie, a Coloured SAP from Bethelsdorp. Here I was handed over. He asked me: 'Klagtes?' and, because of the threat I had received, I said: 'No, but I want to see a doctor.' He asked, 'Why?' and I said 'No, leave me alone, I want to sleep.' I went back to my cell to sleep. I was finished.

While the focus of this barbarity was the young Amabutho, senior men were not spared.

William Velile John says:

The next day Michael Xego, the PEYCO executive member, was brought through to join us [in a cell at Kinkelbos Police Station]. A week later Michael was taken out of our cell by one of the SAP from Kinkelbos. He was taken away for the day, and was returned that night at 4 o'clock or 5 o'clock.

We were horrified by his condition on his return. He was red all over his face – his face, which was also swollen up, was covered in red marks. He couldn't even hold a pair of sentences together in conversation. He just wanted to sleep. The only thing he said was 'This is just a fact of life – I'll tell you about it later. Let me sleep now.' We tried to get him to eat, as he looked weak, weak. He couldn't, just saying 'Gentlemen, it's hard.'

What were the security police trying to uncover?

Of the questions asked, three were repeated and repeated. 'Where are the guns? (and the Scorpions – homemade guns)', 'Who is on the Street and Area Committees?', and 'Who are the Amabutho?' Basic information gathering.

But there were other, more specific, assaults.

Archibald Phumzile Siwisa recalls:

On Sunday 7 December 1986 I was asleep at my house when, at about 4h00 there were loud knocks. I opened the door to find about eight or so security police, six white and two black. They pushed in and demanded 'Where is your mother?' (My mother, Mrs Fazzie, was in hiding from the security police at the time.) They continued: 'This is the last time we will ask you – you will then have to tell us, like it or not. Where is she?'

I replied that I didn't know. They then said: 'Your mother phoned you recently – on Friday – asking you to bring wood and other articles to make African beer. What did you send to your mother and where?'

I don't know.

'OK Archie, now you will tell us the truth.'

They then pushed me into a room at the back of the house. They threw me onto the bed, with my back on the bed. They pushed my hands and feet down and held them down. A black security policeman then brought out a piece of tyre-tube rubber, which was quite large. He then shoved it down, onto and over my face, and pulled it down hard onto me, with his hands down to my ears on the side of my head. I tried to scream but in vain. It stopped my breathing, and I became desperate for breath. After what seemed like ten minutes, he would lift it off, and give me a few seconds' rest while he demanded where my mother was. When I screamed, he said: 'OK Archie, now I'll punish you for trying to call people' and applied the tube again.

This seemed to go on for an hour. I recognise the black security policeman who tortured me like this, as they had been to my house before to look for my parents. But I don't know his name.

After what seemed like an hour, I coughed up some blood, and then realised that they would not think twice about killing me. I decided to tell them where my mother was hiding. I couldn't tolerate it – I believed they would never give me a chance to breathe again.

They put me in an E20 minibus, and I led them to Qhoki Street, in Veeplaas, where my uncle lives who was accommodating my mother. I saw them pull my mother out of this shack, and put her in a van that had accompanied us. I couldn't hear what anyone said. She was then driven off, and, to this day, is in the Paterson Road Jail (Rooi Hel).

That this torture was widespread is indisputable. Laurence Ntlangu: 'I would claim with certain knowledge that all of my cellmates were tortured like this.' Zandisile Faltein: 'In Kinkelbos there were 32 detainees in my cell, and most claimed to have been tortured. The pattern was almost always that they would be transferred to a police station and tortured while being in the police cells, rather than in the prisons.'

And almost always at night. Mncedisi Kondile: 'But it was nearly dawn now – it was the time of going. Security police never want to be seen.' And the aftermath of torture was universally: 'If you complain or lay a charge, we'll come back for you, and you'll get more, and we'll keep you in detention for years.'[371]

McCuen's second guideline for crushing the revolution was the establishment of a new militia, 'not governed by the professionalism of the permanent armed forces'.

Here come the kitskonstabels!

From the beginning, the institution of municipal police was structured to involve a contradiction. This was that the municipal police were designed to use 'more robust' methods than the disciplined armed forces, but they were never given, nor did they receive, indemnity from prosecution.

As we have seen, the security police could withdraw a detainee from cells at a police station (and police stations were the responsibility of the uniform branch) then take this detainee out, torture him (or, occasionally, her), and return the detainee to the uniform branch with broken teeth, bruises, completely destroyed by torture. The uniform policeman would then ask: 'Do you have complaints?', which was universally answered 'no' (as Archbishop Tutu said, 'It is a very brave or mad mouse that reports one cat to another cat'), and there the matter would end, despite clear, prima facie evidence of assault. The security police were immune to investigation, and none were ever charged or convicted of murder or even assault.

The municipal police were not this fortunate, and, if complaints were lodged with the SA Police, they were investigated. Municipal police were charged, tried, and, on occasion, jailed.

Under such circumstances, this 'police force' was destined for disaster.

By June, the Ibhayi City Council had 228 municipal police on their books. Replying to a question in parliament, Minister Chris Heunis admitted that none of them had a Standard 10 qualification, the minimum education level for admission to the municipal police force. In fact, he admitted, 10% had lower qualifications than Std 4. Louis Koch, whose Administration Board had some responsibility for these police, had previously said that they were all matriculants.[372]

Then the Minister of Law and Order admitted, also in parliament, that the South African Police were investigating 49 complaints against Ibhayi municipal police. One complaint against every fourth policeman – surely something of a world record.

Undeterred by such trivial issues, when the State President visited the Ibhayi Council on 2 October 1986, the new Town Clerk, Mr Pullen, presented him with an information booklet on Ibhayi, in which it was stated that 'The municipal police have become a force to be reckoned with. Statistics show that the municipal police is establishing itself well in the townships.'[373]

In that month five Ibhayi municipal police – two white sergeants and three black constables – arrested an African woman and her boyfriend on suspicion of having petrol-bombed another municipal policeman's house. The female suspect was assaulted, smothered with a plastic bag, kicked, stripped naked and spread-eagled on the floor. One white sergeant thrust his truncheon into her vagina. Her nipples were pulled.

Her boyfriend was then brought into the interrogation chamber and was beaten, kicked and made to strip. They were then forced to have intercourse while the policemen forced them on with burning cigarettes.

Eight months later these policemen were in front of Magistrate Gert Steyn, the President of Port Elizabeth's Regional Court. He described these scenes as 'barbarism of the dark ages' while applying long prison sentences to the policemen. In the course of this trial, the white senior sergeant admitted that the Ibhayi municipal police kept no crime registers, no observation books, no cell registers, nor did they have any proper facilities for interrogation.

Another magistrate, when faced with others of the accused, severely criticised the system of municipal police, and suggested it should be investigated. He wanted to know, 'Where are the senior men?'

When Andrew Savage and I met Mr Pullen on 17 November 1986, he said that there were now 600 municipal police compared with a total Ibhayi Council staff complement of 1 500 – i.e. the municipal police was 40% of the entire institution. Pullen expected the number of municipal police to rise to 1 200 early in the new year. Plainly, Colonel McCuen's advice had been swiftly heeded.

As the numbers of municipal police grew, so did the number appearing before courts.

Justice has always been a slow process in South Africa, and it was only in the first half of 1988 that the courts began to fill with municipal police.[374]

On 8 January 1988 five municipal police were charged with the murder of Mr Thembile Sixoto of KwaZakhele, whom it is alleged they beat to death.

Also on that date, a magistrate found that Mr Lungile Gxerwa had been unlawfully arrested, detained and assaulted by municipal policemen acting within the scope of their employment, when, in October 1986, they had placed a rubber tyre over his head and suffocated him while in custody.

Thirdly, on 28 January, six men charged with culpable homicide for the death of a municipal policeman, were found guilty of assault instead, as Magistrate Szewczyk found that they were fighting off municipal policemen who were assaulting them. Five municipal policemen had demanded liquor at the house of one of the accused. When this was refused, the municipal police, who were apparently drunk, began assaulting children and people at the house. While these assaults were underway, others of the accused arrived and fighting ensued. One of the municipal policemen had suffered head wounds, from which he later died. The magistrate concluded that it was clear that the accused had not conspired to kill the policeman.

Fourthly, on 23 March the son of a councillor, who was a municipal policeman, was sentenced to an effective four years' imprisonment for looting and killing a colleague in a shebeen brawl. Passing sentence, Magistrate Naude agreed with defence counsel Gideon Huisamen that the accused had been given the right to possess a firearm when he was not mature enough to do so. The magistrate understood that municipal policemen were not well disciplined and were recruited during a situation of civil unrest. The training they received was for a short period and of an inferior nature, he added. Magistrate Naude said that he did not think that members of the community should suffer the consequences of poor training and the issuing of guns to people who were not well disciplined. He pointed out that the courts were aware of the fact that crimes committed by municipal policemen indicated their lack of training of a high standard.

Fifthly, on 25 March, five municipal police were charged with three counts of assault each. It was alleged that they had picked up three suspects on a charge of arson in October 1986, and that they stripped the female suspect naked and applied shocks to her back, buttocks and legs. Her nipples were pulled, and a white warrant officer had instructed that her breasts be cut.

Sixthly, on 6 May, in a trial in which three people were charged with dealing with dagga, defence lawyer Gideon Huisamen said that while, in this case, a municipal policeman had used his 'colour and position' to persuade the men to become involved in dealing with dagga, he was not an accused because, when things became hot, 'he ran to the police', and was still employed as a municipal policeman.

Seventhly, on 30 June three municipal police appeared on charges of rape, theft of money and cigarettes. This case was postponed.

Eighthly, seven municipal police appeared on charges of theft and attempted extortion on 26 July. The theft concerned a woman who ran a shop from her home, and the extortion was from a man they threatened to arrest for the possession of dagga if he did not pay up. Again, case postponed.

And ninthly, on 29 July 1988, two municipal police appeared on charges of damaging the property of a KwaZakhele businessman, and of pointing a gun at him. Case postponed.

This thinly veneered thuggery probably marks an all-time low in South African policing. The 'instant' policemen, encouraged to ignore the law in dealing with a community in revolt, were nevertheless prosecuted wholesale when they did just that.

Very quickly the system of municipal police began to unravel, and the 'force' repositioned itself as a group of bodyguards for councillors and staff, and as security officials for municipal buildings.

Did all of this, the numerous detentions, widespread torture and brutal clubbing by municipal police, cause the revolution to end?

Data from the Truth and Reconciliation Commission, of the Eastern Cape alone, shows a great reduction in human rights violations from 1986 onward. This information was used by PW Botha to justify the state of emergency. Was that a correct interpretation of the facts?

The Truth and Reconciliation Commission received about 8 000 statements of torture in the period 1975 until 1994 – of these about 6 300 were perpetrated by the South African Police, and over 1 000 of the balance were allegations against the South African Defence Force or the security establishments of the 'homelands'. The same applied to killings and 'severe ill treatment'. Until the Inkatha violence in Natal broke out, in 1986 but particularly from 1990, the dominant killer, torturer and abuser was the South African Police, and they were hardly restrained by the state of emergency. So it was easy for the apartheid state to reduce the level of human right violations – it merely had to rein in its security forces.

With township revolt subsiding, and it did subside from 1987 onward, what then happened to the revolution? Had it been crushed as McCuen proposed?

What happened is not that the revolution imploded, but that, for the second time, it transmogrified.

The revolution began with the formal structures of the UDF (civic organisations and street and area committees) in control. As they were immobilised by killings and detentions, the youth of the townships took control. The pattern of detentions followed this development, as youth were detained wholesale.

What then happened is that the workplace now took a central role. Days lost to strikes and work stoppages rose from 59 861 days in 1976 to 910 000 days in 1988.[375]

The workforce, protected by both trade unions and employers in a way that no civic organisation ever could be protected, now ensured that the intensity of struggle of 1985 and 1986 was not to be lost. There was to be no 'return to normal' until a non-racial dispensation was to emerge.

Mark Bennett sees 'the State of Emergency and the Labour Movement' as having been a trigger factor in a wave of strikes that swept the retail and mining industries in 1986, with workers protesting against the detention of labour leaders.[376]

McCuen's first requirement, the crushing of the revolution, had not happened, despite unprecedented numbers in detention, endless torture and brutal militia.

Stage two: Rebuilding damaged institutions

Incredibly, the government then attempted to blow life back into the Ibhayi City Council's balloon.

Mr Pullen told Andrew Savage and me that, on their recent visits, the State President and Minister of Defence, who only met with the Ibhayi Council and staff, had made it clear that 'it was policy to restore law and order, and that the establishment of black local government through community councils was here to stay, and that alternative structures would not be tolerated.'[377]

This decision proved easier to make than to see through. The Ibhayi City Council was broke, under siege from the community it was meant to represent, bereft of legitimacy and incapable of any significant interventions in the sea of poverty all around it.

Again Mr Pullen gave hints as to the problems. He told Savage and myself that the Council had a number of councillors who had lost everything – their houses had been burnt down, and had now been re-erected 'from state funds in stabilised areas'.[378] All councillors had their 'gat' (gun), and municipal police protected the councillors. They were not allowed out of the municipal building during the day, and their children were sent to school in the Transkei.

What had happened was revealed in parliament the next year: the PFP's John Malcomess presented documents to parliament that showed that Council had misappropriated 24% of the government grant meant to create work for the unemployed at R4 a day, and this money had been used to build 11 houses in KwaMagxaki for councillors, who were renting them for R4.54 per month each. This, despite a previous answer in parliament, by Minister Heunis, that Ibhayi councillors received no 'housing or transport benefits'. Malcomess had further documents that revealed 'a considerable degree of malpractice in the Ibhayi Council'.[379]

In this morass of legal delinquency was another problem which took until January 1988 to be admitted: there were now only two legally appointed councillors in Ibhayi, as the law required a councillor to be resident in the local authority in which they served. The new houses, in the 'stabilised area' of KwaMagxaki, were outside of Ibhayi, and thus the 11 'councillors' resident there were no longer legally councillors. They had been re-hired en bloc, as 'advisers', at the wage of a councillor, and attended council meetings, voted and conducted themselves as before. Included in this package of 'advisers' was once again, Thamsanqa Linda.

It was, of course, in the business of financial management that the real catastrophe lurked.

Here solid information was difficult to obtain, but financial statements as of June 1989 were obtained.[380]

The Ibhayi Council, for the financial year ending 30 June 1989, had an income of R25.6 million (mostly government grants) and an expenditure of R40.3 million, thereby showing a deficit of R14.9 million. This afforded the Ibhayi Council municipal expenditure of R120 per head of the community it served for the year.

In adjacent Port Elizabeth (including the areas of the Coloured and Indian management committees) municipal income was R342.8 million and expenditure was R338.8 million – leaving a surplus of income over expenditure of R4 million, and an annual municipal spend of R1 014 per head, 845% more than Ibhayi, with its bulging deficit. KwaNobuhle/Uitenhage was hardly any different.

The townships of Port Elizabeth were home to about 470 000 people at this time. The Ibhayi Council was providing this community with three libraries containing fewer than 3 000 books in total; no functioning public swimming pools, tennis courts, squash courts, badminton halls, cricket pitches, golf courses, bowling greens or parks. Playground equipment was all of two swings, two slides, two wendy houses and one see-saw. And 12 rugby and soccer fields, three of which were in workable condition. Electricity reached about 10% of houses and bucket toilets were everywhere.[381]

The Ibhayi Council might be light on delivered services, but it was heavy on promises.

In May 1988 the Council announced that it had approved a five-year capital programme of R675 million, including R406 million for the development of a new township, the land for which was not yet purchased ('negotiations are at an advanced stage'). In the current year R58 million was to be spent on KwaZakhele, R7 million for Walmer Township, R25 million to upgrade the KwaZakhele single men's quarters to include flats for the municipal police, and, generously, R4.5 million was budgeted to be spent in adjacent areas not under the control of the Ibhayi Council.

When this budget was published, the source of Council's money, the Cape Provincial Administration, could not but reply. The MEC for Local Government replied tactfully: 'The fact that a project appears on such a capital programme of a black local authority does not imply that it will automatically be approved by government and subsequently funded.' He then announced that no additional funding should be expected for the present year, and next year's budget would be approved in due course. R13.7 million, including all of R200 000 to upgrade Walmer Township, had been approved, 'but there were no funds available to be allocated', he said. With regard to the huge new township proposed in the Ibhayi budget, the MEC replied 'there are no negotiations underway for a land deal'.

There was more, much more. We will just consider one more episode of this Goon Show.

In March 1988 Linda, now back in the fold and straining for action, announced that Council was in a position to put out jobs on government's special job creation programme. Applicants should go to Council's workshop yard in Struandale. Five thousand people responded immediately.

Linda took the names and said they were all on a waiting list. 'Negotiations between the CPA and Council are advanced' for funds for this project.

Five months later – nothing.

Councillor Mpondo described Linda's actions as 'an election campaign'. He had gone to Cape Town with Mayor Nako, Mpondo said, because 'they have been given a mandate by the council to approach the Administration about nine houses belonging to councillors in KwaMagxaki because they were amongst members of the council who felt the houses should be allocated to councillors free of charge'. Their visit, Mpondo said, had nothing to do with job creation funds as Linda had claimed.[382]

At the time, *Monitor* magazine noted: 'The Ibhayi City Council was being left to limp along with government proving "loans" to cover council's salaries, but nothing for township infrastructural development. The conclusions that council was being maintained as an expensive political charade and as a wing of the security forces were inescapable, and future events were to bear these conclusions out.'[383]

Stage three: The propaganda campaign

In October 1986 an anonymous fortnightly fact sheet appeared, and officials distributed it to 8 000 homes in besieged Ibhayi. Clearly pro-Ibhayi Council, *Umyalezo* (The Message) was 'for the people of Ibhayi from an unnamed benefactor'.

Initially the Bureau of Information denied responsibility for the publication. Their spokesperson, Brigadier Leon Mellet, said, 'We do not produce any newspapers under cover.' The paper claimed only to be printed by NKB, 21 De Villiers Street, Port Elizabeth. NKB initially claimed no knowledge of the publication, and expressed concern that someone was using their name.

This feeble cover-up was quickly exposed: Ibhayi's Mayor and Town Clerk, much quoted in the newssheet, were adamant it was a Bureau of Information publication. The local representative of the Bureau then came clean, and what should have been an innocuous enough public relations exercise suddenly became a naïve, disorganised, government propaganda exercise. Again, Council was positioned as being with government and at an increasing distance from Council's citizens. No second edition was attempted.[384]

Stage four: Destabilisation

By now Oliekol New Brighton was looking decidedly threadbare – the security establishment realised that something to restore control was sorely needed.

The idea that arrived was the removal of the people of the Red Location to Motherwell, about 10 km away, on the outer fringe of Port Elizabeth. There, it was doubtless believed, like the citizens of Langa now floundering on the outskirts of KwaNobuhle, this community, historically the most political in Port Elizabeth's townships, would be thrown on the back foot, and spend months rebuilding their homes. All of their disposable income would be spent on additional transport costs. They would be out of the political equation for the foreseeable future and the security forces could move on to stabilise the rest of New Brighton.

In September 1986 a green South African Defence Force van drove around the Red Location, 'it had a voice box… first a white man speaking Xhosa – "you people come here and listen of Red Location… This place is dirty… you are going to Motherwell… So here in Motherwell there is a place with a toilet and a tap and we are going to give you a free transport to remove you … you are going to stay nice there and pay a rent of R21.88" … then it was a Bantu-speaking person… he said he "was from the Ibhayi City Council… they are going to start from block 46 and 47 and 45. They are going to take 20 people to go first to see the place at Motherwell."'[385]

To move the people of the Red Location would, under any circumstances, be a daunting task. Roger Matlock of the Urban Foundation provided some data at the time: the Red Location had 920 official shacks and houses, and 450 'illegals', making 1 370 families of six or seven people in each, between 8 000 and 10 000 people.[386] But their leaders, with the exception of Ernest Malgas, who was still successfully in hiding, were all in detention. A spontaneous leadership to meet this crisis was appointed, led by the redoubtable Mrs Maneli.

There was no time. Already Mr Pullen had put out a press statement that 'lodgers and illegal shackdwellers' were to be moved on 25 November (this was in the *Herald* on 7 November, leaving just over two weeks to marshal a defence). The community did not for a minute believe that only selected persons were to be moved – they had no doubt that the whole community was 'in for it', and they made it clear that there was no appetite to move to Motherwell – this would be resisted, by the community as one, with whatever help they could muster in this difficult time.

With their leadership either in detention or in hiding, they needed all the help they could get. And this help came mostly from white-run organisations.

The community first approached the Black Sash, who called in Andrew Savage, who in turn called in myself. The first meeting of these parties was on 12 November. Two days later, the Ibhayi Council delivered the first removal notices. These were issued in terms of Act 52 of 1951, the Illegal Squatting Act. These notices were taken to Jeremy Pickering, an advocate at the Legal Resources Centre. Pickering saw no easy escape – the notices were, he said, impossible to overturn legally. If the Ibhayi Council decides to act on these notices, Pickering said, 'the people are powerless to resist'.[387]

On 17 November, Savage and I met with Mr Pullen, in the meeting already extensively reported on in this chapter.

With regard to the pending removal, Pullen noted clearly that it was his council's intention to settle the 'illegal lodgers' in temporary accommodation in Motherwell. Many residents, he said, wanted to be rehoused voluntarily in Motherwell. The security forces would provide transport, security and accommodation.

Should there be resistance to the move, the residents would be 'semi-forced' – i.e. personal persuasion would be undertaken. If this, in turn, proved ineffective, 'then I have no comment if they still say "no"'.[388]

Meanwhile it had become clear that the process to upgrade the Red Location when the 'illegals' had been moved was at a very preliminary level. The engineer responsible for the infrastructure, Mr Hector Mackay of Van Wyk and Louw, told Matlock that there was, at that stage, only a preliminary layout plan. This still had to be approved by the Ibhayi Council. Full service plans were to follow. Then an application for funding, if this was forthcoming, then tenders had to be called, contractors appointed and construction begun. He could see nothing happening within nine months. On 20 November, Mr

Mundell of the Ibhayi Council admitted that the move would be delayed because the first sample of 'prefab shacks' for the community to inspect would, at the earliest, be finished on Monday 24 November.

On 19 November between 300 and 400 parents met at the Ascension Church on Avenue C of the Red Location. Attending on invitation were Rev. Brian Bird of IDAMASA, the Ministers Fraternal, Cathy Binnell of Black Sash and myself. Speaker after speaker, with varying levels of emotion, wailed against the proposed move. Two days later Jimmy Matyu of the *Evening Post* wrote that he had approached a group of 400 people at a church. 'The residents unanimously expressed opposition to their forced removal,' he wrote.

A petition signed by 8 000 people from the Red Location was sent to the State President. The petition said, 'We wish to say that we are united in our desire to see nobody from the Red Location moved to Motherwell against his will. All of us sign this petition stating our wish to remain in the Red Location and that our entire community be allowed to stay intact in the Red Location.'[389]

After this it was decided to do a survey of the community, to get detail on a number of issues. Prof. Bill Birkenbach, a professor of Industrial Psychology at the University, Roger Matlock and I did the questionnaire, I pilot-sampled it on 23 November, and three brave youngsters from Walmer Township did the fieldwork on Tuesday 25 November. Despite police harassment, this they successfully concluded. This was the day of the scheduled removal but it did not happen. By this stage a barrage of press publicity was underway, all of it critical of the proposed removal.

The next day, 26 November, Savage, Matlock and I agreed to commission a town plan for the Red Location, to attempt to demonstrate that the entire community could effectively be rehoused in the existing Red Location. The only planner who would touch this project was Gavin McLachlan, a senior lecturer at the University. He had an adequate plan concluded by 1 December.[390]

Things were moving fast. On 27 November the Ibhayi Council called a press conference, at which it was announced that a removal would go ahead. The press was invited to watch this event.

Mr Edward Nyati of the Red Location had a 'brick house' in Motherwell, and he wished to move to it. This was plainly voluntary.

A witness to what followed recorded the following:

To move this tiny shack, there are six or so huge trucks in a row, a Casspir, three or four police vans and about 40 policemen with shotguns etc. The situation is just so sinister. Everywhere terrified people are scurrying to bring down their shacks before their few precious possessions are destroyed.

Mr Mundell makes an appearance, and gets harangued by a group of ladies who can't believe a man they have loved and trusted for so long could betray them so totally.

Everywhere there is the din of hammers at work, the wailing of women, the throb of truck motors, the shouts of policemen. It is a thoroughly rotten scene, of bullying, of threatening, of insensitive, crude thoughtless bureaucrats smashing up people's lives for no reason.[391]

The *Herald* reported the next morning that only one family had been moved.

On 30 November the Human Rights Trust released the results of the Red Location survey.

The results showed that this was a settled community, with 10% of the community having been there for 66+ years. And it was desperately poor – 58% earning less than R100 per month. Nobody wanted to move to Motherwell, but 6% said that, if they were to get a 'cement house', they would move. The press again found much to publicise from this.[392]

On 1 December, with the removal still not having commenced, Savage phoned Brigadier Ernst Schnetler, the head of the uniform branch in Port Elizabeth. Savage and Schnetler had a curiously close chemistry. Savage liked and respected the policeman, and commented that the policeman had passed every exam he had sat at police college, and was always head of the class. Schnetler reciprocated this respect, for Savage had been a very successful businessman and was now an energetic and capable member of parliament. Their mutual respect was to save the Red Location.

Savage asked for an appointment to present the town plan. Schnetler was to be accompanied by Mr Scholtz, previously town clerk of Ibhayi.

It is felt, and recorded in the Red Location diary, that it was during this phone call to set up the meeting that the Red Location removal was called off by Schnetler.

He met Savage, McLachlan and myself courteously the next morning and that afternoon Mr Mundell told the Red Location committee that the move was off. They would be re-housed in the Red Location. Rebuilding would begin in January, he said.

The front page of the *Evening Post* of Wednesday 3 December was covered by a Jimmy Matyu story – 'Reprieve for the Red Location'. Mrs Maneli expressed her delight, and the diary concludes: 'Now all goes quiet in the Red Location.'[393] The removal was off.

It took the men of apartheid less than three weeks to regroup and attempt to recover their lost control. They did this by scouring the Red Location for 'comrades' and detaining anyone even approximately 'political'. This was done in the following way, the notes being taken from a statement in the Human Rights Trust archive, made by Mbuyiseli Zolo, a 20-year-old student whose home was in the Red Location. Other statements confirm what is to follow.[394]

On the 19th December 1986, I was sleeping at home when, at about 2h00 am, a contingent of 10 or even more security police in association with Ibhayi Council law enforcement officers burst into our house. A security policeman named Silulami instructed me and my brother to get up and out of the house.

Outside we found many law enforcement officers with guns in the street. There were similar actions going on in all of our neighbours' houses, and I could see the adult population of many homes being brought out into the streets. I also recognised Jambo, a security policeman, in this area.

We were then instructed to put our hands on our heads, and to keep them there while we were walked to the large open space alongside the disused Avenue C bottlestore. As we started walking I could see that, for as far as I had visibility, the perimeter of the Red Location was ringed with SADF footsoldiers, standing a few paces apart, with their weapons ready. As I met and talked to people from other sections of the Red Location, it appeared as if, in fact, the whole Red Location was surrounded on its perimeter by SADF troops, and that all adult and young residents were being marched to this central area.

As we arrived at the open space near the Avenue C bottlestore, there were two long queues forming – one for ladies, who were walking single file to a caravan, and one for males, who were marching single file to an E20 mini-bus with mirror windows. All residents had their hands on their heads. Many were scantily dressed, and the area was well lit. There were security police, municipal police and soldiers everywhere.

I was forced into the male queue, which was very long, leading towards the E20. As I got to the E20, I was told 'Just look into the mirror!' (it had one-way mirror glass windows, so one could not tell who was inside). A voice from inside said 'Positive!', a black security policeman asked for my name, and, as I gave it, he said 'Climb into the truck!', which I then did. I heard the voice of the informer inside say 'Negative!' to others, who were then allowed to go home.

I understand that the ladies, who I could see forming their queue up to the caravan, were taken into the caravan where there was an informer in a special compartment who likewise said 'Positive' or 'Negative'. The positives were then carted off to jail.

When two trucks of males were full, with over 70 in total, we drove off and, on leaving the Red Location, we could see the ring of soldiers covering the entire perimeter.

There was to be a second destabilisation project, conceived and planned in 1986, but executed four days into 1987. This was to be a combined security force and vigilante attempt to take control of KwaNobuhle in Uitenhage.[395]

The revolution had been creating its own enemies. With the UDF leadership jailed or in hiding, the front line became occupied by youngsters who were out of the control of the jailed leadership. These youngsters knew no restraint, and fire was their weapon. Fire against property, and, horrifyingly, fire against people, perceived enemies of the revolution. This, of course, created great social tension and many animosities.

Two years earlier, Kelman Befile owned three shops in the Langa location. He apparently, for all of the coming detail is hearsay, also owned a farm, on which he had apprehended a poacher, and the youngster had died. To avoid arrest, Befile apparently cut a deal with the police – or so the comrades believed. They burned down his shops in Langa and his father's house.[396]

He then moved to Khayelitsha, in KwaNobuhle, where he again set up shop, and began to prosper. However, the removals that took place in Langa and the resettlement of the Langa people in Tjoksville, the tent town on the fringe of Khayelitsha, brought his old enemies back within striking distance. Again, his new shop was burned. By this time he had apparently, according to the comrades, been involved in the murder of the youth activist Lindile Mente, a member of the executive of the Uitenhage Youth Congress.

Befile and a few friends were now in the firing line so they banded together and formed a group that they called AmaAfrika. Their relationship with another of the comrades' enemies, Rev. Mzwandile Maqina of Port Elizabeth, is convincingly documented. The fight with the comrades began in earnest.

On 31 December 1986 Befile's car was attacked and destroyed, and his brother kidnapped for a short while. Later that day two youngsters were apprehended by Befile's people and were taken to his van, where they were mercilessly assaulted. Fortunately the beating stopped when it was reported that Befile's brother had been found. The youngsters were taken to where he was. There they found three municipal police vans, and again the beating started, in front of the municipal police. The police did nothing.

It took Befile and the security establishment four days from this event to pull together their plan.

And it was devastating.

As the attached map shows, between 3am and 5am on Sunday 4 January 1987, groups of individuals, some masked, awoke all the homes in Tjoksville and Khayelitsha, demanding menfolk to pick up their sticks and other weapons, and to join a crowd that was forming in the area. Those without weapons were later given fence poles – where these came from, nobody was told.

The march began with an address at Kelman Befile's house on the corner of Polana Tini Road and Lawrence Vinqi Drive. Then it went on, gathering men as it went. Eventually it is estimated that the crowd was about 5 000 in number. Even some unionists, known for their pro-UDF position, were seen participating: NAAWU's General Secretary, Makaya Sam, and a full-time shop steward at Volkswagen factory, Tiban Johnson, were in the rapidly growing group. While Johnson, in a later interview with me, claimed that he was coerced, both appeared to believe that the image of AmaAfrika had risen sharply because of the mayhem that was to follow. 'The people' were now tired of necklacing, burning, schools and consumer boycotts and not being able to go to town, both said.

By about 7 am, the group had reached Zamile Motors, at the entrance to 'Old' KwaNobuhle. The group was now thousands strong, and it was followed by two SA Police Hippos. From there they dispersed, all over 'Old' KwaNobuhle. They sought out the homes of the (mostly jailed) UDF seniors – and they removed all the furnishings and possessions, piled them up on the front lawns and torched them.

It was not only the homes of the UDF 'notables' that were attacked – the Methodist minister for KwaNobuhle, Reverend Alec Diko, and the Church of the Province minister, Reverend KS Daba, were both confronted and told never to harbour the UDF activists or meet with 'the PFP', or they would be killed.

And killing did happen that day. John Maya, 14 years old, had his head smashed in, and died before he could get to hospital. And Siphiwo Loom, 20 years old, was pursued in Mtingane Street by a group of four men, armed with pickhandles. They caught up with him, and in the words of witness Mrs Winnie Solomon, one hit him on the legs and he fell. All four struck him, saying nothing, and simply left at the front gate and just walked off up the street, quite unhurried. They didn't even look at the child's injuries.

At the end of the day, these unfortunate two were dead, scores were assaulted, and the total possessions of between 10 and 20 people were destroyed.

And where, in this full day of mayhem and criminality, were the police?

The Human Rights Trust took 27 statements from citizens, ministers of religion, unionists and witnesses over the next few days. Twenty-two of them told a story that none of them contradicted.

There were two helicopters flying overhead for the duration of the criminality – one a police helicopter and one an SADF chopper. They were there from the earliest events, and were clearly anticipating the mayhem. They monitored the entire proceedings and were in contact with a large contingent of police on the ground. The police had deployed troop carriers, Hippos and a number of vans. The municipal police were also there in numbers. While the police did not participate directly in the assaults and destruction of property, they did nothing to stop it, which is as big a crime. Often they appeared to be directing the groups of vigilantes.

It was Crossroads all over again.

And it did not stop on 5 January either. KwaNobuhle was plunged into months of lawlessness and criminality.

In August 1987 four schoolgirls were abducted and brutalised by a group of AmaAfrika. They sought independent medical and legal assistance, and full sworn statements were taken. Their affidavits, naming their assailants, were delivered by their attorney to the Uitenhage headquarters of the SA Police. Five months later the attorney received a terse reply from the station commander. 'Kindly note that the Uitenhage CR 404/10/87 was forwarded to the Senior State Prosecutor for decision, who declined to prosecute in the above matter.'[397]

There was another indignity awaiting the residents of KwaNobuhle.

Oliver Cromwell, when he led a parliamentary invasion from England into Ireland in 1649, was determined to subdue the Irish. In fact he, and his son-in-law who succeeded him as commander of the parliamentary forces, oversaw the killing of between 10% and 25% of the Irish population.

Cromwell had a second agenda – to put down the Irish church. Not only did he execute any Catholic priests who fell into his grasp, but, as a supreme gesture of insult, he stabled his army's horses in Dublin's St Patrick's Cathedral.

A similar gesture of sacrilege was effected in KwaNobuhle in mid-1987. For the people of KwaNobuhle had built a moving Massacre Headstone in the KwaNobuhle cemetery.

On 12 July 1987, the day the state of emergency was reimposed,

Uitenhage vigilantes destroyed this memorial.

They wished their ruthlessness, their authority and their immunity from arrest to be clearly understood.

36

Denouement

A t the end of 1986 the Casspirs and the Buffels whined around Port Elizabeth's townships, in all directions, mostly undisturbed. And in KwaNobuhle in Uitenhage, the bakkies of AmaAfrika youth, brandishing sticks and poles provided by the police, patrolled the township, looking for 'comrades'. God help those they found.

A graph from the work of the Truth and Reconciliation Commission shows clearly that the number of gross human rights violations, mostly murder, assaults and torture, in the Eastern Cape peaked in 1985, dropped considerably in 1986, and dropped again, to a few hundred violations, in 1987.

For much of 1985, the UDF leaders were locked deep in jail; the front line 'comrades', the Amabutho youth, had been picked up, suffocated, detained for as long as necessary to 'teach them a lesson', and were now marked men and women.

Had the 'system' won?

Was the revolution crushed?

The simple answer is 'NO', not at all.

We have seen how the apartheid security police and the SADF's soldiers had thrown everything they had at the revolution in 1985: a massacre in the streets of Langa; a proxy 'war' between the UDF and AZAPO, which was in fact a midnight firefest between the comrades and state-sponsored, armed and assisted vigilantes; Trojan horse ambushes; death squads, again the 'men of midnight', who captured and murdered, as brutally as possible, the leadership of PEBCO (Hashe, Godolozi and Galela) and CRADORA (Goniwe, Calata, Mkonto and Mhlauli) and a large number of other struggle people; a state of emergency that saw mass jailing and security police detention and torture of the entire UDF leadership, and many others, which torture only ended when Dr Wendy Orr laid it out clearly for the public to see; arson attacks on the Watsons' home and targeted commercial attacks on Builder's Market. And so much more, including the tragic but (possibly) not-state-sponsored death of Molly Blackburn, the most courageous and effective of the white opponents of apartheid.

1985 in Port Elizabeth and Uitenhage was the most blood-soaked year in memory, possibly the most blood-soaked in the history of any of South Africa's major conurbations.

All this had not created a clear winner.

The UDF response, including the most effective consumer boycott in living memory, had been more successful than one could ever have imagined: business leaders had pressed the security establishment to release the UDF leadership from detention to negotiate an end to the consumer boycott, and, along with the release of the detainees, again as a result of business lobbying, the SADF had been removed from the townships; the Supreme Court had overturned the only bannings that the state had effected in Port Elizabeth – the bannings of Henry Fazzie and Khusta Jack; pressure to end apartheid in the United States was beginning to become effective, against the position of President Reagan, and disinvestment began with the withdrawal of the biggest American company in South Africa, Port Elizabeth's Ford Motor Company; American banks began refusing to roll over loans to South African borrowers, a trend that became a flood after President PW Botha made the 'Rubicon speech'; anyone wishing to negotiate an issue, from consumer boycotts to bus services in the townships, walked straight past the incompetent, illegitimate and corrupt Ibhayi City Council and dealt directly with the UDF structures; and, as a booster to morale, Umkhonto we Sizwe increased its operations in South Africa.

At the beginning of 1986, the comrades walked the streets proudly as PW Botha ended the first state of emergency and Slabbert abandoned parliament. The Commonwealth Eminent Persons Group arrived and it became clear that their programme involved setting up negotiations between the ANC and the Botha government.

We were an inch from meaningful change.

Of course it was not to be – not yet, anyway. PW Botha was not a 'hensopper' (a Boer war term, indicating one readily willing to surrender to the British) and his performance at the earlier 'Sterrewag' cabinet meeting showed clearly that he was not yet at the stage where genuine negotiations between the government and the ANC were possible. His tolerance of 'foreign intervention' was clearly over when he sent the airforce to bomb so-called 'ANC camps' in neighbouring countries, an effective final 'fuck you' to the Commonwealth Eminent Persons Group and their attempt to create a real stage for legitimate negotiations.

Botha now had a second plan for dealing with the insurrection. The first plan, and the first state of emergency, might not have worked, but this time it would be different.

Colonel McCuen in his writing had laid out for Botha and his ilk a new scenario on how to deal with a large-scale insurrection: first you crush the revolution. This may be messy so it should be effected quickly, using freshly recruited militia who are not restrained by the codes of conduct of the formal security forces. Then you reinstate the organs of government that had been delegitimised by the revolution, and you put endless resources into their hands, to speedily deliver much-needed services to the revolutionary community, thereby rebuilding, also, their lost legitimacy. The delivery of these services is to be accompanied by a massive propaganda campaign, to ensure that the revolutionary populace become aware that their lives are better in the hands of the existing invaders, rather than under the revolutionary control of the murderous 'comrades'. This was the 'WHAM' effect – 'Win Hearts and Minds'. In both the business of putting down the revolution and delivering improved services, an 'oliekol' approach was what was needed – you drop a bit of oil there, and it slowly spreads out, engulfing neighbouring areas. And finally, areas that were irredeemably in the control of the 'comrades' were to be entirely destabilised by mass forced removals, or intense and thorough security force attack.

On paper, this all makes sense – but politics is not played out on paper; instead it is often enacted in bloodshed and mob behaviour in brutally contested streets. McCuen's ideas, designed for the United States' invading forces in Vietnam, and doubtless adapted also for a later war in Afghanistan, never worked in either. How PW and his securocrats believed they could make these ideas work in South Africa is a mystery. But plainly there were no other proposals on the table.

And if one comes to believe that the plan was from another place in a different time, and inappropriate for the South African revolution in 1985 and 1986, when one comes to consider its implementation, one is left breathless in disbelief.

Botha, confident that his newly established National Security Management System had brought all the resources of the state into a unified vehicle to overwhelm the ragtag comrades, convened a joint session of parliament, and on 12 June 1986 announced in the chamber that a second state of emergency was now called. By the time of this announcement thousands had already been detained, and historic numbers were scooped up and incarcerated – certainly more than 30 000 people. And this state of emergency had no time bar – it was to last for over four years.

For 'swiftly-trained militia' read 'kitskonstabels' – they quickly flooded the streets, their victims the hospitals, and their suspects the jails. Razor wire surrounded whole townships, where entry and exit points were accompanied by vehicle and body searches. Truculent communities in Crossroads in Cape Town and Langa in Uitenhage were torn apart, dispossessed of their land and dumped on the periphery of the cities, no longer to mobilise, now just to survive. They were the first 'oliekols', ripped down to the ground so that later development could be unhindered by the intervention of the comrades.

Langa was in for special treatment, and the tent town that became the world of those dispossessed and moved would, after the removal, be beset by police-sponsored vigilantes, as was the whole of neighbouring 'Old' KwaNobuhle.

In Port Elizabeth's and Uitenhage's townships about one person in every hundred tasted detention at this time; some, including particularly the UDF leadership, for years.

PW Botha certainly intended to 'destroy the revolution'.

That's what PW's security forces did do – but it's what they didn't do, or no longer could do, that is even more instructive.

For by the end of 1986 the targeted assassinations had slowed to a trickle, the result of foreign governments, the South African liberal press and local leaders clearly stating that this all had been the stuff of government-sponsored death squads, and many clues were emerging to verify this. Large-scale massacres were also now to be avoided, replaced by vigilante thuggishness and brutality. But this, too, in Port Elizabeth but not Uitenhage, could no longer be effectively coordinated.

Torture, once so routine and widespread, had been curbed by the Wendy Orr revelations. It did reappear as suffocation torture, which leaves no bruises and was much 'safer' in that the evidence of this torture is much more difficult to prove. But this too was under pressure – the Human Rights Trust's Helen Suzman and I took 37 signed statements outlining this 'new method' to Minister Vlok, who appointed the Police's Internal Investigative Unit to investigate. Of course, nobody was charged, but the practice all but stopped. Some things do not thrive in light.

The kitskonstabels were by now despised by the formal security force members, and never gained the opportunity to be the mindless, thuggish wreakers of havoc that McCuen had envisaged them to be. By the end of 1986 they were more likely to be in jail than to be the Taliban of the townships.

The only weapon left to PW's men was detention. Endless detention.

But this too was no longer what it once was. With the prisons now unwilling to continue to be the entrance halls of the torture chambers, conditions in detention began to improve.

As Khusta Jack has written, 'At the peak of the state of emergency, we were squashed into the cells like sardines into a can – often 100 detainees confined in a cell with a capacity of only 45... Time ticked over and the autocratic system itself started to collapse at the edges ... The slow collapse began with letters from relatives and friends trickling in, then came books to read and for those who were studying ... as the years passed, we were allowed newspapers and video movies... By this stage the security police were no longer interrogating people seriously ... by now [the security police] believed that physical torture was futile.'

And, as we were to find out in early 1989, endless detention can also be broken – by hunger strikes.

Then came the determination of the state to resurrect the Ibhayi City Council, which was to be the chosen vehicle for township upgrading, and the home of the 'informal militia'. 1986 saw Minister Magnus Malan and State President Botha both visit the Ibhayi Council and they promised full government support and the resources necessary to make a real difference to the standard of services in the townships.

Of all the extraordinary mistakes made by the iron men of apartheid, this was the dumbest.

By 1986 the Ibhayi Councillors were all living in Council-built houses in KwaMagxaki. The money for these houses had been fraudulently misappropriated from grants provided by national government that were meant to pay for job creation projects. And the fact that the councillors were all now living outside the territory of their municipality disqualified them from being councillors. No worry – they had all been appointed, en bloc, as 'advisers', on a wage identical to their previous council allowance.

The 'councillors/advisers' were under continuous guard, and were not allowed to leave the council building during the working day. Their children were educated in the Transkei. They, as a group, had no following, no authority and no legitimacy. They, fictitiously, headed up a bankrupt government body whose grant money evaporated as soon as it arrived in the council's bank, and whose assets amounted to as little as the council's legitimacy.

It took another two years for this house of cards to collapse, and this collapse was engineered by, of all people, a judge of the Supreme Court in

Port Elizabeth.

Behind this disaster was, of course and again, Thamsanqa Linda, now returned from the Transkei, and an 'adviser' to the Ibhayi City Council.

Linda was by now transparent in his ambition. He had followed Archbishop Tutu around, decrying Tutu's calls for sanctions. The national broadcaster, the South African Television, gave him more time than Tutu. He had made it clear he was for participating in PW Botha's proposed but stillborn National Council, a hare-brained scheme the government had proposed to absorb the political ambitions of 'urban blacks'. It never saw the light of day.

Linda's quest for power, prestige and money had caused him to organise that 'Councillor' Mpondo was voted off the chairmanship of the executive committee of the Ibhayi Council, and also off the Algoa Regional Services Council. Mpondo was replaced by – guess who.

Mpondo then approached the Supreme Court, claiming his now unpaid allowances, and argued that all this was illegal. The matter was heard in the Port Elizabeth Supreme Court by Judge Mullins.[398]

The judge brought the house down, both factually and figuratively:

> It is not often that this court is called upon to enter the world of make-believe. But the facts of this case would be worthy of the attention of the brothers Grimm, Hans Christian Andersen or Lewis Carroll.
>
> There existed within the jurisdiction of this court a local authority established in terms of the provisions of the Black Local Authorities Act No 102 of 1982. It was given the name of the Ibhayi City Council.
>
> In the proceedings at present before me on notice of motion, a lengthy typed document consisting of some 30-odd pages was handed in by consent. It is headed 'Ibhayi City Council – Minutes of the C3/1988 Ordinary Council Meeting held on Monday, 7 March 1988 at 15h15 in the Council Chamber, Struanway, New Brighton.' This document (which I shall refer to as 'The Minutes' because the events recorded therein actually occurred) commences with the names and offices of the various persons at the meeting.
>
> Heading the list is the name of the second respondent with the title 'Administrator'. There follows a list of 'Members of Council', twelve in number. The ninth respondent is shown as 'Mayor'. Fourth respondent is shown as 'Deputy Mayor'. The third, fifth, sixth, seventh and eighth respondents, as well as the applicant, all appear as 'Ordinary Councillors' ... Also shown as being present at the meeting are the names of fourteen 'Officials of Council', including the Town

Clerk, Town Treasurer and various departmental heads and officials. The Ibhayi City Council is cited herein as First Respondent.

The proceedings of the meeting were conducted with proper solemnity and observance of protocol. The Mayor presided. The Mayor and Councillors were described and addressed as such throughout the minutes. Matters were discussed and resolutions were taken. Various financial matters were dealt with and expenditure was approved. The appointment of officials was considered … In fact the minutes record what can only be described as a very model of a model Council Meeting.

Yet, says Mr Dison who appears for the respondents (the Ibhayi City Council), the whole of these proceedings was a charade. That organ of local government, the Ibhayi City Council, does not even exist. There is no mayor, nor, except for the applicant and ninth respondent, are there any so-called 'councillors', entitled to be described as such. The resolutions taken at the meeting are of no force or effect. Nor is there an executive committee.

The proceedings recorded in the minutes, despite their apparent solemnity and validity, were, so it is said, never intended to be more than an exercise in the practical conduct of municipal affairs, with, to use Mr Dison's words, a 'play-play' mayor and councillors of a 'play-play' city council conducting a 'play-play' meeting. All this, says Mr Dison, had the very laudable object of educating the individuals concerned in the functions and duties of elected councillors, but that it was never intended that any legal consequence should flow from their actions. Why it should be necessary to educate persons who had previously comprised the Ibhayi City Council was not explained.[399]

A week later the Ibhayi City Council ceased to exist. By now a desperate government had appointed Barry Erasmus to be its administrator. He announced that he had cancelled all council meetings with immediate effect. 'Advisers' were to stay on, presumably on full pay.

Stripped of all legitimacy in its wars with the UDF, and now of all legality by the Supreme Court, the institution could only limp on, delivering almost no services at a huge cost and sheltering hundreds of kitskonstabels who now had little left to do.

The McCuen formula suggested that this body deliver the vast tapestry of improved services that was required to 'Win Hearts and Minds', and to coordinate a blaze of publicity to accompany this programme. Neither happened, which is hardly surprising considering the state of the institution.

And, when the Red Location proved impossible to subdue, this half-baked council was to coordinate the removal of the entire community to Motherwell. Again, the initial arrangements were cruel and incompetent, and the securocrats called off the ham-fisted removal at the last minute.

Thus, by the end of 1986 the men of apartheid were absolutely not in control of the townships of Port Elizabeth and Uitenhage.

Denied their traditional methods – killing, massacres and torture – and with McCuen's proposals rendered useless by a hapless, hopeless and helpless bureaucracy – they decided to test the water, twice.

Firstly, the Human Sciences Research Council ran two surveys of the opinions of black people 18 years and older, in March 1986 and in September 1986, in metropolitan areas. These surveys followed an earlier and similar survey in May 1985, and the results can be compared.[400]

The results were instructive:

- The percentage of respondents who felt that the 'present unrest is a good thing' had risen from 35% in 1985 to 65% in September 1986;
- The percentage who felt that the security forces could not 'maintain law and order in your township' had risen from 34% to 56%;
- The percentage feeling that the 'outside world should apply sanctions against South Africa' had nearly doubled, from 16% to 30%;
- Apartheid was clearly seen as the biggest cause of 'the present unrest in the black communities', having risen from 17% to 45%;
- Nelson Mandela had risen from 19% to 44% as the chosen 'leader for South Africa'.

These results caused the researcher to reach the following conclusions:

The state of emergency – with its advantages – probably needs to be maintained for some time yet but, while it is in force, genuine and far-reaching change … must be effected through negotiation between the truly legitimate leaders of the respective interest groups in South Africa. If this does not take place, the revolutionary alliance will continue its politicisation of the black masses and steer South Africa into an inevitable 'people's war' from which no party will emerge victorious … A state of emergency … can never control people's perceptions and minds.[401]

The second testing of the water began with a letter dated 13 August 1987. Written by State President PW Botha, it instructed his Minister of Justice Kobie Coetsee to 'consider releasing' Govan Mbeki from his 24-year incarceration on Robben Island. This was done on 5 November, and the somewhat startled elder statesman (he was 77 years old) found himself again living in Port Elizabeth, and addressing a press conference at the Holiday Inn.

In Kobie Coetsee's extensive archive, now kept at the University of the Free State in Bloemfontein, this is candidly described as a 'litmus test'.[402] If this event passed with minimal unrest, Mandela could possibly be released. The revolution would have subsided. Mr Mbeki and Port Elizabeth were plainly chosen because, if quiet was possible here, it was possible anywhere.

Coetsee's archive contains two important reports: firstly, details about a planned 'gathering with Mr G Mbeki in Port Elizabeth' and secondly a 'Security Branch Proposal by Hermanus Barend du Plessis for the mass gathering with Mr Mbeki'.[403]

Apparently it was estimated that the crowd would be of an extraordinarily large size, and of a mood that was impossible to ascertain. The meeting was summarily banned, Mbeki was restricted to New Brighton, and the press was forbidden to quote him. It was to take another two and a half years for the men of apartheid to summon the courage to release Mandela.

Despite outward appearances of calm, it is clear that the striking of a match in the townships of Port Elizabeth and Uitenhage could again ignite an uncontrollable conflagration.

Across the country, strikes and stayaways were 'the struggle in another coat'. The number of people days lost to business rose exponentially: 1983, 125 000; 1985, 676 000; 1986, 1 804 000; and 1987, 5 845 000. While the townships may have appeared quieter, the factories weren't. The situation was unsustainable.

The insurrection of the 1980s was the fifth major confrontation between the apartheid state and the black community it was determined to keep in subjugation.

The Defiance Campaign of the 1950s; the Sharpeville massacre and its associated state of emergency in the early 1960s; the turn to the armed struggle and the sabotage campaign that had immediately followed; the uprising of 1976 that began in Soweto's schools; and now, the war of the 1980s.

This war was the only one that the full resources of the apartheid security juggernaut had not subdued, and could not subdue, for all that it threw at it.

Apartheid had arrived at its own battle of Stalingrad, and, like the Nazi army of 1942, it could not overwhelm an ill-equipped, under-resourced and hopelessly outgunned opponent, the comrades of the townships of Port Elizabeth and Uitenhage, in the battles of 1985 and 1986.

Like the Nazis at the end of 1942, when the battle had clearly been lost, the apartheid army continued to fight on, inflicting incredible suffering in the process, but outright victory was no longer possible, and it was just a matter of time before, finally, the last flag of totalitarianism was to be torn from the final flagpole. As with the Nazis, it took three more years in South Africa. Wasted years of unnecessary suffering and lost opportunities. Of the wasting of precious, limited resources and the emergence of dreadful regional conflicts, mostly in KwaZulu–Natal.

The HSRC report quoted above recommended that the state of emergency was to be continued for some time, enough time for genuine negotiations with legitimate leaders to be undertaken.

As we have seen, Nelson Mandela was visited in hospital by Kobie Coetsee, a visit that Mandela described as an 'olive branch'.[404]

Negotiations had begun.

This was September 1985, a month after PW's Rubicon speech and the ensuing chaos.

Period Four
1987 and 1988

1987 and 1988 were marked by five trends: on and off negotiations between the ANC and the government; a general reduction in township violence, particularly in the Eastern Cape; the workplace becoming more and more the battleground for political and human rights; the beginning of grotesque violence in (particularly) the rural areas of Natal; and the collapse of the apartheid state's 'other' war, the Angolan Bush War.

37

Two years of despair

The year 1987 did not bode well for the UDF, either nationally or in Port Elizabeth.

And the organisation knew it. In early January 1987 the UDF issued their New Year message: 'We enter 1987 devoid of any illusion as to what this government can or cannot do. We do not see any signs that the white minority is ready for a government based on the will of the people. We actually expect 1987 to usher in an era of even greater collaboration between the state president and the military ... We are still committed to waging a non-violent struggle against apartheid even as the state seems bent on closing every available legal space.'[405]

In late 1986 the UDF had attempted three national campaigns – 'United Action against Apartheid', 'Christmas against the Emergency' and 'Campaign for National Unity'. All had been smashed up by the state security apparatus. In the process, in December 1986, the newspapers *City Press*, *Sowetan* and the *Weekly Mail* had each been prohibited from publishing statements about the campaigns. In January 1987 the *New Nation* was added to this unhappy list. Botha had endless powers in terms of the state of emergency, and he was determined to use them.[406]

In December 1986 11 newspapers were banned from publishing all reports, save those distributed by the police, on 'unrest incidents', which now included police or army activity, boycotts, people's courts, street committees or issues about detention.[407]

Another campaign, 'Unban the ANC', which began in early 1987, provided another rough ride.

As part of this campaign, the National Education Crisis Committee (NECC), the South African Council of Churches (SACC) and the UDF jointly placed advertisements in 22 newspapers calling for the lifting of the ban on the ANC, which had just turned 75. PW Botha immediately accused the managing director of First National Bank, Mr Chris Ball, of providing the R150 000 needed to fund the advertisements. This Ball denied, and Botha appointed Mr Justice G Munnik, the Judge President of the Cape Province Division of the Supreme Court, to investigate the funding of the advertisements, and whether or not Ball had been involved.

Munnik interrogated Ball for seven hours, and it emerged that Ball had overridden two of his managers and allowed an overdraft facility of R100 000 to be granted to Mr Yusuf Surtee, who was a managing director of a retail clothing group, and who was described by Munnik as 'a man of no financial substance and an opportunist'. Munnik thus concluded that, as this overdraft had been used to pay for the advertisements, and Ball had been involved in its granting, Botha's allegations were adequately proven.

Later in parliament PFP MP Dave Dalling stated that Munnik should have refused the commission as FNB's predecessor bank, Barclays, had closed Munnik's accounts more than once, and that he had been described by the bank as a 'bad risk'. This Munnik had never declared when taking on the commission.

The controversy saw FNB lose business, and a few years later Ball took up a position with another bank in the UK.[408]

As difficult as these issues were to handle, the biggest difficulty the UDF faced in 1987 was the indefinite detention of its leadership. The Detainees Parents' Support Committee reported that 78% of the detainees they recorded were members of the UDF, and at least 50 of these were senior officials, including the entire Port Elizabeth and Uitenhage executive. Furthermore, the general secretary of the Border region, Rev. Arnold Stofile, was sentenced to 11 years for terrorism in May 1987, and the UDF's acting national general secretary Mohammed Valli Moosa, and its acting national publicity secretary, Murphy Morobe, were detained while hiding at Advocate Dayalin Chetty's house in Port Elizabeth in July 1987.[409]

The 'Delmas' Treason Trial, South Africa's longest-ever treason trial, ground on, and eventually came to judgment on 15 November 1988. The three senior UDF people who were defendants and who had been denied bail repeatedly over the three years of the trial, Moses 'Moss' Chikane (Transvaal Provincial Secretary of the UDF), 'Terror' Lekota (National

Publicity Secretary) and Popo Molefe (National General Secretary), were all found guilty of treason as Judge Van Dijkhorst found that the UDF and the ANC were working in tandem to bring down the government. The defendants were given 10 years (Chikane and Molefe) and 12 years (Lekota) respectively.[410]

With its leadership either in detention or in hiding, the UDF was very constrained in what it could do. One thing it appeared unable to effect was control over its large youth community. While its affiliate in the world of schooling, the National Education Crisis Committee, was making some halting progress with regard to 'people's education', and some in the schools' bureaucracy were going with the idea, the NECC made a call in early 1986 for a return to school. This was not helped by the authorities in 'Bantu Education' now requiring students to carry identity cards and to adhere to new disciplinary instructions. The call mostly failed, most particularly in Port Elizabeth and Uitenhage, where 52 of the 80 national schools whose pupils refused to return were domiciled.[411]

In other respects, young comrades abandoned the front lines. Having tasted detention and suffocation torture, and being leaderless and now becoming unpopular within communities who were tiring of women being made to drink Omo if bought in the wrong shops, the youth went quiet. As Lodge and Nasson wrote, 'By early 1987 black resistance appeared to be at an end.'[412]

With the UDF immobilised and the youth into other things, the townships went quiet. Deaths in political violence dropped considerably.

From a high point in 1986, such deaths dropped dramatically in 1987, and would have been even lower in 1988 had it not been for deaths in the rapidly escalating Natal killing fields. This gave PW Botha the opportunity to claim that the state of emergency was working, and should be allowed to continue. He did not note that his security forces accounted for possibly a third of all deaths in 1986, and Natal accounted for 80% of the 1988 deaths.

But the UDF was not to disappear so quickly.

Attempting to keep the young 'front-trenchers' motivated and yet under some discipline, in April 1987 the UDF created two national organisations, the South African Youth Conference (SAYCO) and the UDF Women's League.

SAYCO was led by Peter Mokaba, a 25-year-old who had already tasted Robben Island. It met under the determined slogan 'Freedom or Death, Victory is Certain', and saw itself as the 'youth detachment' of the broader, veteran-controlled movement. It collaborated with COSATU in calling for a stayaway from the whites-only elections of May, and notched up some limited success here.

To again breathe new life into their threatened UDF, the National Working Committee called 200 delegates to a top-secret destination, near Durban, for a conference in June 1987. This was also to commemorate the fourth anniversary of the founding of the UDF.

At this conference it was agreed to adopt the Freedom Charter, and to consult with all regions about this decision.

The secretary's report was upbeat for such difficult times: 'There has been a shift from what was often youth- and student-led struggles to the exercising of working-class leadership. Particularly over the past few months, workers have dictated the pace and momentum of the struggle.'

It was resolved to work closely from now on with the COSATU leadership. And it was noted that 'our inability to maintain internal structures has impaired the coordination and democratic interaction within the Front'.[413]

Possibly sensing the UDF's vulnerability, the state went in for the kill.

On 9 October 1986 the government issued a proclamation that prohibited the UDF from receiving foreign aid or foreign money. This was devastating. The UDF took a strategic decision to approach the courts and a more strategic one to approach the courts in Durban, where the bench had a liberal gloss. In his court papers Curnick Ndlovu, the executive chairman of the UDF, stated that without foreign funding the UDF could not function.

Their strategic decision proved wise. In May 1987 Mr Justice J Didcott of the Durban and Coast Local Division of the Supreme Court declared the government's proclamation invalid. He nevertheless granted the government permission to appeal his judgment to the Appellate Division of the Supreme Court in Bloemfontein, then the nation's highest court.

Bloemfontein sadly lacked Durban's liberalism, and in September 1987 the Acting Chief Justice, Mr Justice PJ Rabie, upheld the state's appeal, and the UDF was down, but not quite out.[414]

Now for PW's attempted *coup de grace*.

The state of emergency was governed by the Public Safety Act of 1953. This allowed the State President, in any area where a state of emergency had been declared, to, in terms of section 2 of the Act, 'make such regulations as appear to him to be necessary or expedient for providing for the safety of the public or the maintenance of public order'.[415]

Now was such a time for PW Botha. A new proclamation, Proclamation R23 of 24 February 1988, inserted into Proclamation 96, was then inserted into the emergency regulations, and this made possible the dramatic restriction of activities of organisations or people.

All PW now had to do was issue an order by notice in the *Government Gazette*, and he could prohibit an organisation from specific acts, or from 'any activities or acts whatsoever'.

On the day on which this regulation was gazetted, 24 February 1988, the Minister of Law and Order, Adriaan Vlok, issued an order prohibiting 17 organisations from carrying out any activities except preserving assets, keeping books of record and 'taking legal advice and judicial steps'. These organisations included AZAPO, AYO, the Cradock Residents' Association, PEBCO, the Detainees Parents' Support Committee, the National Education Crisis Committee, the Release Mandela Campaign, the new South African Youth Congress, and, of course, the United Democratic Front.[416]

The next month a new organisation, the Committee for the Defence of Democracy, was formed. It too was immediately banned. No emergency exits here.

As Tom Lodge has written: 'In February 1988 the UDF and 17 other organisations were effectively banned. With most of its leadership in jail or forced into hiding, with the struggle against Inkatha in Natal escalating, and with this final prohibition, the fall of the front seemed complete.'[417]

At the time, the UDF leadership, such as was still standing, hardly differed from Lodge's sober assessment. In their 1989 New Year statement, they described 1988 as a year 'of stress, conflict, bitterness and strife'.[418]

38

1987: The year of many strikes

The year 1987 was a year of many firsts in labour disruptions. For the first time in South Africa's history, more than 1 000 strikes were called. Another first – more than half a million workers came out on strike; and another first, by a mile – over five million man days were lost in 1987.[419]

In response to this dramatic escalation, the Minister of Manpower, Pietie du Plessis, informed parliament that now the 'total onslaught had been extended to the labour terrain'.

Three strikes made up much of these statistics: the South African Transport Services Strike (13 March to 6 June 1987); the Postal Workers' Strike (3 April to 3 September) and the really big one, the Mineworkers' Strike (9 August to 30 August 1987).

The South African Transport Services' strike
At the City Deep depot of SATS in Johannesburg, on 13 March 1987, 500 workers downed tools in protest against the dismissal of a colleague, Mr Andrew Nendzamba, who had been dismissed for handing in late the R40 that he had been paid during a delivery.

Within a month the strike had spread to about 80 depots, with 18 000 workers joining in.

Rapidly it became a clash between the unrecognised COSATU affiliate, the South African Railways and Harbours Workers Union (SARHWU), and SATS management.

SARHWU was a union with a long and proud history. Founded by the redoubtable Ray Simons (Ray Alexander's married name) and Johnny Gomes in 1936, it had been crushed in 1965 and been dormant for 20 years. It was revived in December 1985, and shared offices with the newly established union federation, COSATU, in Johannesburg.

SARHWU was denied recognition by the Minister of Transport Affairs. At the time, SATS had 11 registered unions, including one, the Black Trade Union (BLATU), which the minister proposed as adequate for representation of SATS's black staff. For the duration of the strike SATS refused to negotiate with SARHWU, instead conceding to negotiate with a committee consisting of three representatives of the strikers and six from BLATU. This despite the fact that the majority of SATS's black staff were members of SARHWU. It took five more years for SATS to recognise SARHWU and derecognise BLATU.

The strike was no picnic.

In the second week of April, 136 railway carriages were set alight, with 30 being damaged beyond repair, in Soweto and Johannesburg. ANC Radio Freedom applauded this action, stating that, for the first time, fire had spread from the townships to the white areas.

SATS then gave the striking workers until 22 April to return to work or be dismissed.

On the final day of the ultimatum, with workers discussing the issues at SAHRWU premises in Germiston, police opened fire, killing three unionists. Later that day a further three unionists were shot and killed as the left their offices in COSATU House to catch the train to Germiston to inspect the mayhem there.

Police then invaded COSATU House, kicking in many doors and generally creating chaos as they tore open cupboards and briefcases. They arrested 400 unionists in a four-hour raid.

Things got worse. On 27 April four bodies of SATS workers who had been 'necklaced' were found near Kaserne depot in Johannesburg. Another such body was found in Tembisa on the East Rand. The next day police arrested 11 people in COSATU House in connection with these murders. The courts were kept busy with allegations and counter-allegations.

Then, the day after the whites-only general election, 7 May, COSATU House was rendered uninhabitable by two massive bomb blasts that destroyed its structural fabric.

It took eleven years for the truth of this double bombing to be conclusively recorded. Eugene de Kock, commander of the security police's Vlakplaas unit in 1987, told the Truth and Reconciliation Commission on 29 July 1998 how he had pulled off this 'event' on the instructions of his boss, Brigadier Willem Schoon, who in turn said that his instructions came from the 'highest authority in the country'.

De Kock and his team used 50 kg of Russian explosives that they set up in the basement of COSATU House by cutting through the bars at road level before climbing down a rope to set the charges. This took all of four minutes. They watched the explosion as they sped off on a highway east of Johannesburg.[420]

Many years later, then Minister of Justice, Adriaan Vlok, and Commissioner of Police, Johan van der Merwe, admitted this process to the Truth and Reconciliation Commission and applied for amnesty.

The strike was not yet over. It took another month (6 June) for COSATU's General Secretary, Jay Naidoo to announce a settlement. All dismissed workers were reinstated, including Mr Nendzamba, except for those arrested on criminal charges; all detained workers would get their jobs back on release; facilities at the Delmore and Kinross hostels were to be upgraded at the cost of R10 million; workers could now elect their own representatives; and finally, African workers would become permanent employees in terms of the same processes that applied to white workers.

Both SARHWU and SATS claimed this as a victory – no re-employed workers had any disciplinary procedures instituted against them. And SARHWU membership soared to 34 500.[421]

The Post Office strikes

Tensions were visible throughout South African society now, and the Post Office was no exception. Black workers were no longer willing to accept lower wages for doing the same work as their white colleagues. Neither would they accept segregated and unequal change rooms and the repeated non-recognition of the union of their choice, the Post and Telecommunications Workers Association (POTWA).

On 3 April 3 000 Post Office workers from both depots and post offices in the Transvaal went on strike. POTWA's president, Vusi Khumalo, stated that communication with management had proved to be fruitless. His list of unheard demands quickly reached 12.

From today's vantage point it is difficult to comprehend how unequal the capacities for bargaining between management and unions were then. Management simply refused to increase wages and cut off wages to strikers. The strike lasted one month, no wages were increased and resentments continued to build up.

On 29 June about 660 postal workers stopped working again, this time in solidarity with two dismissed workers in Port Elizabeth and East London. The number doubled in just over a week. As numbers increased, so did demands: an end to segregated facilities; the recognition of POTWA; and the removal of apartheid segregation in facilities for the public.

By the end of July about 20 000 workers were out and the demands were being inspected. Management refused to pay workers on strike, and refused to re-employ those dismissed.

The strike was settled on 3 September and management agreed to raise minimum wages by 20%, to R375 a month. Approximately 10 000 workers benefited from this increase, and the department agreed to achieve salary parity over time. Complicated agreements covered the re-employment of dismissed workers – neither side could claim victory there.[422]

The mineworkers' strike

Cyril Ramaphosa was 29 when he got his first job – as an adviser in the legal department of the Council of Unions of South Africa (CUSA).[423]

He had just been admitted as an attorney at the end of a tortuous process of studies and articles, made so difficult by the state's response to his political involvements.

He had started his university career at the University of the North (Turfloop) in 1972, when as a 20-year-old, he had enrolled to study law. He was rapidly caught up in the politics of the time and became chairman of his university's branch of the South African Students' Organisation (SASO) in 1974. He organised a pro-Frelimo rally in that year, and for the first time tasted detention – eleven months in solitary confinement.

After that he gave up Turfloop and found articles with a Johannesburg firm of attorneys.

Then came June 1976, and again detention – this time for six months in John Vorster Square in central Johannesburg.

On his release he kept his head down and in 1981 he earned his BProc through Unisa and completed his articles. Then came the job of legal adviser at the Black Consciousness-leaning CUSA.

The next year, 1982, saw him offered the next challenge in what would become a lifetime of successfully executed challenges. CUSA's national conference resolved to form a union for black mineworkers and Ramaphosa was offered the position of its first general secretary. He accepted this immense task in December 1982.

Initially this new union, now called the National Union of Mineworkers (NUM), had 6 000 worker members on eight mines – by 1986 this had risen to 340 000 worker members. It had become the first registered trade union recognised by the Chamber of Mines as representative of the vast black workforce of this industry.

At the time, the lowest wages paid on South Africa's mines were truly awful. There were differences between gold and coal mines, and between surface and underground workers. Surface workers received R238 per month on gold mines, and R225 on coal mines. Underground workers were paid R431 per month on gold mines and R413 per month on coal mines.[424]

In 1986 the gold mines, in aggregate, declared profits of R8.4 billion, the highest in history. Plainly this was in the mineworkers' minds as the time for negotiations around annual increases arrived.[425]

Mid-1987 was this time. The Chamber of Mines negotiated for the mine-owners and NUM for the lowest-paid workers. The Chamber's offer was 23% for all surface and underground workers on the lowest categories in both gold and coal mines and 17% for the workers on the highest grade that NUM represented. The NUM rejected this, demanding an across-the-board increase of 30%, along with other demands related to leave pay, danger pay and other such matters.

Management unilaterally imposed their offered increases on 1 July. NUM replied with a ballot for a strike on 2 August. A total of 210 000 workers responded and 95% called for a strike. The strike began on 9 August, and by noon of that day 220 000 workers were on strike. The Labour Monitoring Group estimated that, on 11 August, 334 000 workers, 70% of all black coal and gold mine workers, were out on strike.[426]

The rough stuff began very early in the strike. On 12 August the entire regional committee of NUM in Klerksdorp were arrested. Mine security staff were arresting many people, everywhere. The chairman of the gold and uranium division of Johannesburg Consolidated Investment Company claimed that 33 men who had refused to strike had been murdered. When the SA Police said that they had seen no attempts to murder non-striking miners, his company had to withdraw these allegations, made, they said, 'in the heat of events'. They in fact had no evidence of any deaths related to the strike, they admitted.[427]

In the intense environment of the time, violence had, however, become a feature of strikes and this one was not to be an exception.

The largest number of mines, and the biggest employers in the industry, were the many mines owned by the Anglo American Group. This group obtained a court interdict prohibiting mineworkers from intimidation or assaulting non-strikers. Quickly NUM and Anglo American became involved in one-on-one talks. They made halting progress until, in one of the meetings on 18 August, Cyril Ramaphosa was informed of police attacks on miners at Anglo American's President Steyn gold mine. The NUM delegation broke the talks off.

When the strike entered its third week, Anglo American gave its striking workers an ultimatum, 'Return to work or face dismissal'. Bobby Godsell, Anglo's principal negotiator, said that 'The decision to fire was made against the background of technical reports that were coming in from our deep-level stopes – you either had to get people back in the stopes, or we had to write off large parts of the mines.'[428]

The dismissals now began in earnest. Soon 50 000 workers had been dismissed. NUM was powerless, given the law and the balance of forces at the time, to stop this avalanche. Negotiations began, and with the strike less than a month old, on 30 August it was settled.

At the settlement meeting, NUM lowered its demand to 27%. This was rejected. The Chamber agreed only to an increase in the holiday leave allowance and an improvement in the death benefit scheme. Their already-implemented wage increases were all that they would accept. Workers were only to be re-employed on strict guidelines, and in fact more than 50 000 miners lost their jobs.

Marcel Golding, NUM's publicity officer, admitted that the NUM suffered an overall drop in membership from 270 000 to 210 000 over the strike. The balance of power was still in management's hands.

While these strikes, and many of the other 1987 strikes, appear to have given the workers limited gains, in truth it was early days for black trade unions and these unions were operating in an environment where the balance of power, employer vs employees, was totally different from what it is now.

What these strikes did, amongst many worker and societal gains, was to reinforce the reality that progress in a conflictual and divided society such as South Africa was (and still is) best achieved through negotiations between legitimate and mandated parties. The endless flow of strikes also intensified the belief that the status quo in South Africa was unsustainable and that meaningful change, involving legitimate and mandated parties negotiating amongst themselves, was now necessary - in fact, was overdue.

39

Stealthy negotiations with Mandela

T he year 1987 saw the return of a meeting cycle, Mandela with Kobie Coetsee, almost always at Coetsee's house. Senior prison officers were now driving Mandela around Cape Town, on 'orientation' sightseeing trips. Mandela's comforts were, by Robben Island standards, great. But negotiations? Initially nothing.

In late 1987 the government moved up a gear. Botha appointed a four-person 'working group' to liaise with Mandela on an ongoing basis. Chaired by Coetsee, the other three were General Willemse, the Commissioner of Prisons; Fanie van der Merwe, later to be Director General of Constitutional Development; and, controversially, Dr Niël Barnard, the head of the National Intelligence Service. Mandela initially balked at Barnard's inclusion, but later relented.

Mandela's first requests to this group were threefold: he wished to consult with his three friends 'on the third floor'; he wished to consult with Oliver Tambo; and he wished to draft a 'memorandum' to provide to the President, to underpin negotiations. The results of his requests were mixed: he could meet with the 'Penthouse Pals', but only one-by-one; he received a letter from Tambo wanting an explanation as to what was going on (he replied that he had only one objective – to get a meeting together, between the government and the ANC's National Executive Committee); and he began work on his memorandum.

He told his four Pollsmoor pals, individually, that he had begun talks with the government that might lead to negotiations. Sisulu and Kathrada were cautious – they would not stop him, but they 'hoped he knew what he was doing'. Mhlaba and Mlangeni were much more upbeat – they wished him well.[429]

From May 1988 onwards, Mandela met often with Botha's appointed working group. They returned again and again to four topics: the cessation of the armed struggle; the relationship of the ANC with the SACP; the nationalisation of industry and land; and majority rule. The government delegation continued to repeat that the ANC must renounce violence before negotiations could begin. The meetings always stalled on these issues.

In the winter of 1988 Mandela wrote that PW Botha had agreed to see him before the end of August.[430] Shortly after this note, he was visited by his attorney, Ismail Ayob. During the consultation Mandela collapsed and vomited. He was taken to Tygerberg Hospital where tuberculosis was diagnosed. He spent six weeks in Tygerberg, and the proposed meeting with Botha never happened.

After Tygerberg, he became the first black patient ever admitted to the Constantiaberg Clinic, to more fully recuperate. There Coetsee visited, and told Mandela that the government now wished to put him 'in a situation half-way between confinement and freedom'. On 10 December 1988 he was driven to Victor Verster Prison in Paarl, where a staff cottage in the prison grounds had been equipped to be his home. He was even assigned a personal chef, Warrant Officer Jack Swart. He was not told about the plethora of listening devices that had been installed, even in trees in the garden. Presumably however, the worldly-wise Mandela anticipated this. Again the charming Coetsee visited, this time bearing a case of Cape wine as a house-warming gift.[431]

And so 1988 edged to its end. Mandela's memorandum was in process, and there was now a formal structure to begin the talks-about-talks. It may not have seemed much, but it was to be the foundations on which the tumultuous events of 1989 and 1990 were later built. Mandela's bravery and perseverance in the face of obviously duplicitous behaviour by the government, and his willingness to move past his organisation's agreed positions, were remarkable. While his best was yet to happen, the seeds of his greatness were clearly evident in the vision for negotiations that he incubated in the cold and lonely cells of Pollsmoor Prison.

It was not just at Pollsmoor and Victor Verster that strange events were underway. Things were also happening at St Alban's Prison in Port Elizabeth.

At the beginning of the second state of emergency, St Alban's was overwhelmed by the numbers of detainees that had so suddenly arrived. As Khusta Jack has written, 'at the peak of the state of emergency, we were squashed into the cells like sardines into a can – often 100 detainees confined in a cell with a capacity of only 45'.[432] Food was execrable ('powdered egg' and bread), exercise was a privilege easily withdrawn, information from newspapers non-existent. Detention was unquestionably both an enforced isolation and a punishment.

Into this congested, comfortless world, the security police introduced a new nightmare – they told the comrades, loudly and repeatedly, that they were preparing a treason trial for the 'ringleaders', the UDF executive. The model for this had, of course, already been started in Delmas, where 'Terror' Lekota, Moss Chikane, Popo Molefe and 19 others had languished in cells since early 1985. The charge was treason and the evidence to support the charge was that the UDF was in fact the ANC in another set of clothes. In total, the 22 accused spent from mid-1985 until their successful appeal in December 1989, in jail, and only the appeal had allowed Lekota and his team to escape another 10 years of sentence. These sentences, the security police told the St Alban's comrades, would be 'corrected' in Port Elizabeth – they could expect life in prison.

Then came two unexpected visitors, from such unusual sources as to become the source of much speculation in the prison.

Firstly, Reverend Frank Chikane, a patron of the UDF, Moss Chikane's brother, and the Secretary General of the South African Council of Churches, arrived in early 1988.

Ostensibly his visit was to inspect the prison conditions endured by state of emergency detainees. While that made sense, the detainees were still nonplussed that one so publicly critical of the government could have been allowed to meet with them, and share confidential opinions 'from outside'. (It was less than two years later that the security police attempted to kill Chikane by impregnating his underclothes in a suitcase with a contact poison. Both the then Minister of Police and the Commissioner General were later convicted and sentenced to ten years in prison, suspended, for this attempted murder. The Minister, Adriaan Vlok, subsequently washed Chikane's feet as a symbol of his repentance, and has since lived a remarkable life as a penitent determined to atone for his deeds.)

Chikane met a select group of senior detainee leaders. Khusta Jack was one of them and he was astonished at the change in the behaviour of the prison staff when Chikane visited. Instead of the normal 'rude bullies who intervened [in visits from family], mouthing off regulations',[433] now he found 'warders and cops [who] appeared to have been told to be on their best behaviour and politeness was the order of the day. Those warders who were hard-core bigots who could not be reprogrammed to be civil appeared to have been given the day off.' The meeting was in a comfortable office with a table, chairs, coffee, cold drinks and biscuits.

'Chikane gave us messages of support from OR Tambo and the ANC in Lusaka, from Nelson Mandela and the Robben Island prisoners, and from the people of South Africa.'[434]

Chikane briefed them about the situation in South Africa. His analysis was that the confrontation of the previous years had now reached a stalemate. 'In essence he was saying that any further confrontation would not yield positive results for any of the parties concerned ... Pre-negotiation peace settlement talks had begun in earnest between the regime and the liberation movement, notably between Nelson Mandela and various state intermediaries.'[435]

That Chikane had this information at this stage is nothing short of astonishing. The 'negotiation team' that met with Mandela was sworn to secrecy, as was Mandela, and this secrecy in many respects held. FW de Klerk, then the Leader of the National Party in the Transvaal, and Minister Chris Heunis, the minister responsible for constitutional change, only found out about Mandela's manoeuvrings after PW Botha had a stroke and left the leadership of the National Party in January 1989. They knew nothing of these secrets in 1988.[436] And yet Chikane knew!

As did another man. This time it was a mysterious 'retired senior general', by the name of 'General Stevenson'.

Although no such 'general' is in the long list of retired SADF personnel, 'General Stevenson' visited St Alban's some months after Chikane's visit, was billed by the prison staff as a representative of the government and treated by them with much respect.

Shortly after the Chikane visit, detainees began to be released in ever increasing numbers. Releases were now in batches of 20 and 30, and, six months after Chikane's visit, only 'top leadership remained in the cells'. The food improved and newspapers, books and magazines became available.

There were about 20 detainees left when 'General' Stevenson arrived, and he met them individually. He spoke openly of the futility of further confrontation, and he recommended 'speaking around the table as the best way to solve the problems'.[437]

Jack later wrote: 'There was an echo between Chikane's political view and that of the general, namely that South Africa was at a stalemate. Chikane showed us, though not directly, that our structures on the ground were decimated, our people's morale was low, and a clean break to replenish our nation was necessary. The general, it appeared, was essentially saying that the white South African government could not remain in power through the barrel of a gun.

'The next logical thing to do was negotiate a settlement.'[438]

40

Johannesburg to Lusaka

Representatives of South African interest groups in all their many manifestations were also busy meeting Mandela's ANC, as difficult as this was given the fact that the ANC was banned and had no official representation in South Africa.

Michael Savage, who was both a professor of Sociology at the University of Cape Town and a participant in Van Zyl Slabbert's Dakar Initiative of 1987, has compiled a detailed list of such meetings, and has valiantly attempted also to list all the participants.[439] It makes for fascinating reading.

Savage lists 167 'external meetings', South Africans with the ANC, between 1983 and 1990. This involved, Savage writes, over 1 200 South African citizens.

Beginning with four meetings in 1983, three of which were church related, the numbers mount to 27 in 1986, 23 in 2987, 32 in 1988 and 39 in 1989.

News media and journalists are heavily represented, beginning with the irrepressible Max du Preez in January 1984, and continuing with editors and reporters from most South African media (save the SABC). Piet Muller (*Die Beeld*), Barry Streek (SA Independent group), Hugh Murray (*Leadership* magazine), Harald Pakendorf (*Die Vaderland*), Tertius Myburgh (*Sunday Times*), Tony Heard (*Cape Times*) and many others made the trip to Lusaka in these risky years.

Businessmen included Gavin Relly and Zach de Beer (Anglo American),

Tony Bloom (Premier Group), Lord Barber (Standard Bank), Chris Ball (Barclays Bank), and on and on, they all flooded through Lusaka Airport.

Politicians were not to be left behind. Shortly after being made Leader of the PFP, Van Zyl Slabbert took Colin Eglin, Alex Boraine and Peter Gastrow to Lusaka in October 1985. And Mangosuthu Buthelezi reminds us that he met with Oliver Tambo first in 1973 (whereafter his passport was withdrawn), and took a full delegation from the Inkatha yeNkululeko yeSizwe to meet Tambo and his colleagues for nearly three days in 1979. In fact, he writes that Inkatha was founded with Tambo's approval in 1975.[440]

Slabbert, and his academic friend Prof. HW van der Merwe of the University of Cape Town, brokered many meetings. Van der Merwe is credited with the first contact, in August 1984, when he travelled to Lusaka uninvited, and met with Alfred Nzo and Thabo Mbeki.[441]

COSATU, the UDF and many of their affiliated organisations were regular visitors as were church, university and student bodies. Even Prof. Pieter de Lange, then Chairman of the Broederbond and Rector of the Rand Afrikaanse Universiteit, went north.

Another initiative came from a large South African business with a strong British pedigree, Consolidated Gold Fields. Some Gold Fields executives met with Oliver Tambo in June 1986 and asked Tambo what they could do. He suggested that they 'help build a bridge between the ANC and those Afrikaners close to government',[442] and thus was born the 'Mells Park' meetings in the UK. The Stellenbosch academics Willie Esterhuyse and Sampie Terreblanche were the original 'Afrikaners close to the government', and the meetings soon involved regular feedback to the National Intelligence Service (NIS), something Thabo Mbeki, a regular ANC attendee, was kept aware of. This was probably the initiative that led to the meeting between NIS and the ANC in Lucerne in Switzerland in September 1989.[443]

The most well-known of them all was, of course, the IDASA-organised meeting of 47 South Africans (and four 'Honorary Citizens from Outside', Germans who sympathised with the struggle to end apartheid) with a large delegation of ANC top brass in Dakar and Gorée Island in West Africa over a number of days in July 1987.[444]

This conference, commonly known as the Dakar Initiative, was, in the opinion of Slabbert, wide-ranging in both topics and time; 'there never before has been such as extensive exchange of views between South Africans and the ANC'.[445]

After the talks the two delegations issued a joint communiqué which supported a negotiated settlement for South Africa. This included a call for the release of all political prisoners and the lifting of the ban on the ANC and other organisations. The group 'accepted the historical reality of the armed struggle, and, although not all could support it, everyone was deeply concerned over the proliferation of uncontrolled violence ... however, all parties recognised that the source of violence in South Africa derives from the fact that the use of violence is fundamental to the existence and practice of racial domination.'[446]

Did these meetings serve any meaningful purpose?

Slabbert notes: 'the theme that dominated most discussions was: violence vs. peaceful change; revolution vs. negotiation'.[447] Endlessly this topic was ventilated. The delegates from South Africa were predominantly white South Africans, who mostly felt that the 'armed struggle' was counterproductive, cost the ANC more supporters than it gained them and made it impossible for them (whites) to promote the ANC's image as reasonable people with whom one could deal. On the other side, the ANC stated that there was no other option left available with all channels of peaceful change having been exhausted to no avail, and that this action was, in fact, very popular in black communities living under apartheid's jackboot.

Round and round this argument circled, with few changing their position, but never the ANC. As discussions continued, the philosophy increasingly took hold that negotiations like those then underway were more likely to yield a peaceful and acceptable outcome than were the other options. And the people from the ANC were plainly honest participants in these negotiations.

The other result of these meeting was a definite 'upgrading' of the ANC's image with the visiting communities. The old, hoary 'Communist terrorists determined to drive the South African white community into the sea in order to create a Godless, communist world' just did not fit with the people the ANC so carefully presented as its representatives.

Inch by inch, these meetings propelled 'internal' South Africans towards realising that the ANC was black South Africans' 'party of choice'; that the ANC could be negotiated with, that such negotiations could yield a democratic outcome; and that such negotiations were inevitable and, indeed, desirable.

41

The white community
trundles out to vote

I n 1987 the previous whites-only general election was a distant
memory.[448] Held in 1981, it had seen the National Party (NP) win 142
seats in a House of 177 seats. The Progressive Federal Party (PFP) had had
its moment of glory, and returned with 27 seats and the mantle of the Official
Opposition. Only one other party survived with seats: Natal's New Republic
Party (NRP), the straggling survivors of Smuts' once governing United Party,
had eight seats.

The parliamentary system of the time saw parliamentarians elected
individually, to represent individual constituencies. As such, it was legal for
a member of the House to change parties between elections. The party he or
she had been elected as a member of could do nothing to unseat him or her
until the next election.

PW Botha had, of course, in the meantime introduced the tricameral
Parliament. While this had proved to be inadequate to satisfy the political
aspirations of the black community who wanted an equal franchise but got
nothing of the sort, it had proved too much for many of Botha's National
Party members of the House. In 1982, 23 National Party MPs defected to
found the Conservative Party.

The issues on which the 1987 election were fought were threefold: the
racial issue and the future accommodation of black South Africans into South
African formal politics; the security issue, in the midst of a state of emergency;

and the much-resented international campaigns against apartheid, which were of course presented as orchestrated attempts to bully white South Africans.

PW Botha played these up with his usual skill – only the NP could be trusted to handle a set of problems of this size and nature, was the message the NP trumpeted endlessly.

Slogans from the campaign gave clues as to the issues of the time:

- Reform Yes – Surrender No (NP).
- Self-determination Yes – Power-sharing No (CP).
- Rhodesia reformed and surrendered (CP).
- Security through racial harmony (PFP).[449]

For the first time in a long time, this election saw three independent candidates stand, Wynand Malan in Randburg, Dr Denis Worrall in Helderberg (against Chris Heunis, the Minister of Constitutional Development) and Mrs Ester Lategan in Stellenbosch. All were NP 'retirees', seen to be on the left of the NP and close to the PFP. A deal was done by the PFP and the independents that the PFP would not put up candidates to split the liberal vote.

Likewise in Natal, the PFP did not challenge the remnants of the New Republic Party, and eight of the NRP's candidates had no PFP competition.

Election day came, and 67.8% of South Africa's 3 031 414 voters voted. The NP won 52.7% of these voters (1 075 505) and the CP 27% (547 559). The PFP's gamble of not contesting 11 seats failed – the NRP won only one of the eight seats it contested, donating the rest to the NP. Of the independents, only Wynand Malan won.

The score at the end of the day: NP 123 seats; CP 22; PFP 19; NRP one and independents one.

The PFP were no longer the Official Opposition, the Conservative Party was.

The Anglican Archbishop of Cape Town, Desmond Tutu, who had called for the PFP to withdraw from parliament, called these results 'a return to the dark ages'. Chief Buthelezi called them 'the devil's hour of glory'. The UDF said that the election offered 'no solution to the political crisis ... conflict will continue'. Murphy Morobe, standing in as UDF publicity secretary, said that the clear shift to the right of the white electorate was due to 'outrageous and false NP "swart gevaar" propaganda ... as the election heat and dust settles, white South Africans who voted for continued white minority rule will find the crisis and conflict has intensified, and there will be less comfort for all to take home'.[450]

Many commentators said that the CP would become government at the next election.[451]

42

At last, Govan Mbeki is released

ocuments in the Kobie Coetsee archive show that the State
Security Council (SSC) had, as early as 1984, recommended
the release of 'Category 1' security prisoners – those serving life
sentences who were over 65 years of age and who had served 20 years of
their sentences. In fact the SSC had taken the decision to release these
prisoners by Christmas 1984.[452]

It did not happen, and we can only assume that the quickening revolt of
late 1984 caused a rethink.

In fact it took a full three years from then for the men of apartheid to get
their courage up, and on 6 November 1987 the bespectacled, 77-year-old
ANC elder statesman found himself, in a natty suit, standing at a podium
at the Port Elizabeth Holiday Inn, fielding questions from an obviously
excited press corps. Also startled to be free again (but not in Port Elizabeth)
were Messrs Jacob Viljoen and Hendrik Jacobs, members of the Afrikaner
Weerstandsbeweging who had been jailed for 15 years each for terrorism;
Messrs Mike Matsobane and John Nkosi of the Pan Africanist Congress;
and Messrs Walter Tshikila and Thomas Masuku, also of the ANC. All were
freed to dampen the effect of Mbeki's release.

Mbeki immediately made it clear that all those years in jail had not dimmed
his views: 'I am still a Communist Party member, and I still embrace Marxist
views.' He would continue to 'support Umkhonto as long as the ANC deems
it necessary'. He said that solutions without the ANC were not possible, and

encouraged the youth in the townships to 'continue with the struggle'.[453]

If the powers that be in those days thought that Mbeki was to head off to a quiet retirement, they rapidly found that they had misread the Port Elizabeth townships.

Later that month the Dan Qeqe Stadium was booked for his first public rally. Immediately the security establishment commissioned two reports: firstly a 'report on the Planned Gathering with Mr G Mbeki in Port Elizabeth'; and secondly a 'Security Branch Proposal by Hermanus Barend du Plessis for a mass gathering with Mr Mbeki'.[454] These reports told a frightening story.

The meeting was banned under the emergency regulations. The recently appointed Minister of Law and Order, Mr Adriaan Vlok, said that the government had hoped that Mr Mbeki would 'retire quietly', 'but this is not what happened. He is being misused by people around him for political purposes.' The Commissioner of Police then placed an order on Mbeki which prohibited him from taking part in any interview with the media, and confined him to the Port Elizabeth magisterial district. Further, he was prohibited from in any way contributing to 'any material for publication'. All public rallies, either to be addressed by him or to protest his banning, were banned.[455] Later he was also refused a passport, requested so that he could visit his three children in exile.[456]

All of this did not stop him from enjoying the companionship of many of his lifelong friends at the Human Rights Trust's 'Human Rights in South Africa' conference at the East Cape Training Centre in Port Elizabeth in late November 1988. He discreetly set up camp in the projection room behind a thin sheet of glass from the main action, and enjoyed his friends a few at a time!

If the release of his Rivonia comrades was in the planning, it was now put off.

43

Apartheid loses its second war

South Africa 'administered' (ruled) South West Africa in terms of a historic mandate that had come into effect at the end of the First World War, when South West Africa's then German overlords had been pushed out by South Africa's troops. This mandate was fiercely contested and was overturned by a decision of the United Nations. It did not help. South Africa continued its control uninterrupted, and had no intention of surrendering a territory that now had six seats in the South African parliament, all of which voted National Party.

As we have noted, the Namibian War of Independence began in 1962 when Sam Nujoma instructed two men in a SWAPO refugee camp in Zambia to return to South West Africa as SWAPO's first two insurgents.

Incursions began to grow, and on 26 August 1966 the South African Defence Force (SADF) sent Buccaneer and Canberra bombers and paratroopers into Angola to attack and slaughter the inhabitants of a SWAPO base at Omugulugwombashe. This 'operation' is now described as the first battle of the Namibian War of Independence.

Three weeks later, on 6 September 1966, the South African Prime Minister, Dr Hendrik Verwoerd, was assassinated in South Africa's parliament in Cape Town. BJ Vorster was elected to be Verwoerd's successor, and Vorster immediately appointed PW Botha as his Minister of Defence. Botha held this portfolio from 1966 until 1980, when he handed it over to his hand-picked successor, General Magnus Malan, who was at the time the head of the SADF. Malan was Minister of Defence until 1991. Thus these two men controlled South Africa's war machine for the entire period of the Namibian insurrection, the Angolan Bush War, the destabilisation of Mozambique and South Africa's 10-year civil war of the 1980s.

If there is anything commendable in the use of science, technology and lots of money in the creation of new, better and more efficient weapons with which to kill people with whom one differs, Botha and Malan should receive spadesful of commendations. For they created an institution named the Armaments Development and Production Corporation of South Africa, ARMSCOR, and built it into a massive conglomerate of companies, eventually employing 20 000 staff and using about a thousand sub-contractors and thousands of scientists and engineers, until it was the eighth-largest arms exporter in the world, and the biggest purveyor of traumatic death in the southern hemisphere. And all this in the face of a United Nations arms embargo on South Africa, which made illegal (but certainly did not stop) the transfer of new weapon technologies to ARMSCOR.

The most dramatic of the weapons development programmes began in the Atomic Energy Commission, where early work on nuclear energy was converted into a plan to develop a nuclear weapon, and a test site for it, in 1974. The site chosen was a desolate 700 km² semi-desert area near Upington, where between 1976 and 1977 two test wells were dug, for underground testing of a nuclear weapon.

However, a Soviet spy satellite, COSMOS 922, detected these wells on 21 to 25 July 1977 and the Soviet government relayed this fact to the United States. The US officials then organised an overflight by a Lockheed SR 71 spy plane and the existence of the test wells was confirmed.

What happened next remains unknown, but the USA–South Africa negotiations must have been brutal. The test site was quickly decommissioned. Further development of nuclear weapons did, however, continue, but in absolute secrecy at Pelindaba.

A first bomb was completed in 1982. However, because South Africa's aging Buccaneer and Canberra bombers were now obsolete and unable to convey and deliver such a weapon, work went on to develop a rocket delivery system. By 1987 seven nuclear bombs were complete.

There was more. Under the direction of Major-General NJ Nieuwoudt, a prominent cardiologist, Dr Wouter Basson, was employed to develop a range of chemical weapons. These included bacteria such as anthrax, cholera and tetanus, a range of toxins for inclusion in food and drink, and contact poisons for impregnating clothing.

As frightening as these 'exotics' are, nobody was killed by South Africa's nuclear bombs and only a few by its biological weapons. The real killers were the hundreds of thousands of battleground weapons, guns and bombs made by the various ARMSCOR factories.

Huge resources were devoted to weapons systems that were tailored for use in the Angolan bush.

Mobility in bush circumstances was provided by six-wheeled armoured vehicles called 'Ratels', which were fast, stable and capable off-road. Nearly 1 500 were built to a variety of specifications from communication centre interiors to Ratels that could fire armour-piercing rockets to destroy tanks.

'Casspir' mine-proof troop-carriers, which could quickly transport 12 infantrymen, were made and used. Old World War II British Centurion tanks were refitted with new guns, with laser guidance systems provided by the Israelis, and armour that could hold off contemporary anti-tank shells.

In the early years of the Angolan War, the South African airforce had the skies to themselves. Buccaneer bombers from the 1960s and Canberras from the mid-1950s could rain down death and destruction in uncontested horror. Mirage F-1CZs, delivered from the French manufacturer Dassault in 1975 and repeatedly re-jigged to up their speed and their invisibility, were the speed-kings of the skies, reaching 2 335 km per hour. They attacked with impunity.

After Operation Askari in 1983, this all changed.

Neither the Russians nor the Cubans, the military advisers to FAPLA, were consulted in the drafting of the Lusaka Accord and both rejected the wording and the spirit of these 'peace treaties' vehemently. They immediately increased their military aid to FAPLA. The Russians committed billions of dollars of military hardware – eventually as much as six billion in total - including dozens of the latest MIG-23 fighter bombers, much faster and more manoeuvrable than the re-jigged Mirages, and many T-55 and T-62 battle tanks, amongst much else. The Cubans brought in troops by the thousand, and readied them for action. By 1987 there were 37 000 Cuban troops in Angola. Angolans were trained in all these new technologies, including as MIG-23 pilots. Things were changing.

There was, however, another new development that came out of ARMSCOR.

In the first invasion of Angola, Operation Savannah, it became obvious that the South African artillery, which was then World War II G-2 guns with a range of about 16 km, were outgunned by FAPLA's Russian BM-21s. A new gun needed to be developed, and quickly.

South African agents made contact with a maverick Canadian, Dr Gerald Bull. Bull was a remarkably talented weapons engineer, who ran his own company that designed and organised the manufacture of weapons Bull had created.

Bull had designed the GC-45 howitzer, which could routinely place shells accurately enough to land in a 10-metre diameter target 30 km away from the gun. With a Swedish modification to the shell, this could be extended to a 40 km distance from gun to where the shell landed, with this remarkable accuracy.

The South Africans were enthralled. Bull managed to acquire and deliver to ARMSCOR 30 000 155mm artillery shells, each weighing about 45 kg, and 30 gun barrels and plans for the GC-45, and also its necessary radar equipment. The shipments were laundered through Antigua and Spain.

As clever as Bull was, the Americans caught him (he was plainly busting sanctions) and he spent six months in an American jail for this effort. This turned out to be small beer. A later project of his was the building of a super-gun for Iraq's Saddam Hussein, which to the Israelis appeared capable of delivering a nuclear weapon into Israel. As the project started, Bull was assassinated by a three-man hit squad outside his Belgian home. Both the Israeli government and Mossad entirely denied culpability, of course. And nobody was ever arrested.

But ARMSCOR now had what they needed to build a top-range artillery piece, which they quickly did, and affixed it to a wheeled trailer. This was then towed by a gun tractor, and, with 10 additional vehicles to carry shells and victuals for the six-man crew, this combination was called the G-5 and instantly became the principal deliverer of death and mayhem in the South African arsenal. Russian SAM 8 anti-aircraft systems had made it impossible for the SAAF to use their aging Buccaneers and Canberras and the new MIG-23s had reduced the Mirage fleet to quick in-out raids in marginal light (early morning and late evening) – anything else had become suicide. The G-5 filled the gap. Now devastation could be delivered from 40 km off, by guns kept under camouflage in day time, and used ruthlessly at night, to hit targets with a precision a bomb from an aircraft could never match.

Then more weaponry came from another source.

Ronald Reagan had been President of the United States for six years in 1986, and he could now muster the support to repeal the Clark Amendment, thereby opening the opportunity for more CIA aid to UNITA. In that year UNITA's Jonas Savimbi went on a charm offensive in Washington and returned to the Angolan bush with FIM-92 Stinger hand-held ground-to-air anti-aircraft missiles and BGM-71 TOW anti-tank missiles, two world-beating light and easy-to-use weapon systems.

From now on, the FAPLA MIG-23s had to keep to very high altitudes to avoid the Stingers. This made close surveillance of the ground impossible and saved the G-5s from being discovered.

In early 1987 the South African military became aware of the build-up of a massive FAPLA troop strength in southern Angola. Information arrived that the Soviets, who were in a chaotic transition at home, were running out of aid money, and wanted to crush UNITA now, once and for all.

The Soviets had put together Operation Saluting October, which proposed that a number of FAPLA brigades should push out from Cuito Cuanavale to first take Mavinga, and thereafter Jamba, Savimbi's headquarters in the south-eastern Angolan bush. The operation was conceived by, and directed by, a recently arrived Soviet general, variously called Gusev or Shaganovitch.[457]

The plan was conceptualised without any expectation of South African involvement in UNITA's defence. Gusev made no plans to counter any possible SADF arrival into battle.

Castro was completely unconvinced by this plan and instructed his troops to stay out of the fighting. This was a Russian folly and he would have none of it. He later wrote: 'The Soviet advisors thought they were waging the Battle of Berlin, with Marshall Zhukov in command, thousands of tanks and 40 000 cannons. They did not understand, nor could they understand, the problems of the Third World, the setting of the struggle and the type of war that must be waged in that setting.'[458] He was precisely right.

To get from the safety of Cuito Cuanavale to their first objective, the taking of Mavinga, the FAPLA forces had to ford three rivers. This was challenge enough, but worse was that the fording points on these rivers were surrounded by vast stretches of flat, water-logged floodplains, through which the progress of a large number of troops would be intermittent, with delays expected to be frequent. If their movements were anticipated, and their enemy prepared, they could be cannon fodder in these highly exposed areas.

The SADF relied heavily on small reconnaissance teams, called Recces, which were mostly about five soldiers, often in FAPLA uniforms (never in SADF uniforms), who went deep into uncontrolled territory and sent back, by highly sophisticated radio systems, information about FAPLA troop movements, weaponry and other useful information to guide G-5 shells, or simply to alert the SADF of developments. The majority of these recces were Angolan troops, mostly from UNITA ranks, and their courage was beyond comprehension as they sneaked up on enemy columns and weapon positions.

In March 1987 recce groups reported on FAPLA troop movements. By August, eight FAPLA brigades were pushing east from Cuito Cuanavale towards UNITA-held Mavinga. PW Botha was informed and he immediately ordered South African involvement. He believed that should Mavinga fall, then Jamba, SWAPO/PLAN would be unstoppable in northern Namibia. He nevertheless instructed that SADF involvement be concealed, with credit for victories to go to UNITA.[459]

On 5 August the first South African troops entered Rundu and a battery of G-5s was also sent in. South Africa eventually committed their best 'bush-ready' troops – 32 Battalion, the South West African Territory Force's 101 Battalion, and the 61 Mechanised Battalion.

Things were starting to hot up.

A SAAF Bosbok spotter plane was destroyed by a SAM -8 missile, killing the crew. The slow and lumbering Canberras were immediately withdrawn and Mirages used only at first light on low-level bombing raids.

As the FAPLA troops started moving east, they crossed the first two rivers with little resistance.

On 4 September 1987 Colonel Deon Ferreira was brought in to coordinate 20 Brigade in what was now called Operation Modular, and they decided to stop FAPLA's 47 Brigade at the third river, the Lomba River crossing. The FAPLA 47 Brigade then made a fatal mistake – on Russian instructions, they paused just short of the Lomba River in order to take in more troops and supplies. By now the South Africans had arrived and were prepared for them as they entered the Lomba River floodplain.

G-5 bombardments became routine at night, as were dawn bombing raids from the SAAF Mirages. In mid-September the first battles of the Cuito Cuanavale campaign were fought. FAPLA's 22 Russian tanks outgunned the SADF's Ratels,[460] and a dogfight between an SAAF Mirage piloted by Captain Arthur Piercey and a MIG-23 saw Piercey's Mirage damaged, and crash on landing and Piercey's injuries saw him later become a quadriplegic. No further contact between Mirage and MIG was allowed thereafter.[461]

In the first week of September the crack South African brigade, 61 Mechanical, was committed to Angola, and by 7 September they were 25 km south-east of Mavinga. By now the ceaseless G-5 bombardment of the FAPLA 47 Brigade, which had been tasked to establish the bridgehead over the Lomba River, had reduced it from about 1 400 men to about 900 still combat fit.[462]

On 28 September PW Botha, Magnus Malan, Willie Breytenbach and a group of generals flew into Mavinga in a state of panic. They committed another battery of G-5s to the battle, another eight guns, and Operation Modular continued to a final battle at the Lomba River floodplain on 3 October.

It was a massacre. Trapped in the open, FAPLA's infantry was mown down. Those captured proved to be very young and badly equipped, some even lacking boots. Under the intensity of the fire of 3 October, they fled, leaving millions of dollars of Soviet equipment on the battlefield. Much of this was recovered by the South Africans, including an entire battery of SAM-8 anti-aircraft missiles, the first such battery ever to fall into hostile hands.

Mac da Trinidada, a black UNITA recce who did extraordinary work in the bush over the length of the war, remarked: 'I had never seen so many troops as on that day, 3 October. There were hundreds of them running. You could see that some of them were wounded. I really felt sorry for those guys. They had no real chance. We bombed the shit out of them. They were mown down like swathes of grass.'[463]

The FAPLA positions had not been protected by any minefields, and approximately 1 000 of 47 Brigade's 1 400 soldiers were now dead. SADF casualties were minimal.

Angola's President Dos Santos summoned the Russian General Gusev and the head of the Cuban forces, Ramirez, and demanded an explanation. Why had Operation Saluting October failed?

Ramirez replied that they had always known that it would fail and had refused to commit to this folly. Gusev later wrote that it was his 'most difficult task, in moral terms, to inform the President of Angola, whom I had assured that the operation would succeed and that Savimbi would be crushed [of the failure of Operation Saluting October]'.[464]

When the massacre of 3 October was over, Operation Modular was seen to be complete. Now followed a pause in the flow of instructions from the South African politicians to the soldiers in Angola. When the instructions recommenced they were brutally uncompromising: 'clear all enemy forces from the eastern side of the Cuito River ... inflict maximum casualties so that no fresh FAPLA offensive can be launched in 1987 or 1988 – all of this before 15 December'.[465]

Fortunately Colonel Ferreira was not in a position to implement these brutal instructions immediately. General Liebenberg had promised all troops whose two-year national service ended in December that they would be home by Christmas and the new intake was not yet in Angola. Another reason was set out by Commander Jan Hougaard: 'Our troops on the ground were totally buggered. They couldn't give chase. They needed sleep and replenishment. A big effort was made to bring in fresh meat and vegetables, together with cold drinks and beer.'[466]

This enabled the remnants of FAPLA's 47 Brigade to cross the Lomba westwards, to join up with the other FAPLA brigades. Together they retreated to an area between the Cuito, Tumpo and Dala rivers, an area soon to be known as the Tumpo Triangle. Here they were to dig in defensive positions.

On 15 November President dos Santos wrote to Fidel Castro requesting full Cuban commitment in the battles from here on. Castro agreed, but on the condition that all the troops would be under Cuban command, under Cuban General Arnaldo Ochoa Sanchez. The Soviet team would be relegated to the role of advisers. Dos Santos readily agreed.

Castro provided a two-pronged approach. He believed that the only way to defeat South Africa was to open up a second front. He now proposed a flanking manoeuvre, with a significant Cuban force heading south-west, to occupy the uncontested territory in the west of Angola, down to the Namibian border. From here he could threaten an invasion of Namibia.

This he set in motion on 9 March, when he sent a vast force of about 30 000 troops from Lobito south. He described the manoeuvre as like a 'boxer, who with his left hand blocks the blow (at Cuito Cuanavale) and with his right hand then strikes (in the south-west)'.

'This way', he said, 'while the South Africans are being slowly bled dry in Cuito Cuanavale, in the south west 40 000 Cuban soldiers, backed by 600 tanks, hundreds of artillery pieces, 1 000 anti-aircraft weapons and using Mig-23 units that have taken over the skies, advanced towards the Namibian border, ready to sweep away the South African forces.'[467]

At Cuito Cuanavale he proposed an entirely different strategy.

Here he put in 3 000 Cuban troops, and set up three defensive lines. The furthest from the front was his Cuban 13th Brigade, who were settled in on the west bank of the Cuito river, north and south of Cuito Cuanavale itself. Castro was sure that the South Africans would eventually attack Cuito Caunavale, to either take over, or destroy, its airfield. So he positioned his artillery, 60 big guns and the BM-21 Stalin Organs (multiple rocket launchers), also on the west bank, where the ground was elevated, giving better visibility for the gunners. The Cubans spread the guns all round, in small groups, giving the gunners multiple lines of fire.

Just over the Cuito river, to the east, protected by the Dala river in the north and the Tumpo in the south, he stationed his crack 16th and 68th Brigades, with his 360 tank battalion to the south. They were occupying the soon-to-be famous Tumpo Triangle.

Just to the east of this he set up two defensive lines manned by FAPLA troops. All of this the Cubans ringed with extensive minefields, and dug tanks and guns into stationary positions to cover any bottlenecks the South Africans might try to come through. The minefields were latticed with trench lines. They were set out to Soviet military protocols, the intention being not so much to attack vehicles as to channel them into predetermined kill-zones, which were covered by artillery and anti-tank weapons.[468]

On 19 February four Mirages took off from Grootfontein Air Base on a bombing run. It was a disaster. Major Ed Every, in the rear Mirage, was shot from the air and died. This was the first Mirage, after Captain Piercey, to be destroyed.

Three attacks were made on the Tumpo Triangle. Together they were named Operation Hooper and Operation Packer, although they were continuous.

The first attack was by 61 Mechanical Division led by Commander Mike Muller, and included 20 Olifant tanks. They went in on 25 February 1988.

It was hell. An SADF observer counted 1 350 'accurate' artillery shots on Muller's combat group. The minefields were impenetrable, and any mine that exploded gave the FAPLA gunners coordinates to aim at. 'They certainly hammered us that day. Seven of our vehicles were knocked out, and two burned out completely,' said Muller.[469]

Eventually Muller gave the command to withdraw. They would return another day, for a second attack on the FAPLA and Cuban forces in the Tumpo Triangle.

That day was 29 February, and again the leadership was passed to Mike Muller. This time they were to take a northern attack line, and now they were down to 16 tanks.

The result was no different. The tanks had been unserviced for too long, and five had broken down before a shot was fired. And the minefields were equally impassable. They got bogged down, and all the Olifants save five broke down. Similar problems were being reported from the G-5 artillery battalion.[470]

Muller again broke off the engagement.

The third attack followed nearly a month later, on 23 March 1988. This time it was led by Commandant Gerhard Louw, who was the instructor of the tank and armoured car section at the South African Army Battle School in the northern Cape. He was flown in to Rundu at the end of February, in time to see 61 Mechanical and 4 SAI limp past on their way 'home' with their battle-scarred tanks.

Louw was expecting the Regiment President Steyn to arrive with a full regiment of Olifant tanks. In reality he received 11 fewer, or about half of what he expected.[471]

He was to launch in the early morning of 23 March 1988, with instructions to drive FAPLA and the Cubans out of the Tumpo Triangle, and to hold it for long enough for the SADF engineers and others to blow up, comprehensively, the bridge over the Cuito River which was the only surviving route for FAPLA to send troops and weapons from Cuito Cuanavale to attack Mavinga. If this was accomplished, Mavinga and Jamba would be safe for the immediate future.

Just prior to the invasion, the SAAF lost another Mirage, that of Major Willie van Coppenhagen, on his way back to Grootfontein from a bombing run.

The bad fortune did not stop there.

Louw's tanks were in two columns, and he had expected two 'mine rollers' (tanks with an attachment on the front to detonate mines) to lead the way. Only one arrived. He then used two experimental anti-mine mechanisms made by ARMSCOR and called 'plofadders'. These were rockets that were shot over a minefield, to drag a sausage of high explosives behind them. They would automatically explode, thereby detonating mines underneath the 'plofadder' explosion. That was the theory. In reality they did not explode and had to be manually detonated, a very risky exercise.

Quickly three tanks were badly damaged and the columns got bogged down in the minefields under withering artillery fire.

'It was now about 2 pm. The artillery barrage had not let up at all, and with the unexpected exertions the tanks had been guzzling fuel faster than expected. I asked for permission to break off the attack, and Colonel Fouche granted it,' said Commander Louw. They left three Olifant tanks, disabled, on the battlefield.[472]

The Battle of Cuito Cuanavale was over. On 30 April Colonel Fouche departed, and Operation Packer formally ended. The biggest formal battles on the African continent since the Second World War had ended.

Fred Bridgland is a meticulous British journalist who has written much on these battles. Of course it was easier for him to interview South African sources, and this he has done extensively. There is sympathy in his writing for his South African military sources, and yet he is driven to conclude: 'Tumpo Three was the only clear defeat the South Africans suffered in the battles around Cuito Cuanavale. The assault had achieved nothing for the South Africans. Many UNITA soldiers had been killed and wounded. Five Olifants were damaged, and only two of those had been recovered … The capture of the Olifants was a major propaganda and intelligence coup for FAPLA and the Cubans. It enabled them to offer solid evidence for the version of history they were giving to the world – that they were winning the war.'[473]

While the South African troops had been stuck in the minefields of Cuito Cuanavale, just as Fidel Castro had predicted, Castro's second front, the flanking manoeuvre in the west down to the South West African border, had begun. On 9 March 1988 he sent his thousands from Lobito south, much to the consternation of the SADF generals.

At the request of President dos Santos, Castro had replaced a number of his rookie troops in Angola with his top-flight brigades from home. By 23 March, while the third Tumpo Triangle battle was being fought, his forces in the south-west of Angola were upgrading the airfields at Cahama (125 km from the Namibian border) and Xangongo (65 km north of the border). Xangongo airport could soon take both heavy transport planes and MIG-23s. As South Africa's Commandant Jan Hougaard said, 'These were exactly the essential kind of things they needed to do to reactivate the military region and to open up a western front.'[474]

Hougaard was then entrusted with the leadership of the South African forces that were to confront this Cuban onslaught. He immediately sent recce units into the area around the town of Techipa, where it was rumoured that SWAPO had their regional headquarters. He found that the Cubans were now much further south than had been expected. By June 1988 it was estimated that there were 11 000 Cuban troops, who had integrated 2 000 SWAPO guerrillas into their divisions, with possibly 100 tanks and highly sophisticated anti-aircraft systems. Many of these troops were now within 12 km of the border.

Hougaard was ordered to attack Techipa, which by now was seen as the Cuban HQ. He declined. He only had 500 men, which could at best conduct hit-and-run blocking tactics while a larger force was assembled. Mechanical was then readied to join him; their troops had been given a break after Cuito Cuanavale, and some of their tanks had been repaired. Between these battalions, Hougaard said, they could at best slow the Cuban offensive, but could certainly not push it back.

At this stage Castro made an ambiguous statement that could be interpreted as saying that his troops could soon be entering South West Africa. The South African forces replied, threatening a harsh response should this be attempted. Castro responded: 'You are in no position to demand anything.'[475]

At this stage two things happened that showed clearly that the South African military was panicking.

Firstly, General Jannie Geldenhuys on 8 June announced a general mobilisation of all 140 000 South African citizen force reservists, a completely unprecedented announcement. (What he would have got them to do is anyone's guess. His airforce had been grounded by the Russian air-defence systems; the navy was in no way involved in this war; most of his tanks and G-5 artillery pieces were being serviced or, in the case of the tanks, had been immobilised or had been destroyed; ARMSCOR had built only 1 600 Ratels, many no longer in use – they could only have been given a rifle, and sent out as artillery, to be mown down by the armada of Soviet tanks that was building up.)

The second sign of panic was even more dramatic: South Africa in 1988 reopened one of the two test shafts at Vastrap nuclear test site near Upington. Whether this was a genuine attempt at a test, or was just an attempt at improving South Africa's position in the now ongoing negotiations to end the war, we will probably never know. But to test a nuclear weapon when your airforce had neither planes capable of delivering it, nor rocketry to do this, is surely not a sign of imminent battlefield victory.[476]

In Angola the war continued. 61 Mechanical moved their only remaining Olifant tanks, 11 of them, across the Kunene along with a battery of G-5s, two companies of Ratels, eight anti-tank Ratel 90s, and some mortar and multiple rocket launcher units.

In late June the fighting recommenced. As usual, the battery of G-5s created havoc, but this time the Cubans kept coming forward. The Olifant tanks were sent in, but wave after wave of Russian tanks of a considerably more recent vintage pushed them back. The Ratels also had to fall back. Then, on 27 June 1988, when eight MIG-23s bombed and damaged the dam at Calueque, killing 11 South African troopers in the process, the game was up.

Fortunately, diplomatic endeavours now saved the day for the South Africans. Mike Muller got instructions on the 27 June that all troops were to be out of Angola by midnight. This he was greatly relieved to do, even though he had no idea why.

In the writing of Christopher Saunders that we have considered, it became clear that for the duration of South Africa's many incursions into Angola, a dual track of war and diplomacy between South Africa and Angola was being kept up, albeit tentatively. The stumbling block to a wider set of negotiating parties (South Africa, the United States, Angola, SWAPO, Russia and Cuba) negotiating on the full canvas of issues (independence for South West Africa and SWAPO's role thereafter; Russian and Cuban military involvement and the possible spill-over of borders of these armies; South Africa's withdrawal from both Angola and South West Africa) was always South Africa's unwillingness to sit down and talk meaningfully with the 'terrorist' SWAPO and the 'Communist' Cuba.

Possibly the biggest issue was the unwillingness of both Angola and Cuba to provide any assurances that Cuban troops would eventually leave Africa, a repeated South African demand.

In late January 1988, Angola and Cuba gave the United States assurances that Cuban troops were willing to go home, under negotiated conditions. This caused the United States' principal negotiator, Dr Chester Crocker, to accept Cuba as a negotiation partner, while making it clear that the United States would continue to support UNITA until the 'Cuban issue' was finally resolved.

In the same month the Prime Minister of Bavaria, Franz Josef Strauss, who had always maintained cordial relationships with the Russians, met with the Russian Foreign Minister, Edward Shevardnadze. He was given the assurance that the Soviets now wanted a political solution to the 'South West African problem'. This Strauss passed on to South Africa's Foreign Minister, Pik Botha.

In March 1988 Neil van Heerden, South Africa's Director General of Foreign Affairs, met Crocker and Pik got a letter of invitation to meet in London with the Angolans and the Cubans, with Crocker as facilitator. This was agreed. Preliminary talks appeared to elicit a broad understanding that, should Namibia become independent as per the United Nations Resolution 435, the Cubans would leave. This both Pik and Crocker felt was a breakthrough.

On 23 March 1988 the third Tumpo battle happened, and a week and a half later the London meeting sat. It stalled on the Cuban's insistence that they remain in Angola for four years. This South Africa was not willing to concede.

Things were moving fast.

In May 1988 American President Reagan and the General Secretary of the Soviet Communist Party, Michael Gorbachev, met in a summit in Moscow. They agreed that Namibian independence, coupled to the Cubans going home and also the South Africans getting out, and military aid to UNITA being ended, was possible, desirable and now necessary. Crocker had his mandate and a ceasefire was agreed in the Angolan war.

It was not to be a simple process. Between this summit and September six rounds of talks collapsed. It appears now that the Cubans and the Angolans were kicking for touch pending the US presidential election of early November – they hoped the Democrat Michael Dukakis would defeat the Republican George HW Bush, and that their hand would be strengthened.

It didn't happen as they had hoped and three days after the election results were out, with Bush declared President, the negotiations recommenced in Geneva. It was agreed that the Cubans would be out in 27 months and the process then rushed forward to a Tripartite Accord (South Africa, Angola and Cuba) which was signed in New York at the United Nations on 22 December 1988. Less than a year later Namibia held United Nations-supervised elections, and an independent Namibia joined the class of the world's independent nations on 21 March 1990. The ceremony was attended by the one-and-only Nelson Mandela, now a free man – but that is another story for later.

Period Five
1989

1989 was a pivotal year. The apartheid state, having just lost two wars – the first in the Port Elizabeth and Uitenhage townships, and the second in the Angolan bush – did the next obvious thing. They escalated their crudely orchestrated 'black-on-black' violence in Natal and the Transvaal into the largest bloodbath seen on South African soil since the 1899-1902 Anglo-Boer War, in a desperate bid to destabilise the UDF/ANC, for the inconceivable goal of somehow retaining white control of the rapidly approaching 'New South Africa'. Both sides, the apartheid state and the UDF/ANC grouping, were frantically competing to gain control of the approaching negotiation process.

44

Informal negotiations continue

Was it the Nkomati Accord, or was it Fidel Castro's advice?

As we have seen, on 16 March 1984 Samora Machel and PW Botha signed the Nkomati Accord in the Transvaal, near the Mozambique border. This 'agreement' (we use inverted commas, for plainly the South African negotiators had no intention of sticking to what they were signing) saw South Africa pretend to stop support for RENAMO, the price for which was Mozambique's very real expulsion of the ANC from Mozambican soil.

This was a devastating blow for the ANC. Not only did it lose the access to South Africa that MK clearly enjoyed from Mozambique's proximity to the political and economic engines of Pretoria and Johannesburg, but they were reminded most tangibly of the issues that ended the Rhodesian war. The Lancaster House negotiations that ended 'Rhodesia' and began the transition to Zimbabwe were not willingly attended by Robert Mugabe's ZANU. Mugabe had smelt blood and believed that victory over the exhausted Smith regime was inevitable. He had no desire to negotiate a compromise agreement to end a war he believed was almost won. He saw no need for compromises.

Mugabe and ZANU were dragged to Lancaster House kicking and screaming, not by Smith's Selous Scouts, who were almost finished by then; nor were they dragged there by the might of the British empire, nor even the power of the endlessly dishonest South Africans. No, Mugabe ended up at Lancaster House because the Frontline States, his backers, friends and comrades, said that they could no longer afford to support ZANU and he had to now negotiate the best deal he could get to end the years of 'Rhodesia'. Otherwise he would have to conduct his war from whatever other soil he could find to do so. The Frontline States, he was told, had massive and intractable problems of their own. ZANU and ZAPU were on their own.

The same could happen to the ANC, the Nkomati Accord shouted at OR Tambo. And he heard it.

Then there was Fidel Castro.

In 1986 OR Tambo led a delegation to Cuba. Thabo Mbeki was part of the delegation and he recalled the meeting with Castro in a later interview with Luli Callinicos.[477]

Castro drove home many points about the Freedom Charter. Take the clause, 'the wealth ... banks and monopolies, shall become the property of the people'.

'Was this capable of implementation?' he wanted to know. 'If you expropriate them, do you have the people to run the governing bureaucracy, the banks, the mines, the big businesses? If not, this is strategically wrong.' In Cuba after independence, Castro had tried to expropriate the big exporting companies: the cigars and rum businesses. He then found that their owners had registered their trademarks in Florida. He had to bring back the previous owners to run these companies after independence. 'You've got to share power ... you've got to compromise ... You will enter in reality into a negotiated settlement.'[478]

Tambo got the message. In fact, in true Tambo style, he had anticipated these developments.

In 1983 he had encouraged the ANC's National Working Committee to explore proactively scenarios for negotiations.

Negotiations could only come about under three circumstances: 'outright defeat of the apartheid regime; stalemate; or "irresistible pressure from the Frontline States"'.[479]

From this followed Tambo's appointment of a constitutional committee. This included many of the ANC's top legal people: its chair was Jack Simons, and his deputy, who later became chair, was Zola Skweyiya, and it included Kader Asmal, Zingisile Jobodwana, Penuell Maduna, Brigitte Mabandla, Teddy Pekane and Albie Sachs.

Albie Sachs has said how they got their brief: 'OR came to us and he said that there was a lot of pressure on the ANC from various international bodies to produce an ANC constitution. People said, "We know what you are against, but we don't know what you are for. What kind of country do you want?"'[480]

The team produced their first report in 1987. Three issues became firmly established: a multi-party non-racial democracy; a Bill of Rights; and the principle that the final constitution would be negotiated through a constitutional assembly – it would not be the end product of a committee, however clever or well-intentioned. 'Looking back on the process in 1993, Albie Sachs saw the hand of Oliver Tambo on the first two principles.'[481]

The concept of a Bill of Rights emerged from an extensive debate on Pretoria's proposals regarding 'Group Rights'. These were seen as a paper-thin protective covering of the privileges the white community had assembled over so many years; in fact even the concept of a Bill of Individual Rights was called a 'Bill of Whites' in ANC circles. Rather than 'groups' having rights, the team was happy to entrench the individual as the holder of rights to be defended should a bullying state become predatory.

This document became known as 'Guidelines for a Free South Africa'. It went for approval to the ANC's National Executive Committee on 9 October 1987 as a 'statement on the question of negotiations'. It included a lot of what was later to become the 'Harare Declaration'.

The document began with the statement that, while it was obvious that the Pretoria regime was not willing to negotiate, the ANC had never turned its back on meaningful negotiations.

It then tackled head-on the three issues that the regime always threw at the ANC: firstly, until the Pretoria regime ended its bloody, violent war on black communities, the ANC could not be expected to abandon its armed struggle; secondly, the ANC was not the South African Communist Party, and was not a communist organisation – but it would not be dictated to as to who should be its allies in the struggle to end apartheid; and thirdly, the ANC saw the regime's quest to constitutionalise 'group rights' as a weak attempt to entrench existing white privilege and an opaque way to frustrate the universal franchise, an ANC non-negotiable. For the ANC, the best guarantee of rights for all was a bill of individual rights.

Then, and for the first time, the document set out preconditions for meaningful negotiation between the Pretoria regime and the ANC. These included the unconditional release of political prisoners, detainees, captured freedom fighters and prisoners of war. Political trials should cease. The state of emergency should be lifted, and the army and the police removed from the townships and confined to barracks. All laws restricting freedom of speech, assembly and the press were to be lifted.

Then, and only then, could meaningful negotiations begin. The first set of preconditions had been set out.[482]

In the course of the next year, 1988, Tambo refreshed this team by including Neo Mnumzana, Joel Netshitenzhe and Ngoako Ramatlhodi. The terms of negotiations agreed by the NEC were then distributed to the presidents of Tanzania, Angola, Zambia, Zimbabwe, Mozambique and Botswana, for comment, suggested changes and agreement. By now the Angolan Bush War was ending, with the ANC again, as had previously happened in Mozambique, being deprived of its Angolan camps. Tambo knew that things were getting urgent.

1988 ended with Mandela being moved to his 'house' in the Victor Verster Prison complex in Paarl, on 10 December 1988. His comforts expanded exponentially, with personal servants and a personal cook, Warrant Officer Swart, to serve tea and meals to the stream of notables now allowed to visit him. Initially these visitors were mostly 'system' people (his secret negotiating group and others) but as the year progressed his guests took a distinctly left-wing turn, with UDF leaders, trade unionists, senior clerics (the Arch, often, of course), and others. Later in the year he was allowed to phone ANC personnel in Lusaka and Thabo Mbeki became a regular recipient of calls. Most if not all of these meetings and phone calls were recorded, and the transcripts are in the Kobie Coetsee archive at the University of the Free State.

Amongst his first visitors were the 'Pollsmoor Four', his Rivonia Trial comrades, Walter Sisulu, Ahmed Kathrada, Ray Mhlaba and Andrew Mlangeni, who visited in January 1989. Mandela informed them of the 'secret committee' and his regular meetings with them, of his progress in completing his memorandum and of a pending, promised meeting with PW Botha. All four were both excited and nervous.

Then a major shock hit the system.

On 18 January PW Botha had a stroke and was hospitalised. There he remained, recuperating, until his caucus and he concluded that he should be replaced as leader. On 5 February the caucus voted for the Transvaal leader of the NP, FW de Klerk, to take the lead of the National Party, just ahead of PW's hand-picked successor, Barend du Plessis, by 69 votes to 61. Fully expecting to also become State President, FW visited Botha, only to find that the Groot Krokodil had no intentions of surrendering the top job. As he was never an easy man to negotiate with, the best FW could get from PW was an undertaking for PW to resign just at the next general election, scheduled, PW believed, for March 1990. With this undertaking in his pocket, certainly the best he could prise out of the hardened old politician, FW left, and immediately called the next election for September 1989.

The news of PW's condition quickly did the rounds, including through the thick and almost impenetrable walls of South Africa's jails. There about

3 000 political detainees were still languishing 'at the State President's pleasure', and they were surely sick of this.

Maybe here was an opportunity?

On 23 January 1989, five days after PW's stroke, 20 detainees in Diepsloot prison entered a hunger strike, stating clearly that they would not relent until either they were released or charged in a court.

The 20 started a tidal wave. In 1989 there were 53 hunger strikes of 1 429 political detainees and 24 Section 29 detainees, and 34 detainees in homelands prisons.[483] Soon 100 in Port Elizabeth's jails had joined. By 10 February seven of the Diepsloot 20 had to be hospitalised. They were eating nothing and drinking water only, as had the IRA detainees in Northern Ireland in 1981.

Letters were smuggled out to embassies, emphasising that the detainees were to starve until either released or charged. This caused considerable pressure from (particularly) European governments on the recently appointed Minister of Law and Order, Adriaan Vlok. Initially he responded in the traditional way ('We will not be blackmailed ... this is just to cast those in authority in a bad light'), but such intransigence didn't last. Soon he was promising to have signed release orders for 'a substantial number' of detainees, and it was noted that 202 were released by the end of the promised two weeks. When asked if he thought that detainees would starve themselves to death, he replied, 'Personally I hope it will never come to that.'[484]

After 24 days, 24 detainees were in hospital. Minister Vlok then held a two and a half hour meeting with Archbishop Tutu and the Rev Allan Boesak. The clerics emerged and, with careful words, noted that 'Minister Vlok wishes to end this peacefully'. Archbishop Tutu added, 'I do not wish to speak of victory, but it does give our people hope.' Kathleen Satchwell, an attorney for many of the detainees, said, 'It is possible that the majority will be released.'[485]

And so, slowly, they were. By May, Khusta Jack and the last of the jailed senior UDF executives in Port Elizabeth were back 'in town', and those dreadful, long and wasted years in densely crowded cells were behind them. The activists had seized their freedom by risking their lives. Now that they were free, they should have been triumphant.

But they did not come out into an easy world. As Khusta Jack wrote:

All political prisoners were released. Our people were exhausted from five years of intense conflict and people were attempting to move on. Some young activists were looking for work, while others went back to school. Fatigue had set in.

> Back in the townships we did our best to revive the spirit of our
> people ... Political rallies were not well attended. There was, indeed,
> a general feeling of staleness.[486]

But not for De Klerk. On 8 February he made his first speech as
leader of the National Party. He wanted a 'totally changed South Africa ...
White domination, as far as it still exists, must go ... My party strives for
a non-racialistic country'. He now wanted a 'new constitution offering full
participation to all South Africans, white, black, coloured and Indian'. To
this end he called for 'a great indaba, a national convention to negotiate a
new constitution'.[487]

Assistance came to FW de Klerk from an unexpected source, Mrs
Thatcher, Prime Minister of Great Britain.

On hearing De Klerk's stated intentions, she invited, one by one, the
South African Minister of Foreign Affairs, then the Minister of Finance, and
finally De Klerk himself, to meet with her and begin creating proposals for a
negotiated settlement for our country, 5 500 km from her home in London.[488]

'Mandela would have to be released and the ANC unbanned, she stated,
but these steps would have to be accompanied by "assurances from all sides
that there would be no further violence". Buthelezi and Inkatha would
also have to be included in the talks, which should aim for a constitution
incorporating both a universal franchise and safeguards for minorities.
Thatcher embarked on a six-day visit to Africa to garner support for her
proposals, which various African states seemed likely to endorse. She also
hoped for Soviet support, saying she was "pinning her faith on Russia's
glasnost policy to curb the ANC's armed struggle" and pave the way for
constructive talks.'[489]

The ANC knew of this and were concerned. As Thabo Mbeki said, 'If
their plan should be adopted, the ANC would be locked into someone else's
thinking, into somebody else's plan.'

With all this in play, Mandela used his time at Victor Verster Prison
to conclude his manuscript for PW Botha. By the end of March he had
finished. It was a document that he termed a 'non-paper', as it had no status
in terms of ANC ratification, and he had, in a number of ways, stretched
past ANC positions, for instance, in offering to suspend the armed struggle
should negotiations begin in earnest.

Niël Barnard, the head of NIS, read the document thoroughly and
decided to let it 'die a silent death'.[490] It did indeed now disappear and only
surfaced later, as a source of confusion. But it certainly marked out Mandela
as an honest and determined agent for negotiations.

On Tuesday 4 July General Willemse, the Commissioner of Prisons, visited Mandela and told him that he was to meet the State President the next day. Mandela replied that the suit he had been given to use to meet the Commonwealth Eminent Persons Group had long disappeared. Could Willemse help?[491]

Willemse sent a tailor immediately and by the end of the day Mandela was his normal, sartorially splendid self, with a new suit, shirt, tie and shoes.

The next morning Major Marais, the head of Victor Verster, arrived and inspected the cut of the suit now on the world's most famous prisoner. He liked the suit but noticed that Mandela, from long years of no opportunity, had lost the knack of presenting his tie to best effect. Marais took it off and redid it in a double Windsor. Now Mandela was ready for this big day. Marais then drove Mandela to Pollsmoor, where General Willemse's wife served them all breakfast.

Then on to Tuynhuys, the home and office of the State President which is situated adjacent to the Houses of Parliament. It is, as Mandela notes in his autobiography, 'a graceful, nineteenth-century Cape-Dutch style building'. On arrival, their 'small convoy' was spirited into 'an underground garage where we would not be seen'.[492]

Mandela was nervous.

> I was tense about seeing Mr Botha. He was known as 'die Groot Krokodil' – 'the Great Crocodile' – and I had heard many accounts of his ferocious temper. He seemed to me to be the very model of the old-fashioned, stiff-necked, stubborn Afrikaner who did not so much discuss matters with black leaders as dictate to them ... I resolved that if he acted in that finger-wagging fashion with me, I would have to inform him that I found such behaviour unacceptable, and I would then stand up and adjourn the meeting.[493]

Mandela was not alone in being nervous. In the 'grand wood-panelled lobby in front of the president's office' he met up with the other participants for the meeting – Kobie Coetsee, Niël Barnard and a retinue of prison officials. 'While we were waiting, Dr Barnard looked down and noticed that my shoelaces were not properly tied and he quickly knelt down to tie them for me. I realised just how nervous they were.'

The door then opened and I walked in expecting the worst.
From the opposite side of his grand office, PW Botha walked towards me. He had planned his march perfectly, for we met exactly halfway.

He had his hand out and was smiling broadly, and in fact, from that very first moment, he completely disarmed me. He was unfailingly courteous, deferential and friendly.

The meeting lasted no more than thirty minutes, and the conversation was general, non–confrontational, and in fact 'friendly and breezy to the end'. The only point of contention that Mandela records was his request, delivered carefully at the end of the meeting, that Botha release unconditionally all political prisoners. Botha replied that 'he was afraid that he could not do that'.[494]

They then agreed on a bland press statement to be used if news of the meeting broke out, whereafter 'Mr Botha rose and shook my hand, saying what a pleasure it had been. Indeed it had been. I thanked him, and left the way I had come.'[495]

Niël Barnard has provided a second account of the meeting, in the form of a record, in Afrikaans, that is in Kobie Coetsee's archive. Stamped 'SECRET', it is dated 'Tuynhuys, 5 July 1989'.[496]

Barnard's account differs from Mandela's in three significant ways:

- Mandela had offered that, if meaningful steps were taken to 'normalise the situation', the ANC would 'renounce violence and take other steps without either the government or the ANC having to lose face'; and

- Botha had said, in answer to Mandela's request for the release of political prisoners, that a decision had already been taken to release Walter Sisulu, and requested/demanded that Mandela ensure that this release should not be accompanied by unrest or a 'propaganda campaign', and reminded Mandela that 'Mandela's honour is at stake here'.[497]

- Barnard also mentions that, unbeknown to the participants, Botha had ensured that his personal secretary, Ters Ehlers, had secretly taped the meeting. Barnard was later presented with the tape when Botha resigned, and, to Botha's chagrin, had destroyed it. In Barnard's opinion the tape had no issues of state security on it and its presence could have embarrassed participants if it was leaked to the press.

Recollecting the issues of this meeting, Mandela felt that the experience had been very valuable. 'While the meeting had not been a breakthrough in terms of negotiations, it was one in another sense. Mr Botha had long talked about the need to cross the Rubicon, but he never did it himself until that morning at Tuynhuys. Now, I felt, there was no turning back.'[498]

A series of other momentous events were happening at that time, both within South Africa and outside.

Inside South Africa, on 14 August, just over a month from the PW–Mandela meeting, PW blew a fuse when he found out that FW de Klerk was planning a visit to President Kaunda without PW's knowledge. He then went on SATV to announce his resignation from the position of State President as his cabinet ministers were, in his opinion, breaching the necessary collegial trust and playing into the hands of the ANC in the process.

The next day, FW de Klerk was sworn in as acting State President.

Would this change anything? Mandela, initially sceptical of FW's 'liberalism', had made a study of FW's speeches since he became leader of the National Party. Mandela 'began to see that he represented a genuine departure from his predecessor. He was not an ideologue but a pragmatist, a man who saw change as necessary and inevitable.'[499]

If FW thought that the path ahead was to be uneventful, he had underestimated that troublesome cleric, Archbishop Desmond Tutu. FW had been in the job for five days when Tutu announced that he was to lead a large group of black South Africans to a 'picnic' on two 'whites-only' beaches at the Strand in Cape Town. On the day, they were, of course, met with a cordoned-off beach, closed because of a 'police dog-training exercise'. The surrounding roads had also been blocked off.

Tutu et al. were dispersed and Tutu then held a press conference. 'It is incredible that the government is prepared to use arms on people who wish to have a picnic. Instead of getting rid of beach apartheid, they protect it with policemen, dogs and guns.'[500]

And there were more traps awaiting FW.

On 2 September Greenmarket Square was filled with protesters. When the police arrived, they knelt down. The police let rip with water cannons, with the water coloured with a purple dye. With people and buildings splattered with purple, graffiti sprang up with the slogan 'The Purple Shall Govern'. A total of 500 people were arrested that day, including Jay Naidoo, general secretary of COSATU, Allan Boesak, Charles Villa-Vicencio and Essa Moosa.[501] It looked as if nothing was changing.

This protest behaviour was part of a Defiance Campaign called by the Mass Democratic Movement (essentially a combination of the banned UDF and the now Charterist COSATU) to disrupt the 6 September election. This campaign was launched on 2 August, and included acts of defiance drawn from the American struggle for black rights (black people invading 'white' facilities), and banned organisations 'unbanning' themselves – which both the End Conscription Campaign and the UDF did. In the case of the UDF, its self-proclaimed unbanning came on its sixth anniversary, 20 August.

All of these protests were around and about the general election of 6 September 1989.[502]

This was the first, and only, election where all three houses of the tricameral parliament (House of Assembly – white voters; Representatives – Coloured voters; Delegates - South Africans of Indian ancestry) voted on the same day.

Naturally, the action centred on the white House of Assembly.

On the dissolution of parliament in early September 1989, the 166 elected seats of the House of Assembly were divided as follows:

- National Party – 120 seats
- Conservative Party – 22 seats
- Democratic Party – 19 seats
- New Republic Party – 1 seat
- Independent – 1 seat (Marius Barnard in Parktown)
- Vacancies – 3 seats

The results of the 1989 election were as follows:

- National Party – 93 seats
- Conservative Party – 39 seats
- Democratic Party – 33 seats
- Tie (by-election, NP/CP) 1

Thus 32 seats out of 166 changed hands, or 20% of the House, making the 1989 election the most volatile since 1953.

Prior to the September elections, the Conservative Party (CP) had 22 seats in the House of Assembly. All were in the Transvaal, and all were rural or small urban seats. In this election the CP won another 17 seats, sixteen from the NP, and one that had been a vacancy. Five of these seats were in the Free State, two were in the Cape (including Uitenhage) and 10 were in the Transvaal, including one, Pretoria West, in a major urban area. Their percentage of the electorate was now 31.25%. The CP remained the Official Opposition after the election. Plainly they were on the march.

The Democratic Party also had a good election, winning an additional 14 seats. One was from an Independent, one was the last New Republic Party seat in Natal, one had been vacant (Hillbrow in Johannesburg) and 11 were won from the NP, including Walmer in Port Elizabeth and Albany. Of these seats, five were in the Transvaal, two in the Western Cape, two in the Eastern Cape and five in Natal. With the exception of Albany, all were in major urban areas. Their percentage of the electorate was 20.7%.

The NP entered the election with 120 seats and emerged with 93. They won one vacant seat (East London City) and lost 16 seats to the CP and 11 to the DP. They won no seats held by either the CP or the DP. While they still had a majority of the House (54.6% of the seats) this majority was won on 47.8% of votes cast, a minority of votes. The NP had suffered the biggest electoral reverse it had ever experienced. As recently as 1977, just twelve years earlier, it had won 135 of the 166 seats – 82%. In all three elections between 1977 and 1989 they had lost ground. Trouble.

The House of Representatives election was marked by a general adherence to the electoral boycott the UDF had called. In the 21 Cape Peninsula seats, the poll was 9%. In Mitchell's Plain 797 citizens voted, or 1.9% of the enrolled voters. In the four Port Elizabeth seats, two were uncontested and the other two returned polls of about 15%.

The election in the House of Delegates was as extraordinary as was all else in this House, and it quite defies sensible comment. No party ended up with a majority.

It was now clear that the National Party would not survive another election and the tricameral parliament was dead. De Klerk knew this. On 20 September he was inaugurated as South Africa's State President.

It was now time for new ideas, and bold action.

The first opportunity for new thinking was presented immediately, and once again it was that turbulent priest, Desmond Tutu, who was at the centre of the action. This time Tutu was in good company with the Mayor of Cape Town, Gordon Oliver, Allan Boesak, Frank Chikane, Moulana Farid Esack, and 30 000 others. They led a march from St George's Cathedral to the Grand Parade on 13 September to protest police violence, amongst other issues. Twenty people had died in the turmoil around the election boycotts in the Cape, and Tutu was not going to let the government escape responsibility.

By now FW had got the message and the police maintained a low profile. All went off well, to everyone's surprise.

At the Grand Parade Desmond Tutu made a speech, and for the first time South Africans heard of themselves being referred to as 'The Rainbow Nation'. And all this under clouds of ANC flags, and also, dare one mention it, the red flag of the SACP.

Mandela was impressed from his 'house' in Paarl: 'Under President Botha, the march would have been banned, marchers would have defied that ban and violence would have resulted. The new president lived up to his promise to ease restrictions on political gatherings and permitted the march to take place, only asking the demonstrators to remain peaceful. A new and different hand was on the tiller.'[503]

This newly won space was immediately seized.

Massive protest marches happened in Johannesburg (20 000 participants), Uitenhage (80 000), East London (40 000), Durban (20 000) Port Elizabeth (50 000) and Oudtshoorn (8 000).[504] Again, the largest numbers were in Port Elizabeth and Uitenhage. None were disrupted by police action. De Klerk was plainly presenting a different public profile to that of his predecessor.

In Lusaka, OR Tambo was also feeling urgency in the need to stamp the ANC's control on the now inevitable negotiation process, which had begun differently in so many chambers and which, if things went badly, Mrs Thatcher and FW de Klerk could end up controlling.

'Guidelines for a Free South Africa' had gone through the National Working Committee on 9 October 1987. It was then sent on to the heads of the Frontline States, after which it was 'sent home' to be reviewed by selected people, including Mandela, Govan Mbeki, Harry Gwala and leaders of the Mass Democratic Movement. It also found its way to Moscow and Havana.[505]

Now the leaders of the Frontline States needed to be intensively interrogated, to ensure their agreement and that the document was 'a proper expression of the South African people, and then secondly the region'.[506] Hopefully what had happened to ZANU, ominously evidenced in the Nkomati Accord and the agreement that closed off the Angolan Bush War, could be avoided in South Africa.

There was just a week before the Organisation of African Unity's ad hoc committee was to meet, and Tambo wanted the ANC draft, as modified, to be tabled at this meeting. He assembled a team including Steve Tshwete, Thabo Mbeki, Penuell Maduna. Pallo Jordan and Ngoako Ramatlhodi. Fortunately Kaunda put a jet at their disposal.

For three days they jetted and conferred. It was gruelling stuff and Tambo tired. His team of 'youngsters' made him rest in Dar es Salaam, while they met the Tanzanian Foreign Minister, Salim Salim, without him.

Salim argued the details and the team came back to Tambo to tell him that they could not get an agreed wording from him. Tambo was not one to give up. He sat with his team late into the night, fine-tuning the wording of every clause. Only when they believed it would be agreed did they sleep. The next morning Nyerere, on Tambo's exposition of the redraft, signed it off.

Then to Mugabe, and thereafter Masire in Gaborone and Dos Santos in Luanda.

Only when they had a full-house of agreements did they return to Lusaka. It was at 6am the following morning. The 'youngsters' sent Tambo to rest and met at Mbeki's flat to fine-tune the document, yet again, for the ANC's National Working Committee the next day. At 10am in walked Tambo. He wanted to be sure of every comma. 'He literally baby-sat that document, looked after every comma, every word, every spacing and what it looked like on paper,' said Steve Tshwete later.[507]

On the morning of 8 August 1989 the National Working Committee of the ANC approved the document, which went on to be called the Harare Declaration. Tambo guided the debate and the choice of the delegates to take it to the OAU meeting.

That afternoon he went to his office to meet those who had appointments to see him.

Amongst his visitors was Thenjiwe Mtintso, who had recently been appointed as ANC representative to Uganda. On her shoulders had fallen the challenge of finding accommodation for the ANC's personnel who had been expelled from Angola as part of the agreement to end the Angolan Bush War. The ANC again faced the huge burden of a massive relocation, this time complicated further by the inclusion of the inmates of the Quatro detention camp.

She pleaded emotionally to Tambo for help – they had no uniforms, no food, no tents, no training equipment, and it was six months since the personnel had arrived. When she travelled she slept in her Land Rover. And for food for the group, she had to beg the Ugandan army for loans.[508]

She was with Tambo for a long time, often in tears. But she left feeling heard and respected. Something would happen.

After she left, Tambo's driver, Tony 'Gabs' Msimang, heard Tambo's bell ringing. He rushed in to find Zola Skweyiya there, frantically trying to pull a fallen Tambo to his feet. They carried him to their car and drove him to Kaunda's personal doctor. Then he was rushed to a military hospital.

Oliver Tambo had had a stroke.

The next day the Frontline States approved Tambo's document. The Harare Declaration was on its way, while its guardian angel was being flown in mining magnate Tiny Rowland's jet to find medical attention in London.

On 21 August the Organisation of African Unity's ad hoc committee on South Africa agreed the document at its meeting in Harare. The Harare Declaration then went to the OAU Heads of State meeting in Addis Ababa, where it was also approved, and then on to the Commonwealth of Nations meeting in October. Again agreed. At this stage Mrs Thatcher abandoned her rival initiative and it was game, set and match to the ANC. The about-to-happen South African negotiation process had its principles and its guidelines, thanks to a 72-year-old freedom fighter now recovering from a stroke in a Swedish clinic.

10 October 1989 began like any other day in Cape Town. FW de Klerk had

been State President for all of three and a half months. The real excitement of the day was, however, to be in that small house hidden away in the Victor Verster Prison complex in nearby Paarl. It was to be a day of many meetings and much activity.

First to arrive were ministers Kobie Coetsee and Gerrit Viljoen.

Apparently FW de Klerk, when he became president, knew nothing of the negotiations with Mandela that had been going on for nearly four years. Startled, FW had relieved Niël Barnard of his responsibilities on the secret negotiating team and replaced him with the highly educated (PhD in Classics) ex-Professor and ex-Rector of the Rand Afrikaans University, Gerrit Viljoen. Mandela was greatly impressed by the new man and his long curriculum vitae.

Their conversation was secretly and haltingly recorded, and messily transcribed. The record is in the Coetsee archive.[509]

What Coetsee and Viljoen were in Paarl to say, and did say in a very long-winded way, was that the release of Walter Sisulu, Ahmed Kathrada, Andrew Mlangeni, Raymond Mhlaba, Elias Motsoaledi, Wilton Mkwayi, Oscar Mpetha and PAC leader Jafta Masemola had been approved and was imminent. There was an issue on which they needed assurance before this could happen.

Mandela needed to get a commitment from his prisoner colleagues and the leaders of the various structures he was due to meet that evening, that the eight prisoners would 'peacefully integrate' back into society and that their release would not be used as an opportunity to 'raise political tensions'. 'If anything goes wrong, the two of us will have to find other jobs,' said Coetsee.[510]

Mandela gave them the requested assurances, 'they will not do anything to worsen the political situation. I don't have the slightest doubt that they will honour this arrangement between us.'[511]

The two ministers departed. Their job had been to get this assurance and to keep Mandela informed of the arrangements. Both had been done.

Meanwhile, back at Pollsmoor Prison there was much excitement. Albertina Sisulu and her child Nkuli arrived for a routine visit to Walter. Nkuli noted: 'There was a strange atmosphere and wild excitement when we arrived. We asked Tata what was up, but he only told us that he could not spend much time with us that day.' There were, Nkuli noted, 'people from the government' with the prison officials. Somewhat mystified, mother and daughter Sisulu left, for mother Albertina had a very important meeting that evening, at Victor Verster Prison.[512]

The next convoy of vehicles to pull up at 'the house' included visitors

Walter Sisulu, Ahmed Kathrada, Ray Mhlaba and Andrew Mlangeni, Mandela's 'Pollsmoor Pals', now all slated for freedom.

'I was able to say goodbye. It was an emotional moment, but I knew I would not be too far behind.'[513]

At 5:30 pm the Pollsmoor group was moved from Mandela's house to the warders' mess, where they were to have dinner. The mess had a TV, and it was here that the four of them learned again of their impending release.

As the Pollsmoor group was moved out, the third group of visitors arrived: Albertina Sisulu, co-President of the UDF, Cyril Ramaphosa of the National Union of Mineworkers, Cas Saloojee, treasurer of the UDF, and also the UDF's Murphy Morobe.

At 8pm Mandela stopped the meeting, and the five of them watched the news on television.

There it was – De Klerk announcing that he was to free the 'Sisulu Eight', and all unconditionally. It was a de facto unbanning of the ANC. Ramaphosa told journalists that they were all overjoyed and emotional, but very downcast that Mandela was not on the list.

Walter was to be freed at his home in Soweto, so the MDM delegates frantically tried to book flights there. No luck – all flights were full for two days. Cyril tried to convince Albertina that they should request a release in Cape Town instead. Albertina would have none of it. 'I must get back because he must find me at home where he left me.' Ramaphosa booked a rent-a-car, and they drove through the night, 1 400 km.[514]

Bureaucracies do many things, but none of them quickly. It was to take five days for the eight to get released. In between, on day four, 14 October, 50 000 people in Port Elizabeth marched on Louis le Grange Square, the police headquarters in the area, to deliver a petition. Nobody seems to remember the demands of the petition, which were anyway hastily drawn up in the intoxicating environment of a mass march without police harassment. It was a new time and many wished to bask in these new freedoms.[515]

While the nation was revelling in its new-found opportunities to march and protest, Sisulu and his detainee friends were flown on a regular South African Airways flight to Johannesburg on, of all days, Friday 13th. On arrival they were taken to meet Jafta Masemola who was held at 'Sun City', as Diepkloof Prison was sarcastically nicknamed, and spent the night of Saturday 14 October there. They were all told to rise at 2am on Sunday 15 October, to be finally taken home.

Wilton Mkwayi describes these early hours, the last time the Sisulu group were to be in jail together:

On arrival at Sun City reception at 4h00, we saw a forest of plain-clothed men we concluded were policemen. The doors opened minutes after 5h00, and we were each escorted to a waiting car, and driven home in this manner: each one in a separate car, in front of which was another car occupied by several policemen. Behind was a van carrying our prison luggage of 26 years and right behind the van was another car. In other words, the six of us were escorted home in 24 vehicles, four vehicles for each of us.[516]

Walter Sisulu arrived home, unannounced, at 5:30 am that Sunday morning.[517]

As this small grey-haired man, known by name all over the world but by facial recognition almost nowhere, stepped from his comprehensively escorted car, the BBC reporter who had camped for days on site asked him, 'Are you Walter Sisulu?' 'Yes I am, and how are you?' came the well-mannered response from the endlessly courteous Walter.

Albertina was fast asleep. Nkuli was awakened by the noise, and rushed to waken her mother.

'I was so confused. I stood there trembling from head to toe. I was as nervous as a new bride. I had to be dressed like a child.'

And so Walter Sisulu arrived home at No 7372 Orlando West, Soweto Township, Johannesburg.

Pandemonium broke out in the streets around their home, and in fact throughout the country. The MDM, anticipating this, had structured a National Reception Committee, chaired by Cyril Ramaphosa, to handle arrangements.

They decided to reintroduce the Rivonia heroes to the public at a mass rally, to be held at the recently opened Soccer City in Soweto, on 29 October.

This proposed event created wild exuberance in the township communities, and a deep dread in the apartheid establishment.

Kobie Coetsee repeatedly visited Mandela, pleading that the rally should be a 'welcoming event' and not an 'ANC rally'. Mandela played his role responsibly and in turn repeatedly phoned Ramaphosa, requesting a moderate tone. This was agreed, and some newspaper advertisements for the event were cancelled. Walter Sisulu was to deliver the main address and the MDM, COSATU and the ANC in Lusaka were involved in its drafting. There was to be no inflammatory stuff, and Sisulu was chosen because his style of delivery was certainly not that of a rabble-rouser.

A crowd of 70 000 people attended this rally, which lasted 10 hours. Speakers were dwarfed by a backdrop of a 50-foot banner, 'ANC lives, ANC leads'. This was flanked by a forest of ANC and SACP flags. A message from OR Tambo was read. The Rivonia heroes were escorted onstage by platoons of youngsters dressed in khaki, to mimic MK uniforms. In all, dozens of laws were broken and it would have been unthinkable under a government headed up by PW Botha.[518]

Sisulu's speech was carefully worded: he said that the ANC was 'searching constantly for the shortest possible path to freedom', and he presented the Harare Declaration as the guide along this path. He noted that the ANC would discuss the cessation of hostilities on both sides but there could be 'no unilateral abandonment of the armed struggle'. The ANC stood for, he said, 'a constituent assembly elected by universal franchise'.[519]

Predictably, when they met a week later (by now Mandela was so busy that Coetsee and General Willemse had to make appointments to see him), Minister Coetsee presented many complaints to Mandela. Although he had noted that Sisulu had not referred to the SACP in his speech, there were SACP flags on display. Calls were made to intensify sanctions. The *New Nation* newspaper had carried an advertisement calling the event an ANC rally. Nothing positive had been said about the government's many initiatives to root out apartheid.

Mandela politely responded, claiming that if more was expected of him, he should be a free man. And he was not. And that was not his choice.

Less than two weeks after the rally, an event happened that shook the world.

It all began in, of all places, the Roman Catholic Church, when, in 1978, the enclave of Cardinals elected Karol Jozef Wojtyla as pope. Wojtyla, who took the title Pope John Paul II, was the first pope born in that very Catholic country, Poland.

Two years later, under the extremely careful eye of Lech Walesa, a shipyard worker and believer in unionism, the Solidarity Movement was formed. It survived suppression from the Polish state, a client state of Moscow. The new pope backed this movement, and his august patronage gave it the bullet-proofing to survive in this impossible environment.

Then came Gorbachev as Secretary General of the Soviet Communist Party, and his change in government policy that saw Solidarity as legitimate. This led to elections in Poland, and in August 1989 a non-communist coalition government won every seat in parliament. This was the first non-communist government in the Soviet bloc. This in turn drove the change that saw a series of velvet revolutions in the Eastern European states.

This all really came home on 9 November 1989, when the Berlin Wall came crashing down.

This had a dramatic effect on FW de Klerk, who believed that this heralded the end of Soviet socialism and its influence on the ANC. This, FW believed, meant that the ANC would now be less ideological and more open to negotiated compromises, making it the opportune time to negotiate.[520]

At the same time, De Klerk announced that he was phasing out the National Security Management System, which had been PW Botha's fighting response to the perceived 'Total Onslaught'.

The ANC and the MDM both believed that more needed to be done to validate the Harare Declaration, and, as the United Nations was to hold a Special Session of the General Assembly on Apartheid and its Destructive Consequences in Southern Africa in New York on 12-14 December 1989, this presented the organisations with the opportunity to get the highest possible endorsement for that declaration.

To clearly evidence the strength of local support for the Harare Declaration, the MDM pulled AZAPO in to co-organise a massive gathering to consider, and hopefully endorse, the declaration. Called 'The Conference for a Democratic Future', it was scheduled for 8 and 9 December in Johannesburg. In total 4 600 delegates representing about 2 000 organisations attended, and, to emphasise its importance, diplomats from 16 countries attended as well. Sisulu again gave a keynote address, as did AZAPO's Itumeleng Mosala.

While there were many agenda items, the pertinent ones were about negotiations and the constituent assembly. These included, as resolutions:

1. To adopt the Harare Declaration on how the conflict in South Africa could be resolved.
2. To call for a constituent assembly established on a non-racial basis representing all the people of South Africa, to draw up a new constitution for South Africa.
3. That real democracy be given to the freely elected delegates of the people, united in the Constituent Assembly on the basis of one person one vote in a unitary South Africa.[521]

The resolutions of this conference were immediately flown to New York, where they were picked up in the deliberations at the United Nations.

The United Nations General Assembly spent three days, 12 to 14 December, considering the issue of apartheid and southern Africa, and concluded with a declaration. It included the following:

- We would therefore encourage the people of South Africa, as part of their legitimate struggle, to join together to negotiate an end to the apartheid system and agree on all measures that are necessary to transform their country into a non-racial democracy.

- We believe that it is essential that the necessary climate be created for negotiations … accordingly, the present South African regime should, at the very least:
  a. Release all political prisoners and detainees unconditionally and refrain from imposing any restrictions on them;
  b. Lift all bans and restrictions on all proscribed and restricted organisations and persons;
  c. Remove all troops from the townships;
  d. End the state of emergency and repeal all legislation, such as the Internal Security Act, designed to circumscribe political activity;
  e. Cease all political trials and political executions.
- We are of the view that the parties concerned should, in the context of the necessary climate, negotiate the future of their country and its people in good faith and in an atmosphere which, by mutual agreement between the liberation movements and the South African regime, would be free of violence.

There was much else.[522]

All of this began with the document compiled by the eight ANC lawyers at the request of OR Tambo, which went through many layers of negotiations, but ended as it began – a logical, democratic, and thoroughly canvassed document, baby-sat by Oliver Tambo, and bearing his fingerprints all over it. Agreed first by the ANC's committees, then by the presidents of the Frontline States, then by the OAU ad hoc committee and on to the OAU Heads of State, then to the Commonwealth of Nations, then ratified by South Africa's own Conference for a Democratic Future, and eventually encapsulated in a Declaration by the General Assembly of the United Nations - the ideas of the Harare Declaration were now to guide the negotiation process towards the New South Africa, towards Archbishop Tutu's Rainbow Nation.

While the General Assembly was conferring, Nelson Mandela and FW de Klerk were meeting for the first time. This was on 13 December.

Mandela was forewarned of the meeting, and had nearly two weeks to confer and prepare. Then roughly the same procedure ensued as with Mandela's meeting with PW Botha six months earlier. He was picked up and, in a small convoy, was spirited into the parking garage at Tuynhuys. This time it was in the evening, so disclosure was unlikely.

Then to the big foyer adjacent to the Presidential office. There he met Kobie Coetsee, General Willemse, Niël Barnard and Barnard's deputy, Mike Louw. They were ushered into the presidential office, where FW 'was extremely cordial'. Coetzee and his entourage then left, and Mandela and De Klerk conferred alone.

Mandela found De Klerk very different from PW Botha, who was, in Mandela's words, 'another National Party leader who heard what they wanted to hear in discussions with black leaders'.[523]

FW actually listened. In fact, Mandela says, Mr De Klerk seemed to 'be making a real attempt to listen and understand'.

Two issues were discussed: the National Party's commitment to 'Group Rights', and the possible release of Mandela.

Mandela advised De Klerk to drop the 'Group Rights' concept and replace it with a Bill of Individual Rights, and he warned De Klerk that if/and when he was released, he would not 'go out to pasture', but would play a determined role in negotiating a new and just South Africa, as a member of the ANC, banned or unbanned.

Nothing was resolved that day, and Mandela was experienced enough to have expected that.

What is interesting is that both men later wrote of this meeting: Mandela in *Long Walk*, and De Klerk in his autobiography *The Last Trek*, published four years after Mandela's book. Both used the same phrases twice: both recorded that they had 'taken the measure' of the other, and both concluded that 'he was a man we could do business with'. That identical phrases were used is neither here nor there – what is important is that both found in each other a worthy opponent for the future business of negotiations.

Thirty-seven years earlier, a brass plate was put up on an office door in Chancellor House, a building across the road from Johannesburg's magistrates' court. It read 'Mandela and Tambo' and it presented to the public the first, and at the time, only firm of African attorneys in South Africa.

Now these two attorneys, who were such close friends and whose lives had later veered off in such divergent directions, were the two individuals who set the new South Africa on its tracks.

Mandela, locked away in jail, through courage, persistence and wisdom, somehow managed to drag the National Party into a willingness to negotiate. While in jail he met with Coetsee at least fifteen times, and with the Barnard team forty-eight times.[524] Tambo, away in London and Lusaka, set up the preconditions for, and the parameters of, these negotiations, which arrangements would inevitably lead to a non-racial democracy.

It was the old firm, and the first firm, that pulled off this miracle.

45

Apartheid's third and last strategy

I n just more than a decade, from 1985 until and including 1995, best available statistics confirm that 22 456 South Africans lost their lives in politically linked fatalities.[525]

In the twentieth century, only the Anglo–Boer War of 1899–1902 saw a higher death toll – in this war, about 7 000 Boer combatants lost their lives, as well as 27 000 Boer women and children and 14 000 Africans, all of whom died in concentration camps designed and administered by the occupying British forces. A further 22 000 British troops also died – about 8 000 in combat and over 13 000 from contagious diseases (dysentery, typhoid, etc.).

What was going on, in the 1990s, in the decade of revolt and democratic outcome, that caused the return to our soil of such horror?

How could so many people be killed in a country with a functioning police force and army meant to protect them from such lethal violence?

The first thing to note is where and when this happened.

The above statistics show that about half of the deaths happened in Natal, and roughly a third in those areas of the Transvaal where there were concentrations of single men's worker hostels. In other words, these deaths happened in those areas of South Africa where there were significant percentages of Inkatha loyalists. And the greatest numbers of these killings, over 70% of the total, happened between the unbanning of the ANC (1990) and the first South African democratic election (1994).

The then dominant thesis, and this still dominates explanations of these dreadful events, is that the killings were the result of some kind of UDF/ANC–Inkatha conflict. And that this had long roots, going back a long way in time.

Inkatha kaZulu was formed by King Solomon Dinuzulu, king of the Zulu nation, in 1928. It was formed in agreement with the ANC as a rallying point against Prime Minister Jan Smuts' Native Affairs Bill of 1920. In this first iteration it did not last long and went dormant in the 1930s.

In 1975 Solomon's nephew, Nkosi Mangosuthu Gatsha Buthelezi, breathed new life into the organisation and renamed it Inkatha yeNkululeko yeSizwe. Now it was to become a vehicle for Zulu cultural identity, but with time it changed into a political movement with profound cultural roots. In 1994 it changed again, this time into the Inkatha Freedom Party, a conventional political party.

The history of Inkatha is inextricably intertwined with that of its founder, Buthelezi, who was its president from its resurrection in 1975 until he retired in 2019.

Buthelezi is unique as a South African political figure in at least two ways: firstly, he is stunningly durable, having served in formal South African political structures from 1970 to date, an astonishing 52 years, and is still going; and secondly, he has always attracted a large grouping of fiercely loyal followers, matched by an equally vociferous army of determined detractors.

He began in politics in the ANC Youth League while at Fort Hare University, from which university he was expelled for protesting a proposed visit by the Governor-General. He finished his degree at a distance from Alice and it was awarded in the early 1950s, when he was in his early twenties.

He assumed the chieftainship of the Buthelezi clan in 1953, and with that role came the traditional Prime Ministership to the Zulu Monarch and Nation, which he assumed in 1968 and still holds.

Then came formal, Bantustan South African politics.

He became Chief Executive Officer of the Zulu Territorial Authority in 1970, which developed into his becoming the Chief Executive Officer of the KwaZulu Legislative Authority in 1972. Then followed the big one – Chief Minister of KwaZulu in 1976, which position he held until democracy in 1994. In that year he was elected to head the Inkatha Freedom Party caucus in the national parliament. He remains, at the time of this book's writing, a member of parliament at the age of 93.

In the early years, relationships between Buthelezi and the ANC were cordial. Both the re-founding of Inkatha and the assumption of the chieftainship by Buthelezi were contrary to ANC policy, because the ANC resisted tribal mobilisation, but Buthelezi and the ANC conferred on both issues and agreed that he should proceed.

According to Buthelezi, things changed dramatically when, he believed, the ANC tried to kill him at Robert Sobukwe's funeral in Graaff-Reinet in 1978.

At this event he was one of the guests of honour, and had been invited to speak. However, many in the audience were young people from Soweto and Port Elizabeth, including Khusta Jack, and to them 1976 was a very recent memory, as was the 1977 murder of Steve Biko. To these youngsters Buthelezi, now Chief Minister of a bantustan, was 'the system' and had no place at the funeral of a determined non-system man like Sobukwe. They screamed insult at the haughty and proud Buthelezi, who had to be escorted hastily from the event, furious that his dignity had been so trampled on, and by 'children' at that. Worse still, his vehicle was stoned as he left. His Inkatha had just won all the seats in the first election for the KwaZulu parliament, and now, children, the ANC, were insulting him so publicly.

The next year the ANC were furious that Buthelezi released for publication records of discussions he had had with them, and the wave of school boycotts in 1980, agreed by the ANC but repudiated by Inkatha, continued the slide into enmity.

Differences remained verbal until the founding of the UDF in 1983, whereafter the conservative ideology of Inkatha and the revolutionary thrust of the UDF came into sharp contrast. Rivalries deepened and violence began.

Inkatha's ideology was at first dominated by cultural issues – a celebration of 'Zuluness', and a promotion of the pride that goes with being part of a 'warrior nation'. With time, as South Africa changed, so new issues were presented. In all instances, Inkatha adopted conservative positions.

Quickly came the adoption of a notably capitalistic, anti-sanctions, anti-disinvestment and militant unions and anti-armed struggle profile – in all instances, the opposite of the ANC/UDF positions. The Inkatha positions appeared to be designed to delight big business and the white community, whose fawning adoration Buthelezi greatly enjoyed, and received. Alan Paton described him as a man of moderation, friendliness, humanity and Christ,[526] UCT gave him an Honorary Doctorate in 1978, and the *Financial Mail* made him their 'Man of the Year' in 1985.[527]

His attempt to resolve the emerging South African storm was his convening of the Natal Indaba, a constitutional conference held in 1986. In attendance were the PFP, the badly battered New Republic Party, and of course Inkatha; and a wide range of business representatives. A total of 46 organisations were invited. Notable absentees included the UDF, the

National Party, who sent an observer, and the Conservative Party.

Constitutional proposals emerged: a bicameral parliament was proposed. The first chamber would be elected on proportional representation and would choose the Prime Minister. The second chamber would be made up of 10 representatives of 'each racial group', 10 each of Afrikaners, Africans, English speakers and 'Indians'. A further 10 would come from a non-racial 'South African' category, for people who did not wish to be associated with the previous four groupings. Representatives of this chamber would have veto rights on legislation affecting their communities.

Events quickly rushed past these ideas and the 1987 whites-only election suggested that support from the biggest blocks of that community, the National and Conservative parties, was absent.

The Indaba nevertheless gave Buthelezi and Inkatha vocal support from Alan Paton and the Institute of Race Relations, although the ideas were soon lost in the turmoil that had begun.

Through all of this, the ANC in particular, but also the UDF and COSATU, ran an ongoing war of words with Inkatha, which was increasingly seen as being a black hand on PW Botha's tiller.

The language of insult soon gave way to fighting talk, and so began this dreadful period in South Africa's history.

The first recorded massacre happened at the Ongoye campus of the University of Zululand, on 29 October 1983. Inkatha had rallied students to attend a ceremony to celebrate the death of King Cetshwayo and a number of allegedly UDF students protested this event. They were dragged from their rooms, and five were murdered by Inkatha youth with 'traditional weapons'.

Buthelezi, who in his youth had been expelled from Fort Hare for similar behaviour, was entirely unsympathetic that the punishment for such protest had progressed from expulsion to a brutal death sentence, through stabbing and assault:

> I can imagine the deep sense of shock that they [the Inkatha youth] had experienced when cliques of students began abusing me with their swearing ... Our youth, our sons and daughters [are] of a warrior nation and they had gone to the university to commemorate one of the greatest warriors in Zulu history, and the simple fact of the matter is that this violence, so carefully plotted, so carefully orchestrated and so cunningly executed produced the inevitable counter-violence.[528]

Just before this massacre, and prior to the UDF being formed, the Joint Rent Action Committee (JORAC) was formed in several townships south of Durban. It immediately incorporated the Lamontville Rent Action Committee, Lamontville being one of these townships.

It was not only rent issues that this JORAC was to contest – much more dangerously, it also opposed the published plans to excise a number of these townships from South Africa, and to incorporate them into KwaZulu. This was to defy Inkatha, something not to be done lightly.

On 25 April 1983 Lamontville councillor and JORAC chairperson, Harrison Dube, was shot and killed as he returned home from a JORAC meeting. This sparked outrage and a number of councillors' homes were attacked.

These were early days in this conflict and security forces had not yet been taught whose side they were really on. Five people were arrested for Dube's killing, including Lamontville's Inkatha mayor and four of his henchmen. They all received long prison sentences.[529]

Things began to get worse.

In May 1984, in the KwaZulu legislative assembly, Buthelezi, who was both Chief Minister and Minister of Police, laid out the strategy:

> I hardly need to emphasise that we need to be placed in a far better position to defend our property and the lives of our people from those kinds of attacks. We do not intend to be sitting ducks … In fact, I believe that we must prepare ourselves not only to defend property and life but to go beyond that and prepare ourselves to hit back with devastating force at those who destroy our property and kill us.[530]

The pattern of these comments is clear: Inkatha was not the aggressor and whatever violence flowed from Inkatha people was defensive violence – the source of the violence was the ANC/UDF.

The next year, 1985, saw violence spread further. The Inkatha Central Committee took the secret decision that during 1985 'the whole of KwaZulu and Natal must be turned into a so-called "no-go area" for the UDF, regardless of the consequences'.[531]

It was now becoming increasingly difficult to get arrests and convictions. When it was clear that Inkatha was the perpetrator of violence, it became 'defensive violence'. When the UDF parties stated that there was police involvement, this was determinedly denied.

Without a doubt, the most difficult crimes to solve are those where the police, as an organisation and on instructions, have been involved in violence and have instructions to cover it up afterwards. Where will the clues come from, and, if found, where do you present them for investigation?

TRUST FEED IS A small rural town about 20 km from Pietermaritzburg in the Natal Midlands. In late 1988 it had a population of about 5 000 – all fearing removal, as Trust Feed had been declared a 'black spot' (in the charming parlance of the apartheid times), and was slated for removal.

In 1982 the local community formed the Trust Feed Crisis Committee (TFCC) to fight this removal, and to aid development in the area. At the time there were three taps in Trust Feed, and one school.

By 1988, thanks to creative engagement between the TFCC and the Development and Services Board, the community had a reliable water supply, R65 000 had been spent improving the roads, a clinic costing R59 000 was in progress ,and plans were available for a community hall. Construction had created work for 103 local people and, most importantly, Trust Feed had been declared a 'black development area', thereby ending the possibility of a removal.[532]

What was obviously a successful programme had, however, attracted the scrutiny of Inkatha, whose executives wanted Trust Feed incorporated into KwaZulu, and not developed outside of the homeland. Inkatha began mobilising in the area, a space they had not been powerful in before. They formed a committee in opposition to the TFCC, called the Trust Feed Landowners' Committee, and began to attack the TFCC, firstly in words, and then the real thing.

In October 1988 Philip Shange, the chairman of the TFCC, was shot with a home-made gun, as was his assistant. Both survived. On 18 November the home of TFCC supporter BM Nyoka was burned to the ground. Night-time gangs of Inkatha supporters were now going from door to door, demanding that people become members and supporters.

On 23 November buses of Inkatha supporters arrived from Edenvale and Msinga, and plunged into a recruitment drive. For a week, the rule of law was suspended in Trust Feed.

At 11am on 30 November four youths, known to be supporters of the UDF, were killed.

The community got the message and fled. By Thursday 1 December, Trust Feed was virtually deserted.[533]

Using the state of emergency legislation, the area was cleared of journalists in late November. Something was obviously about to happen.

On 2 December about 30 to 40 policemen rounded up known UDF members, videotaped them and detained them under state of emergency regulations. The police then withdrew from the area.

That night a wake of about 20 people was held at house TF83.

At about three o'clock in the morning there was a knock on this door. A mourner opened the door – there in wait was a small group of men, armed with rifles, revolvers and shotguns. They immediately blazed away – inside the house and through its walls and windows. Within minutes 11 mourners were dead, and another two wounded. Thereafter the gang burned down Philip Shange's store and three other homes of TFCC families. This event became known as the Trust Feed Massacre.

On 6 December Buthelezi issued a statement that denied entirely that Inkatha was responsible for the massacre, and he said he would sue any newspaper that published such stories. Later that week he issued another statement which claimed that his lawyers had established that the victims were in fact Inkatha members. Zakheli Nkheli, the Inkatha Central Committee member under whose authority Trust Feed fell, blamed it all on the UDF. 'Now that they have been thwarted in Mpumalanga, they have moved into Trust Feed.'[534]

A newspaper report on 8 December stated that Inkatha now had full control of Trust Feed, and that locals were queueing at the home of Inkatha leader Jerome Gabella to sign up.

'The battle for the control of Trust Feed was won decisively by the vigilantes.'[535]

So there you have it – more 'Black-on-Black' violence, another UDF–Inkatha horror. And, of course, the UDF was the perpetrator.

Or was it?

Eight long years later, in November 1996, a police captain was released from jail, having just been given amnesty by the Truth and Reconciliation Commission.

From his trial, at the end of which Judge Andrew Wilson delivered 11 death sentences, comes a record of these events very different from the preceding notes. Further detail comes from this policeman's application to the TRC for amnesty for these murders. And, between Judge Wilson's sentence and his successful amnesty application, he had spent three years in jail, during which this policeman had had time to consider his life. He had taken on Christianity with humility and determination, and was later to write a Christian testimony as to his crimes. Together these documents make horrifying reading, and tell a very different story.

Captain Brian Mitchell was, in 1988, station commander of the New Hanover Police Station, under whose jurisdiction Trust Feed fell. He was 30 years old. He describes the situation in Natal at the time as a 'low-level civil war'. He was instructed to 'drive a wedge between the UDF and Inkatha … [We] would target and assist the Inkatha members to take out the UDF strongholds.'[536]

Amongst other instructions, Mitchell was sent to 'jack up' the local Inkatha leader, to 'get him to be more forceful with the TFCC members'.[537] He did two things in this regard.

Firstly Mitchell, with his colleague Sergeant George Nichas and two security policemen, got the Inkatha leader in the Trust Feed, Jerome Gabela, to set up the Landowners' Committee in opposition to the TFCC. Gabela was not only the Inkatha leader, he was also a Security Police informer, tasked with informing on the unionists at the bakery where they worked. The committee was duly set up.

Secondly, in August 1988, at the Inkatha headquarters in Edenvale, Mitchell and his senior, Major Deon Terreblanche, met with local Inkatha warlord David Ntombela, Jerome Gabela and two other Inkatha members. The meeting planned a ruthless attack on the Trust Feed community for December 1988. Special constables (kitskonstabels) were to be used. After a police clean-up operation, to disarm and round up UDF supporters ('The aim was to make it easy for Inkatha to wipe out the UDF once and for all?' Judge Wilson asked in the trial. Mitchell replied, 'Yes'[538]) – the police would withdraw, and the special constables would then launch an arson attack, accompanied by a massacre.[539]

On 29 November four special constables were brought to the New Hanover police station. They wore civilian clothes and were lodged with Jerome Gabela, who provided them with a small arsenal of weapons.

On 2 December the known UDF members were rounded up and disarmed. The press had been banned in terms of emergency regulations. Everything was going according to script.

That night was to be the massacre and Captain Van der Heever was transporting and controlling the special constables. An intoxicated Mitchell, accompanied by two police reservists, arrived at midnight to see progress. He was disappointed. Only one building had been torched, and no massacre had as yet taken place. Mitchell gave the special constables instructions to torch the shop of the chair of the TFCC, and gave them an address to conduct their massacre. House TF83.

The massacre duly happened, in all its horror. This horror was compounded by the fact that, as Mitchell said in his testimony, 'the wrong house was hit and 11 innocent women and children were killed'.[540]

The next morning the cover-up began. Three policemen arrived – Major Deon Terreblanche, Commander Davies from Greytown and Brigadier Marx, another of Mitchell's accomplices.

But Mitchell had made a bad mistake. He had brought two police reservists with him the night before to the evening's party. And they spoke to the investigating officer. Mitchell panicked. He phoned Pretoria's Security Police. They told him he had nothing to worry about – they would handle the cover-up. And they knew how to do that.

It didn't work out so easily. The reservists' notes were given to the informal inquest. The magistrate found that there were grounds to believe that the police were involved. The four special constables were summoned, but the local and national Inkatha structures spirited them away, and the cover-up seemed to be effective.

Two and a half years passed, and nothing had happened.

Then a second mistake was made. A Captain Frank Dutton was appointed to investigate another case, that of a series of murders allegedly committed by a deputy minister in the Inkatha cabinet, Samuel Jamile. Dutton was unique in many ways, but most particularly in that he was a straight cop in a bent world. And he did his job properly.

Jamile lived and operated in Clermont, where there was another possible incorporation of an area of South Africa into KwaZulu. This he promoted with enough enthusiasm to instruct the 'taking out' of 12 people who opposed the incorporation. Of these five ended up dead, and seven nearly lost their lives. Dutton did his job and Jamile was found guilty of two murders (in the other three murders key witnesses were spirited away by the KwaZulu police until the trial was over). Jamile got life imprisonment but was freed by President De Klerk within a year on an indemnity, and Jamile's 16-year-old hitman eventually got amnesty from the TRC as he had plainly been working on Jamile's instructions.

While digging his way through the Jamile case, Dutton found the Trust Feed documents and was appointed to take this on.

He was able to find and arrest two of the four special constables, one who was hiding in the home of Chief Khawula, an Inkatha chief on the South Coast. Both admitted guilt in the Trust Feed massacre. The other two were found on Dutton's request by the Commissioner of the KwaZulu police, General Jac Büchner. Büchner then confirmed the cover-up in the Trust Feed investigation, and claimed that there appeared to be many police involved.

Dutton arrested Mitchell on 2 August 1991.

This arrest appears to have caused consternation in Pretoria. General Van der Westhuizen, Colonel Langenhoven and Captain Kritzinger came forthwith to Natal to 'assist the investigation'. Dutton saw through them immediately and got the attorney-general to send them home, which he did.

The trial was sensational, and Judge Andrew Wilson found Mitchell and the four special constables all guilty of murder and demanded an enquiry into the police cover-up. Mitchell got 11 death sentences, and the special constables 15 years each as they had obviously been operating on Mitchell's instructions. Eventually all five got TRC amnesty, Mitchell after a number of successive applications had failed.

All in all, between the massacre and the cover-up, some 10 senior Inkatha personnel were involved, and 19 policemen – four special constables, two other KwaZulu police, and 13 members of the SAP, from a general all the way down to one unwitting constable.

It took two years and eight months, from massacre to arrest, and one principled cop, to bring this witch's nest of criminals and conspirators to book. As we have noted, it is almost impossible to crack crimes committed by the police who are then tasked to investigate their own malfeasance.

Death squads

As difficult as it was to bring to light the Inkatha–SA Police and government collusion in murder and crime against the UDF, was even more difficult it to prove the existence of death squads in South Africa.

It really should have been simple.

On 19 October 1989 Butana Almond Nofomela confessed from death row to a number of murders he had been part of while working for the South African Police.

Less than a month later, on 17 November, that brave newspaper *Vrye Weekblad* ran a front-page article headed 'Bloedspoor van die SA Polisie', which outlined Dirk Coetzee's confessions to a similar set of murders while he ran unit C1 of the security police.

In January 1990 allegations were published that the SA Police had tortured prisoners and supported Inkatha vigilantes against UDF supporters, and had murdered David Mazwai.

It was all pouring out and Kobie Coetsee announced on 31 January that the government had appointed an eminent jurist, Judge Louis Harms, as a one-man commission to enquire into 'certain alleged murders'. This commission was to run from 2 February until September 1990.

The announcement of Harms as the one-man commissioner was greeted generally with relief. He was a respected jurist and went on to become the Deputy President of the Supreme Court of Appeal.

However, his commission, which ended up with nearly 4 000 pages of evidence, started badly and finished even worse.

For a start, one of his investigators, who sat the whole commission out, was Colonel Hermanus du Plessis, who a few short years later applied to the TRC for amnesty for his part in the murder of Sizwe Kondile in 1981. This murder was not admitted to Harms' record.

After all that record and cost, including periods in London cross-examining David Tshikalange and Dirk Coetzee, and 28 individuals in South Africa including Joe Mamasela and Butana Nofomela, Judge Harms came to the conclusion that he 'could not prove that they, the South African Defence Force and the South African Police, had systematically murdered and terrorised opponents of apartheid'. Commission over.

The commission may have been over, but the killing wasn't.

In 1990, with the unbanning of the ANC and the release of Mandela, killings doubled from the previous year and spread beyond KwaZulu to the Transvaal. The TRC believes that the Transvaal conflict was triggered by an ANC rally on 2 July 1990, at which the IFP alleges that speaker after speaker called for the removal of all IFP members from the Vaal townships, ostensibly in response to the ANC speakers' perception that the Natal violence was an IFP construct, and was likely to be exported to the Transvaal. Following this rally, the IFP alleges that ANC youths conducted attacks on IFP councillors' homes and businesses.[541]

Three weeks later, on 22 July, the IFP called a 'peace rally', also at Sebokeng. ANC supporters gathered outside the stadium, hurling abuse, stones and petrol bombs. On the conclusion of the proceedings, the IFP audience moved through the township, killing 27 people. The massacres had started.

What followed now is a development so appalling as to have shaken South Africa into a mood of despair and terror: the earlier wars of 1985–6 had been battles between township comrades, armed with petrol bombs, stones and a few guns, and the security forces, armed with every conceivable weapon. It was an entirely unequal battle, in which the massive disparity in numbers of those killed matched the massive disparity in numbers and quality of arms each side could commit to the battle. But there was a sense of both sides committing to the fight, well aware of the odds and the coming sacrifice.

Now all that changed. The feature of the engagements from 1990 on was that they came to resemble not so much a conflict or a battle, but rather a massacre. One side, having planned the events and being armed to the hilt, attacked unsuspecting, unarmed and unprepared communities, in a determined attempt to murder as many men, women and children as possible.

The TRC has detailed 112 massacres in the Transvaal alone, between 1990 and 1992. The numbers escalated steadily over this period.[542]

Another massacre happened in Sebokeng, on 3 September 1990. Inkatha members carried out the attack, in the early hours; again, more than 20 people were killed. It took the police four hours to arrive, which the locals felt was normal. It fuelled the township perceptions of a police–Inkatha coalition, so vigorously denied by both of these parties.

If the massacre was the new engagement of choice, the collusion of Inkatha–police was its second characteristic, and the centrality of these two organisations in instigating the massacres the third. But proof, again, was not easy to find.

There had been an earlier massacre, on 26 March 1990.

This was of the old-fashioned sort: a large crowd of about 50 000 township people, marching from Sebokeng to the Vereeniging police station to present a list of grievances, was fired on by nervous police: 281 demonstrators were shot and 11 died.

A judicial enquiry was called for and FW de Klerk appointed a judge of the Appellate Division, Judge Richard Goldstone, to do the job. Goldstone castigated the police, and recommended their prosecution. Nine policemen faced six charges of murder and some related charges, but this was postponed indefinitely in 1993.[543]

But Goldstone had made his mark.

As the massacres continued, various initiatives attempted to find solutions. Eventually the National Peace Accord of 14 September 1991 was agreed between a large number of political parties and governments. As a clause in its founding documents, the parties committed themselves to a 'Commission of Inquiry Regarding the Prevention of Public Violence and Intimidation'.

Such a Commission needed a chairperson, and Goldstone was agreed between Mandela, who had been impressed by Goldstone's flaying of the police in the earlier Sebokeng massacre, and FW de Klerk. Thus from 24 October 1991 until 27 October 1994, this commission, with Goldstone at its centre, worked on.

Over this time the Commission delivered 48 reports which varied in degree of completeness.[544]

The commission ran into the massive challenge of getting to the irrefutable truth.

Goldstone's methodology was severe – if allegations did not stand up under sometimes withering cross-examination, he discarded them. And he discarded much.

- Two articles in the *Weekly Mail* of 8 and 15 May 1992, by Drew Forrest, outlined the 'Planning and Instigation of Acts of Violence by members of the SAP in the Vaal Area'. The policemen involved were from the Crime Intelligence Service, and the case of the prosecution was based on two witnesses, Mr Kolesang and Mr Mngomezulu. Goldstone took this up, and after counsel had cross-examined these two witnesses, Goldstone concluded that their allegations were 'totally false', and were supported by 'no credible evidence'.

- Articles in the *Vrye Weekblad* of 30 October 1992, alleging police force involvement in massacres of which a witness, Mr Joâo Cuna, made a series of startling allegations which were taken up in the story. This elicited a Goldstone enquiry and report entitled: 'Allegations of a Third Force'. Again: 'No evidence whatsoever exists for finding that Mr Cuna participated in a massacre as described in *Vrye Weekblad*'.

- When Mandela reported that FW de Klerk was somehow involved in the Boipatong massacre, Goldstone called these allegations 'unwise, unfair and dangerous'.[545]

- On train violence and massacres, again, 'The Commission is unable on the evidence before it to apportion blame'.

- On the Boipatong massacre, he could again find 'no information that suggests any complicity on the part of the South African Police in the attacks'.

And so Goldstone and South Africa stumbled on – investigating presented evidence which so often turned out to lead down a cul de sac. Plainly somebody was behind all this killing, but they knew how to hide their tracks.

Then, with 145 weeks of investigation behind the Commission, and just 11 weeks to go to the scheduled election of April 1994, which essentially marked the end-date of the Commission, a dramatic event happened that was to change all of this.

The Chairperson of the Commission was approached in early February 1994 by a 'senior foreign diplomat', who told Goldstone that there was a serving member of the South African Police who had information regarding 'third force activities' but that this individual would only make this information available to 'an appropriate foreign person'.

Goldstone questioned the usefulness of such a conversation, and instead suggested to the diplomat that this person be requested to meet with, and speak only to, Goldstone himself, and no one else. On 10 February Goldstone got a phone call from 'an employee of the Pretoria branch of IDASA', who said that this person had agreed to speak, but only to Goldstone. Date and venue were then agreed.

On the date, Sunday 13 February 1994, the policeman, named 'Q' in Goldstone's report, arrived with two associates, Majors P du Plessis and E van Vuuren, who both worked in the Department of Efficiency Services at the South African Police, under Major General Fivaz. Q agreed to talk, but only if his identity would never be disclosed. This was agreed.

What followed is termed the 'Interim Report on Criminal Political

Violence by Elements within the South African Police, the KwaZulu Police and the Inkatha Federal Party' and was presented to President de Klerk on 18 March 1994, less than six weeks before South Africa's founding election. The report dramatically changed contemporary history.

Goldstone met Q twice (Sundays 13 and 27 February) and received a written memorandum from him/her. This contained staggering information:

- Unit C1 (later C10) of the security police, known widely as the Vlakplaas unit, which was headed up by Colonel Eugene de Kock, had, from 1989 on, used extreme violence in a determined attempt to destabilise South Africa. This included train and hostel massacres and murders. Willem Coetzee of the East Rand security police had assisted De Kock with the train massacres, which were performed by members of C10, black policemen and askaris, as well as Inkatha youngsters employed by ex-security policeman 'Brood' van Heerden.

- C10 manufactured home-made guns at premises in the East Rand and Silverton. This operation was directed by three warrant officers from C10, Vermeulen, Snyman and Britz. They were then delivered to senior Inkatha men, Themba Khosa and Victor Ndlovu, through Brood van Heerden. IFP members were trained to use these weapons, and 13 named senior police officers were involved: from C10, Murder and Robbery, the security police and including General Büchner, the head of the KwaZulu police.

- De Kock organised large consignments of military weapons from Koevoet in Namibia, including significant quantities of AK-47s. These were brought to Vlakplaas and cleaned in acid and all serial numbers removed, before being put in black bags and distributed to Themba Khosa and Victor Ndlovu for Inkatha's use. Later weapons were also brought in from Mozambique and treated and distributed in the same way. Inkatha paid De Kock for these weapons, and apparently De Kock pocketed the money.

- On 4 September 1990 Themba Khosa was caught by the uniform branch with a car-load of such weapons. C10 paid his bail and legal costs, lifted the weapons and 'cleaned' them so that they could not be linked to any crime and Khosa was released by the magistrate.

- Both Khosa and Ndlovu were paid security police informers. Khosa was given a vehicle by De Kock, and both had false names, as all informers had.

- Despite Vlakplaas having been disbanded in 1990, the C10 officers were merely dispersed through the South African Police. De Kock was paid a severance 'packet' of R1.2 million, but continued with his projects. Many of these operatives had false IDs and false passports – De Kock had seven passports in different names.

- All of this was under the direct control of Lieutenant-General Basie Smit (who was by now the Deputy Commissioner of the SA Police) and Major-General Krappies Engelbrecht, the head of counter-intelligence in the Police. Engelbrecht was intensely involved, and authorised all payments through a secret fund. His payment requests were speedily effected, despite most knowing that he was enriching himself. Lieutenant-General Johan le Roux also, according to Q, knew of all these murders and other crimes.

- Colonel Roelf Venter had been investigating De Kock's arms smuggling when General Krappies Engelbrecht instructed him to stop.

- De Kock, whenever Inkatha ran short of ammunition, would purchase large quantities of whatever was needed from Brooklyn Circle Arms in Pretoria through his company Badger Arms. This was confirmed when the Commission seized Brooklyn's register.

All of the above, and much else, while vigorously denied at the time, was admitted by De Kock in his application for amnesty to the TRC for amnesty.[546]

When this information began emerging, the Commission set about checking it. Firstly the false IDs and passports. Despite blocks within the Home Affairs system around some names, the Commission got sufficient proof of all of this.

As they started these inspections, word of this investigation started flying around.

A Colonel Cronje informed all holders of false documents to bring them in for destruction. And General Krappies sent out an instruction that all files linked to Inkatha should be immediately destroyed. This happened the day after the Commission approached Home Affairs. He also instructed C10 to destroy any records that implicated Inkatha.

On 20 February Goldstone met with the State President and Minister Kobie Coetsee, now Minister of Justice and Defence. Goldstone set out what had been happening, and was given the go-ahead to continue by the State President. Goldstone notes, 'The Commission received all the assistance requested by it.'

Now the dirty tricks started. Major Van Vuuren told Goldstone that General Engelbrecht had instructed members of his units to obtain any information that could be used to compromise Goldstone for the purpose of 'persuading' him to cease the investigation. A series of senior policemen met with Major Du Plessis to request him to inform them of what was going on in the Commission.

To confront what seemed to be the source of these actions, Goldstone got the Commissioner of Police to convene a meeting between himself (Goldstone), some members of his Commission and generals Smit, Engelbrecht and Le Roux, with colonels De Kock, Venter and Bellingham.

Of course, everybody denied everything, except De Kock who admitted to having one false passport, and Venter agreed that Engelbrecht had ordered him to stop his investigation of De Kock. They all also denied putting pressure on Major Du Plessis.

The next day Goldstone had a much more rewarding meeting. This was with C10 operatives Brood van Heerden, Snor Vermeulen, Willie Nortje, David Baker and Chappies Klopper.

Now the admissions were dramatic: yes, huge numbers of Koevoet weapons were obtained, cleaned and handed over to Inkatha; Themba Khosa was an informer, he had been paid and provided with a car and was the principal link with Inkatha; De Kock used to buy large quantities of ammunition for Inkatha from Brooklyn Circle; Krappies Engelbrecht was up to his neck in both Vlakplaas and much else; and many murders were carried out by C10.

Goldstone finished this report with a description of a meeting with the State President, the Minister of Justice and Defence, Minister Kobie Coetsee, and the Minister of Law and Order, Minister Hernus Kriel. It was about hit squads in the KwaZulu police.

Goldstone stated that he had had many leads as to hit squads in the KwaZulu police, but his investigators could get nowhere.

One of these investigators, Captain Scholtz, was at this meeting and said he had over 100 dockets live on this matter. But in late November 1993, Brigadier Du Preez had forbidden any further work on them. This, Goldstone noted, was in direct contradiction to the instruction he had received from the State President.

Scholtz continued: there was convincing evidence that elements within the KwaZulu police had been, and still were, involved in hit squad activities in Natal and the Transvaal. 'Caprivi trainees' (Inkatha had handpicked 200 youngsters and sent them to a special SADF training camp in the Caprivi

Strip, to return to 'protect IFP notables') were involved, and they were kept in two camps in KwaZulu. Then, Scholtz said, some of these Caprivi trainees were sent to Mpumalanga and Bambazi, previously quiet areas. Soon after they arrived, massacres began. And, Scholtz continued, the security police were also in these hit squads.

Goldstone's earlier repudiation of half-truths, plus the obvious integrity which had earned him massive international respect, now served him well. The fact that he was obviously convinced by these revelations meant that when he presented them to President De Klerk, De Klerk knew the game was up. And Goldstone, fearing a cover-up, simultaneously released the report to the press. He was taking no chances at this late stage. This was on 18 March 1994, with just over seven weeks to go to the proposed election.

After these disclosures, it was now impossible for the SA government– Inkatha violence to continue unchecked, to destabilise the election. Like it or not, De Klerk now had to 'retire' Generals Smit and Engelbrecht and order De Kock to be arrested. Who told Buthelezi about the new reality, where and when, we'll probably never know. But he too realised that a new approach was now necessary.

The men of apartheid had just lost their third and final war: the first, the Township War, had been lost in the townships of Port Elizabeth and Uitenhage in 1985–86; the second, the War of Namibian Independence, had been lost in the Angolan bush in 1988; and now the third, the War of Massacres and Slaughter of the Innocents, was lost when Judge Goldstone set its workings out, for all to see.

The Ingonyama Trust

There was a final trick in the conjuror's hat, however. A final deal between the men of apartheid and the IFP. Was it a 'thank you', for 15 000 dead bodies on the failed road to destabilise the ANC? Or was it a great gesture, that enabled the forthcoming election to go ahead, with maximum involvement? Let's see.

The IFP had withdrawn from the constitutional negotiating process in July 1993 and never returned. Their stated difficulties were three: first, the fact that the ANC and the NP had fixed an election date (27 April 1994) and would not countenance postponement; second, the ANC's demand that the final constitution would be drawn up by 'the people' at a constituent assembly, and not by an elite of chosen negotiators; and thirdly, the lack of guarantees as to a federal state. In February 1994 to this trio was added a fourth, when, prodded by his uncle, King Goodwill Zwelithini suddenly became a player, demanding recognition of his 'Zulu kingdom'.

As time drew on, and more and more bodies piled up, the leaders of the negotiations (Ramaphosa, Roelf Meyer and Joe Slovo) hardened their attitudes and by April 1994 were perfectly happy to go into an election without the IFP as a player.

International mediation was, however, agreed, and Henry Kissinger and Lord Carrington made a brief appearance.

Buthelezi was by now being 'advised' by an unusual character, one Mario Ambrosini. Ambrosini was all of 33 years old, came to South Africa from Italy via the United States and claimed a stellar CV in constitutional law. He was seen as an unswerving, uncompromising character who, when the mediation efforts collapsed on his insistence that 'unless the NP and the ANC are willing to talk postponement [of the election date], the IFP will not talk anything else', was apparently elated and rushed from one reporter to another saying 'The tragedy of South Africa is being consumed'.[547]

What Ambrosini did do was to infuriate a few of the audience at the venue where the mediation had happened and failed. This included Washington Okumu, a Kenyan diplomat brought to the process by South African evangelist Michael Cassidy; Danie Joubert, the deputy secretary-general in the KwaZulu government Department of the Chief Minister; and Willem Olivier, an advocate experienced in traditional land practices, used by the KwaZulu government in that field.

The mediation collapsed on 14 April 1994, less than two weeks before the election date.

There was no time. Joubert and his team rushed from idea to new idea, and from Buthelezi to De Klerk, to Danie Schutte (De Klerk's Minister of Home Affairs), and back again. Eventually they had some sort of agreement on three things: firstly, the new constitution must recognise the Zulu king; secondly, international mediation must resume after the election; and thirdly, 'Put the Zulu land into a Trust with the King as trustee, and call it the Ingonyama Trust'.[548] There was a fourth item on which all parties were firmly agreed: the ANC must know nothing about this 'land deal' until after the election.

By Tuesday 19 April, things had moved so well that Buthelezi signed the 'Memorandum of Agreement for Reconciliation and Peace', essentially the IFP's commitment to join the election due a week later. The agreement included the first two of the above conditions, but said nothing about the 'Zulu land' issue.

Buthelezi rushed back to Ulundi on Wednesday 20 April. 'We have a win.'

The KwaZulu parliament was called for Friday 22nd, with only one issue on the agenda, the Ingonyama Trust. Because of the haste, all parliamentary rules were pushed aside (this was illegal, but who cared) and the Bill got three readings and assent. This was the last act of the parliament of KwaZulu.

Now it was De Klerk's turn, and he proved to be as tricky as his predecessor, PW. He called parliament to sit on Monday 25th, with voting in South Africa's election due to begin the next day. Again, the agenda was only one item, and that item was craftily put, all they did was amend the constitution to recognise the Zulu king. Nothing else. No land issues. This was the final act of the tricameral parliament.

That afternoon, FW de Klerk signed, in the privacy of his office, the Ingonyama Trust into law. Nearly 30% (2.8 million hectares) of the landmass of what is today KwaZulu-Natal left South Africa, and was now owned by an unknown trust whose sole trustee was the King of the Zulus.

Mandela found out about this on 20 May from an article in the *Mail and Guardian*. He said, astonished, 'We know nothing of this Trust'. Ramaphosa said he was hearing of it for the first time.

Buthelezi and De Klerk denied having done a deal, and a parliamentary committee of the newly democratic South Africa, set up to inspect this startling arrangement, became overrun by the new mood of reconciliation and decided to 'los die ding'. We still live with its glory today.

Part Three

APARTHEID COMES TUMBLING DOWN

46

2 February 1990

A s 1989 wore to its end, FW de Klerk was feeling the weight of his office. He took a three-week holiday in December 1989, but spent it in 'deep thought and reflection'. South Africa could not remain as it was. The only path forward, he now felt, was genuine, bona fide negotiations. What was left for him to do to get this to happen?[549]

Working with a few trusted ministers, in January De Klerk got a working group to deliver drafts on actions to be taken immediately to a ministerial committee of three, Kobie Coetsee, Gerrit Viljoen and another, who is unknown. This contained a comprehensive analysis of the status quo, and made recommendations for '2 February', which was the date that De Klerk was to address parliament. From this manifesto a shorter 'report' was derived, again directed at '2 February', and stamped 'TOP SECRET'. This report, and the manifesto, are in the Kobie Coetsee archives.[550]

This working group, on reviewing the report, was 'of the opinion that the security situation as well as the importance of negotiations have been fully argued', and that 'The Commissioner of Police called for a security update and then confirmed that there was nothing new to add to the report as it stood'.[551]

What were the recommendations in the report that had apparently satisfied the working group, and which the Commissioner of Police believed would deliver only changes that his force could control?

They were, in summary, the unbanning of the ANC, the PAC and the

SACP, as well as their military wings Umkhonto and Poqo; some loosening of the conditions of the state of emergency, particularly those conditions hindering gatherings and holding back free speech and the removal of press restrictions; the state of emergency was not to be ended until it was obvious that the release of Mandela was not causing too great a turbulence; and, the final recommendation, the release of Mandela at a future but proximate date.

All of this was to be announced on 2 February in parliament.

This package was put to the Cabinet on 31 January 1990, just two days before De Klerk was to deliver it to parliament. It apparently got universal agreement.

De Klerk wrote:

These decisions set the framework for my speech of 2 February. It was now up to me to package them. I cut myself off and started to write. I passed my first draft formulations on to the responsible ministers to obtain their comments and suggestions. When I had received them, I completed the first full draft during the morning of 1 February. I called together a few key ministers, and worked through the speech with them.

He then rewrote it from the beginning to the end, and got Chris Renken to translate it into English. 'At about 6pm on the evening of 1 February, I was more or less satisfied.'[552]

And so it happened.

On 2 February 1990 FW de Klerk stood before parliament to make the traditional opening speech and did something no other South African head of state had ever done: he truly began to dismantle the apartheid system and lay the groundwork for a democratic South Africa … It was a breathtaking moment, for in one sweeping action he had virtually normalised the situation in South Africa. Our world had changed overnight.

So wrote Nelson Mandela four years later.[553]

In fact De Klerk had done the opposite of what most commentators had expected: for we were all convinced that he would free Mandela, and then go home for dinner. As we watched the speech at the Human Rights Trust office in Port Elizabeth, Khusta Jack walked in – 'Wow, he's brave!' he said.

The next morning South Africa awoke with hope for the first time in a decade.

That morning the newspapers were, for once, rapturous. 'South Africa and the world rejoice', 'South Africa breaks through political sound barrier: a new dimension of hope', 'No more reason for violence', 'Politics open to all', 'New steps may open doors', 'Abandon petty politics' (*Die Burger*, 3 February); 'New era for South Africa. Tributes pour in from around the world' (*Cape Times*, 3 February); 'A Rubicon crossed' (*Natal Mercury*, 3 February); 'World welcomes FW's major step forward. Bush wants to review sanctions. Pope may visit' (*The Star*, 3 February); 'Road of drastic change' (*The Citizen*, 3 February); 'NP mothballs old ideas' (*Rapport*, 4 February); 'A page has been turned in history' (*Sunday Times*, 4 February); 'Riding the tide of South Africa's newfound spirit of optimism' (*Business Day*, 5 February).

Newspapers also bill-boarded the opinions of notables: 'FW courageous – Van Zyl Slabbert' (*The Citizen*); 'Buthelezi praises De Klerk's speech: now up to Blacks' (*The Citizen*); '"Takes one's breath away." says Tutu' (*Die Burger*); 'FW has saved South Africa, say business leaders' (*Beeld*); and, for the first time legally quoted in 27 years: '"State President's speech daring" says Mandela' (quoted in, of all papers, *Die Burger*).[554]

As shocked and delighted as so many were, it was immediately asked: where did FW get the mandate for such sweeping reforms? Was his party and the security establishment onside here?

Ten years later Van Zyl Slabbert was at a conference at the Cape and sat next to General George Meiring, who had been the head of the Defence Force for the last years of the apartheid era and for the first few of the Mandela years. One of the speakers was FW de Klerk. Describing the time of the 2 February speech, FW told the conference: 'First I made sure that I had my party, my people and the state behind me. Then I made sure I had the majority of Whites behind me. And then I could release Mandela and face the risk of the negotiations' were approximately De Klerk's words, Slabbert has written.[555]

Meiring was incredulous. 'Over drinks that evening … he said that when De Klerk made his speech, it came as a complete surprise to most in the security establishment.'[556]

De Klerk had called together his generals in November and had spoken to them, but the later scope of his reforms, and the complete lack of consultation to prepare for the consequences, left Meiring nonplussed, and fearing an internal revolt in the defence force. Fortunately, it did not happen.

From Meiring's reaction and other evidence, we can conclude that the police had been better treated because they had been requested to supply, and had supplied, an assessment of the consequences of the announcement.

If Meiring was surprised not to receive communication about the speech, so too was Mandela. There was no instantaneous communication between 'the system' and the world's most famous prisoner.

A direct negotiation

Mandela had to wait seven days to hear that he was again off to Tuynhuys.

He arrived on the evening of 10 February at about 18h00, and was ushered into De Klerk's office. 'A smiling Mr De Klerk' told Mandela that he was to be flown to Johannesburg the next day, and released there.

Mandela's response left de Klerk dumbfounded.

After 27 years in jail, and after an offer of near-immediate release, 'I thanked Mr de Klerk, and then said that at the risk of sounding ungrateful I would prefer to have a week's notice in order that my family and my organisation could be prepared for my release.'[557]

De Klerk was startled. He excused himself and left his office to confer with his advisers.

He returned. His offer was unchangeable, as the foreign press, the diplomatic corps and others had already been informed.

Mandela stood his ground. 'I replied that the plan was unacceptable and that I wanted to be released a week hence at Victor Verster, not Johannesburg.' De Klerk again left the room.

He returned. The date, tomorrow, cannot be changed. But we can release you in Paarl.

Mandela, who wished sincerely to bid farewell to his jailers in a proper and courteous manner, many of whom had become his friends, felt that he had to accept this concession.

'I felt I could not argue with that. In the end, we agreed on the compromise, and Mr de Klerk poured a tumbler of whisky for each of us to drink in celebration. I raised the glass in a toast, but only pretended to drink; such spirits are too strong for me.'

Mandela returned to what he now called 'his cottage' just before midnight. He immediately phoned the National Reception Committee, Winnie and Sisulu. Sisulu said they would charter a plane to bring the Johannesburg notables to Cape Town. Please, Nelson, wait for us to get to Paarl.

Some from the National Reception Committee then arrived, and a statement for the next day was drafted.

'They left in the early hours of the morning and, despite my excitement, I had no trouble falling asleep.'

The next day, 11 February 1990, was, for South Africa and the world, to say the least, momentous.

'I awoke on the day of my release after only a few hours' sleep at 4.30 am ... I did a shortened version of my usual exercise regimen, washed and ate breakfast.'[558]

Walter, Winnie and the Johannesburg team were only due to arrive at Cape Town airport at 2 o'clock, and Mandela's release was scheduled for 3 o'clock. In between his breakfast and this hour, he finalised his address with Cyril Ramaphosa, Trevor Manuel and others of the Reception Committee; they dissuaded Mandela from his determination to make his first speech a speech of thanks to 'the prosperous white burgers of Paarl', and instead to save the moment for 'the people' who were already assembling at the Grand Parade in front of the City Hall in central Cape Town; likewise they dissuaded him from spending his first night as a free man in the Cape Flats, and instead pointed him to the remarkable comforts of Archbishop Tutu's splendid church-owned home in leafy Bishopscourt; and helped him to pack 'dozens of crates of possessions, particularly books and papers'.

His home was the centre of the world on this day, and 'there were dozens of people at the house, and the entire scene took on the aspect of a celebration'. The ever-reliable Warrant Officer Swart 'prepared a final meal for all of us, and a procession of prison personnel just kept coming: the prison doctor gave him an examination and a month's supply of medication; Warrant Officer James Gregory, Mandela's jailor from both Pollsmoor and Victor Verster arrived, as did Warrant Officer Brand. 'Men like Swart, Gregory and Brand reinforced my belief in the essential humanity even of those who had kept me behind bars for the previous twenty-seven and a half years.'

47

Release and welcome

At about 3:15 pm 'Winnie and 30 people with vehicles arrive (four helicopters circle the house). Winnie first enters the house alone – no product [recording] could be made due to the noise. The other people enter the house. Short speeches by various people. 913 [Mandela's official prison number] goes through his speech.' So records the report by the prison's impimpi, in Kobie Coetsee's archives.

Now the real action begins.

At just after 3pm 'a well-known SABC presenter' phoned to ask Mandela to disembark from his convoy just short of the prison gates and to walk his last distance to freedom for an unforgettable photoshoot.

This was agreed, and Mandela and Winnie abandoned their convoy 'about a quarter of a mile in front of the gate', and walked towards the gate. When he got to within 150 feet of the gate, 'I realised we had not thoroughly prepared for all that was about to happen'.

Cameras began clicking 'like some great herd of metallic beasts', journalists, television crews and fans by the thousand 'began crowding in', and Mandela's entourage got him out as quickly as possible.

'As I finally walked through those gates to enter a car on the other side, I felt – even at the age of seventy-one – that my life was beginning anew. My ten thousand days of imprisonment were at last over.'

But his first day as a free man was a long way from over.

It took 45 minutes to drive from Paarl to the Grand Parade. They were instructed to approach the City Hall from the rear, as the crowd was thinner there. Inexplicably their driver drove to the front entrance. 'Immediately the crowd surged forward and enveloped the car. We inched forward for a minute or two but were then forced to stop by the sheer press of bodies. People began knocking on the windows, and then on the boot and the bonnet. Inside it sounded like a massive thunderstorm. People began to jump on the car in their excitement.'

The driver panicked, and appeared to be about to jump ship. Mandela dissuaded him, and there they remained for more than an hour, 'imprisoned by thousands of our own supporters'.

A crowd of marshals managed to clear a path, and the panicky driver then set off 'at great speed in the opposite direction from the City Hall. "Man, where are you going?" I asked in some agitation. "I don't know!" he said, his voice tense with anxiety.'

Mandela kept his cool, and directed the car to Dullah Omar's home, where a startled Omar served them cold drinks. 'We had only been there a few minutes when Archbishop Tutu telephoned. How he knew where we were I do not know; he was quite distressed, and said, "Nelson, you must come back to the Grand Parade immediately. The people are growing restless. If you do not return straightaway, I cannot vouch for what might happen."'

The frightened driver managed the return trip, and Mandela was led to the upstairs balcony. 'I walked out onto the balcony and saw a boundless sea of people cheering, holding flags and banners, clapping and laughing.'

The years of Mandela had just begun.

48

An Eastern Cape welcome

This story is to end where it began – in the land adjacent to Algoa Bay.

When was Mandela to come to Port Elizabeth, to address his faithful? After much toing and froing, the date of 1 April 1990 was agreed.

This was expected to be a big event, but no one anticipated what in fact happened.

The municipality cleared a large area in Motherwell, which is a huge and relatively new black township. It was a site that was zoned for a future school, and as such it was about five hectares in area, and was relatively flat. Hundreds of chemical toilets were rented and they were placed at the end of the site opposite to where the stage was to be erected. As has become usual, all of this happened at the last minute, and by the time they had to be ordered there was only one company that could erect the stage (a building scaffolding company) and one that could provide a sound system to cover this enormous area. Both were ordered, price to be haggled about later. The municipality somehow got power to the site. If it rained, or blew a gale, the event was dead.

It didn't rain, and the wind showed Mandela its respect. The stage wobbled a bit, then settled down appropriately. The toilets were enough, and the PA system did its job. Mandela was indeed a man of magic.

The crowd was huge and was estimated at 400 000. Its size is somewhat captured in a photograph taken by the photographer Peter Auf der Heyde.

When Joe Slovo saw this photograph, he said, 'Heavens, that's bigger than Castro in Havana.' For sure.

The day passed without a disaster, which was a miracle. Mandela's speech will not be reported as one of his greats. It seemed to have been written by a loosely structured team, all trying to get their issues included. But, under the circumstances of so many untried and unpredictable issues, it can all be described as a great success.

Afterword

A great man indeed

Apersonal account and a conclusion.

Clues had by now begun to appear, pointing to the extraordinary personality of this historic person. The rally and the next day's events gave me three clues as to the greatness of the leader we had just uncovered.

Soon after I had returned home from the rally that evening, my phone rang. It was Khusta Jack, the convenor of the committee that had organised the day's events.

Would I like to come to dinner with Mr and Mrs Mandela? Crazy question. Oh, and 'Mr Mandela knows you.'

'No he doesn't'.

'Yes he does – he remembers you distinctly.'

'Nope.'

But I was at the Elizabeth Hotel, then Port Elizabeth's only five-star hotel, two hours later.

There was a long queue, snaking over the hotel's foyer. I joined the back, nervous. The queue took its time, as Mr Mandela insisted in greeting all of his guests individually at the entrance.

Standing next to him, and first in the greeting queue, was his wife, Winnie, around whom no shortage of controversy swirled at the time, and forever thereafter. She was dressed in military fatigues, and my first impression, as I got closer, was that she was overwhelmingly beautiful. On introduction, at last, I found that she was also incredibly charming. She was a phenomenal woman, Winnie Mandela.

Next to her was her husband, and I was introduced by name.

'Oh, Mr Riordan, I remember you.'

Believing a blunt rebuttal would be rude, I carefully replied, 'From where, sir?'

'Possibly 15 years ago you wrote to me through my attorney and requested to know if I was willing to accept nomination for an honorary doctorate from your alma mater.'

It all came flooding back. The 72-year-old had a much better memory than the 43-year-old.

I was in London in 1975, and read in *The Times* that the students' union of the University of London had awarded Mandela, then in jail, an Honorary Life Membership. I had returned home and had written to my alma mater, Rhodes University, to ask what I would have to do to put Mr Mandela up for an honorary doctorate. The proposal was obviously not appealing to the then Registrar, and, like all bureaucrats, he gave me the five million steps necessary. However, he did make me realise that I would have to show that I had Mr Mandela's permission for the application.

I then wrote to Mr Mandela's attorney, Ismail Ayob, and requested him to ask Mr Mandela for such permission. A long delay ensued until I got a short but charming note, signed by Mr Ayob but clearly dictated by his famous client, politely declining the offer. That was then the end of the matter.

Now, in 1990, Mr Mandela reminded me of this 15-year-old correspondence. He continued, 'I was personally keen to take up the offer, but my organisation felt that the state of segregated universities at the time did not warrant it.'

I spent the rest of the evening in a haze, and can remember no details of speeches, food or even company. But I was still sharp enough to realise that all the journalists in the world were falling about desperately trying to get an exclusive interview with Mr Mandela, and, as editor of *Monitor* magazine, I'd also like to try. I approached Mr Mandela's staff and an appointment was made for the next day. Wow!

I waited all of the next day for the interview. Eventually I was at the front of the queue when an aide approached and asked for forgiveness. Mr Mandela could only take one more journalist and, as there was a Norwegian behind me in the queue, could I please allow him my spot? I went home empty-handed but still determined.

My second brush with Mandela's greatness came the next day when Mandela journeyed to Umtata. I had met Bantu Holomisa and knew he answered his own phone. I had his number. I got hold of him and was told to be at his office first thing the next morning. I flew to East London immediately, got a rent-a-car at the airport, and drove to Umtata.

I was at Holomisa's office first thing the next morning, to be told that he and Mandela were at the palatial home of once-upon-a-time homeland leader George Matanzima, addressing a meeting of the local chamber of commerce. I should go there. I did.

I was let in, to a seat behind the head table where Holomisa and Mandela were seated.

The master of ceremonies began with a wonderful story. It was of a girls-only junior school in the rural areas of the Transkei. This school, a church school, was also a boarding school.

A few days after the release of Mandela, a deputation of girls approached the nuns and asked that the nuns get Mr Mandela to address them. In this endeavour the nuns failed. After another few days the girls delivered an ultimatum. Either Mr Mandela comes or they would no longer eat.

The Good Sisters conferred, and concluded that the threat was empty.

That day, lunch was not eaten.

The Good Sisters then realised that more than indifference was needed to solve this problem. One then proved to be as wise as she was good, and left for town. A few hours later she returned – with a tall, thin, elderly man in a suit.

It is not recorded what this gentleman told the girls, nor even who he was – but it worked. The girls scoffed down their dinner that evening. The Good Sisters relaxed and, it is rumoured, Mr Mandela's reputation has survived amongst this not-too-critical audience.

Mr Mandela enjoyed this story hugely when it was told. He then addressed the gathering and thereafter requested each of his audience to introduce himself or herself individually. It soon became obvious, even after those long jail years, that he knew the families of so many of the audience, and he delighted in a quick friendly exchange with each participant. He made every member of his audience feel respected and important. It was astonishing to watch – a wonderful event, a privilege to be there.

What followed this meeting was an extremely long and tiring day and the third example of our new leader's greatness.

I was 30 years his junior, but he endured the vicissitudes of the day better than I did. I followed him everywhere and eventually got my interview. In the Great Man's bedroom, with Peter Mokaba removing his tie and shoes, as Mandela tried the impossible – to give an interview in a condition of exhaustion, very late at night.

I had a long set of prepared questions, and cruelly kept to script despite Mandela's obvious exhaustion. He never flagged and when I eventually ended, he stood, shook my hand, bade me a respectful farewell, and an aide saw me to my car.

I left in no doubt that, in my short experience of this man, he was the paragon of the varied and confusing profession that is called 'politician'. In the midst of our crisis at the final bloody collapse of apartheid, we had our man, the man who could put it all back together, differently and better.

Notes

1   It would be entirely incorrect to compare the violence, intensity and death toll of the Battle of Stalingrad with anything that happened in South Africa, and it is certainly not my intention to do that. This battle, possibly the most ferocious and deadly in human history, saw nearly two million people killed in about five months in a desperately cold Russian winter in late 1942. The dead included about one million Russians, many of whom were civilians (Stalin refused to evacuate civilians, believing that his troops would fight more intensely if they were defending civilians), and a similar number of German, Romanian and 'turned Russian' troops. This number includes possibly 100 000 captured German prisoners of war, most of whom survived only a few weeks of captivity – the Russians did not have enough food and medical supplies to look after their own troops. One can imagine the fate of prisoners of war. The comparison with the Battle of Stalingrad is not meant in any way to diminish the horror of this battle, or the suffering of the troops and civilians involved in this merciless event. The comparison is, as I have noted in the text, a comparison of the turning point both events played in the Second World War and the South African struggle, respectively.

2   Much of this writing on Raymond Mhlaba's early years and of the years of the ANC in Port Elizabeth in the 1940s, relies on *Raymond Mhlaba's Personal Memoirs: Reminiscing from Rwanda and Uganda*, Human Sciences Research Council and Robben Island Museum, 2001, as recorded by Thembeka Mufamadi. Thembeka, under her maiden name, Thembeka Orie, had submitted an outstanding master's thesis to the University of Cape Town in 1993, under the title 'Raymond Mhlaba and the genesis of the Congress Alliance: A political biography' covering also the 1940s, the ANC's early years in Port Elizabeth. This thesis is a very useful document. I have supplemented these sources with an article of mine: Rory Riordan 1: 'ANC Elder Statesmen – interviews with Govan Mbeki and Raymond Mhlaba', *Monitor* magazine, December 1989.

3   Wilton Mkwayi was a reticent individual and there has been, until very recently, little written of him. This changed when Vianne and Michael Bell, two American

citizens who had the privilege of having Wilton as a trustee of their foundation, decided that he needed commemoration. Their biography of Wilton, *Titan without a Profile – The Life and Times of Wilton Mkwayi*, was published in 2020 by the Cory Library of Rhodes University as part of its Eastern Cape Themes series.

4   Bell and Bell, op cit, p 20.

5   Bell and Bell, op cit, p 46.

6   Alan Paton, *Hofmeyr*, Oxford University Press, London, Toronto and Cape Town, 1964.

7   Paton, op cit, p 475.

8   WK Hancock, Smuts 2: *The Fields of Force, 1919-1950*, Cambridge University Press, 1968, p 497.

9   Hancock, op cit, p 497.

10   Hermann Giliomee, *The Afrikaners: Biography of a People*, Tafelberg Publishers Limited, Cape Town 2003, p 475.

11   Allister Sparks, *The Mind of South Africa*, William Heinemann Ltd, London, 1990, pp 175 and 177. Text conflated by this author.

12   Hancock, op cit, p 500.

13   Hancock, op cit, p 485.

14   Hancock, op cit, p 489.

15   Paton, op cit, p 476.

16   Paton, op cit, p 479.

17   Giliomee, op cit, p 481.

18   Paton, op cit, p 482.

19   Paton, op cit, p 489.

20   Luli Callinicos, *Oliver Tambo. Beyond the Engeli Mountains*, David Philip, Cape Town, 2004, p 157.

21   Nelson Mandela, *Long Walk to Freedom*, Abacus Books, 1994, p 128.

22   Albert Luthuli, *Let My People Go*, Fontana Books, 1963, p 97.

23   Paton, op cit, p 493.

24   For the full text of Africans' Claims, consult Thomas Karis and Gwendolen Carter, *From Protest to Challenge, Vol 2, Hope and Challenge 1935-1952*, Hoover Institute, Stanford University, 1973, p 209. For Dr Govan Mbeki's involvement, consult Rory Riordan 1, 'ANC Elder Statesmen – interviews with Govan Mbeki and Raymond Mhlaba,' *Monitor* magazine, December 1989.

25   Gail Gerhardt, *Black Power in South Africa. The Evolution of an Ideology*, University of California Press, Berkeley, Los Angeles and London, 1978, p 51.

26   The full text of the Programme of Action is in Karis and Carter, op cit, p 337.

27   Karis and Carter, op cit, p 337.

28   Elinor Sisulu, *Walter and Albertina Sisulu: In Our Lifetime*, David Philip, Cape Town, 2002, p 117.

29   For a fuller discussion of the core legislation that made up apartheid and its later reform, please read Rory Riordan 2, 'Reform', *Monitor Magazine*, June 1988, from p 17.

30   For brief biographical notes on Dr Njongwe read Gail Gerhart and Thomas Karis, *From Protest to Challenge, Vol 4*, p 116 and Dr Patiswa Njongwe, 'Dr James

Lowell Zwelinzima Njongwe', *Adler Museum Bulletin*, Vol 35, No 1, June 2009.

31   This cameo is from the biographical note by Dr Patiswa Njongwe, in footnote 30.

32   This cameo is from the biographical note by Dr Patiswa Njongwe, in footnote 30.

33   Elinor Sisulu, *Walter and Albertina Sisulu, In Our Lifetime*, David Philip, Cape Town, 2002, p 117.

34   Elinor Sisulu, *Walter and Albertina Sisulu, In Our Lifetime*, David Philip, Cape Town, 2002, p 117.

35   Tom Lodge 1, *Black Politics in South Africa since 1945*, Ravan Press, Johannesburg, 1983, p 41.

36   Tom Lodge 1, op cit, p 41.

37   Elinor Sisulu, op cit, p 141.

38   Rory Riordan 1, op cit, p 23.

39   The full texts of the two letters from Dr Moroka and Mr Sisulu and the reply from Prime Minister Malan's personal secretary are in Karis and Carter, Vol 2, op cit, p 476.

40   Karis and Carter, Vol 2, op cit, p 417.

41   Albert Luthuli, *Let My People Go*, Collins, Johannesburg, 1962, p 115.

42   Luli Callinicos, op cit, p 182.

43   Luli Callinicos, op cit, p 182.

44   Karis and Carter, Vol 2, op cit, p 418.

45   Thembeka Mufamadi, op cit, p 84.

46   Tom Lodge 1, op cit, p 46.

47   Nelson Mandela, op cit, p 127.

48   Nelson Mandela, op cit, p 127.

49   Rory Riordan 3, 'Business Plan for a Performing Arts Centre in the Red Location', Dojon Financial Services, Port Elizabeth, 2012. Original ascription lost.

50   Information about Sr Aidan is from Dr Patiswa Njongwe's article.

51   Rory Riordan 1, , op cit, p 23.

52   Karis and Carter, Vol 2, op cit, p 484.

53   Albert Luthuli, *Let my people go*, Collins, Johannesburg, 1962, p 115.

54   The full text of 'The Road to Freedom is via the Cross' is in Karis and Carter, Vol 2, op cit, p 486.

55   Gail Gerhart and Thomas Karis, Vol 4, op cit, p 61.

56   Thandeka Mufamadi, op cit, p 89.

57   Albert Luthuli, op cit, pp 129–130.

58   Albert Luthuli, op cit, pp 129–130.

59   Tom Lodge 1, op cit, p 43.

60   Tom Lodge 1, op cit, p 50.

61   Tom Lodge 1, op cit, p 43.

62   Nelson Mandela, op cit, p 129.

63   Rory Riordan 1, op cit, p 24.

64   Nelson Mandela, op cit, p 129.

65   Elinor Sisulu, op cit, p 157.

66   Rory Riordan 1, op cit, pp 23-24.

67   Nelson Mandela, op cit p 130.

68   Albert Luthuli, op cit, p 130.

69 Thembeka Mufamadi, op cit, p 74.

70 Thomas Karis and Gail Gerhart, *From Protest to Challenge, Vol 3, Challenge and Violence 1953-1964,* Hoover Institute Press, Stanford University, 1977, pp 9 and 83.

71 Karis and Gerhart, Vol 3, op cit, p 9.

72 Thembeka Mufamadi, op cit, p 93.

73 Thembeka Mufamadi, op cit, p 93.

74 Nelson Mandela, op cit, p 134.

75 Karis and Gerhart, Vol 3, op cit, p 11.

76 Thembeka Mufamadi, op cit, p 103.

77 Nelson Mandela, op cit,p 134.

78 Thembeka Mufamadi, op cit, p 107.

79 Colin Bundy has written the only biography available on Govan and regretfully it is pocket-sized. Colin Bundy 1: *Govan Mbeki,* Jacana Media, Johannesburg, 2012. There is an earlier 20-page biographical note, also by Bundy, in the Introduction to *Learning from Robben Island: The Prison Writings of Govan Mbeki,* David Philip, Cape Town, 1991 (Colin Bundy 2).

80 Colin Bundy 1, p 32.

81 Colin Bundy 1, p 40.

82 Colin Bundy 1, op cit, p 4.

83 Rory Riordan 1, op cit, p 20.

84 Rory Riordan 1, op cit, p 20.

85 Rory Riordan 1, op cit, p 20.

86 Colin Bundy 1, op cit, p 45.

87 Rory Riordan 1, op cit, p 20.

88 Colin Bundy 1, op cit, p 65.

89 Wikipedia, 'Govan Mbeki'.

90 Colin Bundy 1, op cit, p 47.

91 Karis and Gerhart, Vol 3, op cit, pp 40 and 43.

92 Colin Bundy 1, p 80.

93 Colin Bundy 1, p 81.

94 All references to Nkosinathi Benson Fihla are from personal interviews between the writer and Fihla.

95 Govan Mbeki, '30 000 at Funeral of Man who was shot by the Police', *New Age,* 5 April 1956, http://www.historicalpapers.wits.ac.za, reprinted in Bell and Bell, op cit, p 58.

96 Govan Mbeki, '30 000 at Funeral of Man who was shot by the Police', *New Age,* 5 April 1956, http://www.historicalpapers.wits.ac.za, reprinted in Bell and Bell, op cit, p 58.

97 Govan Mbeki, '30 000 at Funeral of Man who was shot by the Police', *New Age, 5 April 1956,* http://www.historicalpapers.wits.ac.za, reprinted in Bell and Bell, op cit, p 58.

98 Ruth First, Preface, *The Peasants' Revolt, by Govan Mbeki,* International Defence and Aid Fund for Southern Africa, 1984, p 9.

99 Colin Bundy 1, p 101.

100 Rory Riordan 1, op cit, p 25.

101 Thembeka Mufamadi, op cit, p 108.

102   Rory Riordan 1, op cit, p 25.

103   Thembeka Mufamadi, op cit, p 108.

104   Karis and Gerhart, Vol 3, op cit, pp 646-647.

105   Rory Riordan 1, op cit, p 26.

106   There is a surprisingly comprehensive Wikipedia article on 'Harold Strachan', and Politicsweb ran a useful obituary by RW Johnson.

107   RW Johnson, op cit.

108   Wikipedia, 'Harold Strachan'

109   RW Johnson, op cit.

110   Rory Riordan 1, op cit, p 26.

111   Thembeka Mufamadi, op cit, p 116.

112   Personal communication from Nkosinathi Fihla and transcripts from the Rivonia Trial.

113   Personal communication from Nkosinathi Fihla and transcripts from the Rivonia Trial.

114   Rory Riordan 1, op cit, p 27.

115   www.justice.gov.za>trc. Mr Harold Strachan.

116   The State vs Zinakile Mkaba, Vuyisile Mini and Wilson Khayinga, Supreme Court of South Africa, Eastern Cape Division – incomplete record at www.historicalpapers.wits.ac.za.

117   Reprinted from *Sechaba, the ANC's journal*, in Wikipedia, 'Vuyisile Mini'.

118   Biographical references to Ernest Malgas and Henry Fazzie are from: Rory Riordan 4: 'Port Elizabeth and Uitenhage – Township Revolt and Political Development, 1976 to 1990', a paper for the conference on 'Port Elizabeth's Place in South African History and Historiography', Vista University, 24–25 September 1992.

119   Rory Riordan 5: 'Attacks on ANC Members, their premises and other such property - 1981 to 1988', *Monitor Magazine* Archives, unpublished.

120   Biographical references to Ernest Malgas and Henry Fazzie are from: Rory Riordan 4: 'Port Elizabeth and Uitenhage – Township Revolt and Political Development, 1976 to 1990', a paper for the conference on 'Port Elizabeth's Place in South African History and Historiography', Vista University, 24–25 September 1992.

121   References to all court issues here are from: 'The State versus Henry Fazzie, James Chirwa, Matthews Makhalima, Maxwell Mayekiso, Ernest Malgaz [*sic*], Jack Ndzuzu and Alfred Khonza', Supreme Court of South Africa, Transvaal Provincial Division, convicted of sabotage by Mr Justice Theron on 30 September 1963. Copies in *Monitor* Magazine Archives.

122   Denis Goldberg, *The Mission*, STE Publishers, Johannesburg, 2010, p 109.

123   For the full text of Operation Mayibuye, consult Karis and Gerhart, Vol 3, p 760.

124   Denis Goldberg, op cit, p 107.

125   Nelson Mandela, op cit, pp 343-344.

126   Quoted in Karis and Gerhart, Vol 3, op cit, p 660. I have heard this attributed to ZK Matthews.

127   Karis and Gerhart, op cit, p 656.

128   Nelson Mandela, op cit, p 335.

129   Rory Riordan 1, op cit, p 28.

130   Rory Riordan 1, op cit, p 28.
131   Denis Goldberg, op cit, p 127.
132   Nelson Mandela, op cit, p 342.
133   Nelson Mandela, op cit, p 346.
134   Nelson Mandela, op cit, p 346.
135   For the full text of Mandela's address, please consult Karis and Gerhart, op cit, Vol 3, p 771.
136   Nelson Mandela, op cit, p 348.
137   Nelson Mandela, op cit, p 348. For much of what is to follow, I am following Mandela's account.
138   Nelson Mandela, op cit, p 348.
139   Nelson Mandela, op cit, p 348.
140   Elinor Sisulu, op cit, p 257.
141   Quoted in Elinor Sisulu, op cit, p 257.
142   Hilda Bernstein, *The World that was Ours*, quoted in Colin Bundy 2, op cit, p xix.
143   Rory Riordan 1, op cit, p 29.
144   Francis Meli, *A History of the ANC: South Africa Belongs to Us*, Bloomington: Indiana University Press, 1989.
145   Rory Riordan 1, op cit, p 29.
146   For the analysis of the closing argument, see Nelson Mandela, op cit. pp 356 and 357.
147   For the analysis of the closing argument, see Nelson Mandela, op cit, pp 356 and 357.
148   For the analysis of the closing argument, I again follow Nelson Mandela, op cit, pp 356 and 357.
149   Thomas Karis and Gail Gerhart, *From Protest to Challenge*, Vol 3, p 57.
150   Karis and Gerhart, op cit, p 61.
151   Karis and Gerhart, op cit, p 62.
152   Karis and Gerhart, op cit, p 73.
153   Bell and Bell, op cit, pp 83–85.
154   Bell and Bell, op cit, p 97.
155   Bell and Bell, op cit, p 106.
156   Bell and Bell, op cit, p 113.
157   Bell and Bell, op cit, p 115 ff, for a detailed assessment of the trial.
158   Rory Riordan 6, *City of Port Elizabeth Capital and Operating Budgets, 1994/95*, private publication of the Transitional Local Council, p 5.
159   The story of South End, and its heartbreaking demise, is well told in Roy H du Pre, 'The Battle for South End: Group Areas Removals in Port Elizabeth in the 1960s', https://journals.ufs.ac.za>jch.article.download. More detail and many memories of old South End can be found in *South End as We Knew it* by Yusuf Agherdien, Ambrose George and Shaheed Hendricks, also edited by Du Pre. Hendricks has added a PhD thesis on this topic, 'Biography of a Vanished Community: South End, Port Elizabeth', Stellenbosch University, 2017.
160   Rory Riordan 7: 'The Great Black Shark, an interview with Chris Hani', *Monitor Magazine*, December 1990, p 10.
161   Rory Riordan 4.
162   Rory Riordan 7: 'The Great Black Shark, an interview with Chris Hani', *Monitor*

Magazine, December 1990, p 10.

163   Mkhuseli Jack, *To Survive and Succeed*, Kwela Books, Johannesburg, 2018.

164   Rory Riordan 8: 'The Watsons', *Monitor* Magazine, October 1988, p 4.

165   Rory Riordan 3.

166   Biographical references to Ernest Malgas and Henry Fazzie are from: Rory Riordan 4: 'Port Elizabeth and Uitenhage – Township Revolt and Political Development, 1976 to 1990', a paper for the conference on 'Port Elizabeth's Place in South African History and Historiography', Vista University, 24–25 September 1992.

167   The murders of Mapetla Mohapi and George Botha are outlined in Truth and Reconciliation Commission of South Africa Report, Volume 3 (TRC3) pp 64 ff.

168   Janet Cherry 1: 'Uitenhage 1804 – 2004: The Struggle against Apartheid' being chapter 7 of 'Uitenhage 200 – 1804 to 2004', edited by Otto Terblanche for the Uitenhage Bicentenary Committee, 2004.

169   The murder of Steve Biko has been extensively documented, beginning famously with Donald Woods' 1978 classic, *Biko*, New York, Penguin. Read also TRC 3, op cit, p 66, and Xolela Mangcu, *Biko: A Biography*, Tafelberg, Cape Town, 2012.

170   Gail Gerhart, op cit, p 260.

171   Xolela Mangcu, op cit, p 125.

172   Gail Gerhart, op cit, p 274.

173   Khusta Jack, op cit, p 81.

174   TRC 3 pp 67 ff.

175   Khusta Jack, op cit, pp 94 ff.

176   Tom Lodge and Bill Nasson, *All, Here, and Now: Black Politics in South Africa in the 1980s*, Ford Foundation and David Philip, Cape Town, 1991, p 164.

177   Rory Riordan 4. All quotes hereafter are from this work.

178   The murder of Griffiths Mxenge, and ensuing issues, are outlined in three articles I wrote for the *EP Herald* on 15, 22 and 29 April 1991 (Rory Riordan 10) and is extensively covered in TRC 3, pp 183 ff.

179   The murder of Sizwe Kondile is recounted in TRC 3, pp 72 ff.

180   The murder of Siphiwe Mthimkhulu is covered in TRC 3, pp 74 ff.

181   Sheena Duncan, 'Riekert Commission Report', *The Black Sash*, August 1979, on SA History Online.

182   Tom Lodge and Bill Nasson, *All, Here, and Now: Black Politics in South Africa in the 1980s*, Ford Foundation and David Philip, Cape Town, 1991, p 48.

183   The notes on PEYCO and Mkhuseli Jack are drawn from Khusta Jack, op cit, and Rory Riordan 4.

184   Janet Cherry 2, 'We were not afraid', being chapter 11 of *Women in South African History*, edited by Nomboniso Gasa, HSRC Press, Cape Town, 2007, pp 287 ff.

185   Allan Boesak: 'Speech at the Launch of the UDF', in *Speeches that Shaped South Africa*, ed by Martha Evans, Penguin Books, Cape Town, 2017, pp 150 ff.

186   Tom Lodge, 'South Africa: Time Running Out', first draft of a later expanded document, which became Lodge and Nasson, p 9.

187   Khusta Jack, op cit, pp 140 and 141.

188   Khusta Jack, op cit, pp 140 and 141.

189   The issues around the Black Local Councils in Port Elizabeth and Uitenhage are drawn from Rory Riordan 9, 'Five Years of the Ibhayi Council', *Monitor*

Magazine, October 1988, pp 13-33.

190 The most complete source on Matthew Goniwe and his later murder is Christopher Nicholson's book *Permanent Removal: Who killed the Cradock Four?*, Wits University Press, Johannesburg, 2004. This readable work gallops along at a pleasant pace, but has a few challenging aspects, for example the interpretation of the death of Molly Blackburn.

191 All notes about Janet Cherry are by the author and much is improved by Janet's comments on an earlier draft of this section.

192 The issues around the Black Local Councils in Port Elizabeth and Uitenhage are drawn from Rory Riordan 9, 'Five Years of the Ibhayi Council', *Monitor* Magazine, October 1988, pp 13-33.

193 Khusta Jack, op cit, pp 158 and 159.

194 Nic J Rhoodie, CP de Kock and MP Couper, 'White perceptions of socio-political change in South Africa', and CP de Kock, Nic J Rhoodie and MP Couper, 'Black perceptions of socio-political change in South Africa', both in DJ van Vuuren, NE Wiehahn, JA Lombard and NJ Rhoodie, *South Africa: a Plural Society in Transition*, Butterworth Group, South Africa, 1985.

195 TRC 3, op cit, p 96.

196 Tom Lodge in Lodge and Nasson, op cit, p 65.

197 Tom Lodge in Lodge and Nasson, op cit, p 67.

198 Mark Swilling, quoted in Janet Cherry 1, op cit, p 154.

199 The issues around the Black Local Councils in Port Elizabeth and Uitenhage are drawn from Rory Riordan 9, 'Five Years of the Ibhayi Council', *Monitor* Magazine, October 1988, pp 13-33.

200 See note 190.

201 SASPU 13, 'Crisis and Struggle in the Eastern Cape – Eastern Cape Activists Speak'. An interview with Stone Sizani and Derrick Swartz. Unpaginated photocopy in Human Rights Trust archives.

202 Khusta Jack, op cit, p 165.

203 The seeming endless list of acts of insurrection has been chronicled in: Rory Riordan 4: Dateline of events, 1984 to 1987, for Port Elizabeth and Uitenhage, and in Janet Cherry 1, for Uitenhage.

204 Janet Cherry 1, op cit, pp 154 and 155.

205 Nicholas Haysom, 'The Langa Shooting and the Kannemeyer Commission of Enquiry' in *South African Review 3*, Ravan Press, Johannesburg, 1986, TRC 3 p 85.

206 Mark Swilling, 'Stayaways, Urban Protest and the State', *South African Review 3*, op cit, pp 20 ff.

207 Allister Sparks, *The Mind of South Africa*, Heinemann, London, 1990, pp 344.

208 Possibly the most comprehensive summary report of the Langa Massacre and the subsequent Kannemeyer Commission is: Derek Catsam, '"Those who Command the Ones that Pulled the Trigger see us as less than Human" The Langa Massacre and State Violence in South Africa', Spring 2000 meeting of the Southeastern Regional Seminar in African Studies (SERSAS), Western Carolina University. see also Janet Cherry 1.

209 Nicholas Haysom, op cit, p 289.

210 Nicholas Haysom, op cit.

211 This description relies on: Martin Murray, *South Africa: Time of Agony, Time of*

Destiny, London, 1987, p 280.

212   Mncedisi Saliso, report in the *Eastern Province Herald* of about a year after the Kinikini deaths. Photocopy in Human Rights Trust archives.

213   TRC 3, op cit, p 109.

214   Mono Badela, 'The Weeks of Rage that led to the First Necklace Death', *Weekly Mail*, 4 September 1987.

215   Martin Murray, op cit, p 281.

216   TRC 3, op cit, p 110.

217   Khusta Jack, op cit, pp 166–168.

218   The continuous pattern of these brutal events is covered in TRC 3, pp 96 ff.

219   Mufson, 'A Tradition of Political Activism: An Interview with Mono Badela', in Lodge and Nasson, op cit, pp 235 ff

220   TRC 3, op cit, p 93..

221   TRC 3, op cit, p 117, and various South African Press Association (SAPA) reports on the TRC's ongoing investigations, particularly those of 9 and 11 March 1998.

222   Khusta Jack, op cit, p 181 ff.

223   Rory Riordan 11, 'Hy is Goed Gebliksem', unpublished report in the Human Rights Trust archives.

224   The Port Elizabeth Consumer Boycott has been the subject of considerable attention, including: Roland White, 'A Tide has Risen. A Breach has occurred: Towards an assessment of the Strategic Value of the Consumer Boycotts', (photocopy in the Human Rights Trust archive; Philip Black, 'Boycott Strategies in the Eastern Cape', a paper delivered at a conference on Development Issues in the Eastern Cape held in Port Elizabeth on 24 March 1986; Kirk Helliker, Andre Roux and Roland White, 'Asithengi! Recent Consumer Boycotts', *SA Review 4*, Ravan Press, Johannesburg 1987; Khusta Jack, op cit, pp 171 ff.

225   Despite its failings, Nicholson's book is a source of much detail here. The TRC notes are brief (TRC 3 p 116). Arthur Chaskalson's masterly summary, presented to the first inquest, is in the Human Rights Trust's archive. George Bizos's description of Advocate Mostert's admissions is in: *No One to Blame?: In Pursuit of Justice in South Africa*, David Philip., 1988.

226   George Bizos' description of Advocate Mostert's admissions is in *No One to Blame?*

227   TRC 3 p 116.

228   Khusta Jack, op cit, p 173.

229   Khusta Jack, op cit, p 176.

230   The section on detainee torture as exposed by Dr Wendy Orr has text from the court application coordinated by the attorney Halton Cheadle which is reprinted in Rory Riordan 11. The notes on Ivy Gcina and her prison warder come from the records of the Truth and Reconciliation Commission. The quotations from Dr Orr come from 'Uncompromised Professional Responsibility in Apartheid South Africa' by Wendy Orr MBChB, in *AMA J Ethics*, 2015: 17 (10) 973–977.

231   Frederik van Zyl Slabbert, *The Other Side of History*, Jonathan Ball Publishers, Johannesburg, 2006, p 22.

232   Military wiki org/wiki/ list of operations of South African border war.

233   Christopher Saunders, 'The South African Angolan Talks, 1976 to 1984 – A

Little Known Cold War Thread', *Kronos*, 37, pp 144 ff.

234   Christopher Saunders, 'The South African Angolan Talks, 1976 to 1984 – A Little Known Cold War Thread', *Kronos*, 37, pp 144 ff.

235   Ken Flower, *Serving Secretly*, Galago Publishing (Pty) (Ltd), Alberton, 1987, p 300.

236   Ken Flower, op cit, p 301.

237   Ken Flower, op cit, p 151.

238   Alex Vines, 'Renamo Terrorism in Mozambique', Centre for South Safrican Studies, University of York, 1991, p 18.

239   Alex Vines, op cit, pp 18 and 19.

240   Alex Vines, op cit, p 19.

241   Wikipedia, article, 'Mozambique Civil War'.

242   Alex Vines, op cit, p 17.

243   William Minter, 'Inside Renamo', *Transformation* 10 (1989), pp 17 ff.

244   Mkhuseli Jack, op cit, p 151.

245   For an understanding of Operation Argon, there is a long (85 minutes) YouTube interview with Wynand du Toit which is easily accessed. Du Toit has written a number of books, the first of which, *Judas Goat,* covers this operation in depth. He has come to believe that Argon was a set-up, designed to create South African prisoners to, somehow, further the cause of the release of Nelson Mandela. For less sensational stuff, Galago Publishing has a number of titles on the Angolan Bush War, of which *The Silent War* by Galago owner Peter Stiff, is pertinent.

246   Hermann Giliomee, *The Last Afrikaner Leaders*, Cape Town, Tafelberg, 2012, p 191.

247   Alex Vines, op cit, p 24.

248   Alex Vines, op cit, p 24.

249   Hermann Giliomee, op cit, p 191.

250   Fanie Cloete, 'Resolving PW Botha'a 1985 Rubicon Riddle', *Historia* 64, 2 November 2019, pp 132-155.

251   Comprehensive excerpts of the speech are in Martha Evans, op cit.

252   Glenn Adler, 'Withdrawl Pains: General Motors and Ford Disinvest from South Africa', *South African Review 5*, Ravan Press, Johannesburg, 1989.

253   An extensive statement of the detention and torture of Archie Mkele is in, Rory Riordan 12, 'Two Irregularities made Possible by the Present State of Emergency', unpublished compilation of 24 statements by detainees of their torture, handed over by Mrs Helen Suzman and Rory Riordan to then Minister Adriaan Vlok in his Pretoria office, 26 August 1987.

254   Rory Riordan 8.

255   Christopher Nicholson, op cit, pp 61 ff. Nicholson repeatedly refers to the business as 'Builder's Market' when in fact it was Builder's Warehouse – no relation to the present giant company. I will stick to Nicholson's usage.

256   Christopher Nicholson, op cit, p 150.

257   Rory Riordan 9.

258   Notes from conversations with Judy Chalmers and George Irvine, and attendance at the funeral.

259   South African Institute of Race Relations, *Race Relations Survey 1986, Part 1*, SAIRR, Johannesburg, 1987, pp 160, 161, and 92 and 93.

260 Ken Owen, 'The man who wasn't there', in Alfred LeMaitre and Michael Savage, eds, *Van Zyl Slabbert: The Passion for Reason*, Jonathan Ball Publishers, Johannesburg, 2010.

261 South African Institute of Race Relations, *Race Relations Survey 1986 Part 2*, p 815.

262 Mark Swilling and Mark Phillips, 'The Emergency State: Its Structure, Power and Limits; in *South African Review 5*, edited and compiled by Glenn Moss and Ingrid Obery, Ravan Press, Johannesburg, 1989.

263 Van Zyl Slabbert, *The System and the Struggle*, Jonathan Ball Publishers, Johannesburg, 1989, p 120.

264 Mark Swilling and Mark Phillips, op cit, p 76.

265 Mark Swilling and Mark Phillips, op cit, p 80.

266 Van Zyl Slabbert, op cit, p 121.

267 Van Zyl Slabbert, op cit, p 123.

268 Van Zyl Slabbert, op cit, p 125.

269 David Webster: 'Repression and the State of Emergency', *South African Review 4*, Ravan Publishers, Johannesburg, 1987, p 142.

270 South African Institute of Race Relations (SAIRR): *Race Relations Survey 1985*, Johannesburg 1986, pp 440 ff.

271 Max Coleman and David Webster: 'Repression and Detentions in South Africa', *SA Review 3*, p 127.

272 SAIRR, *Race Relations Survey 1986 Part 2*, p 516.

273 Brian Pottinger, *The Imperial Presidency*, Southern Book Publishers, Johannesburg, 1988, p 323.

274 Brian Pottinger, op cit, pages 324 and 325.

275 Nelson Mandela, op cit, pp 468 and 469.

276 Riaan de Villiers and Jan-Ad Stemmet, *Prisoner 913, the Release of Nelson Mandela, Revelations from the Archive of Minister Kobie Coetsee*, Tafelberg, Cape Town, 2020.

277 Nelson Mandela, op cit, p 497.

278 Nelson Mandela, op cit, p 502.

279 De Villiers and Stemmet, op cit, p 49.

280 De Villiers and Stemmet, op cit, p 49.

281 De Villiers and Stemmet, op cit, p 49.

282 De Villiers and Stemmet, op cit, p 51.

283 Martha Evans, op cit, pp 173 ff.

284 Martha Evans, op cit, pp 173 ff.

285 Nelson Mandela, op cit, pp 512 and 513.

286 Nelson Mandela, op cit, pp 512 and 513.

287 Joseph Lelyveld, 'Commonwealth Delegates Chart Drive for South Africa Sanctions', *New York Times*, 13 June 1986.

288 Brian Pottinger, op cit, p 331.

289 De Villiers and Stemmet, op cit, p 66.

290 De Villiers and Stemmet, op cit, p 69.

291 De Villiers and Stemmet, op cit, p 69.

292 De Villiers and Stemmet, op cit, p 69.

293 Joseph Lelyveld, 'Commonwealth Delegates'.

294 Brian Pottinger, op cit, p 399.

295 Brian Pottinger, op cit, p 399.

296 South African Institute of Race Relations, *Race Relations Survey 1986 Part 1*, op cit, p 135 and *Part 2*, pp 813 and 814.

297 De Villiers and Stemmet, op cit, p 84.

298 De Villiers and Stemmet, op cit, p 84.

299 Mark Swilling, 'UDF Local Government in Port Elizabeth', *Monitor* Magazine, October 1988, p 48.

300 Mark Swilling, op cit, p 47.

301 Rory Riordan 9.

302 Chris Rennie, 'Court overturns the Banning of Jack', 22 March 1986.

303 Anthony Mathews, *Freedom, State Security and the Rule of Law*, Juta, Cape Town and Johannesburg, 1986, p 127.

304 Lloyd Coutts and other reporters, *Herald* newspaper, 7 April 1986.

305 Janet Cherry 3, 'We are not afraid' being Chapter 11 of Nomboniso Gasa, ed, *Women in South African History*, HSRC Press, Cape Town, 2007, pp 303 ff.

306 Janet Cherry 3, op cit, p 303.

307 Janet Cherry 3, op cit, p 303.

308 Tom Lodge, in Lodge and Nasson, op cit, p 178.

309 The most valuable record of the destruction of the Crossroads squatter camps is that of Josette Cole, *Crossroads: The Politics of Reform and Repression, 1976 to 1986*, Ravan Press, Johannesburg, 1987. This work, written while the embers of the conflagration were still smouldering, is key to understanding the horror. Also: P du Toit and J Gagiano, both then Stellenbosch University professors, 'Strongmen of the Cape Flats', *Africa Insight*, 23, no 2, 1993; and two Truth and Reconciliation Commission reports: 'Vigilantes and Inter-Group Conflicts: Contra-Mobilisation' in Truth and Reconciliation Commission Report, volume 3, pp 463 ff; and the TRC interview transcript of their 11 June 1997 interview with Ulrich Schelhase.

310 Riaan de Villiers, 'The Cape Doctor', *Leadership Magazine*, 1985, 4, no 2, p 52.

311 John J McCuen, *The Art of Counter-Revolutionary War*, London, Faber and Faber, 1969.

312 McCuen, op cit, p 56. 55 Allister Sparks, *The Mind of South Africa*, William Heinemann, London, 1990, p 357.

313 The TRC interview transcript of their 11 June 1997 interview with Ulrich Schelhase.

314 Truth and Reconciliation Commission Report, Volume 3, p 466.

315 Truth and Reconciliation Commission Report, Volume 3, p 466.

316 Rory Riordan 13. Much of the Langa/Kabah history is taken from the Human Rights Trust's submission to the Legal Resources Centre in support of the LRC's submission to, inter alia, the Minister of Constitutional Development and Planning for the purposes of having Langa/Kabah declared, in terms of the legislation of the time, a 'Free Settlement Area', ie an area not restricted to any one racial group. Human Rights Trust archives, unpublished, 1989. This in turn draws extensively from Glenn Adler, 'Trying not to be Cruel: Local Government Resistance to the Application of the Group Areas Act in Uitenhage', paper presented to the Southern African Research Paper Seminar, Yale University, 20

January 1988.

317   Rory Riordan 13, op cit.

318   Rory Riordan 13, op cit.

319   Rory Riordan 13, op cit.

320   Glenn Adler, op cit, p 62.

321   Dr Franco Frescura, 'A Survey of Squatter Housing in KwaNobuhle Extension 4C', University of Port Elizabeth, December 1987, p 10.

322   For the period from the Langa Massacre (21 March 1985) until the razing of Langa (beginning in July 1986) there is a limited literature. For those wanting 'the full Monty', Mark Swilling's PhD thesis, 'Urban Control and the Changing Forms of Political Conflict in Uitenhage 1977 to 1986', University of Warwick, 1994,will keep one awake for some considerable time. A shorter route to much of the same story is also by Swilling, 'Langa: Protest, Urban Change and Defeat', unpublished paper, copy in Human Rights Trust archive.

323   Mark Swilling, thesis, op cit, p 352.

324   The Human Rights Trust, initially 'Operation Real South Africa' was founded by Andrew Savage and myself at the beginning of October 1986. Its first intervention was the horror of the Langa removal, which was well underway at that time the Trust was formed. The Trust approached the issue with enormous energy, and I kept a diary of correspondence and events from 14 October 1986 to January 1987. This work, unpublished, is in the Human Rights Trust archives, and is referred to here as Rory Riordan 14: Langa Diary. The quote from Barry Erasmus's affidavit is on page 55 thereof.

325   Rory Riordan 14: Langa Diary.

326   Rory Riordan 14: Langa Diary, op cit.

327   Rory Riordan 13, Submission to Legal Resources Centre, op cit.

328   Rory Riordan 14, Langa Diary, op cit.

329   David Webster, 'Repression and the State of Emergency', *South African Review 4*, Ravan Press, Johannesburg, 1987, p 144.

330   David Webster, op cit, p 142.

331   Webster and Friedman, 'Repression and the State of Emergency', *South African Review 5*, Ravan Press, Johannesburg 1989.

332   Khusta Jack, op cit, p 200.

333   Tom Lodge, *All, here and now*, op cit, p 88.

334   Susan Collin Marks, a brief introduction to her memoir, *My Mother against Apartheid*, reviewed on the Black Sash's website, www.blacksash.org.za.

335   Mary Burton, *The Black Sash*, Jacana Media, Johannesburg, 2015, p 135.

336   Mary Burton, op cit, p 139.

337   Mary Burton, op cit, p 140.

338   The full results of the 1981 and 1987 elections are in DJ van Vuuren, J Latakgomo, HC Marais and L Schlemmer, *South African Election 1987*, Owen Burgess Publishers, Pinetown 1987.

339   For the results of the 1989 election, particularly in Port Elizabeth, see Rory Riordan 15, 'The General Election of 6 September 1989', private publication of *Monitor* Magazine, 1989.

340   Frederik van Zyl Slabbert, *The Other Side of History*, Jonathan Ball Publishers, Johannesburg, 2006, Slabbert gives a detailed account of the Dakar Initiative in

this publication, and I refer readers to Slabbert's as usual, casual, startling and sometimes infuriating writing.

341   Stephen Ellmann, *Arthur Chaskalson*, Picador Africa, Johannesburg, 2019, p 228.

342   Janet Cherry, *Port Elizabeth End Conscription Campaign: A Brief History*, privately published, November 2009. Most of the facts about the Port Elizabeth ECC I have drawn from this excellent pamphlet. It is unpaginated.

343   Janet Cherry, *Port Elizabeth End Conscription Campaign*, op cit.

344   sahistory.org.za, End Conscription Campaign (ECC).

345   Olivia Forsyth, *Agent 407*, Jonathan Ball Publishers, Johannesburg, 2015, p 139.

346   Janet Cherry, *Port Elizabeth End Conscription Campaign*, op cit.

347   sahistory.org.za, article on Janet Mary Cherry.

348   Janet Cherry, *Port Elizabeth End Conscription Campaign*, op cit.

349   Janet Cherry, *Port Elizabeth End Conscription Campaign*, op cit.

350   Janet Cherry, *Port Elizabeth End Conscription Campaign*, op cit.

351   Olivia Forsyth, op cit, p 122.

352   Olivia Forsyth, op cit, p 122.

353   Anneliese Burgess, presenter, 'Film: South Africa – Apartheid Spy', Transcript of interviews, Journeyman Pictures, 2019, London.

354   Olivia Forsyth, op cit, page 99.

355   Janet Cherry, *Port Elizabeth End Conscription Campaign*, op cit.

356   A quick summary of the economic challenges the apartheid state faced can be found in *Contemporary Economic Policy*, Anton D. Lowenberg, 'Why South Africa's Apartheid Economy Failed', July 1997, XV, pp 62-72.

357   South African Institute of Race Relations, *Race Relations Survey, 1987/88*, Johannesburg, p 406.

358   South African Institute of Race Relations, *Race Relations Survey, 1987/88*, Johannesburg, p 294.

359   South African Institute of Race Relations, *Race Relations Survey, 1987/88*, Johannesburg, pp 324 and 325.

360   South African Institute of Race Relations, *Race Relations Survey, 1987/88*, Johannesburg, pp 406 and 407.

361   Glenn Adler, 'Withdrawal Pains: General Motors and Ford Disinvest from South Africa', *South African Review 5*, Ravan Press, Johannesburg, 1989.

362   Quoted in the *New York Times*, 25 November 1986.

363   South African Institute of Race Relations, *Race Relations Survey, 1988/89*, Johannesburg, p 327.

364   Philip I Levy, 'Sanctions on South Africa: What Did They Do?', Yale University Economic Growth Centre, Discussion Paper 796, February 1999.

365   John J McCuen, *The Art of Counter-Revolutionary War*, London, Faber and Faber, 1969.

366   The Urban Foundation under Roger Matlock commissioned the first properly researched study of the townships of what is now Nelson Mandela Bay, entitled 'Greater Algoa Bay Area – Affordable Housing Research Project'; it was prepared by Executive Projects cc in October 1985, and we use its data here.

367   Rory Riordan 19: most of this is drawn from a Human Rights Trust diary, 'The Red Location Removal', unpublished, in the Human Rights Trust archive. Some

of the material was published in *Monitor* magazine: Rory Riordan 9, 'Five Years of the Ibhayi Council', *Monitor*, October 1988, pp 13 ff.

368 A record of this meeting is in the Red Location Removal diary, and a summary is in Rory Riordan 9, p 20.

369 Rory Riordan 16, 'The Ukuhleleleka of Port Elizabeth', *Monitor* magazine, June 1988, p 14.

370 Rory Riordan 17, 'Some Documented SAP Torture, 12 June 1986 State of Emergency, Documentation June 1986 – January 1987', Unpublished document, Human Rights Trust archive.

371 Rory Riordan 17, op cit.

372 Rory Riordan 9.

373 Rory Riordan 9.

374 Rory Riordan 9.

375 South African Institute of Race Relations, *Annual Survey of Race Relations*, various years.

376 Mark Bennett, 'Recent Trends in Industrial Action', *South African Review 5*, Ravan Press, Johannesburg, 1989, p 296.

377 Rory Riordan 9, op cit, p 22.

378 Rory Riordan 9, op cit, p 24.

379 Rory Riordan 9, op cit, p 20.

380 Rory Riordan 18, *Five Golden Years, Nelson Mandela Bay Municipality 2016–2021*, a publication of the Nelson Mandela Bay Municipality, 2016, p 9.

381 *Monitor* magazine, 'Township Recreational Facilities', July 1989, p 50.

382 Rory Riordan 9, op cit, p 21.

383 Rory Riordan 9, op cit, p 25.

384 Rory Riordan 9, op cit, p 20.

385 Rory Riordan 19, 'Red Location Removal Diary', Human Rights Trust, unpublished document, Human Rights Trust Archives, p 3. This quote is from a report of a meeting between a delegation from the Red Location, led by Mrs Maneli, to the Black Sash Advice Office, notes taken by Shelagh Hurley.

386 Rory Riordan 19, op cit, p 9.

387 Rory Riordan 19, op cit, p 15.

388 Rory Riordan 19, op cit, p 10.

389 Rory Riordan 19, op cit, p 12.

390 Rory Riordan 19, op cit, p 64.

391 Rory Riordan 19, op cit, p 49.

392 Rory Riordan 19, op cit, pp 61 ff.

393 Rory Riordan 19, op cit, p 72.

394 Rory Riordan 19, op cit, p 92.

395 The story of the vigilante attack is covered in detail in Rory Riordan 20, 'The Events in KwaNobuhle, Sunday, 4th January 1987', a Human Rights Trust document, unpublished. From this was drawn Rory Riordan 21, 'Kinikini's Crude Revenge', *Monitor* magazine, June 1988, pp 46 ff.

396 Rory Riordan 20, op cit, p 3.

397 Rory Riordan 21, op cit, p 58.

398 Rory Riordan 9, op cit, p 26.

399 Rory Riordan 9, op cit, p 26.

400 CP de Kock, 'Revolutionary Violence in South Africa: 1000 days after 3 September 1984' in DJ van Vuuren, NE Wiehahn, NJ Rhoodie and M Wiechers, eds, *South Africa: The Challenge of Reform*, Owen Burgess Publishers, Pinetown, 1988, pp 343 ff.

401 CP de Kock, op cit, pp 395 and 399.

402 De Villiers and Stemmet, op cit.

403 Inventory of the Private Collection of HJ (Kobie) Coetsee, PV 357, Archive for Contemporary Affairs, University of the Free State, Bloemfontein, Files 1/ L6/ 12- Mbeki, Govan, 1987.

404 Nelson Mandela, op cit, p 512.

405 South African Institute of Race Relations, *Race Relations Survey 1987/88*, Johannesburg, 1988, p 774.

406 SAIRR, op cit, p 774.

407 Tom Lodge and Bill Nasson, *All, Here, and Now: Black Politics in South Africa in the 1980s*, Ford Foundation and David Philip, Cape Town, 1991, p 88.

408 SAIRR, 1987/88, op cit, p 388.

409 SAIRR, op cit, pages 774 and 775.

410 SAIRR 1988/89, op cit, p 571.

411 Lodge and Nasson, op cit, p 101.

412 Lodge and Nasson, op cit, p 101.

413 Lodge and Nasson, op cit, pp 103 and 104.

414 SAIRR 1987/88, p 777 and 1988/89, p 707.

415 SAIRR, 1987/88, p 583.

416 SAIRR, 1987/88, pp 586 and 587.

417 Lodge and Nasson, op cit, p 109.

418 SAIRR 1988/89, p 709.

419 South African Institute of Race Relations, *Race Relations Survey 1987/88*, Johannesburg, 1988, pp 667 and 669.

420 https://www.justice.gov.za – media, De Kock tells TRC how he blew up Khotso and Cosatu houses.

421 South African Institute of Race Relations, op cit, pp 670 ff.

422 South African Institute of Race Relations, op cit, pp 670 ff.

423 A full biography of Cyril Ramaphosa is Anthony Butler, *Cyril Ramaphosa*, Jacana Media, Johannesburg, 2011. Capsule bios include: Wikipedia; Shelagh Gastrow, *Who's Who in South African Politics*, Number 1, 2, 3, and 4, Ravan Press, Johannesburg, various years; and SA History Online. The Wikipedia and SA History online articles both bear considerable similarities to Gastrow's earlier work.

424 South African Institute of Race Relations, *Race Relations Survey 1987/88*, 678 ff.

425 Coletane Markham and Monyaola Mothibeli, 'The 1987 Mineworkers Strike', SA History. org.za.

426 Coletane Markham and Monyaola Mothibeli, op cit.

427 SAIRR, op cit, p 679.

428 Coletane and Mothibeli, op cit, p 67.

429 De Villiers and Stemmet, op cit, p 89.

430 De Villiers and Stemmet, op cit, p 90.

431 De Villiers and Stemmet, op cit, pp 90 and 91.

432   Mkhuseli Jack, op cit, p 202.

433   Mkhuseli Jack, op cit, p 201 and p 205

434   Mkhuseli Jack, op cit, p 201.

435   Mkhuseli Jack, op cit, p 206.

436   FW de Klerk, *The Last Trek: New Beginnings – The Autobiography*, Macmillan, London, 1998, p 109, and also De Villiers and Stemmet, op cit, p 15.

437   Mkhuseli Jack, op cit, p 206.

438   Mkhuseli Jack, op cit, p 210.

439   Michael Savage, 'A chronology of meetings between South Africans and the ANC in exile 1983–2000', South African History Online.

440   Mangosutho Buthelezi, IFP Statement of 4 November 2014, reprinted in Politicsweb.

441   Mac Maharaj and Z. Pallo Jordan, *Breakthrough*, Penguin Books, Cape Town, 2021, pp 78 and 103.

442   Maharaj and Jordan, op cit, p 126.

443   Maharaj and Jordan, op cit, p 131.

444   Frederik van Zyl Slabbert, op cit (*The Other Side of History*), pp 79–84 provides a surprisingly incomplete list – a better one is in Michael Savage, op cit.

445   SAIRR, 1987/88, op cit, p 707.

446   Frederik van Zyl Slabbert, op cit, pages 49 and 50.

447   SAIRR, 1987/88, op cit, p 707·

448   DJ van Vuuren, J Latakgomo, HC Marais and L Schlemmer, eds, *South African Election 1987*, Owen Burgess Publishers, Pinetown, 1987, p 1.

449   DJ van Vuuren, J Latakgomo, HC Marais and L Schlemmer, eds, *South African Election 1987*, p 1.

450   SAIRR 1987/88, p 778.

451   SAIRR 1987/88, op cit, p 103.

452   De Villiers and Stemmet, op cit, p 48.

453   South African Institute of Race Relations, *Race Relations Survey 1987/88*, Johannesburg, 1988, pp 572 and 702.

454   Both reports are in the Private Collection of HJ (Kobie) Coetsee, op cit.

455   South African Institute of Race Relations, op cit, e 703.

456   South African Institute of Race Relations, *Race Relations Survey 1988/89*, p 578.

457   Fred Bridgland, *Cuito Cuanavale: 12 Months of War that Transformed a Continent*, Jonathan Ball Publishers, Johannesburg, 2017, p 53.

458   Fred Bridgland, op cit, p 44.

459   Fred Bridgland, op cit, p 64.

460   Fred Bridgland, op cit, pp 111-112.

461   Fred Bridgland, op cit, p 139.

462   Fred Bridgland, op cit, p 161.

463   Fred Bridgland, op cit, p 195.

464   Wikipedia article: 'South Africa's Border War'.

465   Fred Bridgland, op cit, p 203.

466   Fred Bridgland, op cit, pp 203 and 204.

467   Fidel Castro and Ignacio Ramone, *My Life: A Spoken Autobiography*, New York, Scribner Books, 2006, p 326.

468   Fred Bridgland, op cit, p 385.

469 Fred Bridgland, op cit, p 351.

470 Fred Bridgland, op cit, p 367.

471 Fred Bridgland, op cit, pp 377 and 379.

472 Fred Bridgland, op cit, p 388.

473 Fred Bridgland, op cit, p 390.

474 Fred Bridgland, op cit, p 407.

475 Wikipedia article: on 'South African Border War'.

476 Wikipedia, 'South Africa and Weapons of Mass Destruction'.

477 Luli Callinicos, *Oliver Tambo, Beyond the Engeli Mountains*, David Philip Publishers, Cape Town, 2004, p 601.

478 Luli Callinicos, op cit, p 601.

479 Luli Callinicos, op cit, p 576.

480 Luli Callinicos, op cit, p 576.

481 Luli Callinicos, op cit, p 577.

482 De Villiers and Stemmet, op cit, p 107.

483 SA History Online, 'Hunger Strikes'.

484 John Battersby in the *New York Times*, 10 February 1989.

485 Scott Kraft in the *Los Angeles Times*, 17 February 1989.

486 Mkhuseli Jack, op cit, p 211.

487 Anthea Jeffery, *People's War, New Light on the Struggle for South Africa*, Jonathan Ball Publishers, Johannesburg, 2019, p 124.

488 Callinicos, op cit, p 604.

489 Anthea Jeffery, op cit, p 125.

490 De Villiers and Stemmet, op cit, p 92.

491 For the descriptions of the Mandela–Botha meeting I refer to Nelson Mandela's *Long Walk*, pp 538 ff.

492 Nelson Mandela, op cit, p 538.

493 Nelson Mandela, op cit, p 539.

494 Nelson Mandela, op cit, p 539

495 Nelson Mandela, op cit, p 539.

496 Reprinted in full, in English translation, in De Villiers and Stemmet, op cit, pp 99 ff.

497 De Villiers and Stemmet, op cit, p 100.

498 Nelson Mandela, op cit, p 540.

499 Nelson Mandela, *Long Walk*, op cit, p 540.

500 'Apartheid Protest at 2 Beaches', *New York Times*, 20 August 1989.

501 Piyushi Kotecha, 'The September 1989 Cape Town Peace March rocked apartheid and reverberated around the World', *Daily Maverick*, 12 September 2021.

502 All comment on the 6 September election is from Rory Riordan, 'The General Election of 6 September 1989', a report compiled for *Monitor* magazine, 1989.

503 Nelson Mandela, op cit, p 541.

504 Jeffery, op cit, p 134.

505 Callinicos, op cit, p 606.

506 Callinicos, op cit, p 606.

507 Callinicos, op cit, p 607.

508 Callinicos, op cit, p 610.

509 De Villiers and Stemmet, op cit, pp 122 ff.

510 De Villiers and Stemmet, op cit, pp 122 ff.

511 De Villiers and Stemmet, op cit, pp 126.

512 Elinor Sisulu, *Walter and Albertina Sisulu: In Our Lifetime*, David Philip, Cape Town, 2002, p 584.

513 Nelson Mandela, *Long Walk*, op cit, p 542.

514 Elinor Sisulu, op cit, p 585.

515 Rory Riordan, *Monitor* magazine, December 1989, 'The Port Elizabeth Protest March, 14 October 1989'.

516 Elinor Sisulu, op cit, pp 588–589.

517 Elinor Sisulu, op cit, pp 588–589.

518 De Villiers and Stemmet, op cit, p 138.

519 De Villiers and Stemmet, op cit, p 140.

520 Dirk Kotze, 'FW de Klerk made a speech 31 years ago that ended apartheid: why he did it', *The Conversation*, 30 January 2020.

521 o'malley.nelson mandela.org, 'Resolutions by the Conference for a Democratic Future on negotiations and a Constituent Assembly'.
     A more complete list, of all the 19 areas of decision, is to be found in projects. kora.matrix.msu.edu.

522 United Nations General Assembly Declaration on South Africa, January 1990, Aluka Digital Library.

523 Nelson Mandela, *Long Walk*, p 544.

524 Maharaj and Jordan, op cit, p 124.

525 South African Institute of Race Relations, *Race Relations Survey 1991/92*, Johannesburg, 1992, p 486; and SAIRR, *South Africa Survey 1995/96*, Johannesburg, 1996, pp 51 and 52. Regretfully the years 1991 to 1995 have not been split between the (then) provinces. These figures agree approximately with those of the Truth and Reconciliation Commission: *TRC Report*, Volume 3, p 670. The three provincial totals are calculations by the author, using the TRC's provincial percentages of 'Numbers of Victims' (Volume 3, p 3) as applied to the full total of fatalities, 22 456, as above. Cape fatalities are: Western Cape, 1 796; Eastern Cape, 2 470.

526 Tom Lodge and Bill Nasson, op cit, p 161.

527 Tom Lodge and Bill Nasson, op cit, p 159.

528 Tom Lodge and Bill Nasson, op cit, p 162.

529 *TRC Report*, vol 3, p 208.

530 *TRC Report*, vol 3, p 219.

531 *TRC Report*, vol 3, p 219.

532 Matthew Kentridge, *An Unofficial War*, David Philip, Cape Town, 1990, p 84.

533 Kentridge, op cit, p 86.

534 Kentridge, op cit, p 88.

535 Kentridge, op cit, p 89.

536 Brian Mitchell, 'Testimony', https://coag.org.za.

537 Scott Kraft, 'Policeman Sentenced to Die for Massacre Order', *Los Angeles Times*, 1 May 1992.

538 Scott Kraft, op cit.

539 *TRC Report*, op cit, p 198.

540   Brian Mitchell, 'Testimony', unpaginated.

541   *TRC Report*, vol 3 p 676.

542   *TRC Report*, op cit, p 675.

543   *TRC Report*, op cit, p 725, and Wikipedia, 'Richard Goldstone'.

544   A useful compilation of these reports is to be found in the Wikipedia article on 'Goldstone Commission'. Individual reports are accessible from links in this article.

545   Wikipedia article, 'Richard Goldstone'.

546   Truth and Reconciliation Commission, Amnesty Committee, AC/2001/225, 'Application in terms of section 18 of the Promotion of National Unity and Reconciliation Act, no 34 of 1995', Applicant: Eugene Alexander de Kock.

547   Hilary Lynd, 'The Peace Deal: The Formation of the Ingonyama Trust and the IFP Decision to Join South Africa's 1994 Elections', *South African Historical Journal*, vol 73, 2021, published online on 19 May 2021.

548   Hilary Lynd, 'The Peace Deal: The Formation of the Ingonyama Trust and the IFP Decision to Join South Africa's 1994 Elections', *South African Historical Journal*, vol 73, 2021, published online on 19 May 2021.

549   FW de Klerk, *The Last Trek*, Macmillan, London, 1988, p 63 ff.

550   De Villiers and Stemmet, op cit, pp 197 and 209 ff.

551   De Villiers and Stemmet, op cit, p 210.

552   De Villiers and Stemmet, op cit, pp 220 and 221.

553   Nelson Mandela, *Long Walk*, op cit, p 546.

554   Willem de Klerk, *FW de Klerk: The Man in his Time*, Jonathan Ball Publishers, Johannesburg, 1991, pages 31 and 32.

555   Van Zyl Slabbert, p 16.

556   Van Zyl Slabbert, p 16.

557   This, and the other notes on this extraordinary meeting, are from Nelson Mandela, *Long Walk*, chapter 99.

558   The description of 11 February is drawn mostly from Nelson Mandela, *Long Walk*, op cit, and, to a much lesser extent, from the report of a spy in the prison service, again kept in the Kobie Coetsee archives, and reported verbatim in De Villiers and Stemmet, op cit, pp 262 ff.

Index